LONDON'S LOCAL RAILWAYS

LONDON'S LOCAL RAILWAYS

Alan A. Jackson

Capital Transport

Dedicated to the Suburban Traveller

First published 1978
Second Edition, revised and enlarged 1999

ISBN 1 85414 209 7

Published by Capital Transport Publishing,
38 Long Elmes, Harrow Weald, Middlesex

Printed by CS Graphics, Singapore

© Alan A. Jackson 1999

ACKNOWLEDGEMENTS

Willing and unremitting help with the original work was received from the late H. V. Borley and G. T. Moody, sadly missed, who gave freely of the fruits of their recording and observation of the London railway scene dating back to the 1910s. Others offering valuable assistance at that time included the late John Faulkner, past President and Librarian of the Railway Club, and John C. Gillham, who has a particular knowledge of west London. In connection with the extensive revision and supplementation involved in preparing this volume, help was again received from John Faulkner and also from Dr Edwin Course, past President of the Railway & Canal Historical Society, who set this student on the road to authorship at London University Extension Courses over 40 years ago. Desmond Croome, collaborator in the preparation of *Rails Through The Clay* and friend of many years, has commented helpfully on those chapters relating to the Underground system, as has another specialist in that field, Brian Hardy. The maps were drawn by Mike Harris.

When working with primary sources, old newspapers and periodicals, the task of a researcher with very limited time to spare was invariably eased and made pleasant by the patience and efficiency of the staff at the House of Lords Record Office, the Public Record Office, the Greater London and former Middlesex Record Offices, the National Newspaper Library at Colindale, the Department of the Environment Library, the Westminster City Library and the Library at the London Transport Museum. Also heavily-used and greatly valued was the access that members have to the special resources of the Railway Club Library. Mention should be made of the ingenuity and the industry of the retailers of old picture postcards and – a special word of thanks – to John L. Smith, of the famous Sutton shop, in unearthing and making available at reasonable cost many valuable images of past scenes which give rise to so much information and inspiration. Last but by no means least, it would be ungracious not to mention the encouragement, prompt decisions and excellent support given by Jim Whiting, a publisher who really cares about this sort of book.

A. A. J.

A NOTE ON SOURCES

An indication of the main sources used is incorporated in the Bibliography. Footnotes have been kept to a minimum; readers interested in sources who remain unsatisfied are invited to communicate with the author through the publisher.

Overleaf: London Chatham & Dover Railway 0-4-2T No. 99 *Mona* on a train of six 4-wheelers ready to leave Greenwich Park c.1895.

PREFACE TO THE SECOND EDITION

This book is a substantially enlarged version of one of the same title written in the 1970s, fully revised and updated. It sets out to examine the history, atmosphere and environment of those railways originating in Greater London which are or were principally used for local passenger traffic. At the publisher's suggestion, a topographical arrangement has been adopted, with a chapter devoted to each quarter, beginning in the south east and proceeding in a clockwise direction to north east London. Several lines omitted in the first edition are now included.

Since outlines of the general historical and geographical background and development of the London rail network are readily available in other books (notably that by the late Professor H. P. White), as indicated in Section 5 of the Bibliography, it has not seemed necessary to include an introductory survey.

Although all the London Underground lines are truly 'local railways', it would be impossible to give all of them adequate and comparable treatment within the bounds of a single volume; again there are suitable works readily available for those seeking information not found here and these are shown in the Bibliography. We have however included those lines which were originally owned by the old steam railway companies.

As in the first edition, the period covered is mainly that before the 1948 nationalisation, though an endeavour has been made to give details of the more important developments up to the end of the 20th century. For further information on recent and future developments on the railways covered, the reader is referred to the periodicals marked with an asterisk on page 452.

Those not well-briefed in London's geography may feel the need for assistance beyond that given by the maps of the individual lines included with the text. This is best met by obtaining a copy of one of the large-scale street atlases mentioned in Section 3 of the Bibliography; such items are not cheap, but their quality is high and their ability to stimulate interest equally so; the outlay will be well rewarded, even for the native Londoner.

The railways finding a place here were an important element in the growth and infrastructure of modern London and many of them continue to play a part in the ever-changing pattern of the capital's development. We have tried to show that even the humblest of suburban lines has a history full of interest, which once appreciated, will enrich the daily or occasional journey over it. Some readers may be surprised to find how little of the Victorian railway heritage has completely disappeared and how, even where the original lines have been closed because the purpose they served no longer exists, their formations and alignments have proved adaptable to easing the construction of new railways serving new roles, not least in improving the environment by reducing dependence on motor transport, with all its attendant noise and air pollution.

In writing this book we have had in mind not just those who enjoy learning more about railways, but all who love the infinite variety and interest of London's complicated modern history. For that reason an attempt has been made to sketch the social backcloth by showing how each line affected its catchment area and how external social factors influenced the levels and the nature of the traffic handled.

DORKING, June 1998   ALAN A JACKSON

CONTENTS

ABBREVIATIONS

BHR	Bexley Heath Railway
BR	British Railways
BTR	British Transport Records
ch	chains
CLR	Central London Railway
District	Metropolitan District Railway
DLR	Docklands Light Railway
ECR	Eastern Counties Railway
EC&TJR	Eastern Counties & Thames Junction Railway
EH&LR	Edgware, Highgate & London Railway
E&SHR	Ealing & South Harrow Railway
f	furlongs
GCR	Great Central Railway
GER	Great Eastern Railway
GLC	Greater London Council
GNCR	Great Northern & City Railway
GNR	Great Northern Railway
GWR	Great Western Railway
H&CR	Hammersmith & City Railway
H&UR	Harrow & Uxbridge Railway
K&R	Kensington & Richmond Railway
L&BR	London & Blackwall Railway
LBSCR	London, Brighton & South Coast Railway
LCC	London County Council
LCDR	London Chatham & Dover Railway
LGOC	London General Omnibus Company
LMSR	London Midland & Scottish Railway
LNER	London & North Eastern Railway
LNWR	London & North Western Railway
LPTB	London Passenger Transport Board
LSWR	London & South Western Railway
LT	London Transport
m	miles
Met	Metropolitan Railway
MDR	Metropolitan District Railway
min	minutes
M&SWJR	Midland & South Western Junction Railway
MRCE	Metropolitan Railway Country Estates Ltd
MWB	Metropolitan Water Board
N&ER	Northern & Eastern Railway
NLR	North London Railway
N&SWJR	North & South Western Junction Railway
PLA	Port of London Authority
RCLT	Royal Commission on London Traffic (1905)
SECR	South Eastern & Chatham Railway
SR	Southern Railway
T&HJR	Tottenham & Hampstead Junction Railway
UDC	urban district council
W&CR	Wimbledon & Croydon Railway

DATES AND DISTANCES

Unless otherwise stated, the closure dates given are the *last full day* of public traffic.

Distances are generally those shown in the Railway Clearing House maps and Junction Diagrams or the railway companies' official publications. With the sole exception of London Transport (and its Underground Company predecessors) who used decimals of a mile, these are always given in miles and chains and are so shown here (80 chains or 8 furlongs = 1 mile = 1.61 km).

CHAPTER ONE

SOUTH EAST LONDON

An SER train from London to Greenwich entering Greenwich station during the final years of right hand running (c.1900). Note the descending gradient from the viaduct and the central through roads. *George Potter*

Railways to Greenwich (map page 18)

Greenwich was the outer terminus of the very first public passenger railway in London, the London & Greenwich Railway, opened in 1836 and completed in 1838. Exclusively a passenger line, its early history has been well documented in other work and need not be repeated here. From 1st January 1845 the whole operation was leased by the SER, though the little company remained in existence until 3rd January 1923 to receive its rent and distribute its dividend.

Thanks to the influential opposition and obstinate prejudices of the Admiralty and the Astronomer Royal, the SER's natural desire to extend this line further east through the important town of Woolwich was continually frustrated, although the latter point had been circuitously reached via Blackheath in 1849 (the North Kent line). There was no lack of proposals for filling the gap east of Greenwich; in 1863 alone three bills were deposited for railways serving the two towns, one each sponsored by the three companies interested in this quarter of London. From the LBSCR camp came the South London, Greenwich & Woolwich Railway, a 6m 62ch branch from the Brighton's line at Peckham via New Cross, Deptford, and a covered way through Greenwich Park to terminate at the Royal Dockyard, Woolwich. The SER supported a Greenwich & Woolwich Railway which sought a 2m 61ch connection between Greenwich and the North Kent line at Charlton, crossing the Park on a viaduct. Lastly the LCDR's No. 1 bill included a 2m 18ch line from the Crystal Palace & South London Junction Railway at Nunhead to Crooms Hill,

Greenwich, the last 319 yd to be in a covered way. Beyond, the LCDR wanted a further 2m 52ch to reach the Royal Dockyard, this to cross the Park in an 843 yd covered way. There were to be connections to the SER and LBSCR where the other two companies' lines intersected. All three proposals met the predictable opposition of Observatory authorities concerned with possible wobbling of their telescopes, but by May 1863 they had conceded there might be a tunnel through the Park on a route defined by them, provided speeds did not exceed 12 mph.

Whilst the three bills were before parliament there was some horse trading between the three main line companies. The LBSCR gave up all territorial claims to Greenwich and Woolwich provided the LCDR showed no further interest in Balham and points beyond. Left with an LCDR invasion of its territory, and facing Observatory hostility to its proposed viaduct, the SER and LCDR reached an arrangement whereby the latter would have running powers over the SER into Woolwich Arsenal via Lewisham and in exchange the SER would be given less valuable running powers to Crystal Palace via new connections at Lewisham, Brockley and Nunhead. This secured the withdrawal of the LCDR Greenwich – Woolwich proposal but the 2½ mile branch from Nunhead to Greenwich, Crooms Hill was authorised to the LCDR by an act of 28th July 1863. In the following year acts of 23rd June and 14th July sanctioned the agreed running powers and connections to allow SER trains to Crystal Palace, both direct from London Bridge, from the company's new Tonbridge main line and from the Mid Kent line at Lewisham. Some work was done on making a Nunhead-Brockley curve behind St Norbert Road, but none of the necessary connections to allow SER access was completed.

In 1865 the SER finally secured an act for filling the Greenwich-Charlton gap by adopting an alignment suggested by the Astronomer Royal, who obtained power to stop the trains. But the SER was not happy with the suggested route and nothing was done until a further SER act was passed in 1872, authorising a line along the north side of London Street, Greenwich and passing along the south side of Trafalgar Road in a cut and cover subway. This removed 'all cause for alarm' at the Observatory. At Greenwich 43 arches of the original viaduct were demolished between Norman Road and the end, and an embankment made which descended to ground level opposite the original terminal. From there the line further descended to the mouth of the new tunnel. The tracks at Greenwich were on a new alignment, requiring complete rebuilding of the station.

The section between Charlton Junction and Maze Hill & Greenwich Park station was the first to open, on 1st January 1873. Temporary platforms on the new site at Greenwich were in use from 11th January 1877 for London trains but the section between Greenwich and Maze Hill was not available for public traffic until 1st February 1878 owing to delays in settling the alignment at Greenwich to the satisfaction of the Board of Trade. Even then most trains terminated at Charlton until 4th March.

The handsome new Renaissance style station house on the south side of the line at Greenwich bore some similarity with its predecessor and some of the Portland stone of the latter was reused in its construction. It was however larger and substantially a new building. Inside were four roads and a bay on the south side. Much to the frustration of the SER, the existing track layout out of London Bridge made it impossible to arrange for normal left hand running between London Bridge and Greenwich and a scissors crossing was installed at Charlton to allow reversion

Westcombe Park station, with an Up train entering, c.1905. *Commercial picture postcard*

to normal running at that point. This superseded the normal left hand running which had been in operation initially between Charlton and Maze Hill. The awkward anomaly was to last until midnight 25th/26th May 1901 when widening works on the tracks into London at last allowed normal running to be adopted through to Charlton Junction. An intermediate station between Maze Hill and Charlton, called Westcombe Park, was added on 1st May 1879 to exploit residential development on the estate of that name. With the connection to the North Kent line at Charlton Junction, the SER line in Greenwich became another alternative route into Kent, no longer just a local railway.

Westcombe Park station, 12th July 1955, looking to Charlton, showing platform extensions at London end for 10-car train scheme under construction. The telegraph poles in the previous photo are still in position. *Alan A. Jackson*

Meanwhile the LCDR was making little progress with its entry into Greenwich. Land was difficult to obtain and the construction work authorised in 1863 was overtaken by the company's great financial crisis of 1866 which landed it in Chancery for five years. An Arbitration Award of 1871 allowed the stricken company, among other things, to spend just enough to complete the branch from Nunhead as far as Blackheath Hill 'with best despatch' and this 1m 55ch length, with an intermediate station at Lewisham Road, was opened to public traffic on 18th September 1871. Finance not permitting anything more, powers for the remainder were allowed to lapse.

A second intermediate station, Brockley Lane, was added in June 1872. All the stopping places were simply and crudely built, largely in wood. Twenty six trains a day each way, about one every 45 minutes, ran on weekdays, with about one train an hour on Sundays. Some of these worked through to and from Victoria but most terminated at Nunhead, connecting into the Crystal Palace services. Things had improved very little by 1887 when there were five connections with Victoria – Crystal Palace trains on weekdays and 15 with the City – Crystal Palace services, plus two morning through workings to Victoria and one at midnight, one through to Moorgate Street, three to Holborn Viaduct, one to Ludgate Hill and seven to St Paul's (now Blackfriars). Sundays saw hourly connections at Nunhead to and from the City or Victoria.

As two of the stations were close to LBSCR and SER establishments on more direct routes to central London (Brockley and St John's), trade was hardly brisk. This no doubt exacerbated the old itch to get a foothold in Greenwich, an itch further irritated by the SER's success at building up a healthy traffic on its new line between Charlton and Greenwich which had encouraged new housing developments east of Greenwich Park. Finally, after many false rumours, a bill was deposited for the 1881 session, a move explained in almost Churchillian terms to shareholders at the half-yearly meeting by the chairman, J. S. Forbes:

> We should not have spent £450,000 to get the bottom of Blackheath Hill. The raison d'être of that expenditure was to get to the heart of Greenwich. Everybody knows what the Greenwich traffic is; it is an astounding traffic. That is a thing that the time has come for doing and we have no hesitation in recommending you to do it.

And do it they somehow did, despite the £225,000 capital required for a sinuously routed line through what was a tightly built-up area. The sanction of Parliament was obtained, extended in time by further acts of 1886 and 1888, for a new alignment, swinging north-east to a terminus at street level in Stockwell Street, Greenwich, set out to allow for a junction with the SER between the east end of that company's Greenwich station and the west entrance of the covered way through the Park. Although the LCDR's intention of making this connection was not included in the 1881 bill, it was mentioned in the Parliamentary proceedings.

The branch started at the east end of Nunhead station, opened on 1st September 1871. Here were two island platforms, the northernmost with Up and Down roads at each side, the other sharing the centre road with an additional Up road on its southern face. The centre road was used by branch trains terminating at the junction. On the Up side was a small goods yard which survived until April 1962. At the east end of the platforms the Crystal Palace lines swerved away to the south,

Greenwich Park
train at Lewisham
Road station
c.1903.
*Commercial
postcard*

View from Lewisham Road Station

BR 31253 running
light between the
former Brockley
Lane and
Lewisham Road
stations, 10th
September 1955.
Alan A Jackson

the Greenwich tracks proceeding almost due east over still open country in a cutting through the south side of Telegraph Hill, emerging to cross the LBSCR main line above the London end of that company's Brockley station (opened on 6th March 1871). West of this bridge, between what are now Pepys and Mantler Roads, were the branch's only freight installations, on the north side Martin's Siding, and almost opposite on the Up side, a GNR coal depot, part of that company's reward for subscribing to the LCDR Metropolitan Extension from Ludgate Hill to Farringdon Street. Martin's Siding, opened in 1885, accommodated 36 wagons and was leased to the LNWR, which sub-let to the coal merchants Charrington, Warren Ltd. The GNR depot, in service in December 1883, held some 40 wagons and was served by GNR coal trains travelling via Farringdon Street and Loughborough Junction. In later years both the yards were worked from Hither Green.

Brockley Lane station was opened in June 1872 to sneak such traffic as it could from the adjacent LBSCR establishment. Both fed on the new district of Upper Brockley, where spacious streets of substantial three- and four-decker yellow brick villas with long gardens were laid out in the late 1860s, for what Charles Booth's survey describes as the 'well-to-do middle class'. Sited on the bridge over Brockley Lane, the LCDR station had wooden platforms, with a small entrance hall at street level. Turning north-east in a deep cutting, the line traversed the southern part of Brockley, then at the edge of London. Falling at 1 in 100, it passed below Loampit Hill into Lewisham Road station, where the brick platforms were connected by a covered iron footbridge. This led to a small wooden booking office building at street level on the Up side, which was so well made that it was still in service as the 1st Lewisham Scouts' hut over a century later.

Crossing St Johns, a villa satellite of Deptford named after its church, the branch very shortly passed over the SER North Kent line near its junction with the Tonbridge main line. Now on an embankment, the branch tracks crossed the Ravensbourne River on a brick viaduct before entering a cutting. Blackheath Hill station was on the south side of that road, its brick platforms served by a booking office on the bridge that carried the street over the line.

The 46ch extension to Greenwich, opened on 1st October 1888, cleaved its way through an area packed with small houses in narrow streets and courts, obliged to twist and turn in steeply-retained cuttings and covered ways to minimise property demolition and compensation to landlords. It started in a deep cutting on the north side of Blackheath Hill and fell at 1 in 80 all the way. After some 200yd it entered a 150yd covered way under Blissetts Hill, continuing through a final section of steeply-walled cutting before reaching Greenwich station. Here the layout comprised a central locomotive run-round road between the Up and Down platforms, the former an island with an Up loop around its outer face. Both platforms and the connecting space behind the buffers were well sheltered by valanced awnings. The main buildings, of brick with round-arched windows, stood across the end of the line level with Stockwell Street, a two-storey house for the stationmaster at the south-east corner. A siding near the signal box provided space for the spare locomotive needed at busy times. The alignment allowed for a connection to the SER in an easterly direction. To avoid confusion after the working agreement between the LCDR and the SER, the station was renamed Greenwich Park from 1st July 1900.

Despite Forbes' ebullience, traffic proved to be light except on Bank Holidays and summer Sundays when the terminus was besieged by crowds seeking the exotic delights of Crystal Palace, whilst in the opposite direction the poorer people from Walworth and Southwark came to relax on the river or in Greenwich Park. But the commuting businessmen and clerks of Greenwich and Lewisham remained loyal to the more direct services of the SER which had opened a station at St John's on 1st June 1873 to compete with Lewisham Road. As for the wealthier men of Upper Brockley, their families and their servants, these found the LBSCR to London Bridge more convenient than the circuitous journey to St Paul's (Blackfriars) via Loughborough Junction.

In January 1899 the through journey from Greenwich to St Paul's or Victoria took about 30 minutes. There were then 43 Down trains between the 06.40 and 00.41 arrivals at Greenwich; in the Up direction, 54 trains left Greenwich between 05.07 and 00.10, whilst on Sundays there were 21 each way. Although some ran through to London, most workings terminated at Nunhead into connections for City stations or Victoria. In 1913 the timetable showed 55 Down and 43 Up, only 11 each way on Sundays, all stopping at each station, taking about nine minutes to traverse the branch.

Until this time the usual formation was four to six wooden 4-wheelers, probably hauled by an LCDR class D 0-4-2 well tank, but in that year a push-and-pull unit consisting of a P class 0-6-0T with a bogie coach at each end appeared on the branch. This ran until the evening of Sunday 31st December 1916 after which as part of the SECR response to a government request to provide extra capacity for war traffic, service on the branch ceased, together with the passenger services on the Crystal Palace line and Sunday trains on the Catford Loop.

Greenwich Park station c.1912 showing one of two 'Sandwich' push-pull units formed that year for working the branch, with LCDR coaches of 1897 and Wainwright P class 0-6-0.

Few were inconvenienced by the closure. LCC electric tramcars, with the multiple attraction of cheap fares, intensive service and ready accessibility, had been operating between Lewisham and Greenwich since 4th April 1908, and between Brockley and New Cross since 26th February 1910, drawing off most of the local traffic that existed. Passenger and parcels receipts at the four stations fell from £13,820 in 1905 to a mere £3,107 in 1915. It was thus no surprise that when the Crystal Palace line was re-opened after the war, the Greenwich branch was left quietly rusting, seeing no trains other than the freights into the Brockley yards and occasional forays towards Lewisham Road for carriage storage. Maintenance beyond Lewisham Road was discontinued, so that by the early 1920s platforms and rails were covered with weeds and rubbish. There was some mild agitation for re-opening, but after hearing evidence in October 1926, the London & Home Counties Traffic Advisory Committee found that the fall in receipts fully justified the SR's conclusion that the bulk of the available traffic had left the railway for good.

The closed LCDR Blackheath Hill station, looking to Greenwich Park, c.1921.
Lens of Sutton

Then someone had a bright idea. In 1926 the infant SR was making a brilliant recovery from the effect of wartime strains imposed on its constituent companies, which had borne the brunt of traffic to and from the Western Front in France. Electrification of suburban lines had been started, but in the congested and busy area around London Bridge there was a traffic problem. Whilst on much of the suburban system electric trains could run unimpeded at close intervals, unimpeded because steam-hauled freights could be accommodated in night hours, the very heavy goods traffic exchanged with the northern companies had to be run in daylight between the electric services. These trains worked to and from Hither Green yards via the City Widened Lines, Snow Hill, Blackfriars Junction, Metropolitan Junction, London Bridge station and New Cross. A particular source of congestion was the section between Metropolitan and Borough Market Junctions, west of London Bridge, where only one Up and one Down line were available to carry all the electric services in and out of Charing Cross together with the 40 or so freight movements daily.

The concept was to join up the North Kent line and the Greenwich Park branch as envisaged in 1863, making a second curve to the main line south of Lewisham, so that goods trains from the north could work from Blackfriars to Hither Green via Loughborough Junction and Nunhead, by-passing the London Bridge bottleneck. This imaginative plan also enabled Hither Green yards to receive another 20 to 30 freight trains daily from the LMSR and GWR via the West London line instead of traffic exchanges at Stewarts Lane, Battersea or Redhill yards.

The first of the two new connections carried freight from 7th July 1929 between the branch at the Greenwich end of Lewisham Road station and the North Kent line on the London side of Lewisham station, crossing the main line on a massive 240ft double span lattice-girder bridge. To reach the main line, the second link (the Courthill Loop) left the Mid Kent about 450yd from the country end of Lewisham, joining the Tonbridge line near Parks Bridge Junction. From Nunhead station (rebuilt slightly further west in red brick with a single island platform, opened in May 1925) to Lewisham Road the old branch was relaid with 45ft 95lb rail and

The bridge carrying the 1929 connection between the former LCDR Greenwich Park branch and Lewisham station over the former SER main line at St John's, looking to Lewisham, with unit 5015 on a Dartford-Cannon Street via Woolwich and Blackheath train approaching, 16th July 1955. The supporting pillar seen on the right was demolished by a collision in fog on 4th December 1957 in which 90 people were killed. *Alan A Jackson*

reballasted. The rest was abandoned by an act of 1929, and the track was taken up in that year. After unsuccessful efforts to sell the land, the cuttings between Greenwich Park and Lindsell Street, Blackheath Hill, were filled with rubble by a haulage contractor who paid the SR almost £1,500 for the privilege, completing the work by 1932. In June 1929 the Traffic Officers' Conference of the SR was recommended to abolish Brockley Lane station, the buildings reported in a bad state and 'no likelihood of a passenger service being reintroduced on the Greenwich Park branch'. At Blackheath Hill and Greenwich Park the buildings were left intact as it proved possible to let them. After the filling work was completed, the sites of the cuttings were used as yards by scrap metal dealers and transport contractors.

It was not long before the enterprising management of the SR was putting the Lewisham connections to passenger use. To allow Dartford Loop and Bromley North trains to call at Lewisham if required, the loop between Lewisham and the main line was electrified from 16th July 1933. Until that time the new route established in 1929 had only been used for passenger purposes by a few summer steam specials to the coast calling at Lewisham. Electrification of the Lewisham-Nunhead section to enable the full potential of the new works to be realised was carried out in the summer of 1935. From 30th September new rush-hour services operated between Dartford and St Paul's (Blackfriars) via Sidcup and via Bexley-heath, affording useful relief to the services into London Bridge, Cannon Street and Charing Cross struggling to cope with a huge increase in traffic from the thousands of houses built between Eltham and Dartford in the late 1920s and early 1930s. Although made more attractive by restricting stops on the inner section to Peckham Rye and Elephant & Castle, bringing Holborn Viaduct within 19 minutes of Lewisham, (just four minutes longer than Lewisham-Cannon Street), the new route was slow to attract passengers. Its popularity was not assisted by charging higher fares and the posting of travelling ticket inspectors to collect this extra revenue. A long period of suspension during the war years and immediately after (from 16th October 1939 to 12th August 1946) did nothing to help, and indeed the six or so trains in the peak periods via Bexleyheath and nine via Sidcup were never over-crowded. In the 1960s and 1970s freight workings over the Nunhead-Lewisham section were much reduced in number, the Brockley Lane yards finally closing from 4th May 1970, the signal box on 7th March 1973.

The substantial 1929 bridge over the Tonbridge line at St John's was very severely damaged by a collision in fog at about 18.20 on 4th December 1957, in which a Cannon Street – Ramsgate steam train ran at about 30mph into a stationary Charing Cross-Hayes electric train, resulting in 90 deaths. The impact toppled the front of the steam train against a steel column supporting the flyover, causing the bridge girders to collapse on to it. Above, two minutes after the collision, the 17.22 electric service from Holborn Viaduct to Dartford, very slowly approaching a red signal, was promptly stopped by its driver when he saw the bridge girders had sagged. This train was not damaged or derailed. The 'temporary' bridge installed to enable the Nunhead-Lewisham line to be reopened on 13th January 1958 is still in position at the time of writing, over 40 years later.

Further alterations to the layout at Lewisham took place from 3rd April 1976 with the opening of a new loop signalled for reversible working through St John's. This formed a flyover, allowing trains from Lewisham for Charing Cross to take the 1929 Nunhead line then descend to the Up side at St John's.

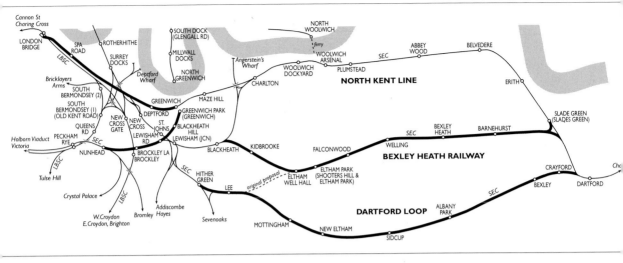

The Dartford Loop

A little to the south east of the railways just described are two others, parallel to and south of the North Kent line and providing alternative routes to Dartford and beyond: the Dartford Loop (also at first known as the North Kent Loop) and the Bexley Heath Railway. Both have long been used for traffic to and from points outside London, but what is now known as the Bexleyheath line was a truly local railway in conception and certainly merits inclusion here. Whether the Loop qualifies is perhaps more debatable but since the 1930s it has carried a great weight of London local passenger business.

In promoting a 9m 50ch railway between Lewisham and Dartford via Sidcup and Bexley in 1861–62, the SER no doubt had concerns about the vulnerability of a gap between its North Kent line and the LCDR main line east of Beckenham which its rival might be tempted to penetrate. There was also talk of providing necessary relief to the North Kent line but subsequent events showed this to be largely spurious since through traffic has never been particularly important.

Construction involved a deep cutting east of Sidcup as the line descended to near sea level when approaching Crayford and Dartford. There were no other serious engineering problems and the new railway, through open country, with intermediate stations at Lee, Eltham, Sidcup, Bexley and Crayford, came into public service on 1st September 1866. There were eleven trains each way daily, about one every two hours, plus a single fast service not calling at the Loop stations; some trains went beyond Dartford at first but after a few years the long distance trains were normally routed via the North Kent line.

All the stations were in the familiar SER rural style; weatherboarded single storey structures, with subways between the platforms rather than footbridges. Sidcup had no subway as passengers passed through the underline bridge over the road to reach the other platform. 'Eltham' was something of a misnomer, since it was actually in Mottingham, about a mile south of its namesake. This anomaly was heightened after the opening of the Bexleyheath Railway through Eltham and the suffix 'for Mottingham' later appeared, with 'for' replacing 'and' at some periods. It was not until 1st October 1927 that the Loop Line station was awarded an unequivocal 'Mottingham'. Between this station and Sidcup, a landowner gave land and money

Top: New Eltham for Pope Street station, looking to London, c.1903. Suburbanisation is already sufficiently advanced to justify a coal office behind the Up platform. *Commercial postcard*

Centre: Sidcup station approach (on the Up side) slumbers in summer haze c.1905. H Gower awaits business with his luggage and parcels van. *Commercial postcard*

Above: Sidcup interior about the same date, looking to London. *Commercial postcard*

to provide another station, duly opened on 1st April 1878. It was known first as Pope Street but this name did not please the developer and it became New Eltham & Pope Street from 1st January 1886 and simply New Eltham from 1st October 1927. This association with building development provided an early pointer to the future major business of the line.

At Sidcup the station was at Halfway Street, half a mile north of the village centre. Bexley station was conveniently near its namesake, as was Crayford, situated less than a quarter mile south of the centre of that community. For many years the Loop line appears to have had little or no effect on the development of the area it served, which remained largely rural, though the railway did attract a few middle class residents around its stations. On 1st June 1895 a new station was opened at Hither Green, where the Loop joined the Chislehurst and Tonbridge main line and this had a separate pair of platforms on the Loop line. Roads of small houses were by then appearing on the London side of the new junction station and more quickly followed.

A double line spur from west of Lee station, running east to south to join the main line was opened in 1899/1900 primarily for freight trains to and from the then new Hither Green yards; it was never regularly used for passenger traffic. At the eastern end of the Loop line, a curve south to north, allowing trains to run from Crayford round to Slade Green and on to the Bexleyheath line came into use much later, on 11th October 1942.

The years from around 1880 up to 1914 saw residential development at Lee, where new roads of houses quickly filled in the area between the original settlement and the station, whilst other residential growth spread southwards towards Grove Park. By 1914, New Eltham although small as yet, was very much a railway suburb, closely grouped around its station. At both places the houses were of medium to small size, in general for the lower middle class commuter. From around 1870 right through

Bexley, the SER main building, on the Down side, surrounded with commuters' motor cars but still gaslit and laced with telegraph poles and wires, September 1963. *BR (SR)*

to the First World War, Sidcup saw steady growth, mainly between the High Street and the line, on either side of Station Road. This was often optimistic in its projection; sales or leases were only slowly achieved, some properties remaining empty for years. At Sidcup some of the houses were larger, aimed to attract the comfortably-off, servanted middle middles who could afford the time and cost of living so far from the City. Station improvements of 1887 – a new booking office on the Up side and platform extensions – may have been a response to the building activity just mentioned. East of Sidcup, there was some new settlement in Bexley village but in general this section of the Loop saw very few commuters before the early 1930s.

Except perhaps at Lee, the arrival of electric trams and motor buses in the Loop's catchment area in the 1900s provided little effective competition then or in later years. Most rail passengers here were commuters to central London and the time factor made the cheaper road fares unattractive for the majority.

Crayford station witnessed an intensification of freight and passenger activity in World War 1. Hiram Maxim's 1888 works at Crayford had been taken over by Vickers in 1897 to become Vickers, Son and Maxim Ltd and after doing well in the Boer War, had suffered some vicissitudes, including for a time manufacture of motor cars, and then complete closure, but from 1914 the firm received huge orders for armaments, notably the Vickers machine gun. By the end of the war, Vickers' Works at Crayford and adjacent Erith (on the North Kent line) were producing 5,000 machine guns a month and aircraft were also being manufactured at Crayford. In a few short years, Crayford was transformed to an industrial town and a total of 600 cottages, including the Barnes Cray estate (1916) were constructed here in 1914–18. All this activity brought much extra freight and passenger traffic to the Loop line.

The Vickers Works, immediately east of the station (employing 15,000 by the end of the war) and two further war factories between there and the Bexley Heath Railway were served by a private siding almost a mile in length, which was opened in January 1915 worked by three small tank engines and the underframe of a LSWR coach powered by a petrol engine, all these owned by the firm.

Wartime traffic also brought about the construction of six holding sidings for Hither Green yards at the west end of what is now Mottingham station. This site became a rail-served United Dairies milk depot for some years from 1948. Another aspect of World War 1 traffic was the ambulance trains bringing wounded men to Sidcup station, whence they were moved in road ambulances to the large new Queen Alexandra Military Hospital in Frognal Avenue.

As on the Bexley Heath Railway, the SR conductor rail electrification was to usher in a new era for the Loop line. Some electric trains started during the 1926 General Strike (on 10th May) followed by a full service from 6th June. The number of trains each way daily was increased from 37 in the last steam timetable to 48, providing a basic frequency of two an hour, with extra workings in the morning and evening peaks. A few steam trains continued to run over the Loop, working fast from London Bridge to Dartford. This new service and a financial climate generally favourable both to the supply and demand caused builders and developers to transform the whole area along the railway from the beginning of the 1930s. By the summer of 1939 continuously built-up London was flowing out along both sides of the Loop line to a point over a mile beyond Sidcup station and on the north side as far as the eastern edge of Bexley village.

Between 1932 and 1938 an entirely new and extensive suburb was constructed between Sidcup and Bexley, with estates sprawling out each side of the line. Almost all these houses were erected by New Ideal Homesteads, who called their handiwork Albany Park. This firm made a £5,000 contribution to the cost of a £15,850 new station of that name to serve their development, also giving land to the SR, and the station, built on a flattened out section of the descending eastwards gradient, was opened on 7th July 1935. Platform buildings, linked by a wide, covered and glazed footbridge were wooden, but the main building, on the north side, was in the Modern style, a flat-roofed brick blockhouse with somewhat lower extensions either side. There was no goods yard. A further agreement made with the developers in 1939 provided for access and station offices, including a passimeter, on the Up side to cost £4,700 against which there would be a £300 contribution and a gift of land from the developer. This scheme was not carried through before the outbreak of war, passengers from the Royal Park Estate continuing to use the public right of way over the station footbridge to reach the Down side ticket hall.

Since a high proportion of the purchasers worked in central London all this new house construction, at an unprecedented pace and selling at very low prices, threw a huge peak hours load on the railway. By 1937 the train service outside the peak hours to and from Charing Cross/Cannon Street had been increased to four an hour and at the busiest peak hour there were a maximum of ten trains, including the service to and from Blackfriars via Nunhead started in 1933 and shared with the Bexleyheath line which has been mentioned earlier. These 'over the top' services to Blackfriars were suspended during the war but returned on 12th August 1946.

Albany Park, provided with assistance from New Ideal Homesteads Ltd and opened on 7th July 1935. Looking to Dartford, with unit 5342 on 4-car Up service, 22nd July 1975. *Alan A Jackson*

Mottingham station, looking to London, 15th August 1969. At this date, the SER buildings survived, apart from some reconstruction of canopies and substitution of SR style lighting on prefabricated concrete standards.
Alan A. Jackson

Freight traffic also benefited from the rapid residential expansion of the 1930s, both in bringing in building materials and later carrying the vastly increased demand for solid fuels to heat the many new houses. In 1933 the Loop saw three freight trains daily and there were trips from one siding to another. Sidcup goods yard was enlarged in 1933 when new housing estates were well under way along the railway at Halfway Street and east of the station. At Mottingham, where a large LCC estate was built south of the station in 1934–7, the goods yard was enlarged in 1935. A postal sorting office opened at Sidcup in 1935, bringing extra mail traffic to that station.

Developments after World War 2 included the introduction of 10-car trains from 1955 and completion of colour light signalling in 1955–70. A reversing siding was inserted at the country end of Sidcup station in 1967, allowing a few trains to terminate there. The summer timetable of that year provided the best services ever, with 13 commuter trains in the busiest peak hour at some stations, many of ten-car formation, and restoration of the four trains an hour off peak frequency. This level of service was subsequently trimmed somewhat but early 1993 saw the full introduction of the slick and smooth-running Networker sets, in a long overdue renewal of rolling stock. As elsewhere, the coal and coke traffic which was almost the only freight handled by the early 1960s, all but vanished with the spread of oil and then gas central heating into suburban homes. Bexley yard closed in May 1963, Crayford in January 1965, New Eltham in November 1965, Sidcup in August 1966 and Lee and Mottingham in October 1968.

Station rebuilding from the 1960s onwards left only Bexley in virtually unaltered SER form. Albany Park received a new ticket office, otherwise retaining much of its 1930s aura. Sidcup was substantially reconstructed in 1987–8 at a cost of around £700,000 to provide a terrazzo-tiled ticket and waiting hall and tenancy and staff accommodation on the Up side. Crayford received the ugly CLASP factory-made components treatment in 1968. Lee, Mottingham and New Eltham saw modest and sympathetic rebuilding under the Network SouthEast regime.

Although still available for services to and from Kent, the Loop is now very much a London local line, linking communities in what is very largely typical 1930s suburbia and carrying a somewhat reduced daily flow of commuters between London's south eastern outskirts and the central area. The 12-car Networker trains, each with a capacity of well over 1,000 passengers, proved more than ample to cope smoothly with peak hour loadings here and on the Bexleyheath line, still two of London's busiest local railways in the 1990s. Slack hours and weekend traffic on the Loop is now confined mainly to the leisure and shopping journeys of the car-less minority, mostly the young and the elderly, but in an attempt to promote it, the service inwards from Sidcup was increased to four trains an hour from June 1996.

The Bexley Heath Railway (map page 18)

'A long and unattractive street of small new shops and dwellings' was how Thorne saw Bexley Heath (or Bexley New Town) in the early 1870s. It then sheltered around 5,000 in houses strung along the main Dover Road amid market gardens, about 1½ miles north of Bexley on the Dartford Loop Line. To the east, at the tenth mile on the Dover Road, was Welling, and closer still to London, the 'suburban village' of Eltham, with its station on the Dartford Loop about a mile south of the High Street. Almost two miles further west, then at the very edge of south-east London, the select suburb of Blackheath offered the pattern that landowners further out wished to emulate, hoping to see the price of their acres rise from £400-£500 to the £1,000 to £2,000 which was usual at Blackheath.

This would require a railway service, but when the private interests petitioned the SER for a line into the Bexley Heath area in 1881 they received little encouragement, being advised to form their own company to minimise opposition and secure land at minimum cost. This was a tactic not unusual for main line companies to adopt in such a situation, in the hope of purchasing a ripening fruit at a discount later, when local effort was exhausted; if prospects were poor, it could be allowed to wither on the vine at no loss to them.

Dr Edwin Course has made a careful study of the genesis and early days of the Bexley Heath Railway in two papers, to which the reader is referred for greater detail than can be given here. He shows how about one-third of the capital of the independent promotion was mustered from local support, principally from active and retired professional and business men living on large and medium sized private estates scattered in the area between the Dartford Loop and the North Kent lines of the SER. Francis Brady, the SER engineer, surveyed a 7m 5f 2ch line from 5ch east of Lee station on the Dartford Loop through Eltham, Welling, and Bexley Heath to a junction with the North Kent about 1½ miles south of Erith. Although this route was sanctioned by the Bexley Heath Railway Act of 1883, the SER, after insisting that the junction be at Lee owing to alleged congestion at Blackheath, now changed its mind and desired the connection to be at Blackheath after all. Delays followed whilst the local company tried to settle terms with the SER for working its line and also sought an acceptable path through the exclusive residential district of Blackheath Park, jealously watched over by Albemarle Cator, who was finally appeased by a promise of a 140yd tunnel extension built solely to obscure the railway from the gaze of the residents.

The 1m 6f 2ch Eltham-Blackheath deviation, which was to meet the original alignment 1m 20ch from Lee, was approved by an act of 1887, but the troubles of the small company were not over. Although it had taken shares and lent money and officials, the SER was distinctly lukewarm about a line which would not only be quite expensive to make, but would abstract traffic from existing stations, whilst adding to the congestion in inner London. Difficulties were therefore made about raising the balance of the capital, involving the promoters in further legislation for extension of time. Eventually the SER was goaded into action by the deposit of two bills, one to abandon the line completely, the other seeking junctions with the SER's rival and neighbour the LCDR. With Sir Edward Watkin still occupying the SER chair, the board was incapable of resisting this sort of blackmail, so in the middle of 1890 an agreement was at last sealed under which the SER was to operate the Bexley Heath for 60 per cent of gross receipts as well as raising the remainder of the

Bexley Heath station with Up train entering, c.1903.
Commercial postcard

Welling station, Down side, in 1895 just before the opening of the line.
Bexley Libraries & Museums

Blackheath Tunnel, an unnecessary engineering work, built up above ground level to conceal the Bexley Heath Railway in its passage through the Cator Estate of Blackheath Park.
E A Course

capital. William Rigby started to make the line, but earthslips and financial troubles caused further delay, and it was not until 1st May 1895 that the service started, with oil-lit four-wheelers provided by the SER, upholstered and antimacassared in the first-class, padded in the seconds, wooden boards in the thirds. There were 14 Down trains and 12 Up, five each way on Sundays, running only between Blackheath and Erith or Dartford, calling at all stations, except in rush hours when some Blackheath–London trains were extended over the new line.

Despite its connection with the North Kent at either end, this 8¼-mile line, so long in the making, was as has been said, essentially a local railway, with a ruling gradient of 1 in 80 and severe curves. To minimise acquisition and demolition of expensive property at Blackheath, it left the North Kent 14ch east of the station on a south-east curve of only 13ch radius, tucked into a steeply-walled cutting. There followed the 437yd tunnel under the Cator Estate, its cosmetic eastern section poking its crown above the level of the surrounding land to avoid too sharp a gradient. Here the double tracks crossed the little Kid Brook, entering an area which the Earl of St Germans had been unable to develop because the Cator Estate, jealous of its privacy, had refused financial inducements to allow a road through Blackheath. St Germans accordingly petitioned against the bills for the Eltham–Blackheath deviation in order to secure a station on his land. This was granted and was connected by a new road across two farms to the Kidbrooke Park Estate, where middle-class villas were slowly grouping around the 1867 church of St James, half a mile north of the line. Kidbrooke's main building, on the Up side, was in the SER standard wooden-boarded style with rectangular sash windows, under a hipped slate roof which was extended over the platform by means of a shallow-curved canopy. On the Down side there was merely a rudimentary shelter. This general pattern was repeated at all the other Bexley Heath Railway stations. A small goods yard on the Up side at Kidbrooke saw considerable expansion and activity in World War 1 when a military depot was placed there, a development which also brought heavy peak-hour passenger traffic to what had hitherto been a very quiet station. Eventually the war depot extended both sides of Kidbrooke Park Road south of the line, served by its own narrow and standard gauge steam locomotives.

Beyond Kidbrooke, on an embankment notorious for slips, the line ran south-east towards Eltham village, swinging sharply north-east on a 12ch curve to skirt the southern boundary of the Well Hall Estate. This cruel kink, many years later the scene of a frightful derailment,* could have been avoided by a deviation to the north but for the success of Well Hall's owner (Sir Henry Page-Turner Barron) in securing a requirement in the 1887 act for a passenger and goods station exactly here, south of the estate at the junction between the original alignment from Lee and the Blackheath deviation. Called Well Hall, (Well Hall & North Eltham from 1st October 1916; Eltham Well Hall from 10th October 1927) this station's passenger platforms were sited above the Eltham-Woolwich road on the west side, just north of Eltham church and in a much more convenient location for the village than the 1866 station on the Dartford Loop about a mile to the south. Goods sidings were provided on the Up side at the London end.

East of Well Hall, the tracks ran through a cutting on the southern side of Shooter's Hill, reaching the summit south of Oxleas Wood, before crossing the Dover Road to enter Welling station. This was on an embankment at the Belle Grove or western end of the village with a small goods yard on the Down side at the country end. At Kidbrooke, builders had nothing much to offer the new line; Eltham's scattered population of 5,600 hardly justified two stations, while Welling, a thin collection of roadside cottages, was to prove no more promising in the early years.

* On 11th June 1972, when a railway staff excursion returning to London from Margate was driven at excessive speed through the 20mph restricted curve; four people were killed, including the driver of the diesel locomotive and two more died later.

Kidbrooke station looking towards Eltham, 30th May 1959, before replacement of the original SER buildings. Unit 4503 on Down train of mixed wooden and steel-panelled stock (8 cars).
Alan A Jackson

Eltham Well Hall, Up side entrance block, as rebuilt by the SR in 1932. The Morris Minor van waiting outside the parcels office door demonstrates that in 1968, when this photograph was taken, evening newspapers were still being delivered by rail to suburban stations.
BR (SR)

A Down train approaches the newly-opened Eltham station, provided from the roadbuilding budget as part of the cost of constructing the new Rochester Way Relief Road seen on the right; 23rd October 1985.
Alan A Jackson

Still on embankment, the tracks continued to a point at the western end of Bexley Heath* where a cutting began. The Bexley Heath goods yard was sited here on the Up side and although this transition point would have provided the cheapest site for a passenger station, the platforms were erected a quarter-mile further east in the cutting at the insistence of Robert Kersey, a BHR director and subscriber, owner of the Brampton Place Estate. Between Pickford Lane and Church Road, the station was thus a quarter-mile north of the Dover Road, a good mile from the centre of Bexley Heath at the Market Place. Most of the promoters' hopes rested on the residential development of this area with its well-drained gravel subsoil, hitherto disadvantaged by the 1½ miles distance from the Dartford Loop station at Bexley.

One further station and goods yard was opened with the line. This was about half-way between Bexley Heath and the junction with the North Kent, in open country between the Erith suburb of Northumberland Heath and Bexley Heath Market Place. It was sited in the middle of a wood on the land of Col. Frederick Barne, a BHR director, and accordingly named Barnehurst. Somewhat paradoxically, this lonely station was for many years the only one to possess a footbridge between the platforms.

Barnehurst was sited at the transition from cutting to the final embankment which carried the line down to the estuarine marshes of the Darenth and Cray, the tracks dividing at Perry Street Fork Junction to join the North Kent at Slades Green Junction (facing Erith) and Crayford Creek Junction (facing Dartford). These connections were made for operating convenience rather than through passenger working – until the 1920s, many trains turned back to London at Bexley Heath or Barnehurst.

Whilst passenger revenues in the early years were about five times those from freight, traffic was light. Despite great activity in the property market, especially at Bexleyheath,* little new housing actually appeared, and soon the SER was expressing its disappointment, all the more hurt because, in the words of the board minutes, 'the line was constructed at the insistence of the landowners'. Absolutely nothing happened at Barnehurst, (where the road to the station was still descriptively named Hills and Holes in the early 1920s), apart from the opening of a golf course on the May Place Estate, which may have produced a few passengers before the members all bought cars. Barnehurst, Bexley Heath, and Welling were all too far from London at a time when white-collar house-seekers could still find attractive and cheap property nearer in at such places as Hither Green or Ladywell. At Bexleyheath the huge Danson Park Estate of the first BHR chairman, Alfred W. Bean, remained very largely intact until it became a public open space in 1924. So miserable was business in the early years of the line that a horse-bus service between the centre of Bexleyheath and the station expired from lack of custom. Despite the anxiety to secure a station for the Kidbrooke Park estate no houses were built south of the church and it became second only to Barnehurst for quietude, at any rate until the war. Some evidence of this was noticed by a writer to *The Railway Magazine* in November 1906 who reported that no first-class ticket had been issued from it to Lewisham Junction until over six years after opening.

* The railway company used the original two-word form but in 1894 the local authority adopted the single word Bexleyheath, emulating Blackheath; railway usage did not catch up for many years.

Eltham Well Hall station looking east in 1926. Newly-laid conductor rails indicate that electric working is about to begin, or has just begun, but the station remains gas-lit and still retains its South Eastern Railway aura almost intact. *E Course*

Board of Trade Inspection of Bexley Heath Railway, 1895 at Bexley Heath station, looking east. No fewer than three Stirling 'O' class 0-6-0 locos occupy the Up line. The lack of residential and commercial development around the station at this time is very apparent. *Bexley Libraries*

Shooters Hill and Eltham Park station (later Eltham Park), erected with contributions from the estate developer, seen here around the time of its opening in July 1908. *Commercial postcard*

One major piece of suburban development did occur in the line's first two decades. In 1899 Cameron Corbett (later Lord Rowallan) purchased 334 acres of Eltham Park either side of the railway east of Well Hall station, with the intention of erecting a villa colony to repeat the success of his father's and his own efforts at Forest Gate and at Ilford. As soon as it learned of this, the SECR lost little time in seeking powers to take over the BHR. These were given in an act of 1900 and the small company was taken up at a discount from 10th July that year. Corbett was soon laying out a grid of streets with Scottish names and on 13th October 1900 he made an agreement with the SECR for 'superior passenger accommodation' for which he offered a valuable consideration. As part of the bargain, the SECR undertook to close Well Hall, which was less than half a mile west of the site of the new station in Westmount Avenue (now Road) at the centre of Corbett's estate. Subsequently the railway authorities discovered that closure contravened the BHR's agreement with Sir Henry Barron, whose heirs were not willing to modify it, obliging the SECR to try to withdraw from the arrangement with Corbett. Suing the railway for breach of contract, he was awarded damages in May 1905, but despite the proximity of the two stations, all ended well because subsequent housing development produced ample traffic for both for many years.

Substantial and capacious like Corbett's houses, Shooters Hill & Eltham Park station, designed by the railway's architect Alfred William Blomfield, was opened on 1st July 1908 (it was renamed Eltham Park on 1st October 1927). A brick booking office building on the road over-bridge was served by gently-sloping covered ways down the cutting sides to the two platforms with their brick waiting rooms, offices, and extensive canopies. In 1922 a footbridge was erected in the centre of the station, allowing the booking office to be transferred to the Up platform and the original street building to be converted to shops. Subsequently a footpath was made on the Up side, giving access from Glenesk Road. Sufficiently far to be out of sight and sound of the railway yet within comfortable walking distance, Corbett erected his most expensive houses, each with servants' annexes attached. Cheaper semis and terraces were sited nearer the line or at the outer edges of the estate. Much of the land had been covered when building ceased soon after the outbreak of World War 1. Occupants paid £26 a year rent for three bedrooms and an 80ft garden, or £38 for four bedrooms; their third-class season tickets to London cost £9 a year, but the early riser could purchase a workmen's ticket for a mere 5d return.

Partly in response to the Eltham activity, the SECR increased the service from 19 each way in 1899 to 32 in the 1900s, with about 11 each way on Sundays. But even as late as 1924 there were still only two Down through trains to the Bexleyheath line between 1700 and 1800 on weekdays, both from Cannon Street. By no means all the new residents used the railway for their journey to work; from 23rd July 1910 there were LCC electric tramcars to Woolwich, carrying many to the Royal Arsenal and other military establishments.

It was this military concentration in and around Woolwich which brought Eltham more houses and population during World War 1. With the Arsenal workforce growing from its peacetime total of 10,000 to over 70,000, the government ordered the erection of a large number of permanent and temporary dwellings around the town. Such was the activity that the three sidings at Well Hall had to be doubled in 1915, when the yard was receiving an average of 75 wagons of building materials daily. Well Hall also saw ambulance trains conveying wounded soldiers for treatment in the Royal Herbert Hospital at Shooters Hill. Although workers in the Woolwich munitions area came to live near the Bexleyheath line, most of their journeys were on a north-south axis for which they could use electric tramways, including the route between Woolwich and Bexleyheath opened on 3rd October 1903. This line offered a certain amount of competition to the railway, which it paralleled between Welling and Bexley Heath stations.

Goods traffic east of Kidbrooke remained very limited, but the passenger stations handled the produce of the many smallholdings, nurseries and market gardens until they were finally extinguished by bricks and mortar. As late as 1930 there were complaints that the waiting room at Bexley Heath station was cluttered with rose trees and crates of chickens.

Great changes were to follow the electrification of the line by the Southern Railway. In preparation for this, platforms were extended in 1924–25 to 520ft and footbridges erected at Well Hall, Welling, and Bexley Heath stations. Some electric working started on 10th May 1926 but the full timetable of three trains an hour in the peak (one Charing Cross, two Cannon Street) with two an hour at other times did not operate until 19th July. Journey time from Bexley Heath to Charing Cross, stopping at all stations, was reduced from 51 to 34 minutes.

Within a year or two the owners of the smallholdings, market gardens, orchards and nurseries were rushing to sell to builders attracted to the area not only by the vastly improved train service, but by the 9½ miles of motor roads from Kidbrooke to Eltham, Welling and Dartford, substantially completed in 1924 at taxpayers' expense, which minimised their road and drainage costs. There was much house-building activity at Bexleyheath from about 1928 but the really dramatic develop-ments in which the firm of New Ideal Homesteads played a leading part, did not begin until the early 1930s, when economic circumstances became highly favourable to the London house building market. Within a decade the whole line from the eastern edge of Eltham to east of Barnehurst was closed in with many thousands of small semis and terraces of four or six.

Between the Edwardian fringe of Plumstead and points well south of the new Rochester Way, New Ideal, Wimpey and Wates and others laid out networks of concrete roads, lining them with little red-tiled houses offered mostly at the cheaper end of the range £425 to £750 freehold. Almost all the purchasers worked in central London and were unable to afford both the mortgage and payments on a car, so unless there were adequate bus facilities, the houses sold most readily if they were within reasonable walking distance (up to ¾ mile) from a railway station with a good service to the City and West End. Knowing the importance of this, New Ideal Homesteads offered the SR £5,000 in cash towards the £7,000 cost of a new station to serve two large estates between Welling and Eltham Park, No. 1 north of the railway, started in 1932 and No. 2 to the south, begun three years later. An agreement signed, the firm boasted in the *Evening News* of 8th January 1936:

> Where NIH build, new stations follow . . . the rapid extension of New Ideal's £1,500,000 Estate at Welling made Falconwood station a necessity.

Taking an optimistic view of the traffic potential, the SR decided to construct a rather more substantial station than at first envisaged for this site, in the cutting east of the bridge under Rochester Way. It included a flat-roofed cinema-style passimeter booking hall in red brick, facing the roadway, a covered footbridge and generous lengths of canopy on both the 540ft platforms, features which increased the cost to £12,500. Practical enough, but without the architectural elegance of contemporary London Transport stations, it came into use with its intermediate colour-light signals, on 1st January 1936.

Falconwood, another station provided with financial assistance from housing estate develop-ers. Opened in January 1936, the Up side entrance block is seen here on 22nd December 1953 still bearing signs of its private company origins. *E A Course*

Some improvement was of course necessary to the existing wooden stations to meet the rapid growth in traffic. After an inspection by the general manager and senior officers in February 1930 the board allocated over £21,000 to reconstructing the main buildings at Eltham Well Hall, Welling, Bexley Heath, and Barnehurst. Eltham Well Hall also received a Down side entrance. Most of this work was finished by the end of 1932 but at Barnehurst, where housebuilding made a late start, reconstruction was not completed until 1935. Canopies were added on the Down side in 1937. During the rebuilding work all the stations were fitted with electric light. The new Up side buildings at Eltham Well Hall, Welling, and Bexleyheath were handsome single-storey structures in red brick under red-tiled roofs, larger than those they replaced, their style harmonising well with the new houses. The quite spacious booking halls were lined with glazed tiles. Finally, as part of a scheme to introduce 9ft wide steel-panelled rolling stock, platforms were lengthened in 1939 to a minimum of 530ft.

Housebuilding brought life to the sleepy goods yards. Materials arrived for roads; bricks, cement, tiles and window frames also came, and later solid fuels to keep the new occupants supplied with warmth and hot water. Enlargement of Welling and Barnehurst yards was sanctioned in 1932 together with an additional siding and car road at Bexleyheath. Two years later, new siding accommodation for 14 wagons was approved for Eltham Well Hall. With its usual eye for economy, the SR management moved the 5-ton crane from the closed station at Sandgate to Eltham Well Hall, and transported a redundant goods shed from Chilworth & Albury to Bexleyheath.

Traffic at Eltham Well Hall fully vindicated the SECR decision to retain it. Manual workers living on the large estates constructed nearby for the Woolwich Borough council in the 1920s went to their Thames-side workplaces by tram or bicycle, but many of their children grew up to find office or shop employment in London, joining the throngs of owner-occupier commuters and their wage-earning offspring. The area between the station and the village had been filled with private enterprise houses by about 1930, some of them dating from soon after the construction of the direct road for the electric tramway in 1910. Additional business was brought by buses which terminated in the large station forecourt, formed in 1952 into a bus terminus for six routes.

Barnehurst station, looking to Dartford, 22nd July 1975. The new brick frontage (right) provided by the SR on the Up side in 1935 has received some BR refurbishment.
Alan A Jackson

At Eltham Park, blank spaces on the Corbett estate, some of them occupied by munition workers' huts of 1915–16, were filled with houses between 1934 and 1939, whilst to the north, on the site of another wartime hut colony, Morrells' Castlewood Estate of 1935–38 offered cosy semis at £575 to £775 freehold. All this brought further business to Eltham Park, already well-established as a season-ticket station.

Welling gained from the eastern fringes of New Ideal's Falconwood and from a large council estate completed north of the line in 1920–26. From about 1928 the whole district to a depth of over a mile either side of the railway at Bexleyheath was networked with countless little streets of small houses whose owners enjoyed especially fertile gardens. By 1938 Danson Park was the only remaining major piece of open space. Typical of the somewhat down-market houses were the three-bedroomed, two reception villas five minutes from the station on the Goldsmid estate advertised in 1931 at £650 freehold. Taking its name from the station, the entirely new suburb of Barnehurst first came to life over Conduit and Three Corner Woods south of the line from 1933 onwards. 'Over 600 satisfied customers' were claimed for the £550 to £850 houses advertised on the May Place estate in April that year. Soon afterwards, New Ideal was at work on the Hill Crest estate north of the railway, while other builders were filling-in between the tracks and the golf course; within five years, Erith and Perry Street were merged with Barnehurst and Bexleyheath.

1929 had not passed before the SR was receiving complaints about over-crowding

The junction of the Bexley Heath Railway and the North Kent Line just east of Blackheath station on 9th April 1955. The substantial concrete retaining wall and sharp (13 chain) curve were required to avoid any incursion into the plot of a pre-existing house and garden (*Claverley*, Pond Road) on Cator's Blackheath Park residential development. *Alan A Jackson*

of rush-hour trains, and a year later the Bexleyheath Chamber of Commerce took up the struggle against what it called 'the continued neglect of the district by the Southern Railway Company'. Waterloo responded by offering the station rebuilding programme already mentioned, also by strengthening the train service. By the summer of 1930 off-peak frequency had been doubled to four an hour and from 30th September 1935 operation of some rush-hour trains over the Lewisham connections to City stations afforded useful relief, as we have seen earlier. Additional peak hour trains on the direct route were provided in the 1930s, so that by September 1935 the peak hour 17.00 to 18.00 saw three departures for the Bexleyheath line from Charing Cross, and two from Cannon Street in addition to the three from Blackfriars via Lewisham. This gave a total of 5,216 seats in the hour compared with 2,608 in January 1933 and 1,956 in July 1926.

During the 1950s and 1960s such limited space as was left inside the Green Belt, mainly at Bexleyheath and Barnehurst, was rapidly used up for private and local authority housing. This added further to the peak-hour congestion already experienced with the resumption of central London business activity after the war. One solution considered by the SR was the adoption of double-deck trains and the two 4-car multiple-unit prototypes, introduced in 1949, spent much of their life on the Bexleyheath line. They provided 1,104 seats (some of the tip-up type) compared with around 700 on a standard train. Often loaded, with standing passengers, to a total of over 1,500 on each journey, they proved a failure, as with one door to 22 seats (say to 30 passengers including those standing) station times were prolonged. Nor did the more sensitive souls relish the claustrophobic upper cabins with their sealed windows, which could be very unpleasant in the rush-hour scrums (though at quiet times lovers found the extra privacy pleasant). Towards the end of 1971 the trains were withdrawn from service after running some 700,000 miles. Long since BR had initiated the alternative solution of 10-car trains, each giving 958 seats. Platform lengthening for these trains started on the Bexleyheath line in 1953, the extra two cars appearing on rush-hour services from 14th June 1954, substantially alleviating overcrowding which was soon to be reduced by the effects of wider car ownership and a decline in the attraction of central London employment. It was the former, together with television's erosion of cinema and theatre patronage, that thinned out the off-peak traffic. The quarter-hour service was accordingly reduced to 20 minutes from 15th September 1958, only to be restored in what proved an over-optimistic gesture in the major timetable revisions of 10th July 1967. From that date, the Bexleyheath line had two stopping trains and two semi-fast (non-stop between Eltham Well Hall and London Bridge) in every off-peak hour. At the same time, the peak morning hour 08.00 to 09.00 was built up to eight London arrivals (two at Cannon Street, six at Charing Cross) and the Down peak (17.00 to 19.00) saw nine departures (five from Charing Cross, four from Cannon Street). On 4th May 1970, the basic service reverted to three an hour, and from 1st November that year working was much improved by the introduction of colour-light signalling controlled from a new route-setting panel at Dartford (Blackheath-Falconwood, worked temporarily from St John's box, had been in place since 15th March). Declining patronage in the evenings and on Sundays following the still increasing ownership of motor cars, saw trains at these times reduced to two an hour, in 1981 and 1983 respectively. In contrast, a welcome innovation, long suggested, was the half-hourly off peak service to and from Victoria introduced in the summer of 1994.

As elsewhere, in an age of declining domestic usage of solid fuels, the small goods yards could no longer muster enough traffic to satisfy Dr Beeching's accountants. Freight trains ceased to call at Welling from 3rd December 1962; Kidbrooke remained busy with Government traffic for some time after the war but changes of use and increased dependence on road transport caused that yard to close from 7th October 1968; and from the same day the freight yards at Eltham Well Hall, Bexleyheath and Barnehurst were also shut.

The SR had planned to rebuild Kidbrooke but other schemes took priority and its rotting timbers were passed to BR unaltered. The construction by the local authority in the early 1970s of a very large complex of tower blocks of flats, shopping precinct and a clinic, all south of the line on the site of the old military depots, promised to put extra traffic through this station and BR responded. In 1971 the SER structures were removed, to be replaced by a new ticket office, heated waiting area and lavatories, all these accommodated within the very ugly CLASP indus-trialised components. On the Down platform a new shelter was erected. As elsewhere the cheap CLASP option proved a poor investment, requiring complete reconstruction of the Up side building in brick and refurbishment of other features in 1994. At that time over 500,000 passengers a year were using this once quiet station.

Further station changes arose from the construction in the early 1980s of the Rochester Way Relief Road, which was somehow squeezed in alongside the railway between Kidbrooke and Falconwood, on the north side as far as Well Hall thence on to Falconwood on the south side, the crossing beneath the line requiring closure of Eltham Well Hall station. A new station, called simply Eltham, was erected at the cost of the road programme on the embankment at the east side of Well Hall Road, trains calling here for the first time on 17th March 1985. Heavily and crudely fashioned in red brick and concrete, with very high flat roofs above the platforms and a large car park and bus station below on the south side, the new structure seemed designed more to resist the worst assaults of vandals and hooligans than to welcome passengers. Staff accommodation and ticket offices at ground level, not completed until October 1988, were placed well away from the gaunt, intimidating platforms from which passengers could ingest the stink and roar of the new road below. As the new site was even closer to Eltham Park, that station saw its last train at 00.08 on 17th March 1985. Subsequent demolition spared the Blomfield building in Westmount Road, which is locally 'listed' and still in use as shops.

After an initial period of disappointing traffic, the BHR went on to fully justify the hopes of its promoters, and remains a very well-used railway as it enters its second century. Had it not existed, it is quite likely that around 1930 the SR would have built a similar line for electric working. At that time, the SR board was looking around for a suitable candidate for the financial aid the government was offering in its desire to relieve unemployment and here, opened up by new motor roads, the market gardens and nurseries around the old Dover Road were obvious fodder for the speculative builder. Had the BHR not been in place, there would have been an irresistible demand for a new railway from Lee or Blackheath through Eltham and Bexleyheath and it would probably have taken priority over the Wimbledon and Sutton and Chessington schemes.

The Mid Kent Railway: Beckenham & Addiscombe (map page 41)

We now reach a railway which was to become local in character, despite the hopes of those who brought it to life; it was also one which spawned several other local lines.

'Mid Kent' seems an odd title for a railway which ran only 4¾m south from Lewisham to Beckenham, but the promoters of what had initially been named the Mid Kent & North Kent Junction had links with the SER and were aware of that company's aspirations for a cut-off line to Tonbridge, avoiding the long way round to Dover via Redhill. After discussions, the SER agreed to staff and work the proposed line, authorised in 1855, for 40 per cent of gross receipts, rising to 50 per cent after two years, when the main line company would take over maintenance costs. This arrangement lasted from the opening day, 1st January 1857, until 29th July 1864 when the SER absorbed the Mid Kent.

Closely following the River Ravensbourne and its tributary the Pool River, the Mid Kent was subject to flooding which hampered both its construction and subsequent operation but there was no major engineering involved. At Lewisham, a new station was provided to replace the old, on the country side of the new junction, with separate platforms for the North Kent and Mid Kent lines. Later the layout here was further modified by the opening of the cut off line through Sevenoaks to Tonbridge, which branched from the North Kent east of Lewisham Junction and in September 1866 was connected to the Mid Kent at Ladywell by a spur from Parks Bridge Junction which allowed Mid Kent services to by-pass Lewisham Junction station.

Decent yellow brick side-platform stations with their main buildings on the Up side were provided at Ladywell (¾m from Lewisham) and at Catford Bridge (1½m), the latter with a goods yard and a substantial two-storey Italianate station house.

Catford Bridge, looking to London c. 1870.

These two stations served and further nurtured the ribbon development that already existed along the Bromley road as far south as Rushey Green. A third station was opened for passengers and goods at Lower Sydenham (2¾m), the unfashionable east end of the plush new suburb on the eastern slopes below the Crystal Palace. The first site was close to the South side of South End Lane, but in 1906 at the behest of the Cator Estate, which contributed, the platforms were resited almost a quarter mile south, closer to the as yet undeveloped northern section of the Estate, with access to its road approaches on the Down side. Despite the Cator link, the new station had no more than the standard SER cheap and cheerful clapboard buildings. In 1854 the Crystal Palace District Gas Company established its works on the Up side just over a quarter mile north of the first Lower Sydenham station. From 1878 this was served by a siding entered from a ground frame controlled from Lower Sydenham Station Box. By 1912 what was now the South Suburban Gas Co. owned three steam locomotives, which operated over three miles of track inside the works. About three quarters of a mile south of Lower Sydenham, the Mid Kent curved sharply eastwards to terminate a quarter mile north of Beckenham village centre. This last section, passing through the Cator Estate, was subject to stringent conditions attached to the sale of the land. One of these was that no trains should stop at stations within Beckenham on Sundays, except early in the morning and late in the afternoon, a restriction not so much based on religious principle but rather to deter invasion of an area the Cator interest had in mind to develop as a respectable residential enclave by rough and noisy Cockney excursionists. This constraint was not finally removed from the railway operators until the end of the Victorian era. At Beckenham, the Cator estate subsidised the station, at first insisting there should be no goods depot but this proviso was modified after the main line was built through the area. Trees and shrubs were to be planted to screen the railway from the view of the sensitive middle class occupants of any houses the Cator Estate might build.

SER building at Lower Sydenham, Up side, c.1968. *BR (SR)*

At Beckenham, the Mid Kent was at first on its own, though soon to be joined by the West End of London & Crystal Palace Railway's eastern extension from Bromley Junction (between Crystal Palace and Norwood Junction) to New Bromley (now Shortlands). Opened on 3rd May 1858 and extended to Southborough Road (now Bickley) on the following 5th July, from the latter date until 1st September 1863 this extension carried SER trains to and from the Mid Kent. Their removal was a consequence of the conversion of the line east of Beckenham into the LCDR's Kent main line, a development which killed all hope of the SER reaching Tonbridge this way. At first SER facilities were maintained, with some difficulty; through carriages to and from the SER Mid Kent line called at stations between Beckenham and Bickley, attached to or detached from LCDR trains at Beckenham. This facility was withdrawn after 30th September 1866.

Beckenham station was jointly owned and maintained by the SER and what became the LCDR. Its main buildings, on the Up side, were in an Italianate style similar to Ladywell and Catford Bridge, the most striking feature an iron and glass train shed which covered much of the two side platforms. There was a small freight yard and a locomotive turntable. Horse bus services were soon feeding in traffic from Bromley, Hayes, Keston and even Sevenoaks, all places (except Bromley) destined to be without railway facilities for some years.

Since the SER was now blocked off east of Beckenham, other schemes emerged for using the strategic position of the Mid Kent. In 1861 the little company successfully promoted a 3¼m extension into the eastern outskirts of Croydon, with a terminus in the Addiscombe Road. And in the 1862–63 Session, in conjunction with the LCDR, the SER sought to use the Mid Kent as a jumping-off point for a 56-mile line from Beckenham to Lewes and Brighton. Both proposals were of course blatant incursions into LBSCR territory.

After two attempts, the Brighton scheme failed but the Addiscombe extension was built and was opened on 1st April 1864, worked by the SER, which secured powers to lease in its act of that year. Suburban speculators were already at work around Elmers End and at Addiscombe. W. Wilkinson, chairman of the Mid Kent, was also deputy chairman of the National Land Co., whose chairman, Charles Gilpin, was an SER director. It is therefore not surprising to find the Land Co. engaged in property transactions in the catchment area of the new railway.

In 1862 the Mid Kent also evolved a scheme for a line leaving the Addiscombe Extension to curve around the west side of Croydon before proceeding south to Caterham. This was effectively stifled by the LBSCR but that company was driven to fend off further attempts to enter Croydon by promoting its own Central Croydon branch, which we shall return to later.

At Croydon, the Mid Kent's main building was on the west side of the line, reached by a short cab approach from Addiscombe Road. The double track ended at a locomotive turntable against the north side of the main road. A four-road engine shed was built to the east of the line at the London end of the terminus.

Two intermediate stations were opened with the line. The first, immediately south of the junction with the original line to Beckenham, was named New Beckenham and had no freight yard. It had been subsidised by the Cator Estate, which intended to develop the district north of the LCDR main line by stringing villas along wide new roads. To avoid confusion, Beckenham station became Beckenham Junction. New Beckenham's original station building, on the Up side, still standing and in use

New Beckenham, looking to London, 23rd February 1963, still gaslit. *Alan A Jackson*

as a private house at the time of writing, was for the time being completely isolated in open countryside. Not surprisingly, it did virtually no business and was closed in the autumn of 1866. At that time defunct railway stations were of sufficient rarity for the Ordnance Survey to print the legend 'Station (Closed)' alongside on its maps. A certain amount of mystery attends this first New Beckenham station as the maps suggest its Up platform may have extended north of the junction, allowing trains from Beckenham to London to call, or possibly work as a shuttle between the two Beckenham stations, although, as is often the case with large scale OS maps, the extent of the platforms is not easy to determine. London to Beckenham trains on the Mid Kent, if they used the station at all, would have needed to indulge in some complex and rather futile shunting manoeuvres. Whatever, from October 1866, if not a little earlier, New Beckenham's platforms were moved north of the Junction, so that trains to and from either terminus might call without complications; there were also some shuttles working to and from Addiscombe in the early years.

The second intermediate station, 26ch south of New Beckenham, was at Elmers End, an area of scattered farm cottages and hamlets also shown on maps as Elm End, Elms End or Elm End Green. Here a freight yard was provided on the Up side and the main passenger station building was on the Down side at the end of a short approach from what is now Elmers End Road. We shall return to these two stations later to note subsequent developments.

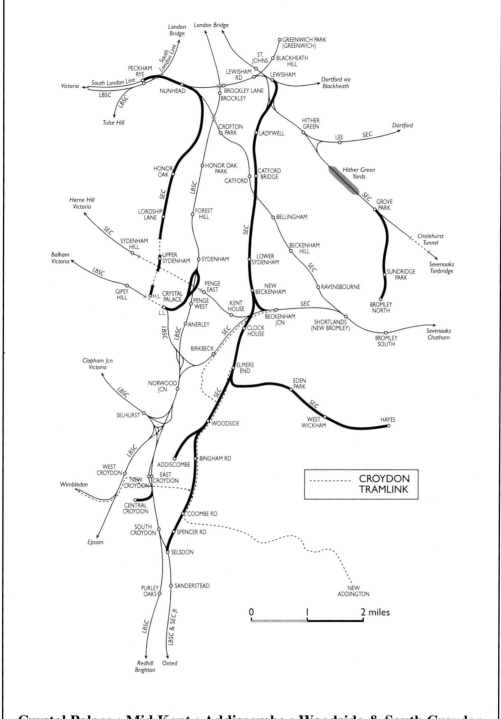

Crystal Palace : Mid Kent : Addiscombe : Woodside & South Croydon
Hayes : Central Croydon : Bromley North : Croydon Tramlink

In the opening month, Bradshaw showed 11 trains each way between Addiscombe Road and London Bridge or Charing Cross, with no service on Sundays. By the following March this had been increased to 16, no doubt in response to the encouraging growth of Addiscombe. That station, less than a mile from the centre of Croydon, and only about a half-mile from the LBSCR station in George Street, was soon to secure a substantial business of its own which might otherwise have gone to the LBSCR, traffic diverted as it were through the back door of this Surrey town, which the SER had hitherto entered only on LBSCR sufferance via New Cross and the main line. The suburbanisation of this side of Croydon had been announced at the time the Addiscombe extension was promoted: on 23rd December 1861 the *Freeholders' Circular* was describing Addiscombe as 'a very eligible situation for gentlemen who wish to build or purchase a house entirely out of the smoke of London and yet within twenty minutes' ride of the City or West End.' These were of course LBSCR times, not to be bettered by the less direct SER route. A magazine called *London Society* also indicated that Croydon was already developing good quality commuter traffic, talking in 1862 of handsome villas springing up on every side 'tenanted by City men whose portly persons crowd the trains'.

Clock House, looking to London, 24th May 1975. Unit 5051 is entering with a Charing Cross–Hayes service. *Alan A Jackson*

Addiscombe Road station (later Addiscombe) exterior, c.1903. A solitary horse cab awaits hire, a canvas sheet thrown over it to keep the interior cool.

The street frontage on the overline bridge at Woodside, c.1905.

Much of the Addiscombe building was on land released by the closure and sale of the Royal Military College for the East Indian Army, whose cadets were transferred to Woolwich in 1862. Laid out by the British Land Company, the College Estate, south of the SER station, had by 1875 become a 'nest of villas' with two churches. South of this, even more spaciously planned, was the Park Hill Estate, started in 1861 by the Ecclesiastical Commissioners, although development here did not really get under way until a reliable water supply was provided in the 1870s.

From around 1870, the Mid Kent line established itself as a suburban route with a steadily growing business. At 69ch north of Addiscombe, a station called Woodside was opened in 1871 with financial assistance from local sources, to serve an extension of South Norwood which was growing down towards the Mid Kent line. Around 1885, to accommodate intensification of this growth and also the working of the extension to Selsdon Road opened in that year, Woodside was rebuilt in yellow brick with a substantial booking hall over the line, its inner wall displaying a clock to the walled, well-canopied platforms below. A bay was provided on the Down side for the shuttle service on the new line. This station secured further but sporadic business from the Croydon racecourse east of the railway, until that closed in 1890. In 1898–99 Addiscombe was rebuilt as a single storey red brick and slate-roofed block, set parallel to the main road across the end of the line. With its spacious concourse behind, serving three well-canopied platforms (two on an island), the reconstructed station made a handsome and commodious suburban terminus.

By 1914 Elmers End had almost joined up with Beckenham east of the railway but the land on the west side was occupied by the Croydon refuse destructor and sewage works, the Beckenham Council refuse destructor and electric power station, two brickworks and the Crystal Palace District Cemetery. The first of this varied group was served by a siding which left the Up side south of Elmers End station, controlled by Sykes' key and ground frame from Woodside box. North of Elmers End station on the Up side, another private siding, dating from the Edwardian years, entered the Beckenham Council site.

To the south of Beckenham Road, lower middle class housing erected in quantity from around 1885 was served by a station and goods yard named Clock House and opened on 1st May 1890. Almost an exact replica of Woodside, (even to the clock on the overbridge), it was sited on the south side of the Beckenham Road overline bridge, which carried the single storey, yellow stock brick building, from which two covered staircases led to well-canopied platforms backed by high brick walls. An opening in the wall on the Down side allowed Post Office vans to be loaded directly off the platform. At the country end of the Up platform an 18-lever signal box controlled the station, the freight siding on the Down side and, later, entry to the Beckenham Council siding mentioned above.

Immediately to the north of Clock House, the tracks passed close above the waters of the Chaffinch Brook, which regularly flooded the line to a depth of a foot or more after heavy rain. This did not cause too much of a problem for steam trains but electric trains taking power from the track were unable to proceed, even after the line had been raised somewhat in 1928, a situation requiring deployment of a standby set of loco-hauled stock shuttling to and from New Beckenham or loco haulage of dead electric trains. Much-handled and very dog-eared posters would be brought out of store to warn passengers of the delays inherent in these emergency procedures. In 1966 the local authority at long last cured the problem by culverting the stream.

Traffic at New Beckenham, much of it first and second class, blossomed under the influence of the developing residential area in the Cator Estate, where roomy villas were laid out along the wide, curving lengths of Copers Cope and adjacent roads in the late 1870s and the 1880s. The articulate residents became impatient about the lack of a footbridge and waiting rooms, the inconvenience attached to the working of the Beckenham Junction services and the increasingly dangerous nature of the Lennard Road–Park Road level crossing south of the platforms. Their complaints were taken up by the Cator Trustees and by the end of the 1890s all parties had agreed to a reconstruction of the station on the same site with a tiled foot subway under the railway in place of the level crossing, and a new road bridge across the two lines further south (Bridge Road) to connect the two sides of the Estate north of the LCDR main line. The spacious brick built station, with long, well-canopied platforms, and its main offices on the Up side, was completed in 1904. There was also a new 50-lever signal box at the country end on the Down side and a third track between the platforms to simplify the process of dividing and combining trains for the two routes to the south. Services had continued to be worked to and from Beckenham Junction over the original line, normally in the form of a portion of London-Addiscombe trains, or after the opening of the Hayes branch in 1882, between London and Hayes. Later there were also some motor train workings, shuttling between the two Beckenham stations. But the middle road at New Beckenham had a short life; the practice of working Beckenham Junction and Addiscombe portions in one train north of New Beckenham was discontinued in World War I and the track between the platform roads was removed in 1926. Sunday services on the Beckenham Junction spur ceased from 3rd April 1916 never to be restored. There were to be further changes following electrification as we shall see in a moment.

Expansion of Lower Sydenham west of the line in the 1890s mostly took the form of housing for local workers; to the east and south, open fields and woods remained either side of the railway, with sports clubs slowly taking up land. Catford Bridge station benefited from extensive villa development east of the line towards Forest Hill, some of which was contemporary with the Mid Kent. Ladywell grew up later, the land west of the line becoming covered with the small terrace homes of third class commuters in the late 1890s and early 1900s.

Addiscombe spread south and east, especially after 1902 when the opening of an electric tramway connecting it to central Croydon encouraged further residential development. In 1908 the large Ashburton Estate around Bingham Road was sold for housing but this was also served by the Woodside to Selsdon Road line which we shall look at later.

Train services were improved with traffic growth. By 1885 there were 25 journeys each way between Addiscombe Road and London, but only four each way on Sundays. In 1910, when there were 30 trains on weekdays and 14 on Sundays, Charing Cross was reached in about 50 minutes, Cannon Street in 40. From 1st April 1880 the SER worked 16 trains between Addiscombe Road and Liverpool Street, using new Up and Down spurs on and off the East London Railway at New Cross (Canal Junction). From 3rd March 1884 these trains were terminated at St Mary's (Whitechapel), using the new Whitechapel Curve, but ceased altogether after the last train on 30th September that year. The 1912 timetables illustrate the considerable variety of Mid Kent service at that time, with Down workings as far as

New Beckenham as follows:

Charing Cross/Cannon Street–Addiscombe/Beckenham Junction	10
Charing Cross/Cannon Street–Addiscombe	2
Charing Cross–Addiscombe	2
Charing Cross–Beckenham Junction	3
Charing Cross–Addiscombe/Beckenham Junction, Orpington	1
Cannon Street–Addiscombe/Beckenham Junction (1 to Orpington)	12
Cannon Street/Addiscombe	4
Cannon Street/Beckenham Junction	3
Cannon Street–Selsdon Road (1 to Edenbridge)	2
St Paul's (Blackfriars)–Beckenham Junction	1

On Sundays there were hourly trains from Charing Cross (two via Cannon Street) to Addiscombe and Beckenham Junction only.

Electrification came to the Mid Kent soon after the formation of the Southern Railway, third-rail multiple-unit trains serving Addiscombe from 28th February 1926 with full service following on 19th July. They gave a half-hourly coverage all day, seven days a week, alternately Charing Cross and Cannon Street, with four an hour at business periods, one Charing Cross, three Cannon Street. Some of the latter, missing intermediate stations, reached London Bridge in 25 minutes from Addiscombe. At the outer terminus on the east side of the line, the SR erected four-road cleaning and inspection sheds for the new trains. Operation was eased by the installation of colour-light signals between New Cross and Ladywell on 30th June 1929. Electrification plans for the Mid Kent encouraged the Metropolitan railway in 1925–26 to try to negotiate for a through electric service between Addiscombe and its system via the 1880 connections at New Cross, but this came to nothing.

Ladywell, looking south, 1890; top hatted commuters prepare to board a morning Up train composed of oil-lit four-wheel coaches.

The investigations carried out in 1925 by Metropolitan Railway officers in connection with this proposal throw some light on contemporary SR operations on the Mid Kent line to Addiscombe. The stations were described as 'old and dingy', the trains (still steam-hauled) as 'infrequent and unpunctual', the stock as 'old, dirty and in bad condition'. Trains arriving at Addiscombe were not heavily-loaded, between 50 and 90 passengers alighting from each arrival between 17.30 and 18.30. This station was said to handle about 1,000 passengers a day, of whom some 300 were taking workmen's tickets. Many residents in the eastern part of Croydon and in South Norwood were stated not to be using the line, preferring the 'faster and more comfortable' services available at East and West Croydon and Norwood Junction stations.

After the electrification of the Hayes branch in 1926 a separate half-hourly service was provided between Beckenham Junction, New Beckenham and Charing Cross/Cannon Street (alternately). But the increased number of through trains to London from Hayes and Sanderstead caused this Mid Kent service to Beckenham Junction to be severely reduced from 1935 and after traffic on 15th October 1939 it ceased altogether. No regular public workings then ran over the spur from New Beckenham to Beckenham Junction for many years but between 1965 and 1983 when the BR Southern Region South East Divisional Headquarters was located in Albemarle Road. Beckenham, some special trains were worked non-stop between Beckenham Junction and London Bridge via New Beckenham for the convenience of railway staff. The spur, which had been singled and signalled for two-way working in 1987, once again carried public trains from 29th May 1995, when an 'experimental' off-peak Mondays to Saturdays service between Cannon Street/London Bridge and Orpington via the Mid Kent line was started.

Housebuilding of any quantity in the post-electrification era was necessarily confined to the few remaining open areas around the Shirley Schools (providing more customers for Woodside); west of the line between Clock House and Elmers End stations; and a large northward expansion of Cator New Beckenham to the east of the railway between New Beckenham and Lower Sydenham. The extensive LCC estate at Bellingham, erected in two phases between 1920 and 1937 also brought a few more passengers to Lower Sydenham. Lastly there was some speculative terrace building at Perry Hill, west of the Pool River, between 1927 and 1935 which provided additional commuters at Catford Bridge. But even in total this was fairly small beans compared with the extra traffic brought to the Mid Kent after 1930 by the intensive private house-building activity along the Hayes branch, which we shall be looking at later.

The 1939 timetables showed the Mid Kent carrying half-hourly Charing Cross–Sanderstead and half-hourly Cannon Street–Addiscombe trains as well as the half-hourly Hayes service. Between 17.00 and 18.00, Hayes branch commuters were offered four trains, Addiscombe three, Beckenham Junction one and Sanderstead three, a total of 11 in an hour for stations to New Beckenham inclusive, ten as far as Elmers End. So busy were the Elmers End signalmen that in June 1939 they asked for more protection in the interest of safety; the minutes record approval of an expenditure of £2,575 on standard SR three-position closed block apparatus between New Beckenham and Addiscombe as a response. Colour light signals did not appear until 4th April 1971 on the Mid Kent, then only between Ladywell and New Beckenham. With the exception of Clock House, where three-aspect intermediate

---

colour lights controlled from Elmers End and New Beckenham boxes had been installed in 1956, the section from Elmers End to Addiscombe retained its upper quadrant semaphores until the opening of the London Bridge Signalling Centre in 1975–76. Then, from 28th September 1975, the signalling from Catford Bridge to Woodside came under the Centre, with New Beckenham, Elmers End and Hayes boxes eliminated. Woodside remained as a fringe box, with the Addiscombe spur unchanged but closure of the line to Sanderstead made it possible to dispense with Woodside box on 24th June 1984, leaving Addiscombe as a fringe box to London Bridge. This lone outpost of low-tech remained until March 1996, when it was gutted by a fire started by vandals. After that the shuttle from Elmers End had to be worked with a pilotman and telephone.

War conditions brought train service cuts. Off peak through services between London and Addiscombe disappeared in the war emergency timetable of 1939 when the station was closed entirely during the middle of the day except on Saturdays. The Mid Kent was reduced to a half-hourly service off peak, working alternately to give Hayes and Sanderstead an hourly interval.

Freight traffic movements on the Mid Kent were dominated for many years by the appetite of the Lower Sydenham gasworks, where as late as 1958 almost 217,000 tons of coal were brought in by rail in a year. In 1951 the regular freight workings were still quite intensive. The day started with four trains between 00.20 and 02.45 carrying seaborne coal from the North End sidings at Erith to Lower Sydenham, a journey which involved reversal at Brockley Lane. Three of the trains returned to Erith. This tranche was followed by the 03.00 Bricklayers Arms–Addiscombe freight, calling at the Catford Bridge and Clock House yards, with wagons and brake for Beckenham Junction at the front. Next came the 04.07 Bricklayers Arms–Hayes, which called at the Catford Bridge and Elmers End yards as required. In the evening, the 22.55 Beckenham Junction–Catford Bridge freight was followed by a Hayes–Bricklayers Arms trip which called at West Wickham, Elmers End, Addiscombe, Woodside, Elmers End Council Siding, Clock House and Catford Bridge. The gasworks sequence then started with the 23.40 Bricklayers Arms–Catford Bridge–Lower Sydenham Gas Siding.

Declining use of domestic solid fuels, Beeching's financial appraisal and closure of town gasworks brought all this to a fairly sharp conclusion in the 1960s. Woodside yard, which had received 11,335 tons of solid fuel in 1958 was shut from 30th September 1963. Clock House and Elmers End followed from 5th October 1964. Catford Bridge and Lower Sydenham, restricted to wagonload coal only from 28th December 1964, were closed completely from 25th March 1968 and 20th June 1966 respectively. The connection to the Lower Sydenham gasworks, long disused, disappeared with the 1971 resignalling. Addiscombe yard survived until June 1968.

Some mention must be made of infrastructure changes since World War 2. Up to the 1990s many of the stations retained their Victorian buildings though canopies had often been shortened in length or removed altogether to reduce maintenance costs. Elmers End, badly damaged by bombs and missiles in the war, underwent some first aid patching-up in which the remains of the old Down side buildings were demolished; then, in 1956, here as elsewhere on the Mid Kent, platforms were extended to 675ft to accommodate ten-car trains, the extensions following the curve of the Hayes branch; new upward-sloping canopies were erected at the south end of the war-damaged Down platform as part of these works. At the same time the

Elmers End, looking to London, 28th April 1962 with a Sanderstead shuttle at the bay platform, left. At this time, the station was still gas-lit and the bomb-scarred remains of the SER Down side buildings are still in evidence. *Alan A Jackson*

tracks used by the Sanderstead and Addiscombe trains were slewed eastwards, the junction moved about 50yd south. After this operation, the signal box, which had been in the angle between the two sets of tracks, had both lines in front of it with sidings and Up bay behind. Vandals set fire to the Up side buildings in 1973 but a boldly-styled glass box entrance hall incorporating a ticket office restored some dignity when completed in 1975. In 1993 the Up bay was shortened to 63yd; the Down bay had been secured out of use in 1985.

At Addiscombe in 1956–57, in connection with the ten-car train scheme introduced on the Mid Kent from 4th March 1957, platform three was abolished, its site given over to a berthing siding; the island platform was at the same time extended up to the signal box. The carriage depot on the east side was closed in 1992 and the associated sidings in 1994.

Another probably deliberate fire severely damaged much of the lavish Edwardian Up side building at New Beckenham in the spring of 1966. A smaller structure replaced the entrance hall and ticket office. Lower Sydenham's timber inheritance from the SER was replaced in 1972 with the ugly factory-made CLASP building components, but after a fire in 1989 the station was rebuilt once more in the more pleasing neo-vernacular style adopted by BR Network SouthEast. Completed in 1991, this provided an Up side building with ticket office, waiting area and staff accommodation as well as new waiting shelters on both platforms. Yet another fire, on the Up side at Catford Bridge in May 1993, was followed by extensive renovations which resulted in the closure of the Up side ticket office in favour of a refurbished one on the Down platform.

From October 1988 staffing at stations was drastically reduced, revenue collection left to ticket machines on platforms and spot checks by inspectors on the trains. This established a pattern soon adopted on other suburban lines.

Modifications to the pre-war electric services have been considerable in recent years, reflecting significant changes in traffic flows. One important development in this area was the growth of Croydon into a major office centre in the 1960s. Another feature has been the way in which since the mid 1930s, the Hayes traffic has dominated business on the Mid Kent.

From 1945 the weekday half-hourly off-peak coverage at Addiscombe was provided by a shuttle service working in and out of the Up bay at Elmers End in connection with the Hayes service to and from Charing Cross (shuttle working on Sundays began the previous year). The summer timetable of 1948 restored a 15-minute off peak service at Elmers End, two an hour going to Hayes, one to Addiscombe, one to Selsdon/Sanderstead. But by the summer of 1950 all four were working through to Hayes, weekdays and Sundays, with Addiscombe and Sanderstead served only by half hourly shuttles on weekdays only. Off peak and commuter loadings on these two services fell off very steeply, making even two-car trains more than adequate. On a weekday evening in July 1975 only seven passengers were seen to alight from a rush hour arrival at Addiscombe. Twenty years after its first attempt had been thwarted, BR succeeded in withdrawing the little-used shuttle service between Elmers End and Sanderstead in May 1983. But not all changes have been negative; as already noted, the revival of a Mid Kent service through Beckenham Junction in 1995, brought an extra off peak facility to the inner section.

With other better-served stations readily accessible by bus or car from its catchment area, the survival of the double track line between Elmers End and Addiscombe seemed more associated with operating convenience than revenue but even this slim justification was removed by the closure of the carriage depot and sidings at Addiscombe in 1992–94. However by that time a new way of serving this district was emerging, one that also seemed likely to provide an alternative to other poorly-used local railways elsewhere in London. Croydon Tramlink was to take over the old SER alignment between Elmers End and its junction with the former Selsdon line south of Woodside station. Using this, a section of the Tramlink system was to replace the Addiscombe shuttle, providing a much more attractive service, since it offered a direct run westwards over street tracks via Addiscombe Road and past East Croydon station into the very centre of Croydon, with connections to the Mid Kent at Elmers End. Quite incidentally, it would also fulfil ambitions first expressed by the Mid Kent and SER in the middle of the nineteenth century.

Conventional rail services to Woodside and Addiscombe ceased after traffic on 31st May 1997 and changes in connection with Tramlink then saw Elmers End converted to a simple through station with the Up bay taken out of use.

The Woodside & South Croydon Line   (map page 41)

This local railway was virtually a southward extension of the Mid Kent line just considered. Croydon is a town well favoured with railways, most of them very busy, but this one was a real backwater. Never properly exploited as a through route and virtually superfluous for the residential traffic for which it was used, the Woodside & South Croydon Railway had its origins in the border battles between the LBSCR and SER. In the early 1860s, the Brighton was seeking to take a share of the Tunbridge Wells traffic from the SER, whilst the latter was casting its eyes towards Eastbourne, even Brighton itself. When the SER planned a direct main line from London (St John's) to Tonbridge via Sevenoaks, avoiding the long detour through Redhill, the Brighton nurtured a Surrey & Sussex Junction scheme, a short cut from Croydon to its Uckfield–Tunbridge Wells line near Groombridge. As this proposal (which obtained an act in 1865 and was incorporated in the LBSCR four years later) was a blatant invasion of what had been settled as SER territory, the latter replied by promotion of a London–Lewes and Brighton Railway in collusion with the LCDR. From junctions with the LCDR and SER at Beckenham, this main line, sanctioned in 1866, would have run south through the very heartlands of the LBSCR. If the scheme ever were a serious one, it was lost in the financial panic of the period, in which the LCDR almost went under. That company was forced to withdraw, and turning to a more amicable attitude with the Brighton, the SER threw the plans into a dark corner.

But for its part, the LBSCR kept the Surrey & Sussex Junction powers alive, just to make sure of staking its claim, and even started to build it, a move soon to be regretted, as the enterprise was attended with many problems and much misfortune. After a number of bridges, viaducts and some tunnels had been begun, the Brighton wished a quick end, seeing no profit in it, nor any virtue, now that it had concluded pooling arrangements with the SER. Denied Parliamentary powers to abandon the line, the LBSCR eventually escaped by paying the maximum statutory penalty for not completing it in the time laid down in the act.

A Down special train just south of Coombe Lane station in 1902, hauled by SECR 2-4-0 No.61A.

The half-finished works were left to nature, but the territory crossed by the route remained the object of contentious schemes and eventually much of the Surrey & Sussex Junction was used for the Croydon, Oxted and East Grinstead Railways. These were authorised in 1878 and taken up as a joint line by the now friendly SER and LBSCR as far as the point where the line from Croydon met the SER Redhill–Tonbridge route (Crowhurst Junctions). The CO&EGR was part of a framework of railways projected at this time to strengthen the LBSCR hold, but with some judicious accommodation of the SER interest in the border territories. Other lines were to link the CO&EGR to the Tunbridge Wells–East Grinstead line at Groombridge and to extend it at either end – to Lewes, and to Woodside, on the SER Mid Kent Line. They thus realised the route of the SER/LCDR joint proposal of 1866, providing the LBSCR with an alternative route between Croydon and Brighton, with the SER allowed access only to the northern section.

The 2m 29ch link at the London end, known as the Woodside & South Croydon Railway, was authorised in 1880. It was taken-over by the LBSCR and SER for joint working from 10th August 1882 under powers given in the original act and confirmed in the SER (Various Powers) Act, 1882.

The joint line from South Croydon to Oxted opened on 10th March 1884 and the link to Woodside, which had been constructed by Joseph Firbank, followed on 10th August 1885, with its intermediate passenger station in yellow stock brick at Coombe Lane. Woodside was rebuilt in brick by the SER, with a bay platform on the Down side for the new service. SER influence predominated elsewhere. All but a few signals at Selsdon Road were of that company's pattern and the junction station at that point, with its separate sets of platforms for the Oxted and Woodside lines, was in the SER timber style. It was the SER which started to work the line, the two companies sharing the local service over alternate years from 1st July 1889.

Diverging from the Mid Kent at Woodside Junction, 12ch south of Woodside station, the new double track was on embankment to a point beyond Bingham Road. For a mile or so the line skirted the eastern edge of built-up Croydon, much of it developed by the British Land Company after 1860. The Addiscombe Park, Ashburton, and other estates east of the railway were to show the first signs of development in the 1900s, but would not be fully covered until the late 1920s. Goods stations were forbidden in this area under a section of the 1880 act which protected Lady Ashburton's estates. Beyond Upper Addiscombe Road, the W&SCR passed into a cutting, skirting the high ground south-east of Croydon known as the

Bingham Road station, Up side 24th May 1975.
Alan A Jackson

Addington Hills, then entering three contiguous tunnels, Woodside (266yd), Park Hill (122yd) and Coombe Lane (157yd). Although the first and last of these were only a very short distance apart, a change in the nature of the soil made it necessary to construct the central section of what might otherwise have been one tunnel on the cut-and-cover principle and this formed what was to become a romantic timbered dell, where the roof of the covered way supported a miniature rifle range, opened before 1914. This part of the route bordered the eastern edge of the Park Hill and Woodbury Farm estates which had already been laid out with artistically-curved roads designed to accommodate large middle-class villas, but to the east, north of Coombe Lane, there was a great deal of open parkland, much of it still uncovered today. From the tunnel the line was on an embankment through Coombe Lane station, which also bore signs of SER origins. Beyond, the line turned south-west towards the Brighton main line, at first in a cutting through the Croham Park estate where villa building started in the 1890s. Emerging at ground level, it entered Selsdon Road station, making its junction with the Croydon, Oxted & East Grinstead at the south end of the platforms.

Most trains ran only between Woodside and Selsdon Road. The 1902 timetable shows 11 each way, worked by the SECR, plus the curious oddity of a Down train which went on to terminate at Dover. Through workings, which had increased to three each way by 1914, never assumed enough importance to remove the predomi-nantly local character of the service, which earns it a place in this book. Daily pick-up freights, two each way in 1902, worked from Bricklayers Arms to Tonbridge via the Mid Kent and Selsdon Road. In its early years the link was used by the SECR as a relief route for excursions between London and the Kent coast which returned to the main system via the Crowhurst spur. Use of this route became less frequent after the opening of the Chislehurst loops in 1902, but it continued well into the SR era.

Traffic through these still half-rural parts of east and south Croydon was very light at first, but Addiscombe gradually lapped up to the west side of the line and during the 1890s there were signs of increased building activity around Coombe Road station and between there and Selsdon Road. Either side of Croham Road, villas were erected close to the line in the 1890s and 1900s. Even so, working expenses normally exceeded revenue and in a creditable effort to exploit new suburban business at low cost, the number of journeys each way daily was increased in 1906 from about ten to 16, using the SECR Kitson steam railmotor units designed by Harry S. Wainwright. Working to and from the Down bay at Woodside, these cars, which were housed at Bricklayers Arms depot, began and ended their day on New Cross–Addiscombe trains. For this service, wooden halts with 100ft platforms were opened on 1st September 1906 at Bingham Road (between Woodside and Coombe Lane) and at Spencer Road (between Coombe Lane and Selsdon Road). Although surrounded by substantial late Victorian villas, Spencer Road Halt, reached only by footpaths, was very close to the existing stations at Selsdon Road and South Croydon. Bingham Road, adjacent to the Addiscombe terminus of the Croydon Corporation electric tramways (4th January 1902) became something of an interchange point, but general business remained very light despite the new housing. During its years of operation, the LBSCR employed pull-and-push units composed of a 'Terrier' 0–6–0T and a single coach, but in the 1910s the one-class Beyer Peacock steam railcars were transferred here from the Eastbourne–St Leonards service. Tickets for passengers boarding and leaving at the halts were issued and collected by the guard.

With its poor loadings easily diverted to alternative routes operated by the owning companies, the Woodside & South Croydon stood out as a clear victim for wartime economies. Railmotor service ceased after last journeys on 14th March 1915, when the halts were closed. Coombe Lane and Selsdon Road east platforms remained open for the few other trains until the evening of 31st December 1916, when these were also withdrawn, although Selsdon Road remained open on the Oxted line side. Empty stock, special trains, light engines and pick-up goods still worked over the line, the latter to and from the Mid Kent to call at the Selsdon Road yard, which was on the Down side of the passenger station at the London end. Local trains were not restored after the war. During 1927 the track was relaid, spawning false rumours that the line was to be re-opened for local traffic. However that summer the section was extensively used for trains from Hastings to Charing Cross/Cannon Street which worked via Tonbridge, Edenbridge and Oxted and rejoined the main line at St John's, a 70-mile journey but comparatively free of traffic. In the same year, mid week excursion trains to Canterbury West, Margate, Ramsgate, Brighton and Hastings starting from Lewisham Junction also ran via Woodside; these called at all stations to Woodside then at Selsdon Road. Similar summer workings probably continued until 1934, the year before electrification. There were also some hop-pickers' specials to and from Kent via the Crowhurst spur.

A 1925 scheme for a Southern Heights Light Railway was to have carried electric trains from Orpington to Sanderstead, connecting to SR lines. To integrate this with the rest of the system, it would have been necessary to electrify Woodside–Sanderstead, which offered a less congested route, with the possibility of convenient interchange at Elmers End with London trains and perhaps some through running via the Mid Kent. Although the Surrey Heights scheme was by then virtually dead, the SR did go ahead with the Sanderstead–Woodside electrification, the general manager cautiously telling the board in June 1934 that it was unlikely to do more than balance the books. This could not but be so, because despite a little more building development, mainly to the east of Bingham Road station, no part of the district served was very far from either Addiscombe or South Croydon stations. One cannot help wondering to what extent this decision was simply an obsession with the neatness of completing electrification of the Southern's London suburban lines.

Half-hourly electric trains, increased to three an hour in the peaks, ran between Charing Cross or Cannon Street and Sanderstead via Woodside from 30th September 1935. 'In view of the development in the area', Bingham Road Halt was replaced by a fully-equipped station at a cost of £10,000. Its brick entrances and covered staircases either side of the underline road bridge led to platforms supported on concrete piles driven into the embankment and sheltered by glazed wood and steel canopies. Spencer Road Halt, only a quarter-mile from South Croydon, was wisely discarded, but almost £7,200 was spent at Coombe Lane, reopened as Coombe Road, with extended concrete platforms and a new red brick, metal-windowed building on the Up side. Selsdon Road, renamed Selsdon (despite two uphill miles to the village) saw no changes, apart from lengthening of the Down platform and closure of the North box. The two-road goods yard here was subsequently enlarged to five roads. Sanderstead's Down platform was extended to 520ft.

Predictably, the electrification was not a success. Drastic cuts were made in World War 2 when trains ran only hourly off-peak, stopping altogether after 19.00 and after 15.00 on Saturdays, when there was no service until Monday morning. Pre-war intervals were restored in 1945 but from 26th September 1949 the through service to Cannon Street was withdrawn outside the peak hours, when two trains an hour shuttled between Elmers End and Sanderstead, connecting at the former with two of the four through trains an hour between Charing Cross and Hayes. This move further depleted the traffic, causing the complete withdrawal of service from 2nd November 1959 between 10.45 and 15.15 and after 20.45 on weekdays and 15.45 on Saturdays. A Railway Club party on Saturday morning 28th April 1962 found a 2EPB set waiting in the Up side bay at Elmers End, where some SER signs still survived. About 12 minutes were occupied in the run to Sanderstead, during which no passengers joined or alighted at the intermediate stations.

Further drastic falls in revenue led BR to propose complete closure from 4th March 1963, one of only two Southern Electric abandonments included in the Beeching Plan (the other was Horsted Keynes–Haywards Heath). After a successful protest lobby had been organised under the local MP, Transport Minister Ernest Marples announced in December 1963 a three-year reprieve followed by a review if the line was still not paying its way; it was stated that despite the existence of alternative routes, some hardship would ensue if service was withdrawn. Despite continuing unprofitability, the 1966 review led only to further pruning; from 2nd January 1967 the half-hourly Saturday peak shuttle (06.51 – 09.11; 11.51 – 14.11) was diverted to Addiscombe, and from 10th July that year, Bingham Road and Coombe Road were served only from 07.52 to 09.50 and between 16.17 and 19.10 on Mondays to Fridays, some afternoon trains reversing at Selsdon instead of Sanderstead. In April 1976 all through trains to and from London ceased, replaced by 2EPB 2-car sets shuttling between Elmers End and Selsdon or Sanderstead.

Selsdon goods yard, reduced to two roads, became a Shell oil-tanker depot in the 1960s. At the adjacent passenger station, the old SER timber buildings were demolished, leaving a station which consisted of short bits of the old canopy on each W&SCR platform and a tiny wooden booking hut on the Down side (Oxted line trains had ceased to call at their platforms in June 1959). When visited in 1975, gas lamps burned all day and the bare platforms still displayed Southern Railway signs (these also survived at Coombe Road and Bingham Road).

This quite hopeless operation, with each train carrying passenger loads which rarely if ever exceeded single figures, was kept going through the 1970s and early 1980s. Latterly there were nine morning Up trains, one starting from Selsdon, the rest from Sanderstead and seven return workings. Evening travellers had the choice of ten each way, including the 18.50 express from Sanderstead, fast from Selsdon to Elmers End. By the early 1980s fewer than 200 passengers a day were using these trains.

The inevitable end, so long postponed, came in 1983, passenger trains concluding with the 19.30 from Sanderstead on Friday 13th May, exploding detonators as it progressed and filled with people who had made little if any regular use of the line. A short length of track, between Selsdon Junction and Selsdon station was retained for working oil tank wagons into the depot on the Down side mentioned earlier. This traffic finally ceased in March 1983.

A scheme for conversion to roads was rejected, to give way to news that the Woodside and South Croydon was not to die completely. Much of the section between Woodside Junction and the site of Coombe Road station now forms part of the Croydon Tramlink light railway route mentioned earlier.

The Hayes (Kent) Branch
(map page 41)

A village of some 600 inhabitants, in Thorne's words 'quiet and respectable and chiefly dependent on wealthy residents', mid-Victorian Hayes was set in one of the prettiest parts of metropolitan Kent. Although touched by several schemes, fully examined in Trevor Woodman's book, it had to wait until 1882 for its railway.

The route from Hayes to the Mid Kent line was revived in 1879 when local interests led by Col. John Farnaby Lennard of West Wickham Court (a Cator Estate trustee) in collusion with an SER anxious to filch what it could from LCDR territory promoted what is now the Hayes branch. This was to pass through a district already unsuccessfully probed by the LCDR, tapping deep into the catchment area of the LCDR's Bromley station through a district which superficially seemed ripe for high class suburban development. Authorised by the West Wickham & Hayes Railway Act of 8th July 1880, the 3m 2f 9ch branch was laid out by Francis Brady, the SER's engineer. Provision was made in the act for the line to be worked by the SER, whose director Alexander Beattie sat on the local company's board; fellow directors included Brady and A M Watkin, the son of the SER chairman. Very quickly the SER took steps to bring the small company into its grasp, securing power to purchase it for £162,000 in 1881. At this time the SER entertained ideas of extending the line to Keston and Westerham but with the realisation that costly engineering work would be involved in penetrating into and through the North Downs, this idea was quickly dropped. Indeed in view of what was to happen regarding the release of land for housebuilding, something on which the local interest amongst the promoters might be expected to have had some foreknowledge, it is remarkable that the SER proceeded with construction of any part of the line.

But proceed it did, and on Whit Monday 29th May 1882, No. 258, a Cudworth outside frame 0–4–4 back tank, worked the ceremonial opening train and the first public services. Provision soon settled down to 13 trains each way, four on Sundays, with connections to the Addiscombe–London trains at Elmers End, where the station had been rebuilt with Up and Down bays and given a new 43-lever signal box. The Up side received a single storey building fitted out with ticket hall, waiting rooms and staff accommodation. There were also new coal sidings behind the Up side bay.

West Wickham, looking to Elmers End, c.1925. *Commercial postcard*

A sleepy country branch line terminus; Hayes in the 1900s.

For some fifty years the Hayes branch was to remain a very attractive country line, climbing some 100ft in a graceful reverse curve towards the Hayes terminus as it skirted around and between the large private estates of Park Langley, Eden Park and Monk's Orchard. At Elmers End, the double track left the country end of the station on a 13ch curve which brought its direction almost due east on to an embankment, climbing at 1 in 76 and 1 in 89. Eden Park, the first station, required by the owner of that estate, William R Mace, had no freight yard. Its building was the familiar cheaply-made SER affair of wooden boards under a slate roof with platform canopies of shallow arch section supported by slim pillars at the platform edge. The Down side had but a small shelter and was connected to the main entrance by an underline subway. Outside there were few signs of human habitation. The mansion of Langley Park was a quarter mile east and the hamlet of Upper Elmers End about the same distance west. A start had been made with some villas along South Eden Park, forming a tentative southward extension of Beckenham, and the southernmost one was sufficiently close to the new station for the tenants to express concern that the signalman might be able to overlook the back of the house. Whilst the line was under construction early in 1882 they succeeded in having the station box moved to the end of the platform. For many years this station was the quietest on the branch and was missed by some trains.

Soon after leaving Eden Park, the embankment ended and the next station, West Wickham, only 67ch further on, was approached in a cutting. Similar to its neighbour, with buildings on the Up side, it was given a goods yard at the London end on the Down side and a covered footbridge connected the platforms. It was sited in the hamlet of Wickham Green and the village from which it took its name, which had 963 inhabitants within its widespread boundaries, was about a quarter mile south. Close to the station a large hostelry, *The Railway Hotel*, was erected in 1882, primarily to serve refreshments and meals to the holidaymakers who arrived by train in fine weather to enjoy the beautiful countryside.

Still on a rising gradient and now in a deep cutting, the railway then ran south east and east into the terminus, with a slight decline at the extreme end of its route. Here was a wide single platform on the south side with a wooden passenger building parallel to the line at the east end, where the track terminated at a locomotive turntable which served the run round road. The building was similar in style to those at Eden Park and West Wickham. Later the west end of the platform was given an additional face, with the bay road terminating against the west end of the station building. A goods yard was laid out on the south side. The 17-lever signal box, on the north side at the west end of the layout was moved in 1935 to the Up side and equipped with a 33-lever frame. Passengers bound for the main street of the village were obliged to climb for a quarter mile up to the Bromley Road. Scattered all round, well ensconced amid the trees of their spacious parks, were the houses of the wealthy residents mentioned by Thorne; *Hayes Place, Hayes Court, Baston Manor, Pickhurst* and *Holwood*.

Here and elsewhere along the branch nothing much changed for many years after the opening. This was no doubt a great disappointment to the promoters and the SER, but the owners of most of the large estates, who had not supported the line, kept their acres inviolate until the early 1920s, speculators not being encouraged. As already mentioned, a few costly villas in ample plots appeared along the west side of the road north from Eden Park station. There was also some building at West Wickham village, and a few more bourgeois 'seats' were cut out of the countryside around Hayes. None of this produced much traffic: indeed business was so poor at Eden Park that it was closed completely on Sundays for a time from March 1905, then reopened with a restricted service until the whole branch lost its Sunday trains as a wartime sacrifice after Sunday 31st December 1916. Although trains ran in the summer from 1920, year-round Sunday working was not restored until Easter 1923.

In such circumstances there was little improvement in the train service on weekdays, virtually unchanged at 15 journeys each way in 1900 and increased only to 18 by 1912. There were no through workings for businessmen until around the turn of the century; even as late as 1912 there were but two up in the morning and one back in the evening. One of these, the 08.37 from Hayes, offered distinguished accommodation in 1909 when it was made up with Continental Boat Train stock. Reaching Charing Cross (14½ miles) in 51 minutes after missing Elmers End, New Beckenham, Lower Sydenham, Lewisham and St Johns, it formed the 10.00 departure for Folkestone. Other oddities were recorded: in the early 1920s the branch was served by a locomotive shedded at Purley which reached its workplace via the then closed Woodside-Selsdon line, making no less than three reversals on the way. As Hayes had a turntable, tender as well as tank engines were seen in SER days. About 1906 the SECR railmotor No 4 was briefly used.

Before the two great rivals made their peace in 1898, the LCDR was offered at least one opportunity to recover such traffic as was leaking out to the SER via Hayes. A 3-mile single line was promoted in 1895 from Bromley LCDR station to a point about ¾-mile short of Farnborough. This railway, which would have given Hayes a second station on the east side of the village, received insufficient support, as did a London Southern Light Railway, which promoted three years later an electric tramway of standard gauge from Herne Hill through Bromley to Farnborough.

It was electric traction, coinciding with economic conditions highly favourable to the large-scale building of small houses for sale to the lower middle-class which was to bring about a complete and rapid transformation on the Hayes branch. The SR laid the third rail* in 1925, operating a public service with a 3-car train from 21st September. This working, for staff tuition, connected with steam trains at Elmers End, not running through to and from London until 28th February 1926. Full electric services started on 19th July, offering a 30-minute frequency seven days a week, connecting at Elmers End with half hourly workings between Addiscombe and London. A small number of through trains ran in business hours between London and Hayes. At Elmers End the train from Hayes ran into the Up bay before the Up train arrived from Addiscombe; after that had left, the branch train crossed over to the Down bay to make cross-platform connection with the next Down Addiscombe service.

The pace of building development was such that before very long it was necessary to augment the service. At last land was being released in quantity for building and the speculative builders' impact on this hitherto favoured area was severe. A Southern Railway residential guide of early 1926 found Hayes 'barely altered from what it was thirty years ago . . . perhaps a few more houses near the station on the London side' and it was necessary to go as far as Keston Park, 1½ miles south-east, a former estate of the Earl of Derby, to find new developments; here 'numerous houses of character and charm' were going up along a new road called Forest Drive, from £800 upwards. It was also noted that the northern part of Langley Park had been sold for building, but the houses were nearer to the old LCDR main line than the Hayes branch. At West Wickham the only signs of activity were a few new houses near the station (Barnfield Road), at Beckenham Road and Hawes Lane, and scattered in Monk's Orchard Park. Early in 1927 the *Sunday Express* dramatically reported the great sense of shock at West Wickham when it was discovered that the recently departed rector had sold some of the glebe land to a speculative builder, a move which made the privileged middle-class residents anxious about the future of their still delightfully rural retreat. This was indeed the year when large-scale building began to get under way, at first in the form of semis and small detached houses on both sides of the railway at the country end of West Wickham station.

Three years later the fields and copses south of the tracks between Eden Park and Elmers End were under the builder, but at Hayes itself nothing much happened until about 1931, following the sale of Hayes Place, Hayes Grove, and other private parks. Then many new streets were laid out south of the station and the large Morrell Coney Hall Estate, somewhat remote from the railway on this side, was completed between 1933 and 1935. By 1938 Beckenham had flowed over the line between

---

* On part of the branch, a *fourth* rail was laid, usually between the running rails and bonded to these, with the object of increasing their capacity to return the earth current.

Elmers End and Eden Park, while new houses, mostly the ubiquitous three-bedroom semis, now covered the area for a mile or more south of West Wickham station and almost two miles westwards towards Shirley. North of the line, long streets of red-tiled 'ideal homes' on the Langley Park estate stretched north towards Bromley whilst at Hayes, where prices tended to be a little higher, some reaching £2,500 when the average semi was between £600 and £800, the station was quite surrounded. To the south the frontier of London had been pushed well into the foothills of the North Downs, cosy suburban sitting and bedrooms looking out over seemingly limitless Kentish countryside at White Shaw Well Wood.

Copywriters for the SR guides enthused, making the best of these raw wounds on the face of what had been some of the finest countryside at the edge of London. They talked rather naughtily of:

> These beautiful estates, yielding to the pressure from the centre and what in the past has been jealously maintained for the pleasure and satisfaction of a few owners, is becoming available for homes in a beautiful country, for innumerable families . . . with a beautiful country village to work upon, and no residue of mean streets to contend with, the creators of modern West Wickham have everything in their favour, and the various estates are being planned and laid out in a tasteful manner so as to secure the best possible advantage from the natural beauties of the district.

Within nine years the railway's traffic increased almost 12-fold, reflecting the builders' bonanza:

	Passenger tickets issued		Season tickets issued	
	1925	1934	1925	1934
Eden Park	8,358	75,841	61	4,188
West Wickham	46,985	251,024	336	18,711
Hayes	21,856	177,424	159	5,831

West Wickham became the busiest commuter station on the branch, with 1,586 season ticket holders in 1935, Hayes running a poor second with 746 and Eden Park almost out of the contest with a mere 300. West Wickham had been transformed from village to small town, with a population in 1934 of 10,080 compared with the 1,301 of 1921. This huge growth produced much of the off-peak as well as commuter traffic as very few of the new home owners had cars and bus services were not well-developed or (to London) fast enough. By 1932 there were three trains an hour through to London, one to Cannon Street, two to Charing Cross, a frequency increased to four in commuter hours. Before another three years had passed, the service was built up to a 15 minute interval through the day, two an hour confined to the branch in the off-peak. The 1939 timetables provided a half hourly service between Charing Cross and Hayes, with another two trains an hour on the branch itself, weekdays and Sundays. Between 17.00 and 18.00 on weekdays there were two trains to Hayes from Charing Cross and two more from Cannon Street. Wartime conditions saw a reduction in the through trains off peak to hourly.

For a few more years people were still coming down by train to the area to enjoy the countryside, despite the relentless advance of suburbia. Whit Monday 1930 saw 21,000 passengers using Hayes station, few of whom would have been local residents, and one Lewisham firm was still bringing its staff by train to Hayes for their annual beanfeast.

To increase revenue and accommodate the swollen business, the SR decided in June 1933 to rebuild Hayes at a cost of £14,000 with shops on the street side and the ticket office and other facilities grouped around a spacious entrance hall. This work, which included a new island platform with a 200ft canopy, was completed in 1935. More coal wharves were added in the following year to feed the thousands of new tiled fireplaces and slow-combustion hot water stoves.

Not all the new building was houses and shops. In June 1928 a trailing connection was proposed from the Up line east of Eden Park for Harold Arnold & Son Ltd, contractors for the Royal Bethlem Hospital to be erected in Monk's Orchard Park. Controlled from a two-lever ground frame released from West Wickham box, this siding was built at a cost of £750, almost all met by Arnolds, whose locomotive worked the ¾-mile line south into the site. All was removed after construction was completed in 1930, this being the last of several examples of railways into large mental hospitals, some of which survived to give regular service.

Although the building boom promised well to spread further south-east into already suburbanised Keston and Farnborough, nothing more was heard of extension beyond Hayes. One reason for this was the Southern's interest in the Southern Heights Light Railway, proposed in 1925 to connect Orpington to Sanderstead via Farnborough and Biggin Hill. After the collapse of that scheme in 1932 there were suggestions that the Hayes branch be extended to Biggin Hill and Tatsfield, where, according to a correspondent to *The Railway Magazine* in February 1935, 'business men have to depend on Green Line coaches and consequently have a bad time when it is foggy'.

Standing in the path of German bombers flying towards London from French airfields, the Hayes branch did not escape damage in World War 2. Bombs fell in the area of Hayes station on the night of 15th/16th September 1940, wrecking the ticket office and the recently rebuilt frontage (Kent House station and Penge tunnel were also hit in the same attack). Then on 10th May 1941 a direct hit was registered on West Wickham station, the bomb landing between the platforms, severely mauling the SER structures. The several serious incidents at Elmers End have already been noted. In all these cases patching-up repairs and restoration of train services was quickly achieved but major reconstruction was to prove another matter.

SER rural style architecture at Eden Park, Up side, 17th September 1980. *Alan A Jackson*

Hayes (Kent) looking east to buffers c.1925 just after the SR electrification, for which the platform has been rebuilt. Otherwise the SER country branch line aura will remain a few more years.
Lens of Sutton

The war-torn building at Hayes became increasingly shabby, so annoying the Chamber of Commerce that in October 1955 volunteers were offered to repaint it, an action which appears to have shamed BR. It was neatly restored in the following year. Seventeen years after its bomb (1958) West Wickham was handsomely reconstructed in brick, with adequate canopies on the platforms. At that time this station had around 1,500 season ticket holders, much the same number as in 1935, but by then it had been overtaken by Hayes, where building in the late 1930s and the 1950s had increased the number to around 2,000.

High traffic levels were maintained throughout the war and for some years afterwards. By 1950 the branch had retrieved its pre-war basic frequency of four trains an hour, weekdays and Sundays, and around that time the Up bay connection at Elmers End was put out of use and the crossover at the start of the branch reversed to allow four-car Hayes trains to work in and out of the Down bay if required.

As almost everywhere at suburban stations, the Beeching regime saw the ending of public freight services. West Wickham yard (where over 11,000 tons of solid fuel had been brought in by rail as late as 1958) was closed from 2nd September 1963, Hayes from 19th April 1965. However the terminus continued for a little longer to handle a rather special type of traffic: greyhound dogs moving between Catford Stadium's local training kennels and Ireland.

With the spread of car ownership, loadings dwindled as many of the declining number of central London commuters drove to join the faster and superior services at Bromley South station and Beckenham Junction. Slack hour trains, which are subject to bus competition for local journeys, were trimmed to three an hour from 15th September 1958 and two from 17th June 1963, reflecting the fall in usage. Suggestions were made in the late 1970s that Hayes might become the outer terminal of a proposed new Fleet Line tube railway, running over the Mid Kent from Lewisham but, renamed the Jubilee Line, that project was in due time diverted to serve the Docklands and Stratford. The line's future as a conventional electrified passenger railway remains questionable.

Elmers End, once the junction of three rail services, is now being served only by Hayes trains and Tramlink. Should traffic levels continue to decline, it may well become a suburban terminus, with Hayes served by an extension of Tramlink over the railway alignment.

The Central Croydon Branch

(map page 41)

Another of Croydon's railway backwaters was created by the pressure of competition in the early 1860s, principally those coming from the direction of the Mid Kent and SER as just described. Between 1839 when the first station opened, and the mid-century railway boom Croydon's population had grown from about 16,000 to over 50,000. At that time it became important to stake out claims in this prosperous district on the edge of London, and SER, LCDR and other schemes for lines to or through central Croydon were on the engineers' drawing boards. As a defensive move, the LBSCR accordingly inserted into its 1864 legislation a half-mile spur pompously entitled the Croydon Central Railway. This was to start close to the intersection of the High Street and Katharine Street, where a small amount of property demolition was necessary, and ran east and north-east to a junction facing London at the south end of East Croydon station, joining the widening to South Croydon that had been authorised a year earlier.

Central Croydon was a modest terminus, its appearance of no particular merit or dignity. There were but two platforms parallel to the south side of Katharine Street, protected by sawtooth canopies, and separated by two centre roads which could be used for rolling stock storage or engine release. Under a glass canopy behind the buffers was a narrow headway connected to the main building by two short flights of steps. At right angles to Katharine Street and served by a small cab yard, this block included a two-storey stationmaster's house at the north end. Beyond the platform, the four tracks converged to two, flanked on the north side by a retaining wall below Katharine Street.

From the opening on 1st January 1868, there were 12 trains from London Bridge, mostly calling at all stations and taking 38 minutes, and 13 trains Up. Another four Down and three Up ran between Central Croydon and Kensington (Addison Road). Sundays saw only one Down and two Up between the terminus and London Bridge, plus three each way to and from Clapham Junction. A year later, this service was augmented when the LNWR Euston–Kensington (Addison Road)–New Croydon trains were reorganised as an LBSCR working between Kensington and New or Central Croydon via Clapham Junction and Crystal Palace. Two of the Kensington trains ran semi-fast, completing the run across the south-western suburbs in 31 minutes.

Central Croydon, looking to buffers, possibly just before re-opening in June 1886.

Looking south from the road bridge at East Croydon c.1890, LBSCR main line to Brighton straight ahead, Central Croydon branch and LNWR train for Willesden Junction at right.

Old habits died hard and as boarding a train at Central Croydon so often meant changing at New Croydon to increase the speed of the journey or to reach the required destination, Croydonians made little use of their new facility. In-and-out working of a much larger number of trains through triangular junctions might have done much to improve matters, but never very enthusiastic about what was to them largely a political line, the LBSCR decided to run it down, reducing the service by the beginning of November 1871 to a mere three each way on the London Bridge route and one afternoon journey from Victoria. Complete closure followed after the last train of 30th November.

Croydon's expansion continued without interruption through the 1870s and 1880s and following a request from the newly-formed corporation, the LBSCR agreed to re-open the terminus from 1st June 1886, demonstrating its lack of interest by leaving it to be served by other companies' trains. Initially there were merely five LNWR workings each way to and from Willesden Junction Low Level via Crystal Palace and Kensington, an extension of a service which had terminated at New Croydon since 1st May 1875. Calling at all stations except Wormwood Scrubs, these trains completed the cross-London run in about 55 minutes. Seven more trains each way used Central Croydon from 1st February 1887, when GER Liverpool Street-New Cross workings via the East London Railway were extended on weekdays, taking about 50 minutes.

Once again, the public made little use of a station that had proved to be less convenient for the expanding residential areas south and east of the town than the older facilities at West, East, New and South Croydon, with their vastly superior services. LNWR and GER trains were cut back to New Croydon after the weekend of 30th–31st August 1890, whereupon the site of the terminus was sold to the corporation for its new municipal buildings. This complex, which included Croydon's third town hall, a public library, and public gardens on the site of the approach tracks, was started in 1892 and completed in four years. In the course of the work a wall was erected across the truncated spur just west of the bridge under Park Lane, the rest of the line forming the nucleus of Fairfield Yard, which was used for permanent way and engineering purposes until February 1933. Soon after that the land was sold to Croydon corporation, which left it as a car park until the Fairfield Halls and other buildings were erected on it in the 1960s. The bridge under Park Lane had been filled in about 1931 and today the only relics of this curious LBSCR appendage are the retaining wall in the Town Hall Gardens and some earthworks near the site of the junction.

The Bromley North Branch   (map page 41)

We have already seen something of the mutual rivalry over territory that existed between the SER and the LCDR before they finally reached agreement to work together from January 1899 as the SECR. As soon as one company served a town of any size, the other did its best to get there too. In Bromley, the story has a twist.

SER trains were in the town first, only to be ousted by the Chatham's, whereupon the South Eastern built a new line to get back. Ten miles south-east of London, Bromley, a market town with some 5,000 inhabitants, was still a quite separate place in the middle of the nineteenth century although the wooded hills around and its coach services to and from London were already securing it some popularity as a residential area for wealthy City men. Railways came first from the north-west in the form of the Mid Kent, opened from Lewisham to Beckenham on 1st January 1857. This line was worked by the SER, but the independent West End of London & Crystal Palace, an LBSCR protégé, also reached Beckenham from Norwood soon after, going on over single track to terminate at New Bromley (now Shortlands) about a half-mile west of the town centre. Over the latter, from its opening on 3rd May 1858, the WEL&CPR worked a shuttle service between New Bromley and Crystal Palace in connection with trains thence to the Pimlico (Battersea) terminus operated by the LBSCR, giving passengers from New Bromley an alternative to the London Bridge service via the Mid Kent.

The SER was interested in using the Mid Kent to get to Bromley and beyond, and a single line called the Mid Kent (Bromley to St Mary Cray) Railway, worked by the SER, was opened from New Bromley to Southborough Road (now Bickley) on 5th July 1858 through a station at Bromley on the site of the Charity Schools which was not ready until 22nd November. Now Bromley South, this was almost as far south of the town as New Bromley was to the west, but gradually the centre of Bromley grew down towards its station. The final developments of this first phase of Bromley's railway history occurred in 1860, when from 1st October it became possible to travel via the WEL&CPR (by then part of the LBSCR) to the new London terminus of Victoria, and when from 3rd December, the western extension of the LCDR reached Bickley, opening a through rail service between London (Victoria) and Canterbury, where there were road connections to Dover. The section between New Bromley (Shortlands) and Bickley, doubled in 1860, was leased to the LCDR from 1st September 1863.

For a while the SER continued to reach Bromley by means of through coaches off the Mid Kent somewhat unenthusiastically attached to LCDR trains at Beckenham, but after 30th September 1866 SER service was not available east of Beckenham.

The SER directors were reluctant to give up Bromley, their interest reviving after the completion of their cut-off main line from Lewisham (St Johns) to Tonbridge in 1868. Nor were the citizens of the town content to remain at the mercy of an LCDR monopoly. As the amenities of the area had attracted many more commuters since the opening of a station, there was much interest in improving communication with the City. An 1863 scheme for a link between the SER main line at Grove Park and the LCDR at Shortlands fizzled out, as did a more ambitious proposal of 1865 for a line from Grove Park, passing under Bromley and the LCDR in tunnel, and going on to Hayes, where it forked, one branch to the west to rejoin the SER near Elmers End, the other through the foothills of the North Downs to serve Keston and Farnborough.

By 1871, Bromley's population had doubled to over 10,000, but there were nearly 2,000 uninhabited houses. Unremitting local pressure for a direct line to the City, with the near certainty that the SER could be tempted back into Bromley produced a bill for a Bromley Direct Railway in 1873, a modest local promotion for a line of only 1m 5f 183yd southwards from Grove Park (where the SER had opened a station on 1st November 1871) to a terminus in 'New Bromley' north of the town centre, close to the main gate of Bromley Palace. The main force behind this scheme was William Dallison Starling, a prominent Bromley citizen and member of the Local Board until his resignation in 1870 over the sewerage question. Horsburgh, the local historian, describes him as 'an arrogant and pompous man', but as is often the case with such people, he got things done.

The 'Direct' in the title referred to the City, for the new line would bring Bromley within 8¾ miles of London Bridge compared with the 11¾ miles run on the LCDR to Blackfriars Bridge. To the West End, the new route gave only a quarter-mile saving to Charing Cross against the LCDR route to Victoria, any time reduction being eroded by the tedious reversals at Cannon Street.

After acquiring its act in 1874, the little company came under the wing of the SER, but although there was power to make agreements with that company for working and use, nothing was signed until 1876; a further act of 1877 extended sanction for agreements to cover maintenance, management, and the fixing, collection, and apportionment of receipts.

An SER director was in due course appointed chairman and the SER engineer acted for the small company. Lucas & Aird, the trusted SER contractors, started to build the railway in March 1877 after signing a £39,500 contract. Stations and signalling followed SER designs and practice. Eventually, under an SER Act of 1879, the Bromley Direct was transferred to that company from 21st July that year, for a consideration of £55,000 worth of SER 4½ per cent Preference Stock, that sum being the statutory capital.

Train service started without ceremony on 1st January 1878, 26 Down and 23 Up, eight Down and seven Up on Sundays, but in the following year this settled down at a slightly lower level, about 19 each way. Except during peak hours, passengers normally changed at Grove Park, where after rebuilding of the station most trains terminated in the Up side bay. Connections were not always smartly made, but the best through trains reached London Bridge in 21 minutes, Charing Cross in 30.

As constructed, the line was only 1½ miles long. At Grove Park, where there were at first only the two side platforms for the main line and branch services, the double track curved away southwards from the country end, on embankment for the first mile and climbing at 1 in 92 along the western edge of Sundridge Park estate. There followed a cutting in which a small station called Plaistow was built to appease the owner of Sundridge Park, E. H. (later Sir Edward) Scott, whose property extended from here to the main line at Elmstead Wood. West of the station, there was already some sign of residential development, small villas in three or four new roads of the 1860s forming a northern satellite of Bromley. For the remaining 35ch to the terminus the line rose at 1 in 74, crossing a busy footpath on the level just before entering the terminus (an iron footbridge was erected here about 1901).

Entirely without shame, the SER accorded Bromley one of those cheap and nasty slate-roofed clap-boarded wooden sheds that it considered adequate for both suburban and country village stations at this period. This shack, with its three brick

Sundridge Park, looking north, 2nd February 1958. At this time most SER features were intact and the only major change in 60 years or so was the SR electric lighting on the platforms.
Alan A Jackson

chimneys and valanced canopy over the alternately dusty and muddy cab approach, was sited alongside the departure platform. The other platform, also occasionally used for departures, just to confuse the customers, could only be reached by crossing the three tracks between the platforms, all of which converged at the south end on to a small engine turntable. A goods yard on the west side had a separate wooden office alongside the passenger building. To supplement the office accommodation and add insult to injury, a disused passenger carriage was later dumped on the footway of the cab road.

Citizens of a town described by Thorne as having a 'quiet air of conscious respectability' were affronted by the crudity of the station. On this there was nothing but prevarication from the SER but their other grievance about waits at Grove Park was mollified by timetable revisions of the early 1880s. Some of the more charitable souls were apt to suggest that the SER terminus at Bromley was of a temporary nature pending extension southwards into the railwayless downlands, but this was merely castles in the air.

To Plaistow's population of over 2,000 in 1871 many more houses were added in the last two decades of the century, some of them small and cheap enough to attract City clerks. By the middle 1890s the district was virtually joined to Bromley and in 1896, no doubt with every show of reluctance, the SER was persuaded to construct brick waiting rooms and lavatories on the Up side and a urinal on the other platform. A covered footbridge in the centre of the station linked the platforms to the usual SER wooden building at the top of the cutting on the Down side. A short cobbled cab road descended past this to a gate on the platform. Perhaps seeking to give the district a slightly more select status, but also to distinguish it from the LTSR station of the same name, the SER used the name Sundridge Park from 1st July 1894. Despite population growth, no changes were made at Bromley, but in the 1880s a bay for the branch was provided at the country end of the Grove Park Up platform. In 1903, with the quadrupling of the main line, Grove Park was rebuilt with three island platforms (the SR later added an Up loop platform). The westernmost faces were allocated to the branch.

From the opening until about 1903 the trains were composed of solid teak four-wheelers. That they were replaced with nothing much more modern is evident from an accident report of 1919, which reveals that the Bromley North Up train which ran into the rear of one from Dartford at Parks Bridge Junction was made up with two sets of six four-wheelers with three six-wheelers. In the early 1890s about half the trains shuttled between Grove Park and Bromley, whilst the remainder ran to and from London as the rear portions (about ten four-wheelers) of slow main line trains. Separate trains to and from London were worked in the rush hours, usually by 0–4–4T. The practice of working on and off the branch into the main line slows continued on a decreasing scale until the early 1920s.

By 1912, when Bromley's population had reached over 33,000, the service had been built up to 30 each way daily (12 on Sundays) to and from Charing Cross or Cannon Street, although the last train of the day was the 00.33 from Holborn Viaduct (the SER and LCDR were of course worked by a Joint Committee after 1st January 1899). At busy times as many as five locomotives could be seen in Bromley station and yard, the passenger locomotives usually 0–4–4T of the SER 'Q' and SECR 'H' classes.

When the SR took over the unfulfilled SER electrification scheme which had included the branch, some thought was given to the stations. It was at first suggested that it the terminus were moved a little to the north, Sundridge Park could be closed (they were so close that the headshunt of Bromley North goods yard almost reached the country end of Sundridge Park Up platform) but this plan was discarded in place of extending the existing Sundridge Park platforms to take eight-car electric trains and giving Bromley an entirely new station on the old site at cost of £32,000. As if the new SR somehow wished to make up for its predecessor's insult to Bromley's municipal dignity, when the new terminus appeared it was a surprisingly elegant and handsome structure, neo-classical in style under a pillared and coppered cupola 60ft above the street. Built in brick with stone facings under a hipped tiled roof, its two large square Georgian windows flanked a high round-arched entrance. There was a 5,000sq ft forecourt on the site of the old locomotive turntable but, as Charles Klapper once pointed out, no attempt was ever made to encourage the bus operators whose many services converged on Bromley to use the front of the station as an interchange point. This situation has been rectified in recent years – the old goods yard is now a bus station.

The 1925 Bromley North station building before and after completion.

The lofty 780sq ft booking hall with its train indicator led on to a 2,360sq ft concourse under a three-span glazed roof. Here there was an exit to Shermans Road, a bookstall and waiting rooms; iron gates guarded a 30ft wide island platform protected for most of its 520ft by a glazed umbrella awning. In the west wing of the main building was a large parcels office. Space considerations prevented construction of a balancing east wing until such time as the road layout was changed. Eleven lock-up shops contributed some revenue to offset the capital cost of this fine station, opened in partly unfinished state on 27th December 1925. During the work, which included construction of a new goods yard, Bromley Council allowed the use of its rail-served depot for public freight traffic, but this siding was taken out of use soon after the completion of the new station.

Electrification on the SR standard 660V third-rail system proceeded simultaneously, the first trial working running down the branch on 19th November 1925. Some services to and from Cannon Street were electrically worked from 28th February 1926, but the full timetable did not operate until 19th July when there were 54 Up and 52 Down trains on weekdays, 32 each way on Sundays, a basic interval of 30 minutes seven days a week with four an hour (alternately Cannon Street and Charing Cross) in the business periods. This replaced the 1925 steam service of 37 Up and 33 Down (16 each way on Sundays). With electric working Charing Cross–Bromley North timings were reduced to a minimum of 23 minutes Up and 21 minutes Down compared with 31 Up and 27 Down by steam haulage.

Bromley North had long been favoured with late night and early morning trains to and from Holborn Viaduct via London Bridge, a convenience which had encouraged newspaper, postal and market workers to live in the town. These were continued for many years after electrification, some of them still steam-worked: thus in 1933 the last electric from Charing Cross to Bromley North at 23.38 was followed down by a steam-hauled 00.40 from Holborn Viaduct, the service reopening with a 03.22 Bromley North–Charing Cross and a 04.20 Bromley North–Holborn Viaduct, both steam trains, the latter a push-and-pull set.

In the catchment area around Bromley North little space remained for new housing in the 1920s, but the excellent electric train service fostered building immediately north of Sundridge Park station. There was also some development in the late 1920s and the 1930s on the western fringes of the Sundridge Park Estate.

Wartime exigencies reduced the off-peak branch service to hourly, but the 30-minute interval was restored on 31st May 1948. The post-war pattern became half-hourly seven days a week, with alternate weekday trains terminating at Charing Cross or Cannon Street (all at Charing Cross on Sundays). Some late night working survived: the 03.30 Bromley North–Holborn Viaduct and the 01.00 down from Holborn Viaduct on Monday to Saturday nights inclusive. Normal times to Charing Cross were 25 minutes, Cannon Street 22 minutes, but some peak-hour semi-fasts reduced this by three or four minutes. Working in ten-car formation at peak periods from 4th March 1957, 4EPB and 2EPB sets had replaced the 4SUBs. The branch still required one freight working daily, usually behind a C2X 0-6-0 or N 2-6-0, to and from Hither Green Yard. There was little or no outward traffic, but domestic fuel and building materials provided inward loads. After a brief period of diesel haulage from June 1961, freight service ceased from 20th May 1968. Bromley North tracks were then reduced to the arrival and departure roads and a single berthing siding alongside the departure road on the north side, was subsequently removed.

From 4th February 1962 electro-mechanical signalling with three-aspect colour lights replaced the manually-worked semaphores but the new signal box at Bromley North became virtually redundant after the closure of the freight yard, opening only when the departure platform or the berthing siding were required for use. At all other times as soon as a train arrived at platform two, the departure route on to the Up side could be set up automatically.

Service changes after the late 1950s reflected the decline in off-peak usage. From 15th September 1958 a two-car shuttle was worked on the branch after 22.00 and all day on Sundays. This was extended to all day on Saturdays from May 1973. Sundridge Park was closed on Sundays from 16th September 1962 and all Sunday trains were withdrawn in June 1981 as well as the late evening services.

Commuter traffic was also declining. A 1977 survey showed a drop in season ticket sales from 1,708 to 768 over the previous ten years. From 14th May 1984, commuters had only one through train (to Charing Cross) with a ten-minute shuttle to connect with other services at Grove Park. All through services to London ceased from 14th May 1990. At the time of writing, the branch remains fully signalled double track, even down to the unnecessary luxury of a platform indicator at Sundridge Park for Bromley North where only one platform is normally used. This extravagance cannot last much longer; various alternative developments, such as a Docklands Light Rail service from Lewisham or an extension of Croydon Tramlink from Beckenham Junction to Grove Park via Bromley centre have already been proposed. Alignments will need to be considered in relation to schemes that commercial pressures will no doubt bring forward for alternative and more profitable uses for the railway land in the centre of Bromley, including the now listed 1925 terminal building and the goods yard site, at present still an open air bus station.

Crystal Palace Railways   (map page 41)

'The most ordinary mode of transit from London to the Palace is by rail . . . special trains are despatched from the principal London stations as occasion may require.' Filled out with much detail on train services and fares, this announcement in Dickens's 1896 guidebook is a reminder that the Crystal Palace, as a permanent feature of London life for over 80 years owed its very existence and its sustenance to railways. After the Great Exhibition of 1851 was over, the board of the London, Brighton & South Coast Railway were very much involved in a proposal to reproduce Joseph Paxton's Hyde Park masterpiece in even more splendid style in their part of south London. With strong backing from Paxton, and in characteristically Victorian manner, they set out with the highest motives; the benefit of the masses, who would have in the new Crystal Palace a great centre of recreation, education and culture; but at the same time they took great care that the maximum returns should come to the shareholders of the railway company. A director of the LBSCR, Leo Schuster, was persuaded without much difficulty to part with his mansion and park, Penge Place, for £86,661. Situated between Sydenham and Norwood this, together with some adjoining land, some 280 acres in all, offered a superb elevated site for the new mecca of the hoi polloi. In May 1852 a Crystal Palace Company was formed under the chairmanship of Samuel Laing MP, the LBSCR chairman, with the LBSCR a majority shareholder. The materials of the Hyde Park building were bought and in the absence of direct railway communication, had to be moved by horses over 20 miles of roads culminating in the cruel one in eight of

Crystal Palace LBSCR station; the 'East Station', looking west about 1914. This view shows the overhead wire electrification which came into use on 12th May 1911, its installation made easier by the removal of the overall roof in 1906. In the background is the 284ft South Tower of the Palace which survived the 1936 fire but was demolished in 1940.

Sydenham Hill. The project was carried out with such expedition that on 5th August 1852 Laing was ceremonially erecting the first column of the new structure. Building by Fox, Henderson & Co. then went ahead in earnest under the personal supervision of Paxton, who took up residence at Rock Hill, a large house in the northern corner of the grounds.

Although the site was close to the LBSCR's Sydenham and Penge stations on the Brighton main line from London Bridge, a new station with direct covered communication to the Palace was planned. This required new railways, the first of which was a 1m 5ch spur from south of Sydenham station to the south side of the grounds, authorised, together with an enlargement of London Bridge station, in the LBSCR Act of 1853. It opened for goods traffic on 27th March 1854 in time to carry some of the final building materials and the exhibits. To handle the heavy passenger movements expected, the LBSCR built two more platforms at London Bridge and widened its line between Bricklayers Arms and Norwood Junction to four tracks. At Sydenham, the Down line serving the new spur was carried over the main lines, an early example of a railway flyover, into a large station to be described in a moment.

Passenger service began with the first of a series of special trains from London Bridge at 10.00 on 10th June 1854, the day Queen Victoria was to declare the great enterprise open to the public. Normal service, usually of 12 four-wheel coaches, was half-hourly from London Bridge (22 trains a day each way).

At first, the Brighton directors were not denied the fruits of their efforts; daily traffic totals reached 10,000, whilst on special occasions such as the inauguration of the fountains on 18th June 1856, the demand was so great that London Bridge was choked with crowds determined to reach the delights of Sydenham Hill. On one day in 1859, 112,000 people were conveyed to the Palace by train, 70,000 via London Bridge and Sydenham.

On 4th August 1853 a second line, the West End of London & Crystal Palace, was authorised to run in continuation of the LBSCR spur via Streatham and Balham to a terminus on the south bank of the Thames opposite Pimlico. An independent promotion, set in a strategic position to attract the attention of the larger companies, it was designed to act as a main line into the West End. Relationships with the LBSCR, which agreed to work it, were cordial and a service began on 1st December 1856 to Wandsworth Common, a temporary station at the north end of the common, which closed on 31st May 1858. Pimlico (on the south bank) was reached on 29th March 1858 and Victoria on 1st October 1860. As it provided the first access to central London for the LCDR, this line is strictly outside the present terms of reference, but a full account of its history is available.*

For the two lines, the LBSCR erected a fine station at Crystal Palace with two terminal roads and two through lines serving the Sydenham spur (the 'East Station'), and two through lines and two bay roads on the West End of London & Crystal Palace (the 'West Station'). The latter line was continued southwards to Norwood Junction on 1st October 1857 and was linked to the Mid Kent (Bromley and St Mary Cray) Railway (later the LCDR) at Bromley (now Shortlands) on 3rd May 1858 to provide the main line access already mentioned. For quick loading and unloading of crowds, the through lines in the East station had platforms either side of each track. In the West Station the bays adjoined the Down through platform. At the western tip of this V-shaped complex was a large street level booking hall under a lantern roof with an elaborate five-bay iron and glass porte-cochère. Either side of this main hall, in square shaped two-storey pavilions were dining rooms, refreshment rooms, stationmaster's office and living accommodation etc., all of this sitting on a bridge over the tracks. A covered way of iron and glass led visitors to the south end of the Palace, its fairly stiff incline moderated by steps and enlivened by statues in niches which those short of breath could stop and pretend to admire. Platforms in the East Station, reached by three wide staircases with stone-capped banister rails and stone newel posts, were sheltered by a twin-span bow section all-over roof set between blind-arcaded, solidly-buttressed walls. Removed in 1906 in a fit of jitters following the 1905 Charing Cross roof collapse, the Crystal Palace roof was replaced by two ordinary centrally-supported umbrella canopies (the centre platforms had by this time been taken away to make room for two carriage sidings). *The Builder* looked at the LBSCR Crystal Palace station and found Gough's design good, although draughty and badly-lit after dark.

* *The Railway Magazine*, October 1956 (Charles E. Lee)

This complicated layout was controlled by three signalboxes: Tunnel, at the north end; South, on the line towards Norwood Junction (also controlling the goods yard); and East, at the Sydenham end of the East Station. Between the two stations, in the opening of the V, was a goods and coal yard supplemented by the Crystal Palace Company's own dock at the entrance to the East Station, where many strange and exotic items, including circus animals, were to be handled over the years.

From the opening, combined rail and Palace admission tickets were issued as authorised in the 1853 act. This facility, which included a substandard rail fare (at first only 5d return) lasted until Southern Railway days and made it necessary to distinguish ordinary tickets by marking them 'Crystal Palace *Station*'.* Similar inclusive tickets were later issued by most of the main line companies serving London, notably the LNWR, which enjoyed running powers to Crystal Palace West Station.

Although the LCDR was given running powers over the West End of London & Crystal Palace Railway into London, the LBSCR jealously guarded its monopoly by refusing to allow the former to share passenger business at its stations between Crystal Palace and Victoria. Nevertheless, at this period the two companies needed each other in central London and their relationship was accordingly harmonious. When the Brighton planned its South London line, linking London Bridge and Victoria stations through the new suburbs of Peckham Rye, Denmark Hill and Brixton, an LCDR protégé, the 6¼-mile Crystal Palace & South London Junction, was allowed to branch off the South London line near what was later Peckham Rye station and also to have the exclusive use of the northernmost pair of four tracks which the LBSCR would build between Cow Lane and Barrington Road Junction, Brixton. In return for these favours, the Brighton had access to LCDR tracks from Barrington Road to Wandsworth Road Junction, where it regained its own territory. All this was authorised in the Crystal Palace & South London Junction Railway and LBSCR Acts of 1862.

The Crystal Palace & South London Junction, which the LCDR agreed to work for 50 per cent of its receipts, was clearly intended to be a rather superior line. Special architectural treatment was imposed by an agreement with Alleyn's College at Dulwich and there was a firm prohibition in section 68 of the act against carriage of any 'Night Soil, Dung, Manure, Compost or other Offensive Matter'.

Seeking its own access to the City from the new branch, the LCDR obtained powers in 1863 for a cut-off between the junction with the LBSCR and their Herne Hill–City line in Walworth. This was to be used by trains to and from a Nunhead–Greenwich branch authorised in the same act, but the state of the Chatham's finances precluded its construction, although as we have seen, the Greenwich branch was painfully achieved.

Peto & Betts' work on the Crystal Palace & South London Junction was sufficiently advanced to allow trains to run through to the terminus at Crystal Palace without intermediate stops, from 1st August 1865. The service was operated to and from Victoria via the South London line between Peckham Rye and Brixton (Canterbury Road) which was opened on the same day.

* A similar notation occurred in north London, where tickets were marked 'Alexandra Palace *Station*', by the GNR and LNER

From Peckham Rye to Nunhead the new branch climbed steadily at 1 in 60 and 1 in 76, continuing up to the Crystal Palace at 1 in 68. Leaving the LBSCR at Cow Lane Junction, 18ch east of Peckham Rye station, the tracks ran east, south and then south west as they mounted the western flank of the Forest Hill–Norwood ridge. As mentioned earlier, at what is now St Norbert Road, an embankment was partially completed in 1865 to carry a chord authorised the previous year for direct running between Greenwich and Lewisham and Crystal Palace. Honor Oak, the first of the branch stations, was entirely timber-built. It served Camberwell cemetery and the northern end of a new villa colony on Forest Hill, sheltered from east winds and facing the setting sun. A small coal yard was placed on the Up side. The booking office was at first in a wooden shed on the Down side of the approach, reached from the west by a subway under the line where a cast-iron notice warned pedestrians of closure on Good Friday, Christmas Day 'and such other days as the Directors may from time to time determine'. In later years tickets were sold on the platform.

Beyond Honor Oak the line kept close to the west side of the ridge, invading the Dulwich College estates, and after crossing Lordship Lane, entered the station of that name. To meet conditions laid down by the College, the road over-bridge was elaborately ornamented and the station house picturesquely styled with two steeply-gabled roofs over its red brick and stone. Elsewhere cost was kept down by using timber construction. A short ¾-mile from Forest Hill station on the LBSCR main line, Lordship Lane had to share what little traffic this villa district produced.

From this point to the terminus the surroundings were romantic and well timbered, remaining so to the very end of the line's existence. Continuing south between a wood and the immense gardens of the huge houses on Sydenham Hill, the tracks passed under an elaborate timber cantilever bridge carrying a public footpath called Cox's Walk. Shortly after, the ridge was penetrated by the 400yd Crescent Wood Tunnel, from which the line emerged briefly within a curve of the ridge known as Hollow Coombe before entering the 439yd Paxton Tunnel (so called because it passed near, but not beneath, Paxton's house). A station named Upper Sydenham, almost lost in the boscage between these two tunnels, was opened on 1st August 1884. Approached by steps and path down the side of the Combe, much prone to landslips, it served an area of very large well-separated villas set in ample gardens. Traffic was always light and by 1910 it was missed by as many as 30 Up and 20 Down trains a day. Immediately south of its platforms the line crossed above the Penge Tunnel of the LCDR Penge Junction (Beckenham) to Herne Hill line of 1863.

Top Right: LBSCR E2 104 at Honor Oak Park on Crystal Palace (Low Level) service, 1926. *O.J. Morris*

Centre Right: Lordship Lane station, looking towards Nunhead, c.1930. The Southern Railway had at this date made virtually no alterations apart from 3rd rail electrification; the platforms remain gaslit. *Stations UK*

Bottom Right: BR(S) unit 4671 at Upper Sydenham on Crystal Palace (High Level) service in the 1950s. Southern Railway signs still survive. Note how the platform extensions have been constructed to a new standard higher level *R.C. Riley*

Opening out from the south entrance of Paxton Tunnel were the approaches to the terminus, built on a shelf alongside the western flanks of the Palace. More splendid in every way than Gough's LBSCR station, Edward Barry's £100,000 train shed of glass, iron and red and yellow brick could stand without shame against the huge bulk of the Paxton building. At each corner were square towers topped by four chateau-style turrets to emphasise the importance of the long carcase. Passenger accommodation, entirely under cover, was divided by a central arcade into two sections served by concourses raised above the tracks at each end of the interior, which carried the booking offices, refreshments rooms, waiting rooms and other offices. Each section had two tracks, the inner ones platformed each side for ease of loading and unloading of packed trains. The four tracks entered the building through small openings at the London end, emerging at the south on to a 44ft 10in turntable on the south side of Farquhar Road, an arrangement which helped locomotives of arriving trains to run round with the minimum of delay. Half of the station was intended for the use of first-class passengers, who were given segregated access to the first-class entrance in the centre transept of the Palace. Direct communication to the Palace, not ready until shortly after the opening of the station, was through a spacious vaulted and tiled chamber beneath Palace Parade, the roadway between the station and the Palace. This Byzantine crypt, devotedly fashioned by cathedral craftsmen especially imported from Italy, was decorated with octagonal pillars of red and cream brick interlaced with stone ribs. Steps led from it to the main floor of the Palace. It survives intact today, almost the only relic of this great structure.

The *Illustrated London News* clearly preferred the LCDR station, talking of its 'superior convenience', avoiding 'the tedious walk up half a mile of corridors and staircases imposed on those arriving by the Brighton company's line'. Nine siding roads between the station and the tunnel together with a run-round road to the turntable outside the blind-arcaded western wall of the train shed provided accommodation for goods traffic and space to store enough locomotives and carriages to move away between 7,000 and 8,000 passengers an hour. Although the names High Level and Low Level were not officially introduced to distinguish the LCDR and LBSCR stations until the formation of the Southern Railway in 1923, we shall use them here to avoid confusion.

At first there were 19 trains daily each way from Monday to Saturday running non-stop between the High Level and Victoria. Lordship Lane station was opened on 1st September 1865, and Honor Oak, Peckham Rye and Denmark Hill on 1st December. With these calls, the throughout journey of 9m 68ch to Victoria took about 40 minutes, and in 1866 there were 33 trains a day each way. A station was opened at Nunhead, 54 chains east of Cow Lane Junction, on 1st September 1871 to serve new housing development.

Large houses set amidst extensive shrubberies and lawns were built in quantity on the east side of the line between Crystal Palace and Lordship Lane in the 1870s and 1880s producing only a trickle of business for the branch, albeit of superior quality. Despite the availability of a City (Moorgate) service upon the opening of a spur from Cambria Road Junction (west of Denmark Hill) to Loughborough Junction on 1st July 1872, the High Level line did not prosper; cemeteries, very low density villa development and the extensive open areas of the jealously-guarded Dulwich College estates gave it precious little sustenance. Nor was the mid-century dream of regular mass excursions to the Crystal Palace ever fulfilled. Indeed, much of the attraction and fashion of the Palace had evaporated before the High Level branch opened; the northern transept was destroyed by fire in 1866, never to be rebuilt, while a strong and successful opposition to Sunday opening further damaged its prospects.

Such was the disappointment that the independent element in the Crystal Palace & South London Junction Co. grew somewhat restive in the mid-1870s, so much so that the LCDR was moved to action, obtaining powers in 1874 for a spur from Kent House on the Beckenham-Crystal Palace Low Level line designed to allow it a direct run from the City and Victoria to the Low Level station. An effective means of bullying the awkward elements on the CP&SLJR board, this move served its purpose and in 1875 the small company was absorbed into the LCDR, under the powers in the CP&SLJR Act of 1864.

The January 1877 timetable shows 24 trains from Victoria to Crystal Palace High Level between 06.55 and 22.52 including two fast trains which completed the journey in 25 and 27 minutes, the first one a non-stop. There were also 30 trains from Moorgate Street, Holborn Viaduct, Ludgate Hill or St Paul's between 08.12 and 12.07, usually missing Borough Road, Walworth Road and Camberwell New Road, the fastest reaching the High Level station in 26 to 28 minutes.

Although the opening of the Palace had encouraged the development of Sydenham and Upper Norwood as quality middle-class suburbs, the Palace itself was very much in decline as an attraction in the last decades of the Victorian era. The LCDR seemed to acknowledge this by renaming the terminus Crystal Palace & Upper Norwood on 1st November 1898, perhaps hoping to attract more residential traffic. A year earlier, Edward Walford had remarked 'commercially, the place has not proved so successful as was at first anticipated. The undertaking was carried out on too great a scale', and Baedeker's Guide to London noticed that '. . . the Crystal Palace no longer bulks so largely among the lions of London as it once did . . .' Indeed, paint was peeling, the roof leaked, the gardens showed signs of neglect, and the Company, feverishly selling off spare land for house building, was fast approaching bankruptcy. Neither the Saturday concerts, nor the regular firework displays by C. T. Brock & Co. did much to stimulate attendances. Only on very rare occasions, such as the Football Association Cup Final, held here from 1894 to 1914, was the ample railway accommodation put to any sort of use. On such days the two companies might share between 20,000 and 50,000 passengers a day, and the LCDR would put on its non-stop service from and to Victoria which brought first- and second-class passengers to the High Level station in a mere 20 minutes.

One of the last great occasions at the Palace was the Festival of Empire and Imperial Exhibition held between May and October 1911, after opening by King George V. This set off a railway race between the two companies. The LBSCR had inaugurated electric services from Victoria on 12th May 1911 and on a trial run had covered the 8¾ miles in 12½ minutes. This achieved, the Brighton started a 17-minute express service for the Exhibition visitors (regular electric service on the Victoria–Streatham Hill–Crystal Palace line began on 1st June 1911). Not to be outdone, the SECR promptly introduced a *15-minute* steam service between Victoria and Crystal Palace High Level, using the 0–4–4T and four-wheel coaches which comprised the normal stock on the line. These ten-coach trains, weighing 120 tons tare, carried passengers of all three classes and the schedule demanded a start-to-stop speed throughout of 39mph, a very commendable performance on a busy line of many curves and junctions, ending with a steady climb.

In the same notable year, the railways were given an opportunity of showing just how the crowd handling facilities at the Palace stations could be used. To celebrate his coronation, the King invited all London school children aged 11 and over to a 'King's Fete' on 30th June. A vast army of over 100,000 children, teachers, LCC staff, journalists and performers were brought from all parts of London in 105 special trains, 58 via the LBSCR and 47 on the SECR. Most came to the Low and High Level stations, but Sydenham Hill and Penge (LBSCR) were also used. Some of the trains bringing the north London contingents came through the City Widened Lines in charge of GNR locomotives. This movement entailed cancellation of 61 regular workings on the High Level line and substantial suspensions of other timetabled services. About 90 additional railway staff were on duty at the High Level station, in the charge of an official who directed operations from the northern concourse bridge, megaphone in hand, like the captain of a great ship controlling emergency disembarkation. All special trains ran to time, not a single child was lost or injured, and if contemporary accounts are to be believed, each trainload of 1,000 individually-labelled brats was discharged in about three minutes.

Normal service on the High Level branch at this period consisted of 21 trains daily from Victoria (usually fast to Brixton) and 28 from the City stations, with similar numbers in the opposite direction. Best times were 22 minutes Up, 25 minutes Down. Sunday service was meagre, with a train about every 80 minutes from Victoria. At the Low Level station 45 trains a day each way ran to and from Victoria via Gypsy Hill and there were also 39 Down and 36 Up London Bridge trains via Sydenham. Electric working between London Bridge and the Low Level via Tulse Hill started on 3rd March 1912, with full service on 3rd June. Like those on the Victoria services, these trains took their 6600V 25c/s traction current from overhead wires through bow collectors.

Loadings on the High Level branch continued to be poor despite the construction in the 1880s, and 1890s of smaller houses on the west side of the line between Lordship Lane and Nunhead, and around Nunhead station. There was severe competition from the LBSCR stations at Sydenham, Forest Hill, Honor Oak Park and Brockley, and also, after 19th December 1908, from LCC electric tramcars running from Forest Hill via Lordship Lane station into Camberwell Green and central London. Some traffic was also lost to LCC tramcars when from 28th November 1907, these reached Homestall Road, Peckham Rye, to tap the little streets between Honor Oak and Nunhead stations. Later, motor bus services from Dulwich Library and Honor Oak to Peckham Rye station took more business from the railway.

With its thin traffic, it is not surprising that when the manpower shortages of World War 1 began to take effect, and when the City Widened Lines were choked with wartime freight workings, the authorities considered passenger services on the High Level branch expendable. The Moorgate Street journeys, which had been severely cut in January 1915 and had ceased to run on Sundays a few years before that, were stopped altogether after traffic on Saturday 1st April 1916. With the last train on 31st December 1916 passenger working was entirely suspended. Wartime exigencies also caused the SECR to abandon after 30th November 1915 the steam railmotor service it had introduced in July 1907 between Low Level and Beckenham Junction. The LBSCR was left to cope with the useful regular traffic from the Palace's wartime role as a naval recruiting and training centre.

Although a City service to Ludgate Hill or St Paul's (now Blackfriars) was restored to the High Level station on 1st March 1919 in time to take some of the traffic generated from the demobilisation centre at the Palace, there was never again any service to Victoria, for which passengers had to change at Denmark Hill. By the beginning of the 1920s there were half-hourly trains between High Level and St Paul's with extra workings to and from Ludgate Hill in peak hours.

The High Level line was included in the SECR electrification proposals of 1920, but nothing was done until the formation of the Southern Railway. That company opened a resited Nunhead station on 3rd May 1925 and in preparation for electric working closed the supplementary signalboxes at Nunhead Bank, Lordship Lane and Upper Sydenham. This left only Crystal Palace cabin and that at Honor Oak, which was retained for working the goods yard, rearranged in 1924 with a siding to accommodate 25 wagons. Platforms at Honor Oak and Lordship Lane were lengthened for the electric trains, but at Upper Sydenham the necessary alterations cost over £1,000. A substation built there had a shaft providing power cable connections into the Penge tunnel below. Staff training runs commenced on 1st April 1925 between Nunhead and Crystal Palace High Level, but the full service of third-rail electric multiple units started on 12th July with a regular 20-minute frequency through the day (30 minutes on Sundays), to and from St Paul's. The all-stations running time was 25 minutes. As Saturday evening loads were lighter than expected, from 19th July 1926 the service after 15.00 was reduced to half-hourly. There was little scope for the capital expenditure to show any substantial returns in increased traffic; the line's catchment area remained unpromising material. A traffic census taken in February 1926 shows what poor business the electric trains were doing: from Crystal Palace High Level the 53 departures between 06.05 and 23.22 carried only 703 passengers (less than one rush hour train load for the busiest London lines), whilst only 653 arrived at the terminus from London during the traffic day. The idyllic surroundings of Upper Sydenham saw only 211 Up passengers and 216 arrivals the whole day; Lordship Lane produced 366 up and 401 down, but Honor Oak did a little better with 654 Up and 560 Down.

The decaying interior of Crystal Palace High Level station, west side, looking to London, 22nd March 1954. *Alan A Jackson*

There was nevertheless some modest growth after electrification. Lordship Lane, for example, issued 30,043 ordinary and 870 season tickets in 1925, but in 1934 the totals were 57,019 and 1,742. Some minor changes were made to the stations; at Honor Oak a passimeter booth, parcel lock-up and retail kiosks were authorised in 1929. Builders did what they could, infilling where it was possible to buy the large houses and demolish them; on the Tewkesbury Lodge estate, for example, west of the tracks just north of Lordship Lane, three- to six-bedroom semi-detached houses were on offer in 1937 at £1,050 upwards.

The Southern Railway very speedily converted the LBSCR overhead wire electrics to the third-rail system; London Bridge to Crystal Palace Low Level, via Tulse Hill on 17th June and the Low Level to Victoria service on 3rd March 1929. On that day the Low Level–Beckenham Junction trains were restored, with electric traction. The London Bridge–Crystal Palace (Low Level) via Sydenham service was electrically-worked from 25th March 1928.

Saved by public subscription in 1913 after bankruptcy of the old company, the Crystal Palace received an injection of new life in 1920 when the King went down to open the Imperial War Museum and Great Victory Exhibition 'with special events culminating in the revived Handel Festival'. But the sad souvenirs of World War I were soon removed to South Kensington, leaving the Palace to subsist on a mixed diet of cat and dog shows, home exhibitions, fireworks, brass band festivals and motor cycle racing, none of which called into action any of the excess capacity at the two railway stations. Then suddenly, on the night of 30th November 1936, it all came to an end; Paxton's great glasshouse melted away in the flames of a spectacular fire, morning light revealing only the two water towers and the railway stations still standing. This occurrence attracted crowds far larger than any seen at the Palace for very many years and prompted the last special train for a Palace event – one was supplied to take home sore-eyed spectators in the small hours. Sets of LCDR 6-wheelers stored in the High Level yard for summer excursions, hop pickers' specials and national emergencies served as an excellent grandstand, withstanding in the true traditions of British workmanship of their age the pressure of the many excited spectators standing on their roofs. Saved then by the intervening roadway and the efforts of firemen through the night, the vast hulk of the High Level station also survived World War 2 with no damage other than the removal of much of its glass by the blast of neighbouring anti-aircraft guns.

After the fire, pleasure traffic to the Palace dropped almost to nothing and when as a wartime measure off-peak and Sunday trains were reduced to hourly from 1st January 1940, local passengers began to drift away to other Southern stations, trams and buses. From 6th January 1941 the branch was worked as shuttle to and from Nunhead, where connections were made into the Catford Loop service every 20 minutes at peak periods and hourly at other times. Storage capacity at High Level was used to hold passenger stock made redundant by the War, notably buffet and second-class boat train cars. A second wartime closure of the branch was predictable, and sure enough 'due to the manpower position' passenger trains were withdrawn after traffic on 21st May 1944, not to be restored until 4th March 1946 when the shuttle service was re-introduced but with some peak-hour workings to and from Blackfriars from 11th August. Finally, on 27th September 1948 all trains ran to and from Blackfriars every 30 minutes, with additional rush-hour journeys, but Sunday trains were withdrawn.

Lordship Lane on the last day of public services, 18th September 1954, Down train entering, unit 4107. The results of German bombing in World War 2 are evident. *Alan A Jackson*

Without some new source of traffic, which was not forthcoming, there could be no hope of recovery from the successive blows received, and for most of the day the trains, now only three or four cars long, ran all but empty. It was a great line for lovers. One estimate put the loading of the 88 trains into High Level daily as 400 – between four and five per train. Rain poured down through the shattered roof at High Level, encouraging a luxuriant growth of ferns and fungi on the rotting timber platforms beneath which rats, far outnumbering the passengers, scurried and scavenged unhindered. For most of the time there was only one platform in use in the huge building, where the northern stairs, concourse and rooms had long since been abandoned to rodents, birds and spiders; adding to the horror film effect, safety nets drooped from the roof to protect passengers from falling debris. At night it was one of the most eerie public places in London.

Senior officers of the Southern who had lived through the Walker electrification era must have found it distressing to recommend the first closure of a Southern Electric line, but it had to be. With all the stations and cabling in deep decay, with no hope of traffic development, and with alternative facilities readily available, the line's fate was sealed, and the local authorities were warned of the closure in January 1954. The last electric train ran on 18th September and the daily freight carrying coal and coke to the yards at Honor Oak and High Level from Herne Hill ceased about the same time. To soak up the displaced traffic, London Transport extended its 63 bus service from Honor Oak to Crystal Palace Parade via Lordship Lane and Sydenham Hill and extra trains (which lasted only a few weeks) were put on between Blackfriars and Nunhead from 20th September 1954. Coal merchants at the High Level station were moved to Gipsy Hill yard, which in turn closed to railborne traffic in January 1969.

Wooden platforms and gas lighting survive until the last day of public service at Honor Oak, 18th September 1954; 4-car unit 4639 is seen on an Up train.
Alan A Jackson

The throat of Crystal Palace High Level station (last day of public service) with an Up train about to enter the 439yd Paxton Tunnel.
Alan A Jackson

Crystal Palace Low Level station, north side, looking to Gipsy Hill, 21st March 1964.
Alan A Jackson

Dismantling the branch proved to be a slow business, occupying much of 1956 and early 1957. When it was done, the LCC bought all 48 acres of railway land from Crystal Palace to Nunhead, subsequently passing much of it to local councils for open space and housing developments. At Upper Sydenham, the sealed-off tunnel mouths became a lasting challenge to adventurous youth. In 1985 a 'Green Walk' was opened alongside and over the line of the railway, parts of which had become a nature reserve.

The High Level station itself remained intact for almost six years after the departure of the last train, patiently awaiting the imagination and finance that might convert it to some worthwhile alternative use. Since it was in London and not Paris, this did not happen and after its demolition in 1961 the vast site lay disused for a further long period whilst its future was discussed interminably. Finally, in 1986–87, the area was densely covered with housing, leaving only the main tunnel mouth and the great retaining wall below Crystal Palace Parade as reminders of what was once here.

So ends the story of a railway constructed at high initial cost in the frustrated hope of snatching some of a rival railway company's profit from the Crystal Palace traffic. As the whole route was fairly closely paralleled by an existing line, once the prospect of regular movements of very large crowds to the Palace was seen as something of an illusion, the enterprise had little else on which to build even modest prosperity. Except on rare and isolated occasions, its huge terminal station proved to be a complete white elephant, far too large for any traffic forthcoming. With the benefit of hindsight we can see that the first line to the Palace and the facilities it subsequently provided would probably have been adequate on their own to handle all the business generated, and that the decision in 1925 to electrify the High Level line was a serious misjudgement.

The Low Level station certainly proved more than capable of coping with the residual rail traffic to the Crystal Palace area after 1954, including that to the National Sports Centre opened in the park ten years later. The cavernous East station was used by the London Bridge trains, latterly running only in rush hours. During the day, the link through it was needed for the transfer of empty electric stock between Victoria and London Bridge and New Cross Sidings. It still remains open and virtually intact at rail level at the time of writing although above there have been some changes. In obeisance to the god of financial economy, BR dismantled some of the Victorian features: the glass and iron porte cochère standing over the road entrance went in the late 1960s and the north tower roof was finally cut down in 1976. The remainder was Grade II listed as of architectural and historical interest. After the collapse of some 1971 proposals carefully prepared by the Clapham Society, the Transport Trust and Sir Robert McAlpine & Sons which would have used the East Station and unwanted railway land as a National Transport Museum, apartments were eventually built in the vee between the East and the West stations in 1990–91. Before that, in 1986, with a substantial grant from the Greater London Council, a new entrance and ticket office were provided above the West station. Reflecting the style of the old Crystal Palace building, this light and pleasing structure of aluminium and glass was finished in bright blue and green.

CHAPTER TWO

SOUTH WEST LONDON

Southfields station exterior, c.1905 *Commercial postcard*

Earl's Court to Wimbledon (map page 165)

At an early stage in its history, the Metropolitan District Railway developed a policy of feeding its capital-intensive inner London section by judicious extensions into potential areas of middle class residential development. In the pursuit of this objective, attention was directed to the well-padded suburban territory occupied by the LSWR, an area which included the favoured Thames-side areas of Surrey and Middlesex.

As early as 12th April 1869 a branch had been opened from west of South Kensington station to West Brompton on the West London Extension Railway in the unfulfilled expectation of attracting LSWR and LBSCR services into South Kensington. This line carried a service to and from Gloucester Road until 1st August 1870, when the trains were extended to Blackfriars.

East Putney station street entrance and cab yard between the two diverging lines, c. 1905. *Commercial postcard*

Wimbledon Park interior, looking north, c. 1905. The four uniformed staff outnumber the passengers in view. *Commercial postcard*

For a while the District was frustrated. A proposal to tap the L&SWR at Barnes was authorised in 1872 as the Barnes & New Richmond Railway, but this was dropped when the LSWR refused a connection. Soon after this, as we shall see later, the District arrived at Hammersmith, making a junction there with the LSWR's Kensington & Richmond line in 1877, an astute move which enabled its trains to gain access to Richmond. It also reinforced the company's expansionist ambitions by enabling it to serve Ealing, the 'Queen of the Suburbs', from 1879, and very soon after that it secured access to Hounslow, both areas we shall consider later. These positions achieved, there remained only one notable gap near the inner part of the District system, the area enclosed by the meander of the Thames past Fulham, long threatened by Metropolitan Railway schemes pushing down from the H&CR Hammersmith terminus. A 1m 67ch thrust from West Brompton towards LSWR territory was authorised in 1878 as the Fulham Extension Railway, a separate undertaking with capital of £300,000.

Built by Lucas & Aird, and engineered by John Wolfe-Barry, this started at the country end of West Brompton station, proceeding in a covered way below the West London Extension and then southwestwards, first in cutting and then on a brick viaduct 'of ornamental character' to the satisfaction of the Ecclesiastical Commissioners, which terminated on the north bank of the river close to Putney Bridge and Fulham church. Putney Bridge & Fulham station (Putney Bridge & Hurlingham 1st September 1902, Putney Bridge 1932) had wooden platforms built out on steel piers and lattice girders from the sides of the viaduct, served on the west side by a large but nondescript flat-roofed entrance building at street level. Built on the eastern part of the garden of a large riverside house called *Willow Bank*, the station incorporated a footway to a new low-water pier where passengers could make connections to river pleasure steamers. Some housing demolition was necessary to make room for the two intermediate stations in the formerly separate residential villages of Walham Green and Parsons Green. Walham Green (renamed Fulham Broadway 1st March 1952), at the site of the Fulham Road tollgate, was in cutting, its platforms partially sheltered by an 'A'-shaped overall roof of glass and iron resting on blind-arched walls. With its booking hall extending out over the tracks from the road bridge, it served the Stamford Bridge grounds, leased in 1876 to the London Athletic Cricket Club & Athletic Grounds. Parsons Green had side platforms sheltered by wooden awnings, with steps down to an entrance hall in an arch of the bridge over the road. Shortly after this, near the start of the remaining 49ch to Putney Bridge, there began the long viaduct, which included a reverse curve to avoid the housing in the Kings Road and the Fulham Refuge & Female Reformatory. As far as possible the whole route was made to pass between housing through the garden land, the viaduct form minimising acquisition and demolition in an area already partially built-up.

The Fulham Extension opened on 1st March 1880 with a half-hourly service from West Brompton, increased on 1st April to quarter-hourly, alternate trains working to and from High Street Kensington. Large numbers were carried to Putney Bridge for that year's University Boat Race, thus initiating this line's strong association with sporting events. As the opening of the branch coincided with a period of rapid housing development in the catchment area, it was not long before a steady daily residential traffic had accrued. Houses 'like serried battalions of a gigantic army . . . marching and counter marching' spread out northwards from the old riverside village centre of Fulham until by 1900 they had all but filled the land between the Thames and the West London Extension and Earl's Court to Hammersmith railways. The new Fulham, which spawned its own entertainment, retail and services area around Walham Green station and a smaller shopping centre near Parsons Green station, brought the district's population from 42,895 in 1881 to 137,289 in 1901. In her *Memorials of Edward Burne-Jones* (1904) Lady Burne-Jones recalled the early 1880s: 'the District Railway had been brought near us and the speculative builder followed . . . the respectable old name of Fulham was taken from us, and West Kensington given in exchange.'

The District's receipts showed a satisfying upward curve, even if there were fewer first-class tickets than might have been wished. In his *Survey of London Life and Labour* (1899) Charles Booth found most of the new inhabitants of Fulham comfortably-off, respectable members of the lower middle class and upper working class: people in the lesser professions, minor theatricals, skilled artisans, shop-workers, clerks, foremen and transport workers, a large number of them travelling by train to work in inner London, taking good advantage of the District Railway workmen's tickets.

From its north bank bridgehead, the District was clearly poised to jump into the LSWR territory on the other side. Opportunity soon came in the form of the Kingston & London Railway, which started life as the Guildford, Kingston & London, looking for District support for its lines to Surbiton, Kingston, Guildford, Ashtead and Bookham. As authorised on 22nd August 1881 this cheeky proposal was reduced to a 7m 45.8ch line from the District at Putney Bridge across Putney Heath and Wimbledon Common to the LSWR Down side at Surbiton (the LSWR simultaneously secured powers for its own lines from Surbiton to fill the Guildford and Bookham gap). Seeing mutual advantage, a West End terminus for the LSWR, lucrative suburban trade for the District, the two companies then combined to obtain equal rights of user over the Kingston & London, the LSWR proposing in its 1882 act to make further connections at East Putney and at Norbiton to allow through running to Kingston and an 11ch branch off the District to its own West End station at Pelham Street, South Kensington. An act of 1882 jointly vested the K&LR in the two companies but it very soon became apparent that the District would be unable to raise its half share of the £650,000 capital. Wimbledon interests, feeling left out, and seeking a cheaper alternative to the West End, had put forward a Wimbledon, Merton & West Metropolitan Bill for what was in effect a branch from the K&LR at East Putney to a two-way junction with the Tooting joint line of the LSWR and LBSCR between what is now Haydons Road station and Wimbledon. Lucas & Aird, the contractors, seeing the possibilities, paid the necessary parliamentary deposit. This new link, over which the District was accorded running powers, was authorised on 18th August 1882 as the Wimbledon & West Metropolitan Railway, without the spur towards Tooting.

Unable to obtain Parliamentary approval to construct the K&LR on its own account, and unwilling to advance capital to the District, the LSWR agreed in 1885 that the K&LR should be abandoned except for the short section between Putney Bridge and East Putney, proposing instead to take over and build the Wimbledon & West Metropolitan, which it would allow the District to use to Wimbledon, where it would provide a separate station, in return for an annual rent of six per cent on cost and maintenance. The District had merely to agree to the preservation of LSWR running powers to South Kensington and High Street Kensington, with the separate terminal accommodation to be constructed at the former if required.

By its act of 25th June 1886 to which the agreement with the District covering the above was scheduled, the LSWR took over the required piece of the K&LR and most of the Wimbledon & West Metropolitan, proceeding to build a double track line together with a flying junction to the Windsor Lines at East Putney (Point Pleasant Junction) facing London, and a deviation to bring the line into the north side of Wimbledon station instead of the proposed junction west of Haydons Road.

Work started in March 1887, with Lucas & Aird getting the contract they had expected. A principal engineering feature, one of the last designs of William Jacomb, the LSWR engineer, was the eight-span wrought iron girder bridge over the Thames. Not given a name (local people dubbed it the Iron Bridge), this structure was never to carry revenue-earning LSWR trains, as that company decided not to take up the running powers and abandoned the proposed Kensington terminus in its act of 4th July 1890. A wide footway on the downstream side was opened to the public on 1st July 1889.

From the bridge, the line climbed at 1 in 70 on a brick viaduct through a partly built-up area, crossing high over the Windsor Lines before entering East Putney. Some houses were demolished. East Putney was a split station, two faces of its well-canopied platforms serving the spur to Point Pleasant Junction, which was graded 1 in 56 downhill and 1 in 60 uphill. A small entrance building in red and yellow brick snuggled in the angle of the two viaducts, fronting its cab yard on the south side of Upper Richmond Road. B. G. Wilson notes that the sharp check-railed curve bearing south-east beyond the station represents the divergence of the 'Wimbledon branch' from the planned alignment of the K&LR, which would have gone almost straight ahead into its Putney Heath tunnel. After this curve, the Wimbledon line entered a 311yd covered way beneath West Hill followed by a cutting containing Southfields station. This had an island platform with stairs at the south end leading up to a small entrance pavilion on the north side of Wimbledon Park Road, with elevations of yellow and red brick in Early English style. Platform buildings under a wide canopy from the staircase were also in red and yellow brick. At the time of opening, a spaciously laid-out estate of large villas was slowly growing on the west side and there were a few houses to the east along the Merton Road. To the south, as far as the LSWR main line there were just parklands and fields.

Now on embankment and curving east to avoid the lake and higher parts of Lord Spencer's Wimbledon Park, the tracks ran under Arthur Road into Wimbledon Park station, in every respect the twin of Southfields except that it faced the other way. Leaving this station there was a facing connection to the carriage sidings before the line curved south to run along the main lines into the 'North Station', two new platforms with a central run round and separate booking office adjacent to the LSWR's platform 1. The coal yard formerly on this site was rebuilt further east. There were signalboxes at East Putney, south of the station on the Up side, and on the platforms of the other two stations.

The District's characteristic Beyer-Peacock 4–4–0T and trains of four-wheelers began to serve Wimbledon on 3rd June 1889, providing 31 journeys a day to and from the City, 11 more than required by the 1886 agreement. A late start and finish to the traffic day (07.27 to 00.09) reflected the middle-class nature of the clientele. On Sundays trains terminated variously at New Cross LBSCR, High Street Kensington or South Kensington; most weekday trains went through to Whitechapel.

This approximately half-hourly service was shortly augmented to give a 15-minute interval at peak periods, while with the opening of the Point Pleasant Junctions on 1st July 1889 there was the additional facility of 12 LSWR trains daily each way between Wimbledon and Waterloo, using the double-track junction with the main lines at the London end of Wimbledon station. This link also had considerable value to the LSWR, both as an emergency diversion and in affording access to and from the West London Extension Railway via Ludgate Junction (north of Clapham Junction station) and Latchmere Junction. This was at its most useful in the Up direction as Down trains were faced with the steep climb from Point Pleasant and a flat crossing of main lines at Wimbledon.

At first the District's revenue was largely confined to Wimbledon and East Putney stations, though this was not to be scorned, especially that from the former with its high proportion of first-class tickets. With Wimbledon Park and Southfields as yet in abeyance, the chairman, J. S. Forbes, was able to say in 1896 that the line had increased the company's receipts by over 44 per cent in six years.

A large part of the Wimbledon Park estate was sold for building during 1898, to be covered within two or three years with a tight-packed grid of new streets east of the line between Wimbledon Park and Southfields stations, streets which were rapidly lined with 'tunnel back' housing for the lower echelons of the middle class. Briefly interrupted by World War 1, the activity here and construction of slightly more superior semi-detached houses further north either side of the railway at Southfields brought much new traffic to these two stations. In the 1910s and 1920s Wimbledon grew north-east towards the southern part of the line, leaving untouched only that part of Wimbledon Park around the lake, the All-England Tennis Courts and the Sports Club. West of the line at Southfields, building continued until 1939, much of it of higher value houses, to be followed after World War 2 by blocks of flats.

To meet the needs of this new population, services and line capacity were augmented, though not all plans were realised. By 1899 the District was working 47 trains a day each way, terminating variously at Whitechapel, Earl's Court or High Street Kensington. Always in the minority on its own line, the LSWR supplied 15 trains to and from Waterloo. District electrification at 600V dc third and fourth rail reached Putney Bridge on 23rd July 1905, trains working to and from High Street Kensington. Arrangements were made for the LSWR to electrify its tracks to Wimbledon in return for District payments of interest on the capital cost, the two companies signing an agreement on 4th December 1903. District electric working to Wimbledon started on 27th August 1905, giving a significant increase in service, most trains running through to East Ham. Current came from Lots Road, Chelsea through a substation at Wimbledon Park.

In 1904, the last full year of 100 per cent steam traction on the West Brompton–Wimbledon line, there were 103 trains a day each way on the East Putney–Wimbledon section, of which 54 were District workings. By 1911 this total had grown to 157, of which 93 were District. This began to stretch the capacity of the manually-signalled double track, but with some skill and the aid of new intermediate boxes at Cromer Road (Southfields) and Revelstoke Road (Wimbledon Park) it was just possible to cope. A further problem for the District was the landlord's propensity to delay or even stop the electric trains at times of stress, particularly on race days. In 1911, when there were 19 race days, 85 District trains had to be cancelled, and January 1912 saw 831 delays to District trains, totalling 2,415 minutes. In these difficult conditions, the District was carrying traffic which had increased by 76 per cent since 1907. The LSWR found itself under pressure to adopt a similar arrangement to that on the Kensington & Richmond; quadrupling between Wimbledon and East Putney was authorised by the MDR Act of 1912, the work to be carried out by the LSWR, which would leave the western pair of tracks for the District's exclusive use, receiving payments of interest at four per cent on capital expended. Improvements were also agreed for Wimbledon station. Although the LSWR board authorised negotiations for land purchase in April 1913, no work on the widening had been done before wartime conditions made a start impossible. With its Wimbledon & Sutton scheme very much in mind, the District obtained powers in 1913 for widening between Walham Green and Putney Bridge, with two island platforms at Parsons Green to facilitate semi-fast working. Again no start was made, although some years later the land purchased was used to make storage sidings either side of the running lines at the country end of Parsons Green station.

Some small improvements were realised. In the early summer of 1910 the District brought into use a third road on the outer (east) side of Putney Bridge station, converting the southbound platform to an island. The old through line became a reversible stub, enabling the operation of a four-minute frequency in rush hours, previously made difficult by terminal movements on the double track. At Walham Green, the single-storey street level building was replaced in 1910 by a two-storey structure in neo-classical style, the work of the District architect, H. W. Ford. This incorporated an arcade leading to a new booking hall and over-line concourse. Extra exits were provided for the Stamford Bridge sports traffic for which there were now ten booking windows, said to permit the issue of 120 tickets a minute. Football traffic had assumed importance with the arrival of the Chelsea FC at Stamford Bridge ground in 1905. Finally, at Earl's Court, from 5th January 1914, eastbound Wimbledon trains used a new flyover which brought them into the station without fouling the Ealing and Kensington (Addison Road) services. Contemporary publicity referred to this as a '£70,000 scheme for catching seconds . . . more trains and more accommodation on the Wimbledon and Putney line'. The original alignment was retained to duplicate the southbound track so that if required, two trains towards Wimbledon could be sent on to the branch, thus clearing Earl's Court station, one train being kept back as desired on the curve, or a fast train could overtake a slow one here instead of in the station. With this improvement and the contemporary addition of an extra terminal platform at the Wimbledon 'North station' by the LSWR, the District was able to start from 9th March 1914 a ten-minute all-day service to Wimbledon, increased to six minutes at rush hours.

Traffic was still growing. The small new houses at Wimbledon Park and South-fields were available for £250-£350 leasehold and typical of the bait which attracted many new District season ticket holders was an advertisement of 1914 which offered two reception rooms, three bedrooms and a bathroom in a new terrace house of 17ft 6in frontage in Wimbledon Park Road, Southfields for £285 leasehold. Here and at Wimbledon Park, the stations were rapidly becoming small suburban centres in their own right, with parades of shops to meet the needs of the new residents.

A further spurt to the popularity of this area (which was also well served by motor buses) was the decision to include the East Putney–Wimbledon line in the LSWR suburban electrification scheme. To allow the running of the third-rail trains, the District's fourth-rail system was adapted by removing the insulation of the negative return and bonding it to the running rails. A special isolating section was installed on the river crossing to prevent bridging of the section gap by the bus-lines of passing trains. This was the first part of the LSWR electrification to open, providing a 20-minute frequency on weekdays only from 25th October 1915 between Wimbledon and Waterloo via Wandsworth Town, six minutes faster than the irregular steam service it replaced. Patronage was not good, and in July 1919 when stock was required to augment busier electric services, all trains were withdrawn except for about half a dozen rush-hour trips which missed Wimbledon Park–East Putney inclusive, reaching Waterloo in 19 minutes. When regular electric working was resumed on 16th November 1919, trains ran only hourly (half-hourly at peak periods), some evening workings not going beyond Wimbledon Park. Three-car sets were sufficient for the loading. The line occupation by these and the various freight and empty stock workings caused no great distress to the District, and with the SR take-over of the Wimbledon and Sutton scheme, (to be considered later) the urgency

West Brompton, 11th May 1963. The site of the West London Extension Railway platforms is at left, with BR D6543 on a southbound empty coaching stock train; District Line station at right. *Alan A Jackson*

was removed from the quadrupling plan. The powers were allowed to lapse, but when rebuilding Wimbledon station in 1929, the SR did provide a new four-bay station for the District with its own concourse below the main booking hall.

Following the Metropolitan's reconstruction of Edgware Road station as an intermediate terminus, 7½-minute District services were started between there and Putney Bridge from 1st November 1926 (15 minutes on Sundays). Some of these trains, particularly on Sundays, went through to Wimbledon. Ten years later, Wimbledon had a four- to five-minute frequency in rush hours, seven to ten minutes at other times, whilst Putney Bridge intervals were respectively two to five and three to six minutes. Trains deceptively labelled WIMBLEDON NON STOP in fact missed only West Brompton and occasionally Parsons Green (and Walham Green in rush hours).

The onset of World War 2 saw the end of regular SR calls at Wimbledon Park, Southfields and East Putney. From 16th October 1939 the service was shaved to half-hourly at peak periods only, ceasing altogether after traffic on 4th May 1941. Through steam passenger workings had become increasingly rare in the 1930s (some LMSR trains were reported by an observer in 1938 as the first through Wimbledon Park for a considerable time). Steam-hauled freight and empty stock remained commonplace until the early 1960s, while occasional SR steam passenger trains and excursions working via the West London line were seen until the late 1950s.

With the end of regular stopping service via Point Pleasant Junction the east side platforms at East Putney remained to confuse passengers, gradually deteriorating until 1959 when the Down side buildings were demolished and the subway was closed off. Through the 1950s and early 1960s, some fast electrics came this way, usually from the Alton line, and running non-stop between Surbiton and Waterloo. Summer Channel Islands Boat Trains also worked via East Putney every year from 1953 to 1962 and it was one of these, in the latter year, which formed the last steam passenger working. Since, a few electric excursion trains have been operated to and from Clapham Junction, or Waterloo, some calling at Wimbledon Park and Southfields. Diesel-hauled excursions via the West London line to and from other BR regions are also occasionally seen. In 1963 the character of the line was further diluted by closing it at night and running milk and freight trains via Earlsfield. Today it is still used for empty stock movement between Clapham Junction or Waterloo and Wimbledon Park sidings, also of course for emergency and engineering work diversions of main line trains.

West Brompton station, London Transport, in the early 1960s with a southbound District Line train entering. The West London Extension Railway can be seen across the centre of the picture. Its West Brompton & Lillie Bridge station, which was alongside the District one, was closed after bomb damage on the night of 19/20th October 1940 and was later dismantled; some remains are visible to the right of the road bridge; a station on the same site was to be reprovided in 1999. *W.H.R. Godwin*

For many years London Transport drivers working south of West Brompton faced violent contrasts in signalling. Manual semaphores on the District's own line, converted to electro-pneumatic working with track circuits and train stops at the time of electrification, were subsequently replaced by colour-lights on the same system. Parsons Green signal frame went out of use from 9th October 1960 when all signalling here came under the control of programme machines. From 20th November that year, these machines, supervised from Earl's Court, replaced Putney Bridge box, and the Parsons Green machines also came under the Earl's Court control room from 12th December 1965. Although East Putney station had track circuits and colour-lights towards Putney Bridge from 20th November 1960 the rest of the Wimbledon line retained its Victorian manual signalling with Sykes' lock-and-block, the Underground crews enjoying in foggy weather the unusual experience of guidance from manually-placed detonators on the rails. Not until 13th September 1970 were further colour-lights installed at East Putney, three-aspect colour-lights with track circuits coming into use through to Wimbledon on the following 29th November, when the boxes at Cromer Road and Revelstoke Road were finally closed (Wimbledon Park and East Putney boxes were retained to control movements into Wimbledon sidings and to and from the Windsor Lines). At Wimbledon itself, the semaphores which remained in the station area until the early 1970s had been fully track-circuited and electro-pneumatically controlled since the opening of the new station signal box on 29th February 1948. Signalling modernisation allowed an effortless four-minute frequency to be maintained in rush hours in all weathers. Edgware Road–Putney Bridge rush-hour workings were all extended to Wimbledon in rush hours on 10th October 1960 and all Putney Bridge off-peak reversals were subsequently similarly extended.

The Up line between East Putney station and the Windsor line at Point Pleasant Junction was closed in 1990 and the retained Down connection was resignalled as a reversible line in February 1991. These changes were part of the incorporation of the Putney-Wimbledon line in BR's Waterloo Area Resignalling scheme, operated from a new control centre on the country side of Wimbledon station. Point Pleasant Junction box was closed in September 1990 and East Putney, Wimbledon Park and Wimbledon 'A' boxes were all taken out of commission on 25th February 1991.

Other than closure of West Brompton on Saturdays and Sundays after 24th/25th January 1970, there was little retrenchment on this busy line. Fulham Broadway and Putney Bridge continued to attract large and often unruly crowds in the football season for home games by the Chelsea and Fulham clubs. At the former, around 15,000 fans could be cleared in an hour by short-working extra trains into the normal service. Putney Bridge still saw an influx on University Boat Race Day, much diminished by the 1970s. Another sporting event which this line sustains is the Wimbledon Tennis Tournament, when well-behaved crowds are carried by extra trains and special bus services to and from Wimbledon and Southfields stations.

Today, with none of its stations much rebuilt, the line retains a certain period charm. The massive Thames Bridge, with its ornamental pilasters and rusticated granite and Portland stone abutments, the sinuous viaducts above the rooftops of Fulham and Putney, and the evocatively Edwardian Putney Bridge station, with its scroll-work lamps and finialled canopies, all combine to give it a special aura. Local business is supplemented by Surrey commuters moving to and from West End workplaces and on Saturdays in winter, Surrey boys give it a two-way football traffic. The line was touched with new fame in 1973 when Marlene Dietrich came this way to her performances at the Wimbledon Theatre, having discovered the journey from her West End hotel took only 30 minutes against an hour by road.

In 1994 the Wimbledon branch of the District line was served by 12 trains an hour at peak periods, four to Edgware Road, eight to Embankment and beyond. At the busiest morning peak hour approximately 2,770 passengers were entering the District station at Wimbledon, 913 at Wimbledon Park, 1,991 at Southfields, 1,854 at East Putney, 1,309 at Putney Bridge, 1,553 at Parsons Green 1,513 at Fulham Broadway and 233 at West Brompton. The journey from Wimbledon to Embankment took 28 minutes compared with 14 minutes from Wimbledon to Waterloo.

A major change occurred from 1st April 1994, when control and staffing of East Putney, Southfields and Wimbledon Park stations was handed over to London Underground. Signalling, which remained a responsibility of Wimbledon Signalling Centre, could be monitored at London Transport's Earl's Court Regulating Room. Under the new regime, the three stations were refurbished and re-signed, their ticket issue facilities modernised. The connections to the main railway system at each end and the ability to use the line for through workings over these junctions were unaffected by this development.

Tube trains may eventually be worked through these stations, operating services over a proposed new link between Wimbledon and Leytonstone via Chelsea and Hackney, whose route across London has been safeguarded.

Croydon train at Merton Park station c.1930. The Tooting platforms are on the right, with the main station building at extreme right.

Wimbledon to Croydon and the Tooting Loops (map page 109)

An important source of water power and pure water, the river Wandle attracted industry to its banks between Croydon and Wandsworth well before the railway age. It was not navigable, and but for the opposition of the mill owners alongside, it would undoubtedly have been canalised before the end of the 18th century. Instead, the district which it served was to get the first public railway to receive parliamentary sanction, the earliest railway of any sort in the London area.

Authorised in 1801, the Surrey Iron Railway, so named because its track consisted of cast-iron plates on stone blocks, ran up the valley from the east side of the river's mouth at Wandsworth through Garratt Green, Colliers Wood and Mitcham to Pitlake Meadow, Croydon, with a 1½-mile branch from Mitcham to the river bank at Hackbridge and another, owned by the Croydon Canal Company, from Pitlake to the canal basin near the present West Croydon station. Serving no less than 38 mills and factories, the line was built by the engineer William Jessop, and its double track was opened for public use on 26th July 1803. The Hackbridge branch and the Wandsworth Basin were ready on 1st June 1804 and the canal spur came into operation on 22nd October 1809.

An extension south of Croydon by the separate Croydon, Merstham & Godstone Iron Railway, authorised in 1803, was opened for public use on 24th July 1805. Although intended to run as far as Reigate, with a branch from Merstham to Godstone Green, this line never got further than the Greystone Lime Works at Merstham, via Purley and Coulsdon.

Both railways were 4ft 2in gauge between the outer faces of the rail flanges. Used only for freight, they owned no rolling stock; horses, donkeys or mules and wagons were all supplied by the users, who paid tolls on a per-ton-per-mile basis. Traffic consisted mainly of coals and manure southbound, lime, chalk and farm produce northbound. Fifty to sixty tons were pulled by one horse without difficulty on the many level stretches.

As the house on the platform demonstrates, Morden was originally a station but from November 1918, with the introduction of a push-pull service, it was reduced to halt status. About the same time, the siding (left) was taken up. This photo of about 1930 looks towards Wimbledon and shows an ex-LBSCR 0-4-2T on a 2-car push-pull unit. *Lens of Sutton*

Business done proved a great disappointment to the owners, as much of the important Croydon traffic went to the Croydon Canal. After 1825 the Surrey Iron paid no dividend, and its total profits over its 40 or so years of life amounted to no more than £10 6s 0d (£10.30) per £100 shares.

The Merstham line lay in the path of the proposed London & Brighton Railway, which obtained powers in its initial act of 1837 to purchase it. This was achieved in 1838 when the tramway was closed for public traffic, parts of it being used during the construction of the main line. The company was wound up by an act of 1839.

Early in 1844 Chaplin and Parsons, the chairmen of the LSWR and the London & Brighton Railway respectively, considered the possibility of a joint terminus near the West End; both were discontented with their respective termini at Nine Elms and London Bridge, the Brighton particularly so, since it was paying heavy tolls to the London & Greenwich and London & Croydon Railways for access. Chaplin was interested in levering away the Brighton from dependence on the London & Croydon as the latter had a scheme for a direct line to Portsmouth which would take traffic from the LSWR. A station was proposed at Waterloo Bridge which it was thought the Brighton might reach by means of a line from Purley (Foxley Hatch) to Wandsworth, LSWR, using the roadbed of the two Iron Railways. In August 1844 the LSWR secured an option to purchase the Surrey Iron Railway, but in 1845 the necessary legislation in the form of a Croydon & Wandsworth Junction Bill was sabotaged by an adverse report from the Board of Trade, while the Surrey Iron Railway Bill seeking powers to sell to the LSWR was also thrown out.

Better luck attended the Brighton in the following session when the London & Brighton Railway (Wandsworth Branch) Act was passed, but by then the steam had gone out of the issue for the Brighton, which had in July 1846 amalgamated with the London & Croydon to form the LBSCR. This abolished the toll burden and the old Croydon element encouraged a cooling of relations with the LSWR.

1846 also saw the end of the Surrey Iron, which obtained its Dissolution Act on 3rd August and then summarily closed on 31st August. The area was not to remain long without a railway. Already, in 1845, seeing the imminent death of the primitive Surrey Iron, local interests at Mitcham had sponsored a 3½-mile Mitcham & South Western Junction Railway from Mitcham Green to the LSWR near the present Earlsfield station. This met defeat from an LSWR still supporting the Wandsworth & Croydon, but was followed by another independent scheme for a Wandsworth & Croydon Railway. That had to be withdrawn when the LSWR and Brighton combined to lean on it, although all three parties did manage to agree that the promoters could build from Wimbledon to Croydon, the LSWR renting as far as Mitcham, the LBSCR leasing the remainder as far as the junction with its line at West Croydon. Subsequently the LSWR withdrew from this arrangement, but the W&CR secured its act in 1853.

As the act only contained provision for working arrangements with the LSWR, the line was built as a speculation by the contractors Peto & Betts and leased to the famous Devonian engineer G. P. Bidder, at that time a resident of Mitcham, who opened the line on 22nd October 1855. It was something of a shambles. Not only had there been two postponements whilst the requirements of the Board of Trade Inspector were satisfied, but on the very first day navvies had to rebuild the track to restore some semblance of stability to the motion of the trains. Two days later, an engine driver was killed when his train completely derailed on a loose piece of track near Mitcham. Commenting on this last incident, *Herapath's Railway & Commercial Journal* acidly observed, "We cannot help noticing that if the rails had been what is called 'fished', the accident could hardly have happened".

At Wimbledon the W&CR terminated in a single-track bay let into the Down platform of the LSWR station, then on the country side of the road bridge, with only a trailing connection to the main line. Soon after leaving this bay, the line turned south-east, taking a more-or-less direct approach to Croydon. Although in fact land was purchased throughout for double track, only a single line was laid.

Two-car push-and-pull unit 982 on a West Croydon to Wimbledon service at Mitcham Junction signalbox c.1930. The guard is surrendering the staff for the single track section south of Mitcham Junction. The Sutton line curves away to the right by the locomotive.

Mitcham, the only place of any consequence on the route, had a station at the south end of the main street where, as at Staines and Enfield, the engineers adopted the economical solution of adapting an existing house, an 18th century building, formerly the country retreat of a City merchant and now listed as of architectural and historical interest. Passengers entered through the front door, purchased their tickets in the hall, passing out through the back door to descend to a platform cut out of the side of the garden. The only other intermediate station was a single platform with low brick shelter called Beddington, but sited rather hopelessly nearly two miles north of that small village, in open country. Its remoteness from the place it was alleged to serve led to its renaming to Beddington Lane in January 1887.

From a point just west of Mitcham station to the site of the present Waddon Marsh platform, the line followed the course of the Surrey Iron Railway on land repurchased from adjacent landowners who had bought it from the old company after 1846. A junction (subsequently removed) was made with the Croydon & Epsom immediately south of the Wandle, but the W&CR single track continued for about ½-mile beside the LBSCR into West Croydon station where it was afforded a short bay let into the country end of the Up platform. Level-crossings over seven public roads are mentioned in the act, but only three survived to the 1990s. It was an easy route to build, rising only slightly at the Croydon end, requiring no substantial engineering other than short stretches of cutting at Mitcham and Waddon Marsh.

A third intermediate station called Morden (Morden Halt, 1st November 1918, Morden Road Halt, 2nd July 1951) was opened in 1857. Whilst it was the nearest station to Morden village, a 1½ mile walk faced anyone unable to secure a conveyance. Its two-storey house, with brick ticket office alongside, and bay window looking up and down the line, survived until November 1982, when both buildings were summarily demolished. The immediate surroundings remained almost entirely rural for over 70 years after its opening.

In a move which put some semblance of order into the operation of the W&CR, the LBSCR secured a 21-year lease to work, manage, and take tolls from 1st July 1856, under an act of that year which also sanctioned additional capital to double the line. Not wishing to remain impotent in an LBSCR enterprise entering its territory, the LSWR obtained parliamentary authority in 1857 for joint operation and under a territorial agreement concluded in the summer of 1859 secured the Wimbledon–Mitcham section for the remainder of the lease, with net earnings and expenses to be shared equally with the Brighton, on the understanding that the latter could continue to work into Wimbledon. By a further agreement of 1862 a joint committee was set up to manage the W&CR. After purchasing the assets of the W&CR and becoming sole owner from 1st January 1866, the LBSCR offered its neighbour a half-share, but with the emergence of a jointly-owned Tooting, Merton & Wimbledon Railway to be opened two years later, the LSWR was content to withdraw, leaving the Brighton with almost all the W&CR to itself.

Rival schemes for the borderland territory of the LSWR and LBSCR in the Wimbledon/Streatham area appeared in 1863–64, with the Tooting, Merton & Wimbledon Extension Railway securing an act on 19th July 1864. This was a nominally independent undertaking with powers to make working arrangements with the two main line companies, but the latter reached an agreement in 1864 which led to an 1865 act dissolving the independent company and vesting its line jointly in the LSWR and LBSCR.

The Tooting, Merton & Wimbledon opened on 1st October 1868 from Streatham Junction (on the LBSCR Peckham Rye to Sutton line dating from the same day). Wimbledon was approached by lines diverging at Tooting Junction, one coming into the town from the north-east, the other from the south-east after forming a junction with the W&CR at Merton. All double track, the TM&W fed the new LBSCR main line through Streatham, but as we shall see, was also to afford the LSWR its long-desired access to the City. The Tooting Junction–Merton–Wimbledon section was justified by promise of freight traffic; William Shears, a director and promoter of the 1864 scheme had copper mills at Merton Abbey (Shears & Sons), where a siding was provided from the opening of the line.

At first only LBSCR trains used the TM&W, working between London Bridge and Wimbledon by both routes to and from Tooting Junction, but the 1865 Act had given the LSWR running powers to Tulse Hill and on 1st January 1869 a Kingston to Ludgate Hill service was started. This used the new Malden–Kingston line, the TM&W and a 74ch Tulse Hill to Herne Hill spur which the LCDR opened that day. The act also allowed LSWR trains to run over the LBSCR via the TM&W to and from the Brighton's freight wharf at Deptford. Most of the twelve trains each way daily between Kingston and Ludgate Hill ran via the Merton line and there were also five trains each way on Sundays. By the 1880s the Ludgate Hill service usually terminated at Wimbledon.

South of Streatham, the LBSCR Peckham Rye–Sutton line did not take the direct route across Mitcham Common but instead swung westwards to pass close to Mitcham, the alignment then curving very sharply round into and out of the W&CR through a shared station called Mitcham Junction. This arrangement, which for many years until they were diverted via Three Bridges, slowed electric coastal expresses to 20mph, gave Mitcham a remotely-situated station which has never developed much traffic. At the country end of the Down platform was a bay used by trains which ran to and from Crystal Palace Low Level (some went through to Wimbledon) in the 1860s and 1870s. Some originating traffic was finally attracted to Mitcham Junction with the opening around the turn of the century of a golf course with a large clubhouse next to the station.

At its opening on 10th October 1868, Mitcham Junction looked very much as it does today, a simple side-platformed country station, although it has long since lost its station signalbox, which stood at the London end of the Up platform, and the bay mentioned earlier.

Returning to the Tooting, Merton & Wimbledon, we must note that there were stations and goods yards at Tooting (just west of the junction), Haydens Lane (Haydons Road 1st October 1889) on the east side of the Merton–Wandsworth road, close to the Wandle, and Merton Abbey on the southern section. A fourth station, at first without any platform on the W&CR, called Lower Merton, was sited at the junction with the W&CR a short distance on the Croydon side of its level-crossing of the Kingston Road. This anticipated the development of John Innes' Merton Park estate, where laying-out of a street grid planted with trees and hollies started in the early 1870s, but housebuilding followed only very slowly. Innes was instrumental in obtaining improvements to the station; the W&CR trains called at a new platform from 1st November 1870 and in response to his persistence, the name was changed to the more socially acceptable Merton Park from 1st September 1887, by which time it was being used by a few middle-class commuters.

As the double track of the Tooting line continued from Merton through new platforms at Wimbledon station to rejoin the northern chord, the W&CR trains began to use this 58ch of jointly-owned line, leaving the original single track to become a siding. In 1881 the LSWR reconstructed the main line station at Wimbledon on the north side of the road bridge alongside the Tooting, Merton & Wimbledon platforms.

The district served by the Tooting line saw some residential growth after 1880. Lower Tooting, which by that year had already a grid of streets either side of the line, filled out, its development eventually to be much stimulated by the arrival in May 1903 of LCC electric tramcars linking it to Westminster and Blackfriars Bridges. Tooting station was resited more conveniently on the east side of the London Road on 12th August 1894, where a more commodious red brick and tile entrance building was provided on the road bridge, with covered stairs to well-canopied platforms. Relics of the original station's Up side building, in use as a house, still survive. Wimbledon grew out towards Haydons Road station in the same period and a new residential colony, with its own church, spread around the little station between 1890 and 1914. There was contemporary development, mainly of small houses for artisans, behind the Tooting–Merton–Wimbledon road, which received an electric tramway, with a branch up Haydons Road, in 1907. Slow for long journeys and for some years requiring a change to LCC cars at the county boundary, the London United tramcars were nevertheless very cheap and frequent in contrast to the Tooting line service, which was complicated rather than lavish.

In 1893 of the 16 Down trains between London Bridge and Tooting Junction, five continued to Wimbledon via Merton Abbey, returning via Haydons Road, the remainder reversing this route. There was a late evening train from West Croydon to Wimbledon which continued via Haydons Road and Streatham South Junction to Victoria, returning to West Croydon, where it arrived about 01.00 by the same route. The contemporary LSWR Up service from Wimbledon consisted of eight trains via Haydons Road and six via Merton Abbey. For some years after the opening of Holborn Viaduct station in 1874, the LSWR trains terminated there instead of Ludgate Hill, using the easternmost platform, but when that was wanted for parcels, the LCDR offered Snow Hill (Holborn Viaduct Low Level). In January 1911 the LSWR was providing two Down trains via Haydons Road and nine via Merton Abbey, with five and six Up respectively. These were supplemented by five trains each way between Haydons Road and Wimbledon, which were mostly extensions of the Merton Abbey workings. At the same time the LBSCR was offering 17 Down to Wimbledon via Haydons Road and nine via Merton Abbey; Up trains to the same number ran in reverse order over the loop. Most of these were motor trains, with first- and third-class seats only, working between Streatham and Wimbledon. At rush hours, both companies' services were fairly well-used, but electric tramcars and motor buses (after about 1910) had secured most of the off-peak traffic by 1914. Howard Turner mentions that in 1912, as the LBSCR locos were far from home (New Cross) for almost 20 hours daily, engine pits were installed at Tooting Junction between the old and new stations to enable ash pans to be raked out.

The Croydon line saw few changes before World War I. In July 1909 Merton Park to Mitcham was being worked by train staff and ticket, Mitcham Junction–West Croydon by electric train staff, with staff stations at Mitcham Junction, Beddington Lane, Waddon Marsh box and West Croydon. There were at this time 12 trains a

West Croydon train entering Beddington Lane c.1906.

day each way and one railmotor working. The 57ch between Mitcham and Mitcham Junction had been doubled in March 1879, probably to facilitate the working of goods trains to and from the sidings and yard at Mitcham, still the only public depot on the line and situated on the south side beyond the road bridge at the Wimbledon end of the station. (Rudely severed by a landslip on the Wimbledon side of Mitcham station in 1971, the double track was cut back to beyond the Croydon end of the platforms).

Passenger business between Wimbledon and Croydon remained very light; Merton Park was the only station that saw even a small increase in residential travel. Elsewhere virtually no houses were built before 1914, apart from a few south of Beddington Lane Halt. At the turn of the century, the passenger trains usually consisted of four to six four-wheelers with open third-class, in charge of a Stroudley Terrier 0–6–0T.

Freight traffic gradually assumed more importance. Between Mitcham and Croydon were a number of sidings of which the most noteworthy was one serving Waddon Flour Mills on the north bank of the Wandle, a single line of almost ¾-mile running due south just over a mile from the Croydon end of Beddington Lane. Near this junction, sidings served gravel pits on both sides of the line, those on the south later rearranged for the British Portland Cement Works, the others for a permanent way depot. Another siding, on the north side, a little nearer Croydon entered a brewery and was followed by another into Croydon Gas, Commercial & Coke Company's works at Waddon Marsh, west of the line. After 1920, these works expanded to the east side, requiring another set of sidings. Also on that side was Croydon Power Station, rail-served from about 1925 and with its own internal system, worked by a small English Electric 500V dc locomotive taking power from an overhead trolley wire. Suffering the combined assault of noxious effusions from the gasworks and spray from the power station's cooling towers, it is not surprising that the tracks here became very corrugated. In 1948–50 a second and very large electric power station (Croydon B) was built on the west side of the W&CR north of the gasworks. This had a large complex of sidings where coal wagons were shunted by Peckett 0–4–0ST and Robert Stephenson diesels.

World War I brought changes to passenger services on both lines. Already much reduced, the LSWR and LBSCR trains between Wimbledon and Streatham via both sides of the loop were among facilities withdrawn after traffic on Sunday 31st December 1916 to make resources available for essential war transport (LSWR trains ceased on Saturday evening as there was no Sunday service). After this, the rush-hour passengers who had made up most of the traffic found their way to and from work by electric tramcar and motor bus, either all the way, or to and from the nearest station open. For Wimbledon passengers there was little hardship as the LSWR's new electric services were in any case more attractive than the 31- to 40-minute steam run to and from the City over the 10½ miles via Streatham. Economies were sought on the Wimbledon–Croydon line by the introduction of push-and-pull sets of two side-gangway coaches and Stroudley 0–4–2T. These trains, which took over the service from 1st November 1918, were manned by conductor guards who issued tickets to those boarding at what were now unstaffed halts at Merton Park, Morden and Beddington Lane. Parcels and other facilities were withdrawn from these points, but Morden, closed on Sundays for some time, was re-opened on that day.

Life on the W&CR and the Tooting loops proceeded uneventfully until the Underground proposed its Morden tube in the early 1920s. One outcome of the row that this provoked was restoration of passenger service on the Tooting loops from 27th August 1923. Seven steam trains ran each way between Wimbledon and Ludgate Hill in peak hours only (three via Haydons Road) hauled by H and M7 0–4–4T. From London Bridge there were about five each way daily in peak hours, all via Haydons Road, from Tulse Hill seven each way (three via Haydons Road)

Haydons Road station looking to Wimbledon, c.1933.

and from Streatham, ten each way (five via Haydons Road). No trains ran on Sundays. Tulse Hill trains reversed on the Herne Hill lines there, those terminating at Streatham used the old short bay on the Down side. Both services were worked by ex-LSWR push-and-pull trains (four-coach bogie sets) and the Ludgate Hill service offered ex-LCDR six-wheelers. Building development immediately before 1914 had created a demand for a station at Streatham Road, between Tooting and Streatham, but this was ignored.

When the Wimbledon–Haydons Road–Streatham line was electrified in 1929, the Merton Park–Tooting section, its traffic now completely drained off by Colliers Wood tube station, was relegated to steam freight only, the last passenger train running on 2nd March. From the following day, electric trains ran half-hourly between Wimbledon and Holborn Viaduct seven days a week (three times an hour at peak periods), 41 each way in all. Until 30th June, Sunday trains worked to and from Victoria via Brixton except for two evening trains each way, but after that, Holborn Viaduct was used all week. St Paul's (now Blackfriars) was reached in 24 minutes from Wimbledon, 19 minutes from Tooting.

Electric service for West Croydon at Waddon Marsh Halt, July 1930.
Lens of Sutton

Initially the electrics regained much traffic from road services, especially in peak hours. At Haydons Road, tickets issued and collected grew from 36,541 in 1928 to 236,845 in 1934 and seasons from 45 to 2,240. This stimulated reconstruction of the station in 1938, when the two-storey station house on the Up side was demolished and new wooden buildings were provided on each platform, that on the Up side including a passimeter booking office. The signalbox, by then open only for freight yard movements and the morning peak, was closed at the same time, and replaced by a ground frame, but it was considered necessary to enlarge the yard to accommodate another 23 wagons. Wooden stations do not of course last long without careful maintenance and further rebuilding in the Network SouthEast brick and tile neo-vernacular single-storey style took place in the 1980s. After the mid-1950s, traffic on the line fell off and today the trains are not heavily loaded even in rush hours. As we shall see when considering the Wimbledon and Sutton line, since 1995 the basic train service has formed part of the Thameslink cross-London operation, working round via Sutton to and from Luton and Bedford.

The Merton Abbey chord remained busy with freight, but the junction at the Tooting end was severed on 10th March 1934, Tooting station obstinately clinging to its 'Junction' appendage until 3rd March 1938. The Up track was removed and the section was worked as a long siding from Merton Park, with control by telephone from instruments in the Merton Abbey goods office. At Merton Park, Croydon line passengers then faced an obstacle course in the form of two closed platforms and the double right of way between their train and the street door. Occasional special passenger workings penetrated to Merton Abbey, where the two-storey station house on the Up side and the two platforms remained in good order for many years. A supplement to the working timetable issued in 1936 indicated that the Down platform could be used by excursion trains, but the line was not to be negotiated at more than 5mph, under the supervision of a pilotman.

In the late 1920s and 1930s, Merton saw industrial expansion and a siding was laid from the Merton Abbey track into the new Lines Brothers Triang toy factory in Morden Road. Other private sidings served the Eyre Smelting Works and the New Merton Board Mills at Merton Abbey. As late as 1960 there were still two return goods workings daily from Norwood to Merton Abbey and one on Saturdays to Hackbridge but, with factory closures and increased use of road transport, loadings fell and after the last revenue train ran coal down to Merton Abbey on 1st May 1975 the track was quickly taken-up.

The Morden tube extension, which passed many feet below the W&CR near Morden Road halt, contributed much clay to the filling of the Mitcham ballast pits served by the latter line. As soon as the tube opened, passenger revenue at Merton Park, Morden Road and Mitcham declined steeply, but the W&CR continued to attract a steady patronage for through journeys and at its southern stations. In 1927 there were 14 push-and-pull workings between Wimbledon and West Croydon, one extended to Crystal Palace Low Level, two from Wimbledon to Sutton via Mitcham Junction, and another from Mitcham to Crystal Palace Low Level. A similar service worked Down.

Reflecting the growth of the West Croydon industrial area, freight workings were quite complex by 1927. In that year ex-LBSCR 0–6–0T and 0–6–2T were normally employed, but the heavier coal workings required Maunsell W 2–6–4T or N 2–6–0. The first run was at 02.50 from New Cross, visiting all the sidings and yards between the two ends, finishing at Tooting Junction via Merton Abbey and returning by the same route at 08.25. This was followed Down by the 05.10 from New Cross to Waddon Marsh, carrying coal for the Croydon Gas Company and returning with empties at 11.25. Traffic for the private sidings at Waddon Marsh and Beddington Lane was carried by the 08.30 from Norwood Yard, which returned from Beddington at 15.10. The large yard at Mitcham was cleared by the 12.55 from Norwood, which returned at 18.05. Last of the booked trips was the 14.37 from Norwood to Haydons Road which left there at 17.10. There was provision for a 16.00 conditional working from Norwood if any coal was left over for the gasworks. At Haydons Road there were private sidings on the Down side opposite the Lambeth Cemetery, where traffic was exchanged with the Wandle Valley Joint Sewage Board's lines, worked by its own locomotive, and on the Down side west of the station, a siding entered the 1897 depot of the Wimbledon Council.

This varied scene was further coloured in 1930 when the LCC was building the 825-acre St Helier housing estate south of Mitcham. C. J. Wills & Sons, the

Waddon Marsh, looking to West Croydon, 13th September 1975. *Alan A Jackson*

contractors, laid an extensive temporary network of flat-bottom rails on cinder ballast to carry materials as required to the building sites. There was a connection to the W&CR through Hall & Company's siding at Mitcham goods yard. This layout, with its 30ft span bridge over the Wandle, was operated by six 0–6–0T dating from 1885 to 1926, shedded at a depot about a mile south of Mitcham. It was one of the last examples in southern England of a major public works contract relying on rail-delivered materials carried to site over specially-laid lines.

As well as the various public and private freight facilities already mentioned, the W&CR also handled the Southern's own needs for its permanent way depot on the north side of the line near Beddington Lane, and for the civil engineer's depot next to the goods yard at Mitcham, a fascinating spot where complicated new layouts were laid down on a trial basis. This depot closed in 1966.

With the sole exception of Woodside–Sanderstead, the W&CR was the only part of the Southern's suburban system not electrified by 1928. Perhaps simply to close this gap, and for no really sound reason, the general manager decided it should be converted, obtaining the board's consent on 7th July that year. With all neighbouring lines already electrified, he thought it could be cheaply done without new substations and there were of course obvious economies in eliminating an isolated steam passenger service. But the board minutes show a sad story of costs rising well above estimates as the bills came in. One reason for this situation was a decision taken following a visit Walker paid with senior officers on 2nd August.

After looking at Dundonald Road level crossing, Wimbledon, which they found 'not particularly busy' though requiring two gatemen as it was open for 18 hours daily, the party proceeded to Kingston Road, Merton Park. Here two signalmen and a porter signalman were on shifts, and a recent census had shown daily passage of 600 buses, 3,400 other vehicles and 5,000 pedestrians. Delays with the more frequent electric trains would be severe, so the chief engineer was invited to report on the possibility of eliminating both crossings by leading the W&CR into the Wimbledon & Sutton at a point south of Merton Park, an ambitious project which no doubt met a quick death once costs were assessed. But the main problem considered by the party was the handling of the important freight traffic after electrification. The existing five booked workings between West Croydon and Mitcham (two extended to Wimbledon) and one or two daily as far as Waddon Marsh would have to be moved to the night hours to make room for the proposed electric service. As such a change would incur almost £2,000 a year in extra costs, not to mention the displeasure of customers, it was proposed to construct another track between Beddington Lane and West Croydon to allow daytime freight working to continue. It was also noted that the Mitcham Ballast Sidings were not used and that much railway land here and near Morden might be made available for factories or housing. Completed in 1930 in time for the electric working, the second line was partly achieved by linking existing sidings parallel to the passenger track on the north side. Between West Croydon and Waddon Marsh the freight line was controlled by electric train staff with a separate set of electric tokens for the block sections; beyond Waddon Marsh the track was operated under permissive working.

By choosing to electrify a single line operated by conductor-guards, the SR ensured that this curious and enduring backwater would retain some character. As no corridor electric stock was available, 2-car electric sets were made up from the original side-gangway trailers of the LBSCR 1909 South London line electrification. Nine feet wide at eaves, with frosted glass vents over the quarter-lights, these vehicles had been taken off the South London line when it fairly quickly became apparent that there was a surfeit of first-class accommodation. Replaced by composite non-driving trailers in 1911, they had been given lavatories and steam heating and placed on main line duty (they were too wide to work anywhere else on the LBSCR electric system). The SR installed new electric traction equipment, forming them into motor/control trailer sets with side gangways retained but no through communication between cars. Some first-class seating was converted to third, but otherwise it was to disappear with the abolition of suburban first-class in October 1941.

Resplendent in fresh green paint, three coats of best white lead on their roofs, these sets started work on 6th July 1930, operating every 20 minutes at peak times, otherwise half-hourly, seven days a week, and sharing the reconstructed platforms 9 and 10 at Wimbledon with the Wimbledon and Sutton service. On the opening day of electric service, a new halt was added at Waddon Marsh, a 170ft island platform attached to the south end of the existing signal box, served by a passing loop which made, with sidings, a spread of four tracks at this point. Passengers approaching by footbridge were offered the bewildering choice of purchasing their tickets from the train guards or from the signalman.

Electric train staffs were used for the single-line working of the passenger trains, with exchanges at Merton Park, Mitcham, Mitcham Junction, Beddington Lane (not a passing place), Waddon Marsh, and West Croydon B box. Using the single line alongside the Croydon & Epsom, the electric trains, like their predecessors, terminated in a bay at West Croydon Up platform, an arrangement which, after the SR had rebuilt West Croydon with a main road entrance at this, the country end, led many a confused passenger to board them for what was thought to be a direct run to London. Traversing the whole length of the W&CR in just over 16 minutes, the electric trains were timed to pass each other on the double track between Mitcham and Mitcham Junction.

The market gardens and other open land in miscellaneous use which made up much of the carriage window scene between Merton Park and Beddington Lane survived electrification. Even today, there are still quasi-rural glimpses, particularly between Merton Park and Mitcham and between Mitcham Junction and Bedding-ton Lane. As late as 1924 milk remained the principal traffic at Morden Road Halt and three years later a *Railway Magazine* writer was describing the surroundings here as 'the most rural and untouched neighbourhood of any within the same radius from Charing Cross'. Houses began to appear in the late 1920s when Merton Park was filled-up south of the W&CR, whilst to the north of the line and east of the main road were the factories already mentioned. The occupants of the houses and the factory workers, however, used the tube railway or road transport in preference to the indirect electric trains with their obligatory change at Wimbledon.

Although there were two or three patches of new housing between Morden Road and Mitcham by the end of the 1930s, the rural atmosphere was preserved when the extensive area of Morden Hall park came under the sympathetic care of the National Trust. From Mitcham to the Junction many small houses were built between 1927 and 1939 and the general residential growth of the Mitcham area required some improvement to the goods yard in 1936, but post-war maps still showed watercress beds south of the line there. Mitcham Common and Croydon Corporation's huge Beddington Sewage Farm kept the next stretch as open land. At Beddington Lane there was a small cluster of new housing close to the station. From here to Waddon Marsh the electric tramway opened in May 1906 between West Croydon, Mitcham, and Tooting with its attendant competing motor buses was probably the main influence on the plentiful new low-cost housing built between 1928 and 1935.

Purley Way, a by-pass round the west side of Croydon, was opened in 1925, crossing the railway at Waddon Marsh and helping to strengthen the growth of the industrial complex here. The 1930 halt was close to Croydon Council's housing estate which filled up land between the railway and Mitcham Road in 1928–31, but it seems doubtful if many of the tenants used the trains in preference to the cheaper and more frequent tram and bus services along the Mitcham Road.

The mixed land uses and street transport competition stunted the growth of passenger traffic that normally accompanied suburban electrification, the nature of the service also proving some deterrent to commuter settlement. Thus the two-car sets continued to provide ample accommodation for the traffic offering right through to the 1950s, when they reached the end of their useful life. In 1954 they gave way to BR 2EPB two-car sets, comfortable and smart enough, but lacking the charisma which brought railway photographers out in some numbers to record the last journeys of their predecessors. Overnight the whole line lost some colour, especially as conductor-guard operation had necessarily to be abandoned and ticket issuing arrangements provided at Morden Road. The versatile signalmen at the other two halts had more work to do.

Mitcham station with West Croydon train entering, 19th August 1957. At this time the entrance and exit of the station were through the house seen at the right hand side of the overline road bridge. *Alan A Jackson*

Goods traffic was still quite heavy in the mid-1950s, bringing on to the line LBSCR C2X, C and Q class 0–6–0, even the occasional E6 0–6–2T or W 2–6–4T. Around 1967, Type 3 (Class 33) diesel-electrics and E6000 (Class 73) electro-diesels took over, by this time on waning traffic, following transfer to road haulage and the rundown of the gasworks. Haydons Road yard closed from 5th December 1966, Mitcham from 1st May 1967, and Tooting from 5th August 1968. After the Croydon gasworks closed, there remained until 1973 two or three daily trips bringing coal from Betteshanger, Kent to Croydon B power station, but in that year a switch was made to Durham coal brought by coastal vessels to Kingsnorth (Kent). There, somewhat incredibly, it was split up into lorry loads and carried over congested urban roads to Croydon. This left gas oil for the power station's auxiliary plant as the only regular freight movement.

With its heavy staffing ratio and lightly-loaded trains, the W&CR was early on the list for closure, coming up for the first time in 1951 when it was decided that with freight still important, passenger abandonment did not make much sense, as signalling could not be much reduced. Instead there followed a series of economy cuts, starting with Sunday closure of Morden Road from 13th September 1964. From 20th June 1965 Sunday trains were withdrawn over the whole line, and from 7th November 1966 Morden Road was also closed on Saturdays. This last date also saw curtailment of evening service with last trains brought back to around 19.45 for departures each end (18.15 Saturdays) instead of 22.45. First trains now started at around 07.15, but frequency remained half-hourly through the shorter day, still with some extras at peak hours (the last of these were eventually withdrawn in May 1971). In common with others on the Southern Region, the halts lost this description in the timetables operative from 5th May 1969, although Beddington Lane's name-board still bore the forbidden word six years later.

With the drastic reduction in freight, it became possible to work the line as a siding from West Croydon, and in 1971 BR decided to test the temperature of the water. Soon after this closure notice was published, an observer found that at 16.30 on a weekday it took him nearly three times as long to travel by car as by train between Wimbledon and West Croydon stations, yet he noticed on arrival at the latter that a train from Wimbledon disembarked only 17 passengers. BR was probably surprised at the extent of the opposition. Sir Richard Thompson, MP for Croydon South, who already claimed credit for saving Woodside–Sanderstead, raised the matter in the Commons on 5th July 1972, suggesting that 1,500 commuters and 1,000 other passengers would have to meet higher fares and a longer and more tiring journey, whilst closure would add to local road congestion. A ministerial reply averred that the average use of the eight stations was about 1,700 passengers each way daily, 'very low for a suburban service of this type'. It was suggested the line was among the heaviest loss-makers in the south-east, but the minister concluded by noting that its future was not yet sealed. At the public enquiry on the same day it was stated that 80 per cent of the users would have up to 26 minutes added to daily journeys, around half having to pay higher fares. Only 11 per cent of users in the Merton area had cars, while some 250 people in Beddington Lane district would be completely isolated, their nearest bus stop 600yd across the Common, a hazard after dark. The Minister of Transport finally announced in July 1974 that the line would stay open, his department following with a statement which admitted severe environmental effects, inconvenience and extra cost to users, and added somewhat gratuitously, that buses would be an inadequate substitute. A year later, BR issued a poster encouraging people to ride the line.

The attractions of this single-track electric line, with its freight workings, manually-operated semaphore signals, varied scenery and country-style stations, were substantially eroded after the 1970s. Although the independent unelectrified freight line between West Croydon and Waddon Marsh was taken out of use from 1st February 1976, the 'as required' oil trains continued to run until some time before the closure of the Croydon Power Station in November 1981. With around a dozen railwaymen on duty at a time on a six-mile line carrying but two trains an hour, further economies were inevitable and so far as signalling was concerned these came about with the phasing of the line into the Victoria Area Resignalling Scheme. From 18th October 1981, West Croydon 'B' box was closed and the section between West Croydon and Waddon Marsh was worked under track circuit block regulations. This was followed by closure of the signal boxes at Waddon Marsh, Mitcham and Merton Park from 23rd May 1982. The level crossings at Beddington Lane, (where the box had been destroyed by fire on 26th April 1981) Merton Park and Dundonald Road, Wimbledon, converted to lifting barriers, were then supervised by closed circuit television from the new Falcon Lane signalling centre at Clapham Junction.

Further cuts were made in the train services. From October 1988 the service was reduced to one train shuttling between Wimbledon and West Croydon at approximately 45 minute intervals, Mondays to Saturdays, finishing early in the evening. By this time something rather better was under consideration: the line was to become part of the Croydon Tramlink light rail system already mentioned. With this, trams were to work into the east side of Wimbledon station, providing it with a direct link to both West and East Croydon stations.

Looking to Tooting from Christchurch Road Bridge, Colliers Wood, 21st June 1975. *Alan A Jackson*

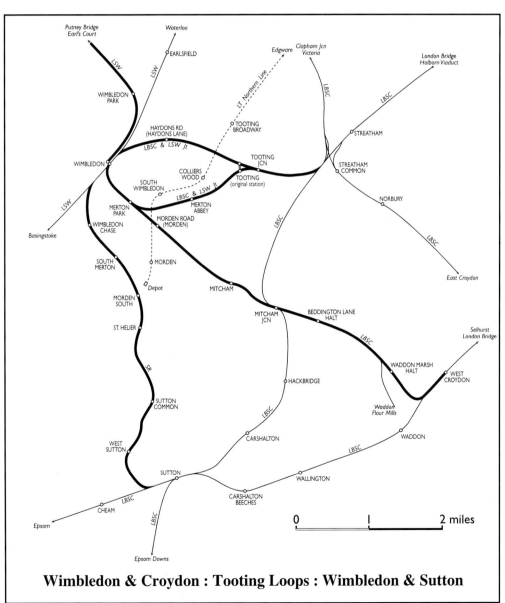

Wimbledon & Croydon : Tooting Loops : Wimbledon & Sutton

Road frontage of Wimbledon Chase station (SR 1929), with BR signage, March 1967. *BR (SR)*

The Wimbledon & Sutton Line

(map page 109)

From the beginning of the 1880s, the small Surrey town of Sutton attracted schemes aimed at breaking the monopoly of the LBSCR. Sited on that company's Portsmouth main line, the town had enjoyed railway service since the opening of the Croydon and Epsom line on 10th May 1847, but its position was much improved with the availability of a direct route to London Bridge and Victoria via Mitcham from 1st October 1868. After this, the district experienced development as a residential area for middle-class commuters and by 1881 the 1851 population of just over a thousand had risen to 10,334.

Attacks on the LBSCR's hold took the form of schemes for branches from the LSWR at Worcester Park (1882) and from Wimbledon (1883, 1888, 1890 and 1891). All failed. 'Sutton', observed the parliamentary committee on the 1882 Sutton & L&SW Junction Bill, 'has to grow into greater importance before it ought to ask for amplification of its railway accommodation'. Grow it did. In 1901 the population, with that of neighbouring Cheam, had reached 20,267 and in *Black's Guide Around London* that year, A. R. Hope-Moncrieff wrote: 'its antiquity is all overlaid by the commonplace smugness of a residential suburb, the fine country round has been much cut up by schools and other institutions'. Sutton was now virtually joined to Cheam in the west, reaching out to touch Carshalton and Beddington in the east and the edge of Banstead Downs in the south. Only the railwayless north, between Sutton Common and Merton, remained neglected by the housebuilder.

Local landowners were restless, considering that if only a railway could be built across these clay pastures and through the elm copses, they stood to gain much. A meeting to consider a scheme engineered by W. Vaux Graham was convened at the Westminster Palace Hotel on 7th October 1908, presided over by landowners Sir

Henry George Smallman and H. D. Searles-Wood. Reporting on this two days later, *The Railway Gazette* considered the promoters 'peculiarly optimistic', especially as there had been no negotiations with the District or the LSWR over the proposed connections at Wimbledon. Nothing came of this initiative, but another meeting of property owners at Merton just over a year later led to a similar scheme by the same engineer being incorporated in a bill for the 1910 session. This envisaged a 5½-mile line from Wimbledon to Sutton through eight intermediate stations, and junctions with the main lines at each end. It was anticipated that the District would work the service with electric traction by extending its trains from Wimbledon. Smallman, Searles-Wood, W. E. R. Innes and other local landowners were prominent among the promoters. These gentlemen were ready to put up some but by no means all the £350,000 estimated capital cost.

From the evidence given to the parliamentary committee by Sir George Gibb, chairman of the Underground Company, and by Albert Stanley, managing director of the District, it appeared that although the District was friendly and would be quite happy to work the line, it had not committed any cash. The LSWR evinced little enthusiasm, expressing concern about further overloading of its Putney and Wimbledon line, also turning-up its nose at the proposed junction arrangements at Wimbledon.

In open opposition to a line which would filch traffic from their territory, the LBSCR, through William Forbes, the general manager, told the parliamentary committee that the railway would be 'a constant source of irritation'. As some indication of the lack of need north of Sutton he put up a Miss Mary Pochin, who solemnly declared that she had once hailed a bus which used to ply between Wimbledon and Sutton but the astonishment of the conductor was so great at being hailed that he omitted to signal to the driver to stop; the driver even turned to see what she was waving at. Forbes then outlined the Brighton's plans for improving the facilities for Sutton: electric trains would reach London Bridge in 20 minutes and Victoria in 18 minutes compared with the promoters' estimates of 32-minute run from Sutton to Waterloo. All in all, he suggested, this was a 'nice little move on the part of the District Railway, first to get to Sutton, then to Epsom, and afterwards on to Brighton'. Although he was of course laying it on rather thickly, the Brighton was without doubt genuinely rattled; in January 1910 it had steam-hauled a South London line electric train to Sutton to test clearances and was preparing plans for widening to four tracks between the western end of Sutton and Cheam (works which were completed in October 1911).

Taking note of the Brighton's attitude, Parliament passed the bill without insisting on the proposed junction at Sutton, although it was stipulated that there should be convenient access between the two stations there. The act gave the MDR powers to run over the Wimbledon & Sutton through an end-on junction with the Putney & Wimbledon line in Wimbledon station. After passing beneath Wimbledon Hill Road, the double tracks were to parallel the LSWR main line as far as the Elm Grove footbridge, just before which there was to be a junction with the LSWR Up slow line, facing London. A station at this point would serve the first site of the All-England Tennis Ground.

At Elm Grove, the line was to swerve sharply, passing beneath the LSWR, to emerge on the south side to receive a connection from the LSWR Down slow. A proposed station at Cannon Hill, closely followed by another at Green Lane, Merton

Park, would serve an area of recent residential development, the line skirting the west side of the Merton Park estate, laid out for building many years earlier. From here, the route would be south to a station serving Morden village and beyond that there was to be another station at Elm Farm on the south side of Love Lane. Sutton Common was next reached, with its station, whence there would be a wide sweep westwards to avoid the already built-up west side of Sutton as far as possible. A station at Collingwood Road (end of Sydney Road) was to be followed by another for Cheam, on the north side of Cheam Road, Sutton. Finally the line would curve eastwards to terminate alongside the LBSCR at Bridge Road, Sutton, next to the Post Office, where a footpath would link it with the LBSCR Up platform.

Despite Forbes' insinuations, the promoters at first found themselves quite isolated, receiving no encouragement from the existing railway companies and unable to raise more capital. In March 1911 they went caps in hand to Albert Stanley, who in turn approached the LSWR to see whether that company would help the District complete the line if the landowners agreed to bear part of any operating losses for a limited period. There was no response, so in October 1911 the District offered to complete the line if the promoters would guarantee about £20,000 a year. This was too much for the landowners to find, and on 8th October 1912 it was finally agreed to limit their guarantee to £6,000 a year maximum for ten years, the District to meet the balance of any deficiency below 4½ per cent return on the capital. Within a few weeks of this agreement, the local interests on the board of the Wimbledon & Sutton Railway Company were replaced by Underground Company nominees, most of the issued shares also passing to Underground representatives or share-holders. From 5th December 1912 all meetings were held at the Underground headquarters, Electric Railway House, Broadway, Westminster.

Whilst the takeover was going through, the District, by agreement with the LSWR, secured powers for a second pair of tracks for its exclusive use between East Putney and Wimbledon, partly for the Sutton traffic. A year later (1913) the District was authorised to widen its own line between Eel Brook Common, south of Fulham Broadway and Munster Road, south of Parsons Green, where there were to be two new island platforms. This work, never started, together with the third track at Putney Bridge station (completed in 1910) would have facilitated working of non-stop trains on the Sutton service.

Alterations were begun on the north side of Wimbledon station in 1913–14 in preparation for the Sutton line, and an extra bay at Wimbledon and additional signalboxes between Wimbledon Park and East Putney came into use on 9th March 1914. Negotiations with the LSWR delayed a start on the Sutton line, but much of the land was acquired and fenced. Wartime restrictions caused further delay. An act of 1913 increased the capital to £550,000 and incorporated the guarantees already mentioned, but a further act of 1915 gave the District powers to guarantee the Wimbledon & Sutton dividends and interest as a working expense.

Immediate post-war conditions were not favourable to a resumption of the scheme, but land purchases continued, including a parcel at Sutton bought in 1920. Opportunity came in the form of the Trade Facilities Act, 1921, which attempted to mitigate unemployment by offering a Treasury guarantee of capital and interest for approved public works. This brought forth a batch of proposals from the Underground Company in October 1921 which included construction of the Sutton line, now estimated to cost, with rolling stock and car depot, a total of £1.7m. The

Treasury agreed to guarantee the package which among other things included modernisation of the City & South London tube railway and its extension southwards to Morden where there would be a link to the Wimbledon & Sutton and a sharing of the car sheds. Bills for all these new works, which also provided for connection of the City & South London with the Hampstead & Highgate tube at Camden Town, were duly deposited in November 1922.

The prospect of tube and District trains busily undermining its traffic at Sutton was too much for the infant Southern Railway. At its Annual General Meeting the chairman, Sir Hugh Drummond, told shareholders it was 'a very serious matter' and in the parliamentary committee on the Underground bill, Sir Herbert Walker, general manager, talked of an 'invasion' of the Southern's territory as defined in the Railway Grouping Agreement. Sir Herbert made it clear to the committee that the SR would not object to the City & South London tube going as far as Tooting and even offered to accommodate the tube trains at Wimbledon via the Tooting & Wimbledon loop if this would secure withdrawal of the District from the Wimbledon & Sutton scheme. But the Underground representatives maintained that a combined depot for both District and tube at Morden was essential and there was no other suitable site. Taking this to mean all or none, the Lords committee rejected the whole of the City & South London extension from Clapham Common to Morden.

Incensed South London MPs, deprived of a much-needed Underground facility, sought to throw all the blame on the SR. Talks between the two parties were arranged and on 25th July a compromise was reached; the Southern agreed the tube might go as far as the north side of the London Road at Morden, with a line beyond for depot access only and no connection to the Wimbledon & Sutton, which the Southern would build and work. Running powers over the Sutton line would be available to the District, with the Southern making the necessary junctions and changes at Wimbledon and Sutton. As a further sop, the SR agreed to restore passenger service between Wimbledon and Streatham over the Tooting & Wimbledon loop, which had been a wartime casualty.

With SR opposition removed, the Morden tube extension was sanctioned and the Wimbledon & Sutton powers passed to the SR from 1st July 1924 under the SR Act of 1st August 1924. This act dissolved the Sutton company, altered the junctions at Wimbledon to the south side of the main line (the District had shown no interest in the proffered running powers) and added the necessary junction with the Epsom line at Sutton. It was altogether a remarkable concession on the part of the Southern, no doubt made under very strong political pressures and eased by an agreement with the Underground Company that there would in future be mutual consultation before competing lines were promoted.

In direct opposition to the spirit of this agreement, the Underground launched feeder bus services when the Morden tube opened in 1926, culling traffic from a wide sector of outer London suburban territory of the SR: Sutton, Cheam, Mitcham, Banstead, Wallington, Worcester Park, even Epsom. These services, combined with very low fares and through road-rail ticket facilities, drew much business from the Southern, quickly depriving it of an estimated four million passengers a year. The loss was made more serious by the rapid residential development of the district after 1928. Around the tube terminus, building of small houses spread wide and in 1929, just to the south, the LCC started to construct its new town of St Helier, over 9,000 dwellings to accommodate some 40,000.

Bridge carrying the Wimbledon & Sutton line over the London–Epsom road c. 1930. Morden South station is just off the picture at the left.

In contrast to the tube extension, progress on the Wimbledon & Sutton was slow. Property had to be acquired and demolished at Merton and at Sutton, negotiations for acquisition dragging on until the summer of 1928. Approval for work to start was given by the SR board on 30th June 1927 and in October the company's engineering staff began operations on the embankment at Wimbledon. At Sutton, the main contractor, Sir Robert McAlpine & Sons, could not make a start until July 1928. Work then continued night and day until September, when a resident secured a restraint on night work from the Vacation Court.

The northern end was sufficiently advanced to allow service of the first two stations, Wimbledon Chase and South Merton, from 7th July 1929, when the Streatham-Tooting-Wimbledon trains (restored on 27th August 1923 and electrified on 3rd March 1929) were extended. Although a double track was laid, this first section was worked with train staff until about December 1929, after which trains ran empty to St Helier station to reverse. The remainder of the line opened for staff training on 1st January 1930, to the public on Sunday 5th January. Late in 1929 742 *Camelot* and other N15 and S15 4–6–0s had tested and ironed-out the track.

Construction through treacherous clay subsoil had been far from simple. Embankments at the southern end had slipped after completion and a vein of blue clay near Sutton required extensive drainage. At the extreme southern end, the engineers had to cut through much chalk and demolish Victorian villas to reach the old LBSCR line. There were no less than 20 bridges over the 5¼ miles and these, together with the drainage works, high embankments and property compensation, pushed up the capital cost to £1.042m. Although hardly justifying the railwaymen's nickname 'Wall of Death' it was a line designed for electric traction, with many sharp curves and only 35ch of level rail in its whole length; gradients were steep. From 50ft above sea level at Wimbledon the line climbed to about 200ft at Sutton.

All intermediate stations were of an economical standard pattern at rail level, a 520ft island platform for eight-car trains, partly covered with a glazed canopy carried on steel stanchions at 38ft centres. General waiting rooms, ladies' and gentlemen's lavatories and separate staff huts comprised the facilities provided. Each station had a passimeter booking office either on the platform or at road level, and at South Merton, Morden South, and Sutton Common there were no other buildings. Divided into two block sections (Wimbledon C–St Helier–Sutton), this was the first SR line to be signalled throughout with upper-quadrant semaphores. One station-master, living in an SR house at West Sutton, supervised the whole line.

In peak hours, eight-car trains ran every 20 minutes between Holborn Viaduct and West Croydon via Wimbledon and Sutton, but the basic service was half-hourly, Holborn Viaduct–Wimbledon–Sutton–West Croydon–Crystal Palace–Victoria, using three-car trains. Connections were available at Wimbledon to and from Waterloo, at Sutton and West Croydon to and from Victoria and London Bridge. The last two trains at night ran only to St Helier, returning to Wimbledon.

Traction current for the third rail came from Durnsford Road power station (Wimbledon) with conversion to 660V dc in substations at Raynes Park and Sutton; later current was taken from the National Grid via a rectifier at St Helier.

At Wimbledon a new through island platform was provided on the south side for Croydon and Sutton trains, the new line running thence for about half a mile between the main lines and the large goods yard and signal works on the south. It then turned south east on a 12ch curve traversing a 1½-mile embankment through Wimbledon Chase station to South Merton. A long siding paralleled the double track towards Wimbledon Chase, where the station served a district which had been built up between 1900 and 1914. Its well-sited frontage on the main Kingston Road was covered with white glazed blocks, but the effect of the curving street elevation was somewhat spoiled by the excrescence of a luggage lift tower which was never used. Showing some evidence of an architect's hand, the general design of this station appears to have been a prototype for new SR 'marine style' suburban stations, setting the pattern for those on the Chessington line. The name Wimbledon Chase for a site in the Merton & Morden Urban District is an interesting example of railway snobbery, matched by the Underground's adjacent 'South Wimbledon', which was in Merton High Street, also outside the Wimbledon boundary.

At South Merton, the tiny passimeter ticket office was on the platform but a concrete base was made alongside the road bridge above for a future entrance building. Although the district was fully built-up by the mid-1930s, this base has never been used. Still on embankment, the double tracks ran south to cross the main London-Epsom-Worthing road on an impressive 120ft skew span of lattice girders which took them into Morden South station, where a subway through the embankment gave access to the island platform. This station has always suffered from its proximity to the tube terminus, and its catchment area was denuded by the large acreages of the tube depot and Morden Park.

A cutting on a half-mile curve of 25ch radius led into the St Helier passenger and goods station, the most important point on the line. Twelve acres of land were conveyed free by the LCC, the SR adding just over two acres more. The freight yard had two roads and a great deal of spare space. On Green Lane, above the tracks, the station building took the form of a concrete blockhouse of quite remarkable crudity, anticipating the products of the modern brutalist school of architects by some 40

Street frontage of St Helier station (1930), still bearing Southern Railway signage 15 years after the formation of British Railways (photo 6th August 1963). *Alan A Jackson*

years. Its sole relieving feature was a narrow glass canopy which advertised the service offered. Some way from the centre of the large LCC estate, it failed to attract more than a tiny proportion of the tenants, most of whom preferred to walk or bus to the tube at Morden, or found employment locally, travelling by bus or cycle.

For almost a mile beyond St Helier, the line was on embankment until the north end of Sutton Common station was reached. Although houses were built each side of the line here in the early 1930s a very large part of the catchment area to the north-east was left as an open space. Facilities were similar to those at South Merton except that the passimeter ticket office was housed in a small hut at road level.

A short cutting and a half-mile embankment carried the line to West Sutton, the last of the stations, also below road level at the start of the deep cutting through the chalk to the junction. Its roadside building was an ugly concrete blockhouse similar to that at St Helier, but with a stubby concrete canopy. East of the station, there was a solid mass of small houses by the early 1930s and some of the streets dated back to Victorian times. On the west were open spaces and a wedge of housing towards the by-pass road, much of it completed by the early 1930s.

Sinuous and steep, the last stretch of the line featured three reverse curves of 15, 20, and 13ch radius, climbing at 1 in 90, and 1 in 49, with a final ramp of half a mile at 1 in 44 into Sutton station. As this area was fully built-up in late Victorian and Edwardian years, it was not possible without undue cost to obtain a suitable angle of slope, so the chalk cutting had in places to be lined with concrete.

Concurrently with the construction of the line, the stations at Wimbledon and Sutton were rebuilt. New road level buildings and staircases at Sutton were finished in 1928, and the enlarged Wimbledon was ready a year later.

From the time the line was opened until the autumn of 1939 builders were busy filling the area near the line with small houses, notably west of South Merton station up to the edge of Morden Park (1934–38), and west of the tracks between St Helier and West Sutton (1927–39) where, apart from some public open spaces, only the valley of the Pyl Brook was left alone. Most of the LCC estate at St Helier had been finished by 1935. Although some traffic was gained from all this activity, the success of the Morden tube with its very low fares and road-rail ticket facilities meant that the hopes of the original Wimbledon & Sutton promoters were never to be fully realised. The fact that the only peak-hour service on the line was to a City terminus, and that over a circuitous route, was a contributory cause of failure, despite the reasonably good interchange facilities at Wimbledon, Sutton and Tulse Hill (British passengers do not like changing trains, however good the connections). Towards the end of the 1950s loadings began to fall off during the day and off-peak trains, never very much used, were carrying only very light loads.

After Sunday 8th November 1959, Morden South closed on Sundays and from 17th June 1963 the line's three night trains disappeared. Originally steam-hauled, these comprised the 00.19 Holborn Viaduct–St Helier, the 01.35 Herne Hill–Sutton (connecting out of the 01.20 Holborn Viaduct–Orpington, also withdrawn) and the 03.40 Sutton–Wimbledon–Victoria (with connection at Herne Hill for Holborn Viaduct). By the late 1950s, the market, newspaper, post office and other small hours workers who had been encouraged by these services to live along the line had all taken to their cars. About 1967 the off-peak service was altered to run from West Croydon to London Bridge instead of to Victoria.

The freight yard at St Helier lost its daily train from 6th May 1963. After this, goods traffic in the form of milk tankers and coal wagons continued to be worked over the line to meet the needs of the Express Dairy's bottling plant at Morden South, where private sidings had been opened in 1954, with a junction facing Sutton at the south end of the station. The loaded milk tanker trains originated at Acton Western Region and there was also some railborne coal inwards until 1970 when the plant was converted to oil brought in by road. Internal shunting was performed by the Dairy's Ruston & Hornsby four-wheel 4B Diesel until 1972 when it was donated to Ashford Steam Centre and replaced by Hunslet Yardmaster four-wheel diesel loco *David*. The siding received its last deliveries of milk in April 1978 but continued to house empty tankers for a few months after that, seeing its final use on 30th December 1978.

Signalling economies were achieved with the line's inclusion in the Victoria Area and Waterloo Area Resignalling schemes. St Helier's signal box was closed after 22nd May 1982 and the southern section passed into the control of the Falcon Lane Signalling Centre at Clapham Junction from 4th October that year. The northern junction came under the new Wimbledon centre in February 1991.

West Sutton's road level building was completely rebuilt in 1989 at a time when all six stations received what was described as a 'facelift' but withdrawal of full time staffing soon exposed all vertical surfaces to almost 100 per cent coverage with mindless spray-painted graffiti and other vandalism. In May 1995 a railway employee described West Sutton in *Railnews* as:

> heavily vandalised and dirty. The waiting room lights still come on at night but the door is boarded up. The station is only staffed in the mornings, so the rest of the time there is no information available and no staff for security.

Left: The unassuming entrance to Sutton Common station, 6th August 1963. *Alan A Jackson*

Below: A four-car electric train climbing the 1 in 44 gradient into Sutton station from the Wimbledon–Sutton line; main line to Dorking and Horsham etc at left, 19th August 1957. *Alan A Jackson*

He added that passengers had no means of knowing what was happening when trains did not appear at the scheduled time. Such problems are not of course confined to this line; in terms of the cost of repairs and redecoration, passengers frightened off by an atmosphere of insecurity and intimidation, and of uncollected revenue from those using the trains, it seems possible that the savings from such staff 'economies' may often be quite illusory.

With bus services and private cars bringing passengers to Wimbledon, Morden Underground and Sutton stations from its catchment area, and other potential users deterred for the reasons just mentioned, off-peak loadings on this line fell away in the 1970s and 1980s. Commuting to central London has also declined, here as elsewhere. Although all Sunday trains were withdrawn after 11th May 1986, the basic two trains an hour were otherwise continued until late at night, Mondays to Saturdays inclusive. A notable improvement was introduced from 29th May 1995, when the basic provision became part of a cross-London Thameslink service to and from Luton, which split at Streatham to give two trains an hour clockwise via Mitcham Junction, Sutton, Wimbledon and Tooting, and two an hour anti-clockwise over the same circuit. Unless a change is made at Wimbledon or Sutton, this provides a painfully slow trundle to central London and traffic remains very thin.

The Epsom Downs Branch
(map page 121)

Regular horse race meetings at Epsom Downs had begun in the early part of the 18th century, patronage of the highest levels of society soon bringing the course to major importance as a centre of this sport. Thorne considered the Derby 'the prime festival of England. For it even legislation adjourned'. Nevertheless, it is somewhat surprising, given that there had been a railway service to the town below the hill since 1847, that the Epsom racecourse was deemed to justify a branch line on its own account, a line which was to serve little else but the unimportant Downs village of Banstead. That the latter community did something to tip the balance is indicated by the presence of its name in the title of the promoting company of 1861. Even more important was the implied backing of an LBSCR worried by LCDR threats for lines from Herne Hill towards Epsom and the racecourse. With a capital of £85,000, borrowing powers of £28,300 and authority to make working arrangements with the LBSCR, the 4¼-mile branch was sanctioned by the Banstead & Epsom Downs Railway Act of 1862. A jolly seal was devised for the company, comprising a locomotive, racehorse, crossed rifles and hunting symbols.

The remote situation of the terminus was well suggested by the wording of the parliamentary draftsman: 'One yard south east of the Gate opening from Epsom Downs into a Field, the property of Mr Gadsden, in the Occupation of Mr Thomas Cook, and part of Longdown Farm'. From here, racegoers were to face a good half mile uphill to the course, about half the length of the climb up from Epsom Town station.

LBSCR auto train at Belmont station (Up side), June 1906.

Sutton station, July 1882, in process of rebuilding – the Up Epsom Downs line platform (left), is still unfinished. The photographer is standing between the main lines looking towards Epsom and the top-hatted stationmaster can be seen at the end of the Down Main platform near the water column.

Leaving the LBSCR at Sutton station, the double track ran southward to the Downs, climbing quite steeply for much of the way, then, as if thinking better of it, turned west through a deep cutting and then south-west along the lower slopes, keeping mostly between the 300ft and 400ft contours. Just over a mile from Sutton, in open country, was the first intermediate station, named California because it served a public house of that name and land bought by a building speculator who had made some money in the gold rush 15 years before. Two three-storey terraces in grim urban style, one with shops on the ground floor, stood empty for many years and still survive as a memorial to his optimistic enterprise. There was in fact to be little or no business here for another 40 years or so, during which time (1st October 1875) the station was renamed Belmont, reputedly at the suggestion of the station-master's wife.

A small freight yard, dating from about 1880, occupied a cramped site between the level crossing at the south end of the station and the bridge under the Brighton Road, access requiring use of a wagon turntable. By 1910 a bridge had been built south of the station to replace the level crossing, its approach road taking up some of the goods yard site. A new yard of three roads was therefore provided to the east of the Brighton Road.

Banstead station, at the western end of the cutting, was a cheaply-made wooden affair, a tiring mile or more below the 550ft high village. A small goods yard dating from about 1880, on the south side, was approached by a steep ramp down from the road, a feature which for many years discouraged coal merchants from establishing a wharf there (in 1892 Rickett Smith was still carting his coal the whole 6½-miles from Sutton to Walton-on-the-Hill). Later two sets of private sidings were built between the yard and Epsom Downs station.

The terminus was 16¼ miles from Victoria via Mitcham Junction, 18 from London Bridge via Tulse Hill. At its maximum extent, it possessed nine platform faces, all without shelter from the elements, a total of 11 tracks including engine roads. All this to handle race traffic on six days a year, traffic which was only intense on two or three of those days. Its situation on the edge of the Downs at the 350ft contour made it a bleak spot in winter. A witness before the Commons Committee on the Epsom Downs Extension Railway Bill in 1892 thought it 'an absolute wilderness and the most god-forsaken place in the world'. Only in that year had a proper road been finished between the station and the Grandstand. Facilities for loading and unloading carriages and for horse box traffic were of course to be expected, and these could be used for handling cattle and sheep, but there was no proper goods yard, not even a crane. A large wooden building to the north served variously over the years as Royal Stables, refreshment rooms, staff canteen and railwaymen's club. The unpretentious station offices and the stationmaster's house sat across the end of the site fronting a small covered concourse.

Whilst construction was proceeding, in 1864, the LBSCR secured powers to absorb the small company, so that when the line was opened for traffic on 22nd May 1865 it was already part of the Brighton system. The initial train service consisted of eight a day each way between about 08.00 and 21.00, four each way on Sundays. Sunday trains, 'which did not literally earn enough to pay for the grease required for the wheels of the engines and coaches' were very soon withdrawn. Otherwise the provision continued without significant change for over 20 years.

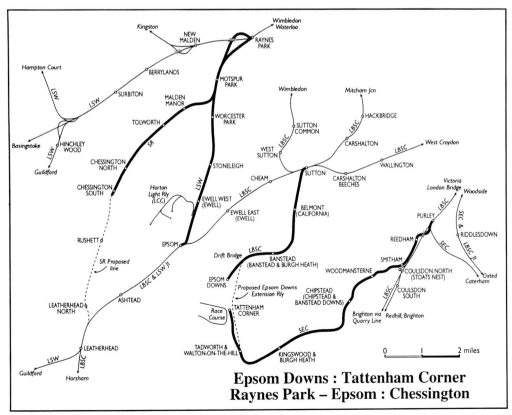

Epsom Downs : Tattenham Corner
Raynes Park – Epsom : Chessington

Even in 1890 there were but 12 trains each way daily, taking about 15 minutes, with first and last departures from Epsom Downs unambitiously placed at 08.15 and 19.50.

Almost from the start, race traffic proved something of a disappointment. Not only were the attendances at the course falling (an LBSCR report of 1869 notes a decrease in visitors to Epsom Races) but many still preferred to travel via the town, where overnight accommodation was available and licensed premises were plentiful. On Derby Day itself the deliciously prolonged pub crawl down from London by road in a vast assortment of horse-drawn vehicles remained popular right up to the motor age. Even so, because it did offer slightly more convenient access to the course for those with little time to spare, the branch did receive a sizeable share of the Derby Day crowds (variously estimated at between 100,000 and 200,000) and of the slightly smaller numbers attracted by Oaks Day. Outside the race weeks, few came on to the line except in the summer, when there was a solid trade in day and Sunday school treats. Many of the children came in special trains which ran on average about once a week at the height of the summer to bring them to the bracing air of the Downs. Near the station, swings, roundabouts, and refreshments were available to attract the children's well-warmed pennies. Acworth, writing in 1899, noted the large covered sheds at the station which offered amongst other things 'donkeys, photography and new milk'. They also served to keep the children out of the rain.

Evidence given to the parliamentary committees on the Epsom Downs Extension and Chipstead Valley Bills of 1892 and 1893 throws some light on the branch at that time. During the winter it was alleged that the terminus saw only about 20 passengers a day, a figure which increased to 30 or 40 on summer weekdays; many of them were golfers. Trains were supposed to connect at Sutton with Portsmouth expresses, which was all right going Down, but they were often late for the Up journey, when harassed schoolteachers had sometimes to endeavour to control their tired and bored charges for half an hour or more. Despite the fact that the LBSCR secretary and general manager (Allen Sarle) used Banstead station every day, the service there was not good, especially on or before race days when the number of trains calling was cut and staff were withdrawn to do duty at Epsom Downs. A Dr Edwin Freshfield related how he once took an Italian gentleman on to the branch; as they got towards the end of the journey, his guest remarked 'This is very refreshing, but it reminds me of railway travelling in my own country' (there could be no worse slur; a British railway compared with some foreign line the British never even built . . .). Sarle told the Extension Bill committee that the working expenses were 2s 7d (12 ½p) a mile and that the profit on working, including Derby Day, was only £90 in 1890 and £204 in 1892; a loss of £550 in 1891 was possibly due to relaying the track. All in all, the branch just about covered its working expenses.

Pleasure seekers and gentlemen commuters apart, there was one more aspect of regular traffic; the airy downlands attracted institutions which supplied freight business and a few passengers. The first of these colonies preceded the railway; the South Metropolitan District Schools, west of the railway alignment near what was to be California station, had opened their doors to pauper children of Camberwell, Greenwich and Woolwich in 1856, and were later to get their own siding (closed about 1889). Similar residential schools for children of the Kensington and Chelsea districts followed in 1880, sited alongside and to the south of the railway between Banstead and the terminus, and also served by a private siding (Crockett's Siding,

1880). Between 1871 and 1877 the huge and ugly bulk of the Banstead Lunatic Asylum rose up on the Downs about half a mile east of the railway, to the south-east of Belmont station. Building materials came in by daily trains from Chelsea Wharf, and were transported over the Downs via a 'tramway' which was nothing more than flat stones laid parallel in the turf to give the horse drawn carts extra purchase, and reduce bad weather difficulties. With the arrival of the motor car, this track became a temptation to drivers, and the stones were removed. Another private siding, Gadesden's, on the Up side about a quarter mile east of Epsom Downs station, was provided in 1886 to service North Looe (Lieu) Farm.

Little residential development appeared around the branch before 1914. Some workers' cottages at Belmont in the late 1880s were followed in the next decade by middle-class villas nearby, building continuing spasmodically until 1915 when a substantial Anglican church was opened at the top of Station Road, by this time lined with small shops. Banstead village attracted large houses for those just one step below the 'gentry', men of business like Allen Sarle, who could afford to run their own carriages to and from Banstead or Sutton stations for their daily trip to London. A colony of new villas began to appear along the Brighton Road, south of the station. But in 1914 there remained a great deal of fine open country, the scenery along the line beyond Belmont little changed from the time of its opening almost 50 years earlier.

We have already noted the disappointing results of race traffic. 'The Derby is not what it was' wrote Acworth in 1899, 'Year by year its importance, or at least its relative importance, diminishes'. A Lords Committee on the Chipstead Valley Bill of 1893 was told by Sarle that race traffic had fallen off in the previous decade bringing in only £2,700 on a mileage basis in 1891 despite the imposition of an 8s (40p) return fare on special trains instead of the normal 3s (15p). Yet Derby Day did remain an important occasion for the branch for over 80 years, reaching its zenith of glamour and bustle in the Edwardian era. Then, around early afternoon, Epsom Downs station presented a lively scene for a skilful photographer, whose postcard remains for us to enjoy: pride of place is taken by the royal train in its special platform on the south side, its resplendent mahogany coaches headed by a gleaming Marsh Atlantic tank engine with the royal coat of arms mounted on the buffer beam, and a gilded crown on the top lamp bracket. Nine other tracks are filled with trains turned ready to go back to London, some of them special Pullman car trains for the private parties of Lord Derby and others, the remainder ordinary suburban coaches for the *hoi polloi*. Although we cannot see them, the station buffer stops are brilliant with floral displays; behind, the station yard is filled with buskers, stalls and sideshows.

A notice of 1896 illustrates the facilities provided: special trains to be worked from both Victoria and London Bridge to Epsom Downs between 11.35 and 13.20, some of the Victoria departures calling at Clapham Junction to pick up passengers booked from Kensington (Addison Road). The company's offices at Trafalgar Square and Regent Street were to remain open until 22.00 for several days beforehand for the sale of tickets, whilst special horsebox trains were to run between Newmarket and Epsom Downs via the East London Railway.

Early in the day, to keep the crowds in some sort of order, large contingents of Metropolitan Police went to Epsom Downs by special train; extra railway staff were brought in and the rest of the branch got short shrift – many ordinary trains were stopped short at Banstead, a practice which lasted until the 1930s. Platform staff disappeared. At Banstead on Derby Day 1893, a witness described to the Lords Committee on the Chipstead Valley Bill that he had had some people down, and his man was obliged to move all their luggage himself. In 1901–02 extra signalling was installed solely for race days traffic, three intermediate block posts controlling signals with detachable arms and no spectacles or lamps. These were Sutton & Belmont Intermediate ('A', 1,408yd from Sutton Junction box), Belmont & Banstead Intermediate ('B', 1,350yd from Belmont station box) and Banstead & Epsom Downs Intermediate ('C', 812yd from Banstead station box). Even in 1923, with the old rivalries extinguished, the Epsom Downs branch carried 42 extra trains on Derby Day, including one reserved Pullman car special.

During the Edwardian years, the outposts of London were brought up to the railway between Croydon and Sutton and the many bright new houses along this frontier kept busy the electric tramway opened in 1906 between West Croydon and Sutton. Rising to this intruder, the LBSCR initiated an auto-train service which provided from 11th June 1906 seven journeys each way daily in addition to the normal service, between West Croydon and Belmont. Consisting of a Stroudley 'Terrier' 0–6–0T pulling or pushing a one-class bogie saloon coach with 50 seats (a form of steam tram in fact) these auto-trains called at all intermediate stations including new halts at Bandon and Beeches. The first of these, between Wallington and Waddon, was opened with the new service, the other, on the site of the present Carshalton Beeches station, was not ready until 1st October 1906. As elsewhere, these special units were perhaps a little faster than the street tramcar and no more expensive, but they could not compete with its frequency and convenience of access.

Belmont's prominence as the only place on the branch showing any signs of suburban growth before 1914 was reflected in the pattern of the train service: in 1910 when the auto-trains (misleadingly described in Bradshaw as 'motor cars' because it sounded trendy at the time) were providing most of the service, Belmont had 36 Down arrivals and 37 departures in the Up direction (eleven and nine on Sundays). But Epsom Downs, in the same timetable, had only 12 trains in and out daily and none on Sundays, whilst Banstead had 22 Down arrivals and the same number of departures in the Up direction (two and three on Sundays). Most of these trains connected at Sutton with services to and from London Bridge and Victoria.

Towards the close of the 19th century the high downland south of Sutton and Epsom attracted a small number of moderately wealthy and influential men who wished to possess small country estates within convenient access of London. Not exactly commuters in the modern sense, they were content to arrive in the City between 10.00 and 11.00. Among these, as we have seen, was Allen Sarle, secretary and general manager of the LBSCR, living at *Green Hayes*, Banstead, whilst another was Henry Cosmo Orme Bonsor, MP for Wimbledon and a director of the Bank of England, who purchased *Kingswood Warren* in 1885. These two travelled up together from Banstead station, and Bonsor, an energetic and dynamic personality, soon developed an interest in railway affairs. In the summer of 1891 he joined two other residents of Tadworth and Walton-on-the-Hill in forming a scheme for a railway from Epsom Downs to Walton-on-the-Hill, principally to enhance the value of the land and promote housing development. Sir John Wolfe-Barry and his nephew Arthur Barry were engaged to lay out a 2m 7f 5ch single-line extension of the Epsom Downs branch rising 240ft on a 1 in 50 gradient from Drift Bridge (between

Banstead and Epsom Downs stations) to a point on Corner Farm about 200yd south of the present Tadworth station. This 320-acre farm had been bought at the low price of £25 an acre by Bonsor's fellow-promoter James W. Benson, who had acquired *Walton Oaks*, Walton-on-the-Hill in 1889. Bonsor had taken a half-share in the land, which it was hoped to develop for building once the railway was begun. A former Tadworth baker, Walter J. Brown, also planned to build on his nearby 200-acre estate. Having ascertained that the LBSCR would be willing to work the Extension, but not to subscribe to its cost, Bonsor put up £55,000 of the required £65,000 capital, Benson the rest.

Opposition came mainly from Frederick E. Colman, owner of the 1,382-acre Nork Park Estate through which the railway was to pass for most of its length, and from the Epsom Grand Stand Association who saw the railway as a threat to their proposal to create a Straight Mile Course, and also likely to frighten horses racing and training on the Downs. Colman had been approached by Bonsor but professed no interest in land speculation, merely wishing no interference with enjoyment of his 'very beautiful and desirable residential and sporting estate' which he had bought in 1890 from the trustees of Lord Egmont. During the passage of the bill this opposition was overcome by the insertion of new clauses. A tunnel would be built for 100yd each side of the Straight Mile with no trains passing through when it was in use. Colman not only gained a private gate to the new station at Tadworth and a personal siding for 20 wagons, but was protected from further stations on his estate and from telegraph wires and poles along the tops of cuttings or over tunnels, and for his benefit all banks were to be thickly planted with trees, plantation style. Wolfe-Barry solemnly assured him that the platelayers patrolling the line (honest men, every one) would be a useful deterrent to the poachers that he feared the railway would encourage.

Once the act was passed, Bonsor and his friends argued with the LBSCR over terms for working the line, then prevaricated whilst they took up the Chipstead Valley scheme (of which more in a moment), which they used as a stick with which to beat the Brighton. This tactic moved the LBSCR to offer a rent of 50 per cent of gross receipts instead of the 55 per cent they had earlier said would barely cover working expenses. Bonsor and his friends also got the Brighton to promise to run a Sunday service despite the earlier failure on the Epsom Downs branch, and a weekday through train each way between Tadworth and Victoria as well as eight Down and nine Up between Tadworth and Sutton, all apparently to reverse in and out of Epsom Downs. Having got this far, Bonsor and Benson now had their sights set higher and refused an LBSCR demand that the Chipstead Valley scheme should be withdrawn as a condition of their working through to Tadworth. As we shall see shortly, a section of the Epsom Downs Extension Railway was to be built as part of the SER's Tattenham Corner branch, which emerged from the Chipstead Valley scheme. The Nork Park Estate siding, for the benefit of Colman's tenant-farmer (who ran a jam factory at north Tadworth as a sideline) was also provided at Tattenham Corner in 1901.

Under Southern Railway management, the Epsom Downs branch saw great changes. During January 1927, the general manager, Sir Herbert Walker, came down the line with senior officers as a prelude to electrification. They decided that the platforms at Belmont would have to be lengthened from 262ft (Up) and 257ft (Down) to at least 500ft, as would the 284ft ones at Banstead. Considering the

Epsom Downs, 18th December 1926 looking to buffers. D1 0-4-T B612 with a train of eight six-wheel coaches and two brake vans awaits departure for London. *H C Casserley*

application made for a halt at Drift Bridge, the officers saw no sign of housing development there and agreed that accommodation would only be provided if paid for by the landowners. It was noted that a full goods station could be made at Epsom Downs if required later by taking out one of the island platforms – an indication that accommodation was already excessive for the traffic offering on race days.

Soon after this, the branch was electrified as part of the Southern's third-rail suburban system. At Epsom Downs, platforms three to seven were equipped for electric working, but at normal times two roads were more than enough and the other three were used to store electric stock. As elsewhere, the train service was transformed. From 17th June 1928 when electric trains replaced steam, a regular half-hourly frequency was supplied seven days a week between London Bridge and Epsom Downs via West Croydon, calling at all stations except Brockley and Honor Oak Park. This was strengthened at peak periods on Mondays to Saturdays when there were three trains an hour. When the direct route from Sutton to Victoria via Mitcham Junction was electrified on 3rd March 1929 convenient connections were made at Sutton to give the branch a faster service to the West End. The circuitous electric service from Victoria to Sutton via West Croydon was extended to Epsom Downs on 4th May 1930, giving the branch a total of four trains an hour throughout the day, strengthened to six an hour in the morning and evening peak and at Saturday midday.

Banstead station exterior, c.1968 with the first late afternoon commuters homeward bound.

This generous and reliable facility, brought in at a time when economic conditions were strongly favouring residential construction around London, was accompanied by a vast amount of new housing in the catchment areas of Belmont and Banstead stations. Ordinary bookings at the three stations grew from 329,778 in 1927 to 927,708 seven years later, with season ticket issues moving in the same period from 2,964 to 12,937. Building on the chalk uplands south of the railway between Banstead and Epsom Downs stations had started in the middle of the 1920s, mostly fairly closely-spaced detached houses selling at around £1,000. Banstead's transformation from a small downland village to a London suburb accelerated with the completion of main drainage schemes in 1927–29. By the mid-1930s the whole area between the village street and the railway was filled with small houses, while by 1939 the mansion and untouched remnant of the Nork Park Estate was surrounded by rather more spacious development. Carshalton and Sutton's outward creep reached Belmont station, whilst Sutton and Cheam spread southwards over the 500-acre Northey Estate, where large detached houses costing between £1,700 and £3,000 were built around the Cuddington Golf Course, reaching Banstead station about 1935 and almost completely sealing off the 750-acre Banstead Downs, which had been preserved against building since the 1860s. To accommodate the traffic arising from this last development, the SR rebuilt Banstead station in brick with extended awnings of glass and steel over each platform.

At the close of the 1930s Epsom's southern outskirts were touching Epsom Downs station and the development of the Nork Estate south east of the branch had brought houses to the edge of Epsom Downs golf and race courses. Much of this housing at the extremity of the branch was in the medium and higher price ranges, but as car ownership was by no means universal even among the owners of the more expensive property, the terminal station was enjoying for the first time a regular all-the-year-round traffic at both peak and slack hours.

This was as well, because the SR had long since begun to concentrate the race traffic on the more convenient and spacious facilities at Tattenham Corner station. Nevertheless, a fair quantity of race business to Epsom Downs survived until the middle 1950s, after which the decline was rapid. The first-class specials, some with Pullman coaches, which brought businessmen down from their offices at lunchtime on Derby Day remained steam-hauled until just after World War 2, when electric locomotives took over. On Derby Day 1952 there were almost 100 ordinary and special trains each way over the branch, over half the workings concentrated between 11.00 and 19.00, all of them electric. Two years later the number of extra staff used on Derby Day was down to seven, and Derby Day 1958 saw only three extra trains compared with the 13 to Tattenham Corner. The intermediate block posts were not used after 1955. Epsom Downs station lost five of its platforms in 1972 and the 1989 changes mentioned below finally removed the branch's capacity to handle race traffic.

When considering the Derby Day service it must not be overlooked that during the 1950s the standard service to Epsom Downs was exceptionally lavish, with six trains an hour each way until early afternoon (three Victoria, three London Bridge), four an hour for the rest of the day and extras at peak periods, in all 87 each way every weekday, or nearly eleven times the number running in 1865. But in an age of increasing car ownership, with television keeping families indoors in the evenings, such generous provision became futile. From 10th September 1958 off-peak frequency came down to half-hourly to and from Victoria via West Croydon. Further changes followed in the late 1960s; the Victoria slack hour service was terminated at Sutton instead of Epsom Downs from 10th July 1967, the branch receiving instead the former London Bridge–Tulse Hill–Horsham/Effingham Junction service every half-hour. On Sundays the half-hourly service was given by trains working between Epsom Downs and London Bridge via Tulse Hill until 4th May 1969, after which day all Sunday working ceased. From May 1973 the slack-hour London Bridge service was turned at Sutton and the branch got a Victoria–Selhurst–West Croydon working every half-hour, with eight peak-period trains between Epsom Downs and London Bridge.

Other retrenchment accompanied service reductions. Banstead goods yard closed on 7th September 1964, and freight trains disappeared with the abandonment of Belmont yard on 6th January 1969. Installation of intermediate colour-lights between Sutton and Epsom Downs (both exclusive) allowed closure of Belmont and Banstead station boxes on 21st December 1969. Belmont's tatty station, showing wounds from World War 2 bombs, gave way in 1968 to one of the Southern's cheap and cheerful modular CLASP pre-fabricated boxes, looking like nothing so much as a very large packing case waiting for a crane. During 1972 the tracks at Epsom Downs were reduced to two (the former platforms 4 and 5) and after the permanent way gangs had departed only one scissors crossover remained, just outside the station. No longer was the terminus to have the artificially busy appearance imparted by the stabling of empty stock at its grass-grown platforms.

In the early hours of 16th November 1981 Epsom Downs signal box was seriously damaged by fire. At first there was hand signalling for a modified service to and from Victoria and London Bridge but after ten days the branch was operated 'one train on line', by a half-hourly shuttle to and from Sutton, using the Down platforms at Banstead and Belmont. From 4th July 1982, apart from short lengths at each end, the line was reduced to single track. This arrangement became permanent from 4th October 1982, when the branch was integrated into the Victoria Area Signalling Scheme and through working to West Croydon and London was restored.

Serious traffic decline was now evident on a line which had once had a ten minute service at peak periods and sold over 2,000 ordinary tickets daily. Thanks to the motor car and dispersal of much central London employment, irrecoverable inroads had been made since the late 1950s into the healthy peak and off peak business once generated by the between-wars suburban growth in the catchment area. By the 1980s, the shrinking army of central London commuters were increasingly using their cars to reach the superior train services at Sutton; children were being ferried to school by car instead of using the trains; cars were carrying those shopping or seeking entertainment and recreation in Sutton and Croydon; and the contra-flow movements to the hospitals and day tripper traffic to the Downs had all but disappeared. That old habits die hard was demonstrated by the trickle of punters still to be seen using the line in Derby week 1988 but these faithful were effectively banished by the 1989 development to be mentioned in a moment. One may wonder how the branch survived the 1970s. Indeed it was not until 1984 that services were given what may prove to be the penultimate cut. Off peak frequency was then reduced to hourly from 14th May, an interval that is inherently discouraging to traffic development.

At this stage in its existence the character of the outer end of the line slipped into a new guise. As a result of a property deal, the spacious site of the terminus and its immediate approaches was sold for development as a housing estate. All tracks were removed over a distance of 374yd, to a point less than a quarter mile from the long-proposed halt at Drift Bridge, where a single platform was opened on the evening of 13th February 1989. Although still called Epsom Downs, a more accurate name for the relocated station would be Drift Bridge or perhaps Nork (there was a footpath to the former). Across the end of the single track Messrs Charles Church, the developers of the housing estate, erected a two storey building which bore a family resemblance to the rather twee neo-vernacular detached houses closely packed all round. To give some indication of its purpose, the frontage was embellished by a length of canopy and supporting posts rescued from the old station.

An early evening visit here in June 1991 found the place completely deserted until the 18.25 arrival from London deposited about 25 commuters. Some seats and a 'train ready to start' button had already been vandalised, graffiti already obtruded and if the little ticket office had ever been manned, it was now firmly shuttered-up. As the tired-looking commuters quickly dispersed and the now empty train returned Londonwards, this strangely unreal railway station resumed its dreamlike air. Its relaxed, totally domesticated environment would look more comfortable with light rail. Perhaps Tramlink will find its way here one day as an alternative to the otherwise seemingly inevitable complete closure.

Tattenham Corner station in the 1930s. *Pamlin Prints*

The Tattenham Corner Branch (map page 121)

Although the Caterham Railway for many years showed little promise, there were signs of residential development in the Caterham valley by the early 1880s. Noting this, and also hoping for an improvement in farm rents depressed by the difficulties and cost of cartage over hilly roads, landowners in the adjacent Chipstead valley projected a branch from the Brighton main line in 1884. This scheme failed to take off, as did a later proposal for a light railway up the valley, but the success of the Epsom Downs Extension Railway Bill revived interest in the route, so much so that by the autumn of 1892 Bonsor and others had persuaded several landowners in the valley to put up the promotion expenses of a bill. Arthur Barry surveyed a single line starting from an end-on junction with the Epsom Downs Extension at Tadworth, running down the valley to Smitham Bottom, where it was to march alongside the main line as far as Purley station. Here there were to be junctions with both the LBSCR and what was now the SER Caterham branch. Bonsor gave the scheme strong support, warming the mutual jealousy of the LBSCR and the SER in the hope of getting one or the other to work both the Chipstead Valley and the Epsom Downs Extension as a through line from Epsom Downs to Purley on favourable terms. He and other landowners looked to these railways to enhance the value of their properties, eventually stimulating residential development, and were prepared to give land in exchange for shares. But neither of the main line companies showed any interest, the Brighton going as far as opposing the Chipstead Valley Bill, averring that the newcomer's trains would interfere with the working of their main line traffic at Purley. Bonsor produced an array of local landowners and residents in support, quietly confident that the LBSCR would be obliged to pick up both schemes and work them as one, refusing to accept a Brighton suggestion that the Chipstead Valley station at Purley should be separate from the LBSCR establishment, the physical link confined to a siding connection. Finally he produced his trump card; the capital of the Epsom Downs Extension and the Chipstead Valley would be pooled, with he and Benson (the other subscriber to the Extension) consenting to take their proportion, almost one-third of the total needed for the two lines, as a deferred charge. With the balance as preferred charge capital, it should not, he suggested, be difficult to raise it from the public, and there were already some promises from landowners. Parliament was persuaded, allowing the bill through, subject to the insertion of a clause protecting the LBSCR against interference with its main line traffic or the prospective widening works at Purley.

Whilst not opposing a junction with the Caterham line at Purley, the SER gave the Chipstead Valley no encouragement, partly because the company doubted its traffic prospects, but also because it feared difficulties in working the trains of both branches into the single bay platform at Purley. In the Lords Committee, the SER general manager, Sir Myles Fenton, firmly denied that the SER was spurning the Chipstead because it was constrained by some kind of territorial agreement with the Brighton – 'We have no territorial arrangement, no agreement by which we could not penetrate into any part of their district, or they into ours'. Wolfe-Barry also declared that he saw nothing to prevent the SER going up to Epsom Downs, except fear of LBSCR retaliation 'in some other way', and the fact that the SER was not contractually or even morally bound to remain east of the LBSCR main line in this district was soon to be demonstrated. Bonsor, not a man to give up easily, was determined to get a railway up to Tadworth and Kingswood. In the year following the Chipstead Valley Act he got himself on to the SER board and a year after that (1895) had reached the deputy chairman's seat. Land was acquired for both the Chipstead Valley and the Epsom Downs Extension, and in 1897 an unopposed Epsom Downs Extension Railway Bill sought powers to abandon 1m 4f 2.5ch between Drift Bridge and a point just north of Tadworth, substituting a 3f 4ch terminal spur from that point to Tattenham Corner, and giving the branch the form in which it was to be built. Any remaining problems were resolved by plans to rebuild Purley station with the widening of the Brighton main line and a bill of 1898, which went through unopposed after a petition filed by the LBSCR was withdrawn, allowed the SER to subscribe to the capital of the Chipstead Valley, which could be built as double track. The final chapters in the Parliamentary story were written in the two following years with unopposed SER bills, which respectively allowed the Extension and the Chipstead Valley to be vested in the SER from 13th July 1899, and gave the SER authority to take up the unexpended borrowing powers of the two companies.

Well before all this legislation had reached the statute book, a single line was opened between Purley East Junction and Kingswood & Burgh Heath. This was served from 2nd November 1897 by trains which called at the intermediate station of Chipstead & Banstead Downs, and during 1899 its track was doubled. A single line onwards to Tadworth & Walton-on-the-Hill, opened on 1st July 1900, was doubled by November that year. Finally, the double track Epsom Downs Extension Railway from Tadworth to Tattenham Corner was ready for Derby Day, 4th June 1901. In open and unashamed competition with the Brighton, the SECR was to have at Tattenham Corner, almost on the race-course, Britain's finest and largest station for race traffic. On that first day the company made a brave start with 13 advertised trains and 35 specials (some coming from as far away as Dover, Margate, Hastings and Reading), bringing in almost 15,000 racegoers.

'Traversing one of the loveliest districts of Surrey, where perfect quiet and beautiful pastoral scenery are to be had within half an hour's journey from London', the Chipstead Valley was certainly a romantic and interesting line. For 5½ miles the climb was steep and continuous, with a final mile of 1 in 80 to a summit ¼m south of Tadworth station. After leaving the Caterham Railway at Purley East Junction ten chains south of the station, the new branch ran for a short distance alongside the Brighton main line before crossing beneath it and continuing parallel on the west side. Just south of the underpass, on the east side was the Reedham Home for

Charing Cross–Tadworth train entering Reedham Halt, 22nd May 1926. *H C Casserley*

Fatherless Children named after its founder the Reverend Andrew Reed, and served by a private siding from the Up track. Reedham Halt, on the west side of the main line, with its 300ft platforms, was opened on 1st March 1911 to enable Chipstead Valley passengers to reach the orphanage and the new housing then sprouting up along the nearby main road; tickets were 'issued by the haltkeeper'. Close to the main line almost as far as Coulsdon North station, the branch finally turned away west through Smitham station, crossing over the Brighton Road and entering the valley. Opened on 1st January 1904, Smitham was but a stone's throw from Coulsdon North (opened in 1899 and then called Stoat's Nest). It had a goods yard but no station house, simply a single-storey wooden building on the Down side and a rudimentary shelter on the Up platform in the usual SER country style. The birth of this station was prolonged, its platforms and signal box completed almost three years before it opened to the public. From a traffic viewpoint it was rendered all but superfluous by the superior facilities of the adjacent LBSCR station, but it was obligatory under section 36 of the 1893 act, in deference to the requirements of the trustees of John Benjamin Smith. The SECR economised by closing it on Sundays from the start until about 1909.

Attacking the Chipstead Valley, the line now followed a sinuous and generally south-westerly course through pretty well-wooded country as yet almost untouched by residential development. Chipstead & Banstead Downs station was sited on the east side of the valley about 200ft below the village of Chipstead and almost a mile to the north of it. Equidistant on the other side was the small village of Woodman-sterne. The station building, on the Up side, was a substantial little structure in a pleasing Domestic Revival style with three dormer windows emerging from its tiled roof on the railway side. A small goods yard was cut out of the valley slope at the London end.

Kingswood station soon after opening. The large number of wagons in the freight yard (left) may be related to railway construction work further down the branch.

After running almost due south for rather more than half a mile, the tracks turned almost west along Chipstead Bottom to climb through what is today some of the best suburban countryside on the former Southern system. At the head of the valley, Kingswood & Burgh Heath station was almost equidistant from the two small villages of its title. As Bonsor's local station, it had the most impressive building on the line, a two-storey mock-timbered station house under a pitched tile roof, sitting above a small booking office and entrance block in red brick, with an impressive arch on the road side. The wide canopy over the Up platform was later railed round with white palings to form a terrace. On the Down side there was a curious pavilion with tall arched windows and roof sloping steeply to the back wall. Also on this side, Bonsor was given a private entrance, beneath the road bridge. Situated at the London end on the Up side, the goods yard sidings extended back into the station approach.

Beyond here the tracks passed through a cutting along the northern edge of Bonsor's *Kingswood Warren* Estate, negotiating the northern tip of Banstead Heath in the 310yd Kingswood Tunnel required by the 1893 act. A second tunnel of 37yd, little more than a bridge, rejoicing in the jolly name of Hoppety, and a northward curve in deep cutting, brought the trains into Tadworth & Walton-on-the-Hill, which at 550ft above sea level, was and is the highest suburban station south of the Thames. Whilst the northern ends of its platforms were at ground level, the station building sat high above the tracks on the road bridge over the cutting. Solidly built in brick and tile, punctuated with tall sash windows, this pavilion was awarded some dignity by a central gable with an arched window which lit the booking hall below. Covered ways led down each side of the cutting to the platforms, each with its small waiting room building. Entered by a trailing connection from the Up line, the goods yard was at the north end.

On an embankment, and almost level, the branch ran to its terminus at the Tattenham Corner of the Epsom Downs racecourse, 21½ miles from London Bridge and 8m 25ch from Purley, stopping just short of the Straight Mile that had proved such an obstacle to the first alignment of the Epsom Downs Extension Railway. It will be convenient to describe this station as it was around 1920, for although by no means complete at the time of its opening, most of the features that will be mentioned were provided by the end of its first year and others were added in the first decade or so. Its passenger accommodation would have been over generous for a medium-sized industrial town; six platform faces (numbered from west to east), consisting of two platforms at the flanks and two central islands. These gravel-covered platforms, each about 20ft wide and completely unsheltered in their exposed position at the top of the downs, varied in length from about 550ft to around 700ft. Between each pair of platform tracks was an engine release road. At the west side, two long horsebox sidings stood in line with the passenger platforms, the outer one serving a brick-built horse dock and stables. On the east was a long siding equipped with a 54ft 10in locomotive turntable, and the layout was completed with the fruit farm private siding on this side and a four-road goods yard on the west at the south end of the site. This layout could accommodate about 24 normal-length trains simultaneously.

Initially the signalling arrangements were very elaborate, but from about 1922 the system was simplified, route indications being given by a main signal through sidings worked by ground levers not controlled by the signalmen. This change reduced the levers in 'A' box, which was situated on the east side at the entrance to the passenger station, from 205 to 125, and in 'B' box, which was at the extreme south end of the layout on the west side and used only on race days, from 50 to 19. The third box, 'C', was a small platform cabin at the buffer end of platforms three and four, used for train indicating purposes with indicators worked in conjunction with 'A' and 'B' boxes. A fire caused by a porter-signalman's carelessness destroyed much of 'A' box on 15th July 1924, requiring complete renewal of its equipment.

Opposite the ends of platforms three to six, behind a spacious concourse was the main booking hall and entrance building, a single-storey structure in the characteristic SER rural close-boarded style under a slate roof. Spaced around the concourse across the platform ends were other smaller buildings containing two refreshment rooms, a staff messroom and a large urinal. In the station approach and in line with the booking hall building was an extensive bungalow which incorporated a third refreshment room, luncheon room, cloak room, cycle store, telegraph office and an auxiliary ticket office. Curving to give direct access to the racecourse, the approach road skirted 'the Mound', a raised lawn which afforded the SER directors and their guests a superb view of the finishing straight of the main racecourse.

Signalling along the branch was Sykes' lock-and-block and the station boxes were supplemented on race days by temporary block posts similar to those on the Epsom Downs branch, although here their equipment was left in place all the year round. These small cabins were at Woodmansterne (1m 7yd from Smitham Station box), Chipstead Intermediate (1m 78yd from Chipstead Station box) and Tadworth Tunnel (1,441yd from Kingswood Station box).

Three distinct types of traffic were expected: racegoers and horseboxes, summer excursionists, and residential. Some effort was expended to attract the second group by providing summer refreshments at Tattenham Corner station but success was limited, hardly justifying the pious sentiments of witnesses in the 1893 bill committees that the poor of London would flock out on Sundays to enjoy the pure air of the Surrey downs, heaths and commons. After the 1902 summer there were no trains to Tattenham Corner in winter and a photograph of about 1920 shows the balcony at Kingswood, which may have been intended as a tea place, decorated with the stationmaster's family washing and bunches of pea sticks drying for his garden.

With the opening to Tadworth in 1900 the branch had about ten trains a day each way, covering the run from Purley in about 23 minutes. The first departure from Tadworth was not until 07.40, the last as early as 20.35. By 1922, with some residential development in the interim, there was a winter service of 17 Up trains and 16 Down, covering the branch in 20 to 21 minutes, while Tadworth's first and last departures had been opened out to 07.06 and 23.12. Except in rush hours, London passengers were obliged to change at Purley into and out of branch trains, worked by Cudworth 2–4–0 and various types of tank locomotive, latterly mainly Wainwright H class 0–4–4T. On race days, particularly for the Derby and Oaks, the branch was alive with trains of great variety, including fast specials from Charing Cross, Waterloo Junction, Cannon Street, St Paul's (Blackfriars), London Bridge and East Croydon, as well as excursions from main towns on the SECR system outside London. In summer, until September 1914, trains were extended 'as required' to Tattenham Corner for day trippers.

If summer pleasure traffic disappointed, estate developers did their best to make up for it. At first almost all development consisted of fairly large houses, mostly detached, in spacious gardens. Most of these Edwardian villas were to be found at Chipstead (where a new golf course proved an attraction), at Tadworth, and at Walton-on-the-Hill, where a small colony of commodious detached houses with servants' bedrooms in the roof spaces (two were designed by Lutyens) appeared around the Golf Club House between 1905 and 1914. None of this activity amounted to very much, but the proportion of first-class passengers produced was very high.

Tadworth station shortly after completion in 1900.

No race meetings were held at Epsom course from 1915 to 1918, but the railways carried military traffic to camps on the downs, where the ample accommodation at Tattenham Corner found a new use. With the cessation of hostilities, the generous siding accommodation provided a temporary resting place for scores of locomotives no longer required by the army.

Race traffic at Tattenham Corner was at its peak in the 1920s and 1930s when on Derby Day as many as 60 specials were worked by tank and tender locomotives of various types and latterly, from London stations, electric multiple-units. Other specials brought punters from such places as Reading (reversing at Purley), Chatham, Dover, Ramsgate and Hastings, whilst affluent businessmen and stockbrokers came down from Cannon Street and Charing Cross, lunching in Pullman cars. Numbers handled grew to more than twice those seen on the opening day; about 38,000, for example, arrived at Tattenham Corner on Derby Day 1923 in the ordinary trains and 54 specials, including two reserved Pullman car trains, and 40,000 returned after the races. Following some problems in handling these larger attendances in 1920 and 1921, on-the-spot improvisation was replaced by London Bridge Control, with all loco and train movements precisely scheduled beforehand.

To accommodate 50 to 60 Down specials on Derby Day it was necessary to restrict the normal branch service, especially as the Down running line between Kingswood and Tattenham Corner was used for stabling some of the trains awaiting the returning crowds. Under the new arrangements introduced in 1923, with handbills advertising 'trains running continuously' between specified times and headways in practice as close as four minutes, arrival, unloading, and clearance of platforms at Tattenham Corner was achieved in four to five minutes. After the formation of the Southern Railway, Tattenham Corner, with its more spacious layout and convenient access to the racecourse, assumed the main burden of the Derby and Oaks traffic, taking all through specials from places outside London as well as the royal trains* from Victoria. On Whit Monday and August Bank Holiday in 1927, for that year only, a number of trains were booked to run to and from Tattenham Corner, at that time normally used only on race days. On the August holiday, 12 trains arrived and ten departed from the terminus.

When it became clear in the early 1920s that the branch would become part of the Southern electric suburban system, estate developers set about their plans with confidence and increased pace, knowing that electrification would bring with it a revolutionary improvement in the train service, encouraging London white-collar workers to settle in this pleasant downland district. Not long after the end of World War 1, Richard Costain bought Bonsor's *Kingswood Warren* Estate to lay out for building. Here from 1923 onwards, in wooded parkland above the 525ft contour just south of Kingswood station, he erected houses on sites of half an acre or more for sale at £800 to £4,000. Nearby, on the Brighton Road between Kingswood and Tadworth, houses with quarter-acre gardens were advertised in 1925, and the adjacent Tadworth Court Estate was under way a year later with detached houses on quarter-acre plots selling at £1,350 upwards. For the time being, commuters buying these new homes travelled to and from London Bridge or Charing Cross in trains composed of two sets of five six-wheelers hauled by H class 0-4-4T.

* Royal trains to the Epsom course ceased after 1924 but royal use of the railway was resumed in 1946 at a time of petrol shortage and has continued ever since.

Into this already active scene came the green electrics, a provisional service from 25th March 1928, the full one from 17th June. There was some disappointment when it was learned that to avoid rush hour congestion, Tattenham Corner and Caterham trains would not be worked across the Eastern section lines to and from the Central side of London Bridge, but would terminate in the low level platforms at London Bridge instead of at Charing Cross as in steam days. (At other times the electrics ran through to Charing Cross). Apart from this blemish, the provision was as excellent as expected; three trains an hour all day long to and from Tattenham Corner, giving that station its first regular all-year-round service since 1902. Sundays saw four trains an hour, two to Victoria, two to Charing Cross, the former being the weekday Coulsdon North trains diverted, a lavish gesture which apart from the summer of 1931 continued until World War 2, when service was reduced to two an hour, one to Charing Cross, one to Victoria. London Bridge was reached in 43 minutes by the electrics, which ran non-stop inwards from Norwood Junction, and in peak hours stopped only at East Croydon between London Bridge and Purley. Tattenham Corner and Caterham trains were combined inwards from Purley, where the joining and splitting of the two branch portions was carried out with all the celerity that multiple-unit operation allows. In peak hours the trains were three three-car sets, one for Caterham, two for Tattenham Corner, the latter with an above-average proportion of first-class passengers. At Tattenham Corner most of the sidings were not electrified, but were used on race days to store electric sets shunted by a steam locomotive. Platform run-round roads were removed, together with the 'C' signal frame. Station lighting was converted to electricity, using current from the conductor rails.

Following electrification, construction of cheaper houses was begun in earnest east of the line between Tadworth and Tattenham Corner and between Chipstead and Smitham. Tattenham Corner's first houses appeared in 1928 when free yearly season tickets were on offer to all who purchased before the end of June. A 'million pound' housing scheme was started here in the early 1930s by Surrey Downs Housing Ltd offering semi-detached and detached designs at £560-£990 'amid the fairyland of Surrey 600ft above sea level on dry chalky soil swept by the sweet air from the SOUTHERN SEAS', whilst another advertisement described it as 'the estate where illness is unknown', a large claim, despite the 'medicinal pines' and the 'absence of fog'. South of the old village and close to the railway, a new Woodmansterne grew rapidly during the 1930s with many roads of small terrace and semi-detached houses and bungalows selling at between £550 and £990. To serve this development, Woodmansterne station, a simple island platform reached only by footbridge from adjacent side roads, was opened on 17th July 1932. Builders conveyed land for it free of charge, also contributing £1,500 of its £7,000 cost.

Higher up the valley, at Chipstead were more detached houses, at prices ranging from £950 to £1,500. By the middle 1930s, the areas around Chipstead, Tadworth and Tattenham Corner stations had assumed the aspect of typical London suburbs, each with its characteristic Tudor-style shopping parade, but none of these places grew large enough to justify the erection of a large cinema. Virtually all the housing, including the down-market terrace blocks, was beyond the reach of railway staff, obliging the Southern to erect a street of cottages near the line about half-way between Tattenham Corner and Tadworth stations. This had to be done in 1928 before Tadworth could be made a signing-on point for the new electric services.

Passenger accommodation was adapted to meet the suburban demand. Reedham Halt, 'inadequate for present-day traffic' was reconstructed in 1936 as a station at a cost of around £8,800. In the same year, Kingswood received a £650 concrete footbridge and a year later improvements were made to the lighting and platform canopies at Tadworth. The hitherto little-used freight yards needed no significant alteration to cope with the loads of building materials and domestic fuel.

Tattenham Corner's spare capacity again proved useful for military purposes in World War 2 when from time to time ambulance trains brought in wounded servicemen for transfer by road coaches to the large hospitals at Epsom. With the resumption of the Derby in 1946, loadings on the main race days returned almost to pre-war levels. On this occasion 34 trains arrived at Tattenham Corner from Charing Cross, Cannon Street and London Bridge between 09.00 and noon. Steam-hauled royal trains from Victoria were seen again on Derby and Oaks Days, with the full support of stand-by engines at Chipstead yard and a breakdown train in steam on the middle siding at Purley. For some years there were also steam-hauled Pullman specials from Charing Cross on Derby Day, with inclusive tickets covering lunch on the train and a seat in the grandstands. All other specials were of suburban electric stock, originating at New Cross Gate, Streatham Hill, Crystal Palace and Wallington. In 1953, when the first race on Derby Day was at 14.00 and the last at 17.20, trains arriving at the terminus between 09.00 and 13.00 totalled 31, six from Charing Cross, 17 from London Bridge, three from Streatham Hill, two from New Cross Gate, three from Crystal Palace Low Level. Returning crowds were offered 25 trains between 17.00 and 19.00, seven to Charing Cross, 16 to London Bridge and two to Cannon Street. Running non-stop, the Pullman special of twelve Pullmans hauled by an N class 2–6–0 left Charing Cross at 12.34, arriving at 13.27. Return times were 17.47 and 18.40. In the early 1950s, crowds arriving and departing on Derby Day reached almost 40,000 at Tattenham Corner station, but towards the end of the decade a combination of lower attendances and increased car ownership brought a severe decline in rail traffic. Race specials dwindled to a level where it was possible to dispense with the intermediate block posts and these were permanently closed after 1970. 1958 saw only 13 extra journeys on Derby Day and a mere two on Oaks Day. By 1976 there were only five extra workings, all on Derby Day. From 1965 the royal train was hauled by electric or diesel locomotives with much less pomp and fuss, and soon afterwards the Oaks Day working ceased. At the time of writing the Queen still goes to the Derby by train, not only because like so many other royal rail journeys in the motor and air age it is traditional, but because rail offers tangible convenience, avoiding road congestion, providing opportunity for refreshment and relaxation en route and facilitating transfer at Tattenham Corner for the ceremonial drive up the course.

Peak-hour traffic on the branch continued heavy in the post-war years, filling the ten-car trains introduced on 20th June 1955. But the general falling-off in slack-hour loadings we have noted elsewhere as occurring from the early 1960s was apparent here, bringing with it rationalisation of facilities and working economies. When on 29th November 1970 the branch was converted to colour-light signalling, a 5m 5ch section was introduced between Chipstead and Tattenham Corner, the box at the latter being the only one left open on the line. At the same time the terminal layout was drastically simplified to three platform roads and two sidings, with 22 instead of 97 levers in the box. From 15th September 1958 off-peak service, which had been

Up train approaching Woodmansterne, 28th March 1959.
Alan A Jackson

Chipstead looking to Purley, 3rd October 1964. SR electric lighting and upper quadrant semaphores are evident but otherwise there is little change since opening date.
Alan A Jackson

restored to three an hour at the end of the war was cut to half-hourly, and an hourly Sunday service was introduced on 13th September 1964, with Smitham station closed all day. As a further economy, from 6th September 1965, the ticket offices at each station were closed at 20.15 on weekdays, all Saturday afternoon and evening and all day on Sundays; at these times conductor-guards issued paper tickets on the trains from portable machines. With this change, off-peak trains reverted to the steam era practice of operating only on the branch. As some compensation, Smitham was reopened on Sundays with Coulsdon North closed instead. Use of conductor-guards was extended from 5th May 1969, when they began to man trains continuously except before 10.00 and between 15.30 and 20.15 on Mondays to

Fridays, when they opened the booking offices but still issued tickets from their portable machines. Some increase in status was granted from May 1970 when off-peak trains again ran to and from Charing Cross, in combination with the Caterham service as before. On the branch, conductor guards changed over from Up to Down trains at Reedham.

Freight traffic, never very important in this agricultural and latterly predominantly residential area, faded away in the late 1950s. After World War 2 one train had sufficed; in 1954 it left Bricklayers Arms at 03.50, returning to Norwood Yard after serving the Tattenham Corner and Caterham branches. Seven years later, when it was working to and from Norwood Yard, three journeys a week were enough and in the early part of 1962 it ceased altogether.

By the mid 1970s, off peak loads had shrunk to a level which might be comfortably handled by a small single deck bus. Pleasure traffic had dwindled almost to nothing; on a fine summer Bank Holiday in 1975, when the Downs were littered with cars, observation showed trains unloading fewer than 20 passengers each at Tattenham Corner. As elsewhere, commuters were also using their cars to reach better served stations such as Epsom and Sutton and the daily flow to and from central London was soon to thin out very considerably.

In these circumstances it was not surprising that further retrenchment and rationalisation followed in the 1980s. From 14th May 1984 the peak hour service to and from London was reduced from four to three trains an hour and the two-car half-hourly off-peak shuttle over the branch was reduced to hourly in the late evening and all day Sundays, most making connection at Purley with the semi-fast Victoria-Brighton trains. A small improvement in the slack hours service was introduced in May 1986 when one of the two trains an hour was extended to work to and from Charing Cross.

Tattenham Corner signal box was abolished on 25th September 1983, control temporarily assigned to Purley. Transfer of all signalling to the Three Bridges centre took place on 14th January 1984. With the loss of horse box traffic to road vehicles, most of the area between platform three and Epsom Lane was sold off. During 1979–80 this site was covered with small houses and garages fronting a road appropriately named Royal Drive – it was used on Derby Day by royal cars after the arrival of the royal train.

The 92-year old 'temporary' SER wooden station at Tattenham Corner was partly demolished on 1st December 1993 when the driver of the 06.16 from Victoria, who was afterwards found to be over the alcohol limit, projected his train through the buffers, over the concourse and into the booking office. Fortunately no one was hurt (the train had no passengers) but the building across the end of the line had to be completely demolished. In its place neat but much reduced facilities were completed at minimum cost in March 1994; near the head of platform three, a modest single storey pavilion in red bricks with a ridge roof of imitation slates housing a small ticket office and waiting area; a separate shelter centrally-placed across the end of the platforms; and on the east side, a small lavatory block. Viewed as a whole, this group, totally subdued by the lengthy unsheltered platforms on one side and a large open area of car parking and approach roads on the other, appeared to bear more resemblance to amenities in a municipal park than a railway station. Careful provision was made, in the form of two gated exits near the buffers of platform three, for the once-a-year passage of royal motor cars.

Motspur Park station from the level crossing, looking to London, 6th August 1960, showing the double footbridge which gives access from either side of the line. The trespass notice on the left still refers to the LSWR. *Alan A Jackson*

Raynes Park to Epsom (map page 121)

After the opening of the main London & Southampton line through Wimbledon in 1838 and the London & Croydon in the following year, Epsom, 'famed alike for purgatives and races', attracted the interest of railway promoters. An unsuccessful London & Dorking Bill of 1839, envisaging a branch south from Wimbledon, encouraged the LSWR to promote surveys by Joseph Locke in 1842–43. This was followed by a LSWR bill of 1844 for a single track branch to Epsom, which Parliament rejected in favour of an extension of the London & Croydon to Epsom because it was thought the Clegg & Samuda atmospheric traction system proposed for that line should receive a fair trial and also because there were fears that slow trains to and from Epsom might interfere with movement over the strategically important main line to Gosport (for Portsmouth).

On 10th May 1847 the LBSCR arrived in Epsom from what is now West Croydon over a 7m 74ch double track along the foot of the North Downs. As atmospheric traction between London & Croydon had proved a failure, the Epsom line was operated by conventional steam locomotives.

What happened next was closely related to the rivalry between the LBSCR and the LSWR for the Portsmouth traffic and their sensitivity about the borderlands of their respective territories. Before long moves were afoot by independent promoters to fill the gap between Epsom and Dorking, astute men who knew they could exploit this situation. An Epsom and Leatherhead Railway was authorised in 1856 over the 3m 54ch from the LBSCR station in Upper High Street Epsom and a terminus on the north side of the Kingston Road at Leatherhead. This was quickly followed by a Wimbledon & Dorking Railway scheme from the same stable, intended to absorb the Leatherhead and open up the area to the LSWR as well as the LBSCR. This new company was to have the same chairman (Thomas Grissell) as the Epsom & Leatherhead and seven of its directors. In Parliament, the proposal was reduced to a link between Wimbledon and Epsom only but the title 'Wimbledon & Dorking' remained to confuse everyone.

Leaving the LSWR at Coombe Lane Bridge west of Wimbledon, the new line was to follow the route to Epsom surveyed earlier by Locke, making a junction with the Epsom and Leatherhead just north of the High Street. *Herapath's Railway Journal* of 20th June 1857 was sniffy about the idea of a second line to Epsom, then a town with only 3,600 permanent residents, albeit swollen by many hundreds more on race days two or three times a year. It considered the LBSCR did a reasonable job with the traffic available, suggesting it was unjust to bring in a competitor 'to aid and assist horse racing, which although rational enough in the abstract has been denounced as the most swindling of all amusements'. In the same issue, a letter signed 'A Railway Manager' described the Wimbledon & Dorking promoters as 'an independent company of landowners', mocking the absurdity of their estimate that 35,000 would be carried on Derby Day over a single line in three hours. Opposition came from both the LBSCR and the LSWR though the latter finally agreed to make a double track and work it for 45 per cent of gross receipts, subscribing for 1,500 shares and nominating two directors. Legislation spanned acts of 1857, 1858, 1859 and 1860.

As for the Epsom & Leatherhead, all attempts by the local interests to secure amalgamation with the Wimbledon–Epsom scheme were frustrated by the LSWR. At the beginning of 1859 when the single line north eastwards from Leatherhead was virtually complete and agreement for the LBSCR to work it secured, shareholders voted for further negotiations with the LSWR, which would be able to provide a shorter route to London. That company, now bothered by schemes to extend the line from Leatherhead to Guildford, showed renewed interest, agreeing to better the LBSCR terms for working and taking a lease from 1st February 1859. On that day, a train service operated by the LSWR was started. Since the LBSCR was effectively blocked out, the unfortunate passengers to and from London were obliged to walk between the new line's temporary terminus at Epsom and the Upper High Street station.

Services over the line from Wimbledon began on 4th April 1859, using the aforementioned temporary station at Epsom (on the site of the present one). It was now possible for the LSWR to provide a Waterloo–Leatherhead service of seven trains Down and eight Up daily and it was also in time to secure some of the traffic for the Spring Race Meeting. Waterloo was reached in 45–50 minutes from Leatherhead, a commendable timing given the single line working south of Epsom.

It was not until 29th July 1859 that the LSWR and LBSCR finally made their peace in an agreement which admitted LBSCR trains to Leatherhead, the section beyond Epsom becoming a joint operation. This agreement established a firm boundary between the two companies' territories which made it possible at some future date for the LBSCR to go on to Dorking and Horsham, the LSWR to Shalford or Guildford. The 30 chains link between the two stations at Epsom, which had been ready early in 1859, was used from 8th August 1859 by LBSCR trains to and from Leatherhead. The company supplied that town with about six trains each way daily but these did not call at the Wimbledon & Dorking's station at Epsom. A further LBSCR/LSWR agreement of 1st January 1862 set up a joint committee to manage the Epsom–Leatherhead line, each company retaining its own receipts and sharing expenses and maintenance costs. Although the tracks from Epsom LBSCR to Leatherhead were jointly owned from 1865, the Wimbledon & Dorking station became LSWR property. This was because that company had effectively been taken over by the LSWR under an act of 1862. In 1863 the LBSCR secured powers, which it was never to use, to work the Wimbledon–Epsom line jointly with the LSWR.

So much for the somewhat tortuous origins of the line south of Wimbledon; it remains to describe it as built. At Wimbledon Junction (also called West Barnes or Epsom Junction), rather more than a mile south west of Wimbledon station, the double track opened in 1859 swerved away south across low-lying mist-haunted fields, more or less level with the land. At 2m 2ch from the junction, the first station, Old Malden, served the small village about half a mile to the west. Malden station on the main line became New Malden & Coombe in May 1859 but confusion was firmly banished when in February 1862 the station on the Epsom line was renamed Worcester Park, after an estate west of the railway. The Up platform here was furnished with a small Italianate house of stock bricks, with arched windows and a barge-boarded, wide-eaved slate roof. This contained the entrance hall, ticket and other offices, with rooms above for the stationmaster and his family. There was a small goods yard at the London end of the Up platform.

Now climbing at 1 in 180 and 1 in 100, the line reached its first summit in a deep cutting through a small wood before descending into the Hogsmill Valley. This descent brought the railway to a point west of Ewell village where, at 2m 18 ch from Worcester Park, a very similar station was provided, though here the house was on the Down side. Some years afterwards, the arrival of a stationmaster with numerous offspring caused the building to be enlarged by the addition of a second gabled two-storey block matching its predecessor in external appearance apart from some slight variations in the fenestration. No doubt anxious to recover some of the cost of this work, the LSWR gave its fecund stationmaster responsibility for Worcester Park as well, a clever strategy since it may also have sapped some of his spare energy. On the Down side, at the London end of Ewell station, a freight siding and a loading dock were provided. Around 1890 a goods shed was added at the London end of the Down platform.

Virtually unchanged after the enlargement mentioned, the passenger station (renamed Ewell West from 9th July 1923 to distinguish it from the former LBSCR establishment) remains today, now a grade 2 listed building. Here, as at Worcester Park, there was no footbridge for many years, passengers crossing the line on the level at the London end under the eyes of the signalmen. Ewell signalmen also supervised the movement of milk churns on wooden flaps erected between the platforms when the line was clear. Worcester Park did not get its footbridge until 1903, when an elegant lattice steel girder job (still in service at the time of writing) was supplied by the Wimbledon Signal Works.

Beyond Ewell, over the 1m 5ch to the junction at Epsom the line climbed at 1 in 100 and 1 in 90, turning south west to avoid the built-up area. The temporary station already mentioned was a crude wooden structure with little or no shelter from the elements but after some years a plain wooden building with gabled roof and canopy at the platform side was provided to accommodate waiting rooms and other amenities. In 1885 a facing crossover was laid between the Up and Down lines at the country end to facilitate reversal of race specials. By that time there were signal boxes at each end of the station, that at the west end controlling entry to a small goods yard on the Down side. More drastic layout changes followed in the 1890s, when two centre roads were inserted, together with a loop on the Up side. The platform on that side, shifted over to make room, was now an island. After this,

LBSCR trains to and from the Sutton line ran through the station, using the centre roads. By the early years of the 20th century, multi-gabled canopies had been added to both platforms to give shelter to the growing number of passengers.

At Worcester Park, a developer had purchased the estate of that name, laying out Great and Royal Avenues west of the railway, roads which were very slowly lined with large villas. At the station end, a small parade of shops appeared. As early as the 1860s, this suburban development was recognised by provision of a semi-fast businessmen's train from Waterloo at around 17.30, but by 1888 the gradual growth around this station and some expansion at Epsom and Ewell had justified an increase to a total of 13 trains each way daily, with Down departures from Waterloo spread between 07.25 and 23.55. Worcester Park experienced further residential expansion in the first decade and a half of the new century, mainly in the form of much smaller houses east of the line either side of the Cheam Common Road. The 1906 timetables provided 23 Down trains between 05.32 and 00.10 and by 1919 there were four trains Down between 06.45 and 08.45 followed by a departure from Waterloo at 45 minutes past each hour (all fast to Wimbledon) until 20.45 with commuter extras at 17.15, 18.15, and 19.15, all fast to Earlsfield, then hourly workings till 23.45. The existence of a considerable residential traffic is evident from the 1919 timetable, which shows five Up trains from Worcester Park between 07.13 and 08.43, all fast to Earlsfield. Sunday services were poor, only eight each way in 1909. By the 1900s, Epsom commuter business to Waterloo was justifying peak hour non-stop trains which covered the 14¼ miles in 25–26 min.

Working on and off the main line was eased by layout improvements. In 1868 the LSWR provided a dedicated pair of tracks for Epsom line trains on the south side between the London end of Wimbledon station and West Barnes Junction, where the old connection to the main lines fell out of regular use. This new double line was extended to New Malden with the opening of the Kingston Loop on 1st January 1869, when additional platforms were provided at Wimbledon on the London side of the overline bridge. After only two years the junction was again altered with the opening of Raynes Park station on 30th October 1871. Richard Garth, who had begun to develop West Barnes Park in 1868, laying out what are now Grand Drive and Blenheim Road, paid £4,000 towards the cost of building and maintaining this station but the name recognises former landowners, the Rayne family, who had long campaigned for such a station. Further changes followed in 1884 when a flyunder was constructed to bring the Up Epsom line to the Up side of the main line, where a junction was made with the Up Slow road (formerly the Up Main). A new Up platform and Up side ticket office were opened on 16th March 1884.

Freight facilities developed beyond the usual yard-to-yard pick-up goods, in a surprisingly varied fashion. In 1909 there were three daily goods trains each way on weekdays, one providing facilities to transport cattle to the Tuesday Market at Guildford. A small brickworks operated by the Worcester Park Brick Company started production on the hill above the west side of the line three quarters of a mile south of Worcester Park station in 1898. This was served by a rope-worked rail incline connected to the Up line via a short siding and trailing points. Known as 'Cunliffe's' after a signatory to the private siding agreement, access was through a ground frame released from Ewell signal box. At Ewell, a siding running out of the goods yard at the London end of the Down platform, installed around 1890 and removed in 1955, carried freight to and from corn mills on the Hogsmill stream.

From the 1920s there was another private siding on the east side of the Ewell goods yard into the Epsom Rural District Council depot. Further south on the Down side, a brickworks was opened by Messrs Stone & Co of Epsom in about 1922. This not only had its standard gauge private siding, entered through a ground frame released from Ewell box, but an internal horse-worked narrow gauge layout. Both the Ewell and Worcester Park brickworks sidings were removed in the early 1950s. Also south of Ewell station was another private siding, trailing into the Up line which gave access to the Horton Light Railway, serving the large complex of London County Council mental hospitals.*

The expected bonanza from the Epsom race traffic* proved something of a disappointment. As we have seen, the LBSCR station at Epsom Downs (1865) and the SECR station at Tattenham Corner (1901), with their extensive accommodation, provided much better access to the race course. Of the three companies in contention for this traffic, the LSWR was always at the bottom of the league, both as regards passengers carried and number of special trains worked. In 1923 only 18 specials were operated between Waterloo and Epsom, compared with 54 to Tattenham Corner and 42 to Epsom Downs and Epsom Town. Cuddington Cutting intermediate box, between Worcester Park and Ewell, specifically installed for race traffic and opened only on the busiest race days, was last used in 1924.

It was London commuters and their families, not punters, who were to provide the bread and butter for this line. By the beginning of the 20th century Raynes Park was showing clear signs of residential development, soon to be further stimulated by the arrival of the London United electric tramcars to link Wimbledon and Kingston via Raynes Park and New Malden from 2nd May 1907. It was these trams rather than the railway which sustained the emerging Edwardian community at West Barnes, later to be served by a new station. Between West Barnes and Worcester Park there was in 1914 nothing but polo and shooting grounds, fields and one or two large houses. To the south, apart from the Edwardian growth at Worcester Park already mentioned and some scattered late Victorian and Edwardian villa building along the Ewell-Kingston road, around Ewell village and on the outskirts of Epsom, the railway still passed through open countryside.

With the formation of the Southern Railway in 1923 it became possible to conceive new route developments using the lines of the absorbed companies. One example of this was the experimental operation of a number of Portsmouth trains via Worcester Park and Epsom in the summer of 1924 but a much more significant development was the inclusion of the Raynes Park–Dorking/Effingham Junction lines in the new company's suburban electrification programme for 1925. Fed through a conductor rail from substations at Raynes Park, Epsom, Dorking North and Effingham Junction, electric multiple-unit trains entered public service on Sunday 12th July 1925, providing three trains an hour seven days a week between Waterloo and Leatherhead, whence two continued to Dorking and the third to Bookham and Effingham Junction. At first both Vauxhall and Wimbledon stations were missed by the electrics but from 1st December, after public complaints, the service was rearranged to call at all stations.

---

* The history of the Horton Light Railway and the Epsom race traffic over the Waterloo-Epsom line are dealt with in the author's book *The Railway in Surrey*, Atlantic, 1999.

Before long the builders of small houses were working hard to fodder the new service. The Edwardian streets at West Barnes were extended to carry London's sprawl southwestwards towards the level crossing at Blue House Lane, where the SR had opened a station called Motspur Park on the same day as the electric working began. A simple 520ft island with a small passimeter ticket office, this was connected to an approach road on the Down side by an uncovered footbridge. Its construction cost of £7,200 was roughly equivalent to the sale price of 11 of the new houses it was designed to serve. At 20 min from Waterloo (9¾m) and with trains every 20 min. all day, sited in pastureland punctuated with hedgerows and lanes, the station formed a potent nucleus for a new residential community. And that was quickly achieved; close to it, east of the line, there appeared shopping parades and a large public house. By 1939 the BBC and London University Sports Grounds were the only reminders of a vanished countryside; the southward view from the footbridge was now dominated by two gasholders and a pumping plant supplying the fuel needs of the new district all round.

Worcester Park expanded rapidly from about 1925. To the west, within just over ten years suburban development had enveloped the village of Old Malden, its 1930s shopping parades dominating one side of the erstwhile village centre with its inn, pond and green. New housing, mostly small semis, had by 1938 flowed out either side of the railway until it coalesced into the surrounding communities of North Cheam to the east, Motspur Park to the north and Stoneleigh to the south, forming a veritable sea of red tile roofs swamping around the Victorian estate and all but obliterating the much older farming settlements.

Most dramatic of all was the appearance at the 12th mile from Waterloo of an entirely new townlet called Stoneleigh, which arose on the pastures and copses of three farms in the course of four short years. A station opened here amid empty fields on 17th July 1932 was handling well over 3,000 passengers a day by 1939. The developers, Stoneleigh Estate Company, were sufficiently convinced of its import-ance to the success of their scheme that on 17th July 1931 they had signed an agreement to contribute almost half the £7,550 cost as well as to give the land necessary to widen the railway. In its original form, with 520ft island platform and unroofed footbridge, Stoneleigh station was virtually a carbon copy of Motspur Park.

By the mid 1930s housebuilding all along the line was imposing heavy pressure on both passenger and freight facilities. Between 1927 and 1937 Worcester Park and Motspur Park stations saw a tenfold increase in season ticket issues while Stone-leigh's 103,742 passengers of 1933 grew in the next two years to an annual total of 313,647, the related gross revenue rising from £4,562 to £13,948. Some attempt was made to increase the train service to meet this growth in traffic. From 5th July 1936, following the opening of the Wimbledon flyover and the track rearrangement thence into Waterloo, the SR inserted another three trains an hour each way (increasing the frequency to a train every ten minutes) between Motspur Park and Waterloo, this in anticipation of the opening of the new line through Chessington to be mentioned later. From the same date, the 20-minute service south of Motspur Park called only at Wimbledon between Motspur Park and Waterloo, running nonstop inwards from Motspur Park in rush hours. Between 1933 and 1938 another five Up trains were somehow squeezed into the service in the morning peak, one starting from Worcester Park. These improvements gave Stoneleigh 13 Up trains from 07.19 until the basic 20-minute service started at 09.27.

Worcester Park station, Up side approach and entrance after the 1936–37 rebuilding.
Raphael Tuck & Son

Stoneleigh station looking to Epsom, 23rd January 1965, showing the 1941 footbridge and booking office and, in the foreground, the foundations of the smaller 1932 footbridge (like that at
Motspur Park), which it replaced. *Alan A Jackson*

Overcrowding reached a very high level in 1934–7, with the SR seemingly taken by surprise by the full effects of the developers' activities. Passengers originating at Leatherhead and Dorking, used to corner seats in the morning but now obliged to stand as far as Stoneleigh or Ewell on the way home after a hard day at the office complained loud and long. Part of the problem was caused by over-provision of first class accommodation; less than three per cent of the new house occupiers using stations inwards from Epsom patronised the 60–78 first class seats in each peak hour train. The resentment this largely empty accommodation aroused when there were eight or more standing in the cramped third class compartments was considerable. Another irritation arose from the variable numbers of seats in each train which resulted from the assorted make-up of the electric rolling stock used at the time. But by the end of the 1930s, with the additional services just mentioned and with the new stations at Malden Manor and Tolworth siphoning off some passengers from Stoneleigh and Worcester Park, things began to improve somewhat.

The provision of more peak hour trains owed much to the lobbying of the very active local residents' associations at Stoneleigh and elsewhere. These bodies also campaigned for station improvements, another matter in which they had some success, though much was done by the SR without external prompting. By the early 1940s all the stations except Ewell West had undergone some rebuilding. At Raynes Park, noting the extensive residential development south of the station, the SR board authorised extensive new works in June 1933. These comprised: new ticket and parcels offices and a parcels and van yard on the Up side abutting the main road; a footbridge connecting the totally rebuilt staggered platforms (four faces serving from north to south, Up Epsom, Up Slow, Down Slow and Down Epsom lines); a new passimeter ticket office and entrance on the Down side; a post office; and eight lock-up retail premises to provide some revenue against the outlay. This work was completed in 1936.

Motspur Park's footbridge was enlarged in 1932 to allow access to the platform from new residential roads on the west side of the line. In 1937–38 the platform canopy here was extended at the London end and other improvements were made to a station destined to become the junction for the new line through Chessington to Leatherhead.

Worcester Park's little country station of 1859 was reported to the SR Traffic Committee in June 1935 as 'totally inadequate' for current needs. An almost total reconstruction was duly ordered. This included raised and widened platforms; slewing of the Down line; a new Up side entrance building in concrete and red brick with metal-framed windows and a flat roof to accommodate the main entrance hall and various offices; and a back-tilted steel girder canopy along much of the Down platform with a new exit from the street below. All was in place by the end of 1937 but further expenditure had to be agreed in 1939. The freight yard here was swamped by deliveries of building materials, not to mention a vast increase in solid fuels for the new houses. A very necessary enlargement was completed in 1934 and further works were undertaken in 1935/36. Even so, when the General Manager and senior officers inspected in December 1936 they found the yard filled to capacity, ordering two more sidings to be laid with a cart road and also a shunting neck to avoid delays to the passenger service.

As early as May 1935 Stoneleigh Residents' Association had started to prepare a case for reconstruction of the three year-old station. The little footbridge was already slowing down clearance of the platform in the evening peak period, making it almost impossible for incoming passengers to reach trains without unacceptable delay. In October 1937 the SR board authorised major rebuilding. This involved the erection of 12ft wide covered stairs with a railed off section for contra-flow passengers, leading to a covered bridge of the same width which was to incorporate an enlarged ticket office. Delayed by war preparation works, this project was not completed until 1941/42. Its traffic still presenting some problems, in 1946 Stoneleigh station was given intermediate colourlight signals controlled from the boxes at Worcester Park and Ewell West.

At Epsom, the pre-grouping arrangements, with two stations a mere half a mile apart, four signalboxes and two freight yards, demanded early rationalisation. The first step was the concentration of all freight traffic at the former LBSCR yard from 2nd January 1928, a year in which total reconstruction of the old wooden LSWR passenger station was begun. The sturdy and workmanlike replacement received only the most cursory architectural treatment, confined to the road frontage on the Down side. Two island platforms were provided, each 650ft long and 35ft wide, canopied with steel and glass for 300ft. The northernmost face was used by Waterloo trains and the opposite one by the Up Victoria and London Bridge services. The second island accommodated Down Waterloo line trains at its inner face and Down services from London Bridge and Victoria at its outer face. This arrangement allowed easy interchange for passengers desiring alternative routes at a station where good connections were for many years available throughout the traffic day, a facility inexcusably eroded in the early 1990s and further damaged by the fragmentation of responsibilities which followed rail privatisation. Wide covered stairways at the London end led to a subway and a spacious entrance and ticket hall cut into the south side of the embankment. One side of the underline subway was fenced off to allow unimpeded movement of parcels, luggage, mail and other passenger train traffics to and from electric lifts which gave access to the island platforms. The main frontage to the approach road was plain-faced and flat-roofed.

A new 60-lever signal box straddled the centre roads, controlling a rearranged layout which included a siding and a 200ft horse and carriage loading bay on the south side parallel with the passenger platforms. All the through lines were signalled for reversible working to allow terminating trains to return from the same platform. At the country end, each side of the running lines, two new berthing sidings were provided for electric trains, equipped with staging to allow carriage cleaners easy access. Although not yet completed this new station, which unforgivably lacked a buffet, was brought into use on 3rd March 1929, the LBSCR station (renamed Epsom Town on 9th July 1923) having closed the previous night. On the same day new electric services were begun between London Bridge and Dorking/Effingham Junction via Tulse Hill and Sutton. Main line services to and from the South Coast continued to pass through without calling, despite a 25 mph limit through the new platforms. a matter which caused considerable irritation to the late Cecil J. Allen when an Epsom resident.

After World War 2, peak hour congestion did not revert to the high levels of the 1930s. Overcrowding inwards from Epsom was ameliorated by the introduction of more spacious new rolling stock, wartime abolition of first class on local services and the new stations on the Chessington branch. As the pre-war building activity between Epsom and Raynes Park had left very little land uncovered there was

Ewell West, looking to London; Up train leaving with unit 4693, 22nd June 1963. Signal box, semaphore signals, gas lighting and freight yard are all still present at this date. *Alan A Jackson*

virtually no additional traffic to be had from this source. From the late 1950s off peak loadings were thinned out by the inexorable rise in car ownership and the use of television as a substitute for spectator sport, cinema and theatre visits. This fall was recognised from 7th January 1963 when the 20 minute frequency was reduced to half hourly in the middle of the day and evenings, all day at weekends. Even so, this line suffered less than many since the lack of parallel bus services between its stations and a wayward road layout that frustrated speedy motoring helped to sustain

The 1929 station at Epsom looking to London, 17th September 1987. *Alan A Jackson*

all day patronage, especially at Worcester Park and Stoneleigh. A notable intensification in track occupation started on 29th May 1995 when for much of the day the half hourly all-stations service was supplemented by two trains an hour working to and from Guildford/Horsham (Dorking from 30th September 1996) which did not call at intermediate stations between Epsom and Wimbledon.

Signalling modernisation began with the installation of automatic colour lights between Raynes Park and Epsom from 27th February 1966, allowing closure of the boxes at Worcester Park and Ewell West. This work included colour light starters at Epsom station Up side. Motspur Park (originally Blue House Crossing) box was retained for operating the level crossing (converted to controlled lifting barriers from 4th November 1974) and the electrically-worked points at the junction of the Chessington branch. From 30th January 1972 until 21st July 1990 when it was closed and replaced by control from the Wimbledon Signalling Centre this box assumed control of the whole of the Chessington branch. The neighbouring West Barnes Lane Crossing box was closed and the level crossing controlled by cctv from Raynes Park box from June 1978. That box was in turn closed in May 1990 when control was moved to the Wimbledon Centre. Epsom's unusual overline signal box was closed on 25th July 1990, its responsibilities assumed by the Wimbledon Signalling Centre from 29th July. Demolition did not take place until April 1992.

Colour light signalling and installation of the BR automatic warning system (January 1978) came too late to prevent the line's first serious accident, which occurred in thick fog on the evening of 6th November 1947 when the 16.45 Up from Holmwood to Waterloo ran into the crowded 17.16 from Waterloo to Chessington South whilst it was crossing from the Down side on to the Chessington branch just south of Motspur Park. Four passengers were killed and 34 injured. Some lives were probably saved by the presence of a more modern steel coach in a crucial position. The driver of the Up train, unable to see the semaphore signal, had relied on a fogman who had shown a green light, under the false impression that he had heard the signal arm move to the 'off' position.

Freight, latterly hauled by SR Moguls and Q1 0–6–0s and then diesel locos, declined rapidly after the late 1940s and was eventually almost wholly limited to domestic solid fuels. That traffic was reorganised in the 1960s. Ewell West yard was closed from 1st May 1961 and Worcester Park from 6th May 1963 though this yard had to be temporarily reopened for coal and coke traffic in the winter of 1963–4. After 1963 solid fuels for the area were handled by new depots on the Chessington branch as mentioned later. Raynes Park freight depot, in the vee between the Up and Down Epsom lines, was closed at the end of 1969 but until the end of 1983 a remnant survived in use as a civil engineer's depot, requiring occasional opening up of the ground frame housed in a small cabin on the Down side just north of Motspur Park station. This cabin had been used to control a minor level crossing, reduced to a foot crossing in December 1965. After 1983 the ground frame remained to operate an emergency crossover between Raynes Park and Motspur Park.

Peak hour overcrowding is now a thing of the past on this quintessential commuter railway, but passenger loadings have held up well in recent years despite economies that (with the exception of Epsom) have produced unwelcoming stations without staff and train running information for much of the day. Staff cuts have also engendered boarded up waiting rooms and lavatories and encouraged the mindless vandalism that breeds on lack of supervision.

The Chessington Branch   (map page 121)

As the perceptive reader will have already observed by the several references in the foregoing account, the history of the Chessington branch is closely related to some of the events just described. By the late 1920s, builders had brought the edge of London to a depth of 1–1½ miles south of the former LSWR main line between Raynes Park and Surbiton, a growth which owed much to the Edwardian electric trams of the London United Tramways and the LSWR electric services. Further south, the clay meadows and pastures in the valleys of the Hogsmill and its tributary the Rythe, and the higher woodland and commons towards Ashtead remained almost untouched by suburban building. In this extensive territory between the Raynes Park–Leatherhead and New Guildford lines there were but three villages (Hook, Chessington, Old Malden) and a sprinkling of Victorian and Edwardian villas at Motspur Park/West Barnes and Worcester Park. During 1927 the bright raw concrete strip of the Kingston By-Pass road seared the fields across the northern fringes of this district, almost at once attracting at its London end new bus services, small houses, shops and even factories.

This development was not unnoticed by the Southern Railway's passenger-conscious management. Early in October 1929 Sir Herbert Walker was reporting to his board on the desirability of a railway through the territory between the existing lines south of Surbiton. Like the Metropolitan's proposal for Stanmore, the bill prepared for the 1930 session was designed to catch government assistance under the Development (Loan Guarantees and Grants) Act of 1929. It proposed a line from a junction with the Raynes Park–Leatherhead railway 617yd south of the Blue House Lane level crossing at Motspur Park, across the Hogsmill Valley, passing north of Old Malden and west of Chessington, then running parallel to the Kingston–Leatherhead road on its east side before rejoining the existing railway 270yd north east of the Kingston Road bridge at Leatherhead, near the site of the first Leatherhead station. Seeking shareholders' consent at the February 1930 meeting, the chairman explained that 'it may be a very valuable railway to us if we get the powers to do it, because it is outside the effective bus area for people coming into London'. Certified for quick passage through Parliament in view of its expected contribution to the relief of unemployment, the bill received Royal Assent on 1st August 1930.

A long delay then ensued before any work could be done. Although the board authorised purchase of land for the first 4m 75ch of the 7m 3f 2ch route in November 1930, it was soon discovered that much of it was already being broken up into small parcels, moving through the hands of speculators who were forcing prices up in anticipation of large-scale housebuilding. As at Golders Green and many other places around London, the railway found that its own plans for extension had encouraged profiteering in land it wanted to build the line. Complicated by appeals, the process of property acquisition was to last over six years. In one case the SR was obliged to pay £7,347 after arbitration for little more than two acres, a figure seven or more times the land's value in the mid-1920s. Meanwhile, in November 1933, the board agreed that the remainder of the land should be bought as far as the junction at Leatherhead.

As we have seen when looking at other areas, the early 1930s were a propitious time for the rapid erection and sale of small suburban houses around London. By 1934 the district south of Surbiton was being well worked by builders under the additional stimuli of the Kingston By-Pass, its bus services, and the promise of the new electric railway. From 1933 Wates and others had started to fill up the land between the new railway and new motor road as far as Tolworth, leaving to nature only the immediate valley of the Hogsmill. South of the new line's route, between the Motspur Park junction and Old Malden, many small builders laboured mightily from 1932.

This activity led the general manager to suggest to the board in June 1934 that construction might start at the London end. Sir Herbert Walker estimated that with four stations and two goods yards, an electrified double track on this section to the usual SR standards of 600V dc third rail could be managed for £440,000 excluding land. Another £120,700 would be needed for five eight-car trains to work the proposed 20-minute service. This was agreed, subject to clearance with the LPTB in accordance with the understanding reached after the Battle of Morden. With land still being purchased, the first contracts were let in May 1935. Three months later the finance for the new line was included in a scheme submitted by the SR under the Railways (Agreement) Act, 1935, another unemployment relief measure, which secured the capital at a very low rate of interest guaranteed by the Treasury. The section south of Chessington was to be left until building development in that area justified its cost of construction.

Working under George Ellson, the SR chief engineer, Sir Robert McAlpine & Sons began at Motspur Park early in 1936, sharing the earthworks contract with Edmund Nuttall, Sons & Co Ltd. During April, the junction was completed with a short length of permanent track to feed the contractors' temporary way. This track also facilitated the reversal of an additional train service (three per hour) between Motspur Park and Waterloo, which started on 5th July 1936. During the following December, the general manager visited the works with other senior officers, deciding on the spot that such was the progress of the housing development they would provide 540ft side-platform stations instead of the 520ft islands of the Motspur Park and Stoneleigh type originally planned.

Construction through the very heavy and corrosive clay of the Hogsmill basin

Facing Page: Tolworth station under construction in 1938, viewed from the goods yard on the south side, looking towards Malden Manor. *F Foote*

---

proved both onerous and costly. Its instability required piling, dry-fill around the clay cores of the embankments, and cutting slopes as gentle as 2½ to 1, with the floors covered with ash, or even in some places concreted. Presence of sulphates in the clay caused the engineers to prescribe the use of aluminous cement wherever the work was in contact with running water. For most of the distance to Chessington the line was on embankment, but there were cuttings near the junction, between Malden Manor and Tolworth, and between Chessington South station and its goods yard. Climbing towards the country end, the line had gradients of 1 in 91 and 1 in 98 for a quarter-mile between the junction and Malden Manor and in the descent from that station on to the Hogsmill viaduct. There were seven overbridges across public roads, one underbridge at Chessington South and a three-span 140ft viaduct over the Hogsmill at the country end of Malden Manor station. All were built of steel plate girders encased in concrete (in the erroneous belief that this would save maintenance) and were supported on mass concrete piers and abutments.

Concrete was also much used in the four stations, which were an outstanding feature of this railway. All were of the same basic design, derived from Wimbledon Chase, but here for the first time SR architects attempted to integrate the street buildings of a suburban station with its platform structures. This was something that London Transport had been doing on its Underground extensions under the inspiration of Charles Holden, but the SR's success was limited, failing to emulate the calm elegance of the Holden buildings. The smooth lines and simplicity of the Chessington line station elevations, much influenced by cinema and marine architecture, certainly produced a striking effect, at its best whilst the materials remained unweathered. On the platforms, the style was set by the graceful 200ft long 'Chisarc' cantilevered concrete canopies, illuminated by porthole glasses and a mixture of blue, white, amber, and pink GEC fluorescent tubes, an early use of this type of lighting in a transport environment, and certainly revolutionary for the Southern, where electric trains often served stations lit by gas or even oil lamps.

Each street-level structure, flanked by a very small car park, included ticket office, bookstall, lavatories for each sex, parcels office and a small lock-up shop. Towers were erected for luggage lifts which were never installed. To gain the platforms, passengers traversed subways and stairs but all the Down platforms also had a separate ramp giving access from the road, intended for milk and luggage. On each side, behind the canopies, were general waiting rooms with oak furniture and an enclosed heating stove, and, on the Up platform, a porters' room. There were detail differences. At Chessington South, where the road building was above the line, the Up platform and footbridge were not completed. Both Chessington stations had less massive supports to the canopies, and street buildings with facing bricks in place of the cement-faced stock bricks used at Tolworth and Malden Manor.

The first 2½ miles to Tolworth, with the intermediate station at Malden Manor on the northern edge of the old village of Malden, was opened on Sunday 29th May 1938, served by three six-car trains an hour seven days a week, a projection of the July 1936 Motspur Park workings mentioned earlier. Tolworth station was well-sited on the west side of a 94ft span bridge over the Epsom-Kingston road close to its intersection with the By-Pass, where since 1930, builders of small semis and terraces had been busy closing the gap between the new road and the Edwardian fringes of Surbiton. At this temporary terminus all trains used the Down platform, returning to the Up line on the London side of the road bridge.

Chessington North, looking to Tolworth, May 1939.
SR Official

Malden Manor exterior, 1938; a not wholly successful attempt to create an integral design in the 'Modern' style. The entrance block shows an affinity with Wimbledon Chase, built almost ten years earlier.

From the start a buoyant commuter traffic was obtained from the new housing estates although a good deal of it was extracted from other SR stations. Useful relief was given to the Raynes Park–Epsom line which as we have seen had been somewhat overwhelmed by the rapid south-western growth of London since 1930. Many of the new house owners from the estates built from that time either side of the Kingston Road between the Hogsmill valley and Worcester Park transferred their allegiance from Stoneleigh station to Tolworth, whilst those living in the extensive accretions around Old Malden moved from Worcester Park station to Malden Manor. Tolworth also gained some passengers from Surbiton, especially those who preferred a seat to non-stop runs in crowded trains, and finally there were some new customers from buses feeding the Morden tube (belated retribution!). As noted earlier, in recognition of its new junction status and traffic growth, improvements to the 13-year-old station at Motspur Park were completed in June 1938.

Chessington South station on the first day of public service, 28th May 1939. The people are heading in the direction of the Zoo. *Lens of Sutton*

The remaining two miles to Chessington South, with an intermediate station at Chessington North, were electrified on 14th May 1939 and opened to the public on Sunday 28th May. On the preceding Friday the deputy mayor of Surbiton performed a ceremonial opening. As the official party emerged from Chessington South station, it was greeted by a baby elephant which returned with them to Chessington Zoo, where a lunch was given by the proprietor. This was a demonstration of the importance of a traffic which has ever since been encouraged by joint publicity and combined rail and admission tickets.

Some housebuilding between the line and the Leatherhead to Kingston road had started about 1934, but on the east side of the railway, with the exception of the Copt Gilders estate near the old village of Chessington, there was little building until after World War 2. Even today a very large amount of open land remains south of the line east and west of Tolworth station. Beyond Chessington South, all was still open country in 1939 but large tracts had been sold for building, notably the Chessington House Estate and 166 acres between Malden Rushett (the first station site after Chessington South), and the Leatherhead golf course. These areas were subsequently sterilised by the creation of the post-war London Green Belt.

After an inspection in May 1938 the general manager had criticised the station naming agreed with the local authority (Chessington Court and Chessington Grange), expressing the hope that the word Chessington could be omitted from one. Chessington North and Chessington South were finally adopted, but the confusion foreseen by Sir Herbert Walker persisted, as evinced by notices on the Down platform at Chessington North warning NEXT STATION FOR THE ZOO.

With the completion of the second station, the three trains an hour were extended to Chessington South, taking 31 minutes for the 14 mile all-stations run from Waterloo. Quarterly season tickets for the full distance were £4 8s 0d (£4.40), rather less than two weeks' pay for the average adult clerical worker.

Tolworth was given a goods yard sited at the country end on the Down side, its four roads increased in 1940 to seven, providing room for 218 wagons. The three-road yard at Chessington South, also on the Down side and a short distance south of the passenger station, opened to goods traffic on 1st July 1939.

Electrically-worked points on the Down line at the junction were controlled from Motspur Park box, but the Up track had unworked trailing points protected by a 20mph restriction. On the branch itself, upper-quadrant semaphores were worked from boxes on the Down platforms at Tolworth (20 levers) and Chessington South (18 levers) using Stevens & Sons frames recovered from LSWR boxes and instruments of standard SR three-position, 'closed-block' pattern.

At the terminus, passenger trains went in and out of the Down platform using a crossover north of the station. An Up platform had been built, complete with 'Chisarc' canopy, but no footbridge, lighting, fencing, or accommodation were provided. Electrified track continued some 20ch beyond the platforms, extended later with plain track for a further 13ch. During construction the contractors dumped spoil from the cuttings to form the embankment beyond here almost as far as Chalky Lane. In 1941–42 the embankment was carried further towards Leatherhead by Royal Engineers as a training exercise, using chalk excavated for wartime works at Andover Junction and Basingstoke, until they reached Chessington Wood, only a quarter-mile north of the next intended station. This work can still be seen today, with the remains of the railway fences.

An RAF barrage balloon station was opened near Chessington South station in 1939, followed shortly after the war by erection nearby of single-storey government office buildings on two sites and a further complex at Tolworth station. These developments helped to create a valuable contra-flow of peak-hour traffic, strengthened in 1946 by the opening of an office tower block with accommodation for some 2,500 workers close to Tolworth station.

Post-war railway planning for London, enshrined in the grandiose 1949 Report of the London Plan Working Party, included a scheme categorised as lower priority for a route 'E' tube line paralleling the Northern line between Kennington and South Wimbledon, there branching into two routes, one to go on to Chessington South via Raynes Park, using the SR tracks on the branch and taking over the service, which would be supplied from a new car depot at Chessington South. Whatever the future of the Chessington branch, it now seems unlikely that this scheme will be resurrected.

Very soon after the war, the line experienced its first serious accident as described earlier. Mishaps of this type were eliminated by the introduction of track-circuited colour-light signalling, eventually to be provided on the branch from 30th January 1972. The two manual signalboxes were then demolished and the branch was worked directly from Motspur Park box with a ground frame at Tolworth goods yard. The BR automatic warning system was installed in January 1978.

In addition to its regular-interval passenger trains, the branch has seen a fair variety of operations: steam and later diesel-hauled excursions bringing customers for Chessington leisure attractions from all over Britain, the usual SR nocturnal freights,

Chessington South station seen from the overline bridge, looking to London, 3rd March 1962. Note the uncompleted Up platform and the opening made in the brickwork at the top of the staircase for a footbridge, which was never completed. Upper quadrant semaphore signals, telegraph wires and SR electric light fittings of 1939 remained at this time but all the housing dates from after 1945. *Alan A Jackson*

parcels trains and, on at least one occasion (1954) a royal train, carrying the Queen back from the Derby via Chessington South to avoid the returning crowds at Tattenham Corner.

Freight traffic, hitherto mostly small loads of building materials, domestic coal and coke, assumed new importance in the early 1960s. The thrice-weekly working was retimed to mid-day in 1963 to allow the line to be shut at night, but this frequency was soon inadequate for in May that year a mechanised solid fuel distribution depot was opened on the site of Chessington South yard, where public traffic ceased from 18th March. Two freight trains daily were then required, usually hauled by SR Moguls, Q 0–6–0s, and even on occasion, Bulleid Pacifics. This new facility was operated by Messrs. Charringtons and together with the Tolworth depot opened later, replaced goods yards at Claygate, Surbiton, Hampton Court, Esher, Walton-on-Thames and Worcester Park. One of the more positive achievements of the Beeching era, it was served by block trains coming direct from the Notts & Derby coalfield. A similar, larger fuel depot was opened on the site of Tolworth goods yard on 4th January 1965 under the auspices of the National Coal Board. This was big enough to require internal motive power, at first a small green Barclay 0–4–0 diesel shunter, later ex BR Drewry D2310. This depot was fed by two and sometimes three trains a day in addition to the daily working to Chessington South. Motive power in the first years was usually a Class 5 4–6–0.

As domestic consumers converted in droves to oil and gas central heating in the late 1960s and the 1970s, traffic into these two depots fell away but in 1974 there were still 17 trains of 21-ton hoppers each week to Tolworth and six to Chessington South, mostly moved by SR electro-diesel locos as trip workings from Wimbledon yard. The 1980s saw further decline, with Chessington latterly served by Class 37 and even Class 58 diesels bringing in a few hoppers, sometimes just one, from Didcot. These workings ceased altogether in 1988, when the Chessington South rail-hauled coal was diverted to Purley. The depot was closed on 4th November.

Tolworth depot also began to handle aggregates traffic from about 1981, additional plant for this coming into use from March 1984 following a Government grant. Coal trains did not run after 1989, but the ex-BR diesel shunter remained in use. There were still two stone trains a week in 1992 but after July 1993 the Tolworth facilities were abandoned and freight workings over the branch ceased.

Towards the end of the 1950s the branch suffered the general decline in off-peak traffic noticed elsewhere and from 15th September 1958 frequency was reduced from three to two trains an hour. Sunday trains, for a long time sparsely used, were reduced to hourly in winter from October 1976. Further cuts were made in 1993 when evening services were also reduced to hourly intervals. The population in the catchment area has in recent years shown a slight fall and this, together with the other factors operating to reduce central London commuting, brought peak hour services down from four trains an hour to three from 1976–77, further cuts following later.

Chessington North station (1939) on 23rd April 1962, viewed from the Down side. *Alan A Jackson*

In the late 1970s about 28,000 tickets were issued on the branch each month and 1,540 season tickets, with Tolworth the busiest station at 9,800 and 460 respectively. By the early 1990s passenger numbers had fallen quite steeply, a count of passengers boarding between 06.00 and 21.00 showing not only the extent of the decline but a shift in the station league table:*

Chessington South	238
Chessington North	662
Tolworth	558
Malden Manor	836

Staffing economies had been made as early as 1971 when tickets at Chessington South were issued by the duty railman from his office on the platform and the street level booking office was closed. By the end of the 1980s the ticket offices at the other three stations were manned only in the morning peak period with no staff at all on duty at other times.

Powers for the completion of the line to Leatherhead were kept alive until 1961, after which the alignment remained zoned for railway use in the Surrey Development Plan for a further ten years. Since most of the countryside south of Chessington is part of the London Green Belt, protected from the swathes of small suburban houses that would have otherwise covered it around the proposed station sites at Rushett and Leatherhead North, the fulfilment of the SR scheme of 1929 is now very much a dead duck. Suggestions have been made for an extension to give better access to the Chessington World of Adventures, a very popular theme park establishment on the Zoo site in 1987, which even without this has boosted off-peak traffic to Chessington South especially in school holiday periods. New housing developments on the former LCC mental hospitals estate west of Epsom might also be served if a further mile or so were built, but such projects will never materialise without the (very remote) possibility of large injections of capital from interested parties.

In the sixth decade of its existence this half-finished railway continued to carry on a much reduced scale the traffic for which it was built: movement of office workers into and out of central London daily. It is interesting that this was a railway constructed when much of the new housing it was intended to serve was already in place and in use; and it is certain that without it, an intolerable strain would for many years have been thrown on road services and the existing rail facilities at Stoneleigh, Worcester Park and Surbiton. But after 60 years it had all but outlived its purpose. Passenger loadings off-peak, except at those times when the theme park is in heavy demand, had become very light; in winter trains carried much less than a busload and inter-station fare-paying traffic on the branch had all but disappeared thanks to the high tariff for local journeys. With such a scenario, the financial pressures for rationalisation and economies seemed likely to increase; proposals had already been made to demolish the Modern style SR stations (initially those at Chessington South and Malden Manor), replacing them with bus-stop style basic facilities so that land might be released for development. For the future, track singling and shuttle operation seemed possibilities for the medium term but the best solution might be integration of much of the line in a Kingston area light rail scheme, involving total abandonment of conventional electric railway operation.

* Source: Surrey County Council

Exterior of Kingston-on-Thames old station buildings, c. 1907. *Commercial postcard*

The Kingston Loop
(map page 165)

Perhaps the most important of all places around London not touched by the main lines was the ancient borough and market centre of Kingston-on-Thames, strategically placed at what was for many years the last Thames bridge before London, on the main road to Portsmouth. At the end of the 1830s there were over 8,000 living in this Surrey town, served by over 60 daily road coaches to London. With the moral support of the coaching interest, the opposition of Lord Cottenham, owner of much land between the town and Wimbledon, secured the diversion of the London & Southampton Railway to the south. Francis Giles had engineered a line in 1831 which would have passed about midway between the town centre and the present Surbiton station, but the opposition caused Parliament to approve a route in 1834 which although in a sense more direct, entailed a long embankment across Norbiton Common and a deep cutting through Surbiton Hill, about a mile south of Kingston. Trains began to run between London (Nine Elms) and Woking on 21st May 1838 calling at a station named Kingston, situated just east of the present Surbiton station, where the line passed below the Kingston-Epsom road.

Within two years, speculative builders had established the beginnings of New Kingston, or Kingston-on-Railway, the middle-class villa suburb later to become known as Surbiton. There were some non-stop trains to and from London and it was not long before Kingstonians were regretting their isolation both as regards passenger and freight traffic. Grain which had formerly reached Kingston's important maltings by water was now going direct to London by rail and there was a noticeable depression in the town's retail trade. By the 1850s influential people in Kingston were ready to support almost any scheme which promised to end the indignity of a town with almost 11,000 people but no railway station nearer than one mile from its centre.

Some proposals touching the town came forward in this period, but surrounded as it was by royal parks, the Thames, and Wimbledon Common, the scope for direct links to London on useful through routes to points outside the capital was somewhat restricted. There were strong interests working to have Kingston connected by rail to the GWR and LNWR main lines, but naturally enough this met with little enthusiasm in the town. In 1857 there was a bill for a broad gauge branch from the GWR through Brentford to Richmond, offering the promise of further extension southwards to Kingston, but this was easily defeated by LSWR opposition. A bill from the same direction two years later sought powers for a Southall-Brentford-Kingston-Merton line, which would give access to Croydon via the existing Wimbledon & Croydon railway. The LSWR successfully countered by offering to construct a 3¼-mile branch from the Richmond-Windsor line at Twickenham following the Thames, to end at the west side of Kingston bridge. This was duly authorised in August 1859. After much agitation by the Kingston interests, another act in the following year sanctioned its extension for 72 chains into a terminus at Richmond Road, Kingston. Somewhat to the disgust of the LSWR, Parliament insisted that a station still be provided on the opposite bank at Hampton Wick, a mere 700yd west of the Kingston station. When the double-track branch opened on 1st July 1863 there was a second intermediate station, Teddington & Bushy Park, between the village and the north gate of the Park.

At a level just above that of the present booking hall, the three-bay, four-platform terminus under its all-over roof was at first known as Kingston New, or Kingston Town. The name Kingston soon sufficed because from the opening day of the branch, the main line station was called Surbiton & Kingston instead of Kingston Junction. A bridge of five cast-iron arches of 75ft span carried the tracks 24ft above Thames high water just north of the old road bridge. There were no other features of interest between here and the junction with the Windsor line west of Twickenham station.

It was not long before there was considerable grumbling at the roundabout approach to London, a journey of 15 miles for which some trains required as much as 57 minutes. To make matters worse, the LSWR fares were seen as expensive compared with those of the more direct horse buses (9d second-class rail to Richmond, only 6d by bus) and of the NLR, which also served the new branch. The *Surrey Comet* declared on 4th July 1863 'These fares, we feel convinced, will be as prohibitive to the development of short traffic as if a protective tariff had been framed for the very purpose'. A further irritant was a small reduction in the service required to make room for the Shepperton trains when that line opened in November 1864. Fortunately for the Kingstonians, the LSWR was not to be left in peace. From 1863 several proposals came forward for lines eastwards towards London and although all were defeated by LSWR opposition, that company was obliged to consolidate its position by obtaining powers in 1865 for a line from Kingston through New Malden to Wimbledon. This was to begin with an end-on junction with the Twickenham line, crossing the Richmond and London roads on the level, going on to the main line just west of Coombe & Malden station (now New Malden). Here the double track passed below the Southampton line, continuing alongside into Wimbledon, where end-on connection was made with the new Tooting, Merton & Wimbledon Railway described earlier. As there were misgivings about the Kingston level crossings, powers were obtained in 1866 for an alignment which brought the tracks over both roads into a high level station. This was to have two side platforms, parallel and to the north of the 1863 station and about 15ft above it. The junction was steeply made between the west end of the new platforms and the river bridge.

Built by John Aird & Sons, the Kingston & Wimbledon opened without ceremony on 1st January 1869, all trains from the high-level station running to and from Ludgate Hill, calling at the one new intermediate station of Norbiton, three quarters of a mile east of Kingston on Coombe Lane (now Road), and at new platforms at Coombe & Malden. Norbiton's large yellow brick station house on the north side of the line was similar in style to that on the west side at Teddington. In 1880 a double-line junction was made with the main lines west of Coombe & Malden station and four years later a connection was put into the new Up slow (former Up main) on the north side of the embankment so that the flyunder subsequently carried only the Down Kingston road.

Despite some continued dissatisfaction with the train service, which encouraged further railway schemes involving Kingston, the LSWR loop stimulated steady suburbanisation of the riverside area between Kingston and Twickenham in the late 1860s and 1870s, much of it taking the form of large middle-class houses. Around 1875 Teddington had many 'villas and genteel dwellings' and a new village centred on the station 'already has a church, schools, hotel and shops of a more showy description than those of the mother village'. Landowners and developers, led by Sir Thomas Freake, tried hard to persuade the LSWR to open a station to serve the new district of Strawberry Hill between Teddington and Twickenham, finally moving it into action with cash offers of one-third of its £1,500 cost, put up by those who stood to gain most. A vaguely Italianate two-platform station distinguished with some delicate-looking ironwork under its canopies was the result. This opened on 1st December 1873 and at first only Kingston and Twickenham trains called to serve 'the curious village of Strawberry Hill, made up wholly of *villas*', but by 1877 almost all the Shepperton branch trains were also stopping there. A useful aid to train working in the area was opened on 22nd October 1883 in the form of a flyover carrying the Up Kingston line over the Windsor lines into a new platform at the north side of Twickenham station, joining the Up Windsor line at the east end. In 1899, carriage sidings were constructed near the Fairfax Road level crossing at Teddington, on the Down side.

Exterior of Hampton Wick station c. 1907. *Commercial postcard*

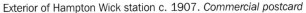
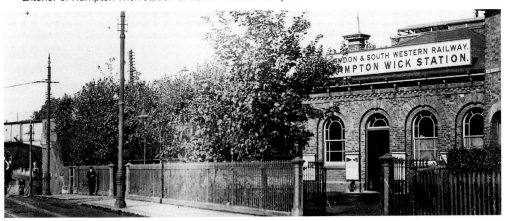

As mentioned, the discontent in Kingston persisted after the opening of the loop in 1869. Envious eyes were cast from the town at Surbiton's excellent main line service and at favoured Richmond, with its fast trains to Waterloo and services north and north east provided by no less than five other companies. Prominent among the foreign elements anxious to penetrate the juicy LSWR territory in the Thames Valley and northern Surrey was the impecunious but ambitious Metropolitan District Railway. At one time it seemed likely that this initiative would bring Kingston its long-desired direct route to London. An independent bill deposited in 1880 proposing a Guildford, Kingston & London Railway stirred up great optimism and enthusiasm in the town, with the mayor sitting on the formation committee and the corporation offered a statutory right to appoint a director. To the consternation of Waterloo, the District was pulling many of the strings. Eventually, after much negotiation, there emerged in 1881 a Kingston & London Railway Act. In its final form, this 7½-mile line would have run from Surbiton to join the District at Putney Bridge, with connections at Norbiton to allow running from Kingston to Putney Bridge and to Surbiton. To be worked by a joint committee of the promoters, the LSWR and the MDR, this line would give LSWR trains access to High Street Kensington and South Kensington, and have intermediate stations at Coombe & Kingston (just east of the Fairfield), Roehampton (near Robin Hood Gate) and at Tibbett's Corner, Putney Heath. So interested was the LSWR that in 1882 it obtained powers to build a West End terminus at the corner of Pelham Street and the Fulham Road alongside South Kensington station. In that year the whole project was transferred to the District and the LSWR equally, but the Kingston directorship was retained. Some work was started, but with the District unable to raise its proper share of the capital and the LSWR unwilling to help it, the scheme was dropped in 1886 in favour of a shorter link between Putney Bridge and Wimbledon, for which the Kingston & London supplied the northernmost section from south of East Putney to Putney Bridge, as mentioned at the beginning of this chapter.

As something of a sop to the disappointed Kingstonians, the LSWR in the 1880s undertook substantial rebuilding of the inconvenient two-level station, making a large concourse between the buffer stops of the low-level terminal platforms and the Richmond Road with a new staircase between the two sets of platforms.

When Kingston station first opened in 1863 there were 15 Up and 13 Down trains on the Twickenham and Waterloo route and nine each way to and from Fenchurch Street, most of these involving a change at Hampstead Road (Primrose Hill). These North London Railway trains were an extension of the service started on 20th May 1858 between Hampstead Road (Primrose Hill) and Twickenham. About half of them were composed of LSWR stock, the rest of NLR; LSWR and NLR locomotives were transferred at Kew. Further variety was evident after the opening of a junction at Longhedge, Battersea, on 3rd April 1866, when trains also began to work between Kingston and Ludgate Hill.

After the opening of the link between Kingston and Malden, the NLR trains were diverted to terminate at Richmond over a new line between Richmond and South Acton opened on the same day (1st January 1869). The Kingston high level platforms saw eleven trains daily to and from Ludgate Hill, passengers from Waterloo changing at Wimbledon and those from Victoria at Herne Hill. Demand for direct service to and from Waterloo soon made itself felt; there were only two trains each way in November 1869 but the pattern gradually changed until eventually

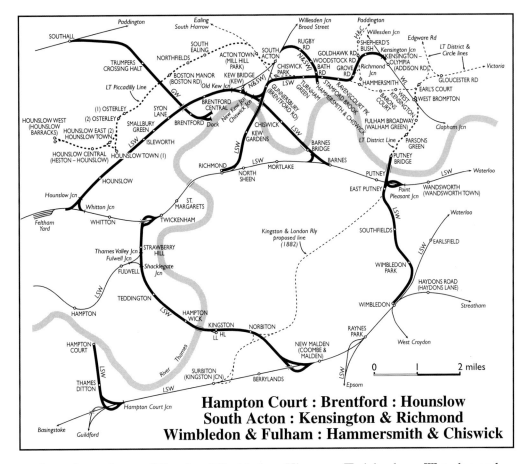

**Hampton Court : Brentford : Hounslow
South Acton : Kensington & Richmond
Wimbledon & Fulham : Hammersmith & Chiswick**

the main service was Waterloo–Wimbledon–Kingston–Twickenham–Waterloo and vice versa, referred to officially in the timetables as the *Roundabout*. By 1909 there were 39 trains from Waterloo to Kingston via Wimbledon each weekday, most of them stopping at all intermediate stations, with a running time of 37 minutes over the 12 miles. In the rush hours, when some stations were missed, the best time was 25 minutes. There were by this time only two trains (both in the evening) from Ludgate Hill. In the same year there were 35 trains from the high-level station to Waterloo, most of them coming through from Teddington. Strawberry Hill also had the Shepperton trains, which ran to and from Waterloo via Twickenham.

At this time there was a daily milk train and six freight workings between Malden and Teddington, serving the yards and sidings at Malden Crossing, Norbiton, Kingston, Hampton Wick and Teddington. Only four goods trains ran the opposite way round the loop, including two from the Midland Railway's Brent yard at Cricklewood (there was also a return working to Brent). A substantial part of the traffic was movement of coal into the Hampton Court Gas Company's works on the Up side between Hampton Wick and Teddington and those of the Kingston Gas Company in the Lower Ham Road north of Kingston station. The yard on the Down side at Malden Crossing was used by the Surrey Coal & Coke Company, which later shared it with the Twisteel Reinforcement Co. In the 1920s and 1930s the Kingston Gas Works sidings also gave access to the depot of the Anglo American Oil Co.

Hackney Carriages in attendance at Twickenham station, c.1905.

LSWR 'torpedo' front electric set on Waterloo via Wimbledon train entering Norbiton in the 1920s.

Freight traffic continued to be important until the 1950s when the Teddington, Kingston and Norbiton yards and depots were served by daily pick-up freight trains working to and from Feltham and Nine Elms yards. Through trains ran from Kingston to Feltham to convey wine traffic for other BR regions from the VP works at Villiers Road, Kingston. Facilities were curtailed in common with those of most other London lines in the 1960s: Norbiton and Teddington yards saw their last trains in May 1965, while Kingston yard closed in September 1966, apart from the siding to Fyffe's banana warehouse.

Passenger trains serving Kingston were among the very few inner suburban operations of the LSWR and as such were very vulnerable to the competition offered by the road service improvements which followed the introduction of the electric tramcar and motor bus in the first decade of the century. Clifton Robinson's London United Tramways reached the area through Twickenham, Teddington and Hampton in April 1903, crossing the bridge into Kingston and Surbiton in March 1906, finally reaching Wimbledon through Malden and Raynes Park in May 1907. Running along roads which paralleled the entire length of the railway from Twickenham to Wimbledon, the electric cars seized local traffic to an alarming extent. Another threat appeared in 1911–12, when the local authorities, banded together in the Thames Valley Councils Association, were working to get an apparently interested Central London Railway to extend its tube service over new surface lines into the area. At the beginning of 1912, under these combined pressures, the LSWR was dusting-off earlier plans for electrification. An announcement that March indicated that the Kingston Loop would be electrified 'as a dramatic answer to the appeals made from various quarters to the Central London Railway to invade the South Western preserves'. Despite this, the local authorities, Twickenham, Teddington and Hampton Wick among them, were said that month to be welcoming the prospect of competition and doing all they could to induce the CLR to alter its proposed bill for a Richmond extension to allow for working further into the Thames Valley.

An official announcement about the LSWR proposals followed in December 1912, in which it was stated that Waterloo–Wimbledon–Kingston–Richmond–Waterloo would be tackled first. For reasons of economy, the multiple-unit stock would be restricted to first- and third-class. To simplify connections with the East Putney–Wimbledon section already in use by District Railway electric trains, that company's voltage of 600dc would be used, with third-rail current collection.

Characterised by semi-streamlined 'torpedo' fronts, the electric trains of converted steam stock worked the Kingston Roundabout and Shepperton services from 30th January 1916. The three-car units (motor-trailer-motor), which ran singly in slack hours, were coupled together at peak times. They each seated about 180, some of the first-class sections including a smoking saloon formed from three old second-class compartments. Kingston Roundabout got four trains an hour each way plus two more each way between Malden and Teddington for the Shepperton branch. At peak hours there were two extra steam trains (electrics from 2nd April 1917) between Shepperton and Waterloo via Strawberry Hill. Trains ran at regular intervals past each hour, and Kingston's electric train every ten minutes compared with gaps of forty minutes to one hour in the former steam timetable. The electrics were lively both in speed and acceleration, reaching Waterloo in 28 minutes from Kingston instead of 35 (Teddington–Richmond–Waterloo, 40 to 49 minutes by steam train, now took only 32 minutes). With the new trains, all stations on the loop received electric lighting. The generous level of service introduced with the 1916 electrification remained virtually unchanged until the outbreak of World War 2, but in the 1920s Kingston–Wimbledon–Waterloo journey time was reduced to 27 minutes.

Traversing as it did an area which had seen substantial residential growth in the Victorian and Edwardian years and which possessed large acreages of royal parks, the electrification was not accompanied or followed by any large scale housebuilding although there were many small schemes to fill pockets left by the pre-1914 villa builders, much of this on the low-lying riverside land at Teddington, to the north of Kingston either side of the Richmond Road, and either side of the railway between Norbiton and Malden. Traffic on the loop grew steadily in pace with this further activity, and although the frequency remained adequate, the SR decided in 1929 that the time had come to clear away the inconvenient muddle of Kingston station. Assistance was forthcoming from the local authority, and after a delay caused by the national financial crisis, a £40,500 scheme was approved in October 1934. In the following year, all the old street-level buildings were replaced by an imposing red brick entrance and shop block prominently sited at the corner of Richmond Road and Wood Street. During the reconstruction of the high-level platforms a 520ft bay was added to replace the old low-level station, whose lines were shortened to form a loading dock, and whose site became a bus station. Some of the old cast-iron supporting pillars survived reconstruction of the high-level platforms, both of which got additional accommodation lit by steel-framed windows curving round at the ends, a buffet on the Up platform and opposite, a ladies' room with stained glass in what is now known as *art deco* style. A small passimeter booking office was added at street level for passengers proceeding from Richmond Road to the Up platform.

Teddington station also received attention in 1938, the improvements including a new building on the east side. Strawberry Hill's old wooden buildings on the Up side were replaced by a brick-built waiting room and booking office in 1935, the original booking hall becoming the Down side waiting room. Further station works have been undertaken in more recent years. Hampton Wick was completely demolished in 1968, to be reconstructed with steel and concrete platforms and the CLASP system modular buildings. A considerable amount of work was carried out at Kingston in 1988–90, providing a new ticket office and shops around a thoroughly refurbished ticket hall and entrances; rail level structures were also renovated at the same time. The elegant 1863 building at Teddington was completely restored to its original external appearance in 1991; internally the waiting rooms and ticket hall were modernised and a shop added.

Norbiton signal box, redundant after closure of the goods yard, was taken out of use from 27th July 1969. A major resignalling, in which all semaphore signals were replaced by colour lights, Kingston box was closed and Strawberry Hill and Malden Crossing boxes became gate boxes was completed on 10th November 1974. From that date, the whole of Kingston Loop came within the control of the new signalling centre at Feltham.

In an era of increasing car use, the lavish off peak service over the Loop was superfluous. From 15th September 1958 Kingston was served by four trains an hour, with a half hourly service between Teddington and Twickenham. The Sunday frequency of six trains an hour between Malden and Teddington was reduced to two an hour to Shepperton and two 'Roundabout' trains on 10th September 1962 and after September 1964 the half hourly Shepperton trains terminated at and started from Kingston. Sunday services were further modified from 5th October 1987, when Kingston via Richmond trains ceased and a Waterloo–Twickenham service ran hourly, connecting with the Shepperton shuttle.

Although for some years occasional through special excursions were still worked, the 1930–37 experiment of regular Sunday trains (also Fridays in 1930 only) between Kingston and the Kent Coast resorts was never revived.

The original Teddington Down side exterior of 1863 photographed in its centenary year with 1930s Southern Electric signs still exhibited. In recent times this building has been completely restored. *BR (SR)*

From 2nd October 1899 the Kingston Loop had had a few trains through the night except on Saturday/Sunday nights. Until World War 2, these were steam-hauled to allow traction current to be switched off for track maintenance. Calls were made at all stations Norbiton to Strawberry Hill inclusive except Hampton Wick but Norbiton and Teddington were omitted after 1st June 1981, by which time very drastic cuts had been made. With patronage fallen to very low levels, the night services were completely withdrawn from 2nd October 1989.

As an important retail centre, Kingston has in recent years become increasingly plagued by road traffic congestion and car parking problems. In an endeavour to alleviate this situation and encourage shoppers on to public transport, from 13th May 1991 the Borough Council financed a doubling of the off peak service to four trains an hour between Teddington, Kingston and Waterloo in the middle of the day from Mondays to Saturdays inclusive. The town's retail and entertainment attractions continued to provide a buoyant off peak traffic for most of the day into the 1990s, especially on Saturdays.

The entrance to Shepperton station, 31st October 1967. This building, on the Down side and now demolished, exhibits the virtually standard architectural style of all the original stations on the branch. *BR (SR)*

The Shepperton Branch (map page 171)

We now turn to a branch off the Kingston Loop that, like the Chessington branch, was really intended to go further. Chertsey's railway situation bore some similarities to that of Kingston but on a smaller scale. A small market town on the Thames, about 19 miles south-west of London, it found itself left 2¼ miles north of the London & Southampton Railway main line which here turned more sharply south-west towards a suitable gap in the Chobham Ridges. Although a branch from Weybridge was opened as early as 14th February 1848, access to London remained indirect, and the completion on 1st October 1866 of a loop through the town to the Staines & Wokingham line at Virginia Water did little to improve matters, despite the new and more convenient station that came with it. Chertsey hankered after something better for another 50 years or so.

Hope flared briefly in 1861 when a Metropolitan & Thames Valley Railway seemed about to give the town some sort of direct link to London. From a terminus on the north side of Chertsey Bridge, the M&TVR was to run through Shepperton, Sunbury, Twickenham and Isleworth and over part of the new Brentford to Southall branch to the GWR main line near Hanwell. Junctions were proposed with the LSWR Twickenham–Kingston–Malden line near the present Strawberry Hill

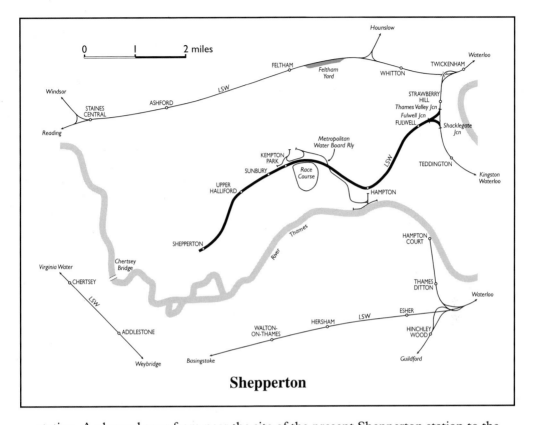

Shepperton

station. A planned spur from near the site of the present Shepperton station to the Thames (presumably to serve Walton Bridge) had been dropped by the beginning of 1862. It was hoped that the GWR would agree to build and lease the line, allowing the LSWR and the Metropolitan Railway to work over it with their own trains. The promoters were local residents and landowners, together with parties interested in increasing the prosperity of the Southall–Brentford line. As the GWR terms were not acceptable to the promoters, they turned to the LSWR. In the euphoria of deliverance from a Paddington invasion, that company conceded more favourable terms for leasing and working – retention of 50 per cent of gross receipts, guaranteeing the small company four per cent on capital up to £110,000; but the LSWR did insist that the line be restricted to 6m 52ch from the junction with its Kingston line to a point near Shepperton. An agreement with the LSWR dated 1st May 1862 scheduled to the Thames Valley Railway Act of 17th July 1862 confirmed the abandonments of the inner and outer sections of the original scheme, and required ballasting to be 'gravel at least eighteen inches deep' and the rails to be 'eighty pounds per yard and fished'. William Schaw Lindsay MP, chairman of the Metropolitan & Thames Valley Railway, lived at the Manor House, Shepperton, and the proposed terminal section to Chertsey Bridge would have crossed his land, but it seems likely that the dropping of this section was due more to LSWR opposition than to second thoughts on his part. The word *Metropolitan* was now removed from the title of a scheme successfully reduced to a 'blocking' line serving a few unimportant Thames-side villages.

John Aird & Son received the construction contract, taking £95,000 of the £110,000 issue of four per cent stock instead of cash. Airds had their eyes firmly on Chertsey; not only did they get the Shepperton terminus built as a through station, but they drummed up support from the remnants of the original promoters, and late in 1864 offered to build a connection between Shepperton and the LSWR near Addlestone at no cost to that company. But the LSWR sensed a new threat and stifled the gift horse, refusing the necessary approval for a junction.

The curious creature of all this activity was a meandering single line through small communities of which Shepperton was one of the least impressive, with a population of less than a thousand. The Reverend W. J. Scott described the branch as crossing 'a flat and somewhat dreary region of Middlesex' to terminate 'to all seeming – in a potato field, as if weary of going further in such country'. Leaving the Kingston Loop about a mile south of Twickenham, the track ran almost due west, then almost due south just beyond the western edge of Bushy Park. Before reaching the river, it turned northwest to skirt the northern boundary of *Kempton Manor,* an estate which together with that of *Sunbury Court* prevented the seemingly logical and otherwise unimpeded route along the riverside to Sunbury. For its remaining length, the direction was generally southwest to the terminus on the northern outskirts of Shepperton village. Passing loops were provided at Kingston Junction (also known as Thames Valley Junction) and at Hampton, Sunbury and Shepperton stations.

Fulwell (for Hampton Hill), the first intermediate station, stood in open country, taking its name from *Fulwell Park,* seat of the deputy chairman of the Thames Valley Railway Co, over half a mile north-west. Although the line passed close behind the large village of Hampton Hill (sometimes called New Hampton) the expense of a separate station was avoided. Hampton station was on the western edge of this riverside community, notable for its extensive waterworks. For the reason already given, Sunbury station was about a mile north of its village amid fields near the Staines to Kingston road. The terminus, about three quarters of a mile north-west of Shepperton village centre, in the aforementioned potato field, was rather nearer the smaller community of Halliford, and 18¾ miles from Waterloo via Richmond.

All stations except Fulwell received small goods yards, and all had decent yellow brick houses in a standard design that featured heavily pedimented gables and round arch windows in groups of three, quite different from anything on the LSWR. An Up platform at Shepperton soon fell into disuse, never gaining either footbridge or subway.

Passenger trains started on Tuesday 1st November 1864, worked by a single-line staff, signals being provided only at the loops. Although the Thames Valley Company, nine-tenths owned by Aird & Son, was sold to the LSWR under an act of July 1865 and wound up on 11th January 1867, the name Thames Valley line survived on OS maps and on the lips of the staff for another half century.

Under the new owners, the line (which had been built for double track) received its second road between the junction and Fulwell about 1867. Further progress had to await a stimulus, which came with the sale of the Kempton Manor Estate for conversion to a racecourse in 1869. At first unconvinced, the LSWR refused improvements, but eventually approval was given for further doubling which reached Sunbury on 17th July 1878 and the terminus on the following 9th December. The Preece single wire signal instruments then installed lasted into the British Rail era.

Sunbury, looking to London c.1921 with a Shepperton service unloading. The industrial complex (left) enjoyed a small network of private sidings and the gated siding below the signal arm serves a modest establishment at the right signed 'Fear Brothers'. There are milk churns awaiting an Up train. *Commercial postcard*

Soon after the racecourse opened on 18th July 1878 a platform was erected on the south side of the line about half a mile east of Sunbury station, near the grandstand. A second platform was added in 1879 but for the next ten years the station was available only to members. Complete rebuilding took place in 1890 and in its final form the Kempton Park racecourse station had three platforms sheltered by long canopies and connected by a covered footbridge (the third platform road, never electrified, served the outer face of the Up platform). The extra-long Down platform was able to take two LSWR first-class only Members' Special trains composed of American Line saloons. A covered way connected the station to the racecourse. Some further improvements were carried out in 1930. After 1890 the station was opened to the public on race days, when it was served by the branch trains as well as the race specials, but it could not be used other than to gain access to and from the racecourse.

To facilitate the working of race traffic, and to some extent freight movement as well, the LSWR constructed the Fulwell Curve, opened on 1st July 1894 from Fulwell Junction to Shacklegate Junction on the Kingston line about a quarter of a mile south of Strawberry Hill station. Race trains could then work over the rather longer route to Waterloo via Kingston (20m 68ch from Shepperton) but the curve was not used by ordinary passenger trains until 1st June 1901, when a single Down working (18.07 from Waterloo) was routed this way. Inside the triangle formed by the three junctions a locomotive depot known as Fulwell was built to replace the small shed at Twickenham and to service the Shepperton and Kingston lines. Opened on 1st May 1897 and enlarged in 1908 to accommodate 30 locomotives (mostly tanks), this depot eventually employed over 500 men, but it was in turn replaced by the new Feltham yard depot in 1922. From 1916 the site was partly used as an electric train depot, wholly so from 1923. Enlarged in 1936, it could accommodate up to 11 eight-car trains overnight. As an electric car depot it was known as Strawberry Hill.

Although Chertsey's population of about 3,000 hardly seemed large enough to justify the fuss, the desire for further railway accommodation persisted. There was some optimism in 1884 when the LSWR included a connection between Shepperton and the Weybridge–Virginia Water line in its bill for the next session, but once again the citizens of Chertsey were to be frustrated as the item was withdrawn from the bill soon after it appeared. In 1906–7 agitation flared up again; the Chertsey UDC petitioned the LSWR board, only to be told that the company did not see any return for the outlay. Others were persuaded to join the battle, and in 1911–12, the local authorities of Weybridge, Sunbury, Hampton Wick, Hampton, Twickenham, Molesey and Teddington tried hard to persuade the Central London Railway to bring tube services to the area (the CLR had plans to go as far as Richmond via Gunnersbury, depositing a bill in 1912 for this). The tube company did ask the LSWR whether it might run its trains over the line to Shepperton whilst assuring the local authorities 'most emphatically' that it had decided to enter the Thames Valley. By this time (November 1912) the LSWR, which already had modest plans to electrify the inner suburban services, had read the danger signals and promptly blocked such aspirations by including the Shepperton, Hampton Court and Hounslow lines in its own scheme. It also soon became apparent that the CLR's Thames Valley manoeuvre had been little more than tactics against the background of a prospective merger with the Underground Group; once the takeover terms for that had been agreed late in 1912, the Thames Valley councils were dropped like discarded toys.

Before going on to look at the LSWR electrification, a word should be said about the branch service in steam days. The first entries in Bradshaw are outside the LSWR pages under the special heading 'Thames Valley Line', not that there was much to offer – the initial service was but seven trains a day each way, all between Shepperton and Waterloo, with very long gaps. Thus anyone missing the 13.15 from Shepperton would cool his heels until 17.15 whilst the unfortunate seeing the tail of the 12.00 departure from Waterloo would have to wait until 16.10 for another. On Sundays there were four journeys each way, working only between Twickenham and Shepperton. The run from the outer terminus to Waterloo took from 50 minutes to over an hour and the luckless poor with money for no more than a third-class ticket were obliged to catch the first train of the day each way, waiting till the next day before returning. Dissatisfaction with the train service simmered for the next 40 years, partly because of the irregular sequence, but also because of the frequent need to change trains at Twickenham. In 1866 there were ten trains a day each way (five on Sundays) and 20 years later, although the number of weekday trains had increased to sixteen, ten involved a change at Twickenham or Strawberry Hill for London and the average running time for the full journey was still 50 or 55 minutes (one journey took 67 minutes). By late 1915, just before electrification, there were 23 trains each way on weekdays but even the best still required 48 minutes for the 18¾ miles to Waterloo. With the single exception mentioned earlier, all regular passenger trains ran via Twickenham and Richmond, and several combined with Kingston or Windsor services between Twickenham and Waterloo. Freight workings, which had started with one train a day, had increased to two daily by 1909.

Whether it was the poor train service, or the flat, unpromising nature of the district served, there was no really significant residential development along the line before 1914. Teddington crept westwards towards Fulwell station, mostly in the form of

Hampton Station, looking to London c.1905. The coal siding and yard by the overline bridge supplemented a freight yard at the country end of the station. *Commercial postcard*

low-cost housing for workers at the large depot of the London United Tramways, and others. There was some industrial development in the Fulwell area, accelerated in World War 1, but none of this brought much traffic to the branch. At Hampton, a large estate called *Marling Park* north of the station was laid out for building in mid-Victorian times but filled only very slowly. Housing began to appear around Sunbury station at the turn of the century, some of it associated with the arrival of the Lincrusta-Walton wallpaper factory. The immediate surroundings of Shepperton station acquired a mere sprinkling of villas, a row of shops and a Railway Hotel.

This scene was enlivened on Sunday 30th January 1916 by the arrival of the 'torpedo end' electric trains bearing the easily-remembered headcode 'S'. For the first time, almost all the service was routed via Kingston, a change made to balance the Hounslow Loop service on the Richmond line and to give a combined 10-minute headway all day between Waterloo and Teddington. Altogether it was a revolutionary improvement, 35 trains a day each way, every day of the week, running at 30-minute intervals on weekdays between 05.55 and 22.55, with an extra Down train from Wimbledon at 05.09 and another at 23.53 from Waterloo. On Sundays, trains worked every half hour between Twickenham and Shepperton with headcode 'S̄'. As previously mentioned, rush-hour trains were lengthened from three to six cars, and there were steam (later electric) trains via Richmond. After 1919 all weekday trains ran via Kingston with peak-hour non-stops from Norbiton to Wimbledon covering the Shepperton–Waterloo run in 44 minutes. Rush-hour working via Richmond reappeared in 1920 and the fast trains on the other route were gradually removed. From 1916, following the electrification, Fulwell Junction signal box was open all day, (the Station Box was closed in July 1917) and the Up platform at Shepperton became a carriage siding. Stabling at Shepperton was improved in 1925 by the installation of an electrified siding and cleaning stage.

After 1926 the basic service settled down to half-hourly via Kingston calling at all stations and taking 48 minutes. Some peak-hour trains ran via Richmond, missing stops, until 1958, and some Sunday trains went that way until the same year. At various periods, as an economy, or to relieve summer congestion on the main line out of Waterloo, the branch was worked as a shuttle to and from Kingston, a practice which had been a feature of Sunday working from the early 1920s. The new timetable of 15th September 1958 gave a basic half-hourly service for seven days a week, taking 47 minutes and calling at all stations via Kingston; three peak-hour workings each way via Richmond completed the throughout journey in 40 minutes. Sunday trains reverted to the half-hourly Kingston shuttle from September 1964 and the running time of the basic weekday service was extended to a dreary 50 minutes. Improvements came with the Southern Region's radical new timetable of 10th July 1967. By missing Vauxhall, Earlsfield and Raynes Park, the basic all day half-hourly service ran from end to end in only 44 minutes, later increased to 45 with the Raynes Park stop restored. The Kingston–Shepperton half hourly Sunday service remained, as did some peak-hour runs via Richmond.

For many years after electrification steam locomotives continued to work freight and certain race specials. In LSWR days race trains were operated from various parts of the system but the post-grouping service was invariably to and from Waterloo. Until September 1939, first-class race trains made up from SECR and LBSCR compartment stock hauled by LSWR M7 0-4-4T, ran between the electric services, whilst other race trains were electrically-worked. The branch goods locomotive was employed in term time to haul a school train between Hampton and Twickenham until 1939, an unusual working which no doubt created many conversions to the railway cult. Another occasional sight was steam coming to the rescue when electric traction was in difficulty, as in the summer of 1957, when after a night of heavy rain the line was under water at Fulwell and an M7 was summoned from its empty stock chores to work a shuttle service between Teddington and Hampton for most of the next day (13th August). In more recent times, diesel locomotives have been used when this vulnerable section is flooded.

As elsewhere, the electric service stimulated housing development, but the generally flat and unattractive aspect of the district, pock-marked by gravel pits and reservoirs, its inaccessibility, and the lack of fast trains outside peak hours combined to discourage intensive development beyond Hampton. At Fulwell in the late 1920s and early 1930s large housing estates were built north-west, south and south-west of the station and there was much filling of the empty spaces left by the Victorian and Edwardian developers at Hampton and Hampton Hill. At Sunbury bungalows and low-cost houses appeared in haphazard groups between the railway and the river, and a belt of new housing linked the Staines Road north of the station with Feltham. Shepperton station became the centre of a small but fairly cohesive new suburb, and there was another much smaller group of new roads to the west at Shepperton Green. In 1931 the building activity at Shepperton was sufficient to justify the provision of a siding on the down side for materials coming in for the builder W. J. Lavender.

Freight traffic to and from the yards and private sidings at Shepperton, Sunbury and Hampton was handled by one or two trains daily, usually worked in the 1930s and 1940s by Adams '0395' and Drummond '700' 0-6-0 locomotives. In 1952 the one morning train ran from Twickenham to Shepperton and back to Feltham and a light engine worked from Twickenham to shunt Hampton yard. Although depleted traffic and rationalisation caused the closure of Shepperton and Sunbury yards on 7th October 1960, at Hampton, with its small yards on both sides of the line and where accommodation had been extended in 1930, freight working, which latterly included frozen horseflesh carried in Hungarian State Railways vans all the way from the plains of Central Europe, survived until May 1965. Another special traffic was coal and materials for the Metropolitan Water Board's pumping stations at Sunbury, Kempton Park, and Hampton. The private water companies which had established themselves at Hampton twelve years before the opening of the branch had received their coal via Thames river barges and horse carts, but the East London Water Company which had come to Sunbury in the late 1860s used the LSWR. After the Metropolitan Water Board took over the installations in June 1904 it was decided to build a 2ft gauge railway system with transhipment sidings alongside the LSWR Up line at Kempton Park and at the riverside at Hampton. The 3½-mile system opened in 1915 was worked by three very trim Kerr, Stuart 0–4–2T named *Hampton*, *Kempton* and *Sunbury*, joined by the 0–4–2T *Hurst* some years later. Eventually there were about 140 tipping, hopper and other wagons and the little trains were a pleasant surprise for the untutored traveller between Hampton and Kempton Park. With the conversion to oil-burning in the pumping stations there was no work for the railway; in 1947 the locomotives were cut-up and the line dismantled. Until 1956 the MWB also maintained a private siding on the Up side between Sunbury and Kempton Park (Hanworth Road).

Metropolitan Water Board Railway locomotive *Sunbury* in the 1920s, at Kempton Park Pumping station. *Locomotive Publishing Co.*

World War conditions produced special traffics. In 1914–18 there was a large camp at Sunbury and the racecourse was used as a motor transport store, both bringing extra work to the line. World War 2 also provided much interest for the observer, including the transport of Italian prisoners of war to and from Kempton Park camp in eight-car sets of Maunsell corridor coaches. British Thermostats built a war factory near the point where the line passed under the Feltham–Walton road, and to serve this a concrete platform with small brick buildings called Upper Halliford Halt was opened on the Down side east of the road on 1st May 1944. There was no need at this time for an Up line platform as during the war years the branch was worked as a single track, the other line serving as a parking place for crippled wagons. An Up platform and concrete footbridge followed after the war. On 29th December 1940 a bomb completely demolished the Up side at Sunbury station.

Single-line working, which lasted from 1940 to 1946 was an extension of a practice which had long applied on race days. On those occasions (and there was a meeting in eight of the twelve months during the height of the course's popularity) the Down line between Sunbury and Shepperton was worked in both directions in accordance with Electric Train Tablet Regulations, the other track being used to park race specials end-to-end, awaiting the time when they were called forward to Kempton Park station for the homegoing crowds. To facilitate this intensive working, the 1½-mile section between Hampton and Kempton Park boxes was shortened by the manning of temporary block posts at Mark Hole (on the Down side, 949yd from Hampton) and Hanworth (on the Up side 920yd from Kempton Park station). The box on the Down platform at Kempton Park was otherwise only manned when access was required to the MWB siding. There was a third temporary block post at Fulwell Cutting, between Fulwell and Hampton on the Down side, one mile from Fulwell Junction box. Using these boxes, electric race trains were operated at intervals as close as four minutes at the busiest times (Easter Mondays), working by both routes from and to Waterloo. A standby steam locomotive was stationed at Sunbury in case of emergency. Increased car ownership and television killed this business and by the later 1950s single-line working was seen only on Easter Mondays. A few special trains continued to run to Kempton Park until the early 1960s. Horsebox traffic, once a great feature on the day before the first races and the day following the last ones, with steam locomotives working through from the LNER and other lines, also dwindled to nothing in the 1950s as horse owners turned to the more convenient motor boxes.

After the mid 1960s there was a decline in commuter traffic. Season ticket issues on the whole line fell for example from 1,367 in 1967 to 1,041 in 1974. Peak hour workings were accordingly thinned out from May 1977. Further economies, this time in weekday evening and Sunday coverage, were put in place from 1st June 1981. Signalling modernisation produced more savings. From 9th March 1969 Sunbury box was closed, Fulwell Cutting box following on 1st April. In 1974 the whole branch was moved to control from the new Feltham panel box, with colour light signals replacing the old semaphores; this operation, which saw the closure of the remaining manual signal boxes (Shepperton, Shacklegate Jc and Fulwell Jc) was substantially completed on 10th November but Hampton survived as gate box until 3rd January 1975, when cctv allowed operation of the level crossing to be supervised from Feltham panel.

Station reconstruction started inauspiciously with installation of the ugly CLASP

Packing case architecture at Sunbury, Up side, 1968. The Southern Railway seat (left) has more aesthetic appeal than CLASP, but it has to be admitted that the predecessor structure here was no more elegant. *Alan A Jackson*

system building at war-damaged Sunbury in 1967. Freight yard land on the Down side here was used for an office development which formed part of the passenger station from 1989. Shepperton's semi-rural aura was disturbed in 1963 when the two-storey headquarters offices of the Ian Allan organisation were erected across the end of the tracks, their drabness subsequently given some colour when the firm purchased the first class Pullman car *Malaga* for hospitality accommodation, stabling it on the site of the old carriage dock.

Following a development deal, Shepperton station was totally rebuilt in 1988, the new structure incorporating further offices for Ian Allan Ltd. The new building's end elevation, which included a clock, was in somewhat awkward Post Modern style, intended to recall the attractive Italianate lines of its predecessor on the same site. At ground level there was a glazed waiting area and ticket hall, with a canopy on the platform side. The forecourt was attractively landscaped.

By the early 1980s the unmanned premises at Upper Halliford had inevitably succumbed to vandalism and graffiti scrawling; the adjacent concrete, noise and stink of motor road infrastructure and use added further to its repulsiveness. Somewhat surprisingly, in view of the rather thin catchment area, substantial funds were found for its total reconstruction. Completed in 1991, this featured a Neo-Vernacular ticket office and staff room on the Down platform and a large arched waiting shelter on the other side, the whole watched over by cctv cameras.

No major changes have so far been made at Hampton and Fulwell. Whilst Kempton Park no longer saw special trains, the ordinary branch services continued to set down and pick up the depleted ranks of punters at appropriate times on race days. By the mid 1990s, the branch had lost much of the character it once had; local journeys had long suffered serious depredation from a network of bus services and later from the spread of private car ownership. Outside commuter hours, passengers were very few. It seems doubtful whether this rather hopeless enterprise has ever paid its way except perhaps briefly in the 1930s and 1940s. Writing in 1918, long before anyone dreamed that it would be paralleled over part of its course by the frenzied roaring of a motorway, the Reverend W. J. Scott found the outer section as 'bearing an odd likeness to bits of the Midland & Great Northern Joint'. Well, we all know what happened to that . . .

Hampton Court station at 13.50 on a wintry day around 1908. The nature of the traffic suggests commuters returning from a Saturday morning stint at their London offices. The Tudor style goods shed is just visible at the left. *Commercial postcard*

The Hampton Court Branch (map page 165)

The magnificent State Apartments and grounds of the royal palace at Hampton Court were thrown open to the public by the young Queen Victoria in November 1838 without charge or restriction, and in the next decade visitors arrived by road and river steamer at the rate of some 178,000 a year, many of them on Sundays when there were few other comparable attractions open to them. With its main line passing only just over a mile to the south, the LSWR management thought this too good an opportunity to overlook and a bill was prepared for the 1846 session. Everyone was quite certain what it was all about: *The Illustrated London News* referred to it as 'this holiday railway' and W. J. Chaplin, the LSWR chairman, spoke of it somewhat patronisingly as affording 'a fresh means of cheap and legitimate recreation to the poorer classes'. A double line of 1m 52ch, running north from the main line near Long Ditton to the southern approach of Hampton Court road bridge was sanctioned by the LSWR (Hampton Court Branch) Act of 1846. There was some delay whilst it was considered whether the route might be used as the first part of a line to Staines and Windsor but, this proving unnecessary, work began in January 1848.

Engineering was straightforward, as the line for almost its entire length was on an embankment about 18ft high with only one major bridge (over the river Ember at the south end of Hampton Court station). Although named Hampton Court, the terminus also served the south bank riverside village of East Molesey (then spelled Moulsey) and there was a renaming to 'Hampton Court and East Moulsey' on 1st June 1869. But all the emphasis was on the Palace, even to providing the station buildings with architectural treatment in keeping, red brick and stone dressings and Jacobean curved gables (the locomotive shed was lovingly styled with steep pitched roof and prominent buttresses). The terminus was between the mouths of the rivers Mole and Ember on an artificial island created by a creek which served a watermill and connected the two rivers. A new engine shed erected about 1895 south of the Ember bridge survives today, heavily disguised as a plastics factory.

There is some evidence that for a short period after the branch opened on 1st February 1849 certain trains, if not all, were horse-drawn, with journey times far in excess of those advertised. In a letter to *The Times* of 13th February 1849, the use of a horse is described by a local doctor as 'a daily (not single) occurrence' and he relates that on 9th February the 12.45 train left Hampton Court in charge of 'an old grey horse . . . saddled and bridled' under the guidance of 'Evans, the Moulsey flyman', taking 20 minutes to reach the junction, where a main line train had been standing for 28 minutes waiting for the Hampton Court coaches to be attached. Kingston (now Surbiton) was reached in about 30 minutes from Hampton Court instead of the five shown in the time bills. In his *Short History of East Molesey*, Herbert Adams mentions that the 'flea-bitten grey' drew only one carriage, which included the guard's van. Whether this expedient arose from a shortage of locomotive power or uncertainty about the settlement of the embankment is not clear, but it does demonstrate that historians cannot always rely on published timetables as evidence of what was happening on a railway at any given time.

The first timetable, for what it is worth, gives five trains each way on weekdays, plus two more from Hampton Court with connections to Waterloo trains at Surbiton. The five through trains took about 45 minutes between Hampton Court and Waterloo – the somewhat incredible allowance of only five minutes between Hampton Court and Surbiton has already been noted (today's electric trains, with an intermediate stop at Thames Ditton, take seven). Sunday service was sparse, despite the fact that this was the only day when ordinary people could visit Hampton Court, but no doubt the three trains each way on the branch and one through working each way were duly increased in the summer months.

A little short of half-way along the branch the western fringe of the pretty riverside village of Thames Ditton was passed. This was a modest holiday resort, with some middle-class settlement, and it was not long before a demand arose for a station. Passenger facilities were provided in November 1851.

As time passed, Hampton Court gained in popularity as a pleasure resort; thus on Whit Monday 1850 some 2,000 were carried on the branch, but in the late 1860s and early 1870s the average attendance at the Palace each year was well over 200,000 and on Whit Monday 1872 there were almost 30,000 admissions, a high proportion of which would have come by train. Ordinary weekday service in 1867 was 15 trains daily each way, taking ten to eleven minutes from Surbiton to Hampton Court, calling at Thames Ditton. On Sundays about nine trains ran each way. By 1880 there were 19 trains Down on weekdays and 16 Up, taking about 42 minutes to and from Waterloo.

Houses began to appear just west of the terminus in the late 1860s and early 1870s, principally on an estate called Kent Town, which in accordance with the Victorian custom, was provided with its own church. East and West Molesey, together with neighbouring Thames Ditton were by the turn of the century firmly established as middle-class residential areas. Train service was accordingly increased, with 29 Up and 27 Down weekday trains in 1910 although the throughout timing was still between 41 and 48 minutes. A daily goods train worked the yard at Hampton Court but Thames Ditton never dealt with more than parcels traffic. A racecourse opened alongside the river at Hurst Park in 1889 brought the line more business. Horsebox traffic for this continued well into the 1930s, and punters used the branch in considerable numbers until the course closed in October 1962. Just before that, on

Whit Monday, they would give the branch its busiest day of the year, with trains running at five-minute intervals or less, a service facilitated by the opening of a special six-lever intermediate block post in the staff room on the Up platform at Thames Ditton.

The LSWR Thames Valley electrification scheme, already noticed, provided the branch with a regular service of three trains an hour for the greater part of each weekday from 18th June 1916 (service was half-hourly until 07.00 and after 21.30). Hampton Court–Waterloo time was reduced to 33 minutes despite calls at all eight intermediate stations. From 20th November 1916, for no particularly good reason, service was boosted to four trains an hour for the main part of the day. Daylight Saving, or 'summer time', introduced as a wartime measure on 21st May 1916, was used by LSWR publicity. Tired war workers and soldiers on leave from the Western Front, with girl friends, were enticed to summer riverside delights with a booklet entitled *Long Evenings on the Silver Thames* which showed them that by going to Hampton Court or other riverside stations on the new electric trains they could get in several hours on the water before darkness really set in: should the river-rocked kissing and fondling be prolonged, the electrics would still be there very late at night to take them back to town.

To facilitate the working of the intensive electric service, the LSWR built a new 1½-mile approach to the branch on the south side carrying the Down Hampton Court line on brick viaducts of 336yd and 100yd to a 160ft lattice girder span over the main lines. This was ready for traffic on 4th July 1915, in the midst of World War 1. By coincidence, the vicinity was to suffer serious damage from a German missile in World War 2, when on 2nd November 1944 the formation at Hampton Court Junction was put out of action for two days. Electrification caused the removal of the Prentice equipment for radio-controlled cab signalling, used for experiments on the branch in 1913 and 1915.

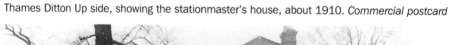
Thames Ditton Up side, showing the stationmaster's house, about 1910. *Commercial postcard*

Throughout the 1920s and 1930s Hampton Court had three trains an hour working to and from Waterloo in 32 minutes, calling at all stations. This excellent service fostered residential growth around Thames Ditton station and on the riverside land west of the terminus, a process further assisted by the opening in 1933 of a motor road from a new Hampton Court Bridge to the Kingston by-pass. Low land prices on the flat gravel plain between the branch and the reservoirs at West Molesey and the favourable economic conditions for housebuilding in the early 1930s generated the construction of low-cost houses at some distance from the station, though the developers liked to use its name. Nearer the line, in East Molesey and Thames Ditton, prices for small detached and semi-detached properties were a little higher.

All this activity led the commercially-aware SR management to look to the exploitation of its assets at Hampton Court station. Between 1935 and 1936 the platforms were shortened and the goods yard brought into a smaller area, but a proposal to use some of the land so released for the construction of an Odeon cinema which the SR was prepared to subsidise to the extent of £3,000, did not materialise. The rearrangements of this period, which also included lengthening of the platform canopies, were in part to accommodate the alignment of the approach to the new river bridge; tracks were cut back at the river end, where a handsome ornamental wall was erected across the width of the station in 1934.

Changes since World War 2 followed a pattern which has become familiar to the reader. After road competition had reduced traffic to a trickle and solid fuel distribution had been rationalised, the goods yard closed on 3rd May 1965. Wider car ownership combined with higher standards of living worked to erode the long-standing summer and bank holiday pleasure traffic. Off-peak frequency was reduced to two trains an hour on 15th September 1958, but with rush-hour loadings sustained by a post-war increase in housing density and the overbuilding of Hurst Park racecourse in 1967, peak service was increased to four an hour from 10th July 1967. With an additional call (Berrylands, opened on the main line for new housing north-east of Surbiton in 1933) the Waterloo journey now took one minute longer than in 1916, but working was eased by the introduction of colour light signals on the branch from 22nd March 1970, controlled from a new power box at Surbiton. Hampton Court, reduced to a gate box, was abolished from 23rd September 1979 when cctv was installed to enable the level crossing to be operated from the Surbiton panel.

Reductions in train services followed a continuing decline in traffic: cuts in peak hour services from June 1981; Sunday trains in winter running only hourly from October 1992; and late evening frequency also widened out to hourly from October 1993. the branch still handles one special traffic, that produced by the annual Garden Festival and Flower Show at Hampton Court, an event inaugurated in 1990 and initially subsidised by Network SouthEast. An enhanced service is operated on this occasion to and from Waterloo and some special trains from elsewhere are worked through over the branch.

As the only British railway ever built expressly to serve a royal palace, the Hampton Court branch provides the fastest public transport link to this tourist attraction from central London but this fact is little known; for many years the rail service has received no properly-focussed publicity with the result that, as at Windsor, most visitors travel by motor coaches and cars, imposing extra strains on an already overloaded road system.

Ex-GWR AEC railcar at Staines West; looking to buffers, 18th July 1955. *Alan A Jackson*

West Drayton to Staines

Serving the very fringe of the Metropolitan Police District, the Staines & West Drayton Railway had much more of the country branch about it than most other London railways. Its beginnings were complex, evolving as they did from the not uncommon scenario of local interests seeking to improve railway accommodation by trading upon the rivalry between two or more main line companies. A small market town on the London to Exeter Road at an important crossing of the Thames, Staines had lost status with the arrival of the railway age, but the opening of the Windsor, Staines & South Western Railway, linking it with London on 22nd August 1848 had encouraged local industries. By the mid-1860s, these included a large brewery, mustard mills, a papier mâché factory and the world's first linoleum works, producing the floor covering invented in the town in 1860–63 by Frederick Walton. With the GWR main line only some six miles to the north across easy railway country, the business interests in the town, hoping to lower freight rates and open up new outlets, were turning their attention to a route first selected by three unsuccessful Uxbridge & Staines bills of the 1840s. After the failure of a bill deposited in 1863 for a West Drayton & Staines Railway, one of two similar schemes deposited in November 1865 became the Colnbrook Railway Act of 1866, a single standard gauge line southwards from the south side of the GWR station at West Drayton to the LSWR Windsor branch at Staines Moor, half a mile north-west of the town. The proposals included a line passing below the GWR at West Drayton to allow through running from Uxbridge to Staines. On 13th July 1866 the GWR agreed to work the line for half the gross receipts, but the powers to build it expired before the £60,000 capital could be raised.

A second act of 7th July 1873, with one of the 1866 promoters still in play, authorised a 5m 2f 9.2ch Staines & West Drayton Railway over the same route, joining the LSWR 43ch northwest of the bridge over Staines High Street, but omitting the through link to the Uxbridge branch at West Drayton. This time the LSWR reacted with some vigour to the invasion of its territory, opposing the bill by alleging that the proposed junction at Staines would be dangerous and the extra traffic impossible to accommodate at Staines station. These objections produced a clause in the act which required that the line should be built only to standard gauge, which would restrict any expansionist tendencies on the part of a still largely broad gauge GWR.

The Staines & West Drayton Railway company formed by the 1873 act suffered a long period of negotiations and frustrations before giving birth to its line. Extensions of time had to be obtained in 1878 and 1881, the last act also altering the GWR junction to one on the north side of the main line at West Drayton, a change required by the widening into Paddington. Still without much hope and forlornly casting about for sustenance, the S&WDR directors even wooed LNWR share-holders early in 1882 with a proposal that their line might form part of a *Grande Ceinture* round the west side of London which would bring LNWR trains from Watford via the proposed Uxbridge & Rickmansworth Railway, the GWR branch to Uxbridge and new lines south of Staines, on to the SER and LBSCR via Leatherhead and Dorking. This move did nothing to improve relationships with Waterloo, driving the S&WDR deeper into the embraces of the still somewhat reluctant GWR. An agreement was at last signed on 13th November 1882, which secured that the GWR would work and maintain the line after the first six months, in return for half the gross receipts. Perhaps not wishing to upset its neighbour unduly, the GWR protested that the sharing of Staines station would cause delays, insisting that there should be a 'proper and sufficient independent terminal pas-senger and goods station'. A bill deposited in the same month included provision for this separate Staines station and approach, also for a connection to the LSWR nearer to that company's Staines station coming off the West Drayton line on the south side of the Windsor branch. Also in the bill were a line into the linoleum factory and extensions to Egham and Chertsey. Predictably the LSWR opposed, but local interests were able to convince the parliamentary committees that their town required further railway accommodation after the S&WDR agreed to drop the proposed extensions. In that form the act was passed on 2nd August 1883.

Although a start was made with construction during 1882, the little company's troubles were not yet over. A squabble with the contractors drained away funds in legal action, culminating in the appointment of a receiver. When the GWR came to the rescue with more capital, all seemed well, but that was soon exhausted and no more was forthcoming.

Somehow the section between West Drayton and Colnbrook was finished in time to allow the GWR to start six passenger trains a day on weekdays from Saturday 9th August 1884. Further progress was retarded by the financial crisis, exacerbated by the withdrawal of labour when wages could not be paid. In this dark time, the engineer, A. Thuey, saved £1,150 by adapting a house owned by Charles Waring Finch (of Finch & Rickman's Mustard Mills) as the Staines terminus. Opened for public traffic on 2nd November 1885, the completed line was served by nine trains each way to and from West Drayton on weekdays. At first passenger business was distinctly thin; few wished to cross this relatively underpopulated stretch of outer London, and apart from a sprinkling of commercial and professional liaisons between Uxbridge and Staines, or those seeking destinations on the GWR west of London, the trains were all but empty. Freight traffic was also slow to develop, despite the provision of yards at Colnbrook and Staines, but things gradually improved. In May 1887 the authorised line was built across the river into the works of the now prosperous Staines Linoleum Company, yet even this had to be shared with the LSWR, which was also invited into the factory premises.

The 6½-mile single track left the GWR Uxbridge branch 21ch west of West Drayton station, falling at 1 in 104 and curving sharply to get beneath the main line. After bridging the Colne, a south-westerly course was pursued, bringing the track into Colnbrook station, which was north of the Bath Road and east of the village. Between the platforms was a passing loop and, on the Down side, dutch-gabled, the 'proper and sufficient dwelling house' required by the 1882 agreement. A signal box to the south controlled the goods yard, loop and level-crossing of the Bath Road, which was spaced wide enough for the second track that was never added.

Now going due south, the branch skirted the eastern boundary of the Poyle Explosives Works before crossing the lonely Stanwell and Staines Moors between the Wyrardisbury and Colne rivers. After climbing at 1 in 133 to bridge the Windsor line, it ran south-east, parallel to that line, before making a final curve southwards into its terminus just north of Church Street, Staines. A single long platform with a short canopy at the south end together with loading dock, run round road, goods shed and small engine shed, filled the back garden of Mr Finch's house. Behind the house another canopy sheltered passengers as they passed through the back door into the hall and out again through the front door. From the booking hall, stairs led to what remained of the domestic rooms.

With passenger business stagnant, there was a need to clutch at every straw. After closure of the ranges on Wimbledon Common, a Metropolitan Rifle Range Company was formed in 1890 to build ranges near London for those Volunteers who did not wish to go out to Bisley. That these new ranges were sited on Staines Moor, just west of the S&WDR was not unconnected with the existence of a shared director-ship. Subject to the S&WDR paying 4½ per cent interest in accordance with the 1882 agreement, the GWR agreed to construct a halt, which was opened with the ranges on 1st March 1892. A simple timber platform about 20ft long, devoid of shelter and furnished only with a seat, lamp and back fence, its only access was by field path from the range pavilion in Moor Lane. During its whole life it remained a conditional stop, where for many years trains set down and took up in daylight on weekdays only. Tempted away from geographical accuracy by the empty charm of alliteration, the Rifle Range Company preferred Runemede Range and the halt was so-called until 9th July 1934 when it became simply Runemede. Exactitude was finally established from 4th November 1935 with the renaming to Yeoveney.

By then possessing over eighty five per cent of the S&WDR issued stock of £161,640, the GWR acquired powers in its 1900 act to take over and dissolve the company, exercising them from 1st July that year. At this time there were still only about eight trains daily to and from West Drayton, where they shared the north side island platform with the Uxbridge trains. One of the Down workings ran mixed traffic, restricted to six vehicles, a feature which lasted until the 1930s. Sunday service started in 1887 with four trains each way. Once the GWR assumed full

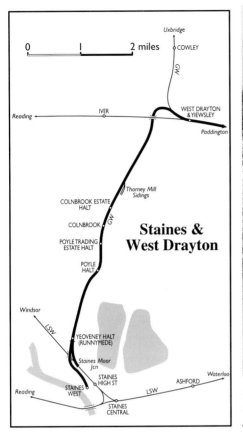

Colnbrook station, looking north, with loco 1436 on
Staines train, 25th September 1956.
Alan A Jackson

control there were some improvements, so that by 1912 there were 14 workings each
way, a few to and from Paddington and Aldgate (between 1904 and 1911 there were
even through runs between Staines and Victoria). One-class steam auto-trains,
introduced on Sundays from 1st October 1914, were later extended to weekdays, so
that by 1st January 1916 all but one train was of this type. In October 1921 there
were 16 journeys each way daily between departures from West Drayton at 07.23
and 22.28. On Sundays there were seven each way between 10.12 and 21.52.

Use of the Staines Linoleum Factory for military purposes and opening of camps
around Staines provided new traffics in 1914–18, but afterwards the more relaxed
tempo of what was essentially a country branch quickly returned. Freight remained
more important than passengers, not that the latter were neglected. At the time when
the GWR was trying to extract the last ounce of business from its investment in
branch lines by opening many new halts, the Staines line was not overlooked. On
1st June 1927, Stanwell Moor & Poyle Halt (renamed Poyle for Stanwell Moor on
26th September 1927) was opened 65ch south of Colnbrook to serve the Explosives
Works, Stanwell Moor village and scattered farmhouses west of the line. This had
a crude wooden shelter, lacking the elegance of the more usual GWR 'pagoda'.
Service on weekdays remained at about the same level through the 1920s and 1930s,
but rush-hour workings of five coaches, generally hauled by 2–6–2T, ran to and from
Paddington, missing the branch halts. Sunday service was built up to 14 each way
between 09.02 and 21.58 from West Drayton.

A solitary passenger enjoys the spartan facilities of Yeoveney; the post for raising the signal lamp to stop a train after dark can be seen at the corner of the platform. Looking to West Drayton, 25th September 1956. *Alan A Jackson*

War again brought change. In a move which recalled the wildest dreams of the harassed S&WDR board, the authorities decided that the line had some strategic potential, seeing a role in bringing traffic from the north and midlands safely round into Feltham Yard or other points in south and south-east England should the London river crossings be severed by enemy action. To achieve this, a curve closely following the 1873 act alignment was built from a point south of Yeoveney Halt to the SR Windsor branch at Staines Moor Junction near Staines GWR station. At West Drayton double track was installed from the junction with the Uxbridge branch to the bridge under the main line, where a small signal cabin was erected. All was ready in June 1940, but no use was made of the new link until 15th September 1940 after the Metropolitan Extension at Snow Hill (Holborn Viaduct) had been blocked by bomb damage. Thereafter for a few years, surprised train crews found their freight trains routed this way to and from the GWR at Greenford, but this ceased with the end of the war and the junction at Staines Moor was taken out on 16th December 1947. Whilst saplings grew strongly between the rails there was some talk of closing the old GWR terminus (known as Staines West since 26th September 1949), diverting the West Drayton service to the SR station over the wartime link. No doubt Waterloo again showed resistance to this, pleading it could not be done until capital was available to improve the cramped Staines Central.

A traumatic change in the character of the whole area came with the establishment in 1946 of London Airport (Heathrow) when the once sequestered frontiers of Middlesex and Buckinghamshire became ever more befouled by the incessant row of low-flying aircraft with their attendant fumes. Factory estates also appeared along

GWR 0-4-2 tank loco at Staines West, 20th July 1952. The main station building here (not shown) began life as a private residence and is now in use as commercial offices. *R. C. Riley*

the branch between Colnbrook and Poyle. To serve one of these, Poyle Estate Halt, with a 50ft platform and tiny canopy supported on concrete posts was opened on 4th January 1954, just over ¼ mile south of Colnbrook. Trains stopped at rush hours, but at other times by request only. On the same day, two extra journeys were provided, making 18 each way daily, 12 on Sundays. Steam remained supreme on this untypical London line where most trains were push-pull units of two saloons (some former GWR railmotors) powered by 14xx 0–4–2T. Freight was usually handled by 57xx 0–6–0PT and 61xx 2–6–2T. South of the factory estate belt, the line retained much of its rural character through the 1950s, although its peace was increasingly threatened by aircraft noise. Yeoveney Halt, a miraculous survival from a more gentle, romantic era, was now frequented only by occasional fishermen and lovers. Stopping a train here as evening mists rose over the fields was an experience unique in the metropolitan area. Once light had faded, it was necessary to raise the lamp on the post provided; somehow the driver always *did* stop, even if occasionally he had to reverse and trundle back because the passenger was noticed only as the engine passed the platform. This choice relic of GWR country branch line practice was finally closed 'due to the cost of repair' after the last trains had called on 13th May 1962.

Other more important changes were made in these post-war years. Freight movements south of Colnbrook ceased on 30th October 1953 when all consignments were transferred to Staines SR yard. By some bureaucratic oversight, the signal box at Staines West was left open although there was never more than one train on the line at a time south of Colnbrook and the engine shed had closed in June 1952.

GWR AEC-type diesel cars appeared on some passenger workings in January 1954, taking over all weekday services outside peak hours in the following year. Steam survived otherwise until 5th October 1958, after which the whole service was operated by new BR diesel cars. Passenger traffic reached its peak; although daily journeys remained at 18 each way on weekdays, on Sundays there were now 16 trips to and from Staines West with a last departure from West Drayton at 22.43. Except for the first three weekday trains in the morning and two in the evening which called at Poyle Estate and Yeoveney halts, notice to the guard at West Drayton or Staines West was necessary if one wished to alight at these places at other times; 'passengers desiring to join should give the necessary hand signal to the driver'. Yet another halt was opened on 1st May 1961 about ½ mile north of Colnbrook. Worked on a conditional stop basis, Colnbrook Estate Halt had a short platform and shelter much as those of its immediate neighbour.

Traffic results in 1960 were such that BR could not make a convincing case for closure when this was suggested as a means of reducing the cost of the Staines By-Pass road then under construction. But as Beeching's accountants were able to show in 1962 that by their standards the branch was not 'paying its way' passenger closure was listed in the *Reshaping of British Railways* report of 1963. Extra workings at rush hours were taken off in October 1964 and the last passenger train ran on 27th March 1965 (Sunday working had ceased late in 1961). Alternative public transport was provided by buses which followed a meandering route between West Drayton and Staines.

Meanwhile freight underwent a minor revival. During 1964 the Staines West goods yard was dismantled to make room for an oil storage depot served by a siding accommodating 12 tank wagons. From October that year freight trains were again seen south of Colnbrook, bringing oil from Purfleet to the new depot. In 1975 there were 15 trains a week carrying between 1,200 and 1,500 tons of oil. Colnbrook itself was in that year receiving oil trains at an average of 75 a week (6,000 to 7,500 tons) and also about 10 tons of scrap metal a week. At the same time oil was coming into Thorney Mills, between Colnbrook and West Drayton, in an average of 24 trains a week (1,000 tons) and ten trains a week of stone (3,000 tons) were also arriving. This depot also sent out scrap metal at the rate of 360 tons a week. Traffic to and from the Cory/Shell heating oil depot at Staines continued until 16th January 1981 when the tracks south of Poyle were abandoned to the construction works of the M25 motorway. The Staines oil depot was then connected to the Staines-Windsor branch and the oil was brought in that way from 30th January 1981 until 24th June 1991, after which this rail traffic ceased.

At Colnbrook the public freight yard was closed in January 1966 and the station buildings and signal box were razed to the ground in January 1979. But the railway as far as Colnbrook and just beyond remained open for private sidings and oil trains, having its revenge on the government's roadbuilders, who were obliged to incur large sums of taxpayers' money to provide for its path under the vast concrete clover leaf junction of the M4 and M25. Oil tanker workings continued until 1982, then resumed from 1st March 1990 to 1993 when aviation fuel was delivered to a rail terminal just north of the Bath Road.

History shows the usefulness of this line for freight. Colnbrook oil terminal was again re-activated in September 1997 to receive fuel and there is also a possibility that its formation may one day be useful for rail access to the nearby Heathrow Airport.

Isleworth station, LSWR, Up side building, c.1905. *Commercial postcard*

The Hounslow Loop (map page 165)

J. N. Brewer, in his 1816 *Beauties of England & Wales* wrote of Hounslow, 'the chief dependence of the place is on the immense tide of road traffic, which rolls to and from the metropolis with surprising vehemence and bustle'. The first stage out of London, nine miles from Hyde Park Corner, and either side of the main route to Bath and the West, Hounslow was to be left stranded between the main railways to the west and south-west, and very quickly suffered a decline in business and status after these lines had opened. More self-sufficient was semi-industrial Brentford, river port and transhipment point for the Thames and Grand Junction Canal (later Grand Union Canal). Both places were obvious calling points for any railway attempting to fill the gap between the main lines; equally obvious was that the Richmond Railway (to be opened from Wandsworth to Richmond on 27th July 1846) was the most likely base for such a line, and that Staines and Windsor were the desirable objectives at the outer limits of this Thames Valley sector. There was however a slight geographical difficulty in serving all four points in a direct line from Richmond as a glance at a map of the area will show.

An 1844 proposal for a railway from Richmond to Staines received support from the Richmond Company, but this and rival schemes did not emerge from the Parliamentary session of 1846. A new enterprise, the Windsor, Staines & South Western, formed late in that year with LSWR support, was authorised in 1847 to build from Richmond to Windsor (Datchet) via Staines, together with a 7¼-mile double-track loop from the Richmond Railway at Barnes through Brentford and Hounslow, rejoining the main line at Hounslow Heath.

In a race with the GWR to reach the royal town, the main line was pressed ahead, opening to Staines and Datchet in August 1848. There was less urgency about the loop in a time of some financial difficulty, so it was not until 22nd August 1849 that the first passenger train ran between Barnes Junction and Smallbury Green, a temporary terminus a quarter-mile east of the present Isleworth station. The remaining section to Feltham Junction opened on 1st February 1850.

Joseph Locke engineered the loop line and Brassey contracted to build it. From Barnes Junction, it ran north-west, traversing the western end of the then very small village of Barnes and crossing the Thames on a cast iron bridge. Chiswick, the first station, was between the two estates of *Chiswick House* and *Grove House*, and almost a mile west of the village. Located on the Duke of Devonshire's land, its construction was enforced by the 1847 act, though for many years it was said to be of less benefit to the railway than the station that might otherwise have been built in Barnes village. After running behind Strand-on-the-Green, the line turned west to reach a station named Kew, sited on the main road from London to the west and opposite the road bridge to the village of that name on the Surrey bank. Running west and then south-west to avoid the built-up area of Brentford town, where a station was provided on the Hanwell road, the loop recrossed the main Bath road, into a station called Isleworth at the point where that parish ended and Hounslow began. Opened on 1st February 1850, it replaced Smallbury Green, closed the previous day. The station at Hounslow was 13½ miles from Waterloo, in open country to the south of the town on the road to Whitton village. Goods and coal yards were provided at Chiswick, Brentford and Hounslow.

At the opening of the line to Hounslow there were about 15 trains each way on weekdays and nine on Sundays, the Hounslow-Waterloo journey taking between 50 and 60 minutes, calling at all stations (there were a few semi-fasts taking slightly less time). For a short period (3rd April 1866 to 31st January 1867) users of the loop were able to travel between its stations and Ludgate Hill via Clapham and Longhedge Junctions, but there were only about two trains each way daily. The daily Down service over the loop in January 1867 terminated at Windsor (three) Feltham (seven) Hounslow (21, including two from Ludgate Hill) and Kew Bridge (one). There were also six North London Railway trains between Hampstead Road (Primrose Hill) and Kingston via the eastern end of the loop, a service to be mentioned in a moment.

As early as 1847 the promoters of the Richmond Railway, led by William Chadwick, had seen the importance of a connection between the loop and the northern main lines, enabling freight, particularly coal, to flow from the midlands and north on to the LSWR, and they hatched a scheme for a North & South Western Junction Railway from the loop at Brentford to join the LNWR at Harrow. Such a proposition required a great deal of careful political footwork to bring it to life, and after various adventures, alarums and excursions well described by R. A. Williams, a 3m 5f double track was opened between Kew Junction, on the loop about a quarter-mile west of Kew Bridge station, and West London Junction at Willesden, LNWR. Authorised by an act of 24th July 1851, this North & South Western Junction Railway was to be jointly worked and guaranteed by the LSWR and the LNWR. Freight began to pass over it on 15th February 1853, but passenger trains, operated by the NLR, did not appear until 1st August, working from separate platforms at Kew to Hampstead Road (Primrose Hill) or Fenchurch Street. A joint LSWR/LNWR service between Hounslow or Brentford and Euston was mooted, but it seems doubtful that it ever ran. Only slightly more substantial was the NLR service started on 1st June 1854 between Hampstead Road (connections to Fenchurch Street) and Windsor via Brentford and Staines. Infrequent, and not encouraged by the LSWR, it came to an end on 31st October that year.

To meet various threats of invasion from the north, the LSWR allowed trains of NLR stock to run from Hampstead Road to Twickenham from 20th May 1858 via Kew Junction (reverse), Chiswick, Barnes Junction (reverse) and Richmond. LSWR locomotives worked as far as Kew, the NLR taking over inwards from there. An equal number of trains worked over the same route were composed of LSWR carriages, and each company's trains called at both the Kew stations. In the summer in some years there were Sunday through workings from and to Bow.

This gesture was not enough to secure the LSWR's position and when further threatening schemes appeared in the 1859 session, the southern company pushed them away by promising (amongst other things) to build curves to eliminate the reversals at Kew and Barnes. Both curves, of 26ch double track, were opened on 1st February 1862, the first from Kew Curve East Junction on the N&SWJR to New Kew Junction on the LSWR, whilst the other joined the loop to the Windsor line just west of the Beverley Brook at Barnes (Chiswick Junction to Mortlake Junction). As already noticed, from the opening of Kingston station on 1st July 1863 the service was extended to there. The curves were not needed long for their intended purpose as they were rendered redundant by the opening of the LSWR's Kensington & Richmond Railway on 1st January 1869, a line which allowed a direct run between Willesden and Richmond via a new junction at South Acton. Although little used, the Barnes Curve was not removed until about 1881 and its site remained indicated by a row of cottage property known as 'Railway Side'. In contrast, the New Kew Curve continued busy with freight and special passenger workings and was also used by North London trains, which terminated on it at platforms opened on 1st February 1862 alongside the LSWR Kew station and connected to it by subway.

A steadily heavier freight movement passed over the original link between South Acton and Old Kew Junction, especially after connections had been made with the new Midland main line at Brent (Cricklewood) via the Midland & South Western Junction Railway, on 1st October 1868. Although a connection was opened between the N&SWJR and the GWR main line at Acton Wells on 1st January 1877 this did not prove of much use for through freight to and from the LSWR. More fruitful was a link between the M&SWJR and the new GCR main line at Neasden opened on 1st August 1899 which gave LSWR trains access to the GCR sidings at Neasden.

These links made the Hounslow loop the southern end of a strategic belt line joining the LSWR to the London docks and all the main lines north of the Thames, a circumstance which influenced the LSWR's choice of Feltham as a site for a large new marshalling yard completed in 1921–2. Before that, on 31st March 1870, the growth of freight traffic had required a third track between Kew Bridge and Windmill Road, Brentford, to accommodate trains coming off the N&SWJR. Nine years later, this track was signalled for two-way working. A second goods relief road was opened along this stretch by the Southern Railway on 7th May 1932, providing access to Brentford yard without fouling the loop tracks. Further widening between Brentford and Isleworth, authorised in the SR Act of 1930, was never completed, but in 1932 the SR extended the Up road loop at Kew from New Kew Junction to Chiswick Junction so that longer coal trains could be accommodated.

A second connection between the loop and the northern lines was made at the request of a House of Commons committee. This was the so-called Chiswick Curve opened on 1st January 1869, allowing working from the loop east of Kew Bridge (Chiswick Junction) to the Kensington & Richmond line just south of what is now Gunnersbury station (Brentford Road Junction). Passenger trains used it from 1st June 1870, running between Waterloo and Hounslow via Kensington (Addison Road), but from 1st November this circuitous service was diverted to Richmond via Kew Gardens, with a shuttle train affording connections between Gunnersbury and Hounslow.

To meet a District Railway move towards Twickenham, to be mentioned later, a line known as the Whitton Curve was opened on 1st January 1883, giving the loop its final form. This was a double track from Hounslow Junction just south of the station to Whitton Junction on the Windsor line, allowing a direct service to be worked from Hounslow to Twickenham and Richmond. From its opening day it carried trains running from Gunnersbury through Brentford, Hounslow, Twickenham, Richmond, and Kew Gardens back to Gunnersbury, replacing the Gunnersbury–Hounslow shuttle. On weekdays there were eight trains round each way increased in February 1883 to 15, with seven then added on Sundays, but from 1st November these trains ran only between Gunnersbury and Twickenham, via Hounslow.

Perhaps the most outstanding physical feature of the loop was the Thames bridge at Barnes, which the LSWR and SR put to good use during the annual Oxford and Cambridge boat race. On that day, train services over the bridge were stopped at the time of the race to allow spectators brought down from Waterloo in first-class only special trains to view the classic struggle from a comfortable grandstand. These workings continued into the 1930s; a note in *The Railway Gazette* of 29th March 1935 records that three trains were to be run that year from Waterloo, at 13.50, 13.59 and 14.06 for a return fare of half a guinea (52½p) inclusive of entertainment tax. With the increasing weight of locomotives and freight trains, it became necessary to strengthen the bridge, which was rebuilt in 1894–5 with wrought-iron bow-string girders and new brick abutments and piers. A public footpath was then added on the down train side. As on the Shepperton branch, the catchment area showed no strong residential development during the era of steam traction, when both the frequency and speed of the London service remained a constant source of dissatisfaction, especially amongst the inhabitants of Hounslow.

This town expanded only very slowly and unsuccessfully. In 1870 there were said to be 'many hundreds of empty houses in the neighbourhood' solely on account of the 'high railway fares and time wasted on the journey to London'. At this period most trains took about 55 minutes to reach Waterloo, it being a matter of complaint that the journey sometimes lasted as much as half an hour longer than that from Twickenham. Some improvements were made as the century drew to its end. By 1885 there were 29 Down and 26 Up trains on the Chiswick route to and from Waterloo, taking 35 to 45 minutes, and 21 each way on the Twickenham–Hounslow–Gunnersbury service, giving connections at Gunnersbury with the Richmond to Waterloo or Ludgate Hill service via Kensington (Addison Road). In June 1888 the Down loop service terminated variously at Staines (two), Feltham (13), and Hounslow (14) plus a half-hourly frequency between Gunnersbury and Hounslow with alternate trains going on to Twickenham.

Chiswick for Grove Park station, looking to Barnes, about 1950. *Lens of Sutton*

The latecomer: Barnes Bridge (1916) looking towards the rail bridge over the Thames, 30th March 1974. *Alan A Jackson*

Hounslow started to expand towards the railway and the Heath in the 1890s, so that by 1914 it was spilling over the line towards Whitton. A second public house, the *South Western*, had been opened south of the station to supplement the original *North Star* which dated from about the opening of the line. During the same period some of the large estates around Chiswick station were broken-up for building, houses appearing north of the station and between there and Kew Bridge. Around the bridge on the north bank, development was primarily commercial, centred on a market for local fruit, vegetables and flowers which after 1893 was housed in a building provided by the local authority. Brentford itself expanded very little but at Isleworth a new district called Spring Grove was laid out west of the line not long after it opened and there was also some villa development close to the station on the south side. The urban district of Heston-Isleworth, covering most of the line's catchment area at the outer end, experienced a 40 per cent growth between 1901 and 1911, from 30,863 to 43,313, but this owed more to the District Railway electric service and the London United tramcars than to the line we are considering.

These two powerful agents of suburban growth had both appeared in the Edwardian era. The District service will be described later, but the influence of the electric tramway was also significant. On 4th April 1901 the London United electric tramways reached Kew Bridge from Shepherds Bush and on 6th July the service was extended through Brentford and northern Isleworth to Hounslow. These tramcars, trundling along the main road every five minutes from 04.00 until 02.00, inevitably attracted much local custom away from the LSWR line which they virtually paralleled all the way from Hounslow to Gunnersbury. Almost overnight the receipts at Kew Bridge, Brentford, Isleworth and Hounslow stations dropped by a third. Nor was this the full extent of the attack, for on 13th August 1902 the LUT cars were plying along the road between Isleworth and Twickenham. It was not only the local traffic, such as that associated with the Pears Soap factory at Isleworth, the Brentford Market and shopping journeys into Hounslow and Brentford which the LSWR lost. Some London workers soon began to find it more convenient to take a tram from Brentford, Kew Bridge or Chiswick to Shepherds Bush or Hammersmith where new electric railways were available to convey them swiftly and comfortably to a large variety of destinations in the West End or the City, a route made all the more attractive by the availability of through booking facilities.

From 1st March 1910 the LSWR attempted to cut its losses by introducing steam railmotors on the long-established Twickenham/Feltham-Hounslow-Gunnersbury service. These cars had a lower carrying capacity than the LUT tramcar, having only eight first-class and 33 third-class seats, although it was possible to haul a trailer coach if business was brisk. Twickenham was reached in 20 minutes from Gunnersbury, about the same time as the more direct tramcar, and the road times to Isleworth and Hounslow were marginally bettered, but of course the trams at Hounslow were in the High Street, whilst the station was some distance to the south. In any case, as there were only 18 journeys each way (13 on Sundays) the railmotors offered no serious competition to the very frequent trams. However, the LSWR was planning something which would be more effective; by the beginning of 1912 it had decided to include the loop in its suburban electrification scheme.

In the meantime the London service, which had remained little changed since the 1880s, was slightly augmented and improved. In 1910 there were 37 Down trains terminating variously at Feltham (most often), Hounslow, Staines, Windsor, Twickenham or (one only) Ashford. In the Up direction there were 30 journeys and on Sundays 14 trains ran each way over the loop. Although a few semi-fasts reduced the through time from Hounslow to Waterloo to 37 or 39 minutes, most trains took 44 to 47 minutes. Five years later, the best time from Hounslow was 34 minutes in the Up direction and 29 back, but these were isolated examples and the average time was around 45 minutes. The 1914 Bradshaw showed only 11 railmotor runs each way between Gunnersbury and Twickenham or Feltham via Hounslow and this subsidiary service ceased altogether on 22nd February 1915. From that day, apart from Bank Holiday workings for several years, the Chiswick Curve saw only occasional excursion trains, troop trains and horsebox specials. On 29th May 1930 the SR Traffic Committee decided that these could be worked via Old Kew Junction,

LSWR steam rail motor car No. 9 at Hounslow, Down platform, c.1912 on the Gunnersbury–Hounslow–Twickenham/Feltham service, which operated from 1910 until 1915.

allowing closure of the curve together with the two controlling boxes at Chiswick Junction and Gunnersbury West. Tracks were eventually removed in July 1932 and two years later the land was sold to Chiswick Estates Ltd to be filled with blocks of flats.

Electric trains arrived on the loop on 12th March 1916, giving a substantial improvement in service. The route followed was a circular from Waterloo to Hounslow via Chiswick, returning via Richmond (headcode 'O') and also outwards to Hounslow via Twickenham, returning via Brentford (headcode '$\overline{\text{O}}$'). By the former, Hounslow was reached in 35 minutes and trains ran every half-hour from 05.22 to 00.05, every hour on Sundays. In the peak period some via Brentford ran non-stop between Barnes or Putney and Waterloo (these were steam-hauled until 31st July 1916).

With the electrification, Barnes at last received a centrally-sited station. Barnes Bridge, two 400ft platforms with timber buildings, was opened on the first day of electric working. It was situated by the riverside, at the south end of the bridge over Barnes Terrace and the river. A pleasing street level entrance pavilion in stone and red brick with an iron and glass awning blended well with the balconied Georgian and early Victorian houses of the Terrace. The booking office windows were in a tiled subway through the embankment, giving this part the appearance of an Underground station of the period. In recent years the street-level facilities have been replaced by a small ticket office on the Up platform, enabling the station to be worked by one man.

During World War 1 the loop was very busy with special traffics. Military camps were established at Chiswick and Hounslow, together with an airfield on Hounslow Heath. In the early months of the war, very heavy troop traffic passed on to the N&SWJR via Hounslow, and troop trains and military freight movements continued to keep the line busy for the next four years.

A substantial amount of residential development was fostered by the electric trains, principally between Brentford and the outer end of the loop in the late 1920s and early 1930s. Immediately south-west of Brentford, this growth was also associated with the opening in 1925 of the Great West Road and the factories which that new artery attracted. To serve this new district, a cheaply-built station with two 400ft side platforms was opened at Syon Lane on 5th July 1931. On both sides of the line between Isleworth and Feltham Junction large estates of small houses were erected for private sale by R. T. Warren, Wimpey, and others in the 1930s, so that by 1939 the whole area between the Staines Road at Hounslow and the Windsor line just west of Twickenham was a sea of new houses sold at prices between £500 and £1000. The hamlet of Whitton, transformed to a new suburb, received its own station on the Windsor line in 1930, but many of the new residents on the northern side of the district used Hounslow station.

North of Old Kew Junction a new Kew Bridge goods yard was opened in 1929 and enlarged in the following year, whilst a new goods yard opened at Hounslow in 1931 at a cost of £14,500 had to be enlarged in 1937–8. Hounslow passenger station received in 1933 a passimeter booking office for the new business on the Down side, with additional parcels accommodation, and extra sidings for electric stock stabling were completed here in 1939.

Wood Lane Crossing, Isleworth, 30th March 1974. *Alan A Jackson*

London's Local Railways

Down side buildings, Brentford, LSWR, disguised as Brentford Central, BR, 11th January 1975.
Alan A Jackson

Use of the loop by freight trains moving between the northern and southern lines continued to be brisk until well into the 1960s, making it a mecca for engine-spotters or railway observers (according to age). In the 1950s for example, as many as 30 different types of steam locomotive could be seen between Old Kew Junction and Feltham Junction, originating from all the old companies other than the GWR. The pattern of freight movement at this time varied little from that which had prevailed in earlier decades: domestic and industrial fuels southwards, cement and manufactured goods northwards. In 1953 there were some 30 trains each way between the Feltham yard and the yards at Neasden, Temple Mills, Brent, Cricklewood, Willesden and Ferme Park (Hornsey). Some journeys to and from the latter were worked via the Metropolitan Widened Lines; Chiswick and the section of the loop between Kew Bridge and Barnes was also used by 11 trains a day each way between Battersea and Hither Green and Brent yards.

Local goods traffic ebbed in the late 1950s. Chiswick yard was the first to go (14th June 1958) with Brentford Central following on 4th January 1965 and the old yard at Kew Bridge on 3rd April 1967. Hounslow New Yard closed on 6th February 1967 but the Old Yard lasted until 6th May the following year. Movements to and from Feltham Yard also declined in importance and during 1965 the connection to the third and fourth (N&SWJR) tracks east of Brentford was taken out of use. Closure of Feltham Yard followed in January 1969. Inter-regional movements by no means disappeared, and after June 1966 there were summer Saturday through passenger workings between Sheffield and Portsmouth and Bournemouth via Brent, Acton Wells, Old Kew Junction and the loop. The other arm of the Kew triangle via New Kew Junction had no advertised passenger service since the summer Saturday Nottingham–Ramsgate trains of 1965–8, but during the spring and autumn it saw twice-weekly trains of senior citizens from Newcastle and other northern towns on their way to and from cheap holidays at Eastbourne, Hastings and the Kent Coast resorts.

The Hounslow Loop

Off-peak passenger traffic on the electric services had been light for many years; three-car and even two-car trains have on occasions sufficed to carry it. Until the end of World War 2, the maximum train length was two three-car sets, but from 15th November 1948, eight-car trains could be accommodated at all seven stations.

'Rationalisation' and economy cuts have been very much to the fore on the Loop in recent years. From 19th August 1987 the ticket offices at all the stations except Chiswick (open in morning peak hours) and Hounslow (open most of the day) were closed and all station staff withdrawn. For a time conductor guards issued tickets on the trains but these were subsequently withdrawn after automatic ticket machines had been installed at the stations and penalty fares introduced. Alas, the prevalent late 20th century youthful vandalism which is encouraged by leaving stations and structures unsupervised soon set about persistent wreckage of the machines, causing conductor guard ticket issue on trains to be restored from mid-1994. The closure of ticket offices did however make it possible to rescind another economy measure; from 17th May 1987 Sunday trains were restored at Barnes Bridge and Syon Lane. Unstaffed stations, intimidating at night, do not encourage traffic and the management's reflex action of reducing the basic hourly service to hourly in late evening from 4th October 1993 seemed hardly likely to improve patronage at those times.

With its procession of steam-hauled freights and other special workings to and from north of the Thames now gone, with colour lights and track circuit block replacing semaphore signals in 1974 and with lifting barriers at level crossings instead of manually-worked gates, the Loop has lost much of its special atmosphere.

Further depredation of the somewhat old-fashioned aura of this line, with its many reminders of the LSWR, took place in 1989–90 when all the stations were subjected to a drastic economy treatment, euphemistically known as 'refurbishing'. At Barnes Bridge the roofing was removed from the platform approach ramps, the waiting rooms were opened out and the street level buildings were converted to offices. Surprisingly, the old platform canopies were spared. The Tite station house on the Up side at Chiswick was quite pleasingly restored and let out as offices, its platform canopy retained. A converted outbuilding housed the ticket office. At Kew Bridge the handsome Italianate street level building was sold out of railway use; the footbridge, retained without its glazing, was reached by a new entrance alongside the old station house. Brentford suffered a severe mauling. Both platforms were stripped of their canopies and small shelters with glazed arch roofs installed in their stead. The covered footbridge here was completely removed, obliging passengers to take the long way round via the road bridge and approach yard. The station house on the Down side was left in a much mutilated state. At Syon Lane all the SR structures were removed, basic shelters and a new footbridge appearing in their place. Isleworth lost its Up platform canopy and its neglected empty station house on the Up side soon became a victim of vandalism and graffiti daubing. At Hounslow the station house, also on the Up side, was let for non railway use, the ticket office moved to a converted outbuilding. Here platform canopies were retained on both sides. In 1981, further south, at the two-way junction with the Windsor and Reading line, a steeply-graded overline bridge was erected on the east side to allow development inside the railway-bound triangle.

This now rather colourless but useful line no doubt has an assured future especially as it has some value as diversionary route for through services but the decline in traffic at most of the intermediate stations is a cause for concern.

The crude corrugated iron and timber of the first District Railway provision at Northfields, just before the rebuilding of 1911. An eastbound train is leaving. *London Transport Museum*

Hounslow and Heathrow Airport

Railway promoters were much attracted to the yawning gap between the LSWR line to Staines and the GWR main line. Although it contained little population but the contiguous settlements of Hounslow, Isleworth and Brentford, served since 1850 by the LSWR loop already considered, Windsor lay temptingly to the west, while the inner end was sufficiently close to west London to make the more optimistic dream of suburban development.

Parliament had authorised a second line to Hounslow as early as 1866. This Hounslow & Metropolitan Railway formed a 3½-mile Western extension of the Acton & Brentford Railway which had been sanctioned a year earlier to run from the GWR at Acton to pass south of Ealing and join the Southall-Brentford branch just north of Brentford. Leaving the Acton & Brentford at Boston Lane, the Hounslow & Metropolitan would have passed over the Brentford branch, throwing off on the west side a four-furlong spur towards Southall. Then proceeding south-west, parallel to the LSWR Hounslow loop but about ¾-mile to the north, it kept clear of the built-up area along the Bath Road, turning west at Hounslow to terminate on the Bath Road opposite Hounslow Barracks. The act allowed for mutual facilities for passenger and goods traffic between the new line and the GWR.

In the financial panic which followed the failure of Overend, Gurney & Co it proved impossible to raise capital for this speculative venture into territory already served by the LSWR. Although extension of time was obtained in 1869, the scheme failed, but the attraction remained and similar lines were sought in unsuccessful bills deposited for the sessions of 1875 and 1876, the first with connections to the MDR and the Hammersmith & City instead of the GWR, and the second to join the H&CR only. After the Metropolitan District Railway had succeeded in obtaining powers for an Ealing extension in 1877, the landowners who were behind the Hounslow schemes sought to connect their proposed branch with that railway in unsuccessful bills in the 1878 and 1879 sessions. Commenting that the 1878 scheme was intended to go on to Windsor, *Herapath's Railway Journal* thought that the Hounslow line would not pay.

A similar bill was finally authorised by the Hounslow & Metropolitan Railway Act of 26th August 1880. In this the first directors and subscribers were named as Henry Daniel Davies (a landowner and building developer of *Spring Grove*, Isleworth), Jason Gurney (of *Percy Lodge*, Hounslow) and James Oliver Mason (of Grosvenor Road, Pimlico). Their company was to build a 5½-mile branch from the MDR Ealing Extension just south of the present Ealing Common station to the Bath Road opposite Hounslow Barracks over virtually the same route as the 1866 scheme and the western part of the unbuilt Acton & Brentford. Capital was £210,000 with borrowing powers for a further £70,000. An agreement made with the MDR on 3rd June 1880, scheduled to the act, provided for that company to work, manage and maintain the Hounslow & Metropolitan as a passenger line in return for half the gross receipts after deduction of passenger duty. The H&MR also got ten per cent of the MDR portion of fares passing from its line on to the MDR system. Both payments were limited to 4½ per cent of the H&MR's capital outlay, set at a maximum of £250,000.

At this time the MDR was flushed with enthusiasm for suburban expansion, which it saw as a means of increasing the return on its heavily capitalised inner London lines, although the company was by no means always clear how to raise money for suburban adventures. The MDR looked with particular envy at the supposedly rich residential territory of the LSWR, and with the Ealing Extension opened in 1879, and the Hounslow line secured in 1880, it spent some time in 1881 brooding on how to use the latter to reach Twickenham and Kingston. The company's intentions were clarified in a bill deposited in November which sought a 2½-mile line southwards from the H&MR at Hounslow, passing east of Kneller Hall to join the LSWR Kingston loop between Twickenham and Strawberry Hill. For good measure a spur to the LSWR 750yd east of that company's Hounslow station was included. It was apparently intended that the line should be used to work a circular service to and from Earls Court via Hounslow, Kingston, Wimbledon, and Fulham. Not surprisingly this bill met fierce opposition from the LSWR, which was able to kill it on promising to build a Hounslow–Whitton curve to provide the Hounslow–Twickenham facility. Construction was nevertheless begun in 1882 from the northern end, on land which had been bought in the name of the H&MR early that year: this may seem something of a paradox, but it was always possible to build a railway without parliamentary sanction on land obtained by voluntary agreement, provided the tracks did not cross a public highway or infringe on tidal waters. In this case the tracks were brought into a station high above Hounslow High Street's northern pavement where the rails pointed menacingly towards the first-class riverside territory of the LSWR – but although the bridge abutment was built, the lines did not cross the road. In fact parliamentary authority for this 2f 5ch spur from the H&MR was obtained in the Hounslow & Metropolitan Railway Act of 29th June 1883, by which time the work was completed and trains were running into the station at its southern end.

This first section of the H&MR, from the Hounslow High Street station to the junction with the MDR near Ealing had been given priority and its 4m 37ch of double track were in public use from 1st May 1883. At the inner end most trains terminated at Mill Hill Park (Acton Town from 1st March 1910) but until 31st December inclusive some ran through to Mansion House. Thenceforward, for most of the period of steam operation, through workings terminated at Earl's Court. Most trains on the new branch called at the intermediate stations of Boston Road (Boston Manor from 11th December 1911), Osterley (later sometimes called Osterley Park or Osterley & Spring Grove) and South Ealing, all of which opened with the line. Boston Road station was in open fields on the west side of the main road between Brentford and Hanwell; Osterley, also in open country, was near the southern gate of Osterley Park and close to the northern part of Davies' ambitious Spring Grove villa colony which had grown only very slowly since its beginnings in the early 1850s. South Ealing was on the main Ealing to Brentford road at a point already touched by the outskirts of the Queen of Suburbs.

Dull things in grey stock bricks and slate, lit by round arched windows, these stations had little architectural merit. The only other feature of note was the double span lattice girder bridge over the canalised river Brent and the GWR branch. Hounslow terminus, later to be called Hounslow Town, was reached by a brick viaduct of some 20 arches which ended abruptly at the unfinished bridge over the High Road. Two side platforms here were protected by wide wood and glass canopies; a signal box, and locomotive siding with pit, coal storage, and water tank completed the rail-level installation. Below was a substantial station house in brick, its second floor and roof reaching rail level.

Hounslow Town station, District Railway, 1905. A bus station occupies this site today.
LT Museum

Exterior of the first Osterley station (Osterley & Spring Grove) on the west side of the overline bridge in Thornbury Road, 2nd May 1959. *Alan A Jackson*

The remaining 1m 44ch from Lampton Junction with the northern end of the Hounslow spur to Hounslow Barracks (renamed Hounslow West 1st December 1925) offered little promise of traffic. It was nevertheless opened as a single line on 21st July 1884, at first covered by a shuttle service of 12 trains a day each way which worked from Osterley, where a lay-by and locomotive run-round road was provided between the running lines west of the station. Hounslow Barracks had the usual H&MR stock brick station house and booking hall, but only a single platform. There was a signal box, and another at Lampton Junction which also controlled the convergence of double and single track 200yd to the west of the junction.

Traffic results were poor in the early years, but it is amusing to reflect that many of the passengers were extracted from the LSWR stations at Hounslow, Isleworth and Brentford, only to be carried to London over that company's property between Hammersmith and Turnham Green.

No doubt the Hounslow High Street spur was completed because it was far advanced before the bill was lost, but as the awkwardness of operating this not particularly remunerative appendage soon niggled, it was closed after traffic on 31st March 1886. In its place the District opened next day a one-platform station named Heston-Hounslow on the single line at Lampton Road about half a mile to the west. This station, with its corrugated iron building, was a good deal less convenient for the centre of the town.

The District's enthusiasm for the line waned so much that until the beginning of the twentieth century it was left to languish on a diet of one train an hour (two in peak periods); in 1900 there were still only 22 trains daily each way. Building was discouraged; a District driver recalled in his old age that 'builders got it in the neck properly', so much so that some were obliged to let rent-free to keep their property from deteriorating and 'many DR men got nice little houses this way'.[*]

* Memories of District driver Membery, *TOT Magazine*, February 1929.

A *Railway Magazine* contributor visiting the branch in 1901 thought it must be one of the most cheaply-worked lines in the United Kingdom. Although each station was manned with ticket collector, porter, and a youth, seldom was more than one of these visible, while the stations seemed to have received no paint since their opening 18 years earlier. Only one five-coach train ran each hour for most of the day, and single line working seemed a possible further economy. He did have a good word to say about the connections at Mill Hill Park (now Acton Town): the Up branch and Down main line trains arrived here about the same time, after which the branch train went forward, the locomotive running round whilst the Down train left for Ealing; the branch train then entered the Down platform to await the arrival of the Up train from Ealing. The writer had visited the derelict Hounslow Town station, finding that the platforms outside the covered portion had disappeared, their old supporting pillars fast decaying. A short section of the spur was still connected at Lampton Junction but all other track had been removed. Beneath the roof of the station, over the remains of the platforms, the laundry of the occupants hung above their strolling rooster and his hens. In the station yard and arches of the viaduct were Urban District Council dustcarts, steam rollers and other vehicles.

This account also mentions what appears to have been an experimental installation of automatic signalling in preparation for the planned electrification of the MDR. The writer noted starting signals without arms and signals not connected to the station boxes, which remained 'off', only changing to 'on' after the passage of each train, when they were so held until the section was clear, an event announced by the ringing of an electric bell. He wrongly surmised that the numerous ramps he saw between the rails were to operate station indicators in the carriages, commenting sarcastically that none of the trains were fitted with such indicators.

It was indeed a portent, for this sleepy backwater was soon to see great changes. The opening of the London United electric tramways through the Brentford and Hounslow area which has already been noticed also caused serious depletion in MDR local traffic. The new American owners of the MDR quickly decided to buy the Hounslow & Metropolitan from Charles Morris and others, and to electrify it with the rest of the MDR. Both measures were authorised by the MDR Act of 21st July 1903. Vesting of the H&MR in the MDR took place on 1st July 1903, following acquisition for around £166,000 of a railway that had cost the original owners almost £330,000 to build.

In the face of electric tramway competition priority was now given to passenger traffic and a scheme to use the line also for freight was dropped. Preparations for this had been made in the MDR Act of 1900, which allowed the agreement of 1880 between the MDR and the H&MR to provide for the carriage of merchandise over the H&MR. The intention was to operate through goods trains between the GCR and the LSWR via a curve at Rayners Lane and a reopened Hounslow Town spur extended to join the LSWR at Hounslow. Instead, the Hounslow Town spur was reopened for passenger traffic only on 1st March 1903 with a service of two trains an hour, supplemented in the peak periods. These three-coach trains were joined at Osterley to five-coach trains which had started from Hounslow Barracks, the eight cars going through to Mill Hill Park or Mansion House. In the opposite direction, the three coaches for Hounslow Town were detached at Osterley for working to the High Street terminus by a second locomotive. These movements were facilitated by the restoration of the old loop siding between the main running lines at Osterley.

A permanent automatic signalling installation of the standard open-air Underground type was switched-in on 11th June 1905 preparatory to electric train working on the four-rail dc system from 13th June. The new services operated between Hounslow Barracks and Mill Hill Park or South Acton, trains running in and out of Hounslow Town via the original eastern curve and a new 7ch western curve (first proposed in the 1883 Bill) which rejoined the through line at Kingsley Road Junction. From this time no passenger trains ran on the through line between the two junctions.

Very soon the electric service, which was much more frequent (over 76 trains a day each way in 1907 compared with 22 in 1900) as well as faster and more reliable, was encouraging the construction of small houses at Hounslow, and between Brentford and Ealing. This growth was particularly rapid along the southern fringes of Ealing and at Little Ealing, its satellite south of the line, where a crudely-built halt with booking office hut on Northfield Lane bridge was opened on 16th April 1908. Despite the spread of little houses and the ugly bulk of the Ealing District Steam Laundry behind the eastbound platform, there were still some pleasantly shaded fields west and south-west of the new halt which attracted the patronage of Sunday School outings in high summer. But this did not last long, and in 1911 Northfield Halt was transformed to a full-scale station with concrete platforms and a spacious well-glazed entrance hall on the road bridge, named Northfields & Little Ealing on 11th December that year. Houses hereabouts, fitted with gas and venetian blinds, some of them in 'tree-lined roads', were advertised between 1904 and 1913 at £200-£300 leasehold or rents of 11s 6d (57½p) and 12s 6d (62½p) weekly.

Boston Manor for Brentford and Hanwell, looking north east, c.1912, with a two-car train at the eastbound platform.

London's Local Railways

From 1st January 1909 the basic service of two-car trains worked every ten minutes, connecting at Mill Hill Park with all Mansion House-Ealing Broadway trains. This ten-minute frequency was subsequently extended over the 1m 31ch single-line section at the western end of the branch, in and out of what was now a single platform line at Hounslow Town, where all points, sidings, the run-round road and signal box had been removed. To simplify operation it was decided finally to abandon the Hounslow Town spur, the terminus being closed after traffic on 1st May 1909. From the following morning its place was taken by a new station of the same name (renamed Hounslow East from 1st December 1925) 336yd to the north of the old, on the through line. This was less pretentious but more attractive than its predecessor, but although its garden-city style buildings by the District's architect H. W. Ford were eminently right for the surrounding suburban scene, the layout made no provision for traffic growth. The main building, of timber and brick under steeply pitched tiled roofs decorated with Tudor chimneys, snuggled tightly into the northern side of the embankment, hidden from the town centre.

A bus garage, opened by the London General Omnibus Company on 14th July 1912 on the site of the old terminus lasted until 1954 when London Transport resited it further north, adding a bus station, but missing the opportunity to provide a fully integrated road-rail interchange at this busy point despite the availability of owned land. The railway station, as we shall see, was little altered then, despite its inadequacy.

With the completion of the new Hounslow Town station, work began on extending the double track westwards from the country end of its platforms. Double-line working reached the east end of Heston-Hounslow on 24th April 1910, that station being converted to an island platform on 19th October 1912, and worked as normal double track from 1st November. This left 62ch of single line at the extremity of the branch which was soon required to carry 300 trains a day, in rush hours at intervals of six minutes but by that time train staff had been replaced by non-token working.

Another Edwardian improvement was the reconstruction of Mill Hill Park as Acton Town in 1910, providing two island platforms separated by a single track in the centre. When this was ready on 20th February, Hounslow trains shuttled in and out of the single central road, departing within three minutes of arrival. Passengers for London alighted on the left-hand platform, those for South Harrow or Ealing Broadway using the westbound platform at the right-hand side. To the north of this new station, from 10th February 1910, the Down Ealing trains used a new flyover above the two Hounslow roads.

One aspect of the road-rail co-ordination which followed the acquisition of the LGOC by the Underground Company in 1912 was the operation of a bus service between Hounslow Barracks station and Windsor via Colnbrook and Slough, realising an old District dream. This began on 14th July 1912 as an hourly Sunday service but such was the public response that it was quickly built up to a five-minute frequency for much of the day. By the autumn of 1912 it was running daily and other Sunday services to Staines, Burnham Beeches and Virginia Water had been added.

Several factors contributed to the early start of suburban development in this part of London after the end of World War 1: the opening of the Great West Road in 1925; the existence of extensive market gardens and orchards whose owners were ready to sell at low prices; and the well-established electric railway service via Acton

Town, with its frequent trains to the West End and the City. After a large housing estate had been started on the south side of the Bath Road opposite the terminus in 1926, building in this district continued until the early 1930s, by which time the formerly isolated Hounslow Barracks were completely surrounded by streets of small houses except in the south-west corner. Between the railway and the Great West Road, from Hounslow to Osterley, and either side of that road at Osterley, house building started in earnest in the early 1920s so that by 1935 the spread of development south of Osterley Park covered most of the area between the MDR and the former LSWR Hounslow Loop.

Nearer to London, the soggy valley of the Brent was left to golf courses, parks and sewage farms, but by the early 1930s there was a strip of building south-west from Hanwell past Boston Manor station into Brentford; Little Ealing had by then merged with South Ealing and the Underground's 'Northfields', whilst South Ealing had spread south of the railway for half a mile eastwards from its station.

As early as 1926 Hounslow East and Osterley stations were handling almost a million passengers a year, totals soon to grow substantially. The Underground Company's publicity of this period invited readers of the *Evening News* 'Why not live at Osterley?' quoting a house price range of £650 to £1,500, or plots at an average of £5 10s (£5.50) per foot frontage. Builders and buyers came forward after that in sufficient numbers to produce the results already sketched, so that between 1921 and 1939 the population of the larger part of the area served by the branch (Heston & Isleworth) increased from 47,500 to 102,000.

For its part, the Underground Company and its successors the LPTB, carried through a substantial amount of rebuilding and improvement between 1920 and 1939, gradually bringing the traffic capacity of the branch, with a few minor blemishes, well into line with the increased needs of the catchment area. Doubling of the remaining 62ch of single track at the outer end was completed on 28th November 1926, together with the reconstruction of the interior of Hounslow West, where from 11th December 1926 there were three tracks, one each side of an island platform and the other serving a platform capable of easy conversion to an island should traffic require. The dreary entrance building and station house of 1884 were swept away, to be replaced from 5th July 1931 by a striking Portland stone-dressed heptagonal hall with shops, in the early style of Charles Holden. Its impressive interior, decorated in gold and light scarlet, was floodlit at night. A bus lay-by and car park were provided outside.

By the late 1920s, when the Hounslow branch was carrying 170 trains each way daily, District Line capacity was severely taxed. With the availability of Government guaranteed cheap money in 1929 for projects which would relieve unemployment, the Underground Company decided to lessen the District's burden by extending Piccadilly line tube services over the branch as far as Northfields where a site was available for a much-needed rolling stock depot. To give unimpeded access to and from the depot, a second pair of tracks was to be laid between Acton Town junction and Northfields, and these were ready for use on 18th December 1932. At Acton Town the westbound Ealing & South Harrow line was carried over all the Hounslow branch tracks except the southernmost westbound road. The new depot, which could be entered from either end, was designed by Stanley Heaps, the Underground Company's staff architect, in co-ordination with Adams, Holden & Pearson. West of the overline road bridge the westbound running line was carried beneath a depot approach track. Completed early in 1932, the depot housed 304 tube and District line cars, about half this total under cover. There were 19 tracks, 450ft long, in the sheds, two allocated to car washing and two for maintenance, these equipped with lifting bays and travelling crane.

As the depot site was south of the running lines between Northfields and Boston Manor stations, the existing Northfields platforms blocked the area required for the depot approach tracks, requiring the reprovision of Northfields station on the east side of the overline road bridge. Two island platforms (District trains on the outer sides, Piccadilly on the inner) were brought into use on 19th May 1932 although the new station was not fully completed until December that year. For the street level, Adams, Holden & Pearson designed a lofty rectangular entrance hall in glass and brick, with a flat concrete lid and integral shops, all in similar style to the other new stations then being erected on the suburban extremities of the Piccadilly line. This fine structure was placed on the statutory list of buildings of special architectural interest in 1994, although its original lines had by then for some 14 years or so been cruelly marred by open steel stairways erected to meet modern 'belt and braces' safety requirements.

As the resiting of Northfields brought the London ends of its platforms a mere 265 yards or so from the country end of South Ealing, the relocation of that station further east was considered. The first proposal was to move it to the London side of the overline bridge, but by November 1930 a recommendation had been made to provide a new station about 710 yd east at the Ascott Avenue bridge. As a result it was thought necessary to make an eastern exit from Northfields into Weymouth Avenue. Accordingly a footbridge was built at the London end, together with a 6ft-wide uncovered footway along the north side of the cutting leading to a small and very basic ticket office building in Weymouth Avenue. However, as we shall shortly see, South Ealing stayed where it was, making this provision somewhat unnecessary and it was closed from 4th May 1942. The footway and little entrance building were demolished in 1959 but the associated footbridge at the eastern end of Northfields station survived until the end of 1985.

Piccadilly tube trains reached Hounslow West on 8th February 1932, but this was merely in substitution for some District workings to and from South Acton and Acton Town; the full service of Piccadilly trains running through to stations in north London did not start until 9th January 1933 to Northfields, and 13th March 1933 to Hounslow West. The basic frequency was six trains an hour, some not stopping at South Ealing and Boston Manor. District workings were confined to rush hours only, when there were eight an hour plus 15 Piccadilly trains to and from Northfields, with eight to and from Hounslow West. On 13th March some 70,000 free tickets were issued to persuade the public to sample the new service, many of the recipients using them for the 48-mile return journey between Hounslow West and Enfield West (now Oakwood) which was opened on the same day.

This was not the end of the modernisation programme. A new station was opened at Osterley on 25th March 1934, 200yd west of the original, with an entrance on the north side of the Great West Road. Although one of the least successful of the Adams, Holden & Pearson designs, marked by an ugly 70ft brick 'sign tower' carrying a concrete and glass lighting beacon, this is now a listed building. A pleasing feature was the curving of the glazed footbridge as it merged into the low booking hall. Until 1957, when some demolition took place, the old buildings in Thornbury Road remained intact, the entrance hall serving as a fruiterer's and greengrocer's shop, later as a bookshop.

Boston Manor was rebuilt with less enthusiasm. Something had to be done as the old H&MR buildings stood in the path of the proposed western approach tracks to the Northfields depot, so a new glazed hall was erected on the road bridge together with a modest brick sign tower. This opened on 25th March 1934, but the rail level saw little change and the original MDR pitched roof canopies with their period wooden valancing remained in place.

South Ealing was to suffer from the irresolution of senior management. In 1931 the old station was completely demolished, and the side platforms were converted to two island platforms to serve the new four track layout. Pending a final decision on the Ascott Avenue site mentioned earlier, a temporary wooden ticket hall and entrance was erected on the south side of the overline road bridge, which of necessity had to be rebuilt to straddle the wider alignment. Very small wooden shelters were placed on the new platforms.

Then in 1935, with traffic levels at South Ealing stabilising, perhaps even growing, the management settled on leaving it in position. Evidence of this appeared within a year: a 141ft long flat-roofed concrete canopy structure terminating in a waiting room with a glazed, semi-circular wall was added to the eastbound island platform. However total rebuilding was delayed by higher priorities and then by the outbreak of war, and the westbound island, with its small pitch-roofed waiting hut, was left quite unaltered, as were the 'temporary' footbridge and street level building of 1931. As a result of this 'as you were' decision, South Ealing attained the dubious distinction not only of having some of the longest-lived temporary buildings on the London Transport system but of being the surface station closest to its neighbour – the centre of its platforms was a mere 0.24 mile from the centre of Northfields.

After a lapse of over 50 years, a new station building was eventually erected on the site of the 1883 one, served by a new footbridge which had a diminutive canopy where it debouched on to the westbound island. This reconstruction, in use from 3rd May 1988, included a refurbishment of the 1931 platform hut on the westbound side and of the 1936 building work on the other platform. Both structures were left intact as a memorial to uncharacteristic vacillation on the part of Frank Pick and Lord Ashfield in the 1930s.

In the years immediately before World War 2 the service to Hounslow was built up to a 7½-minute frequency off peak, running through to Wood Green and stations beyond. At peak hours with the additional District workings, intervals ranged from two to five minutes. Thus at Hounslow West between 08.00 and 09.00 in 1936 there were nine Piccadilly Line departures for Wood Green or beyond and five District, terminating at East Ham, Barking or Upminster. Piccadilly Circus was reached in 32½ minutes, Mansion House in 46½ minutes. On Sundays there were Piccadilly Line trains every eight minutes. This pattern saw few significant changes until 10th October 1960 when some District trains were taken out, leaving roughly about four an hour through the peak periods. To compensate, in June 1961 some Piccadilly Line trains were altered to start from Hounslow West in the morning peak. As reasonable connections could be made by simply crossing the platforms at Hammersmith, no great hardship was caused when London Transport decided to remove the somewhat anomalous District workings in the interests of rationalisation. The last District train on the branch left Hounslow West for Acton Town at 18.00 on

9th October 1964. For many years the centre pair of tracks between Acton Town and Northfields were used during the day for testing stock from Acton Works. In rush hours all four lines returned to normal passenger service. From north to south, these tracks are designated: eastbound local (ex District line); eastbound fast; westbound fast; and westbound local (ex District line). Withdrawal of District service enabled the eastbound local to be entirely dedicated as an engineers' test track from November 1985 and although the westbound fast was normally used by Piccadilly line trains, it could also be occupied for the same purpose when required, with the public service diverted to the westbound local. In 1995 the eastbound local line was restored to use by normal passenger services. After the cessation of District trains, track and platform works at Boston Manor restricted the operation of the larger loading gauge District Line stock to the section east of Northfields depot (the airport extensions, mentioned below, were built to tube loading gauge).

The omission of Hounslow East from the pre-war rebuilding programme was to be regretted soon enough as the 1909 accommodation proved pitifully inadequate for a rush-hour traffic swollen by the build-up of feeder bus services into the bus station on the site of the old spur. Complaints led to an Adjournment Debate in the House of Commons in 1961 when the local MP, Richard Reader Harris, described how in the evening peak the congested westbound platform could not be cleared before the arrival of the following train. Fault was also found with the mean little waiting shelter on the uncanopied eastbound platform, which was compared in size to the Government Front Bench. In his reply, the Rt Hon Ernest Marples, Transport Minister, mentioned plans for rebuilding, and conceded that the platform widths were two feet less than the normal twelve. Despite this minor fuss and various announcements about rebuilding in conjunction with hotel or office projects, nothing was subsequently done apart from the construction of a new waiting room and a long canopy on the eastbound platform in 1964. Thirty one years after that some rebuilding work was undertaken on the westbound platform.

The opening of London Airport (Heathrow) in 1946 produced a new traffic magnet at the outer end of this line, which was in a position to provide the nearest rail access to central London. Connecting buses were available and passengers with only hand luggage found this a cheaper and often slightly faster way to and from central London than the alternatives of airline coach, taxi or private car. In 1973 a *Daily Telegraph* reporter established a 66 minute timing from Holborn station to an airport check-in desk, 43 min on the rail journey, 12 on the bus, which waited seven minutes before leaving. On return he managed to travel from the airport arrival gate to Holborn station in 74 minutes.

To cater for this type of lightly-loaded passenger and also 'meeters and greeters' and airport and airline staff, an extension from Hounslow West to a station under the central part of the airport was started in April 1971 after almost a quarter of a century of planning, discussion and consideration, such a delay being about par for the course for public transport expenditure of any significance in Britain in the second half of the twentieth century.

The new line branched off at the London end of Hounslow West station, where the roadside building was retained but the platforms were reprovided at subsurface level. Platform three of the terminus, on the north side, was taken out of use on 22nd October 1971 to allow work to proceed. For most of its 3½ miles, the extension was in a cut and cover trench excavated at the side of the Bath and Great South West

Roads but beyond the intermediate station at Hatton Cross there were deep level tube tunnels under the airport. The old platforms one and two at Hounslow West were closed after traffic on 11th July 1975, the new ones coming into use three days later. On 19th July 1975 trains ran as far as Hatton Cross, a spacious building close to the maintenance facilities and offices at the east end of the airport. This station was massive in appearance and costly in construction, allegedly because someone decided it must be able to withstand the impact of a jumbo jet crashing on to it. Delayed by labour problems and other difficulties, the remainder of the extension, into a terminus named Heathrow Central, was opened on 16th December 1977, 31 years after the airport, providing a destination and a traffic role far beyond the wildest imaginings of the promoters of what had now become the 'Airport & Metropolitan'.

In its first full year, traffic on the extension fell below the several estimated figures, capturing only about one fifth of the total passenger throughput of the airport in 1978, a proportion which remained little changed in the 1990s (most air passengers arrive and depart by private car, hire car or taxi). Office and other airport workers were also not to be separated from their cars in any significant numbers, a factor which led to disappointing business at Hatton Cross. Furthermore, although the service was good (up to 15 trains an hour), the journey to London, with 12 station stops before the fringes of the central area were reached, tended to be tedious even for Londoners and no doubt daunting for air travellers from other countries not accustomed to using public transport. Many, having tried it once, probably never came this way again. Nor was it possible to use the tube service for all flights, since the airport check-in and arrival times extended well beyond the Underground's traffic day. Even so, in 1979 8.8 million passengers were handled at Heathrow Central (clumsily renamed 'Heathrow Central Terminals 1,2,3' from 3rd September 1983) and 7.6 million in 1981, an economic recession accounting for the decline.

A further extension including a station serving the new Terminal 4 was opened on 12th April 1986, the trains travelling direct to it on a single line loop diverging from the 1977 line just beyond Hatton Cross and returning to the beginning of the loop via the original station, then renamed 'Heathrow Terminals 1,2,3'. The continuing growth of passenger traffic at the Airport itself produced a little more business, raising the annual total moving over the tube line to around 15 million by the mid 1990s, of which almost 2.5 million were using Heathrow Terminal 4 station.

Although the tube facility just described had the advantage of distributing airport traffic through much of central and Greater London, a fast direct service to the centre was also needed if more passengers were to be wooed away from the congested road approaches to Heathrow, where over 30 million passengers a year were requiring surface access by the early 1990s, most of them to and from London. Conventional railway services to the passenger terminals of what was to become the world's busiest international airport had been debated since the mid-1950s, initial schemes favouring a branch to join the Hounslow Loop at Whitton, using dedicated new tracks thence alongside existing lines into London (Victoria), via Putney and Clapham Junction. The opening of the tube extension in the 1970s tempered the wind behind such schemes and when the subject was taken up again in the late 1980s attention had turned towards a northern link to the old Great Western main line.

Discussions between the British Airports Authority plc and the British Railways Board produced plans for a joint venture (respectively 70 and 30 per cent later altered to 80 : 20) which received Government blessing in July 1988. This proposal was for

A Heathrow Express train at Heathrow Terminal 4 station in July 1998, a month after the full service opened.

a line into the airport from a flying junction (Airport Junction), just west of Hayes & Harlington station. It offered a seamless journey in fast electric trains to and from dedicated platforms (nos. six and seven) at London Paddington, non stop in 15 minutes, departing from each end every 15 min. At the airport, a station would be provided at the central terminal area (14.6m from Paddington) the line continuing to a station serving Terminal 4 (16.4m). The service would offer a strong contrast to the leisurely station to station trundle of the often crowded tube trains, notably in its endeavour to project the much vaunted air travel ethos beyond the airport by use of specially-designed ribbon-glazed trains, a lavish staff to passenger ratio and airline check-in facilities at Paddington. Although all four tracks out of Paddington were electrified at 25kV with overhead catenary, with the relief lines upgraded to allow speeds up to 100mph, the airport trains were normally to be confined to the 125 mph fast lines. Construction was not without its problems. The airport branch was planned to be partly in cut and cover and partly in bored tunnel but in an area not noted for its environmental attractions, the local authorities insisted on a greater length of underground line than the physiography required. Then, in October 1994 there was a disastrous subsidence during construction of the station area at Heathrow through London clay using a shotcrete lining. This not only halted airport tube services temporarily but set back the Heathrow Express construction programme by six months.

Full services on the completed line, London's newest 'local railway', started on 23rd June 1998. Should a fifth terminal be agreed for Heathrow it is intended that both Heathrow Express and the Piccadilly tube lines serve it with short underground branches from the existing lines, additions which would produce quite a complicated net of railways beneath the centre of the airport, in total estimated to bring the ground public transport share of passenger traffic to 38 per cent. Also for the future is the further complication of a rail link to the south for air passengers and others originating in Surrey, Hampshire and south west England.

GWR auto train 88 at Brentford station, c.1920, looking to Brentford Dock.

Southall to Brentford (map page 165)

Quite soon after the opening of its main line out of Paddington in 1838–41, the Great Western Railway found its freight connections to the London port and markets far from adequate. A transfer depot had been set up at Bull's Bridge, near Hayes, where the railway and the Grand Junction Canal came together at the confluence of the canal's Thames arm. Here, in the 1850s coal was being moved from rail wagons into barges at the rate of some 50,000 tons a year, but the water transit to Brentford, involving negotiation of eleven locks in six miles, was slow enough, even when not 'enhanced in winter by frosts, and in summer by droughts'. Schemes for railways between the GWR and Brentford were deposited each year from 1845 to 1848, including elaborations in the form of extensions to Hounslow, Staines, Westminster, or to the LNWR at Pinner. None reached fruition, partly because the inhabitants of Brentford and Hounslow were loyal to the LSWR, which had arrived first, giving them reasonably direct access to central London. Attention was subsequently concentrated on a freight link to replace the canal. An 1854 proposal for a Great Western & Brentford (Thames Junction) Railway, which included the construction of a Thames-side dock on the 'Town Meadow and Ozier Bed' received parliamentary approval as the Great Western & Brentford Railway Act of 14th August 1855.

This 7ft gauge line and dock was the last railway project engineered by I. K. Brunel, now pre-occupied by his ill-starred maritime enterprises. The GWR was sufficiently sympathetic towards the scheme to suggest that there should be no difficulty about its leasing and working the branch. Some of the subscribers were GWR shareholders, but there was no finance forthcoming from the main line company despite the convenience offered, and no agreement was reached in time for the act. This lack of support was all the more difficult for the small company to bear in that they had to face fierce opposition from the canal company which added considerably to the expense of construction and secured access for the latter to the railway dock. As sitting tenants of Brentford, the LSWR also opposed, but with a good deal less effect.

Work began in the spring of 1856, but as building of the dock proved troublesome and Brunel's estimates far too conservative, further capital had to be raised after powers had been obtained in acts of 1857 and 1859. The act of 1857 mentioned the need to provide more facilities for traffic in 'Welsh Smokeless Coal' while that of 1859 also confirmed an agreement of 1st February 1859 with the GWR under which that company undertook to lease the branch for 99 years for a rent based on tonnage carried (in the case of passenger and horse and carriage traffic, a rent rising after five years to £500 a year). The main line company was to provide locomotives and stock and maintain the installations after the first year. In return for a payment by the Brentford company of £6,000, the GWR agreed to transfer the cranes and other machinery from their Bull's Bridge depot to the new Brentford dock. Except in what were described as 'urgent or extraordinary circumstances' all goods and mineral traffic arising below or at Southall or at any point on the Brentford line, which was destined for points on the branch or on the Thames, and all traffic from such points was to be routed over the Brentford Railway.

Although the narrow and twisting approach road from Brentford High Street, with its bridges over river and canal, was not ready, a formal opening ceremony took place on 15th July 1859. As the steamers *Venus* and *Jupiter* reached Brentford from London Bridge, the official party was greeted with a 19-gun salute whilst bands on each vessel played *See the Conquering Hero Comes*. Travelling to Southall and back in their special train, the guests were impressed by 'the permanence and solidity which characterises the construction'. At the banquet which concluded the proceedings, Charles Eley, secretary of the GW & Brentford, commented on the inadequacy of the canal 'for the greatly increased traffic which the opening up of the Welsh coalfields has brought upon it', adding proudly that the railway project had been completed 'despite the difficulties and obstacles greatly increased by the Russian War and the money panic which followed'.

Goods flowed along the line from the following Monday, 18th July 1859, but preparations for the passenger service were accorded low priority. A nondescript station was erected at Brentford, trains starting to work between Southall and there from 1st May 1860. To save money, the plans for a terminus at the river edge serving a ferry to Kew Gardens were abandoned.

Built for double track but at first only a single 7ft gauge track on the Down side, the 3m 77ch line fell at 1 in 102, 1 in 110, and 1 in 120 towards the river. At the east side of Southall the branch was connected indirectly to the main line through sidings, then shared the Down side island platform with the Down main line. To reach the Brent Valley without violating Osterley Park, the alignment had to go almost due east from the station until it intersected the canal and Windmill Lane at a point later known as Windmill Bridge or Three Bridges, where the roadway was carried above the canal in its 8ft deep cast iron trough and the railway passed beneath both.

South of this curious confluence of transport modes, the railway turned south-east to run between the canal and Osterley Park, closer to the former, reaching after 1½ miles the point where the Hounslow & Metropolitan would later cross it and the canal on a two-span bow girder bridge approached by brick arches. There followed after 1925 an impressive girder bridge which carried the tracks over the new Great West Road. Beyond, the line ran on an embankment to Brentford High Street, passing over the LSWR Hounslow Loop on the way; a connection between the two, authorised by the LSWR (Additional Powers) Act of 1866, was never built. Brentford's platforms were on the north side of the High Street bridge, at the western end of the town; its only building, a wooden shelter, was on the west or Up side. This platform, with signalbox at its south end, was connected to the roadway by a wooden staircase which a dissatisfied director described in 1866 as 'impracticable for ladies in rainy or windy weather'. The shocking scenes in the era of crinolines when the slightest untoward movement revealed delicate pantaloons or pantalettes are best left to reader's imagination. A separate footpath from the road to the Down platform fell into disuse after the introduction of railcars and auto-trains.

From the High Street with its box girder bridge, the line turned east on arches, twice crossing the river Brent before entering the dock area. This was at the northern tip of the Syon Park estate where the Brent joined the Thames, and eventually contained six large warehouses, a riverside wharf with a 2,270ft quay and the main dock, which had a covered basin at the west end.

Goods traffic, always the mainstay of the branch, built up rapidly from 58,000 tons in the first six months of 1860 to 66,000 in the same period following year. Whilst the importance of Brentford as a GWR London freight terminus was considerably diminished by the subsequent opening of outlets via the Metropolitan and North London Railways and the West London Extension Railway's Chelsea Dock, the Brentford installations remained sufficiently busy to justify gradual improvement.

Freight movement was facilitated by the addition of a mixed-gauge track on the Up side of the branch from 1st October 1861, this coinciding with the inauguration of mixed gauge between Paddington and Reading. Until 1875 the two tracks were worked as separate single lines, but between 4th and 7th June that year the broad gauge was removed from the Up line and the Down track was narrowed to standard. Ordinary double-line working began in March 1876. These later developments took place under GWR ownership which became effective from 1st January 1872, having been authorised by the GWR (Additional Powers) Act of 5th July 1865.

Before the independent era ended, the Brentford directors had sought to increase their empire and income by promoting or encouraging various schemes which made use of their property. The Acton & Brentford proposal of 1864 fits into the story of the Hounslow & Metropolitan, already related; the other schemes, which involved extensions towards Isleworth and Twickenham (with running over the LSWR to Richmond), and lines over the river to serve Kew Gardens, all failed.

Passenger services comprising some ten to 12 trains a day each way did not prosper, and the area served showed no tendency to develop in a way which would be helpful to a line pointing away from London. On the trains of three or four coaches, with their three-man crews, the average number of passengers 'did not exceed half a dozen' a situation that the GWR endeavoured to mitigate by including the branch in its steam railcar scheme. These cars, with seating capacity varying from 52 to 64, began to work on the line on 2nd May 1904, providing a half-hourly service weekdays and Sundays for a fare of 2d all the way. It was soon discovered that these newcomers could not haul an additional coach should this be required, so from about 1905 they were replaced with auto trains, push-pull units of 517 class 0–4–2T with one or more trailers. Apart from a brief and unsuccessful experiment with a BTH-Maudslay petrol-electric car in 1912 this was the normal mode for the rest of the period of passenger working.

GWR auto train (loco 1165) for Brentford at Trumpers Crossing Halte, c. 1906.
Locomotive Publishing Co

As part of the improved service, an intermediate stop was made from 1st July 1904 at an occupation crossing 39ch from Southall. With its pagoda-roofed huts on each of its timber platforms, this place was named 'Trumper's Crossing (for Osterley Park) Halte'. Trumper, the owner of the nearby Warren Farm, was no doubt much tickled, remembering the difficulty that the company had experienced in acquiring his land. Although in open country, the halt was reasonably close to the western edge of suburban expansion at Hanwell, and to the back entrance of the LCC mental hospital (Hanwell Asylum) but it was a good half-mile from the Wyke Green Golf Club it was alleged to serve.

The passenger potential of the branch, never very great, was neatly undermined by the opening of an electric tramway along the Boston Road between Brentford and Hanwell on 26th May 1906. As the 1904 improvements had generated little extra traffic, the line proved an easy victim for wartime economies, all passenger trains being withdrawn from 22nd March 1915. Single-line working of the freight traffic was then considered, but it is not clear whether it was in fact adopted. Under pressure from local interests, the GWR restored auto-trains on weekdays only from 12th April 1920, but with intervals extended to hourly (half-hourly at peak periods), 11 trains in all each way. In 1921 the service, which started with the 05.30 and 06.15 departures from Southall, was then half-hourly until 09.18, hourly to 17.15 and half-hourly to 20.45. At this time the intermediate stop was known as 'Trumper's Crossing for South Hanwell and Osterley Park'. A half-hourly Sunday service introduced in the summer of 1923 was withdrawn at the end of September and never again restored. From 1929 weekday trains were restricted to early morning and early evening and early morning and midday on Saturdays but the 1938 timetable showed 14 trains each way daily at these times, 11 on Saturdays. Trumper's Crossing, closed after last trains on 30th January 1926, had by then been demolished. During the empty midday hours from 1933 onwards, the branch was used by the Associated Equipment Company for testing the diesel-mechanical railcars being built at its Southall Works (between the main line and the branch). The AEC's successor, Associated Commercial Vehicles, similarly used the branch for trials of its experimental four-wheel diesel units in 1951–52.

A second wartime closure came after the last train on 2nd May 1942, but this time service was not restored with peace, although the ACV trials just mentioned excited rumours that passenger trains would run again. The ramshackle station and signal box at Brentford remained as a reminder until 1957. Other than the spread of Hanwell westwards in the 1890s and 1900s, somewhat inadequately met by the opening of Trumper's Crossing Halte, and some 1930s development west of the line near Brentford station, much better served by the new SR station at Syon Lane, no new housing appeared along the course of the branch in the whole of its 82 years of passenger working.

There was, however, a late flowering of freight business from new factories at Brentford, a development which owed more to the opening of the Great West Road on 30th May 1925 than the existence of the railway. As they were completed, from 1926 onwards, private sidings were built into the extensive premises of Macfarlane Lang (biscuits) and Firestone (motor tyres and rubber), both of them north of the new road and west of the line. Brentford Town goods yard, north of the new road where it passed under the branch, was opened on 3rd November 1930 to serve the new industrial area. During the early 1920s there were five booked freights a day with extra runs as required, but the new business caused the number of workings to more than double by the mid 1930s. Land on the Great West Road purchased for the new depot but surplus to railway requirements was subsequently developed by the GWR as an industrial estate.

More work for the Docks appeared in 1928 when the GWR assumed transport of the whole Morris Motors export output. 'Knocked down' and in packing cases, the vehicles were moved by rail from new private sidings at the Cowley, Oxford factory to Brentford, where a 150ft by 80ft shed was erected to house them whilst they awaited transfer to the Thames lighters which would carry them down-river to ships in the Port of London. During the export season from October to May, special trains were run for this traffic and the total business reached between 12,000 and 20,000 cars a year. Also at this time, the GWR augmented its accommodation at Brentford Dock by constructing a four storey warehouse fitted with overhead runways on the ground floor and electric cranes on the upper floors. This building, extended in 1938–9, enabled the company to lease accommodation to traders requiring it for bulk storage.

In 1951 there were still 25 freight trains over the branch daily, and as late as 1960 there were seven regular workings to and from Brentford Dock, some calling at Brentford Town yard. Traffic in the late 1950s was both substantial and varied: in the year ended November 1956 Kirkland records that the dock imported 52,888 tons of general merchandise and 10,960 tons of minerals, exporting respectively 127,766 tons and 9,612 tons. That year saw 20,769 tons of general merchandise and 169,077 tons of minerals (mostly coal and coke) brought into Brentford Town Yard by rail, whilst 17,586 tons of general merchandise and 24,433 tons of minerals were forwarded. Goods coming into the dock on lighters and small coasters included iron and steel, timber, wood pulp, flour, animal feeding stuffs, starch and cork; goods outwards by rail and water consisted mostly of motor vehicles and accessories (Morris cars), steel tubes, copper wire, tinplate, china clay and food products. Freight trains at this time were normally hauled by 57xx 0–6–0PT.

As an economy, single-line working using tablet apparatus was introduced in 1952, trains travelling over the former Up line between Southall and Firestone signalbox which controlled the Town yard and access to the private sidings. Traffic was transferred to the old Down road in 1956, worked under electric token regulations, and the Up line was then dismantled.

The somewhat optimistic picture painted by Kirkland in his 1960 article on this line was soon to be clouded. Drastic reductions in use of solid fuels, containerisation of shipping traffic into London, and greater use of road transport for freight movement all combined at around the same time to undermine the main livelihood of the branch. Brentford Dock, which also suffered from poor road access, was closed on 31st December 1964 after a rigorous Beeching appraisal which took into account the need to renew infrastructure and equipment. A deal was done with developers who transformed the 21 acre site into *The Dock*, an imaginative estate of high class apartments, yachting marina and riverside gardens, completed in 1978. A year after the closure of the railway dock, the tracks south of the Great West Road had gone but the Town yard remained open for public traffic until December 1970. Freight for the private sidings then continued. In 1975 Day's Roadstone terminal at Brentford was receiving an average of five trains a week (3,500 tons in total) and some ten trains of cinders, slag and coal ran weekly; in addition around 600 tons of scrap metal were taken out by rail every week.

A future for the line was firmly underwritten by the Greater London Council, which opened a solid waste transfer station on the site of the old Town freight yard early in 1977. This facility received domestic and other refuse which was compacted in the plant and loaded into box containers, each holding up to 12.5 tonnes. Fork lift trucks then placed them on Freightliner type carriers for transport by rail in up to five trains a week to a landfill site (worked-out gravel pits) at Appleford, near Didcot. Two diesel locomotives were usually required to move the 800 tonne trains up to Southall.

The LSWR bridge over Hammersmith Grove, looking north from Beadon Road, c.1905. The street level entrance to the station was on the right just before the bridge. *Commercial postcard*

The Kensington & Richmond Railway (map page 165)

Richmond, leading river resort and desirable place of residence for affluent City men, attracted numerous railway schemes in the boom years around 1860, many with the objective of undermining the LSWR's hold by providing access to west London, the West End, or the City via the North London Railway or the Metropolitan. All this activity caused the North & South Western Junction Railway to promote its own line from Kew Bridge to Richmond, with a feeding connection from its Hammersmith & Chiswick branch into the proposed Hammersmith & City Railway near Shepherds Bush. Anxious to keep the juicy Richmond fruit in its own basket, the LSWR persuaded the N&SWJR that it would fill this dangerous vacuum itself, providing connections and running powers for the N&SWJR and its users.

The result was a Kensington & Richmond Railway, a six-mile branch from the West London Railway north of Kensington (Addison Road) station, through Shepherds Bush and Hammersmith to meet the N&SWJR south of Acton and carry its trains over the Thames on a new line into a separate terminus alongside and to the north of the existing Richmond station. This separation, intended to force other companies to continue using the circuitous access to the LSWR proper via the Kew and Barnes curves, upset the LNWR, which was in a position to make difficulties about the proposed junction at Kensington. A batch of further schemes for the area drove the LNWR and LSWR into each other's arms, easing the passage of the Bill which was to receive royal assent on 14th July 1864. As authorised by the act, the Kensington & Richmond ran into the Hammersmith & City from Kensington, leaving it again just north of the Hammersmith terminus, an arrangement designed to allow GWR and Metropolitan trains to run to Richmond (the GWR was to pay for adding broad gauge to the K&R if wanted). A joint H&CR/LSWR station was to be built on the portion of the H&CR used by the LSWR trains, the H&CR to be dual-gauge at this point. At South Acton, an 'Acton Junction Line' would allow trains to work from the N&SWJR to Richmond. A second act in June 1865, extending time, rearranged the Hammersmith layout to provide a separate through line from Kensington with junctions on and off the H&CR, the intention being that some K&R trains would run over the H&CR to call at the joint station whilst others would by-pass it. This act also sanctioned a 'Chiswick Curve', to allow direct running from Hounslow LSWR onto the Kensington line just south of the present Gunnersbury station. A 'Kew Bridge Curve', for direct running between Richmond and Hounslow, authorised by the LSWR (Additional Powers) Act of 1866, was never built.

Further modifications at Hammersmith, agreed with the GWR and Metropolitan on 13th July 1867 and confirmed by the LSWR General Act of that year, provided for one junction north of the H&CR terminus, allowing trains to run from the H&C towards Richmond, and abandoned the proposed joint interchange station. In its place, the LSWR would build a station at Hammersmith Grove, south of the proposed junction, which GWR and Metropolitan trains would be able to use on payment and which would be connected by 'a convenient passageway', enclosed and covered and at least 10ft wide, passing over the H&CR into its Hammersmith terminus.

Another 18 months passed before Brassey & Ogilvy had the line ready. From 1st January 1869 LSWR trains began to run over it, working approximately hourly between Richmond and Waterloo via the Latchmere and West London Extension Junctions at Battersea (LSWR trains had been running between Kensington and Clapham Junction since 2nd March 1863, and, with the LNWR, between Kensington and Waterloo from 6th July 1865). Also from 1st January 1869, the new line carried NLR Broad Street-Richmond trains using what are now South Acton and Gunnersbury Junctions, then known as Acton and Brentford Road Junctions. A third service, operated by the LSWR from the same day, ran between Richmond and Ludgate Hill, an extension of a Kensington–Loughborough Junction–Ludgate Hill working which had started on 1st February 1868. This last very circuitous service, taking from 58 to 62 minutes, was for many years covered by about ten trains a day each way. The North London trains, which ran half-hourly as far as South Acton, splitting there, with alternate trains going to Kew Bridge, remained almost unchanged until 1909 when it was increased to half-hourly to Richmond (Sunday trains had been half-hourly since 1906).

Leaving the West London Railway 24ch north of Kensington (Addison Road) station at Richmond Junction, the K&R curved westwards in a semi-circle to pass beneath the H&CR viaduct, then going due south, following the H&CR on its west side for 700yd, its tracks rising at 1 in 108 on a low viaduct to enter the station known as Hammersmith, Grove Road. Wooden platforms here, 15ft above the H&CR, were sheltered by generous canopies supported on decorated cast-iron columns. At street level on the east side was a plain two-storey station house with round-arched windows. Complying with the act, the LSWR provided a connecting footbridge to the H&CR terminus and the eastern entrance to this can still be seen at the time of writing. The junction, which ran from 15ch north of Grove Road into the H&CR, was not used until 1st June 1870 when GWR trains started to run approximately hourly from Bishop's Road, Paddington to Richmond. From a point on the London side of Grove Road the direction changed to west, on a 1m 23ch brick viaduct, 20ft high with arches of 20ft span. At its west end was an embankment and a station at the east side of Chiswick Common named Turnham Green. This had a street building of one storey in similar style to Grove Road, situated alongside Turnham Green Terrace north of the line. For the next 75ch the tracks were mostly in cutting at 1 in 120 down, turning due south into Brentford Road station (renamed Gunnersbury 1st November 1871) where the station house, almost a replica of that at Grove Road, stood in an approach from Chiswick High Road at the west side of the line. North of the bridge under this main road was Brentford Road Junction where the important connection from the N&SWJR came in.

After passing above the Hounslow loop, the K&R was carried over the Thames on a five-span wrought-iron lattice girder bridge, which although approved by the Thames Conservators as required by the 1864 act and decorated with gothic capitals on its red brick abutments, successfully disfigured the attractive riverside hamlet of Strand-on-the-Green. On the south side, the line ran on a 22ft embankment east of the Kew Bridge-Richmond Road, entering Kew Gardens station, which was required by the 1864 act. On the Up platform was a two-storey house in the standard style, and also, to cater for the visitors to the Gardens a quarter-mile to the west, a pavilion containing a licensed refreshment bar. For another 1m 16ch the tracks ran due south to Richmond Junction, whence there was another 14ch into the separate six-track three-platform terminal on the north side of the Windsor line. The N&SWJR maintained its own booking office and clerks there until 1917.

Although completed at the same time as the rest the 30ch Chiswick Curve, from 8ch south of Brentford Road station to Chiswick Junction 23ch east of Kew Bridge station, was not regularly used until 1st June 1870. From that date the LSWR Waterloo–Kensington–Richmond trains were diverted over it to terminate at Hounslow and the Richmond connection was covered by LSWR Ludgate Hill trains and the GWR Richmond service already noticed. This arrangement was short-lived. From 1st November 1870, the GWR trains were withdrawn, the LSWR resuming a Richmond–Kensington–Waterloo working, supplying Hounslow connections by means of a shuttle service to and from Brentford Road. The subsequent history of the Chiswick Curve has already been noted in the account of the Hounslow Loop.

Housing expansion at the London end of the line by the late 1870s justified two more stations. Shaftesbury Road, opened on 1st April 1873, 64ch east of Turnham Green, served a new district called Ravenscourt Park whose name it adopted from 1st March 1888. Shepherds Bush station (1st May 1874) was 35ch west of the junction with the West London Railway, conveniently placed near the south corner of Shepherds Bush Common. Covered steps led down to each platform from the west side of the bridge carrying Shepherds Bush Road over the line. The undistinguished platforms were mostly wooden.

Further westward expansion of London either side of the line occurred in the last quarter of the nineteenth century, most notably in the form of Britain's pioneer garden suburb, Bedford Park, just north of Turnham Green station, from 1875 to 1881. Although the house building which had virtually shut in the line as far as Turnham Green by 1901 owed something to the horse tramways along the roads west of Shepherds Bush and Hammersmith to Kew Bridge after 1882–3, it was primarily succoured by the increasing variety and intensity of the train services worked over the K&R.

Ravenscourt Park station, LSWR, looking west, c.1903. *Lens of Sutton*

Turnham Green station and signalbox, LSWR, looking north along Turnham Green Terrace (Chiswick Common at left), c.1905. The entrance to the station is on the far side of the bridge, on the right. *Commercial postcard*

By its act of 11th August 1875, the Metropolitan District Railway, which had reached Hammersmith Broadway in 1874, secured passenger and coaching traffic running powers over the LSWR line to Richmond New station in return for giving up 'other routes' to Richmond, Kew, Barnes and Putney, including its Earl's Court–Barnes extension, authorised in 1872. Under the same act the District constructed a 39.5ch link from its Hammersmith station to the K&R, climbing at 1 in 46 to what was to be known as Studland Road Junction. The engineering, which included the rebuilding of Hammersmith station, was substantial. On what was to prove an enduring service, District trains reached Richmond on 1st June 1877.

Traffic was good from the start, with 54,000 carried in the first month, but some distress and a few unpleasant accidents were caused by the 2ft or more difference between the levels of the District carriage floors and the low LSWR platforms. R. A. Williams has recorded in some detail the events of this period, when ladies were sometimes obliged to sit on the floor in order to negotiate their exit to the platform; tightly sheathed in whaleboned corsets, covered in voluminous petticoats, and blushing with middle-class propriety, their dilemma must have been considerable. These difficulties were overcome, and with the opening of a further westward extension of the District from Bedford Park Junction, Turnham Green, to Ealing Broadway on 1st July 1879, the MDR became the major user of an important part of the K&R, the running powers for its 'western branches' enshrined in the MDR Act of 1877.

The District's great rival, the Metropolitan, had also been exploiting the potential of this part of suburban west London, feeding from 5th July 1875 the H&CR Shepherds Bush station with a horse-bus service to and from Turnham Green (the buses ran to Hammersmith H&CR from 12th June 1876). Further efforts were stimulated by the District's success, and using the existing running powers, the Metropolitan started an hourly service between Moorgate Street and Richmond via Hammersmith Grove Road from 1st October 1877. The eastern terminus was soon after altered to Aldgate. These trains worked in the path of one of the 10-minute Aldgate–Hammersmith trains, the diversion to Grove Road making little difference to the Hammersmith passengers who could use the interconnecting footway between the two stations.

Another company to exploit the K&R was the Midland, which gained access via the Brent Junction (Cricklewood)–Acton Wells Junction line of 1st October 1868 and the N&SWJR. Running powers were exchanged with the LSWR, which acquired the useful ability to pick up freight at Brent Sidings. From 3rd August 1875, Midland passenger trains began to work between Moorgate Street (or Kentish Town or Childs Hill & Cricklewood) and Richmond via Acton. Few passengers were attracted to this circuitous service, which ceased on the evening of 31st January 1876, but the Midland tried again on 1st May 1878, offering an even more devious route from St Pancras to Earl's Court via Cricklewood and Acton, using a new 20ch curve from the South Acton–Gunnersbury line at Bollo Lane Junction to the K&R at Acton Lane Junction, 47ch west of Turnham Green station. This curve, authorised by the LSWR General Act of 24th July 1871, was primarily intended to carry coal trains feeding the many fireplaces of west London through the Midland's own coal yards at Kensington High Street (opened 4th March 1878) and West Kensington (25th March 1878); another yard at South Kensington, for which running powers were granted from Earl's Court, was never built. Midland coal trains were the only regular freight traffic ever worked over the K&R, which had no goods yards along its route. Attended with no more success than its earlier venture, the Midland's 'Outermost Circle' passenger service between St Pancras and Earl's Court ran for the last time on the evening of 30th September 1880. Still undeterred, the Midland made a further bid for west London traffic on 1st January 1894 when it extended its Childs Hill & Cricklewood–Stonebridge Park trains to Gunnersbury, some eleven workings each way daily. Defeat was acknowledged by final withdrawal of Midland local trains on the evening of 30th September 1902, but from 1st July 1905 to October 1908 the Midland ran passenger trains from Bradford (with through coaches from other northern and midland cities) to Portsmouth via Hendon and Richmond, while in the summer of 1911 there were also LNWR Manchester–Southampton trains running via Gunnersbury.

New Year's Day 1894 saw GWR rolling stock on the K&R again, that company starting a joint service with the Metropolitan between Aldgate and Richmond via Hammersmith, Grove Road. These trains (seven Metropolitan and ten GWR each way on weekdays and 13 GWR each way on Sundays in 1903), were worked at a loss, which was increased latterly by the competition of new electric tramways parallel to much of the route. The GWR was however reluctant to give up and suggested the service might be worked more economically by railmotors connecting with the H&CR trains. The through steam workings to Aldgate were therefore withdrawn in place of a GWR steam shuttle between Richmond and Notting Hill (now Ladbroke Grove) from 1st January 1907. This ran every half hour for most of the day, hourly on Sunday mornings and half hourly on Sunday afternoons. To facilitate terminal working, a loop and crossover were provided on the Up side east of Notting Hill station. The losses continued and traffic was discouraged by the necessity of changing trains, causing the Richmond service to be withdrawn after traffic on 31st December 1910 and leaving the Metropolitan to consider whether it should run electric trains to Richmond.

Since the electrification of the H&CR in 1906, the Metropolitan had toyed with the idea of using its existing running powers to work an electric service to Richmond via Grove Road and Turnham Green. Provision was accordingly inserted in the MDR Act of 1910 (mentioned below) to allow the Metropolitan and GWR to run over and use the northern pair of tracks between Hammersmith and Turnham Green which the LSWR was to electrify if the Metropolitan or GWR wished to run an electric service to Richmond. Furthermore it was provided that the LSWR would build northern platforms at the proposed Stamford Brook station if the GWR and Metropolitan required this. Negotiations between the Metropolitan Railway and the LSWR, begun in 1911, had reached an advanced stage by the middle of 1914, but in the previous year the London Electric Railway had obtained powers for a connection between the Piccadilly tube line and the LSWR at Hammersmith with the intention of running tube trains through to Richmond. Sir Albert Stanley (later Lord Ashfield) offered the Metropolitan financial compensation in return for giving up its running powers to Richmond and this was accepted. In November 1914 the 15ch curve between the Hammersmith & City line and the LSWR at Hammersmith was severed at its north end and the rails were completely removed in May 1916.

Few changes were made in the LSWR's own services. In June 1888 the Waterloo–Richmond journey was taking about 46 minutes on trains running approximately hourly between 08.45 and 22.15. Ludgate Hill–Richmond occupied 62 to 65 minutes, again about hourly, between 08.29 and 20.55. By June 1906 this had been little altered, but there were now departures from Waterloo up to 23.40 and an additional Clapham Junction–Kensington–Richmond service taking about 50 minutes and running roughly every hour between 05.40 and 23.17. Another new facility, lasting only from 1st October 1901 to a date in 1909, was a weekday service between Clapham Junction and Twickenham via Kensington, the Chiswick Curve and Hounslow. The LSWR was now very much the minor operator on its own line; in the early 1900s it was working about 28 passenger trains each way daily, compared with 61 by the other companies between Richmond and Gunnersbury (25 District, 17 Metropolitan/ GWR and 19 NLR). In the busiest 50 minutes of the morning peak at Richmond this combination produced trains of five different companies serving six different destinations (Broad Street, Waterloo, Ludgate Hill, Whitechapel, New Cross, and Aldgate). On Sundays from 1902 some of the LSWR Clapham Junction–Kensington (Addison Road) trains were extended to Richmond and Kingston, a practice which lasted until 30th June 1912. An unusual feature of the summers of 1907 and 1908 was the operation of a daily train each way between Richmond New station and Salisbury via Hammersmith Grove Road and Clapham Junction.

As can be judged from the proliferation of services, Gunnersbury was an important station for many years. It had five tracks serving two island platforms and an extra face on the west side, all converging to double track at the south side of the bridge under Chiswick High Road. South of the station, two pairs of tracks continued for about 400yd until the westernmost pair swung away to form the Chiswick Curve.

It was in these Edwardian years that the future of the K&R was shaped. One of the sections of the MDR Act 1902 authorised the MDR and LSWR to make agreements regarding electrification, but when serious planning began it was soon realised that there would have to be separate tracks for the intensive electric service proposed by the District over the 75ch between Hammersmith (Studland Road Junction) and Turnham Green, even then carrying 148 trains each way daily. These two extra tracks were originally included in the MDR bill for the 1903 session, but in January 1903 the MDR and LSWR reached an arrangement regarding terms and conditions for working the MDR 'western branches' traffic between Studland Road Junction and Turnham Green. Sealed in an agreement dated 23rd July, these provided for the District to withdraw the quadrupling proposal in return for a certain amount of freedom in regard to the number of trains that it could run over the LSWR lines, and the fixing of fares. This agreement, designed to last to the end of 1912, could only be in the nature of a stopgap. Electrification of the Hammersmith– Richmond track by the LSWR, with the MDR paying interest on the capital, was covered by another agreement dated 4th December 1903.

After the electrification of the District's Ealing, South Harrow and Hounslow services had been completed in 1905, the 75ch of common user LSWR track was carrying some 500 steam and electric trains daily. Determined to release itself from a situation which inhibited the development of its western electric services, the MDR sought and secured a new agreement with the LSWR, dated 11th April 1910 and confirmed by the MDR act of that year. This provided that the LSWR line between Acton Lane (west of Turnham Green) and Studland Road Junction, Hammersmith, would be widened on both sides to accommodate four tracks east of Turnham Green, the two tracks on the south side to be designated for exclusive MDR and Midland use in perpetuity. The MDR was to have the use and maintenance of the southern platforms at Turnham Green and Ravenscourt Park, and the access to them; the LSWR was to control the booking offices and entrances to these stations, but both the LSWR and the MDR would appoint station staff and ticket collectors for their portions. Even such small details as the right of the MDR 'to electrically illuminate' the southern platforms and direction signs and to receive revenue from all advertisements and automatic machines were recorded. Most of the new works were to be undertaken by the LSWR, which was to receive four per cent on its outlay as well as its annual rental for running rights.

Turnham Green as rebuilt in 1911, still very much in its original condition apart from lighting and seats; looking towards Acton Town, 14th July 1994. *Alan A Jackson*

The new tracks, all LSWR property apart from two short sections, but signalled throughout by the MDR, came into use on 3rd December 1911. In the alterations, Studland Road ceased to be a physical junction and at the Turnham Green end non-conflicting junctions had been made between the LSWR and the new lines. Turnham Green had a new box with two locking frames, one a Westinghouse, pneumatically operated, under a District man, the other manual with Sykes' lock-and-block, in charge of an LSWR signalman.

Turnham Green station was rebuilt with two steel-and-concrete island platforms. The old Bedford Park Junction between the LSWR and the MDR west of the station was moved 150yd west to Fishers Lane where a bridge allowed LSWR trains to and from Richmond to pass under the Ealing line to gain access to both sides of the new northern platforms. A second island platform had also to be built at Ravenscourt Park, where the northernmost faces were now used exclusively by LSWR steam trains, and a new street-level building was provided on the south side of the viaduct. On 1st February 1912 the District opened a new island platform for its own use on the leased tracks between Ravenscourt Park and Turnham Green. Called Stamford Brook, this had a small street building south of the line at the west side of Goldhawk Road, providing convenient interchange with the London United Tramway services. This station, to be maintained and staffed by the MDR, had been included in the MDR Act of 1910.

In December 1911 and January 1912, the MDR introduced a much improved service over the new lines, 198 trains daily to Ealing instead of 119, 144 to Hounslow instead of 121 and 96 to South Harrow instead of 68. The LSWR, facing increasing competition from alternative electric rail services, electric tramcars and motor buses, now began to prune its steam services over the K&R; by 1910 the weekday Waterloo service was down to 13 each way (ten on Sundays) and Ludgate Hill to ten (one of them to and from Hounslow). There was also one train daily between Richmond, Kensington and Clapham Junction and a few between Battersea and Richmond.

Shepherds Bush, LSWR, looking east in June 1916, just after closure.

Hammersmith Grove Road, LSWR, looking north in June 1916, just after closure. Posters advertise the new LSWR electric services and exhibit names of employees killed on active service.

Stopping at all stations, Kensington was reached in 21 minutes from Waterloo, Richmond in 46 minutes. In 1912 the service to and from Richmond via the K&R ran to Clapham Junction instead of Waterloo; by July 1914 there were only two trains each way between Ludgate Hill and Richmond, a year later only one. The year 1915 saw the Richmond–Kensington–Clapham Junction service severely slashed and converted to push-pull operation (two coach bogie sets, first- and third-class only). On Saturday evening 3rd June 1916 all LSWR service over the K&R ceased, and Shepherds Bush, Hammersmith Grove Road and the northern platforms at Turnham Green and Ravenscourt Park were all closed.

Cable laying on the LSWR at Turnham Green in 1911 in connection with the provision of extra tracks for the District Railway. *Lens of Sutton*

However, 1916 was not all gloom for the K&R. From 1st October the NLR was able to introduce its electric service between Broad Street and Richmond or Kew Bridge, using the same four rail system as the MDR. Richmond–Broad Street time was cut from 56 to 44 minutes but the basic service remained half-hourly on weekdays and Sundays with some extra peak workings. There were now District trains to Richmond every 15 minutes daily including Sundays, a frequency subsequently increased to ten minutes. From 1920 the NLR electrics gave summer Sunday pleasure-seekers a fifteen-minute service, an interval extended to weekdays in 1922 and to winter Sundays in 1925.

For some years the Underground companies had planned further services to Richmond over the K&R. In 1913 the Central London Railway Act had sanctioned a 2½-mile extension under the Goldhawk, Stamford Brook and Bath roads and Chiswick High Road, to surface at Gunnersbury station, where a junction was planned, and as already mentioned, a London Electric Railway Act of the same year authorised a connection between the Piccadilly tube and the LSWR line at Hammersmith, which would enable Piccadilly Line trains to run through to Richmond. No work had been started on either scheme before World War 1, but with the return of peace, a much less costly proposal was evolved for the Central London. Sanctioned by the Central London & Metropolitan District Companies' (Works) Act, 1920, this provided for a short south-westerly extension from Shepherds Bush, the tube tracks rising either side of the K&R near Richford Street (west of the bridge under the H&CR). From there it was intended to run tube trains over electrified tracks of the K&R to Turnham Green and on to Richmond, perhaps beyond (*The Railway Magazine* talked wildly of tube race specials from Liverpool Street to Ascot). This scheme also came to nothing, which was perhaps as well because by 1927 the SR, as successor to the LSWR, had been obliged to increase its rental charges to the District and the LMSR (successor to the North London) to meet the wear and tear caused by electric trains on the Richmond–South Acton section.

The Kensington & Richmond Railway   229

In 1926, after the K&R tracks between Kensington and Turnham Green had lain disused for ten years, the SR board authorised the recovery of permanent way, telegraph and signalling equipment and told the West London Railway that it did not propose to continue the £165 annual payment still being made for maintenance of Richmond Junction (Kensington) and its signalling. Despite speculation in *The Railway Magazine* that the War Office had vetoed any obstruction of the alignment between Kensington and Studland Road Junction in view of its possible strategic value for military traffic, the course of the disused line north and east of the H&CR Hammersmith car shed, seven acres in all, was offered on a 98-year lease in a *Times* advertisement of 13th December 1929.

But if the War Office was no longer interested, the Studland Road Junction–Turnham Green section was certainly of immense strategic importance to the Underground, now its only user apart from the two or three LMSR coal trains each day. In 1925 the 1913 proposals for the Piccadilly extension over it were revived, but now the intention was to project the tube trains to South Harrow and Hounslow rather than Richmond, using the former LSWR between Hammersmith and Turnham Green as a four-track electric railway and quadrupling the Underground's own surface tracks between Turnham Green and a point beyond Acton Town. A new agreement was reached between the MDR, the SR and the London Electric Railway. Dated 10th June 1926, this was scheduled to the London Electric & Metropolitan District Railway Companies' Act of 1926 authorising the new works. It allowed the Underground companies to take over and electrify the disused pair of tracks on the north side between Turnham Green and Hammersmith, together with the stations, reserving to the SR the right to run 'occasional and special' passenger and goods trains, but not so as to 'unreasonably disturb' the Underground traffic. Just where these SR trains were going to go is not clear, but it is certain that had railway enthusiasts been as well organised in the late 1920s as they are now, there would have been SR steam trains running to their occasional delight as far as the London end of Ravenscourt Park station. The London Electric as well as the MDR were by the agreement authorised to run over the Acton Lane–Richmond line, thus opening the way for Piccadilly Line services. The SR was to continue to maintain and operate Acton Lane Junction signal box, plus the earthworks and bridges on the Hammersmith–Turnham Green line. Increased rents were payable to the SR as residual freeholders in return for what was in effect a long lease to the Underground giving it almost complete control. The Metropolitan, GWR, SR, London Electric Railway and District Railway also made a new agreement (31st July 1926) for the by now almost academic purpose of securing the Metropolitan and GWR running powers over the newly abandoned layout and to preserve the route for a Metropolitan electric service to Richmond.

Once all four tracks were electrified and the remains of the LSWR replaced by Underground equipment, the running arrangements were altered to make the centre pair of tracks fast for Piccadilly trains working non-stop between Hammersmith and Acton Town, with the outer pair slow for the District trains, which called at all stations. These alterations, which included some rearrangement of the junctions west of Turnham Green and a new eastbound platform at Stamford Brook for District trains (in use from 5th June) came into full operation on 4th July 1932. After the new junctions had been made with the Piccadilly Line, the viaduct round to Grove Road was fully restored, in a fashion which would have made it possible to re-establish a connection, presumably against the remote possibility of a Metropolitan service to Richmond. Any speculation about the future of the Kensington end of the K&R was effectively dispelled in 1937 by the erection of a large block of flats across the alignment on the east side of the LSWR's Shepherds Bush station. Around 1950 an office block was built across the old line at Grove Road and in 1954 it was blocked by a new bus garage at the country end of Shepherds Bush station. Some relics survived for a long time. At the end of the 1950s it was still possible to see the canopies, platforms and stairs of the then isolated Shepherds Bush station; the lattice girder bridge over Hammersmith Grove Road, and the LSWR station building, latterly used as a banana warehouse, were not demolished until June 1954.

Richmond station frontage shortly after completion of the Southern Railway rebuilding in the Modern style, 1938. As well as the Southern services, this station was served by the Underground (District Line) trains using the former LSWR Kensington & Richmond line as far as a point east of Ravenscourt Park and the LMSR North London electric services to Broad Street, also using that line as far as a point just north of Gunnersbury. *BR(SR)*

Left: Richmond train entering Kew Gardens station, 29th June 1957. The LSWR style canopies are prominent, along with SR type electric lighting and the 1911 ferro-concrete footbridge.
Alan A Jackson

Right: Exterior of Kew Gardens station (Up side) with Underground and BR symbols prominent on the canopy, 12th October 1967 *BR(SR)*

Below: Gunnersbury in the early 1960s showing the by then disused eastern island platform and the temporary roofing erected after the cyclone damage of 1954. The original LSWR station house can be seen at the right by the side of the footbridge.

Long before that, the SR had rationalised its heritage at the western end of the K&R. Gunnersbury station was reduced to two tracks in July 1932, leaving only the western or Up island platform in use. At the end of the year the refreshment room was closed. With these alterations came the closure of the Chiswick Curve and a consequential reduction to double track south of the station. Gunnersbury's appearance was sadly mauled on 8th December 1954 when its platforms formed the focal point of a small cyclone. Some of the damage was patched up in rather ugly fashion, but in 1967, BR completed a new station in combination with an 18-storey office tower at the north end of the site. At the same time the LSWR station house was demolished and double deck car parks were made on the original station area either side of the new island platform. Further rebuilding took place in 1994 in conjunction with the British Standards Institution, which was to occupy a new headquarters building next to Gunnersbury station. This work provided a new entrance and cladding of the existing ticket office, walkway and footbridge to match the adjacent offices. Today the place is virtually unrecognisable to those who knew it in the 1950s and earlier. Only Kew Gardens survives more or less intact as an example of a K&R station; although Turnham Green's street level building is the original one, its interior has been completely altered by London Transport.

Recognising the *de facto* position which had existed since 1932, the British Transport Commission formally transferred the Turnham Green–Hammersmith section to London Transport from 23rd January 1950. No longer was it necessary to show on Southern maps what W. H. Bett so neatly described as a piece of line 'petering out rather indecisively and mysteriously in the Turnham Green neighbourhood'. BR completed the severance on 28th December 1972 by closing the connections with the SR Windsor lines at Richmond.

At Richmond in 1994 the busiest peak hour saw eight District Line trains leaving, all running via Embankment, these sharing tracks as far as Gunnersbury with four North London Lines trains to Willesden Junction, Stratford and North Woolwich. The maximum number of passengers hourly entering these trains at Richmond was 1,946; the largest hourly total entering Kew Gardens station for both services 947, and Gunnersbury 618. At Richmond, the terminal platforms numbered 3 to 7 were available for use by the two services.

CHAPTER THREE

NORTH WEST LONDON

LNWR steam railcar at Woodstock Road Halt, Hammersmith & Chiswick branch, at the inauguration of the railcar service in 1909, looking to Hammersmith & Chiswick station. *Lens of Sutton*

The Hammersmith & Chiswick Branch
(map page 165)

At the opening of the railway era Hammersmith was little more than an overgrown village extending from the crossroads at the present Broadway to touch the outskirts of the smaller communities of Chiswick and Turnham Green. Its houses, and its inns, which provided much of its living, bordered the main road to the west country but at the riverside were the genteel villas and summer retreats of affluent Londoners who gained access by the numerous river steamers. All around were the market gardens, orchards and small dairy farms which sustained west London. Like Hounslow and Brentford, Hammersmith had been left high and dry between the two main railway arteries west of London, and it arrived at the middle of the nineteenth century with nothing better in the way of railway accommodation than the moribund freight-only West London Railway on its eastern borders.

In its opening year (1853) the North & South Western Junction Railway (N&SWJR) obtained powers to build a 1¼-mile branch from Acton Gate House Junction to a station called Hammersmith situated in a market garden on the north side of the main road, almost exactly half-way between the centres of Hammersmith and Turnham Green, but within the parish of Chiswick and nearer to that village than the Chiswick station we have already noticed on the Hounslow loop. The exact object of this initiative is somewhat obscure, but as there were only two or three houses blocking further progress to the riverbank it may have been intended to make a riverside wharf when more capital could be arranged. At all events the financing of this little branch was very soon a matter of controversy, the shareholders forming an investigatory committee when they discovered that the directors had authorised construction outside the company's guaranteed capital. Not surprisingly, the committee found that the capital had been grossly misused and could see no sound reason for building the branch.

This assertion was certainly a reasonable one as far as passenger traffic was concerned, for the line offered only the most inconvenient and indirect access to any place of importance. A traveller proceeding from the centre of Hammersmith would first have to go for one mile west along the main road to reach his train; once seated in it he would find himself moving further west then north, east, south and west again before arriving at the somewhat inconvenient City terminus of Fenchurch Street. Should he choose the alternative of Waterloo via Kew, it would still be necessary for him to navigate almost a full circle before reaching the West End. No-one in his senses would do it; the horse buses and even the river steamers were far more direct.

The south-facing junction with the N&SWJR main line reflected an expectation that the LSWR might be persuaded to work the branch but that company, together with the other main line operators, showed an understandable reluctance to provide passenger services to this 'Hammersmith'. So although there were freight movements from 1st May 1857, it was not until 8th April 1858 (after the N&SWJR had in desperation considered using horses and then managed to acquire its first and only steam locomotive especially for the purpose) that passenger trains could begin to run. This little Sharp, Stewart 0–4–0 saddle tank, which spent its nights in a tiny shed at the north end of Hammersmith station, hauled a composite coach nine times a day (five on Sundays) to and from Acton Gate House Junction, where the NLR trains stopped to pick up the coach. In the Down direction, the North London enginemen very often did little more than slow down at the Junction whilst the guard detached the Hammersmith coach by snatching the coupling, an unofficial procedure which led to frequent derailments. With the delays at the Junction, the best time from Hammersmith to Fenchurch Street was 55 minutes.

From the Junction, which was 22yd north of a level-crossing over what is now Acton Lane the single line dropped at 1 in 69, curving in a semi-circle through open country, running east and then south into the terminus. No substantial works were necessary for there were no intermediate stations and only two small bridges over a stream, whilst at the terminus an existing two-storey house on the main road served as stationmaster's residence and offices. From the road, the intending passenger saw nothing of the railway, but walking through the front door, he bought his ticket in the hall, moving through the back door into the garden, where he boarded his train from the single long platform.

The somewhat risky and illegal goings-on at the Junction came to an end on 1st November 1865 when the branch train began to run through to Acton (now Acton Central) after reversal at Gate House. In the Down direction it was propelled from Acton to the Junction. A further change took place on 1st January 1880 with the opening on that day of South Acton station and a separate 19ch line alongside the N&SWJR main line between it and the Junction. This enabled the Hammersmith trains to terminate in a bay platform at South Acton in connection with the North London service. At this time the branch trains were normally composed of three four-wheeled oil-lit coaches hauled by inside-cylinder NLR 4–4–0T of the 105 class. Two of these locomotives were housed in a two-road shed near the Junction; later on, the branch locomotives were shedded at Willesden, but the building survived to be blown down in the great 'Gunnersbury Whirlwind' of 8th December 1954.

In 1897, whilst residing at 62, Bath Road, Bedford Park, the great French impressionist artist Camille Pissarro (1830–1903) immortalised this little line, which ran alongside the house. Notable amongst several of these oil paintings is *Train at Bedford Park*, now in the Ashmolean Museum, Oxford, which depicts locomotives shunting freight wagons between Bath Road and the bridge carrying the LSWR Kensington & Richmond line. The LNWR semaphore signals then in use are faithfully reproduced.

Hammersmith's rapid growth, from 25,000 in 1861 to 72,000 in 1881 was entirely related to its transformation into a London suburb following the establishment of direct links; the Hammersmith & City Railway in 1864 and the Metropolitan District Railway in 1874. A third link, less direct, was the LSWR Kensington & Richmond line (Chapter 2) of 1869, which crossed the little Hammersmith branch immediately north of its terminus. From the many hundreds of new houses which crept out towards its tracks in the late Victorian and Edwardian years, the branch gained little or no business. Any workers using it to reach 'Soapsud Island', the laundry colony at South Acton, were hardly enough to create rush periods.

Freight movement was rather more substantial, serving the coal yards at the terminus and near the Junction. At the latter there were also private coal sidings for Eastman's Dye and Cleaning Works, and for an asphalt plant. These demanded a daily train with an additional trip for the private sidings in the evening.

Soon after taking over management and operation of the NLR on 1st January 1909, the LNWR sought economies in working the branch by replacing the trains with a one-class 48-seat steam railmotor of the type designed by its chief mechanical engineer, G. Whale. *Little Jenny*, as it was named locally, ran half-hourly on weekdays from 4th January 1909. At Hammersmith & Chiswick terminus a raised wooden platform protected by a crude canopy was erected to facilitate access to and from the car, while to encourage maximum use of the more frequent service, simple timber halts were built at all points where the line crossed roads or paths. Named Rugby Road, Woodstock Road, and Bath Road, all three were opened on 8th April 1909. On the same day, the booking office at the terminus was closed and tickets were issued on the car by a conductor-guard whose ticket stock was limited, making

Looking north from the buffer stops at the Hammersmith & Chiswick terminus of the N&SWJR on 18th June 1955. A District Line train is seen on the former L&SWR Kensington & Richmond viaduct. *Alan A Jackson*

it necessary to re-book at South Acton for all destinations off the branch other than Kew Bridge, Acton or Willesden Junction.

On 9th March 1913 the steam car was replaced by LNWR petrol-electric railmotor No. 9, operating from Willesden North Shed, but traffic, which continued to be very light, had now been further damaged by the opening in 1912 of the adjacent Stamford Brook station on the Metropolitan District Railway, so that the line was a clear candidate for a wartime closure list, its last passenger workings being made on 31st December 1916.

With the end of passenger working, the terminus became a shop and dwelling house but the platform line and run-round loop remained intact until May 1958. A daily freight ran down the branch for another 40 years, but by the late 1950s the line was worked as an unstaffed siding subject to a 10mph speed limit, train crews operating the level-crossing gates at Bath Road. Although the timetable provided for a daily train, three visits a week usually sufficed for the traffic offering. Steam power in the form of Willesden-based ex-LNWR 0–8–0s and Fowler Class 4F 0–6–0s gave way to diesels around 1962. Before then, on Saturday 10th November 1956, the branch saw its most heavily-loaded passenger train ever in the form of a special working carrying over 200 railway enthusiasts. This train of four packed BR compartment coaches, hauled by BR Class 4MT 2–6–4T 80065, was not allowed to enter the platform road at Hammersmith & Chiswick, but came to a halt on a goods road just behind the still extant N&SWJR platform.

Beeching's accountants did not take long to discover this sleepy backwater. The last freight workings were made in 1965, the yard at the Junction closing on 3rd January and that at the terminus on 2nd May. For over ten years the large area of land around the branch terminus remained uncovered but eventually houses were erected and what is now Ravensmede Way covers the site.

Site of the Bath Road Halt, with Bath Road level crossing and signal box, looking north, 4th February 1956. The timber supports of the halt platform can be seen on the left. *Alan A Jackson*

The Ealing Branch (District Railway) (map page 260)

We have seen in the previous chapter how a short connection at Hammersmith allowed Metropolitan District Railway trains to run over the LSWR's Kensington and Richmond Railway to Richmond from 1st June 1877. In hot pursuit of further suburban business, the District obtained an act in 1877 for its own 2m 75ch line to run north west from Turnham Green through stations at Acton Green (later Chiswick Park), Mill Hill Park (now Acton Town) and Ealing Common to a terminus adjacent to the GWR station at Ealing. Construction under the engineer J. Wolfe Barry was set back three months by severe winter weather and the line was eventually opened on 1st July 1879.

Barry's stations at the places named were all in a similar somewhat plain brick style, with two storey houses for the stationmasters and single storey entrance buildings. Entrances and ground floor windows featured protruding brick surrounds. Before long the frontages were in several cases distorted by the conversion of some of the ground floor to shops and all were heavily disfigured with advertising hoardings with a jumble of messages mostly about the railway's services and fares. At Ealing, the terminus was on the east side of Haven Green, a little to the north of the GWR station. Here the road level building consisted of a pair of the standard two-storey houses linked by an entrance frontage with two tall arch-roofed doorways. Behind, at a lower level, was a small train shed with two platforms, the southernmost with a face each side at the outer end. A major rebuilding was undertaken in 1911–13, when H. W. Ford, the District's architect, provided a two-storey classical frontage in Portland stone with a wide central entrance flanked with small shops. There was a substantial steel and glass canopy, initially adorned with a clock. A fourth platform face added at this time on the north side was later shortened to accommodate an uncoupled two-car set or locomotives. There was also a bay on the south side from about 1905.

Ford also supplied the design for the 1910 reconstruction of Mill Hill Park where the new building, placed over the line, consisted of a single storey hipped-roof stone-frontaged block dominated by an arched central entrance. Extra income from retail lettings was now much to the fore and provision was made for a small shop each side of the doorway. At the same time the double line and side platforms were replaced by three tracks serving two islands. This allowed trains to be run into the centre reversible local road (with a platform face either side) to await the arrival of eastbound and westbound services on the outer faces. A new flyover bridge west of the station allowed westbound Ealing and Hounslow trains to leave at the same time. From 1st March 1910, with these new works largely completed, the station was renamed Acton Town.

Ealing's 1879 railway brought what was soon to be dubbed 'The Queen of the Western Suburbs' within 48 minutes of the City of London (Mansion House), with two trains an hour provided all day, four an hour in the peaks. This District Railway facility was very soon making a substantial impact on the area's growth and prosperity. Between 1880 and 1914 residential streets spread out south and north of the GWR main line, whilst to the east, Ealing had by the 1910s coalesced with neighbouring Acton. With a constantly growing population (over 30,000 by the early 1890s) Ealing became the first municipal borough in Middlesex in 1901.

Following the excursion into suburban areas ripe for steady development, not least Ealing, the aggregate total of ordinary and season ticket journeys on the District

The original building of Mill Hall Park station (now Acton Town), on the east side of the railway, in 1908. The overline road bridge is at the extreme right of the picture.
London Transport Museum

increased from 30.26 million in 1877 to 34.1 million in 1882. This did not however bring any great financial rewards. Although the company was able to pay its first dividend on ordinary shares in 1878 and reach the dizzy height of 1½ per cent on ordinaries in 1880, this period of prosperity soon fizzled out.

Whilst in the full flush of its expansionist mode, the District sought powers to reach Uxbridge, depositing bills in 1879 and again in 1880, but both were thrown out after fierce GWR opposition. As a sop, the GWR conceded running powers to Windsor over the junction authorised in the MDR's Ealing extension legislation of 1877. This venture was not successful. After the junction east of Ealing station had been made in 1883 a District service of 11 trains a day each way on weekdays and nine on Sundays, using its own locomotives and rolling stock, was begun between Mansion House and Windsor on 1st March 1883. It attracted little business and from 1st October 1884 was reduced to four each way daily, ceasing altogether on 30th September 1885. The reactions of the few passengers originating in the still sparsely populated area west of Ealing to the harshness of the ride in the little four-wheeled carriages of the day no doubt contributed to this failure. Any subsequent resumption was prevented when a rebuilding of the GWR station at Ealing in 1898–99 extinguished the connecting line.

The opening of the London United electric tramway from Shepherds Bush through Ealing to Southall on 10th July 1901 and the electrification of the District Railway between Ealing and Whitechapel from 1st July 1905 further lubricated the residential growth and general prosperity of the area. Although comparisons of the census figures are misleading because of boundary changes it is clear there was a very substantial increase in population in the Ealing area between 1901 and 1911. In 1913 Ealing Broadway was offering 11–12 District trains an hour at peak periods and eight an hour (at six-ten minute intervals) for most of the remainder of the day. To attract the lucrative first class season ticket traffic, the so-called *Ealing Express* had been introduced. Leaving Ealing Broadway at 09.10 (there was a return working in the late afternoon) this passed all nine stations between Ealing Common and Sloane Square exclusive. There were other less ambitious 'non-stops' in the middle of the day. By 1921 the evening *Ealing Express* was timed to leave Mansion House at 17.07, taking 30 minutes to reach Ealing Broadway (it ran non-stop Sloane Square to Acton Town). Such was its popularity that it was then lengthened from six to eight cars.

To accommodate the Ealing & Shepherds Bush Railway, carrying Central London Railway tube trains to Ealing Broadway from 3rd August 1920, new platforms were inserted that year between the GWR and District stations. At this time a wide covered footbridge was erected to link all platforms in the three Ealing Broadway stations; the train shed of the 1879 District terminus was retained and it still survives at the time of writing, substantially unaltered. A new signalbox for the District and Central Lines was opened on the north side of the terminal tracks on 30th September 1952. In the following decade a further major reconstruction at Ealing Broadway put Ford's 1911–13 station building out of railway use. Passengers for both BR and London Transport trains were to use a single entrance and a new ticket hall with a glass-fronted ticket office situated just below street level. This was built on a concrete raft over the former GWR platforms. Above it rose a nine-storey office block with a shopping parade opening to the street. A new covered footway linked all platforms. Although the new entrance and ticket hall were opened on 5th December 1965 and the District line entrance and ticket office closed on 13th November 1966, all the new work was not completed until the end of 1968. The LT platforms were numbered in with the rest of the station from 1st July 1967, platforms 1, 2 and 3 becoming 7–9.

Ealing Common station was handsomely reconstructed in the Charles Holden 'Morden Extension' Portland stone-clad style in 1931. Its heptagonal ticket hall, under a stubby tower, opened for public use on 1st March, was decorated by the interior designer Basil Ionides in grey, green and cream, the floor inlaid with a black star motif. The rebuilt platforms included concrete canopies with clerestory illumination, the first example of this in a Holden station.

The rearrangement of tracks west of Hammersmith mentioned earlier required total reprovision of Chiswick Park station, undertaken in 1931–33. It was a difficult site and one objective was to command attention from the High Street, a short distance to the south. The new station, with four tracks but side platforms serving only the District line trains, was completed in 1933. Design here was in the hands of S. A. Heaps, the Underground's staff architect, in consultation with Charles Holden, whose 'family style' for the Underground's new 1930s stations was adopted. The street level building, on the south side of the viaduct, was dominated by a lofty and spacious semi circular ticket hall in hand-made, sand-faced, multi-red bricks. This had a flat concrete lid and very large windows, the brickwork left exposed inside. At the west side, a tower in the same bricks carried the Underground bullseye symbol and the station name. Below were three wide entrance openings and several shops set in a lengthy flat-roofed frontage. More sand-faced multi-reds backed the platforms on the viaduct and behind this, the canopies were curved and cantilevered, their concrete showing the board marks of the shuttering. As elsewhere, works in connection with the Underground Ticketing System of the late 1980s seriously eroded the careful architecture of the entrance hall.

Acton Town underwent its second rebuilding in 1932–33, with Heaps again working to Holden's new 'brick box and concrete lid' style. Here Holden's sketches had suggested a rectangular entrance hall with tall narrow windows facing the street and a long low flat-roofed entrance and shop line at road level very similar to that at Chiswick Park, extended to provide an auxiliary entrance from Bollo Lane on the east side. The entrance hall, lined with quarry tiles. led out to footbridges and gangways designed to separate inward and outward passenger flows. The platforms and tracks were also rearranged and rebuilt to accommodate the contemporary quadrupling, the new layout becoming, east to west: South Acton terminal road; District eastbound; Piccadilly line eastbound; Piccadilly westbound; District westbound (i.e. five platform faces, with two islands, and a side platform on the east).

A study of the catchment area of the Ealing extension suggests that until the 1920s and 1930s, most of its traffic originated at Ealing and to a lesser extent at Chiswick Park. The residential development around the latter was mostly in place by the time the station opened, notably the estate immediately to the north, whose name was assumed by the station from February 1887. Curiously the place is not in Chiswick at all, but the developers wanted a suitable cachet. Beyond here, the market gardens west of the line defied the builders for many years. Then in 1921 part of the site was covered by the Chiswick Works of the London General Omnibus Company and from 1922 the rest, on the north side of the N&SWJR, by its cousin, the Underground Company's Acton Works, provided to centralise the overhaul of all the undertaking's trains.

Mill Hill Park was another residential estate giving its name to a station. This was laid out north east of the railway, on the east side of Gunnersbury Lane, in 1877–80 but was not filled up until the early years of the twentieth century. West of the line here, the more compact housing of the Gunnersbury Lodge Estate and Gunnersbury Park Gardens, respectively north and south of Gunnersbury Lane, both date from 1925–27 and other housing between Gunnersbury Avenue and the railway up to Ealing Common is of similar date. What is now Acton Town station did however benefit from the start from its reasonably close proximity (just over a quarter of a mile) to the town centre of Acton, a circumstance which justified the later renaming.

The Ealing Common works and car sheds of the District Railway, on the east side of the line just south of the station, were erected in 1904–05 for the electrification. They occupied 25 acres bought from Leopold de Rothschild of Gunnersbury Park. Most of the housing east of Ealing Common station was built in the 1900s and early 1910s but that to the north west, towards Ealing itself, appeared in the 1880s and 1890s.

In the Appendices to the 1905 Report of the Royal Commission on London Traffic (vol III, p.547) we find a carefully compiled record of a typical commuter journey via Ealing Common station in 1904, just before electrification. Walking from the house to the tram stop took 7½ minutes (4mph), the electric tram to Ealing Common one mile in 7½ minutes (8 mph) at a fare of 1d, Ealing Common to Mansion House by train, (3½d workmen's fare), 9½ miles in 45minutes (12.6mph), and walking at the London end another 7½ minutes, a total of 11.5 miles in 67½ minutes (10.25 mph) at a cost of 4½ old pennies. In terms of purchasing power, the total fare may be illustrated as the cost in 1904 of five copies of *The Daily Mail*, or nine pounds of potatoes, or two small (2lb) loaves of bread. Taking into account the five minutes expended in waiting for tram and train, the average speed was 9.25 mph. A year later, after electrification, the running time on the railway would have been reduced to 35–36 minutes, even less after the subsequent introduction of the 'non-stop' working mentioned earlier. In 1996 the District Line Journey took 33 minutes, at a single fare of £1.80. Ealing's terminal platforms, still not entirely without their Victorian aura, remain well and efficiently served by the District Railway's successors.

South Acton Branch (District Railway) (map page 260)

Whilst its Turnham Green to Ealing extension was under construction in 1878, the District Railway obtained powers to build a spur from it (the Acton Loop Line) so that trains could run from the Willesden direction off the N&SWJR towards Ealing. A similar curve in the opposite direction (Bollo Lane Junction to Acton Lane Junction) was used from March 1878 by Midland Railway coal trains running to yards on the District. Although the N&SWJR had opened a station to serve the newly developing district of South Acton on 1st January 1880, the District was in no hurry to build a line whose purpose was more closely connected with the development of the western part of its system than short-distance traffic within Acton. This delay entailed a considerable amount of parliamentary cost in obtaining legislation for extension of time and revival of powers; although Ordnance Survey maps of the early 1890s reveal that some earthworks had been started near Bollo Lane, a serious beginning with the Acton Loop Line had to wait until 1898. Construction was then placed in the hands of C. J. Wills & Son, contractors for the Ealing & South Harrow Railway, the incentive for completing the link being its value in transporting construction materials to the E&SHR works. One of these trains first passed over the completed line on 15th May 1899.

It seems likely that the District saw the main use of the line as providing access to coal yards it might eventually persuade the northern companies to provide free at its western suburban stations, but this came to nothing and by 1902 it had been decided to electrify it as a projection of the E&SHR, with a station alongside the N&SWJR at South Acton for easy interchange with the NLR services to Richmond and Broad Street. This proposal was also dropped and once again the Acton Loop Line was left; although the E&SHR was opened on 23rd June 1903, no passenger trains appeared on the Loop until 13th June 1905 when a South Acton–Hounslow Barracks electric service was started, using the American-inspired 'A' stock. London passengers changed into steam trains at Mill Hill Park (now Acton Town) until the inner part of the District Railway was electrified on 1st July 1905. Connections at South Acton were indifferent; for example, in 1909, trains arrived from Hounslow at 21 and 51 minutes past each hour, and trains for Willesden and Broad Street left at 28 and 58 minutes, but passengers arriving in NLR Down trains at nine and 39 minutes past waited 13 minutes at South Acton before the District train left.

Until electric working started, the Acton Loop Line had only a single track, although the works provided for double. At the South Acton end, the junction was controlled by an N&SWJR box and working was by pilotman. When the District doubled the line early in 1905 a crossover was laid on Palmerston Road bridge and a District signalbox was opened on the new South Acton platform.

The Loop left the London end of Mill Hill Park station at South Junction, running parallel to the main line on the east side before curving round to cross Bollo Lane on a plate girder bridge and run alongside the N&SWJR on embankment into South Acton station. Here the District provided a platform of six car length and the rudimentary corrugated iron hut it considered adequate for its less important western suburban stations. This building backed on to the N&SWJR Up side at slightly higher level, steps leading the passenger to a small entrance hall which contained the District ticket office and doorways to the street and the N&SWJR platform. After a few years, ticket issue was more economically carried out from the signalbox on the platform above.

By the time the District passenger service started, the area around South Acton station was fairly well built-up, with small houses inhabited by the upper ranks of the working class, though a few larger villas and nursery gardens survived from the previous development phase. In the 1880s and 1890s, Acton had spread south towards Bollo Lane and contemporaneously the separate suburb of Acton Green had swamped the area between South Acton and Turnham Green stations. There were also some laundries and drying grounds ('Soapsud Island') serving the middle-class families of Kensington.

Both the LNWR and the Midland had obtained running powers over the Acton Loop Line, the former to Ealing Common Junction, the latter to Mill Hill Park only. Working timetables showed early-morning paths 'as required' for stores or ballast trains, but this seems to have been a survival from the construction of the E&SHR; freight traffic was virtually non-existent. All non-passenger working ceased in 1914, District Junction box closing in the following year, when the points into the N&SWJR were clipped out of use. Everything was left intact for possible use at short notice until about 1930, when the points were taken out; the box was demolished in 1934.

By 1913 the through workings between South Acton and Hounslow had been replaced by a 20-minute shuttle service working between 05.55 and 00.40. Through journeys were later restored and in 1922 there was a 15-minute service (30 minutes on Sundays), most trains running to and from South Harrow (some Uxbridge) and, on weekdays, about half a dozen over the Hounslow line. Traffic at South Acton, much of it interchanging with North London trains, reached 349,000 a year in the mid-1920s, well over twice that of some stations on the Ealing & South Harrow.

In conjunction with the projection of Piccadilly Line tube trains over the western section of the District Railway, the layout at Acton Town was considerably altered and the station completely rebuilt. A short platform (No. 5) was specially provided on the east side for the South Acton trains. The Acton Loop Line was now reduced to single track with 'one train on line' working and when this came into effect in February 1932, the District box at South Acton station was closed and demolished. For training purposes some Piccadilly Line tube trains were operated between South Harrow and Acton Town and between South Acton and the Hounslow branch, but tube car operation lasted only from 8th to 14th February 1932, when double-line working ceased. From the next day the Loop was operated by a shuttle service using either a 'B' stock motor car (No. 37, which had been specially converted to work as a double-ended unit) or a two-car unit of 'B' stock motor plus control-trailer. The latter was observed soon after the start of the new service bearing at the respective ends the absurd legends ACTON TOWN NON STOP and SOUTH ACTON ALL STATIONS.

Tunnel-type telephone wires, allowing the driver to cut off traction current without leaving his cab, were erected alongside the line on concrete posts during 1938. This paved the way for one-man operation. Two 'G' stock driving motors (4167 and 4176) were accordingly modified to operate as double-ended units; each had air doors worked from the driving cabs, two 240hp motors and 44 seats. This single-car working, known to the staff as 'the Pony', ran between 06.00 and around midnight. In the 1950s the frequency was about every ten minutes (every seven minutes in peak hours) and despite popular belief that departures from Acton Town were influenced by the staff's tea-making activities (there and back whilst the kettle boils), a timetable was observed.

District Line single car train from Acton Town arriving at South Acton station 21st February 1959. It will take up a return load of only two adults and three children. The North London line platforms, at a slightly lower level, appear behind the corrugated iron architecture of the District Railway. *Alan A Jackson*

Those who used the interchange facility at South Acton increasingly favoured bus or private car, and in the 1950s rarely were more than half a dozen passengers seen on the train. Sunday working ceased after 8th June 1958 and in a search for system-wide economies, London Transport proposed complete closure. It was suggested that connections between the North London trains and Piccadilly/District services might be made by taking a bus between Acton Town station and Acton, where Acton Central station could be reached by walking 330 yards. Those unfortunates who lived near South Acton station, where some new flats had been built and more were planned, had to walk the equivalent of the full length of the Acton Loop Line to reach a bus road. In November 1958 the London Transport Users' Consultative Committee opposed the closure, suggesting weighted fares as an alternative, but were overruled by the central committee. The last car ran at midnight on Saturday 28th February 1959.

London Transport customarily wastes little time in extinguishing rail facilities after closure, and South Acton was no exception. The crossover connecting the branch to the eastbound fast road south of Acton Town station was taken out of commission from 19th March 1959 and by 13th May all track on the Loop Line had gone. Demolition of South Acton LT station followed soon after. At the end of 1963 the embankment between Bollo Lane and South Acton was levelled preparatory to the erection of blocks of council flats. The bridge over Bollo Lane was dismantled in the following January, during which process it collapsed into the road, blocking it for several days while the wreckage was cut-up where it lay. At South Acton station about the same time a recreation ground was extended over the site of the line so that today there is virtually no trace of it beyond Bollo Lane and very little elsewhere. Had the North London line been incorporated into the London Transport system, it is conceivable the Loop might have survived, as it would have offered useful cross-town routes, including a less-congested connection between Heathrow Central and the northern main line termini.

The Ealing & Shepherds Bush Railway (map page 260)

Not long after its opening in 1864, the Hammersmith & City Railway, a joint enterprise of Metropolitan and Great Western, providing through trains to the heart of the City, was beginning to encourage residential spread west of Notting Hill. December 1868 saw the opening of Latimer Road station on the western edge of the smart new district of North Kensington, whilst still further west, Hammersmith was growing northwards, the pace of building hampered only by the absence of railway facilities.

To remedy this omission, a Latimer Road & Acton Railway was promoted in 1881 with a capital of £180,000. A branch from the H&CR, it was to follow a route somewhat south of the present line of the A40(M) motorway, to join the GWR near Friar's Place Green, east of that company's Acton station, 2m 15ch in all. Serving north Hammersmith and east Acton, it could hope for a steady growth in commuter traffic similar to that experienced by the H&CR; the whole area traversed lay ripe to receive the housebuilders.

Authorised in 1882 to a nominally independent company, the Latimer Road & Acton sought a working agreement with the Metropolitan and the GWR, but its potential was somewhat damaged when on grounds of alleged traffic congestion, the H&CR allowed it only an interchange platform where the two lines came together at the H&CR bridge over Wood Lane. To make matters worse, the GWR insisted on a separate station at Acton.

Enough cash was raised or promised to permit a start on construction in 1883 at the Acton end. A house standing on the site of the proposed Acton station near Friar's Place was demolished and an iron bridge erected over the N&SWJR near the present motorway bridge. This activity ceased when the money ran out; neither the GWR nor the Metropolitan were prepared to come to the rescue, and desperately seeking other suitors, the promoters were to submit bills for the 1887 session which provided for an independent terminus at Notting Hill Gate near the Metropolitan station and a link with the District between West Kensington and Earl's Court. At the Acton end, an extension towards Gunnersbury was mooted. None of this was authorised and a Notting Hill & Acton Railway Bill of 1888 for a similar route was also lost.

Much effort and money was spent on legislation after this. No less than four acts, mainly for extensions of time, were obtained between 1885 and 1893. An unsuccessful bill of 1890 sought a curve at Shepherds Bush which would have allowed direct running from Hammersmith H&CR on to the Latimer Road and Acton, though it is difficult to appreciate what the value of this might have been. Agreement was eventually reached with the GWR and Metropolitan for joint working, and this was confirmed in yet another act (1895). Despite this, capital was shy, and the veil was drawn by an abandonment act of 1900. Only the lawyers, parliamentary agents and engineers had profited.

Much the same route was revived by the Ealing & Shepherds Bush Railway, authorised to the GWR in 1905. This was primarily intended to give that company a suburban services terminus north of Shepherds Bush Common against the west side of the Central London Railway tube terminus, to which there would be subway connection. A junction with the West London Railway north of Uxbridge Road station was also proposed, mainly for freight purposes.

The Ealing & Shepherds Bush was to serve north Hammersmith and east Acton in much the same way as the Latimer Road & Acton would have done, but its route passed a little further north and its access to the GWR main line was more devious because it was arranged to touch the new Wycombe main line. In 1911 the Central London Railway got powers for a half-mile connection between its Wood Lane terminus (near White City) and the Ealing & Shepherds Bush, over which its tube trains were to run to Ealing GWR. The much improved facility which this scheme offered caused the GWR to abandon its proposed suburban lines terminus at Shepherds Bush.

In a 1912 bill, the Metropolitan tried to get into the game, seeking powers to make a connection with the Ealing & Shepherds Bush between Wood Lane and Latimer Road. This failed because both the GWR and the Central London opposed through running by the Metropolitan over the Ealing & Shepherds Bush, protesting that it would obstruct the CLR service. The District added its weight, objecting to the Ealing competition. The Metropolitan finally gave up its ambitions in this area in return for a GWR agreement to a 1912 scheme for capital improvements on the Hammersmith & City Railway.

Construction of the double-track Ealing & Shepherds Bush was started by the GWR in 1912 but work was delayed by World War I and it was not possible to open it until 16th April 1917, when freight trains passed over it to and from the West London Railway at Viaduct Junction. No regular passenger working started until

North Acton, GWR, looking to London, c. 1938; the Central Line (Ealing & Shepherds Bush Railway) platforms are just off the picture on the right.

3rd August 1920 when the GWR received the boon of a through tube service between its Ealing station, the West End and the City. The tube trains called at the new station of East Acton, serving an LCC housing estate which had been started in 1912. Two other intermediate stations on the Ealing & Shepherds Bush, West Acton and North Acton, were added on 5th November 1923. All three were cheaply built and without architectural distinction; West Acton even had the standard GWR halt 'pagoda' shelters.

Motor roads called Westway and Western Avenue were carved through the area in 1922 and 1924, while during the 1920s most of the district between the GWR main line at Acton and Wood Lane was covered with LCC and Hammersmith Borough Council housing, this over 40 years after the promoters of the Latimer Road & Acton had hoped for such development. During 1937 the GWR quadrupled the section between Wood Lane and North Acton to separate tube and freight movements in anticipation of extension of Central Line tube service alongside the Wycombe line as far as Denham. GWR trains ceased to use the electric lines from 19th June 1938. Until that year they had carried one regular GWR passenger service, workmen's trains between Greenford and Kensington (Addison Road), started in 1922 and extended to Clapham Junction in 1933. These trains came very close to the site of the inner end of the Latimer Road & Acton as they passed on and off the West London line at Viaduct Junction.

The four tracks of the Ealing & Shepherds Bush Railway near Wood Lane, looking west, 6th April 1957. Wood Lane Jc signal box is beyond the concrete footbridge and the freight lines to Viaduct Jc with the West London Railway are seen between the Central Line tracks and Du Cane Road (right). An eastbound Central Line train has just passed through the flyunder which was built at this point to change the direction of running between the two tube lines. *Alan A Jackson*

The Ealing & Greenford Line (map page 260)

When the GWR secured powers in 1897 for the section of its direct Birmingham line from Old Oak Common West (Acton) to a junction with its Maidenhead-Princes Risborough line at High Wycombe, the legislation included a two mile 24.55ch double-track line between the new main line at Greenford and Brunel's London & Bristol at West Ealing. To this the GWR Act of 1903 added an eastern curve at Greenford (26.4ch) and a western one at the southern end (36.6ch); these were something of an afterthought and parliamentary sanction followed their construction.

The initial reason for linking the two main lines at a point so close to their junction at the London end was principally to allow freight trains to run off the new High Wycombe direct line through Ealing Broadway on to the Midland, LNWR and North London lines via Acton Wells Junction and also to provide for expresses on the new line to call at Ealing Broadway. But in practice it became very much a local line, hence its inclusion here. Indeed from the start the possibility of developing suburban traffic was not overlooked; the additional curves authorised in 1903 were largely designed for this purpose.

From its junctions with the old Bristol main line the Greenford line ran in a cutting through the higher ground north of Ealing, emerging at Castle Bar Park to cross the claylands of the Brent Valley on a high embankment, passing over the Ruislip Road and the Brent on a 320ft brick arch viaduct. It continued northwards above ground level as far as South Junction, where the Greenford East and West Loops diverged. At the time of construction, most of the area traversed was open country. Only at the southern end did built-up London touch the new railway. Greenford, then a small crossroads settlement, was away to the west on the country bank of the River Brent, near the point where the river turned south, and almost a mile from the railway. Its new station, sited at the junction between the West Loop and the new main line, was about halfway between Greenford village and the then separate community of Greenford Green to the north.

By the beginning of 1903 work on the new railways was sufficiently advanced to permit operation of trains between Old Oak Common and Ealing or Hanwell via the north-south connecting line. Some urgency was evident as the Royal Agricultural Society had prepared 100 acres of show grounds at Park Royal (so named by Edward VII when he performed an opening ceremony on 25th May 1903) and to serve them the GWR had erected a substantial station with long stone platforms on the new main line about halfway between the present North Acton and Hanger Lane stations. Almost immediately after the royal visit, freight trains began moving in materials and equipment for the first Show, some coming in via the new north-south link. A service of passenger trains, 14 each way daily, weekdays, was started on 15th June 1903 between Paddington, Westbourne Park, Park Royal, the Greenford East Loop and Ealing Broadway. During the period of the Agricultural Show (23rd – 27th June) this was augmented to provide a 20-minute service. Over those five days, some passenger trains were also worked between Southall and Park Royal via the Hanwell curve and the Greenford East curve. Not surprisingly in view of the lack of development in the Brent Valley, passenger traffic fell sharply once the Show-ground closed and all these trains were withdrawn on 4th July 1903.

Indeed the Show itself was something of a flop, despite the combined efforts of the GWR, the LNWR and the District Railway to serve the new grounds with dedicated stations. Nor was the event any more of a success in 1904 and 1905, a sequence which caused the Royal Agricultural Society to give up the site in despair. Possibly the farmers and traders felt ill at ease in a place which was neither town nor country and no doubt the limited interest of Londoners in matters agricultural was not sufficient to bring them out in any quantity for what was for many a difficult journey across the city. In an attempt to rescue something from its large investment in Park Royal, the GWR made some use of the sidings as a freight depot and also enticed Queens Park Rangers FC to play in the showground from August 1904. When this move proved unpopular with the football fraternity, the GWR built QPR a new ground on railway land immediately north of the station, leasing it to the club on favourable terms. This venture proved moderately successful, producing a steady flow of winter Saturdays football traffic until 1915, when the whole area north of the station was taken over for war purposes.

The combined effects of very heavy rain and the pounding of freight trains for the 1903 Show wrought such havoc with the earthworks of the newly-built railway that it was closed between Old Oak, Park Royal and West Ealing from 10th August 1903 to allow an army of over 500 men to rebuild the works and construct new halts. After passenger trains returned on 1st May 1904 a complex pattern of workings developed, to be much varied from time to time. The intricacies so fascinated the Rev. W. J. Scott that he contributed an article on the subject to the 1908 *Great Western Railway Magazine* which ran to no less than four instalments.

The first service (1st May 1904) operated between Westbourne Park, Park Royal and Southall, calling at new halts erected at North Acton (adjacent to the present LT station), Twyford Abbey (by the Hanger Lane bridge), Perivale (on the west side of the Horsenden Lane bridge), and Castle Bar Park for Greenford (1m 1ch north of West Ealing at the point of transition from embankment to cutting). This last halt could only be reached by a fieldpath but it served the 17-acre GWR sports ground east of the railway, and on the west side, the Central London and West London Schools for Pauper Children, where Charlie Chaplin spent some time as a pupil. All four halts had short timber platforms with centrally sited corrugated-iron 'pagoda' waiting huts. With no other amenities beyond oil lamps and name boards, and without staff, they set a pattern for the many which were to follow all over the GWR system. They were expressly designed to accommodate the 52-seater steam railcars which the company had chosen to use in the as yet undeveloped districts west of London and on its rural branch lines.

The initial train service was worked by one such car ('rail motor-car' in GWR parlance), based at Southall shed and operating about 14 trips daily (about every 70 minutes) from the 07.00 ex-Southall to the 22.42 ex-Westbourne Park. Although built, the eastern curve at West Ealing was for some reason not available for use, hence the choice of Southall as the outer terminus. At the London end, Westbourne Park was the starting point because Paddington did not have the capacity to take the railcars, though they did start and finish there on Sundays, when there were nine trips each way.

In a commendable effort to stimulate traffic, leaflets about this service were distributed to London property auctioneers for onward transmission to developers and landowners. A second railcar, which arrived on 1st July 1904, was put to work to run ten times daily each way (roughly hourly) between Park Royal and Acton via Castle Bar Park. After Greenford station had opened for regular traffic on 1st

October 1904, most of the railcar trips worked in and out of there using the Greenford West Loop, and some of the Acton journeys were extended from the same date via Acton Wells Junction to Willesden Junction High Level. A further halt was opened on 1st March 1905 at Drayton Green, 57ch south of Castle Bar Park and just north of the triangular junction. Close to existing housing in north east Hanwell and the western edge of West Ealing, this attracted a trickle of residential traffic. Later the area was enlivened by the construction of an engineer's depot inside the triangle and a four-road coal yard east of the halt to serve the domestic needs of West Ealing and north Hanwell.

Changes made to the railcar services on 10th October 1905 saw the end of the lightly-patronised Southall via Castle Bar trips apart from a few Sunday workings this way between Paddington and Southall. The basic service now ran Westbourne Park–Park Royal–Greenford–Castle Bar Park–Acton–Willesden Junction. 1906 saw further alterations, set out in great detail by Scott, but which it would be tedious to relate here.

With the opening of the Uxbridge (High Street) branch on 1st May 1907 the service was changed again, eventually settling down to run between Denham (or Gerrards Cross from July 1909) and West Ealing via Uxbridge (High Street), Denham (again) and Greenford. The Westbourne Park–Park Royal–Castle Bar Park–Acton–Willesden Junction trains were cut back to Acton GWR during a coal strike in March 1912 and never again ventured beyond that point.

Twyford Abbey Halt closed completely from 1st May 1911, giving way to a new halt called Brentham & North Ealing a short distance further west, better placed to serve the 1901–14 housing estate south of the line known as Brentham or West London Garden Village. Also, immediately west of the junction between the two main lines, at Old Oak Lane, a halt of that name, with full length platforms came into use on 1st October 1906 mainly for the convenience of railway staff at the adjacent engine and carriage depots.

Loadings in these early years did not tax the limited capacity of the steam railcars. On the first day, 1st May 1904, a fine Sunday, about 400 tickets were sold on the Westbourne Park–Southall service, a figure only subsequently approached on sunny weekends and Bank Holidays when west Londoners were tempted to taste the rural delights of the Brent Valley. Such trippers were encouraged by cheap fares and, from August 1904, a Sunday and Bank Holiday railcar service by both routes between Kensington (Addison Road) (now Olympia) and Greenford. From 16th April 1905 this was extended back to Clapham Junction and later in 1905 into the GWR side of Victoria station. Brent Valley trains were not seen at Victoria after 1915 but from about 1930 the GWR worked unadvertised workmen's trains from Clapham Junction to Ealing Broadway via Greenford, services which were mostly patronised by staff employed at Messrs J. Lyons' factories at Cadby Hall (near Olympia) and Greenford.

Regular use of the route via the Hanwell and Greenford East loops ceased after 1905, this then seeing only football and other specials. The two western loops were followed in combination by occasional weekday trips until 1910 and by some summer Sunday trains until August 1914. After that, all regular passenger trains to various destinations used the Greenford West Loop and the West Ealing Loop, as is still the case at the time of writing.

It has taken some time to describe even the main pattern of the services up to 1914 but in practice they did not amount to much in terms of frequency. Thus in 1910 there were 20 railcar trips each way daily between Greenford and West Ealing or Hanwell (one), offering either connections or through working to Westbourne Park, Uxbridge (High Street), Denham, Acton, Willesden Junction and Southall (one). Sundays saw four each way between Victoria and Greenford via Castle Bar Park, five between Paddington and West Ealing via Castle Bar Park and two between Uxbridge (High Street) and Acton/Southall. The Acton–Westbourne Park service ceased in 1914, after which the stops between Greenford and Old Oak Lane were served by main line local trains and the West Ealing–Greenford section was covered by trains between Ealing Broadway/West Ealing and Greenford or stations north west of Greenford.

It did not take the GWR very long to realise that use of a small tank engine (usually a 517 class 0–4–2T) with one or two trailers fitted for push-pull working offered greater flexibility and economy than the steam railcars. Like the steam railcars, these so-called 'motor trains' or 'auto trains' could be staffed with a conductor, saving the cost of ticket offices. By the early 1920s they had taken over almost all the Brent Valley services.

With some new housing appearing between West Ealing and Greenford on both sides of the line from 1925 onwards (most of it in the 1930s) trips were increased to

Greenford auto train (BR loco 1456 and car *Thrush*) at platform 3, Ealing Broadway, 17th April 1954. *Alan A Jackson*

around 32 each way daily, taking 10–12 minutes. The Elthorne Heights Estate, west of the line between Castle Bar Park halt and the river Brent was started in 1923/4 by the Great Western Land Company (which had no direct links with the GWR). Here detached four bedroom houses were advertised at £1,000–£1,250. Immediately north of this, also bringing some business to Castle Bar Park halt from 1932, was the Cuckoo Estate, where small three-bedroom houses were sold at £750. Three years later the LCC started its Hanwell Estate, making use of the large area occupied by the Residential Schools and by 1938 some 5,300 were living here. Between the wars, Ealing advanced up to the east side of the railway and the edges of the GWR Sports Ground.

To the north, Western Avenue, one of the state-funded unemployment relief roads, was opened through the Brent Valley as far as Greenford in 1927 and on to Uxbridge in 1935–37. This main road construction soon hastened the development of estates of small houses between the old village of Greenford and its station, which had started in the 1920s. Light industries were also encouraged by it and a whole new district grew up around Greenford station, where season ticket issues rose from 469 in 1923 to 4,068 five years later. This development stimulated the GWR into providing South Greenford halt, 61ch north of Castle Park. Approached by footpaths either side of the embankment leading from Western Avenue, the new facility was opened on 20th September 1926. At first the main users were road construction workers and patrons of the Perivale Park Golf Course and the West London Shooting Grounds. The 'South' in the name was a typical piece of railway management geography, accurate only in relation to the 1904 Greenford station, as the site was three quarters of a mile *north east* of the old village centre.

House and factory building led to some improvements (from 20th June 1932) along the main line through Greenford, including the opening of another halt, at Park Royal West (just west of the District Railway bridge) on that day. Another feature of the 1932 summer timetable was a sensible extension into Ealing Broadway of all services through Greenford and Castle Bar, providing connections to main line services and the Underground. This 1932 timetable brought 27 more trains each way, most of them turning round at Northolt. At Ealing Broadway, a siding was built for the auto trains between the Up and Down Relief lines and equipped with an engine inspection pit and a water crane. A further innovation was the provision of two late night theatre trains departing Ealing Broadway at 23.02 and 23.52. From this time the auto-trains were worked by the new 48xx 0–4–2T or by 54xx 0–6–0PT. At rush hours, a second trailer was added (the halt platforms between West Ealing and Greenford had been lengthened to allow for this in 1930).

In part these improvements were designed to counter the bus competition which had started in 1930 when residential development had attracted a Royal Highlander service between Ealing Broadway and Greenford, passing close to West Ealing station and Drayton Green halt and tapping the new housing south of Ruislip Road to the west of the railway. From 1933 London Transport perpetuated this service, which has always operated much more frequently, if more slowly, than the trains. Trade at South Greenford and the halts on the main line was drawn off by a General bus service along Western Avenue which provided a connection to Park Royal Underground station from May 1932. Another bus service started at about this time served the roads on the west side of Castle Bar Park and Drayton Green halts, passing through West Ealing to Ealing Broadway.

The main line featured in the 1935–40 London Railways New Works Programme, and after the delay caused by World War 2, Central Line tube trains were projected alongside it from North Acton to Greenford from 30th June 1947. These trains were carried above the Greenford East and West Loops on single track concrete and lattice girder viaducts which left the original GWR double track junctions unaltered. A single line spur was built from the Greenford West Loop to allow the Ealing auto-trains to ascend between the east and westbound electric lines to terminate in a bay set into the eastern end of the island platform which formed the new Greenford Central Line station. This platform, 33ft above the roadway, was reached by a single escalator of 30ft rise, the first on the Underground carrying passengers up to their train. The old GWR halts on the main line were replaced by new stations at Perivale and Hanger Lane, both on new sites.

At first the 35 trains a day each way over the Greenford–Ealing Broadway line (22 on Sundays) continued to use the old GWR platforms at Greenford which were connected to the Central Line ticket hall by an underline subway but when the tube service was extended to West Ruislip on 21st November 1948, all auto-train trips west of Greenford were withdrawn and an hourly train (with additional workings at the peak periods) then ran each way in and out of the unelectrified bay road at Greenford Central Line station, using the spur mentioned earlier. Until 17th June 1963 the old GWR station at Greenford remained open for parcels trains and some main line calls.

Class 54xx 0-6-0PT No.5401 propels an afternoon Northolt to Westbourne Park train on 16th June 1947. Old Oak Lane Halt was closed two weeks later. *J.J. Smith*

Throughout the 1950s the Greenford–Ealing line retained much of the delightfully relaxed aura of a GWR country branch line. That regressive GWR attitudes remained very much alive at Paddington was demonstrated in 1951 when a new series of steam-hauled auto-trailers of saloon type with large windows and sliding ventilators were introduced. Two of them, named *Thrush* and *Wren* were allocated to the Ealing–Greenford service, which continued to be operated with a mixture of BR and GWR cars for another six years. Diesel power reared its smelly head on Monday morning 25th August 1958 in the form of four new two-car sets (double-ended power cars plus single-ended driving trailers). On the previous evening, the steam auto trains trundled off to Southall and were never seen on the line again. The new arrivals maintained the hourly frequency with peak hours extras which their predecessors had provided before the economy cuts of June 1958. Subsequently cuts were made in Saturday services and there were no Sunday trains after 6th September 1964. Before long, most trips were undertaken by single cars. The diesels completed the 3½m run in 13 min.

Until the Beeching cuts of the early 1960s, Drayton Green and Castle Bar Park were under the supervision of the West Ealing stationmaster. The former was unstaffed but at Castle Bar Park there were two women porters taking turns for two shifts. South Greenford, supervised by the Greenford stationmaster, was unstaffed. These arrangements ensured that the passenger facilities were kept tidy and free from vandalism.

After the withdrawal of staff and supervision in the 1960s, the three halts were all reconstructed with concrete platforms. The nostalgic pagodas at Drayton Green and Castle Bar Park were replaced with ugly red brick shelters and those at South Greenford with the flimsier bus stop type, very soon to lose their glass. The small wooden ticket offices erected by the GWR for commuter service at Drayton Green and Castle Bar Park gave way to brick and concrete accommodation strongly fortified with steel shutters and heavy duty padlocks against youthful vandals. The word 'Halt' did not appear on the new nameboards but the GWR heritage tenuously survived in the form of that company's seats, their wood soon heavily scored by the sharp knives of the vandals, who also quickly did their best to wreck and disfigure everything else newly-provided.

The two loops at Greenford were singled in about 1970 and the connection at Hanwell was also reduced to a single line junction. Although all four loops remained in use, the West Ealing coal yard was closed to public traffic from 4th January 1965. An interesting change to the appearance of the line occurred in 1976–77, when the cutting north of Drayton Green was converted to a covered way to allow construction by the GLC of houses (Copley Close) over the line, part of the process of infilling land between Cavendish and Browning Avenues to provide 639 new homes.

Train services have been substantially improved in recent years. From 1980 the basic frequency was increased to half-hourly off peak, 20 minutes at peak times. To achieve a reduction of two minutes in the running time, the three halts were converted to request stops. From 16th May 1988 the Greenford–Ealing Broadway shuttle was extended into Paddington. On Saturdays there were three trains an hour (20 min intervals) from Greenford, respectively fast from Ealing Broadway to Paddington; Paddington all stations; and Ealing Broadway only. October 1993 saw replacement of the odoriferous and rattly first generation diesel cars by smooth and good-looking Class 165 turbo sets.

Greenford auto train (BR loco 1474) at Drayton Green c.1955.
Lens of Sutton

BR 2-car diesel set for Greenford leaving South Greenford, 18th June 1960. At this date, apart from the train, this was in every respect a typical GWR rural halt.
Alan A Jackson

BR 2-car diesel set from Ealing Broadway entering the central bay between the two tube line platforms at Greenford, 5th September 1959. The Old Oak-High Wycombe main lines are at the left of the picture, which looks towards London.
Alan A Jackson

Train approaching Wembley Exhibition station in July 1925. Just visible on the right are cars of the 'Never Stop' railway. *H C Casserley*

The Wembley Stadium Loop (map page 260)

In the years immediately preceding World War 1 the idea of a British Empire Exhibition came forward several times but it was not until 1920, when the government and others had agreed to contribute to a fund which would guarantee the organisers against loss that sufficient force built up to bring the concept to fruition. Its objects were then stated to be to 'take stock of the resources of the Empire' . . . to 'make the peoples of the Empire better known to one another, . . . to display scientific practice and research', and . . . to 'enable established industries to show what they have to offer'. The chosen site was Wembley Park, six miles from Marble Arch, served by three railway stations; the Metropolitan's Wembley Park, the GCR's Wembley Hill and the LNWR/Underground at Sudbury & Wembley (later Wembley Central). Electric trams and several bus services also passed close by.

The 280-acre Wembley Park estate had been purchased by the Metropolitan Railway in 1890. An attempt to open up the area as a sports and leisure centre to increase rail revenues had flopped badly; in particular its main feature, Sir Edward Watkin's English version of the Eiffel Tower, erected here in 1892 had not reached above the first platform level and was ignominiously dismantled in 1906. After that, the Metropolitan set its mind to developing the area 'as a building estate in the interests of the railway company'. By 1914 just over 100 houses had been erected in the western part of the site but activity had then ceased and was slow to resume after 1919. There was thus a large area of land still uncovered within the fork formed by the Metropolitan Railway and the former GCR Neasden–Northolt line. In January 1922, 216 acres here were sold to the company organising the Exhibition.

Sir Sam Fay for the GCR and R. H. Selbie for the Metropolitan had agreed in 1921 that the GCR might construct a 'siding' into the Exhibition Grounds following a promise by the GCR that most of the freight brought in over it would be routed via Quainton Road and the Met & GC Joint line. Later the GCR decided to build a loop about a mile long, diverging from the Down Main of the Neasden–Northolt line just east of Wembley Hill station, crossing the Up line, then running north into the Exhibition site before turning back north-east and then south east to rejoin the former GCR Up Independent line at Neasden North Junction, then the Up Main at Neasden South box. This new line was to be signalled for this clockwise direction only and both connections were to be controlled by Neasden North Junction box. When the LNER, as successors to the GCR, decided to build a passenger station on the new railway, which would give it the only station actually inside the Exhibition Grounds, the Metropolitan protested in 1923 that this action was opposed to the spirit, if not the letter of the agreement made between the two companies in 1913 that the GCR would not seek to exploit local traffic between Marylebone and Harrow. But the LNER insisted that the Wembley Loop was connected to its own Neasden–Northolt line, to which the agreement did not apply. The Metropolitan, taking legal advice, was firmly told it had no case to pursue.

Construction of the single track loop, started in December 1922, required removal of around 40,000 cu yd of clay as the station area was approached in a deep cutting. Here a single platform, as yet without any shelter or other buildings, was provided on the west side of the single line. At 600ft long and 22ft 6in wide, it was just big enough to hold a nine coach train of suburban steam stock. As a three minute service was planned between Wembley and Marylebone, the LNER installed automatic colour light signalling and ac track circuits between the London terminus and Wembley Hill station and also around the Loop, closing two manual signal boxes. This allowed very close working, including a maximum of four trains on the Loop at any time.

The first part of the Exhibition Grounds to be completed was the Empire Stadium, which still stands today, on the highest part of the estate, occupying the site of Watkin's ill-fated tower at the southern edge of the area and very close to the north side of the railway between Neasden and Northolt. The largest building of its type in the world at the time, it was selected by the Football Association as a permanent home for its Cup Finals from 1923. The Stadium, which could seat 120,000, and the new railway were ready in time for that event, Bolton Wanderers v. West Ham United, held on 28th April. The railway managers had reckoned on the Cup Finals attracting far more people on one day than the Exhibition would normally see, but even they were to be surprised: over 200,000 made their way out to Wembley and when the Stadium was filled, football-besotted men and boys continued to surge in until the pitch itself was swamped. After herculean efforts by the police, it was cleared to allow the match to start somewhat later than planned.

The LNER had timetabled 51 trains from Marylebone to the Loop station, 15 between 13.00 and 14.00 and nine between 14.00 and 14.30. Mostly of eight bogie coaches and monopolising platforms 3 and 4 at Marylebone, these were filling to capacity from around 11.00. Arrived at the new station, in trainloads of 800–1,000, the crowds very quickly exited through 16 gates on to a road leading directly to the Stadium, about five minutes walk away. All worked smoothly in the outward direction.

However, following the chaos mentioned, the thousands unable to gain access to the Stadium drifted back to the station, anxious to return home. As they pushed in, loaded trains were still arriving. These had to be promptly reloaded and despatched, but many trains had already proceeded to Neasden sidings to await the end of the match. Hurried arrangements were improvised to recall them to take the frustrated spectators back to London. Inevitably the major dislocation of the booked arrangements that ensued caused some delay to the returning trains. As the match finished late, the trains taking back the lucky spectators were also heavily delayed as the timetable fell apart. Some of the crowds were dealt with by the LNER at its Wembley Hill station and large numbers used the Metropolitan at Wembley Park station.

The British Empire Exhibition was opened on 23rd April 1924 and with it, the Loop for a second time, now with a completed station, equipped with a lengthy canopied brick and concrete shelter and other small buildings in an architectural style similar to that adopted for the Exhibition generally. Every day through the Exhibition season, eight-ten trains of five-six coaches an hour were worked to and from Marylebone, mostly with ex GCR 4–6–2T, covering the journey in 12 minutes, the loop eliminating the delays involved in reversal. When the Exhibition closed on the evening of 1st November 1924, 17.5 million people had paid to enter the grounds, providing a special traffic which the LNER had of course to share with the Metropolitan, the LMSR, the Underground and the road services. Despite a reduction in the cost of the combined rail fare and admission charge, there was a great deal less interest for the second season in 1925, with a total of only 9.7m tickets sold between 9th May and 31st October. During the 1925 season, the LNER operated a similar service to that of 1924 round the Loop mostly using its new suburban N7 0–6–2T.

On Cup Final Day in 1925, the LNER was greatly put out to find employees of the Metropolitan Railway distributing leaflets at Marylebone station suggesting the Metropolitan route from Baker Street was the best way to the Stadium. Alex Wilson, for the LNER, wrote to Selbie, the Metropolitan's general manager, protesting:

> When all is said and done, your company get the lion's share of the Wembley traffic and you must not begrudge us any few odd crumbs that may fall from the rich man's table . . .

But the LNER did have the advantage of sidings which ran right into two of the largest Exhibition buildings, the Palace of Engineering (with its railway exhibits) and the Palace of Industry, as well as another along Commonwealth Way serving the Canada and Australia buildings. These enabled it to gain much of the freight traffic involved in erecting the structures, making the roadways and other features and setting up the displays. After the final closure in October 1925, rail access gave the LNER a lever towards obtaining the dismantling business and the traffic involved in the subsequent conversion of the site into industrial units and warehouses. An Exhibition Goods Yard here survived until 3rd December 1962.

The LNER, with its Loop and Wembley Hill stations, was also best placed to serve the Stadium, which was now converted to accommodate greyhound racing as well as other sports. After 1924 (118,000), Cup Final attendances settled down to 90–95,000, almost all travelling by public transport and of which the Metropolitan carried about one third, leaving the balance to the LNER and the other alternatives.

After closure of the Exhibition in 1925, the loop and its station (renamed Wembley Stadium in 1927) were regularly reopened for passenger services to principal events at the Stadium, notably the FA and Rugby League Finals and the England v. Scotland International Matches. These occasions provided a feast for trainspotters as there were many special workings from distant places supplementing the Marylebone service. Some use was even made of the loop during the war, as for example for the FA Cup Final of 1943. On the occasion of the April 1948 FA Cup Final, 14 trains ran, carrying 9,500 on to the loop and 12,500 away after the match.

Station and Loop were renovated for the 1948 14th Olympic Games, held at the 1923 Stadium and the adjacent 1934 Empire Pool. By the 1960s, diesel multiple unit sets were able to cope with a reduced level of patronage on the special services round the loop from and to Marylebone. The 1923 line and its station were last used for the Rugby League Cup Final of 18th May 1968 but the official date given for closure of the Loop was 1st September 1969. Rails from a point just north of the platform were lifted at around that time and the connection at the Wembley Hill side was broken early in 1970.

In recent years, following use of the Empire Pool (renamed the Wembley Arena) for entertainments and other events as well as swimming, the opening of the Conference Centre in 1976 and later the Exhibition Centre, Wembley has seen traffic more evenly distributed through the year. Although some still passes via Marylebone and Wembley Stadium (formerly Wembley Hill) station, the majority is handled at Wembley Park station. The long battle to win extra revenue from Wembley has in the end gone to the Metropolitan, the originators of the whole exercise.

The LNER Wembley Stadium loop and passenger platform, looking north east in the mid-1950s.
Lens of Sutton

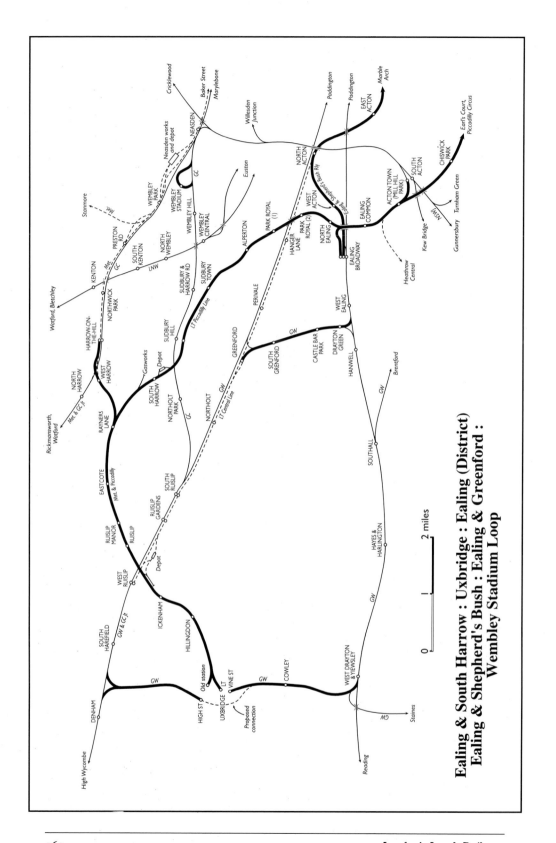

Ealing & South Harrow : Uxbridge : Ealing (District)
Ealing & Shepherd's Bush : Ealing & Greenford :
Wembley Stadium Loop

Cowley station, looking to West Drayton, almost ready for public opening, September 1904.

The Uxbridge Branches (Great Western Railway)   (map page 260)

Like its Middlesex sister Hounslow, the town of Uxbridge was a place of some importance at the beginning of the nineteenth century. A staging point on the Oxford road 15 miles from London, with breweries, corn mills and market, it was also well served after 1798 by the Grand Junction (later Grand Union) Canal, which not only moved freight to its metropolitan markets, but took passengers up, if somewhat slowly. Although a focus of many railway schemes, Uxbridge passed the Victorian era with only minimal railway accommodation, a fact which surely contributed to its contemporary decline. Then, at the turn of the century it quickly found itself with two more stations and an electric tramway link to west London. All three railway services were essentially of a local nature and did little to revive the town's prosperity; we shall examine later the facilities provided by the Metropolitan and District Railways; here we are concerned with the contribution of the Great Western, by whom the burghers always considered themselves poorly treated.

Whilst Brunel could have brought his London to Bristol line into the southern part of Uxbridge without too much difficulty, he preferred not to cut across the lower part of the Colne valley, taking instead the level route through West Drayton, some 2½ miles south. After the opening of a station there on 4th June 1838, road conveyances plied from Uxbridge High Street for those choosing the faster if less convenient alternative to the Oxford road coaches. Local interests were soon seeking a rail connection, finding it necessary to get up an independent scheme. A 2½-mile single line along the Colne from West Drayton was authorised in 1846 as the Great Western & Uxbridge Railway, but capital could not be raised and although the GWR took powers in the following year to purchase the undertaking, it had no incentive to build and allowed the scheme to lapse.

Finally goaded into action by local support of the Oxford and Brentford schemes of the early 1850s, the GWR secured a third act in 1853 authorising a 2m 51ch single line of 7ft 0in gauge over the 1846 route with a deviation at the Uxbridge end to a new terminus near the Vineyard. Leaving the main line west of West Drayton station, the branch was to climb at 1 in 116 to cross the canal and the valley road, soon afterwards passing behind the east side of Cowley village into a cutting, terminating on a short rise of 1 in 66. In a central position on the south side of Vine Street, the terminus had two tracks with four platform faces and a very narrow headway beyond the buffers. Over it all was one of the timber and glass A-shaped roofs favoured by the GWR at this period, a feature which lasted until 1932–3. The side platforms were removed when the roof was replaced with a conventional umbrella canopy protecting about two coach lengths of the widened island platform. The single-storey, hipped roof building across the headway, in local yellow brick, had a wooden canopy on the outer side until 1941 when it was demolished by a bus. West of the passenger station was the small goods yard, awkwardly situated for shunting at the top of the gradient.

Public traffic on this, the first GWR branch in the London area, began on 8th September 1856 when there were 15 arrivals at Uxbridge daily and 13 departures (ten and 11 on Sundays). All connected with Up and Down main line trains, and the balancing workings were goods trains which may have carried passengers. By 1870, with most trains into Paddington operating over standard gauge rails, re-gauging became increasingly desirable, especially for the working of freight. The job was completed on 9th October 1871. Doubling followed in 1880/1881, probably in response to the first threats of District Railway invasion of this part of the GWR monopoly.

Initially most of the trains, some of them mixed, were confined to the branch, but from an early date there were daily through workings to and from Paddington for the convenience of businessmen. Working over the Metropolitan Railway to the City via Bishop's Road, Paddington, was started in 1879 to meet the competition and threat of the District Railway, which had reached Ealing Broadway that year. Although there were rarely more than three trains Up in the morning and a similar number back in the evening, these Uxbridge (Vine Street)–City workings were continuous from 1881 to September 1939.

After the electrification of the Metropolitan in 1905, electric locomotives of that company hauled the GWR carriages between Paddington and the City, a somewhat piquant situation since the Metropolitan was by then in direct competition with the GWR for Uxbridge traffic. For a few years from July 1897 there were also through trains between Vine Street and Victoria via West London Junction and Latchmere Junction, Battersea.

As well as the 20 trains a day each way on the branch, there were around 1900, 12 Up and ten Down journeys to and from Paddington or the City and two between Uxbridge and Victoria with Paddington coaches. A 1911 timetable shows 31 trains a day each way, mostly confined to the branch, plus 14 Up and 13 Down through London workings of which two Up and one Down were Victoria trains taking one hour ten minutes, while five Up and three Down were Liverpool Street workings. The best time from Uxbridge to Paddington was 20 minutes. Apart from an early morning working which appeared in 1906, the line saw no steam railcars until these took over most of the Sunday service in October 1914.

Cowley, an agricultural community of some 500 inhabitants (1871), 1½ miles north of West Drayton, did not get its station until 2nd October 1904. With its characteristic liberality, the GWR then provided wide 400ft platforms and decent brick buildings; the main structure, single-storied, with an ample canopy, was on the Up side and a small waiting room and men's urinal in similar style on the Down. Since there was no goods yard, a block post was dispensed with and the whole line continued to be worked as one section. Another economy was the absence of a footbridge, the porter on the Down side having access to a lockable box of Uxbridge tickets. By 1913 this station was handling around 40,000 passengers a year but its best period of growth was during the 1920s and 1930s when there was some housing development, mostly west of the line. In 1937 over 65,500 passengers were handled. Even then, much of the catchment area was taken up by nurseries, cemeteries and a sewage works.

One of many proposals for cracking the GWR monopoly of Uxbridge was the long-lived scheme for a link between Uxbridge GWR and Rickmansworth LNWR, mainly to provide for freight transfers. First authorised in 1861, the Uxbridge & Rickmansworth lived in paper and talk for about 40 years, providing sustenance for lawyers and politicians through no fewer than 11 acts of parliament.[*]

But Uxbridge was far more interested in getting itself on to a main line, or at any rate in achieving a direct link to London, and every encouragement was given by the town to the many schemes which emerged after 1879, most of them with open or covert support from the District or the Metropolitan. When the 1891 census revealed a fall in population this was attributed to the deficiency in railway accommodation and used as evidence of the need for something better.

At the end of the 1890s the GWR found itself facing District-inspired schemes linking Uxbridge and the Chiltern towns to London, and worse, a proposal for an independent railway from London to South Wales via High Wycombe and Denham which might make use of the District as one means of gaining access to central London. GWR powers were accordingly secured in 1897 to block this by constructing a direct main line between Acton and High Wycombe, affording a shorter route to Oxford and Birmingham by using the existing line from Wycombe through Thame to Oxford. Although a connection with the unbuilt Uxbridge & Rickmansworth was included, this proposal again by-passed Uxbridge and when a protest deputation from the town waited upon the GWR board they were told that although a line nearer the town had been investigated, use of the Alderbourne valley route would affect too many interests, not least the scenic Burnham Beeches. As a sop, Uxbridge was promised a branch from the new line, which would join the existing branch to form a loop which would carry circular services to and from the City section of the Metropolitan Railway via Greenford and via Ealing Broadway, a proposition which was eventually mentioned to the parliamentary committee on the GWR Bill of 1897. Not all the Uxbridge representatives found this an acceptable substitute for the sting of competition from a second railway company in the town; one was churlish enough to cast doubts on the GWR's intentions, asserting that although it might build the promised line, it would not use it. He was not far wrong. Parliament, also apparently convinced of the merits of competition, passed the 1899

[*] Useful summaries of this saga will be found in *The Railway Magazine*, January-February 1945 (H Langford Lewis) and December 1959 (J Spencer Gilks).

Uxbridge High Street station, 1907, looking to buffers and the half-built underline bridge for the proposed connection to the West Drayton Line.

Harrow and Uxbridge Act, the final step for a line first proposed in 1881 and opened in 1904 and one which now provides the town's only railway connection. We shall be looking at this shortly but it should be noted here that, aided by the extension of the London United electric tramways to Uxbridge in the same year, it reduced the 162,000 tickets issued at Vine Street in 1903 to 120,100 in 1913.

In fulfilment of its promise, the GWR sought and obtained powers for the northern branch into Uxbridge in 1898, a 2m 7f 2.2ch line, which was to have junctions with the new Wycombe route facing both London and Denham. Following the Colne valley to join the existing branch in the town, it was in effect a substitute for the southern part of the long-planned Uxbridge & Rickmansworth, for which powers finally lapsed in 1901. A longer but cheaper route for this GWR branch, detouring west of the town to join the West Drayton line 34ch south of the terminus, near Walford Road, was authorised in 1899. Work started on the whole 3m 2.35ch, but when it opened on 1st May 1907, trains ran only to a second Uxbridge station (High Street) on the east side of the main road between the Grand Union Canal and Fray's River. Construction work south of this point which included a cutting, an embankment, a 1,275yd brick viaduct and an iron girder bridge over the High Street was stopped before completion. Sensibly, the GWR decided that there was not enough traffic potential to justify the proposed circular service now that both District and Metropolitan electric trains served Uxbridge. Powers for the uncompleted section were formally abandoned in 1914.

Denham West Junction with the new Birmingham line was immediately east of the Grand Union Canal Viaduct; the 2f 6.76ch spur to Denham East Junction, opened at the same time as the branch, was never used for regular passenger workings. Nine steam railcar trips worked each way daily between Denham, Uxbridge (High Street), and West Ealing, with some going on to Ealing Broadway or Willesden Junction. Sunday railcar working between Uxbridge (High Street) and Kensington (Addison Road) via Park Royal or Ealing Broadway was started in July 1907, continuing sporadically on summer Sundays until 1914. Some weekday journeys were extended to Gerrards Cross in July 1909; the cars then ran down the main line from London to Gerrards Cross, ran back to Uxbridge (High Street) and returned to Gerrards Cross before working up to London along the main line.

Freight working on the branch did not start until 11th May 1914, when a small coal yard was opened at street level to the west of the passenger station, approached by a spur from a junction about a quarter-mile north of the terminus. Tracks on the little-used east curve at Denham were removed for war purposes about 1916 and never again laid throughout. From 14th May 1942 a single track was opened over the alignment from Denham South Junction to serve an oil tank depot.

From Denham South Junction the branch ran on an embankment almost due south to cross Fray's River near Denham Lock, then following the west bank of the river, coming to an end at a bridge across the north end of the High Street. North of this bridge, at the west side of the line, there was a single timber platform with a canopied wooden building, cantilevered at the back from the embankment and containing ticket office, waiting rooms, lavatories and the stationmaster's office. Access from the street was by a covered stairway to the south end of the platform. At street level, under the bridge, the GWR erected a flat-roofed brick building most of which was leased out as a café.

Since very little business was attracted by the slow and restricted passenger service of steam railmotor cars, it was no surprise when the GWR offered suspension of passenger trains as a contribution to economies required to help the war effort at the end of 1916. Much of the line was also singled to supply rail for Army use. Passenger services were resumed, on weekdays only, from 3rd May 1920 over what was now a single track branch through an area never able to generate even the scanty settlement that might justify an intermediate halt. Apart from the demolition in 1922 of the bridge over Uxbridge High Street, there was little to disturb the sleepy between-wars life of the branch until the construction of a bridge carrying the Western Avenue arterial road over the line in 1939–40. Train services in this period, normally working between Uxbridge High Street, Denham and Gerrards Cross, a 13 min journey, continued as steam railmotors until the mid 1930s when they were replaced by typical GWR auto trains, latterly powered by 54XX 0–6–0PT. After the signalling had been removed in the early 1920s, the branch was worked by use of a small metal token, with one engine in steam at a time, or two coupled together. By 1938 there were just nine services each way daily with a surprising five extra workings at midday on Saturdays, thought to be justified by shopping traffic. At the end of the 1930s, when the station was staffed with two porters under the supervision of the stationmaster at Vine Street, about 10,000 tickets a year were issued at High Street, say around 30 a day, this figure almost certainly including season ticket journeys.

Uxbridge Vine Street station, looking to buffers, in the 1930s. *Lens of Sutton*

For the second and last time all passenger trains were withdrawn after traffic on Thursday 31st August 1939; on the following day, the GWR was heavily engaged in the evacuation of schoolchildren from London and this and the immediately following outbreak of war provided convenient justification for not resuming a little-used service. Freight trains, mainly incoming coal, continued to run daily if required, reversing in the engine run-round loop of the old passenger station by means of ground frame levers. To enable the tracks in the former passenger station area to be removed, a run-round loop was installed a short way up the branch in 1956 but in post-war conditions the depot here had become superfluous and all freight working to High Street ceased from 24th February 1964. Some trains continued to use the track between Denham West Junction and the oil depot until a final working on 30th April 1965.

In contrast to this decline, from the late 1920s the original Uxbridge branch enjoyed a modest prosperity in an area experiencing steady industrial and residential development. By 1938, when there were 46 trains daily each way and 26 on Sundays, the whole route, apart from a stretch at Cowley, was clothed with houses and factories. Seventeen trains, three on Sundays, ran through to and from London, discerning passengers finding them more comfortable and marginally faster than the London Transport services via Rayners Lane. On the branch, auto trains with one or two cars in charge of fussy little 0–4–2T or 0–6–0PT ran to and fro, taking seven minutes for the journey. On the outbreak of war in 1939 the two trains each way between Uxbridge and Liverpool Street (Metropolitan Line) were withdrawn, running for the last time on Saturday 16th September, but Paddington workings continued. Wartime demands brought additional freight traffic to the branch.

At the end of the 1950s the line was still quite busy, with 35 trains each way daily, about a dozen of them to and from Paddington at peak hours, taking about 30 min. GWR AEC railcars replaced the steam auto trains in the mid 1950s at a time when freight business still required three workings daily. The aura of the GWR was still very apparent but it was to be an Indian Summer both for the line and those at Paddington striving to maintain GWR traditions. The appearance on the line of new BR diesel railcars in 1958 raised hopes of a new era which were soon to be dashed. From 27th July 1962 passenger workings were reduced to peak hours only and after Saturday 8th September that year ceased altogether. The next month saw the line reduced to single track. Any residual London traffic via West Drayton fell away quickly; the alternative bus route (available on the parallel road since the 1930s) was not only slower but exposed passengers to the elements as they transferred between road and rail. For journeys to London, Uxbridge was soon relying entirely on the latter-day intruder.

Cowley station closed completely with the end of passenger trains but at Vine Street parcels trains continued to visit the platforms until 11th July 1964. Freight traffic into Uxbridge yard ceased on 24th February that year. One small section survived for a while; a 26ch length at the southern end was used until 1976 by trains serving a siding added about 1964 for the Middlesex Oil & Chemical Works at Yiewsley. Beyond that point, all tracks and railway structures were quickly demolished and before many years had passed, much of the alignment had been built over.

The Ealing & South Harrow Railway bridge over Twyford Abbey Road, looking north west, c. 1912. The entrances to Park Royal & Twyford Abbey station (1903–31) can be seen at the right hand side of the bridge. *Commercial postcard*

The Uxbridge and Harrow Branches (Met and MDR)   (map page 260)

A substantial wedge of Middlesex between the LNWR and GWR main lines remained without railways until the very end of the nineteenth century. As late as December 1901, the Reverend W J Scott was able to hope that 'this wooded country, so close to London' would not be covered 'with rows of the small yellow brick houses one sees at Wood Green or Leyton'. It is true that the Metropolitan reached Harrow in 1880 and was at Pinner five years later, but this merely scraped the north-western edge of the area. Several reasons may be cited for the slow exploitation of land so near the western edge of London: the GWR and LNWR, for many years content to enjoy their profitable long-distance traffic, were able to postpone the hazardous task of developing suburban business through their inconveniently-sited termini; speculative builders were deterred by the lack of railways in an area mostly covered with deep hard clays that discouraged house construction until main drainage schemes were implemented, while industry was notably absent, except on a few sites alongside the Grand Junction Canal.

During the final quarter of the nineteenth century this railway desert began to attract a variety of schemes, some supported or directly promoted by the MDR in expansionist mood, others put up independently by parties who wished to challenge the GWR monopoly at Uxbridge, with its unsatisfactory branch line access; or to develop land for housing; or even to form possible corridors for new main lines coming to London from the north and west. But it was the District that took the lead role.

On 1st July 1879 that company reached Ealing, a vantage point from which it could contemplate further objectives: Harrow to the north, Uxbridge and High Wycombe to the north-west. The boardroom mood at this time was quietly optimistic; ordinary shareholders had received their first dividend (if only ½ per cent) in 1878, receipts and traffic were climbing, and there were high hopes for the new lines to Ealing, Richmond and Fulham. A new policy was announced in the chairman's report of 30th January 1880:

> The enormous outlay of the parent line can only be fully utilised and made ultimately profitable by judicious and comparatively cheap lines constructed in direct continuation of those already existing; and into districts possessing not only a present considerable population but also affording attractive outlets for the denser population of London constantly moving westward.

These remarks introduced a proposed extension from Ealing to Uxbridge, then served only by the little GWR branch of 1856. In 1861 an extension of that branch northwards to Rickmansworth had been authorised to an independent scheme, and there had been other earlier proposals which would have given this important Middlesex town direct access to London. The District's Uxbridge Extension Bill deposited in November 1879 provided for an 8m 5f westward extension from Ealing which for its last five furlongs would run into Uxbridge alongside the GWR, a brazen assault on its territory which that company successfully opposed. Notwithstanding this defeat, the District board deemed it 'necessary and prudent' to try again the following year with a route only slightly different. Again the bill was thrown out.

Railway interest in Uxbridge remained strong, with the business community working hard to secure some competition for the GWR, which reacted by doubling its branch as a precautionary measure in 1880/1881. November 1881 saw the deposit of no less than four bills affecting the town, none directly promoted by the District. Two of the proposals followed much the same route as the earlier District bills: the Uxbridge & Rickmansworth (Ealing Extension), and the High Wycombe, Beaconsfield, Uxbridge & London, which was to be linked with the GWR at High Wycombe, with the Uxbridge & Rickmansworth near Uxbridge, and the District at Ealing. The other two bills went further north. The Harrow & Uxbridge was a straightforward branch from the Metropolitan at Harrow-on-the-Hill via Ruislip, but the Beaconsfield, Uxbridge & Harrow, the only bill of the four to succeed, was more ambitious, proposing a line westwards from junctions with the LNWR and the Metropolitan at Harrow to Beaconsfield through Ruislip. Uxbridge would be reached via the Uxbridge & Rickmansworth, which was to be joined near Denham. Although the junction with the LNWR was deleted, the rest emerged as the Beaconsfield, Uxbridge & Harrow Railway Act, 1882. No capital was raised; the powers, which lapsed in 1887, were not renewed.

Harrow, about four miles north of Ealing across Alperton Vale was an obvious target for the District. Until the arrival of the Metropolitan from Baker Street and Finchley Road on 2nd August 1880, its only railway accommodation was a poorly-served station on the LNWR at Wealdstone, over a mile north of the town. There had been some attempts to remedy this deficiency. An unsuccessful London, Harrow & Rickmansworth Railway Bill of 1864 had proposed a line from Rickmansworth through Pinner, Roxeth (now South Harrow), Greenford Green, and Alperton to join the LNWR at its crossing of the Brent, with a spur to the GWR at Old Oak. At its northern end this line would have joined the existing Watford and Rickmansworth branch and the authorised Amersham & Chesham Railway. A few years later the GNR was making unsuccessful attempts to reach Harrow from Edgware, but nothing more happened until 1876 when a Harrow & West End bill was deposited. This was a branch from the GWR at Ealing to Roxeth and Harrow, London Hill, hoping to carry District trains from that company's Ealing Extension, which was in the same session, as well as GWR workings. The bill was rejected as were no less than four similar ones promoted in 1877, 1878, 1879 and 1884. Of these, the first three were entitled Harrow & District and included junctions with the Metropolitan at Harrow, whilst the last three also provided for connection to the MDR at Ealing. The 1884 scheme went on to join the GNR, its ambitious promoters seeking running powers over the GNR into Farringdon as well as over the District, Metropolitan and GWR, arrangements postulating some interesting circular services.

The next proposal to affect the still railless claylands of West Middlesex came from a new direction. A Harrow, Ealing & Willesden bill, deposited in 1886, sought a line from junctions with the LNWR and Midland & South Western Junction at Willesden, west through Alperton and then north-west, through Sudbury to terminate at Roxeth (South Harrow), throwing off a branch from Alperton to Castle Bar Park, Ealing. It was hoped to run into London both via the Midland and the LNWR, carrying passengers from the houses whose construction the railway's promoters hoped it would stimulate. New housing at rents of £250-£300 per annum on the southern slopes of Harrow Hill was mentioned in evidence, and one promoter was an Alperton builder and contractor who told the parliamentary committee that he had houses to let at £40-£60 per annum, so that there appeared to be scope for both first- and third-class traffic. On a technical objection skilfully raised by its counsel, the LNWR rid itself of the proposed connection, bringing the whole bill to grief, but the committee recorded that it did not wish it to be thought that its opinion was that no further railway communication was required in the district.

Although now in a far less buoyant state, the MDR was still concerned about the vacuum which remained so near to its western extremity. The board authorised survey of an extension to Uxbridge in November 1892, but decided not to deposit a bill. An Ealing & South Harrow Railway bill was however deposited the following year, ostensibly by local interests anticipating District support. A 5m 2f 9.7ch line, this was to run from the MDR Ealing Extension at Hanger Hill Farm, Ealing, to Roxeth, now for the first time christened 'South Harrow'. Arthur J. Barry was the engineer, and agreements were sought with the District, whose shareholders approved the bill. It passed unopposed, obtaining royal assent on 25th August 1894. The preamble to the act explained that construction estimates were based on double track to MDR standards, but until goods traffic could be brought onto the line, it might be made cheaply as a 'single track light railway' for £75,000 instead of £160,000.

This goods traffic was expected to arrive from outside London. At the MDR half-yearly meeting of 9th August 1894, the chairman, James Staats Forbes, spoke obscurely of 'some other railway company northwards' having sufficient interest in the E&SHR 'to materially assist construction', adding that the idea seemed to be 'a connection between a great northern railway and this little railway' to enable the former to use District access to central London. In these circumstances, he slyly suggested, it would be necessary for the District to subscribe capital.

Forbes' reference was probably to the London extension of the Manchester, Sheffield & Lincolnshire Railway (later the Great Central). Work on this had begun that year with the intention of entering London over the Metropolitan Railway as far as Finchley Road, a move facilitated by the fact that both railways shared the same chairman, the famous Sir Edward Watkin. Watkin fell ill in 1894, resigning his chairmanships, and his successor on the Metropolitan made things less easy for the London extension of this 'great northern railway'. It seems likely that Forbes was hoping to profit by this, offering an alternative route into central London. But in the event the newcomer obtained powers in 1895 and 1896 for a second pair of tracks alongside the Metropolitan, thus removing a major cause of friction. Forbes had a second string to his bow. another trunk line scheme, the London & South Wales Railway, aiming to break the GWR coal monopoly, deposited its bill in autumn 1895. Engineered by J. Wolfe Barry, this was to enter the London area via High Wycombe, Denham, Ruislip and Harrow, with junctions to the Metropolitan at Great Missenden and to the Midland at Welsh Harp, Hendon. Neither of these two companies could be relied upon to afford the newcomer access to central London, so Forbes set out to attract this further prop for the E&SHR, promoting an extension from South Harrow to Uxbridge and High Wycombe, and a small terminus for it at South Kensington. These proposals were however withdrawn before the end of 1895 when the South Wales apparently showed no interest. In any event the new main line scheme collapsed a few weeks afterwards, with the GWR promising to improve its access to South Wales.

Despite this setback, the District still felt impelled to make its bid for Uxbridge and High Wycombe, promoting in 1896 through a nominally independent company an extension of the E&SHR through Ruislip, Ickenham and Uxbridge, passing south of Chalfont St Peter and north of Beaconsfield. At Uxbridge it would have junctions with the diuturnal Uxbridge & Rickmansworth. The terminus at High Wycombe, which required property demolition, was to be higher than the GWR, without physical connection. By this time it had been decided that the E&SHR should be part of the District system, built by that company, and the 1896 bill included spurs at Alperton to the M&SWJR at Neasden and also from North Ealing to a proposed GWR Acton–Wycombe line, facing towards London. An extension of time was sought for the E&SHR, also running powers over that line for the High Wycombe's trains, over the GWR into Acton, and over the Uxbridge & Rickmansworth. Business interests in Uxbridge, ever keen on breaking the GWR monopoly, subscribed towards the expenses of the High Wycombe Bill. Once again we read of the District Chairman talking about 'judicious and timely extensions', now pointing to the example of the Metropolitan Railway, enjoying 'relative prosperity' from the same policy. A new threat to the inner London lines, motor bus and electric tramway competition, added further urgency. Thus persuaded, the MDR shareholders agreed the new bill in February 1897, with working by the MDR.

Now very much alive to the dangers of competition from the Oxford–Princes Risborough–High Wycombe direction, the GWR promoted in the same session a bill for a main line from Acton to High Wycombe, and it was the powerful opposition of the GWR that secured the deletion of the Uxbridge–High Wycombe section of the District-sponsored bill. The remainder, from South Harrow to Uxbridge, was authorised as the Harrow & Uxbridge Railway Act of 6th August 1897, which included confirmation of an agreement dated 19th July in which the District undertook to manage and work the double-track line. The District's own act of that year also confirmed an agreement to work the E&SHR, so that on paper at least the District was in Uxbridge at last, although that is by no means the end of the story.

A loop between the original GWR main line and the new route from Acton to Wycombe, included in the act for the latter, was in effect a final mutilated realisation of the several Ealing–Harrow and Ealing–Uxbridge proposals already mentioned. In the following two years the GWR secured powers for the Denham–Uxbridge branch and the Great Central Railway was authorised to link Northolt on the new GWR main line with Neasden on its original Metropolitan entry into London. These lines, subsequently built, completed the final pattern of the railway network in West Middlesex, with one small exception.

Attempts to raise capital for the South Harrow to Uxbridge line met with no success. As the shaky finances of the District were over-extended on the E&SHR and the capital-intensive Whitechapel & Bow, it became all too clear in the autumn of 1898 that unless a saviour could be found, Uxbridge would not get its competitive line. After informing Forbes, who raised no objection, the Uxbridge parties began to woo the Metropolitan, receiving sufficient encouragement to promote a bill for the 1899 session which sought powers to link that railway at Harrow with the Harrow & Uxbridge at Rayners Lane, with a curve at the latter which would allow through running from South Harrow to Harrow-on-the-Hill, and a flyover for the Down line at the point of junction with the Metropolitan. At the committee stage, Forbes began to object, seeking to make the Harrow & Uxbridge a joint District and Metropolitan enterprise, but he soon had to admit that the District was quite incapable of raising half the capital and had in any case decided to concentrate its efforts on the Whitechapel & Bow. It was finally agreed that the Metropolitan would manage and work the line from the date of Board of Trade authority, taking all receipts and paying the Harrow & Uxbridge Company three per cent on the capital cost of what the H&UER were to build as a 'first class double line' for passengers and goods.

From the wreckage of its hopes the District secured running powers for up to three trains an hour each way daily and eight goods trains each way in return for a minimum annual rent of £2,000. Some anxiety was expressed that having no interest in it, the H&UR would not make the Rayners Lane to South Harrow portion of the original act, but counsel for the promoters gave an assurance that it would be built and worked, whether or not the District used its running powers. The arrangements described were incorporated in the Harrow & Uxbridge Railway Act of 9th August 1899, the 1897 agreement with the District was repealed, and the way was at last clear for some real progress to be made on what now seemed to be a reasonably viable group of railways.

That summer, C. J. Wills & Son had two steam navvies and 325 men at work on the Ealing & South Harrow, the stations were started, and most of the bridges were completed. Work then tapered off and by the end of 1899 seems almost to have stopped, probably owing to the parlous financial state of the District. In his report of 8th February 1900, Forbes cautiously told shareholders that the E&SHR and the Whitechapel & Bow would be open 'within two years', sugaring the pill with a promise of freight business for both.

Under the MDR Act of 1900 the E&SHR was transferred to the larger company from 1st July that year. This act also sanctioned further capital, which was some-how secured, enabling work to proceed until the project was brought to virtual completion in the spring of 1901. On 4th April that year the Board of Trade inspector passed the line for public traffic, but the District was in no state to open it. Its main London system, increasingly vulnerable to competition from electric tramways and tube railways, was in dire need of modernisation and electrification, yet the board could hardly muster sufficient cash for day-to-day running costs. At the time when the clouds seemed at their blackest, deliverance arrived from the west. Whilst the E&SHR was being prepared for Board of Trade inspection in March, the District had passed into the control of the dynamic American railway and tramway financier and entrepreneur, Charles Tyson Yerkes and his associates. In that summer Yerkes formed the Metropolitan District Electric Traction Company to finance the electrification of the whole system, the money coming entirely from the USA.

As the E&SHR was lying ready for use, Yerkes and his advisers decided it would form an ideal test bed for the District electrification, but there was at first some delay whilst the District and the Metropolitan, who shared operation of the Inner Circle, decided which system they would use, and who would supply the electric power. During the winter of 1902–03, electrification was completed between Mill Hill Park (now Acton Town) and South Harrow using the 550V dc system with centre positive and outside negative conductor rails which a Board of Trade arbitration tribunal had chosen, much to Yerkes' satisfaction. A generator used for the Inner Circle electrification experiments of 1899–1900 was installed on the canal bank at Alperton where coal could conveniently be brought by barge. Yet another act was required to sanction electric working of the E&SHR and this, which also included the purchase of more land to ensure the stability of cuttings through the Middlesex clay, was passed in 1903.

Two seven-car trains, built by Brush of Loughborough from drawings prepared in the USA, were straight-sided, monitor-roofed, arch-windowed and of distinctly transatlantic appearance. Each train consisted of three motor cars and four trailers, one having British Thomson-Houston Sprague multiple-unit control, the other Westinghouse pneumatic control. After the trials on the E&SHR it was the former which was eventually selected for the main District fleet. When delivered on 11th March 1903 the cars, with their gate platforms and central sliding doors, were in bright yellow picked out in maroon, with the company's name in full over the windows, USA style. During the year three were painted white above waist, red below, and six others bright red, but very soon all were in the red livery finally chosen for the District electric stock. They were kept in a shed at the London end of South Harrow station, where the electrical equipment was fitted and various experiments made, including an unsuccessful attempt to set one alight by starting fires inside and below it with electric arcs. In the shed and sidings the rails were of the American flat-bottom type, spiked to the sleepers, but elsewhere on the E&SHR the traditional British bullhead laid by the contractors was left undisturbed.

By May 1903 conductor rails had been installed on the running lines, with the negative return protected by boards. Yerkes' plans to make the District a true American 'rapid transit' operation called for a completely new approach to signalling and the system now installed on the E&SHR was later adopted with only minor modifications for the whole of the Underground company's network. Basically this consisted of electro-pneumatically operated signals (lower quadrant semaphores in the open air, colour-lights in tunnel) held in the line clear position until operated by 110V track circuits, and protected by train stops. Similar to that proved on the

Boston Elevated Railway, it was designed and manufactured by the Westinghouse Brake Company under the patents of H G Brown. On the E&SHR it replaced the conventional mechanical system with Sykes' lock-and-block and station boxes which had originally been provided, requiring only two boxes, at Hanger Lane Junction and South Harrow, to control junction, terminal and siding movements.

From Hanger Lane Junction where the authorised north to west curve towards Ealing was not built, the line turned sharply to the north-east, reaching the first station, North Ealing & Hanger Hill, which had a substantial house on the Down side and a crossover at the country end, enabling the line to be worked independently during the trial period. The site was close to Hanger Lane in a part of Ealing so far almost undeveloped, with Hanger Hill Farm close by. After skirting the eastern boundary of Hanger Hill House grounds (later a golf course) the tracks crossed above the new GWR Wycombe line before entering Park Royal & Twyford Abbey station, where there was nothing but a simple corrugated-iron shack on the Up side reached by a flight of steps from Twyford Abbey Road below. The surroundings were open, but Park Royal, the new 102-acre permanent London showground for the Royal Agricultural Society, was immediately to the east. From here the line crossed Alperton Vale, the Brent and the canal before entering Perivale–Alperton station in the centre of Alperton village. Here the corrugated-iron booking office was in the roadway below platforms partly protected by clumsy wooden canopies. The surroundings were a little more lively than at the first two stations, a few houses and some long-established factories on the canal banks, but Perivale was over a mile across fields to the west.

Park Royal and Twyford Abbey station, District Railway (Ealing & South Harrow Railway), soon after opening in 1903, looking to London. Note that the construction materials are almost entirely timber and corrugated iron, to reduce costs to the minimum.

The line now turned north-west, soon running into Sudbury Town for Horsenden, another corrugated-iron hut, this time on the Up platform, which was more or less level with the surrounding land. Its name was rather a joke as Sudbury at this time consisted of nothing more than a few well-dispersed houses, a farm and a brewery set around the Priory, all a good half-mile north of the station. At the western end of this settlement was another iron hut station, set in open country, Sudbury Hill for Greenford Green. Later the GCR Northolt to Neasden line was built beneath an E&SHR cutting just beyond here, a cut and cover operation not without difficulty in the unstable heavy clay. North of the cutting, on the Up side, were the electric car sheds and sidings at the London end of South Harrow station, which was almost five miles from Hanger Lane Junction. The well-built station house on the Up side was similar to that at North Ealing and there was a crossover at each end of the platforms. At the northern end, on the London side of the bridge over the Harrow to Northolt road, the rails met those of the Metropolitan Railway's Uxbridge line at what was known as Northolt Road Junction. 'South Harrow' was a railway renaming of Roxeth, the community on the southern slopes of Harrow Hill whose inhabitants served the needs of Harrow School, the big houses higher up the hill, and the works of the Harrow District Gas Company.

Invited with other reporters to see Mr Yerkes' American style railway, *The Times'* man thought the cars more like trams than railway carriages, with far fewer seats than comparable steam suburban trains. Told that they expected to carry almost as many standing passengers as seated ones during the busy periods and that this was the usual thing on American railways, he remarked 'whether the London traveller will take kindly to this arrangement remains to be seen'.

Following a satisfactory Board of Trade inspection on 16th June 1903 it was intended to open to the public on Monday 22nd June, but heavy rains shifted the earthworks so much that it was only possible to run between Mill Hill Park and Park Royal on 23rd June, the opening day of the Royal Agricultural Society Show. Until the show ended on 27th June, a shuttle service of four trains an hour worked to and from Mill Hill Park, but although the weather cleared up, the attendance at the Show was the lowest for 28 years. Despite the electric rail service and special GWR workings on their new line, the shows of the following two years were similar failures, causing the Society to give up Park Royal as a bad job in 1905.

Restoration of the line north of Park Royal was speedily accomplished, enabling the full length to be opened on Sunday 28th June 1903, but the clay continued to give trouble for a long time, requiring speed restrictions and even on occasion, single-line working. The 08.05 departure from South Harrow that Sunday inaugurated the District Railway's first permanent electric service on London's first surface electric railway. At first only hourly, with some extras in the mornings and evenings, the frequency was soon increased to half-hourly with connections into the steam service at Ealing Common and Mill Hill Park. Few passengers were attracted, and the lack of any service beyond South Harrow did not help matters. Sudbury Town saw only 60,000 bookings in its first year and the stationmaster, who had a house at Alperton and was, American-fashion, responsible for these two stations and Park Royal, was not exactly busy.

Although the Metropolitan had reached South Harrow at the end of 1903 there were no regular services over this section until 1910. Pending further developments, the MDR protected itself with trap points, but when the Metropolitan's first electric

'Underground to Anywhere: Quickest Way: Cheapest Fare' is the enticing message at the door of the corrugated iron shed that was the original station at Sudbury Town, portrayed here on a commercial picture postcard published around 1908. The London platform is nearest the camera and the stationmaster's house can be seen at the right. The direction of the shadows and absence of activity suggest that the picture was taken early on a Sunday morning.

cars were delivered early in 1904 it was arranged that they should be tested on the South Harrow–Rayners Lane section, for which purpose a short section of the Down road was electrified, using power from the Alperton plant.

The contractors, Bott & Stennett, had begun to build the Harrow & Uxbridge in September 1901, but it was not until 4th July 1904 that the public were able to ride between Harrow-on-the-Hill and Uxbridge. As the Metropolitan's new power station at Neasden was not yet ready, steam trains were used, running to and from a bay platform at Harrow-on-the-Hill, some to and from London in the peak periods. At the formal opening on 30th June a decorated train of two saloons, two bogie firsts and two brake coaches hauled by 0–4–4T No. 1, its coal painted white, left Harrow, backed down the South Harrow line to show the flag, and then took the guests on to lunch in a marquee at Uxbridge station. A *Financial News* reporter remarked that 'the line passes through a charming rural district, which looked its best and suggested infinite possibilities of snug residences to spring up in due time'. And spring up they did, though not in any great numbers until the 1920s and 1930s, as we shall see.

Leaving the Metropolitan's main line west of Harrow-on-the-Hill, the branch ran south-west to Rayners Lane Junction, where the South Harrow line came in from a viaduct of 71 brick arches and three iron bridges which covered most of its 1.17m. About half-way between Rayners Lane Junction and Uxbridge was Ruislip, the only intermediate station, with a large station house on the Up side, a half a mile below the village. Its yard had facilities for coal, cattle, horse and carriage traffic and (appropriately) furniture vans. Passing east of Ickenham village, the line then ran south-west to terminate at Belmont Road, Uxbridge. Here the plan was that of a through station with two 473ft side platforms, 20ft wide, firmly placed on the alignment of the 1897 High Wycombe proposal. (With suggestive imagery, *The Railway Magazine* of September 1903 had remarked 'The Fulmer Valley lies temptingly open . . .'). To the south of the station there was a large goods yard and shed. The main passenger building, in red brick, which included a refreshment room, was also on this side of the line.

Other than the Roxeth viaduct there were few features of interest, as the line passed through fairly level open pasturelands for most of its length, with few houses to be seen until Uxbridge was reached. Signalling was the usual Metropolitan Railway Spagnoletti electric lock-and-block, controlling mechanical semaphores from boxes at Rayners Lane, Ruislip, and Uxbridge. Conductor rails had been laid in anticipation of electric working through a substation at Ickenham. Electric trains composed of end-platform stock designed for urban service on the Inner Circle worked incongruously through the fields to Uxbridge from 1st January 1905, but steam trains did not entirely disappear from the branch passenger services until the end of May.

With the completion of the District's main electrification in 1905, the E&SHR was integrated with the rest of the system, taking its power from the huge new plant at Lots Road, Chelsea, through a substation at Sudbury Town. Until the summer of 1909 there were no public workings beyond South Harrow, but then the District running powers on to the Uxbridge line were exercised in the form of pleasure party specials worked from Ravenscourt Park and West Kensington and hand-signalled between South Harrow and Rayners Lane Junction. Regular service of District trains to Uxbridge started on 1st March 1910, remaining hourly for most of the day until 1919. Sunday trains were about every 45 minutes but in summer, when cheap tickets were issued, frequency was increased to half-hourly in the afternoons for the benefit of pleasure traffic. As the District trains were short, the Metropolitan waived its statutory right to a minimum payment of one shilling (5p) a train-mile. Towards the end of 1910 the District tried out late-night theatre trains to Uxbridge on Wednesdays and Saturdays, and for a short time an Uxbridge portion was included in the 17.15 Mansion House–Hounslow Barracks. This had disappeared by 1911 when the only through District working between central London and Uxbridge was the last train Down at night.

Since its opening in 1855, the South Harrow works of the Harrow & Stanmore Gas Co. had received its coal in road carts coming up from the canal wharf at Greenford Green, then from Harrow (Met) yard, but in 1910 a siding, crossover and signalbox were provided just north of Northolt Road, South Harrow. From 4th October, Metropolitan steam locomotives propelled a coal train daily (at first averaging seven trucks) from Rayners Lane to the works, returning with gas coke. A minimum 14,000 tons of traffic annually was guaranteed by the gas company.

Varying at first at four, three or two trains an hour, the basic E&SHR service settled down to every 20 minutes in 1911. Running time between Acton Town and South Harrow, at first 24 minutes, became a mere 14 after 1906 when single-car operation was introduced in the middle of the day and all intermediate stations except Alperton were treated as conditional stops. Park Royal, the least used, closed earlier and opened later than the others. In the hope of attracting pleasure traffic, Sunday service was increased from two to six an hour in 1911, but wartime constraints brought this down to four in 1916 and three a year later. South Harrow trains usually ran to and from South Acton or Acton Town, but at peak periods some worked to and from central London. By 1913 South Harrow was generating a trickle of commuter traffic, which justified the introduction on 1st January 1915 of a morning business 'express' named *The Harrovian* in the timetable folders (the staff called it *The Pansy*). Leaving South Harrow at 08.15 and missing some intermediate stations, this covered the congested 15¼m to Mansion House in 39

The Ealing & South Harrow Railway did have decent brick built stations at each end of its line. South Harrow's street frontage to South Hill Avenue, Roxeth is seen here on a commercial picture postcard published about 1908.

minutes, and although it survived until the introduction of tube trains on the line in 1932, it was never matched by an evening return train. Between London and Acton Town, rush-hour trains normally consisted of eight cars, five working to and from Hounslow, three to and from South Harrow.

In the early years there were about 25 trains daily each way between Harrow-on-the-Hill and Uxbridge (15 on Sundays), some running through to and from London in the rush hours. The fastest train in 1911 was the 07.22 from Uxbridge which reached Baker Street in 38 minutes, Liverpool Street in 54. By 1916, with suburban growth just evident, the service had been increased to about 48 trains a day each way, 28 on Sundays; most trains terminating at Harrow had London connections.

At the MDR meeting on 6th August 1903 the chairman had looked forward to rapid suburbanisation of what was 'almost an unknown territory to Londoners, even of the West End', but in the event house building along both routes to Uxbridge was at first very slow. A few streets of small houses appeared close to South Harrow station around 1910–14, with similar developments at Sudbury Hill and Sudbury Town, and Wembley spread towards Alperton station. Traffic between Harrow and Uxbridge was at first extremely disappointing, and despite efforts at promotion, which included a Metropolitan booklet on the residential and holiday attractions of the district, in 1908 the Metropolitan was losing £3,000 a year, not counting interest on capital. Economies made late in that year included removal of through trains to and from Baker Street, leaving the line worked by a three-car shuttle service which allowed closure of Ickenham sub-station. To build up traffic, the Metropolitan opened a series of halts which it was hoped would attract pleasure seekers until housing development got under way.

The first of these simple structures, asked for by the parish council, was at Ickenham, close to the old village. Constructed at minimum cost, its timber platforms on concrete pillars, only three-car length, opened on 25th September 1905 with nameboards reading *Ickenham Halte*. Holidaymakers formed the main traffic here for many years, the villagers serving lunches and teas in their gardens or cottage rooms, sending them home with cut flowers at 6d (2½p) a bunch. Delayed by a 1918 proposal to resite the halt near the Air Board Stores, platform lengthening, by then much needed for the quite heavy summer traffic, was finally completed for the 1922 season.

Two more halts came into use on 26th May 1906, sited in the rural seclusion between Harrow and Ruislip, both of them at first conditional stops. Eastcote, on the Northolt Road, about a mile south of the village, rapidly assumed popularity as a destination for children's treats and summer excursions, so much so that it had to be extended from three-to six-car length in 1910. In July 1913, 93 children's parties were dealt with, 16,000 in all or up to 3,000 a day, a statistic which caused the board to sanction some modest improvements to the structure. Building of estate roads started here at the end of 1912, materials subsequently coming in through a wagon siding worked by Annett's key until a signal box was opened in 1913. Another intermediate block post was established at the Ickenham Ground Frame about 1914. The second of the 1906 halts was at Rayners Lane, just west of the junction with the South Harrow line, serving nothing but two or three well-dispersed houses, a sewage farm and a rifle range. Operating convenience rather than traffic demand was the reason for extending its platforms from three to six car length in 1918.

Responding to pressures from Ruislip Manor Ltd, which gave land and started to develop a 133-acre estate between the Eastcote Road and the railway in 1911, Ruislip Manor halt, at first only accessible by fieldpath, was opened on 5th August 1912. A siding to bring in building materials was laid from Ruislip station, extended into the estate area with light railways. By 1914 roads had been laid out and some 200 houses built, many of them unsold. More successful was West Harrow halt, a delayed response to the quite considerable amount of house building west of Bessborough Road which had begun around 1905. Only a quarter mile west of the junction with the Metropolitan main line, West Harrow, perched on an embankment and entirely in timber, built at a cost of just over £1,000, a little more than that of two of the new houses served, was opened on 17th November 1913. Within three years, it was handling 40,000 passengers a month. Noting that receipts had grown from £3,770 in 1915 to £16,308 in 1927, the board agreed to a minor reconstruction in 1928 which included concrete platforms of eight-car length.

Thanks to the economy measures described, and the small additional traffic generated by the halts opened up to that year, the Metropolitan's Uxbridge branch showed a small credit balance for the first time in 1912. Further progress was checked by the outbreak of World War 1; house building then slowed down and before long stopped altogether, not to resume for some time after the return of peace.

During the war years, railwaymen quietly cultivated potatoes alongside these still very rural lines, grateful not to be in Flanders' trenches. When the railway had been built, sufficient land was taken for four tracks between Harrow and Uxbridge, and this provided six acres within the fences which in 1917 were turned over to cultivation, together with Metropolitan fields at Eastcote and Ickenham.

For some time after the war, pleasure traffic remained the major feature at Eastcote and at some of the other stations. In 1919 one train ran all the way from Surrey Docks to Eastcote with a children's outing, and between April and August 1925, 40,000 arrived at the halt in pleasure parties. Reporting in December 1926 that drawing-up at the six-car length platforms was endangering the children, the general manager persuaded the board to extend them to 420ft (eight cars); a 120ft shelter was provided on the Up side at the same time. South Harrow was another popular resort for children's excursions, special trains coming in the 1920s from Shepherds Bush, Ravenscourt Park and elsewhere to the Roxeth fields and sports paddocks, bringing up to 3,500 a day in high summer.

The Metropolitan's Harrow & Uxbridge Railway terminus at Belmont Road, Uxbridge was built as a through station aligned for further extension to High Wycombe, for reasons explained in the text. This view, apparently taken just before the opening in July 1904, also shows (right) the spacious goods shed and yard. *Commercial postcard*

The tiny pavilion of a design that served as entrance and ticket office for several Metropolitan Railway suburban stations, seen here at Eastcote in 1933 attracting some new suburban house-wives. The tobacco kiosk looks rather out of place on the bridge over the line, and not particularly waterproof. The tea shop on the right is a relic of an earlier era of pleasure trippers – at this time the countryside they sought is rapidly being covered with houses.
London Borough of Hillingdon Libraries

The Uxbridge and Harrow Branches (Met and MDR) 279

One of the first pointers towards the coming residential boom was the sale of the 400-acre Swakeleys Estate at Hillingdon in September 1922 and of the 200-acre Hillingdon Court Estate in the same year. By the end of that year, the Halden Estates Company, which planned to erect £750 detached houses at Hillingdon Court was negotiating with the Metropolitan for a siding and passenger halt. This was agreed subject to the donation of land for a future goods yard and a guaranteed minimum annual income representing 10 per cent of the cost of construction and staff wages. Hillingdon halt opened on 10th December 1923, its siding following soon afterwards. No longer needing the 7½-acre plot that it had bought at the Swakeleys sale for a goods yard, the Metropolitan sold this in 1927 to its subsidiary, the Metropolitan Railway Country Estates Ltd, for its Hillingdon Mount Estate.

During the 1920s residential development along the Metropolitan line was steady, if sporadic. That at West Harrow has already been mentioned, and when local authorities pressed for service enhancements there in 1925 the response was to extend trains terminating at Harrow to Rayners Lane, making minor improvements at the latter point. At Eastcote, serious building started in 1923, soon taxing the capacity of the ten-wagon siding. After it had been told of wagons held back at Harrow daily for lack of room, the board authorised improvements in September 1923. Land bought by the railway company next to the station in 1923 was sold for development three years later to Metropolitan Railway Country Estates Ltd.

Ruislip Manor was slow to start. As the Ruislip Manor Co did not prosper, much of its land was sold off in large blocks, but when nothing had happened by mid-1926, the Metropolitan threatened to close the halt. This was averted when the owner of the Windmill Hill Estate agreed to make an annual grant of £50, and he and others began to use the spur siding adjoining the halt to bring in building materials towards the end of 1926.

For reasons analysed in another book* suburban growth around London took off at the end of the 1920s. One of the most favoured sectors in the following decade, the whole catchment area from Harrow to Ruislip and from Ealing to Rayners Lane then experienced large-scale construction of small houses by private firms until most of the fields and woodlands were covered by semis and short blocks. West of the line at North Ealing the Hanger Hill estate appeared from 1928, while at Twyford and Alperton the activity was intense from the same time. Between Sudbury's two stations new streets either side of the line were largely filled up between 1930 and 1936. By 1939 there was very little open land left between South Harrow and west of Ruislip, where Nash, Crouch, Davis and other firms had carpeted the fields south of the railway with a patchwork of new streets; north of the tracks, the whole area up to the Metropolitan main line was suburbanised by about 1936. A major contributor to this last was the Metropolitan's offspring, the Metropolitan Railway Country Estates Ltd, whose 213-acre 'Harrow Garden Village' around the once-isolated Rayners Lane station, was begun in May 1929 on land acquired in 1928 with loans from the railway company. A Metropolitan Railway advertisement in the *Evening News* of 24th January 1931 invited readers to 'view the development of this delightful estate on the Metro . . . houses by well known builders available at popular prices. Free first class return tickets from Baker Street'. For those tempted by this offer there were 110 trains daily to Rayners Lane and the same number back, a

* Jackson, Alan A., *Semi-Detached London*, Wild Swan, 1991

journey of '21 minutes from town'. Other MRCE schemes along the line evolving about the same time were Hillingdon Mount, already mentioned, Eastcote Hill, Manor Farm (Eastcote Road, Ruislip) and Elm Grove (Ruislip). Among those aiding MRCE in the creation of the new suburb of Rayners Lane were T. F. Nash Ltd, who acquired the 250-acre Tithe Farm Estate. A long siding was constructed into this during 1931 to bring in building materials, the Metropolitan receiving £1,600 in six annual instalments for the cost of connection at Rayners Lane.

During the two decades after 1931 the population of Ruislip & Northwood Urban District grew by almost 326 per cent, the largest accretion in London for the period, most of it logged up by the end of 1939. London Transport estimated that the number of residents served by the Harrow to Uxbridge line rose from 48,300 in 1931 to 95,000 in 1938; at Rayners Lane alone, traffic jumped from 22,000 in 1930 to 4,000,000 in 1937, marking the transition from a tree-girt country lane to bustling suburb with large shopping centre and super cinema. At Ruislip Manor, the 17,000 passengers of 1931 grew to 1,262,500 in 1937. Nearly 1,500,000 more journeys were made from South Harrow in 1936 than two years earlier, whilst at Park Royal the 1,300,000 travellers of 1936 were three times the 1933 total.

As most of the new householders were London office workers, train services and station accommodation had to be reshaped to cope with peak movements. In 1931 the 1920 service of four trains an hour with rush-hour extras on the South Harrow line was increased to six and then in the autumn of that year to eight (six on Sundays). From 1920, two trains an hour ran through from the District line to Uxbridge, weekdays and Sundays, but this was increased to three in 1932. On the Metropolitan line in the 1920s there were some 50 to 60 trains each way daily between Harrow and Uxbridge, but as early as 1928 the general manager foresaw that the need to strengthen this substantially would require additions to substation capacity. As Ickenham and Harrow substations were 4½ miles apart, voltage was low between them and in March 1928 the board agreed to a new substation at Eastcote with two 1,200kW rotary converters. Taking advantage of a government grant of interest at five per cent on the capital, under the 1929 Development (Loan Guarantees and Grants) Act, the Metropolitan resignalled between Rayners Lane and Uxbridge in 1930, installing long-range Westinghouse automatic three-aspect colour-lights which required signalboxes only at Rayners Lane, Eastcote, Ruislip and Uxbridge, with a ground frame at Hillingdon yard. At Rayners Lane, the original 22-lever mechanical locking frame at the intersection remained until the early hours of 22nd November 1934 when it was severely damaged by a runaway ballast train. A replacement box at the country end of the Up platform controlled the whole layout including the South Harrow gasworks siding and a new reversing road between the Up and Down lines west of the station. At the gasworks, the 14-lever mechanical frame was abandoned, replaced by a plunger operated by the engineman's foot, which gave a 'train ready to start' indication in the new Rayners Lane box when the once or twice daily steam working was ready to return to Harrow-on-the-Hill. In full operation from 17th November 1935, Rayners Lane cabin had a power frame of 35 levers incorporating route lever working. Its opening allowed removal of the lock-and-block on the South Harrow–Rayners Lane section, the last example of this on lines wholly worked by London Transport.

As pressure increased, it became impossible to find more paths over the District line for the Uxbridge, South Harrow and Hounslow trains into central London, so when cheap government money was on offer to combat unemployment, it was decided to extend Piccadilly tube trains to South Harrow (and, as we have seen, Hounslow). Work on this started in 1930, in conjunction with an extension to Cockfosters at the other end of the Piccadilly Line. Tube trains reached South Harrow on 8th February 1932, shuttling to and from Acton Town. Through services began on 4th July, providing the Ealing & South Harrow line with its first all-day through workings to and from inner London; the old 7½-minute District shuttle with two through morning Up City trains and four back in the evening was replaced by tube trains at 5½-minute intervals, supplemented in rush hours, a total of 170 each way daily between South Harrow and the Piccadilly tube. Six- or seven-car trains were used at peak hours, three at other times, all composed of new rolling stock fitted with four air-operated sliding doors each side of each car. Between South Harrow and Uxbridge, a 20-minute District service replaced the half-hourly workings to and from Ealing Common, but from 23rd October 1933 Piccadilly Line tube trains ran to Uxbridge, where like their predecessors, they were relegated to the almost unsheltered platform on the north side. These trains ran every 20 minutes, soon increased to four per hour (three on Sundays), with extra workings at peak periods. Tracks were raised at stations to give a suitable compromise platform height for both types of stock. Many tube trains ran the full 31½ miles from Uxbridge to Cockfosters, at that time the longest tube train journey in London. The tube extension was fed through a distribution station, control room and substation at Alperton, and unmanned substations at Sudbury Hill and North Ealing. Car sidings were laid at South Harrow on the site of the 1903 installation.

Publicised by such naive slogans as 'Live at Ruislip where the air's like wine, it's less than half an hour on the Piccadilly Line', further house building followed these service improvements, much of it either side of Field End and Victoria Roads south of Eastcote and Ruislip Manor stations. Not three years elapsed before an MP was asking in Parliament about overcrowding on the Piccadilly Line in north-west London. New rolling stock was promised, but nothing appeared, apart from the 1936 experimental trains, which started work on the Uxbridge line on 8th April 1937.

All the District's outback stations of corrugated-iron and timber disappeared in a modernisation programme in response to the huge increase in passengers. Park Royal & Twyford Abbey was closed after traffic on 5th July 1931 to be replaced the following day by a temporary station just under a mile south on Western Avenue, better placed to serve the new housing and factories which had appeared in this area from 1929 onwards. With traffic showing a growth from an initial annual total of about 60,000 to almost 1,300,000, Sudbury Town was chosen for the prototype of a new generation of surface stations for the Underground system. Designed by Charles Holden and others working under his supervision, these were to gain recognition as some of the finest examples of British public building of the inter-war period. In restrained functional style, with meticulous attention to detail and passenger flow, graceful and appropriate, the new Sudbury Town which opened on 19th July 1931 was built around a large flat-roofed passenger hall in Buckingham brick and white reinforced concrete. Similar but less confident rebuilding of Alperton and Sudbury Hill followed in 1932. At South Harrow the new station of 5th July 1935 had an entrance on the main road, the architects solving the problem of an embankment site with a design of some elegance. Park Royal got its new

Like the District Railway, the Metropolitan was for some years reluctant to spend more than the minimum on new stations for suburbs that had yet to develop; their provision may be compared with that of the GER on the Churchbury and Fairlop loops. This is Ruislip Manor, looking north, on 26th April 1934. Timber platforms and crude wooden sheds are still thought good enough, despite the arrival of new housing on both sides of the line (which seems to form a frontier of quality here). Note too the interesting mixture of Metropolitan diamond and Underground Co bullseye symbols still awaiting standardisation by the new London Passenger Transport Board.
London Transport Museum

permanent station on the site of the temporary one on 1st March 1936. Also in the Holden style, its 40ft diameter passenger hall, marked by a rectangular sign tower, dominated this part of Western Avenue. Only North Ealing remained unaltered, retaining its original signs and early Underground ambience up to the end of the 1950s, when some minor refurbishment took place.

During 1937–38 the Metropolitan Railway's formerly rural halts at Rayners Lane, Eastcote and Ruislip Manor were transformed into modern Holden style stations. The Metropolitan had considered plans as early as 1928 for complete rebuilding of Rayners Lane with two island platforms to form an intermediate terminus providing cross-platform interchange with the District, but nothing was done apart from the provision of an additional waiting shed on the old wooden side platforms. The opening of a timber building on 14th March 1935 to replace the tiny roadside booking hut of 1906 was an expedient pending agreement of road widening plans, which finally allowed the LPTB to go ahead with a new station, opened on 8th August 1938. Designed by Holden and Uren, this had as its main feature a tall rectangular hall astride the railway, jutting 25ft from the building line, so that pedestrians could walk in and out of it from the footpath and flanking shops. Rather less impressive new buildings in Holden style at Ruislip Manor and Eastcote were completed in 1938 and 1939 but at the former, the work at rail level was left unfinished. At Hillingdon, where receipts moved from £2,025 in 1924 to over £12,000 in 1930, the board ordered some improvements in the latter year. Building pace at Ickenham did not justify reconstruction before 1939 and although platforms were lengthened, this remained very much the country halt, with its homely little booking office on the road bridge. In the mid-1960s London Transport slowly transformed it to a suburban station, opening a passenger hall built on a raft over the line on 19th September 1971.

Bold decisions had to be taken at Uxbridge where, using the entry provided by the existing large goods yard, the LPTB erected an entirely new rail and bus station fronting the High Street. Approached through a deep cutting, this had three tracks with four platform faces under an impressive overall roof of glass and concrete. At the High Street end, a spacious passenger hall with a licensed refreshment room was linked to the roadway by a shopping arcade. When this new facility was opened on 4th December 1938 the tube service to Uxbridge was increased from four to eight trains an hour.

Suburban growth also required expansion of freight installations. At Ruislip, where the 1904 passenger station remained unchanged apart from a new covered footbridge and roofing and shelter extensions in 1928, the yard was enlarged in 1928-29. After the board heard reports of an average of 17 wagons blocked daily at Harrow unable to get into Hillingdon, that yard was improved in 1930. Nash's private siding at Rayners Lane has already been noted, but this was preceded by another laid in 1929 for the builder E. S. Reid, who met its £1,000 cost. For the new suburb the Metropolitan opened a public yard west of the station in July 1929 where by the end of the year traffic had risen from 230 to 1,157 tons a month, requiring expansion in 1930.

At Uxbridge the wholesale grocers Alfred Button & Sons had leased buildings in the goods yard since 1913 on condition that the Metropolitan would get a minimum level of traffic, but when the firm wanted to expand this property in 1926 whilst sending the bulk of their traffic by road, the Metropolitan insisted that the company withdrew all but one of the road vehicles that had been used to carry goods from the London docks and markets, consigning the bulk via the railway. This was agreed, and for some years much of it passed through the Metropolitan's Farringdon goods depot, but when the LPTB took over in 1933 this movement was seen as an embarrassment to the rapidly growing passenger traffic. Reconstruction of Uxbridge station brought closure of the yard at the end of April 1939.

Freight movements over the Uxbridge line survived well into the postwar years, ex GCR class N5 0-6-2T giving way in the 1950s to BR standard class 4 2-6-0s and these in turn, in 1963 to diesel locomotives. The closure of the South Harrow gasworks on 4th April 1954 brought to an end the local trips described earlier and a Beeching rationalisation killed off the remaining public freight workings, diverting all railborne solid fuel (virtually the only residual business) to a new concentration depot at West Drayton. As a result the yards at Rayners Lane, Eastcote, Ruislip and Hillingdon were closed from 10th August 1964.

At West Harrow, where the ugly station structures of timber and old rail had become unstable on their embankment perch, a total reconstruction was completed in September 1990. Clad in white vitreous enamel metal panels, the new platform buildings included small waiting rooms. At street level, the Metropolitan Railway's garden shed-like ticket hut gave way to a ticket and entrance hall in brick and glass which bore a passing resemblance to a very large greenhouse. This new building was sited below the London platform and passengers for the Uxbridge direction, having bought their tickets, were still obliged to pass under the railway bridge and climb the separate staircase to the westbound platform.

Somewhat more splendid was the replacement of the shabby station at Hillingdon, long overdue for rebuilding. Here some forward-looking architecture from the Cassidy Taggart Partnership won a design competition. Completed in 1992-3 and funded from the roadbuilding coffers of the Department of Transport, this trans-formation came about because the 1923 station most fortuitously stood in the way of a desired realignment of the A40 London-Oxford road (Western Avenue). It was a rare and precious example of public expenditure in the interests of speeding up motor traffic being obliged to benefit rail transport facilities. The new platforms, moved 71 metres nearer to Uxbridge, with ticket office above their London end, were reached by a lengthy elevated covered walkway from the former ticket office site in Long Lane. Two hydraulic lifts with a 16ft 6in rise were installed to facilitate access by those with impaired mobility. This end of the platforms, the footbridge over the line and the new ticket office area were protected by a graceful ridged overall roof and a second similar roof at a slightly lower level covered a further length of the platforms with their waiting areas enclosed in glass block walls. These stepped roofs, reminiscent of the Victorian trainsheds, created a bright and airy space beneath, luminous with direct and reflected light from their fritted glass and white metal framework. Since the pattern of the glass was varied to correspond with the changing angle of the sun's rays, it provided protection from solar heat and radiation without degrading the light. Visually, the whole structure formed a creditable adornment to the Uxbridge line, in its own generation standing comparison with the fine 1930s architecture elsewhere. Unfortunately, any contemplation of its interesting and pleasing design, from within or without, was assaulted by the persistent roar which arose from the malodorous chasm enclosing the adjacent A40 road.

The elegant 1993 station at Hillingdon, looking to Uxbridge. *Capital Transport*

Further modernisation of signalling was undertaken in the post-war period: on 17th October and 12th December 1948 the Metropolitan's 1930 installation between Harrow and Uxbridge was replaced by standard London Transport two-aspect colour-lights, increasing line capacity to 30 trains an hour. On the Ealing & South Harrow, the original semaphores were gradually replaced by standard colour-lights until the last, at Hanger Lane Junction, went out of use on 21st November 1953, a date which marked the end of semaphore signals on wholly-owned London Transport electric running lines. Some points at South Harrow remained mechanically-worked until 14th November 1957 when the signal box there was closed in favour of remote control from Rayners Lane. The South Harrow–Ealing section was controlled from the Earl's Court Regulating Room after another programme of signalling improvements, completed on 17th July 1978.

On the Metropolitan Line between Harrow and Uxbridge, a further signalling modernisation scheme was started in 1987. Uxbridge box was closed and its work transferred to an auxiliary panel at Rayners Lane from 4th May that year; under this scheme, supervision and operation of the whole line was eventually to be moved to the Signalling Control Centre at Baker Street station.

To give permanent way trains from Ruislip depot better access to the LT system and to increase operational flexibility in movement of empty stock, a single line connection, unelectrified and hand-signalled, was laid through sidings from the Uxbridge line west of Ruislip station into the Central Line Ruislip depot between Ruislip Gardens and West Ruislip stations. This came into use on 24th July 1973. From 28th September 1975, mainly to facilitate its use for reversing Piccadilly Line trains at Ruislip, it was signalled and electrified.

Train services underwent some modification from the late 1950s onwards, partly to reflect the general decline in off peak loadings and later the severe staff shortages experienced by London Transport in the mid 1970s. Frequency after 21.00 was reduced to 20 min Mondays to Fridays and before 09.00 and after 19.00 at weekends. Piccadilly Line tube trains were progressively withdrawn west of Rayners Lane: between 10.00 and 16.00 on weekdays from 2nd March 1959, on weekday evenings and Sundays from 16th/22nd October 1967, after midday on Saturdays from 5th December 1970 and all day Saturdays from 5th October 1974. By 1995 the number reaching Uxbridge had declined from 106 a day in 1958 to 30.

Things then improved. From 30th May 1995 the midday Metropolitan Line service Mondays to Saturdays was increased to six trains an hour (8/12 min. intervals); a 15 minute service was introduced on Sundays in shopping hours in response to changes in Sunday trading legislation; and from September 1996, Piccadilly tube trains once again ran through all day to Uxbridge. The important point to absorb is that even at its lowest point, the service given to Uxbridge and intermediate stations through north west London's 1930s suburbia was always better than that received by comparable areas south of the Thames, such as Waterloo–Raynes Park–Epsom. Although post 1948 traffics would never at any point have come near to justifying commercially the ambitious line capacity advancements put forward in that year, the London Transport services through South Harrow and Rayners Lane to Uxbridge continue to make a substantial contribution to the success of the popular residential and retail centres they serve and in whose development they have played such a large part. The shades of Henry Raynes, C. T. Yerkes and R. H. Selbie must view the outcome of their initiatives with continuing satisfaction.

The Stanmore Branch (LNWR)

(map page 293)

Like the Chipstead Valley, the Harrow–Stanmore branch owed its existence to the drive and pertinacity of a single capitalist. With a population of only 1,400 and three stations within little over a two-mile radius, Thorne's 'neat, clean, genteel' village of Great Stanmore seemed a poor candidate for a railway of its own, but in the 1880s, this picturesque district of north Middlesex, already a favourite place of residence for the moderately wealthy, attracted the attention of the hotel and restaurant magnate Frederick Gordon (1835–1904). The particular object of Gordon's interest was Bentley Priory, a mansion set in a vast richly-timbered estate, once the home of Queen Adelaide, latterly of Sir John Kelk, the prosperous railway and building contractor. In 1882 Gordon bought the estate with the intention of converting it into a country resort for his London hotel guests, a project which could not be expected to prosper without some improvement in railway communication. Meanwhile the Priory opened as an hotel on 6th June 1885.

Edgware, Stanmore & Harrow Railway and Edgware & Harrow Junction Railway Bills deposited by other interests in November 1881 had failed, as did the Ealing, Harrow & Edgware Bill deposited in 1884. Obliged to promote his own line, Gordon engaged William Beswick Myers to survey a route from the LNWR at Harrow. Opposition from Lord Wolverton of the Glyn banking family was overcome when Gordon purchased part of his estate, land which he opened as a golf course in 1893.

The 2m 4f 7.25ch branch was authorised in 1886 as the Harrow & Stanmore Railway, to a company consisting of Frederick Gordon, Edward Hegley Byas, John Pound and Charles Edward Keyser, with a capital of £60,000 and borrowing powers of £20,000. From a junction with the LNWR Up slow line at Harrow, facing away from London, the branch was to run due north between Kenton Lane and the west side of Stanmore Park, finally passing through the southern part of the Bentley Priory estate to terminate on the west side of Green Lane, 190yd north of St John's parish church.

When Gordon failed to raise capital for this line he promoted a second bill in 1887 for a shorter route of 2m 1f 2.25ch, which left the 1886 alignment 2f 6.25ch from Harrow, passing to the east of Stanmore Park to terminate 375yd south-east of the parish church on the west side of Old Church Lane. In its new act of 1888, the Harrow & Stanmore's capital was reduced to a more manageable £36,000 with borrowing powers of £12,000. Gordon took up 3,180 of the 3,600 £10 shares and 40 more went to his relatives.

Myers settled a junction with the LNWR which agreed to work the line, leaving Gordon to find the money. By its act of 1891 the main line company was authorised to enter into agreements with the Harrow & Stanmore, and an agreement dated 29th January 1891 scheduled to the act required the H&SR to build and maintain for one year a single line with passenger and goods station at Stanmore and interchange sidings at Harrow, also an intermediate station if this were required by the LNWR. In return, the main line company would work the branch in connection with its system, provide staff and rolling stock and after the first year undertake maintenance and repairs, all this for 60 per cent of gross receipts. The LNWR (Additional Powers) Act, 1899 confirmed the purchase of the H&SR by the LNWR on 1st July 1899, and an agreement scheduled to the act revealed the price as £34,000 in cash with H&SR liabilities as £36,000 in £10 shares, £12,000 in debenture bonds, and a mortgage of £2,800.

The pretty conceit that was Stanmore LNWR station, of which only a small part survives. Since the LNWR van carries a poster advertising the new line to Watford, this photo probably dates from 1912. *Commercial postcard*

Meanwhile, at 12.17 on 18th December 1890, the first train left Harrow for Stanmore, inaugurating a timetable of ten Down and nine Up trains Mondays to Fridays with one extra each way on Saturdays. The first departure from the terminus was at the reasonably gentlemanly hour of 08.20, but the last Down run from Harrow was at 20.15. To secure his railway, Gordon was obliged to pay careful attention to local feeling; one demand was that there should be no Sunday trains, although he did manage to obtain a concession that the ban should be limited to 40 years. Stanmore's station building, as we shall see, was another costly obligation in this direction.

At Harrow station the branch platform, labelled HARROW JUNCTION CHANGE FOR LNW RAILWAY, differed in fittings and appearances from the rest of the building, an indication of the line's independent origins. For the first part of its route, the branch descended at 1 in 95 and 1 in 528, but just before half-way started to climb at 1 in 80, 1 in 85 and entered the terminus at 1 in 285. Situated about a quarter of a mile from the village centre and 94ft above the junction, Stanmore's station met the sensitivity of the privileged and affluent residents with truly delightful gothic elevations intended to blend into its surroundings of leafy parklands and expensive mansions. A low red brick and tile building with freestone embellishments, it bore a strong resemblance to a tiny country church, its principal feature a square tower decorated with spire, stone-faced clock and buttressed portico. The interior consisted of a single platform 310ft long, protected for most of its length by a cast-iron and glass awning supported by stanchions bearing the arms of the Gordon family. Facing the platform was a locomotive run-round road; behind it, on the east side, a goods shed and four sidings.

As working was on the single-staff system, the only signals were at each end, those at Stanmore two arms on a single post controlled from an open ground frame at the buffer stops (this was later replaced with a standard LNWR frame at the London end). Push-and-pull operation with Webb 2–4–2T started about 1907, after which the locomotive was invariably at the Harrow end of the train. The redundant locomotive line at Stanmore was used to stable stock. Freight trains were also propelled on the branch, latterly under a 13-wagon restriction. There was no intermediate goods yard but a siding was provided just north of Kenton Lane, where until about 1920 Marylebone's refuse was unloaded to deposit on the fields of Marsh Farm. Another change in the early years was the complete reconstruction of Harrow & Wealdstone station in connection with the LNWR widening and suburban electrification scheme. Completed in 1912, this work included a 540ft island platform (No. 7) for the Stanmore trains, with the Up slow line on the opposite face (No. 6). The position of the new suburban lines at the extreme west side of the station combined with the nature of the junction rendered it unduly costly to include Stanmore in the electrification scheme, a circumstance which to a large extent sealed the fate of the line, allowing other railway companies to exploit the district during the building boom between the wars.

As yet there was no sign of any traffic potential. Gordon's enterprises at Stanmore failed and the line's business was very light. A few houses appeared near the station, some built by Gordon but the Bentley Priory hotel flopped and Gordon moved in with his second wife and 11 children. He became a regular passenger on the 08.20 Up train, returning home from London in the evening. After his death in 1904, Bentley Priory became for 20 years a school for young ladies, before passing to the Air Ministry. Gordon laid out a road named after himself across the part of Stanmore Park that he had bought and three-bedroomed houses here were advertised in 1906 at rents of £26 a year, but there was no general development of small houses at this time in the country between Stanmore and Harrow & Wealdstone stations.

Some inroads were made into such traffic as did exist on the branch by the establishment of motor bus services in the area. In 1922 an hourly service was started between South Harrow and Golders Green via Harrow & Wealdstone station, Stanmore and Edgware, and since 1913 there had been a 20-minute bus service between Kilburn and Watford via Stanmore Hill. From 1924 the South Harrow–Edgware buses, increased to half-hourly frequency, were feeding the new Underground terminus at the latter point, with through tickets to London available which were cheaper than the Stanmore–Euston fare via Harrow & Wealdstone.

From about 1923 a number of roads were made east of the branch at Stanmore station, and in the late 1920s and early 1930s Kenton was creeping north to fill the triangle between the branch, Kenton Road and Kenton Lane. This last development, of semi-detached and terrace blocks, was soon to provide extra loads for the Stanmore branch. In response to demands from the builders, the LMSR opened a halt called Belmont on 12th September 1932, sited where the branch passed under Kenton Lane about 1¼ miles from the junction. The single platform, on the west side of the line, supported an ugly wooden waiting shelter and a wooden ticket office under a pitched roof. Branch trains called here on weekdays between 07.00 and 22.00, and soon the somewhat primitive facilities were proving inadequate. Wealdstone spread eastwards to the branch in the early 1930s, whilst Davis Estates and others built north from Belmont towards Stanmore Park, selling at prices between

£595 and £865. By this time a second competitor was in the field. The Metropolitan Railway had opened its branch to Stanmore on 10th December 1932, but although this had the advantage of through rush-hour trains to and from the West End and the City, initially the fares were at main line rates leaving the road-rail facility via Edgware Underground as the cheapest route for Stanmore residents.

With building of low-cost houses proceeding apace, Belmont became and was to remain the main traffic centre for the Stanmore branch. Bricks for house building were brought in to a temporary siding nearby. A reconstruction scheme announced in 1935 was completed on 5th July 1937, when a 300ft island platform station with centrally-heated waiting room replaced the halt. A wooden booking office, built out on stilts at the side of the road bridge was linked to the platform by an uncovered footbridge. The passing loop, with its spring-loaded points and ancillary sand drags, controlled from a signal box on the platform, made it possible to have two trains on the branch at a time, providing a ten-minute service in the peak. As a further refinement, electric token block working with long and short section tokens started in September 1938; the extraction of the long section token from the Belmont frame locked it, also securing the slip points at Harrow to prevent a second train from entering the branch. The signals were then set to give one through road on the west side of the Belmont loop. With the long section token placed in the Belmont frame to unlock it, it was possible to withdraw a blue section token to give to the driver of a Stanmore train. This done, the Harrow No. 1 box signalman was able to take out a red token which allowed a second train as far as Belmont. The two trains met there and the tokens were exchanged after being used to unlock the appropriate starter signals and crossover locks. Should any driver attempt to pass the Belmont starter signals at danger, he would find his train in the sand drag.

Before serious building began in the 1920s, 30 trains a day each way sufficed, but the service was then gradually improved so that by 1933 the morning intervals were only 15 to 20 minutes with service after that irregular, gaps varying from 15 to 65 minutes. Sunday trains were started on 6th May 1934 at approximately 20-minute intervals between 09.00 and 23.00. With the new loop in operation, the 1938 timetable showed 71 trains each way on weekdays leaving Stanmore between 06.43 and 00.25 and Harrow between 06.43 and 00.54. A ten-minute service applied in rush hours and at Saturday midday. A similar pattern was operating in 1946 but with earlier and later trains (05.45 to 01.05 from Harrow) and on Sundays there were half-hourly departures from Harrow between 07.35 and 00.05.

Webb 2–4–2T pushing or pulling one, two, or three coaches were replaced about 1934 with new 2P 0–4–4T which were also used on the daily freight run. Fowler 2–6–2T arrived in 1935, to remain the usual locomotives for most of the rest of the branch's life. The only other type of steam locomotive regularly seen were Ivatt 2–6–2T which were allocated to the line from their introduction in 1946. Webb tanks reappeared after World War 2, finding some difficulty in propelling three modern bogie coaches up the hill to Stanmore.

British Railways experimental ACV diesel railcar units took over the passenger service from 15th March 1954, and with some breaks these rattling and uncomfortable sets of three four-wheeled vehicles remained on the branch until 13th June 1955 when they were moved to the Watford–St Albans branch. Diesel car working was resumed on 6th August 1957, using both the ACV and the then new BR Standard types, steam locomotives coming to the rescue from time to time.

LMSR class 2P 0-4-4T 6409 ready to return from Stanmore, c.1938. *J G Dewing*

Sunday working was a victim of the coal shortages of winter 1946–47, but was restored the following June. Patronage was so light that Sunday trains were withdrawn permanently from 27th July 1947. In these early post-war years the LNWR rubber doormat at Stanmore station still showed little sign of wear and by 1952, with daily loadings on the branch averaging 700, it was not difficult for the BR accountants to establish an annual 'loss' of £4,000, which made it eligible for closure. Not surprisingly, the many rail user residents of Belmont rose up in anger, securing the retention of the section between there and Harrow.

After 13th September 1952 the delightful little station at Stanmore saw only the daily freight train, which brought in bananas and domestic fuels, and later, stores for the main line electrification. Holders of unexpired season tickets from Stanmore were allowed to use them on London Transport buses between Harrow & Wealdstone station and Stanmore church (route 114) or between Belmont station and Stanmore church via Wealdstone (routes 18 and 114). In 1955 the west side of the Belmont loop was taken up, working on the branch reverting to one train on line from 9th July. Freights to Stanmore continued until August 1964 when the last of the engineering stores were moved away. Track lifting began soon afterwards.

Despite the introduction of the diesel cars which brought some increase in

Experimental ACV lightweight diesel railcar set at the Belmont island platform, ready to leave for Harrow & Wealdstone, 17th April 1954. An LMSR 'Hawkseye' station name sign, a type stand-ardised in 1938, survives at right. *Alan A Jackson*

loadings, off-peak travel became very light towards the end of the 1950s for the usual reasons. Only some 900 ordinary tickets were issued each month for journeys between Harrow and Belmont in 1957, but this figure, which related only to local issues, was about twice that of steam days. Peak-hour patronage remained fairly heavy, with some trains in 1958 loading to over 100 passengers.

Ordinary bookings to and from Belmont faded away almost completely in the early 1960s when rail fares were allowed to climb above those of competing bus services, whilst operating difficulties brought frequent cancellations. Belmont duly appeared in the sad and lengthy list of potential casualties included in Dr Beeching's *Reshaping of British Railways* of 1963. During that summer a 15-year-old schoolboy collected 1,080 signatures in favour of retention, but was obliged to admit to the enquiry that only some 450 of these were regular users of the line. The Beeching decision was duly confirmed, the last train running on 3rd October 1964, after which the remaining passengers had to seek the alternative bus services which had already drained off most of the business. This was not quite the end. BBC television films were made on the branch in 1965 and 1966 and the first few chains out of Harrow & Wealdstone were used as a siding and as a tamping machine test track until 1968.

Few clues remain for the railway archaeologist. Belmont station was demolished in July 1966. This was no loss architecturally, but it is sad to record that despite the efforts of local residents, the planning authorities allowed the pretty little building at Stanmore to be incorporated in a housing and garage development. What survives is almost unrecognisable and the delightful Victorian atmosphere has gone. Harrow Council bought most of the track bed, using it for a variety of purposes including electricity substations, housing, car parks and schools, even a cemetery extension. Solid reminders of Gordon's enterprise remain in London's Northumberland Avenue, but there is little enough to see at Stanmore.

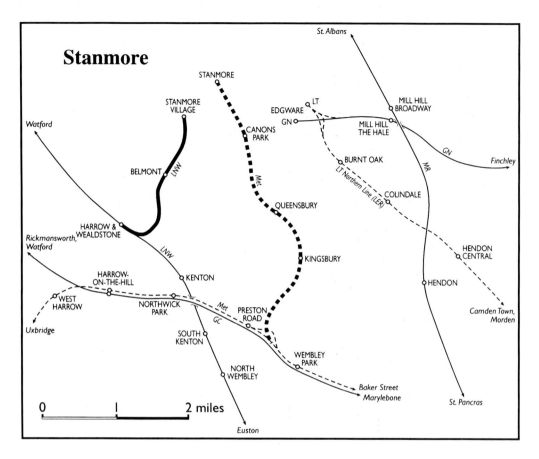

Stanmore

The Stanmore Branch (Metropolitan Railway)   (map above)

As early as 1892 a Metropolitan extension from Wembley through Stanmore to Watford had been suggested, and it came up again in 1908 when the Watford & Edgware interest saw it as a means of getting its line built; the idea was revived by Bushey residents in 1911, but on each occasion the Metropolitan shunned the advances. Although it later reached Watford by another route, it did however retain interest in Stanmore as an objective. A second railway to that place might seem an extravagance, even in the 1930s when the area was becoming thoroughly suburbanised, but the LNWR branch just described left untouched the western side of Edgware which had begun to grow in the late 1920s, also missing a large district west of Edgware Road which had seen industrial activity in World War I and which now seemed ripe for intensive housing development. So, thinking that there might be some pickings to be had, reinforced by the prospect of getting substantial parcels of land free or at nominal price from All Souls' College and the promise of government assistance with finance under schemes to relieve unemployment, the Metropolitan began in the summer of 1929 to look at possible extension in this direction. The aim was to draw from the Underground Company some of the business that it was at last getting from its 1924 Edgware extension, at the same time staking out a rival claim to the still open country north of Edgware in which the Underground had long had an interest. London was on a northward march, nothing seemed likely to halt it, and the Metropolitan had no wish to be left behind.

In September 1929 the Metropolitan board was told that all landowners along the route had been approached and serious opposition was unlikely. Property demolition could be confined to a few houses in Whitchurch Lane, Edgware. The picture of low land costs proved to be too rosy, as after work had started, it was necessary to compensate some developers at Canons Park and around Kingsbury for disturbance to housing estates already in the process of being laid out. Basing his assumptions on traffic growth at North Harrow and Preston Road between 1923 and 1928, the general manager forecast to the board that the new branch should produce a net profit of at least £20,000 a year within a few years. Again this was somewhat optimistic, as we shall see.

A bill for the 1930 session proposed a 4m 3.7ch branch from about half a mile north-west of Wembley Park station to a terminus on the eastern side of Stanmore, passing through potential suburban areas around Kingsbury Green and western Edgware. At the February meeting shareholders were told that the Stanmore catchment area, which was being rapidly developed for housing, was legitimately 'their territory'. An astute questioner from the floor made the awkward point about adding to the already serious congestion between Finchley Road and Baker Street, fears that the chairman tried to assuage with talk of more rolling stock and longer trains. He did not mention that the board had been concerned with this problem for over ten years, having tried earlier to secure government assistance for a 1925 scheme for a main line size tube between Willesden Green and Edgware Road. This had however come up against the difficulty that the Ministry of Transport's new 'Requirements for Tube Railways' would have prevented the operation of compartment stock on the planned line; the Metropolitan's long-distance services were entirely worked with such stock, which was preferred by the passengers. Nothing was done, although alternatives were considered and some stopgap measures taken; the misgivings of the questioner were to be justified and, as we shall discover, London Transport eventually had to undertake surgery.

Understandably, the LMSR objected to a second station in Stanmore on the grounds of wasteful competition, but were not in a very strong position as the Metropolitan could show without difficulty that it wished to serve a different district and also that its facilities would offer greater convenience to Stanmore travellers.

The Stanmore bill was one of four for new London lines in the 1930 session whose passage was facilitated because they were certified as likely to contribute substantially to the early relief of unemployment. Royal assent was given on 4th June and Treasury approval to a grant under the 1929 Development (Loan Guarantees & Grants) Act followed just over a month later. This was to amount to five per cent of the net expenditure for five years and 2½ per cent for a further five years. Petitions against the bill from the Wembley Urban District Council secured among other things that the abutment walls of the road bridges should be faced with brindle bricks up to dado height and bricks of 'varied and approved tints' above, whilst the de Havilland Aircraft Co. wanted any embankment past its Stag Lane airfield to be not more than 25ft high, with no obstructions more than 25ft above existing ground level.

In its *Metro-Land* annual for 1931, the company enthused over the new line, which the writer noted would pass through a district little known in the first part of its course except to the 'Sports Grounds players who use Preston Road station'. The central part was described as 'open pastureland crossed by a few footpaths' whilst the last section, approaching Stanmore, would pass through pleasant parkland. 'Houses there are at present practically none, but they will speedily follow the line . . . the work presents few engineering difficulties, the district for the most part being fairly level and of an altitude varying from 135 to 220 feet'. This statement about ease of construction was no doubt recalled with a bitter smile later. Substantial earthworks were required through the area's heavy clay and some short cuts were evidently taken to keep costs within estimates, since the formations subsequently required expensive maintenance and remedial treatment. In 1995 the whole length of embankment between Canons Park and Queensbury had to be stabilised.

In a 1933 advertisement the Metropolitan suggested that the district served, 'essentially pastoral in character' (they liked the word, but there was more hay than sheep) would 'provide room, under healthy, happy conditions, for a considerable population', an assertion somewhat at odds with the conclusion that 'the pleasant lanes, meadow tracts and byways that abound' would become 'deservedly popular with the pleasure-seeker'.

Hendon Rural District Council was less enthusiastic. Examining the bill in December 1929 it remarked somewhat sourly that the new railway would cut through 43 football and hockey grounds, would displace 14 houses each side of Whitchurch Lane, some of them only six months old, and would cross a fine avenue of trees, a dairy farm, the avenue to Canons Park and land scheduled as an open space.

Construction by Walter Scott & Middleton started early in 1931 under the Metropolitan Railway's chief engineer, E. A. Wilson. Temporary railways served by Manning Wardle 0-6-0T dating from 1876-1908 were laid along ground level, eventually to be linked to a siding alongside the main line at Wembley Park, and serviced by a depot west of the proposed Kingsbury station. Public roads were crossed on the level, with traffic controlled by flagmen. Delays caused by the prolonged wet weather in 1931 were recouped by 24-hour working during the following spring, summer and early autumn. On the first Sunday of December 1932 two Metropolitan Railway K Class 2-6-4T arrived to consolidate the new permanent way.

An official ceremonial opening took place on Friday 9th December when the Minister of Transport, the Minister for the Colonies (the local MP), and other notables joined the Metropolitan chairman, Lord Aberconway in a six-car train of new multiple-unit compartment stock, to which was added the company's official saloon and a Pullman car. This train ran to allow an inspection of the new stations and a formal 'switching-in' of Stanmore signals from Wembley Park signal box, returning the company to luncheon at Baker Street's new Chiltern Court restaurant. One of the speeches, by J. H. Thomas, Dominions Secretary and former GWR engine driver, was notable for the sentiment, still apparently tenable, that in the development of the nation, prosperity had run side-by-side with the prosperity and development of its railway system.

Public service started the next day, 10th December 1932, worked with multiple-unit compartment stock. Except in rush hours, when some trains ran to and from Baker Street, passengers were obliged to change trains at Wembley Park. There were 72 trains each way daily on the branch with a reduced service on Sundays, the best travelling time for the 11¼ miles from Stanmore to Baker Street being 22 minutes.

Left: The handsome station building provided for its Stanmore terminus by the Metropolitan Railway, seen here just before opening in 1932. Designed by the company's staff architect, C W Clark FRIBA, its Domestic styling was in keeping with the high quality housing of the area it served.

Right: Interior of Stanmore Metropolitan Railway terminus, with special train for Press inspection, December 1932. The unsuccessful goods yard is at the right. *C F Klapper*

From the junction, seven miles from Baker Street, the new line ran north-east on embankment, traversing its sharpest curve (15ch radius) and twice crossing the Wealdstone Brook which had been diverted into new channels. At this point, the alignment was to some extent determined by the presence of a new housing estate north of Preston Road station, the site of Uxendon Farm, Barn Hill, and the watercourse. Continuing north-east towards the Edgware Road and the still small communities of Roe Green and Kingsbury Green, the line entered a deep and wide cutting, passing below the Kingsbury-Kenton road. Here was Kingsbury station, which strictly should have been called Kingsbury *Green*, as that place was but half a mile east of the line, whereas Kingsbury itself was well over a mile away, close to Neasden station, which was called Neasden & Kingsbury until the new station opened. The entrance block, on the south side of the road bridge, was in the centre of three cottage-style red brick-and-tile two-storey blocks of shops, with flats above. There were five shops in each of the side blocks and three each side of the main entrance. From the entrance hall with its passimeter ticket office, covered stairs led down to platforms either side of the cutting, each platform with a short canopied red brick building containing a neat waiting room with tiled fireplace and wooden bench seats along the walls. Electric lamps held in pretty iron scroll work lit the platforms at night. When the station was opened there were no significant population centres nearby other than the small settlement at Kingsbury Green and, a little to the north, Roe Green, the interesting 1917 garden village for workers in the adjacent wartime aviation factories.

Crossing open land and skirting the east side of Willesden Isolation Hospital, the branch now turned north-west on embankments which continued almost to the terminus, encountering its maximum gradient of 1 in 70. Passing between the western boundary of Stag Lane airfield and the Hendon Isolation Hospital, the direction changed to almost due north. After crossing above Whitchurch Lane, where some suburban building was already in evidence, Canons Park (Edgware) station was entered.

At street level on each side of the northern abutment of the bridges was a canopied entrance to a booking hall beneath the first arch of the six-span masonry viaduct supporting the platforms. Either side of the entrances were small two-storey blocks of shops with flats over. Platform structures were similar to those at Kingsbury.

London's Local Railways

For its final section the line turned slightly north-west, entering the ancient Canons Park. Here it was closest to the LMSR branch, just over half a mile to the west. Encountering the upward slope of the Elstree Ridge, the tracks entered the terminus in a cutting. The station itself, the summit of the line, was scooped out of the side of the hill, its main building fronting on to the south side of the London Road, almost half a mile east of Stanmore village centre. Any extension towards Elstree and St Albans was going to involve expensive tunnelling through Elstree Ridge, but the terminus was planned to require very little alteration should that be required. The terminal platform was an island protected by a canopy which also covered the waiting room, staff accommodation and the lower landing of the covered staircase to the roadside building, a large three-storey block with its first floor at ground level. East of the platform was the only goods siding on the branch, together with two stabling roads. As traffic in domestic fuel and building materials was well entrenched with the LMSR, freight business at uncompetitive rates did not justify working a train up the line, and the facility was withdrawn on 31st March 1936.

The roadside buildings at Kingsbury and Stanmore were executed in a domestic style of 'pleasing and unassuming simplicity' by the company's architect, Charles W Clark, who also designed houses on Metropolitan land at Pinner and elsewhere. Stanmore, with its handsome hipped roof, four chimneys and Georgian windows would not have looked out of place on a country gentleman's estate. Both buildings were in red multi-coloured bricks set on a few courses of dark brindled bricks which formed a mock plinth. Their long red-tiled roofs were broken by dormer windows, one of which lit the entrance hall. These halls were tiled in khaki tone below plaster friezes, whilst the doors, clock and other features were elegantly framed in hardwood.

Canons Park was less impressive; here the roadside buildings were flat-roofed, the horizontal motif of bridge and roof emphasised by the pattern of the brickwork and a dark granite plinth. All three stations had platform buildings in matching red brick with workmanlike glass and steel canopies valanced in metal.

Spoil from the station area at Stanmore and the Kingsbury cutting provided much of the fill for the embankments. There were seven underbridges, the largest with a span of 89ft, and eight overbridges (four of them footbridges). All main bridges apart from one in steelcrete were of plate girder construction with concrete slab floors. Set in a 30–32ft wide formation, the double track consisted of 45ft 95lb bullhead rails and in accordance with Metropolitan practice, the 600V dc conductor was placed outside the inner running rails, current returning to a negative conductor between the running rails.

Signalling was conventional, with three-aspect colour-lights, ac track circuits, train-stops and short-range colour-lights or electric discs for shunting, but there was one novel feature. All points and signals were worked from Wembley Park box, using a Westinghouse centralised traffic control system for the first time in Great Britain (first in the world for a suburban application).

Power from Neasden at 11,000V three-phase ac was converted to traction voltage in new rotary substations at Preston Road ($3 \times 1,500$kW) and Canons Park ($2 \times 1,500$kW). Publicity for the opening made much mention of 65 new multiple-unit compartment cars which could be used to form seven complete eight-car trains or be broken up into four-car formation for slack-hour working. Five of the third-class cars were used to bring existing seven-car MW trains to eight-car length. This steel-panelled stock by Birmingham Railway Carriage & Wagon formed the cere-monial train described earlier, but the branch passengers also saw much of the older type of compartment stock. From January 1934 until November 1938 the off-peak shuttle was operated by single-unit 52-seater compartment cars converted from older stock in 1910 for the Uxbridge branch. Thereafter, until the arrival of tube stock, a two-car set was made up to accommodate traffic increases. The 1934 timetable shows three off-peak shuttle workings to and from Wembley Park each hour and three through workings composed of three- or four-car trains.

As it was constructed at just the right moment to coincide with the London suburban housing boom, building development did 'follow the line' as had been prophesied. Between 1931 and 1938 the population served between Kingsbury and Stanmore increased from 17,800 to 33,100, producing a 253 per cent increase in tickets sold (742,000 in 1933 to 2,622,000 in 1938). Train services were augmented accordingly so that by 1935 there were 98 each way on weekdays (45 of them to and from Baker Street) and 50 each way on Sundays.

Neither Stanmore nor Canons Park reaped anything like the maximum from their burgeoning catchment areas for reasons to be discussed in a moment. Kingsbury's trade became fairly brisk in 1933–38 when the whole of the surrounding area was clothed with small houses. After 1933 the station shopping parade was joined by others of varying styles and ugliness on both sides of the road, also by a cinema, the whole forming the focus of an entirely new community centred around the railway.

But perhaps the branch's greatest success in its early period was the new district built on and around the Stag Lane airfield after it closed for flying in October 1933. Plans for this 'new township of 100,000 houses and 150 shops' had been announced in local newspapers as early as April 1932 as 'awaiting the railway'. As there had been nothing there other than the flying field and hangars (they remained as factories) a name was required, and the not too imaginative choice of an estate agent was Queensbury. A station to serve it had been a condition of free conveyance of land by All Souls' College in 1929 (which wanted it to be called Kingsbury Downs) and on Sunday 16th December 1934 a wooden halt was opened. In 1936, with the growth of the surrounding area justifying something better, London Transport built a spacious new entrance hall and access passage through a large neo-Georgian block of shops and flats erected alongside the line by John Laing & Son. In the 1950s, the crude platform shelters were rebuilt in brick and concrete, leaving some evidence of the original halt in the timber platforms beyond the canopied sections until they too were rebuilt in 1978–9. With the station and the opening of other large blocks of flats and shops, followed in 1938 by a 1,500-seat cinema, this western end of the 80ft wide boulevard through the new suburb became its focal point. West of the railway, in the last three years before World War 2, Kenton grew northwards and houses and factories appeared alongside the 1935 dual carriageway motor road which replaced the tree-shaded Honeypot Lane. As there was no facility for railborne freight and as their workforce depleted the ranks of those who used the railway daily, these factories, with others (some of World War 1 origin) near the Edgware Road, much reduced the impact of Queensbury on the health of the branch.

A second influence militated against complete success for the new line. The Underground Company had encouraged its subsidiary, the LGOC, to operate feeder buses based on the Edgware extension stations. Providing a frequent service, together with road-rail bookings, these buses exploited to the full the new housing areas west of the Edgware Road, passing the entrances of the Metropolitan stations at Stanmore and Canons Park. The convenience of this road-rail facility, with its direct access by a shorter route to both West End and City via Euston, and above all its cheaper fare structure, encouraged a substantial proportion of the new home owners to use the Edgware tube in preference to the Metropolitan, some of them even coming to it from the west side of the Stanmore branch. The fare anomaly arose because the Metropolitan had in 1928 aligned its outer district fares and season ticket rates to those of the LNER; its ordinary fares were thus 1½d a mile, whilst the Underground's were closer to bus and tram fares, averaging 1d a mile with special reductions to encourage settlement at the outer ends of tube extensions. The single fare from Edgware to Charing Cross was 7d (3p) compared with 1s 2d (6p) from Canons Park, the latter route of course somewhat longer. This gave more than enough margin to cover the cost of the feeder bus ride whilst still offering the daily traveller a worthwhile saving over walking to a much nearer Metropolitan station.

After much agitation, London Transport took the opportunity of a general five per cent fare increase on 11th June 1939 to even out the rates. Fares on the former Metropolitan services came down to 1d a mile (no less than 700 fares from Stanmore branch stations were reduced) whilst the old Underground Company's substandard fares on the Edgware tube were increased to 1d a mile. But old habits die hard, and diversion of traffic to the Stanmore branch stations was not significant. Even in the 1950s many commuters were still using the very frequent (three to four minute) 18 bus across to Edgware station from places as far west as Belmont, and the former Metropolitan stations were never crowded even at the busiest times.

As expected, the imposition of Stanmore through trains inevitably worsened the existing peak-hour congestion between Finchley Road and Baker Street, where the Metropolitan's four-track main line came down to double. A variety of proposals had been considered by the Metropolitan Railway from 1915 onwards, but the solution finally adopted by London Transport used a plan formulated by the Underground Company in the early 1930s. This took the form of a 2.14-mile small-diameter tube railway from the Bakerloo Line at Baker Street which would surface for cross-platform interchange with the Metropolitan Line services at Finchley Road. By extending the Bakerloo trains over the existing Metropolitan tracks to Stanmore, capacity would be released on the old inner section. It was thought that the Bakerloo could accommodate dual termini north of the Thames because the original service to Queen's Park and beyond was not heavily loaded and could sustain a reduction in frequency if trains were lengthened from six to seven cars. Works for this scheme were duly incorporated in the 1935–40 London Railway Programme, construction starting in April 1936. A burrowing junction north of Wembley Park was included to allow Stanmore trains to reach local roads rearranged in the centre of the four tracks between Preston Road and Finchley Road, and this came into use on 6th November 1938 together with a rebuilt station at Wembley Park.

Operation with tube type rolling stock began on 27th March 1939 when three-car trains ran between Stanmore and Wembley Park for staff training. A through service over the 14.8 miles between Stanmore and Elephant & Castle started on 20th November 1939, six-car trains operating the whole route all day, reaching a maximum of seven an hour at peak periods on the Stanmore branch section. Not all went smoothly. Wartime commitments delayed the delivery of train describers and until 12th December 1939 when paper stickers showing 'M' over the background of the old Metropolitan diamond device appeared in the front windows of Stanmore trains, there was much confusion at inner London tube stations as to the destinations of trains. Drivers unfamiliar with the new route were hampered by blackout conditions, with the result that irregular running continued well into 1940. Nor were tube train drivers accustomed to such rural features as the electrocuted stag spotted after dark on the line between Canons Park and Queensbury in the autumn of 1944.

Platforms at the branch stations were altered to a compromise tube/surface stock height of 2ft 9in above rail, despite the fact that there was to be no more regular working of full-size stock over this line. Signalling was also changed to conform to LPTB practice, two-aspect signals replacing the old (some were retained with one lens covered), repeaters added and electro-pneumatic train stops installed. Centralised traffic control was discarded, a new 47-lever power frame with mechanical interlocking opening at Stanmore in 1939. Six new stabling sidings laid on the site of the old goods roads at Stanmore were used during the war years to house tube cars surplus to requirements pending completion of the 1935–40 New Works Programme. In 1949 land alongside these sidings was purchased for the construction of a new Bakerloo Line car depot in connection with the scheme authorised that year to extend the southern section from Elephant & Castle to Camberwell Green. Revised cost estimates led to the deferment of this proposal in September 1950. The 1939 resignalling of the branch proved unsatisfactory in that it restricted train intervals to a minimum of 3½ minutes, so delays building up in central London could not be rectified by retiming trains on the branch. To remedy this, complete resignalling for a minimum two-minute interval was undertaken in 1955.

Such a close frequency was not dictated by traffic levels. Patronage began to decline in the 1950s when the timetable was rearranged to provide for alternate trains to work only on the branch. The construction of a large complex of government offices close to Canons Park station in the late 1940s added a useful element of contra-peak flow until growth of car ownership removed most of it.

From 1st May 1979 Stanmore services were diverted away from the Bakerloo Line through new tunnels between Baker Street and Charing Cross via Bond Street and Green Park. Two thirds of the 2½–3min peak hour service at Charing Cross (formerly Strand/Trafalgar Square) then ran through to Stanmore, the remainder reversing at Wembley Park, Willesden Green or West Hampstead. Stanmore had a 3½–4 min frequency at rush hours and 7½ min during the middle of the day. This development, given the name Jubilee Line, was a belated recognition of the fact that although it made good sense to integrate the 1932 Stanmore branch with the central area Underground system it had been a mistake to do this by overloading and complicating the Bakerloo Line.

Although it is doubtful whether traffic on a branch line built in the very last years of competition between London railway operators has ever justified its construction and maintenance costs in the narrow financial sense, Wembley Park–Stanmore does continue to play a useful role in relieving the strain on the north London road system. For the perceptive visitor, the branch still retains some of its original atmosphere, rewarding the attentive eye with delightful reminders of Metro-land suburbia, particularly at Kingsbury station.

Edgware GNR, in August 1920 looking to buffers. The sign (left) reads 'EDGWARE FOR CANONS PARK'. The proverbial man and a boy are the only sign of life on the single lengthy platform.
H J P Rutherford

The Edgware, Finchley and Barnet Branches   (map page 304)

To the north of Kings Cross and Euston, a low range of hills with a moderately steep southerly slope runs across from Willesden through Hampstead and Highgate to the western outskirts of Wood Green. Behind there is high ground northwards through Finchley towards Barnet, where the town centre is at the summit of a 430ft hill. This barrier, long known as the Northern Heights, was carefully avoided by the early main lines. The London & Birmingham of 1837 passed it on the west; the Great Northern, completed in 1850 to Maiden Lane, swung to the east, seeking a ruling gradient of 1 in 200. Barnet, a coaching town on the Great North Road with an important cattle market, had to make do with a station 1½ miles from its centre.

Other places left unserved in the Northern Heights gap included the straggling villages of Edgware and Finchley, agricultural communities whose farms provided hay for London's huge army of horses. Edgware, as the first stage out of London along Watling Street, had also been a place of some importance in coaching days, but with the eclipse of road transport, its many inns and drinking houses saw little trade except at haymaking time, and by the middle of the nineteenth century its population of around 1,500 was slowly declining.

Proposals to connect Edgware to London by rail were brought to Parliament in 1860 and 1861, but these poorly-engineered schemes failed. Coming up with something rather better, including a station in the centre of Finchley, the Edgware, Highgate & London Railway obtained an act in 1862. Intended to attract GNR interest, it succeeded in getting that company's agreement to a junction at what is now Finsbury Park, and the main line company also consented to staff and work the railway for 50 per cent of gross receipts, subscribing one-third of the £220,000 capital; in return, it was awarded three of the eight seats on the board.

Imbued with a desire to retain some measure of independence, the little company was soon in financial difficulties, its situation aggravated by the appearance of the Midland Railway, whose authorised main line of 1863 kept very close to the western edges of the Northern Heights and attacked the south Hertfordshire plateau at Elstree, cutting right through the district the EH&LR hoped to serve. This threat the Edgware company countered by sponsoring a scheme for a 6¾-mile single-line extension to Watford and a branch from Highgate to Muswell Hill. (The latter's objective was Alexandra Palace, and we shall be returning to it in chapter 4). Both lines were to be worked by the GNR, and both were authorised in 1864. In a further attempt to strengthen its prospects, the EH&LR promoted another line from Finchley to Barnet along the east side of the Dollis Brook valley, for which it gained GNR support after a brief row with 'big brother'. An act for the Barnet line was finally obtained on 16th July 1866, not before Parliament had had to consider a rival Midland branch from Cricklewood and a GNR counter-thrust in the form of a strategic loop to the main line from Potters Bar through the western edges of Barnet to a junction with the EH&LR just west of Finchley. To consolidate its position, the GNR now made a good offer for the Edgware company and its offshoot the Watford & Edgware, the takeover coming into force on 1st August 1867. Despite the fact that some land had been bought, the GNR had little desire to trespass in LNWR territory, so the Watford line was formally abandoned by an act of 1870.

After all the financial, political and engineering delays it had suffered, the 8¾ mile EH&LR was eventually opened on 22nd August 1867 from Seven Sisters Road (now Finsbury Park) to Edgware through stations named Crouch End, Highgate, East End Finchley, Finchley & Hendon,* and Mill Hill. The line began each side of the GNR main lines, the Down track climbing on arches between the two Down slow tracks to join the Up line from Edgware, which was carried over all the main lines before descending to the extreme east side of Seven Sisters Road station.

All the intermediate stations had two side platforms except Mill Hill, which had but one, on the north side. Edgware, built as a through station in anticipation of the extension to Watford, had its main platform on the west and another side platform opposite, which before long fell into grass-grown disuse. There was also a large station house on the main platform, and a sizeable goods yard on the west side, together with a small engine shed, which was to be blown down in the Great Blizzard of 1881.

Beyond the north end of Highgate tunnels the line was single, but the 13-arch brick viaduct over the Dollis Brook between Finchley and Mill Hill was built wide enough for double track, as were the other structures on this section. Starting to climb at Finsbury Park, the line's gradients steepened to 1 in 60 east of Crouch End

---

* Renamed 'Finchley' February 1872; 'Finchley, Church End' July 1896.

station, 1 in 59 east of Highgate, reaching a summit north of the Highgate tunnels. The station here, attractively sited in a fold of the hill between the two pairs of single bore tunnels, was set out as an intermediate terminus, the tracks splaying to allow a central shunting road long enough to accommodate a short train. Of the 18 trains each way daily, eight reversed at Highgate, the rest going through to Edgware. Some served Kings Cross, others ran only to and from Seven Sisters Road station.

The double line was brought to East Finchley on 1st December 1867, Highgate then ceasing to be a terminus for some trains. Doubling was extended to Finchley & Hendon on 1st November 1869 this station then becoming the intermediate terminus, rebuilt with an island platform on the Down side, the western face used by Edgware trains in both directions. Meanwhile, in February 1868, trains from the EH&LR began to run through to Farringdon Street, and from March to Ludgate Hill, using the newly-opened City Widened Lines. As operations were somewhat inhibited by the absence of a direct connection from the Down line to the single line at Finchley & Hendon, Edgware's through trains to and from London were very few.

Northwards from Finchley, the double track to Barnet was opened on 1st April 1872 through stations called Torrington Park Woodside and Totteridge. Approaching its High Barnet terminus, the line mounted the side of the Dollis Valley at 1 in 61, cutting right across the former horse race track (once a feature of Barnet Fair) and crossing the Great North Road before coming to an end on the east side of Barnet Hill. Cabs and pedestrians from the hilltop town had to negotiate a steep approach from the main road, a feature which, in icy weather, was to cause many a dignified season ticket holder to complete an unwisely hurried progress to the morning train on his backside. The terminus, 11m 17ch from Kings Cross, had two platforms, the eastern one taking the form of an island. Carriage sidings on the east side and a goods yard to the south completed the layout. From the opening day there were 24 trains each way daily, all but one terminating at High Barnet, the exception going on to the Edgware line, which was otherwise now worked entirely as a shuttle to and from Finchley.

From the late 1860s these facilities encouraged suburban growth as far out as Finchley and within the next decade or so built-up London was pushing beyond Finsbury Park, requiring station accommodation at Stroud Green, where a wooden building on the embankment was in use from 11th April 1881. Finchley's high ground and good drainage attracted the better-off middle class commuters and their families; the village of 7,416 in 1871 had by 1901 become a small town of over 22,000.

A gradual increase in the train service, with morning and evening peaks becoming a feature in the late 1870s, threw considerable strain on the congested approaches to Kings Cross, a situation somewhat relieved when North London Railway trains to and from Broad Street all day appeared on the branch on 18th January 1875.

Increasing traffic led to layout changes. About 1880 Highgate station was rearranged with a central island platform instead of side platforms, served by a new booking office on the footbridge which gave access to entrances both sides of the line. At Finchley a double-line junction was laid in June 1896, facilitating through workings between Edgware and London, but although these were then increased, they never exceeded six each way daily. A new villa colony near Torrington Park Woodside, caused this station to be renamed Woodside Park for North Finchley in the public timetable dated 1st May 1882. Seven years later, waiting rooms were

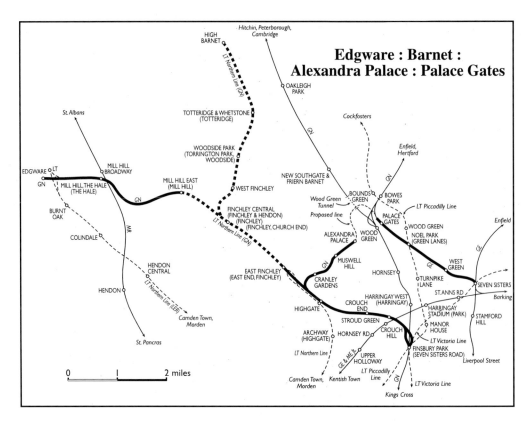

Edgware : Barnet :
Alexandra Palace : Palace Gates

erected on the Down platforms both here and at Totteridge & Whetstone. Further
south, suburban snobbery required the renaming of East End, Finchley, which
became East Finchley from 1st February 1887. From 1889 onwards there were
sporadic campaigns to secure a station in the 1½-mile section between this station
and Finchley. Such calls were still being made in the 1940s, but as before, they fell
upon deaf ears.

At High Barnet in 1896 a new entrance and ticket office (still in use over a hundred
years later) were provided halfway down the pedestrian approach slope from the
town, at the level of the footbridge, but the original cab entrance at platform level
remained in use at peak periods.

The Edgware line remained a sleepy backwater, for some obscure reason known
locally as 'the Pig'. Its relaxed atmosphere was hardly affected by the addition of a
wooden halt at The Hale, a single platform on the north side just west of the Midland
main line bridge, on 11th June 1906, an optimistic attempt to divert some traffic
from the new suburb that was growing around the Midland Railway's Mill Hill
station. A goods yard was added at The Hale in August 1910, when a booking office
was placed on an extended platform and a man was posted to look after both goods
and passenger business.

Goods traffic on the Edgware line received a boost in 1886 with the opening of
the North Middlesex Gas Works, served by sidings at the south side of Mill Hill
station. Further business came here with the construction of an infantry barracks
north of the station; the sidings put in for the building work were retained for army
traffic after the depot opened in 1904.

The precipitous approach to High Barnet terminus, with the original buildings at the lower level and the later ticket office in the middle foreground. This commercial postcard was published around 1905 but the buildings shown all survive in only slightly altered form almost a century later.

H. A. Ivatt's steam railmotors 1 and 2 were tried out on the Edgware–Finchley service from 19th February 1906. The diminutive 0–4–0T mounted on the same frame as a 53-seat car was fine for most of the day, but at holiday times when more capacity was required, the steam unit was not powerful enough to draw an extra coach. After just over a year, locomotive-hauled trains once more reigned supreme.

Suburban development on the Barnet–Finsbury Park line after 1870 required additional freight facilities. Loads were mostly house coals, building materials, perishables, and of course the ubiquitous milk churns (Down full, Up empty) as more and more of the local dairy farms were built over. By May 1879 additional sidings had been laid at Finchley and the accommodation there was further expanded in 1880 and 1907. More goods roads were added at East Finchley in 1898 and 1902, the business there becoming sufficient to justify a separate daily train.

Finchley's population reached 39,419 in 1911 when Church End station (now Finchley Central) had 60 trains each way daily, 14 of them to London between 06.00 and 09.30 serving Kings Cross, Farringdon Street, Moorgate, and Broad Street. After the opening of the tube railway from Charing Cross to Golders Green in 1907, some of the rush-hour traffic of the High Barnet line was extracted by electric tramcars and motorbuses which fed the tube from North Finchley, offering through bookings to tube stations from 1914. From March 1907 electric tramcars running parallel with the steam railway all the way from Highgate to High Barnet provided a more convenient, frequent and cheaper facility which drained-off most of the railway's purely local traffic. Motor-buses joined the trams in this activity from around 1914.

When the building boom of the late 1920s and 1930s filled up most of the open land remaining around the line, rush-hour services came under severe pressure and the LNER, not altogether enthusiastic about its GNR inheritance, dusted-off the latter's electrification plans only to find finance eluding its grasp. Changes were therefore few and undramatic.

From 1931 F. J. Ingram laid out the Woodside Park Garden Suburb west of the Dollis Brook and its name was added to the boards at Woodside Park station. Southwards, between the Dollis Brook and Ballards Lane, new houses appeared in large numbers between 1925 and 1936 over the fields and nursery gardens in an area known as Nether Street. Considering this description unattractive, the developers preferred West Finchley, which became the name for the new station they persuaded

Woodside Park station, GNR, looking to High Barnet about 1905. A small crowd including three nuns in full garb awaits an Up train. Apart from the fashions, the advertisements, the goods yard and the absence of conductor rail, this scene is little changed over 90 years later.
Commercial postcard

Highgate station GNR, looking to Barnet, *c.* 1903. The little hut behind the fence houses a representative of the Imperial Property Investment Company of Moorgate, no doubt anxious to interest prospective commuters in desirable residential prospects in this well-wooded middle-class area.
Commercial postcard

the LNER to open on 1st March 1933 where Nether Street crossed the line. As this was the LNER, construction was done as cheaply as possible, using second-hand materials from closed stations. A final improvement, which assisted running during the fogs to which the area was prone, was the introduction in 1932 of multiple-aspect colour-light signalling over the two miles between Finsbury Park No. 7 box and Park Junction, Highgate, allowing closure of the manual boxes at Stroud Green, Crouch End, Archway and Highgate.

During the 1930s passenger trains usually consisted of two Gresley 'quad-art' sets (two four-car articulated sets), some still gaslit. D. S. Barrie recorded that the Gresley N2 0–6–2T used to reach speeds up to 33mph with fully-loaded evening rush-hour trains on the climb to Highgate. Earlier, the GNR had deployed sets of 11 or 12 large four-wheelers with upholstered third class, hauled by Sturrock and Stirling 0–4–2 well tanks and 0–4–4 well and side tanks. The early years of the century saw the arrival of Ivatt 4–4–2T and the first of the Gresley 'quad-art' coaches appeared in 1911. By about 1914 the most usual passenger engines were H. A. Ivatt's N1 0–6–2T of 1907. Broad Street trains, confined to rush hours from the early 1920s, were for many years in the charge of the NLR 4–4–0T, but the LMSR introduced Fowler Class 3F 0–6–0T in the 1930s. Passenger accommodation on these trains was even less comfortable than the spartan 'quad-arts' as almost until the outbreak of World War 2 Broad Street commuters suffered the joys of NLR four-wheelers with half-partitioned thirds. Second-class facilities were withdrawn on the Barnet and Edgware lines at the end of 1937.

A 1938 timetable shows 57 trains a day from High Barnet, terminating variously at Kings Cross, Finsbury Park, Moorgate (13, confined to morning peak), and Broad Street (12, morning peak). Some of the Up peak-hour trains passed stations between Finchley Church End (now Finchley Central) and Finsbury Park, whilst the evening rush hours saw some non-stop working between Finsbury Park and East Finchley. Notwithstanding cheap off-peak fares, the irregular steam service proved utterly unattractive to a population still largely dependent on public transport. Compared with the adjacent Golders Green–Edgware line, which had generated 181 annual journeys per head of population served, the High Barnet/Edgware/Alexandra Palace group of lines produced a miserable 26 per head. As we shall see, London Transport hoped to change all that.

High Barnet station, LNER, looking to buffers, about 1938. Work has not yet started on the electrification for Northern Line tube services and LNER and LMSR steam trains, respectively bound for Kings Cross and Broad Street, stand peacefully at platforms 1 and 3.
Lens of Sutton

Freight traffic, almost entirely inwards, remained buoyant in the 1930s, although by the end of that decade road-making and house-building materials were becoming less important. In 1938 there were some eight goods trains daily to Barnet and Edgware behind GNR 0-6-0 and 2-6-0 tender engines. Edgware goods yard had been enlarged in 1926 to deal with building materials and domestic fuels for the suburban growth which had followed the arrival of the tube trains from Golders Green two years before. The Underground extension encouraged the LCC to site a large housing estate immediately south of Edgware. Watling was given its own station on the new Underground line, but much of the estate construction material was brought over the LNER line from Finchley into special sidings at The Hale, installed in 1926 to serve the contractor's temporary site railway system. Another aspect of the vast suburban expansion of the inter-war period was a revolutionary change in the distribution of milk. Large combines absorbed the many small dairy firms, introducing road and rail tankers and glass bottles instead of the unhygienic inefficient churns from which milk had been ladled into the housewives' jugs. In 1928 the United Dairies' milk depot at East Finchley was adapted to receive milk brought nightly from Staffordshire in trains of glass-lined tank cars, each tank carrying 3,000 gallons. This traffic, which even at the start fed some 750,000 suburbanites on the Northern Heights, continued for 20 years before giving way to road tankers.

The single-line Edgware section, its passenger business further diluted by the Underground extension, continued its relatively quiet existence. In 1938 there were 26 trains a day each way, only four more than in 1901 despite the fact that Edgware's population had grown in that period from 868 to almost 15,000. New housing had certainly brought a few extra passengers to The Hale, and rather more to Mill Hill (which had been respectively renamed Mill Hill for The Hale and Mill Hill East from 1st March 1928) but through trains to London were reduced, and in 1938 there was only one in the Up direction with no corresponding evening return. Rolling stock on the line varied from LNER vestibuled main-line stock to ancient GNR four- and six-wheelers, but in September 1929 there was some local excitement when the brand-new Sentinel steam railcar *The Rising Sun* appeared. This seated 59 passengers in some comfort, but like its GNR steam railmotor predecessors it suffered from an inability to cope with sudden surges of extra traffic, and was withdrawn during the following year. During its stay, *The Rising Sun* covered a single trip to High Barnet and back at midday, whilst a tank engine took over passenger working on the single line and placed wagons in the goods yards. At the end of the traffic day, the railcar worked in revenue service back to Finsbury Park.

Between Finchley and Edgware operation was by train staff with one engine in steam, signals being confined to an ancient fixed distant outside Edgware and a tall post on the platform there to prevent drivers from crashing through the buffers on dark nights. Unusual measures were therefore necessary when the line was required to cope with the exceptionally heavy traffic generated by the annual Royal Air Force display at Hendon aerodrome. Thus on 25th June 1932 through trains were running from Kings Cross and Moorgate to Mill Hill for The Hale every few minutes starting at 13.30 and during the afternoon normal service had to be suspended because some 1¼ miles of the single line were occupied by the trains which were to return to London from 17.24 onwards. Flagmen were present to control moving up, which was conducted at a very low speed.

In this 1937 view, Mill Hill East for Mill Hill Barracks, gaslit, sleepy and deserted, awaits the arrival of construction workers to provide double track for the proposed tube train service to Edgware and Bushey Heath.
Lens of Sutton

Totteridge & Whetstone station, LNER, looking to London, probably in the 1930s.
Lens of Sutton

East Finchley LNER, looking to London, probably in the early or mid 1930s. The nameboard has received a supplementary indication 'And The Hampstead Garden Suburb' but there is little else in the scene to indicate that this is already a thriving residential area with an electric tramway and Edwardian shopping parades just outside the station. All the railway infrastructure shown here was soon to be swept away and replaced with the impressive 1939 station for the Underground, designed by L H Bucknell in the Holden style.
Lens of Sutton

The Edgware, Finchley and Barnet Branches

The proximity of the Northern Heights lines to the Underground routes terminating at Edgware, Highgate (now Archway) and Finsbury Park led to their being incorporated in the major railway development plan drawn up by the London Passenger Transport Board and the main line companies north of the Thames soon after the formation of the Board in 1933. In view of its contribution to the relief of unemployment, this plan, announced in 1935 and modified two years later, received government blessing and a Treasury guarantee for the principal and interest involved. An important share of the finance was to be devoted to the Northern Heights. From the tube railway terminus at Highgate, tunnels were to be built to bring the trains to the surface alongside the LNER just south of East Finchley station, which would be rebuilt. A connection to be made between the LNER line and the Underground terminus at Edgware would allow trains to run into London via East Finchley from a new extension to Bushey Heath along the alignment of the Watford & Edgware Railway, which had been protected from house-building. At Drayton Park, the Northern City lines were to be brought up to run into the east side of Finsbury Park LNER station. The intention was to operate three new services of tube trains: between Moorgate and Alexandra Palace or East Finchley; between Bushey Heath and Kennington via East Finchley and Charing Cross; and between High Barnet and the Northern tube line via Camden Town. For the Bushey Heath service, the Edgware line was at last to be doubled and the junction station at Finchley Church End (Finchley Central) was scheduled for complete reconstruction. All LNER lines involved would get power-operated signal boxes with automatic colour-light signalling to tube railway standards, and the tube stock used would be partly owned by the LNER, which was to retain the freehold of its lines. Work on all this began in November 1936, but completion of the scheme was frustrated by the outbreak of World War 2.

To allow doubling and electrification to proceed, trains between Finchley and Edgware were replaced by a 'railway bus', complete with railway ticket structure, on some Sundays from the autumn of 1938, and completely from 11th September 1939. Tube trains reached East Finchley on 3rd July 1939 but the very impressive new station, with its two island platforms and Eric Aumonier's statue of an archer firing his rapid transit arrow towards London, was not fully completed until the following year. Thanks to the slow start of active hostilities between Great Britain and Germany, it proved possible to finish the electrification to High Barnet, and on 14th April 1940 tube trains began to operate a vastly improved service to and from that terminus. In peak hours there were trains every ten minutes from High Barnet and every five minutes from Finchley Central (so renamed from Finchley Church End on 1st April 1940). On weekdays 212 tube trains served High Barnet and there were 396 at Finchley Central and stations south in comparison with the 114 each way in the LNER 1938 timetable. All the electric trains ran via Charing Cross, but a service to the City branch of the Northern Line was started on 24th January 1941 and was increased to a ten-minute interval in peak hours from 19th May 1941. As we shall see in the next chapter, steam trains continued to run up to Alexandra Palace, and they also worked temporarily between East Finchley and Finsbury Park (Kings Cross, Moorgate and Broad Street in peak hours). They ceased to soil East Finchley's bright new concrete on Sunday 2nd March 1941, after which passengers requiring stations between Highgate and London on the surface could use the newly-completed tube station (opened on 19th January 1941) beneath the surface platforms at Highgate and the steam service between Alexandra Palace and Finsbury Park. The planned reconstruction of Finchley Central with a building on the overline road bridge was not started and the old GNR station remains in use today.

With some pressure from the War Office, Mill Hill barracks were served by reopening the Edgware branch as far as Mill Hill East on 18th May 1941. Despite the fact that a second track had been laid with conductor rails as far as Mill Hill for The Hale, the tube trains used only one line and the other was removed soon afterwards. The service was to and from Morden until 19.00 on weekdays; at other times the branch was shuttle-operated. Although the railway bus was withdrawn, rail tickets were available on ordinary service buses working between Edgware Underground and Mill Hill East. Tickets for journeys via Finchley Central were also issued at Edgware Underground and Mill Hill LMSR stations, which provided the curiosity of railway tickets headed LNER issued at an LMSR booking office for travel on an LPTB bus.

About 1942, to accommodate army traffic, the goods yard on the north side of the line at Mill Hill East was extended. Since the cessation of steam passenger services parcels had been carried by road, and depots for road collection were established at all stations except West Finchley. At Edgware, however, parcels continued to be brought in and taken out by rail.

In general, passengers were well pleased with the improved service although it was much more difficult to get a seat for the first part of the journey home in the evening. They missed too the 'Minute Bell' which had stimulated generations of City men to break into a trot down the steep slope of the High Barnet approach road; more romantic travellers were saddened to see LPTB roundels replacing the old black-and-white nameboards; 'Totteridge & Whetstone' had been contracted to 'Totteridge'; 'Woodside Park and North Finchley for the Woodside Garden Suburb' was replaced by 'Woodside Park'; and the imposing 'Finchley Church End change here for Mill Hill, The Hale and Edgware' was now just 'Finchley Central'. As for the latter, 'No one could ever imagine anything but tube trains calling at such a station' a reader of *The Railway Magazine* sneered in 1940.

For a few more years, goods trains brought steam locomotives (latterly N2 0–6–2T) over all the LNER lines, and after the war, tender engines were seen on occasional seaside excursions or railway enthusiast trips. Working of freight trains amidst the busy tube service presented some difficulties and curiosities. As the signal overlaps at the two-aspect colour-light signals were arranged to fit the braking performance of the tube trains, the goods trains were restricted to a 20mph limit and 14 wagons, while disc distants were installed in the rear of the colour lights to give a minimum braking distance of 500yd. All steam locomotives were supposed to be fitted with tripcocks to allow the London Transport train stops to bring them to a halt should they pass a signal at danger, but this rule was sometimes ignored. To penetrate beyond Mill Hill East it was first necessary to procure the key of the Edgware ground frame from Finchley Central signal box (an earlier procedure had been to carry a train staff normally accommodated at the Mill Hill East ticket office). The Mill Hill East platform signal was then passed at danger and after the tripcock had operated and been re-set, the train proceeded westwards with the driver keeping a sharp outlook for children on the track. If, as sometimes happened, the train became derailed, or the locomotive failed, the guard would take the ground frame

East Finchley as rebuilt for Underground train services in 1939/40, looking to London 23rd March 1957 with a Morden train at platform 4. The centre roads provide access to and from Highgate depot. *Alan A Jackson*

key (or the train staff) back to Finchley Central by bus, returning in due course on the rescue locomotive. Tube cars moving between the Northern City Line and Acton Works were attached to goods trains made up at Highbury Vale Yard, often travelling right through to Edgware and back before returning to London Transport hands at Highgate depot. This was the former Wellington Carriage Depot, used in steam days for storage of spare main line coaches and minor repair work, and was situated just north of the Highgate tunnels on the east side of the line. With openings made at the north end, the buildings were converted in 1939–40 to serve as tube car sheds, further stabling being provided in open sidings on the east side. In exchange the LNER got a new depot sited alongside the main line at Wood Green.

With the full revival of road transport after the War, freight traffic was soon mostly solid fuels and building materials. Nevertheless in 1956 there were still nine trains each way daily to East Finchley and seven beyond there, including coal for the lineside gasworks at Mill Hill East. In 1953 the old GNR station at Edgware still employed about 20 staff on goods and parcels work; passenger enquiries and bookings were also dealt with, bringing in a revenue averaging £100-£200 a month. But all this was in the nature of a swansong; the Mill Hill gasworks was closed in 1956 and in the following year all domestic fuel traffic was transferred to a new centralised distribution depot at Enfield Chase. From 1st October 1962 the yards at High Barnet, Totteridge, Woodside Park, Finchley Central, East Finchley (West Sidings) and Mill Hill East were all closed to rail traffic. When erection of a tower office block at Edgware in 1961 required demolition of the old station buildings, parcels and passenger agency facilities there were withdrawn, although the goods yard and that at Mill Hill The Hale remained open until May and February 1964 respectively. Freight working beyond Finsbury Park ceased with the closure of the yards at East Finchley and Wellington Sidings in June 1964 and the track beyond Mill Hill East was lifted later that year.

The London Green Belt, a feature of post-war planning, enshrined in government-approved development plans, made it unlikely that the proposed tube services beyond Mill Hill East to Edgware and Bushey Heath would generate a sufficient traffic. A preliminary announcement was made in 1950, foreshadowing the death sentence proclaimed in February 1954. As the proposed Moorgate-Alexandra Palace tube service was also dropped at the same time (for a different reason), the little stub of the Edgware branch and the High Barnet line north of East Finchley now became a simple appendage of the Northern Line out of Camden Town, with the short section south of East Finchley retained for access to the car sheds at Highgate Wood.

Recent decades have seen several changes immediately south of East Finchley station. The old LNER sheds which had been converted to a Northern Line car depot were completely rebuilt in 1969-70 to provide eight covered tracks under a single ridged roof, with improved access at the north end which considerably facilitated empty train movements. Following train service cuts, Highgate Wood stabling sidings were closed from 6th December 1982; tracks at the south end of the car shed had been removed shortly before this. In declining use, this almost new depot, housing nine trains, was itself closed after 25th March 1984, together with the 1939 Park Junction signal box, the last manual box on the Northern Line. Apart from one reception road retained for engineer's trains, the whole site was mothballed. This somewhat secluded, wooded area with its abandoned buildings was soon discovered by drop outs and vagrants who, unable to believe their luck, took it over. Arsonists and vandals also enjoyed themselves. Then, after a few more years had passed, their occupation and amusement was brought to an end. In connection with an increase in train services on the Northern Line, the installation was renewed, coming back to life from 23rd January 1989. Eight covered tracks, one open track, engineer's train siding and a tamping machine siding were then controlled by electric interlocking in a new relay room, train drivers operating trackside plungers to initiate movements. Park Junction box was demolished in 1995.

There has been little significant change to the rest of the infrastructure in recent years. Closure of West Finchley station was considered and rejected in 1983 and in 1992 some rebuilding was undertaken. Platforms were reconstructed and a new brick-built entrance and ticket office were provided on the northbound platform. The secondhand footbridge and the pretty timber waiting shed on the southbound side, with its valanced canopy, imported by the LNER, were both carefully restored and retained. Further north, at Totteridge, serious ground movements occurred in the station area in the summer of 1982, entailing temporary closure of the southbound line and platform. Subsequent stabilisation work was accompanied by a certain amount of rebuilding of the station but the original Victorian scale and style were very largely retained.

This is typical: even today, the transformation into another part of the Underground system is incomplete. For the seeing eye, once the East Finchley's stunning 1930s architecture is left behind, there is still a strong flavour of the past; the Great Northern Railway country branch comes alive, not only in the stations, where, as elsewhere the steam railway heritage is commendably cared for by London Transport, but even in the survival of several Victorian manual signal boxes, well-maintained and put to other uses. Woodside Park station, in particular, is worth travelling a long way to see; it has hardly changed in appearance since the 1890s.

CHAPTER FOUR

NORTH EAST LONDON

Alexandra Palace after the fire of 9th June 1873, showing the extreme end of the branch railway, apparently unaffected by the conflagration despite its timber platforms.

Railways to the Alexandra Palace

(map page 304)

The psychological impact of the Crystal Palace on its new site was such as to ensure north London interests would inevitably seek to emulate it, and an 1860 scheme, involving GNR directors was the first of several. Capital could not be raised, but the 1862 International Exhibition held in the Cromwell Road, Kensington provided a new stimulus. A group of businessmen purchased 240 acres of open country on and around the 310ft knoll that rises between Hornsey and New Southgate, their declared intention being to erect a north London Crystal Palace, using the materials from the International Exhibition, and naming it Alexandra Palace after the wife of the Prince of Wales (later Edward VII). The park was opened to the public on 23rd July 1863 and a year later work started on a building designed by John Johnson and Alfred Meeson. Financial problems and the unstable nature of the subsoil (gravel over soapy clay) caused many setbacks and the builders, Kelk & Lucas, were not finished until 1866. As the original enterprise had by then collapsed, the Palace was to remain empty and unused for over six years. Work on completing the park went forward, and the associated racecourse was opened in June 1868.

To serve the Palace, the Edgware, Highgate & London Railway had obtained powers in 1864 for a 1m 11ch branch starting near its proposed Highgate station and terminating at Muswell Hill near the boundary of the new park. Section 23 of the act, which contained sanction for the collection of one sum for railway fare and admission to Palace and park, noted that the railway was 'chiefly intended for the Conveyance of Passengers to and from the Alexandra Park at Muswell Hill belonging to the Alexandra Park Company (Limited)'. Two years later new companies had been formed, and an act of 1866 noted in its preamble that the landowners, the Muswell Hill Estate Company Ltd, had let for 999 years to the Alexandra Palace Company Ltd land which was 'being laid out in an ornamental manner and for public resort and recreation' whilst another part was 'being laid out as building ground'. This act authorised railways in the park, one extending the EH&LR branch from Muswell Hill alongside the northwest wall of the Palace, and others (which we shall come to later) linking the Palace to the Great Eastern Railway.

A third party seeking access to the supposed goldmine on the Northern Heights was the North London, Highgate & Alexandra Park Railway, whose Act of 1865 authorised a line from Caledonian Road station NLR to the EH&LR at Highgate, with running powers thence to Muswell Hill. This would have given a slightly more direct route to inner north London and the City, to which the GNR was understandably opposed, and no more was heard of this scheme once the EH&LR had been absorbed into the main line company. Yet another interested company was the Metropolitan & St Johns Wood Railway, a line authorised in 1864 from Baker Street to Finchley Road; a year later this company had promoted an extension from Swiss Cottage to Hampstead, with plans to go on to Highgate and Alexandra Palace, but the section beyond Hampstead, involving cuttings across the Heath inevitably encountered powerful opposition, and was not sanctioned.

In pace with the slow gestation of the Alexandra Palace there was no hurry to build the branch, although land was bought from 1867 onwards. Eventually, in the autumn of 1871, when there was some assurance that the Palace was at last to open, a start was made on the railway. About the same time work also began on the separately owned line from Muswell Hill to the Palace, and that was completed before the rest, in the summer of 1872.

The double track from Highgate, with its intermediate station at Muswell Hill, opened with the Palace on 24th May 1873. As the Muswell Hill Estate Company possessed no locomotives or coaches, the line was worked throughout by the GNR, the Estate company recovering what it could by imposing an exorbitant 2d single fare for the half-mile from Muswell Hill to the terminus. Issue of such tickets was however not frequent, the most popular ones being the shilling (5p) returns from Kings Cross, which included Palace admission.

By far the most convenient, if rather roundabout, access to the Palace, the branch at first enjoyed a very satisfactory traffic, indeed on the opening day there were so many passengers in the first-class compartments that they were deemed 'unfit to be entered at all by ladies or delicate persons', and on the following Whit Monday the largely rail-borne crowd of over 60,000 exceeded that at the Crystal Palace.

Alas, a few days later, on Monday 9th June 1873, North London's proud new attraction was completely destroyed by a fire which originated in a charcoal brazier used by workmen on the roof. Within 1½ hours the building was transformed to a 'melancholy and gutted ruin', despite the efforts of the GNR which, with an interest in the fate of the Palace not entirely altruistic, despatched two of its fire engines by rail from Kings Cross which reached the scene before any of the road appliances. Indeed the loss was a bitter blow to the GNR as well as to the underinsured Palace proprietors; at this period there was no suburban development to support the branch apart from a scattering of large villas whose owners could well afford to go down by carriage to the better-served stations at Wood Green or Highgate. So it was that once public interest in viewing the blackened ruins had waned, the train service, already reduced from 18 to seven each way, ceased altogether. After 31st July 1873, the only activity was a daily pick-up goods to Muswell Hill yard, if traffic required.

Although some half million pounds of assets had been lost it was decided to try again. Designed by John Johnson, a new palace, seven acres in extent, rose from the embers in only ten months. Grandiloquent in aspect, it lacked the delicate elegance of its smaller predecessor. For the opening on 1st May 1875 the full train service was restored, together with North London trains working to and from Broad Street via Canonbury. Only 21,000 attended the opening, but the following Whit Monday brought 94,000 to the Palace and Park, most of them coming by rail. *The Builder* reported journeys of over an hour from Kings Cross to the Palace on that day, and a chaotic evening with a derailment at Copenhagen Tunnel which blocked the whole line back to Alexandra Palace, causing many to walk off the railway at Holloway station, and others to spend the night on the trains.

The reopening revived interest in providing access from the Metropolitan Railway. In 1875 and again in 1876, bills were presented for a branch from Swiss Cottage to Highgate, with stations at Childs Hill, Hampstead Village and The Spaniards, but although the Metropolitan was sympathetic, that company was deterred by a lack of GNR interest and the scheme failed.

After autumn events in 1876 the Palace remained closed through the winter and with it the terminal station, but in those early years it enjoyed a modest success and the Muswell Hill Estate Company, as owners of the railway in the grounds, paid dividends of 2½ and three per cent in 1878, a year when almost 500,000 were carried on their section of the line. Like its sister south of the river, the 'Ally Pally' did not sustain public interest sufficiently to make it profitable. Despite its huge Willis organ (one of the largest concert instruments in Europe), the Japanese, Egyptian, and Moorish villages, the Italian garden, the 200-seat circus and the many other attractions and amenities inside the building or in the Park, the place gradually lost popularity and fashion, attracting large crowds only on the three Bank Holidays. Its owner, the London Financial Association, was itself inhibited by the possession of great quantities of unmarketable securities in hopeless railway enterprises. The Association went into decline in the late 1880s, its misfortunes exacerbated by lack of success in developing parts of the Park for residential purposes.

In 1877 the Association had secured parliamentary powers to sell 80 acres north of the Palace for house building (legislation was necessary as the 1866 act had authorised the railway on the understanding that the 240-acre Park was to be devoted to public recreation in perpetuity). A small amount of the 80 acres was sold-off in March 1878, but development was slow and Bacon's map of 1880 shows empty roads marked 'Alexandra Park Muswell Hill Estate'. Further sales in 1881 and 1883 found no buyers. In the 1880s and 1890s the London Financial Association wasted much money in promoting unsuccessful bills to secure powers to sell the whole of the Park for building.

Stroud Green GNR, c.1905. The station entrance and ticket office is behind the horse van on the right. Note the competition between coal merchants handling railborne fuel for suburban grates (left). The wooden station structures have long since gone but the underline bridge and railway alignment either side are still accessible for pedestrian exploration. *Commercial postcard*

The midday sun shines on an anorexic looking horse and ancient cab awaiting custom outside Muswell Hill station in the mid-1900s. Houses are offered to let or for outright sale and Gray Brothers have 11 types of railborne coal to sell householders, the most expensive (Inland Wallsend) at £1. 3s (£1.15p) a ton, a sum roughly equivalent to the weekly wage of the labourers who built the houses around here. *Commercial postcard*

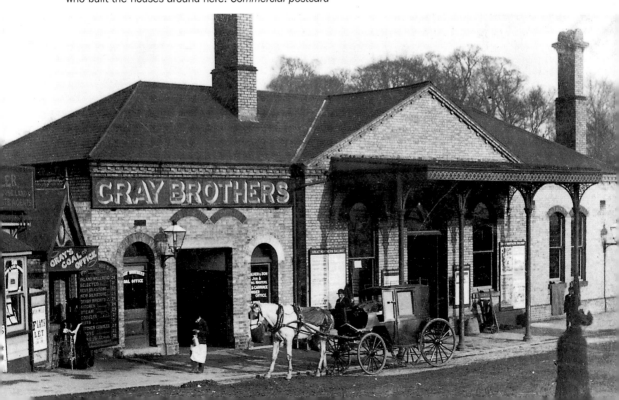

During the early years, access to the terminus was restricted to those holding the combined rail and admission tickets or prepared to buy entrance tickets on arrival. With an eye to future residential development, the Muswell Hill Estate Co. obtained parliamentary powers in 1886 to incorporate the holders of stock and shares in the railway undertaking into a separate body to be known as the Muswell Hill & Palace Railway. This had the effect of enabling the terminus to be operated as a public railway station although as someone sourly remarked, there were perhaps not more than 20 souls in the vicinity to make use of it. Plots still sold only very slowly and for a few more years the station was closed when the Palace was shut to the public.

For the Palace things went from bad to worse. It was closed from late August 1882 until March 1885 and there were further periods of continuous closure between September 1885 and May 1889. During these times the racecourse remained open for a few days' racing each year and other events were organised in the racecourse area, all this bringing sporadic bouts of traffic to Muswell Hill station. When the Palace closed in August 1889 after a none too happy season, it was to remain lifeless until March 1898. Hoping to encourage some residential traffic, the GNR nevertheless opened the terminus in March 1891, but receipts were so low that it was shut again in April 1892. In 1898 the GNR, perhaps seeing that suburban development was at last a definite possibility, agreed with the owners that the station should remain open continuously. Trains ran into the terminus again from 1st April that year when the Palace reopened from its long sleep, and almost 100,000 travelled on Easter Monday to see a balloon ascent, a parachute race, fireworks and other events.

After unsuccessful attempts in 1897 to enhance the attraction of its building land by promoting costly railway connections from Alexandra Palace station to the GER and GNR stations at Wood Green, and a fairly disastrous season in 1899, the owners in desperation offered the whole property to the local authorities. By an act of 1900 under which trustees were constituted, the local authorities were allowed to borrow money to contribute towards the purchase. The transactions were completed in February 1901, when 173 acres passed to the trustees and the balance was sold off for building. Under the new regime the white elephant perked up a little, enough for a short time to keep the annual revenue account in balance. Perhaps deceived by this temporary revival, the GNR made an agreement with the Muswell Hill & Palace Railway Company on 3rd April 1911, under which the main line company was to purchase the undertaking from 14th August 1911 for £18,416, releasing the small company from its obligation to pay five per cent interest on the £1,584 which the GNR had spent on improving the Alexandra Palace station. This agreement was confirmed by the GNR Act of 1911.

After swamping Crouch End, Hornsey and Stroud Green in the last two decades of the nineteenth century, the outward tide of London moved on strongly towards the isolated villas amid the trees on Muswell Hill. By 1901 roads had been laid out towards Hornsey, either side of the road called Muswell Hill, and on the east side of Muswell Hill Road to the south of the branch. This activity led to the opening on 2nd August 1902 of a second intermediate station, named Cranley Gardens after one of the new residential avenues. Through the 1900s and 1910s, the new suburb of Muswell Hill grew rapidly north of the railway, filling up at last many acres of the old Alexandra Park north of the terminal station. For a short period all this building brightened the fortunes of the GNR branch, providing it with a regular daily traffic for the first time. There was also a useful freight movement in the form of building materials, domestic fuels, and goods for the new retail centre at Muswell Hill Broadway. So intense was the building activity around Muswell Hill station about 1900 that a network of light railways was laid down, spreading out from a junction with the branch. Over these lines, contractors' locomotives hauled main line wagons along the housing frontages, pausing at each plot whilst the requisite quantities of bricks, timber, ironwork and so forth were dumped.

But scarcely had the new passenger traffic established itself when it was seriously diminished by improvements in road transport. First came electric tramways: in December 1905 from Turnpike Lane to the bottom of Muswell Hill and through the Park to the Palace doors; and in April 1906 from Wood Green to the east entrance to the Palace. Then, with even more effect, motor buses began to penetrate the very heartland of the branch, establishing direct communication between Muswell Hill and the new tube railway stations at Highgate (now Archway) and at Finsbury Park, with their direct services to the West End and the City. In April 1914 a four-minute service of small single-deck buses was started by the London General Omnibus Company between Finsbury Park and Muswell Hill via Crouch End, and shortly afterwards, an eight-minute frequency was available between Highgate (Archway) Underground and Muswell Hill, passing Cranley Gardens station. The GNR hounded the General into court with charges that excessive loads were being imposed by the buses on its overbridges at Cranley Gardens and Crouch End stations, a move which at least kept down the size of the buses used, for even a five-tonner was alleged to be dangerous for flimsy structures built to carry farm carts. In those days of cheap labour there was little difficulty in intensifying the service to make up capacity, and as the buses offered the attraction of through bookings via the Underground the hold they established strengthened steadily through the 1920s.

Curiosities of railway working such as through trains between the Alexandra Palace branch and Woolwich via Ludgate Hill and to and from Victoria were also affected by the competition from tube railways and motor buses. Both workings had disappeared by 1910, when the branch supported 61 trains each way daily, 15 more than seven years earlier. Not all these worked through to the terminus at Alexandra Palace while 20 of them were NLR trains to and from Broad Street. The GNR workings ran either to Kings Cross or Moorgate Street via the City Widened Lines. Last arrival at Muswell Hill was 00.16 but the first departure, as late as 07.14, provided firm evidence of the middle-class nature of the area. Eight minutes were taken from Alexandra Palace to Highgate, seven more to Finsbury Park. In the Down direction an additional two minutes were allowed to give the steam locomotives time to tackle the climb up to Highgate. These timings were to remain virtually unchanged for the next 30 years.

The special passenger traffic which had long been a feature of this line, trains for Sunday school treats, boy scout rallies, and other Palace events, was given a new twist with the outbreak of war in August 1914. The Palace closed on the 8th, briefly becoming a holding centre for mobilising army reservists who arrived and departed by rail; no sooner had these left for France than their place was taken by Belgian refugees who came in their hundreds from October onwards, many in special trains which worked through to Alexandra Palace station from Tilbury, Folkestone and Dover. In May 1915 when the refugees had gone, the Palace became an internment camp for 3,000 enemy aliens, and immediately after the end of the war it housed 4,000 civil servants engaged on clearing up the administrative aftermath.

Heavy use of the City Widened Lines for wartime freight caused off-peak cancellations to and from Moorgate and Kings Cross and from 11th January 1915 most of these trains disappeared, leaving only a shuttle between Finsbury Park and Alexandra Palace in slack hours. North London Railway off-peak trains also ceased, briefly reappearing after the war before succumbing to an early LMSR economy campaign. After 1919, GNR services were fully restored, continuing with little change for the next 20 years. Thus in 1939 there were 43 Up trains on the branch between 07.10 and 23.12, including departures from Alexandra Palace for Broad Street between 07.59 and 09.45. The Down service was similar. Although Sunday trains were fully restored on 1st February 1925 after suspension from 1st October 1915, they had finally yielded to bus competition by 1930.

In the early days, the GNR used Sturrock 0–4–2 well tanks and Stirling 0–4–2 and 0–4–4 well and side tanks. These were displaced in the early 1900s by Ivatt 1500 (later C12) 4–4–2T which in turn gave way to the powerful Ivatt N1 and Gresley N2 0–6–2T in the 1910s and 1920s respectively. North London trains were normally headed by William Adams' outside cylinder 4–4–0T, but these were superseded in the 1930s by Fowler's ubiquitous Class 3F 0–6–0T. First and third class was still provided in 1939, the second having disappeared at the end of 1937. On the Broad Street services the old NLR four-wheeled coaches were made to last well into the inter-war period. The articulated bogie stock of the LNER trains, comfortable enough whilst no standing passengers intruded into the very restricted leg room, remained gas-lit to the end.

Highgate in LNER days; N2 0-6-2T 4741 bursts out of the eastern tunnel with an Alexandra Palace train in the mid-1930s. The sign hanging below the station nameboard gives no additional topographical assistance, but merely advertises 'The Daily Mirror'. *H C Casserley*

Alexandra Park reopened to the public in March 1920, the Palace in 1922. On 7th October in the latter year, a huge boy scout rally saw the arrival of 60,000 by train through the three stations serving the Palace; 12 special trains were somehow inserted into the ordinary service on the GNR branch. But the popularity of the Palace, which the trustees were unable to keep in good repair, was again in decline. A writer in the 1924 *Hornsey Journal* blamed the poor transport facilities; after remarking that trams on the hill were few and far between at night, he continued:

> There is a railway station actually inside the building it is true, but it is dirty, dark and dismal, and the trains are so infrequent that this means of access scarcely counts on the few days when crowds are expected. Everyone avoids the station who can possibly do so, for the railway service does not even offer the attraction of cheapness.

In evidence to the 1930 parliamentary committee on the Underground bill for a tube railway extension through Wood Green which would compete with the LNER, the vice-chairman of the trustees correctly averred that the LNER service to the Palace had not seen any improvement for over 20 years. On Sundays there were often as many as 6,000 visitors to the Park, but the LNER provided no trains. A recent Bank Holiday had seen 30,000 at the Palace and Park but only some 150 had arrived at the station as the service was slow and inadequate.

At this point we can turn to look at the line as it was in the 1930s. From Park Junction with the Barnet and Edgware line north of Highgate station, the double track curved east alongside Gravel Pit or Highgate Wood, soon entering Cranley Gardens station. This served the southern parts of the Muswell Hill district and its two side platforms with their small wood and brick buildings were on the west side of Muswell Hill Road. There was a wooden booking office building on the bridge with an open footbridge to both platforms immediately behind it. A second entrance, guarded by a ticket collector's box, led directly from the Down platform to the main road. Discreetly hidden by a line of trees behind the Up platforms was the goods yard, opened on 29th June 1897.

Beyond the road bridge, the tracks crossed from the west to the east side of the Highgate/Wood Green ridge, emerging on to a 17-arch brick viaduct which offered extensive views across north London. After passing under Muswell Hill itself and now heading almost due north, the train entered Muswell Hill station, only one minute's walk from the Broadway, the centre of this middle-class suburb. From the brick booking office building on the road bridge, stairs led directly to each of the side platforms. On the Down side there was a short canopy and a rush-hour entrance from Dukes Avenue; the Up side had a canopy of about four coach lengths and behind it was a small goods yard which required a back shunt by trains coming from Highgate. Like the other two stations, Muswell Hill had a small signalbox. The busiest on the line, it was given a passimeter ticket office in 1927, the first on the LNER.

The final 40 chains were mostly in a shallow cutting with the Palace coming into view on the right. After passing over a small road into the Park, the train arrived at the little terminus, heavily overshadowed by the huge bulk of the Palace's north-west face. Lacking even a hint of the grandeur and scale of the Crystal Palace stations, it had little to show other than some architectural styling on the street frontage and the signalbox. When opened, its platforms were beneath a terrace alongside the north-west front and this structure, with its blind-arcaded outer wall, survived the 1873 fire. The interior, with its wooden platforms was in such an advanced state of decay and rot by the 1900s that the GNR had to set about rebuilding it. The terrace was demolished apart from the flight of entrance steps near the station and what had been a long island platform was shortened to about two train lengths and given conventional umbrella awnings. The old Up side bay road with its side platforms became a carriage siding. At the Muswell Hill end, alongside the passenger lines on the north side, was a two-road yard reached by a facing connection placed between the platform end and the signalbox. The main traffic here was coal for the Palace heating system which consumed vast quantities of fuel – as much as five tons were required to take the chill off the Great Hall for a single concert or organ recital.

This little line, together with the longer branches to Barnet and Edgware, received the promise of a bright new electric prosperity in June 1935. It was to become part of the London Underground system under the five-year new works programme then announced, carrying tube trains projected from Drayton Park via Finsbury Park and Highgate. A rush-hour service of 28 eight-car tube trains was proposed between Moorgate (Northern City) and Finsbury Park, with 14 onward to Highgate (LNER) and thence seven to High Barnet and seven to Alexandra Palace. For the rest of the day, there would be 12 eight-car trains an hour between Moorgate and Highgate (LNER), six going on to Alexandra Palace, six to terminate at East Finchley.

London Transport's publicists carefully pointed out that the Barnet/Edgware/Alexandra Palace group of LNER lines was attracting only 26 annual journeys per head of population served compared with 181 on the adjacent Golders Green–Edgware tube line. A substantial traffic increase was forecast once tube trains were running to the three LNER suburban termini.

This 1935 scheme was in fact largely a re-hash of old plans. A northern section of the Highgate tube as far as the surface railway station at Highgate had appeared in a bill as early as 1901 and during the 1920s, projections further north had been publicly mooted by Underground officials. The Finsbury Park and Moorgate tube line, originally the Great Northern & City Railway, had in fact been planned to carry electrified services to and from GNR suburban stations and had been built to main line loading gauge for that reason. Its 1892 act, supported by the GNR, provided for a connection climbing to the surface between Drayton Park and Finsbury Park, where the tube trains would have shared platforms with the GNR. But the two companies squabbled over terms and eventually the GNR bottled-up the GNCR in an underground terminus which it built beneath its Finsbury Park station, isolating it from the outside world except for a back shunt connection for rolling stock purposes into the Highbury Vale sidings. In 1924 the LNER revived the idea of electrified suburban trains using the Moorgate tube and obtained powers for the necessary connections south of Finsbury Park. Delayed by the difficulty of raising capital on acceptable terms, the scheme was dusted-off in 1929 when government legislation designed to relieve unemployment afforded an opportunity to finance it. The LNER, however, had to fight for this government assistance in competition with the Underground Company, whose scheme for extending the Piccadilly tube from Finsbury Park to Cockfosters eventually won the favour of government and Parliament.

Work on the 1935 Plan for the Northern Heights lines, due for completion in 1940, came to a halt at the beginning of that year having already been slowed down by wartime conditions. As described in Chapter 3, only the sections from Highgate (Archway) to High Barnet and Mill Hill East were brought into use.

With the outbreak of war the Alexandra Palace branch trains were reduced by as much as 62 per cent on Mondays to Fridays. Through working to and from Moorgate and Broad Street ceased from 10th September 1939 in the expectation that wartime commuter traffic to the City would fall heavily after firms had evacuated their staff to the countryside. Broad Street trains returned on 4th December, but ceased for good after the night of 3rd October 1940 when they were interrupted by severe bomb damage to the North London lines. In 1940 the branch once again played its wartime role of carrying refugees from the Low Countries to temporary shelter at the Palace. Troops returning from Dunkirk were also brought up the hill by train for billeting in the Palace and Park.

When tube trains reached High Barnet in April 1940, LNER steam trains ran only to East Finchley in the rush hours, the rest of the service diverted to Alexandra Palace. Trains called at the new Highgate tube station below the LNER station from September 1940 for air raid sheltering, but public traffic here did not start until 19th January 1941. Escalators were then available from tube level to a new booking hall under the LNER lines, but the escalator for the further climb to street level had to await the post-war era (25th August 1957). From 3rd March 1941 all steam trains west of Finsbury Park worked to and from Alexandra Palace, giving the branch an enhanced service for a time.

There can be little doubt that had the war been delayed for only a year the Alexandra Palace–Moorgate electrification would have been ready at the end of 1940 and the branch would be open today. The only major work unfinished was the completion of the northbound connection at Drayton Park and, at Finsbury Park, the additional platforms, with their underline bridges at each end. Conversion of the GNCR tube to give it signalling, platform height and current collection standard with the other tube lines was completed in May 1939 and at Drayton Park the civil engineering work for the southbound line from the surface was finished, including a 10ft 6in diameter covered way descending beneath the Broad Street lines at 1 in 50. Earthworks for the northbound link were well advanced, whilst at Finsbury Park the abutments for the road bridges were formed and the girders for one lay ready for rolling-in. Structural steelwork to support Finsbury Park's additional island platform had been erected over the site for the new ticket hall and was to remain in position, steadily rusting, until September 1972. Conductor rails had been placed in position for much of the distance to Alexandra Palace and East Finchley, together with lineside cabling. By 1941 substation buildings were in place at Muswell Hill station and Crouch Hill. A new signal box building (not equipped and put into use until 1953) was finished at Drayton Park and the London Transport box at Park Junction, just beyond Highgate, came into daily service from 30th July 1939. At Crouch End and Highgate, platform edges had been reconstructed in concrete with the platforms lowered to compromise tube/main line height, whilst Highgate had also received a Holden style building with flat concrete canopy on its island platform, its walls embellished with LT bullseye roundels.

'To conserve motive power and fuel', further cuts were made to the Alexandra Palace steam train service from 7th September 1942. All through trains to London were then withdrawn, leaving only three an hour shuttling to and from Finsbury Park at peak hours Monday to Saturday. On Mondays to Fridays the last train was at 19.00, on Saturdays at 17.00. With the return of peace there was some improvement, so that by 1950 the midday gap had been reduced to 11.30 – 15.30 but there were still no trains later than those in the September 1942 timetable. More damage was done to the line's image in the winter of 1951–2 when the branch was closed completely to passenger traffic after the last train on 27th October, allegedly as an economy measure in a period of manpower shortage. Local pressures secured a restoration of train services from 7th January 1952 and after a slight augmentation the following month there were 15 trains Down (one to Highgate only) and 17 Up daily (two from Highgate). After the 09.42 from Alexandra Palace there were no Up trains until 17.05 and there was a corresponding gap in the Down service from Finsbury Park. Saturdays saw 15 Down workings and 16 Up between the 07.00 from Finsbury Park and the 17.25 from the Palace. The seeds of destruction were sown.

In this last decade of operation, the usual formation was a couple of gaslit coaches and N2 or N7 0–6–2T working push-pull. From time to time trainspotters (an easily bored breed) were given variety in the form of C13 4–4–2T and ex GCR F2 2–4–2T. Punctuality was erratic, especially in winter weather and a contemporary traveller remembers explanations for delays and cancellations which varied from the mundane 'breakdown' or 'fog' to the trendy 'export freight on the line'. It was not a service to inspire traffic despite the existence of through bookings from all Underground stations, introduced in anticipation of the tube conversion. This facility was not publicised and in traffic circulars London Transport booking clerks were periodically exhorted to warn any passengers requesting such tickets about the limited nature of the train service. In the 1950s requests at Finsbury Park for stations on the Edgware or Barnet lines by changing at Highgate were still met with printed tickets, but persistence was required as the clerks often tried to sell an LT ticket via Kings Cross. Any casual travel which still survived must have been finally smothered by the introduction of mileage fares in 1952; after then, the circuitous nature of the route caused fares from Alexandra Palace from Broad Street or Kings Cross to be 50 per cent above those to nearby Wood Green & Alexandra Park station (now Alexandra Palace) on the main line.

In contrast to all this discouragement, London Transport was working single deck buses at 35 journeys and hour between Finsbury Park and Muswell Hill stations, with a further 17 an hour on the inner section from Crouch Hill. Between Muswell Hill and Highgate stations two bus routes provided no less than 40 journeys an hour.

Interior of Stroud Green station, with LNER N2 2663 on a two-coach train for Alexandra Palace, 11th August 1945. The conductor rails were laid in 1939–40. *H C Casserley*

Alas poor Highgate! Looking west from the top of the tunnel on 5th July 1981. This view shows the partial conversion to a surface station for the proposed Northern Line extension from Drayton Park to Muswell Hill and Alexandra Palace, on which work ceased in 1940, never to be resumed. Although there is little sign of it here, below this site is the present Northern Line Highgate tube station. As can be seen, the area is even more thickly wooded than it was in the 1900s. Not surprisingly the place is alleged to be haunted, perhaps by the spirits of frustrated commuters who once dwelt at Muswell Hill. *Alan A Jackson*

When there was no sign of restarting work on the 1935–40 Railway plan local interests grew restive. Parliamentary questions in 1948 received the reply that there was need to restrict capital investment. Before long a reassessment had begun. Wartime bombing had severely reduced the quantum of offices in the City, adding impetus to a drift to the West End which had started before 1940. Post-war Labour governments did not exactly encourage rebuilding of City offices and the consequent heavy fall in commuter traffic between the branch and Moorgate and Broad Street, combined with the successful diversion of most other business to road services, influenced the decision-making. Buses were doing well on roads as yet uncluttered by large-scale car ownership and a surfeit of lorries, and the pre-war philosophy that electrification would generate suburban traffic, exemplified by the Barnet line results, was conveniently forgotten at 55 Broadway.

In the autumn of 1953, for what London Transport unblushingly called 'reasons of reduced traffic', this part of the 1935–40 Railway plan was announced as cancelled. The local authorities and the Alexandra Palace Trustees, the latter protesting that the Palace had yet to be restored and reopened, were solemnly told that the average of 700 passengers Monday to Friday (45 a train), or 22 a train on Saturdays, did not justify keeping the line open, let alone electrifying it. A dubious assertion that although £300,000 had been spent on the works another £2m would be needed to complete them was not challenged.*

* Both figures are at 1939 prices.

Cranley Gardens station, 3rd July 1954, the last day of passenger service; the two-coach train with its N2 0-6-2T is bound for Alexandra Palace. *Alan A Jackson*

It was easier in 1953 than it would be nowadays for such a decision to be imposed without proper discussion and analysis and the Transport Users' Consultative Committee duly applied the rubber stamp. On 3rd July 1954, just before 17.00 eight gas-lit coaches, packed with railway enthusiasts and sentimental local residents stood at Finsbury Park under the stern eyes of police dog handlers and their charges. The N2 hauling this last train made a spirited attack on the Northern Heights, but some jerky starts from Stroud Green and Crouch End resulted in a drawbar fracture beneath the leading coach when the departure from Highgate was attempted. After some delay the train was propelled to Alexandra Palace by the N2 from a following freight. Arrival back at Finsbury Park, with the original locomotive restored for the downhill run, was a mere 35 minutes late. A punctual arrival would of course have been something of an anti-climax for the final journey on this line.

Those conductor rails still remaining had been removed by February 1955, when only the discerning eye could detect what might have been but for Hitler's strategy. With the end of the rail service, bus frequencies were heavily strengthened to eliminate all opportunity for criticism, the peak-hour frequency of the 41-seat single-deckers between Muswell Hill and Finsbury Park becoming 46 an hour, one of the most intensive in London. A so-called 'express' bus with a 6d (2½p) minimum fare and through season tickets to tube stations appeared in October 1955 on this route. In icy weather, this and the other buses left passengers to fend for themselves on the one in nine gradient of Muswell Hill.

Goods trains and the occasional enthusiasts' special kept the branch alive a little longer, but Muswell Hill yard closed from 14th June 1956 and Cranley Gardens from 18th May 1957, after which coal and coke came to the area by road from the rail-served concentration depot at Palace Gates, to be mentioned later. When the line closed, the bridge over the railway at Muswell Hill station was filled in, allowing use of 56-seat double-deck buses from 6th January 1960, running at 38 an hour in peak periods. From October 1967 the through bus-tube season tickets were limited to existing holders and on 6th September 1968 the 'express' bus disappeared. In May 1969, with the conversion of the Muswell Hill–Finsbury Park route to single-deck flat-fare buses running at 18 an hour in the peaks, the through road-rail tickets were completely withdrawn. On the Muswell Hill–Cranley Gardens–Highgate route at this time, two services provided a peak frequency of 20 buses an hour. Such was the fall in traffic.

When all freight working to Edgware and High Barnet came to an end in May 1964, the tracks between Finsbury Park and the tube car sheds at Park Junction, became semi-derelict, coming to life only occasionally to transfer tube cars between the Northern Line and the Northern City at Drayton Park. There were also some trials of tamping equipment by London Transport. The section between Finsbury Park No. 7 box and Park Junction was latterly operated as a single line and progress of the LT battery locomotives with BR pilot on board was at walking pace whilst a sharp lookout was kept for old prams, oil drums, car tyres and other detritus of inner London civilisation. Bridge maintenance on this section had been neglected for some years and this, together with plans for electrification of the suburban services through Finsbury Park, hastened the end. The final LT rolling stock transfer was on 29th September 1970, these movements being made with greater complication from 5th October via Kings Cross and the City Widened Lines until London Transport gave up working the Drayton Park–Moorgate tube in October 1975. At the end of 1971 the rails between Finsbury Park and Highgate were removed and the tunnel mouths at Highgate sealed, leaving the London Transport depot at the end of a stub from the through line south of East Finchley.

Through electric trains from the GN to Moorgate via Finsbury Park and Drayton Park began on 8th November 1976, at last fulfilling the 1892 plan for electric working between Moorgate and Great Northern suburban stations . . . except for those on the Northern Heights.

After closure, Haringey Council eventually adopted much of the railway alignment between Finsbury Park, Highgate and Alexandra Palace as a 'Parkland Walk' but by the time this was achieved, some buildings had blocked the route on the site of Cranley Gardens and Muswell Hill stations. Suggestions for using the route as a light rail scheme came forward from time to time, initially from London Transport itself and this may yet become a reality. Meanwhile, although much of the Victorian railway infrastructure and the physical preparations for electrification have disappeared or been altered beyond recognition, some relics of what was 'Almost a Tube' may still be found, though it is advisable to explore in broad daylight and preferably not alone.

We now turn to the second aspirant for the rewards of the expected bonanza in Alexandra Park. The Great Eastern Railway responded in almost reckless manner to the advances of the Muswell Hill Estate Company, which was seeking all the access it could get. That company's act of 1866 included powers for a 1m 2f 9ch line curving north west and then north through the Park to a point just south of what is now the North Circular Road, where it would make end-on junction with a 3m 1f 7ch branch authorised by GER Act of the same year from the proposed Enfield Town line at Seven Sisters (Tottenham). The loop round the back of Alexandra Palace (where the Muswell Hill Estate and Railways Act included a chord which would have allowed through running from Highgate to Seven Sisters) would have entailed some interesting engineering to bring the tracks down from the top of the hill into the Lea Valley. When a financially embarrassed GER came to parliament in 1869 with a bill to discard various schemes of dubious merit, it is not surprising to find the Alexandra Palace branch in the list of abandonments. Accepting the realities of the situation, the Muswell Hill Estates & Railway Company obtained powers in 1871 to abandon the bits of railway in its 1866 act rendered useless by the GER withdrawal.

A BR diesel car set on a special working from Hitchin via the Cuffley Loop at the still gaslit Palace Gates station, looking towards the end of the line, 13th September 1958. *Alan A. Jackson*

Although the GER was no longer interested in a mountain railway up to the Palace, it did feel the need to fill the gap between the Enfield Town branch and the GNR main line, territory in which others were beginning to show interest, especially as it was now in the path of the tide of bricks and mortar seeping northwards from London. Thus the GER Act of 1874 included a branch from Seven Sisters more-or-less on the 1866 alignment but stopping short after 2m 5f 4.5ch at a point in Bounds Green very close to the GNR Wood Green station (now Alexandra Palace) although with no provision for a connection. That there was still some intention of catering for Palace traffic was seen in the extra spaciousness of the terminal station, which was somewhat deceitfully named Palace Gates. Until the coming of electric tramcars in the early years of the twentieth century passengers arriving here for the Palace were faced with an uphill walk of all but three quarters of a mile before they were in sight of the eastern entrance doors.

The double-track branch opened as far as Green Lanes station on 1st January 1878, the first train leaving Liverpool Street at 09.10 to arrive at the temporary terminus 30 minutes later. The remainder of the branch to Palace Gates was ready for public traffic on the following 7th October.

At Seven Sisters the wooden branch platforms were on an embankment, curving away to the west at the country end. On the Down platform a small brick building housed waiting rooms etc; the Up side was linked to the Enfield Town platform by footbridge between the two embankments but it was also possible to walk round the platforms at the London end where they came together under a small canopy. A subway connected all four platforms to a footpath which led to the main booking office and entrance in West Green Road, but at the west end this subway opened into Birstall Road, where a small booking office was established in 1906. Latterly only used for workmen's traffic, this closed in 1942. Over the 53 chains to West Green station the line fell at 1 in 100, passing under West Green Road to enter platforms sited in a wide cutting. This station, which served the hamlet of that name, still separate from Tottenham when the line opened, had low buildings in yellow stock brick and timber boarding on the north side of the road bridge and a signal box and goods yard on the Down side, with sidings which came almost to the road, above and behind the platform.

Beyond here the branch continued on a north-westerly course, now climbing for the rest of its distance with gradients as steep as 1 in 51 and 1 in 66. Green Lanes station was on an embankment with wooden platforms and platform buildings served from a small brick booking office at street level close to the centre of the village of Wood Green. Its signal box was on the Up side at the country end of the bridge over Green Lanes and the goods yard was also on that side of the line, at ground level a little to the south east. Palace Gates station, 7m 66ch from Liverpool Street, had generously-proportioned yellow stock brick buildings connected by a wide covered footbridge. With its 750ft platforms (260ft under canopies) and main entrance on the west side, it was built as a through station, and was at ground level, in open fields almost exactly half-way between what is now Bounds Green Road and the GNR Wood Green (now Alexandra Palace) station. At the country end the tracks led on to a small engine shed and carriage sidings on the Up side, and to a goods yard on the west, the whole site occupying eight acres. The signal box was on the Up platform and two sets of staff cottages were built near the station entrance. Saxby & Farmer lower-quadrant signals and Tyer's block telegraph system lasted the branch the whole of its life with only minor modifications and renewals.

As we have seen, the Alexandra Palace proved a miserable failure as a popular resort, so the branch's pleasure traffic never amounted to very much except on special occasions such as Bank Holidays and exhibitions. There was however a significant flow of commuters as the fields between Seven Sisters and Green Lanes filled up with small terraced houses in the late 1870s and the 1880s. By 1914 streets of such houses clothed the line half a mile deep each side for the whole of its length except for a short stretch north of West Green. East of Green Lanes station, the extensive Noel Park Estate of the Artisans', Labourers' and General Dwellings Company was laid out under architectural supervision in 1883, though not fully completed until the 1900s. During its construction, sidings were extended from the north end of the 1883 Green Lanes freight yard into the site. This development was thought important enough to justify a change in the station's name from Green Lanes to Noel Park from 1st May 1884. Building activity along this line was not uninfluenced by GER fares policy, for although the 2d workmen's return was not available, 3d returns to the City were issued before 07.00 and 4d returns (4½d from Palace Gates) between 07.00 and 08.00.

Nor was the GER ungenerous with the train service. By 1908 a total of 41 Up and 38 Down through trains between Palace Gates and the City alternated with Enfield Town–City trains. Off-peak service was half-hourly, with strengthening in the peak periods, so that there were, for example, six trains from Liverpool Street to Palace Gates between 18.00 and 20.00. Stopping trains averaged 31 minutes for the 7¾ miles, but some rush-hour trains, missing stops, did the run in 25 minutes. In peak hours the formation at this time was all four-wheelers, eight six-a-side third-class coaches, six second-class, and three firsts, offering a total of 888 seats, but some of the early morning trains were all or nearly all third-class with a total of 972 seats. At other times 12-coach trains were worked. After 1910 through trains between the branch and Liverpool Street were gradually reduced; Sunday trains worked only on the branch from 1912.

As elsewhere, the Jazz Service of 12th July 1920 brought major alterations. The principal feature was the introduction of two two-car 'auto' or push-and-pull sets which provided the half-hourly slack period working and at peak hours connected with Enfield line trains at Seven Sisters, alternating with through trains between Palace Gates and Liverpool Street, making up a combined ten-minute frequency. Special signalling arrangements were necessary at Seven Sisters to allow the auto-trains to terminate at the Up branch platform, thus affording the maximum convenience for passenger interchange. A 'Syx' electro-mechanical train stop protected the main line, not only preventing over-running, but allowing Enfield line trains to approach the junction without a check. Access to the branch platform was controlled by a calling-on arm at the country end.

At the rear end of the second of the two compartment coaches in the auto-trains was a cab containing compressed-air equipment which enabled the driver to control the regulator, brake and whistle of the F7 2–4–2T at the other end. Through trains, hauled at first by 'Buck-Jumper' 0–6–0T, were composed of 16 four-wheelers including two firsts and two seconds, but during the 1920s Gresley 'quint-art' bogie articulated sets and N7 0–6–2T took over. After 1926 travel on the auto-trains was given added interest by the importation of clerestory-roofed GER main line bogie stock complete with lavatories (later boarded up). In the 1930s there were three auto-trains in use, one with three clerestory-roofed vestibuled bogie coaches, the others each made up with a composite bogie suburban carriage and an ex-GER main line bogie coach. School children, often the only passengers outside peak hours, enjoyed such unwonted luxury with less vandalism than it would now provoke, but the author recalls that the faded comforts of the main line cars did much to encourage teenage dalliance on long summer afternoons, when it was always better to travel to Palace Gates than to arrive.

Palace Gates push & pull auto train No.2 in the Up branch platform at Seven Sisters c.1939.

A North Woolwich–Palace Gates train under the capacious footbridge at Palace Gates, in charge of BR 67205, 24th August 1950. *E A Course*

An interesting traffic surviving until the 1930s were the trains of horse boxes carrying grooms and racehorses from Newmarket to the racecourse at Alexandra Park, which was reached by walking the horses through the streets from Palace Gates station. Latterly these trains were usually hauled by B12 4–6–0s in charge of Cambridge crews.

Through trains between the branch and Liverpool Street had ceased by 1939 but until 6th July 1942, when it was withdrawn under the exigencies of wartime, a frequent shuttle service was maintained. Restored with some brave publicity on 31st May 1948, it disappeared for ever from 15th January 1951 'owing to fuel cuts'.

The branch supported another service, not so far mentioned. With the opening of a curve from Seven Sisters to the Tottenham and Hampstead Junction Railway at South Tottenham on 1st January 1880, trains were worked over this and Tottenham West and South Junctions from Palace Gates to Stratford and Fenchurch Street. On the following 1st September the service was diverted to Blackwall, but ceased after traffic on 28th February 1881. Six years later, on 1st June 1887, a most useful cross-London facility was established by operating trains from Palace Gates to North Woolwich. This proved of great value to dock workers and railwaymen employed at the vast Stratford complex; the trains were also used by North Londoners employed at Woolwich Arsenal, especially during World War 1. In the opposite direction, on Sundays and Bank Holidays, East Londoners came this way to relax at Alexandra Palace. Eleven trains each way, roughly at hourly intervals, were provided in 1910, with six each way on Sundays. Calling at all stations, they accomplished the 12½-mile run in 42 minutes. In 1938 there were 14 trains each way on weekdays, with a generous Sunday service of hourly trains from late morning to early evening.

Reductions came with wartime and from 5th July 1942 there was no service outside peak hours on Monday to Saturday apart from a few trains for Sunday workers. The latter ceased from 23rd March 1947 but about a half dozen peak hour trains ran each way daily until 7th January 1963 when the service was cut back to run between Tottenham Hale and North Woolwich.

These North Woolwich trains were similar in character to those working between Palace Gates and Liverpool Street, but after the departure of the 'Buck-Jumpers' in the 1920s they were usually hauled by F7 2–4–2T, N7 0–6–2T or G4 and G5 0–4–4T. From 1st January 1962 some of the workings were handled by Rolls-Royce three-car diesel sets, but N7s continued to appear, making this the last outpost of steam on the Great Eastern sector of BR in the London area.

Declining passenger patronage, which caused the eventual withdrawal of services from the branch stemmed from two factors: changes in employment patterns (local road journeys to new factories instead of radial rail journeys to inner London workplaces), and the vastly improved road transport provision with the arrival of the electric tramcar and the motor bus in the 1900s and 1910s. Electric trams were working between Wood Green and Finsbury Park from 22nd July 1904, and between Wood Green and Tottenham on 20th August, whilst a branch tram service from Wood Green to Alexandra Palace East, passing close to Noel Park and Palace Gates stations, started on 11th April 1906. At Finsbury Park, tramcar passengers could make an easy transfer to new electric tube railway services to the City and West End. Between 1910 and 1914, motor bus services were started along the road between Seven Sisters and Wood Green, passing West Green station, and also between Noel Park station and the West End. Further damage followed the 1932 opening of the Piccadilly tube from Finsbury Park through Turnpike Lane (less than a mile west of West Green station) and Wood Green to Bounds Green, the last two stations being very close to Noel Park and Palace Gates. This drew off any remaining passengers whose workplaces were in the West End, the Finsbury, Holborn, or Kings Cross areas.

Some rush-hour traffic remained both to the City and the Stratford, docks, and North Woolwich stations. Indeed, the LNER had sufficient confidence in the future to announce in June 1937 that Noel Park station was to be rebuilt, noting that it had been used by 250,000 passengers in 1936. Later in 1937 the underline bridge here was renewed in connection with a road-widening scheme and although a small start was made on reconstructing the station, work stopped on the outbreak of war in 1939.

Destruction of City offices and other workplaces in the inner area by the German air attacks of 1940–41, the serious damage to the Royal group of docks and the evacuation of many businesses to outer areas reduced the traffic to a trickle and led to the cuts of 1942. With road services back to peacetime standards and a very slow reconstruction in the City and East End, the restoration of the shuttle service in 1948 proved to be a short-sighted extravagance.

In these declining years of passenger traffic the completion of a link with the former GNR lines at Bounds Green brought about a substantial change in character of other train movements. Although a connection had been authorised by the LNER Act of 1924, the powers were allowed to lapse in 1929 before any work had been started, but in the following January, mainly to allow GE section suburban stock to move to and from a washing plant at the new Bounds Green carriage depot, a single-line connection was made in the sidings between the depot and the former GER terminal yard at Palace Gates. This soon proved useful for other purposes, even carrying some east coast excursion trains from former GNR suburban stations during the summer of 1939. Two years later to relieve the normal routes, the LNER started to work coal trains to Temple Mills (Stratford) through Palace Gates, usually splitting the trains in two for movement over the branch in charge of two 2–4–2T or a J39 0–6–0. At best this was awkward and time-consuming, so under the pressures of wartime demands it was decided to build a through connection between the GER branch and the Hertford loop. This was a single track signalled for two-way working, controlled from Palace Gates and Bounds Green boxes by direction levers associated with track circuits. It came into regular daily use from 9th July 1944, carrying four through freight trains each way between New England (Peterborough) and Temple Mills. Loaded southbound, empty northbound, these were limited to 50 wagons by the curvature and gradients of the branch. From the summer of 1953 the connection was again used by excursions from GNR suburban stations to Clacton and Southend, usually calling at stations on the branch, whilst in May 1959, when major engineering work blocked Broxbourne Junction, Cambridge line trains were worked to and from Liverpool Street via Palace Gates, Hertford North and Royston.

Goods traffic only briefly outlasted passenger services: West Green yard closed on 5th October 1964, Noel Park on 7th December, while through freights ceased from 28th December. Palace Gates yard and the 1944 connection survived the branch, thanks to the construction of a domestic fuels concentration depot in the old GER yard. This Charrington depot, opened in July 1958, was one of the first of its kind, handling coal and coke in full trainloads and equipped to bag the fuel ready for road distribution over a wide area. It dealt with up to 55,000 tonnes a year, replacing the coal yards at New Southgate, Oakleigh Park, Noel Park, West Green, Stoke Newington, South Tottenham, Hornsey, Cranley Gardens, Muswell Hill and Highgate.

With the declining use of solid fuels, traffic fell away causing closure and demolition of the depot in 1984. Even then the Palace Gates branch did not completely disappear hereabouts; the area from a point just north of the demolished Palace Gates station to the junction with the Hertford line was retained as part of the layout of the Bounds Green Inter City trains depot of 1976–77.

Following closure and dismantling of both the GNR and GER branches and the rebuilding of Wood Green main line station for the Kings Cross suburban electrification scheme, little survived to remind the visitor of the extensive railway accommodation which had once existed for North London's Palace of the People and its Park. Such rail traffic as remained, further diminished when the Jockey Club deprived the race course of its licence in 1970, was to pass through the main line station. In recognition of this what had been Wood Green & Alexandra Park was duly renamed Alexandra Palace from 17th May 1982. Ugly and brooding on its hill, victim of yet another disastrous fire in July 1980, the great building piled up a substantial debt liability for its initially enthusiastic new owners, Haringey Council. Under that regime, it was eventually restored to meet modern entertainment, recreational and commercial needs. If sufficient traffic can be generated by the new facilities behind the Victorian frontage, the future may yet see some restoration of more convenient rail facilities in the form of light rail, as suggested above.

Up train entering the island-platformed Bowes Park station c.1905. *Commercial postcard*

The Cuffley Loop (map page 365)

Although intended as a by-pass for the vulnerable Great Northern London approaches and built to main line standards for much of its length, the Wood Green–Hertford–Stevenage loop has never carried regular long-distance passenger services despite the capital lavished upon its outer section. Left for 47 years as a suburban branch, it was operated as two separate passenger branches even after completion as a loop. For these reasons it earns mention in this book.

We shall see later how the Middlesex market town of Enfield was at first reached, somewhat circuitously, by the Eastern Counties Railway and subsequently more directly by its successor, the Great Eastern. In 1865, a year after the GER Act for the direct approach, the GNR sought and obtained powers to build a relief loop to its main line, which would extend from the north end of Wood Green station through Enfield to Hertford, whence trains would return to the main line via the existing Hatfield to Hertford branch and a new spur from that towards the Welwyn Viaduct. Probing into this borderland, the GER in the same year received authority to build a branch from Tottenham on the proposed direct Enfield line, to Winchmore Hill. Before any work was done on the GNR line, the board reconsidered what it could afford, obtaining a Board of Trade certificate in 1869 to abandon the section beyond Enfield.

The GNR then started construction of what was nothing more than a country branch aimed into potential middle-class suburban territory threatened by the Great Eastern. The local character of the line was well illustrated by the wicked curving ascent out of Wood Green, where Down trains had to storm a 1 in 55 grade to reach the three-span plate-girder bridge over the main lines. Up trains were brought in more gently on the opposite (eastern) side of Wood Green station. At Bounds Green the Up and Down lines came together, running northeastwards on embankment to Palmers Green station. This place was then nothing more than 'a little gathering of houses on the road to Enfield' but the station was placed on the road to Southgate, a village ¾-mile away to the northwest on the foothills of the Barnet Ridge, much favoured by wealthy businessmen, for whose benefit a privately-operated horse-bus feeder service was started. At the transition from embankment to cutting on the north side of the road, the station house was a pretty barge-boarded, twin-gabled bungalow, with covered staircases at the back leading down to the platforms. Run-round facilities were installed to allow trains to terminate here, together with a small goods yard on the Up side at the London end, all controlled from a signal cabin under the stairs to the Up platform. When the goods yard was enlarged about 1936 this cabin was replaced by a box on the Down side, where a goods shed and siding had been added. Other than extension of the Up platform canopies and the provision of a separate canopied waiting pavilion on the Down platform this station was to remain virtually unchanged for over a hundred years.

After traversing the foot of the high land along the edge of the Lea basin in a cutting, the branch reached Winchmore Hill, almost the twin of its predecessor in siting, layout and architecture except that its goods yard was north of the passenger station on the Down side. Today the street-level building is but a remnant; elegantly carved wooden finials and barge boards on the gables have long since rotted away, and in 1965 subsidence caused the whole of the Down side wing to be demolished. At the time of the opening, the country at Winchmore Hill, 'undulating, abundantly wooded and agreeable' was already a favourite place of residence for City men 'whose comfortable houses are seen on every hand'.

A final stretch, mostly on high embankment on a falling gradient, brought the line

Winchmore Hill station GNR, c.1910. A solitary cab awaits hire to a destination in this well-scattered middle-class residential district. *Commercial postcard*

to its terminus at the western edge of Enfield. This was at street level, with a two-storey twin-gabled house in the same style as the others, placed firmly across the end of the tracks, as if to emphasise that all thought of further extension had been abandoned. Inside, an island platform, sheltered by a wide canopy for much of its length, was flanked by engine run-round roads and sidings. There was a goods yard at the London end.

An evocative portrayal of the impact of this line on the quiet gentrified country at the northern edge of London is found in a book written by the observant daughter of Winchmore Hill's doctor. Miss Cresswell watched the generally well-behaved navvies building a tall embankment across the valley of the Salmons Brook, noticing how, when exposed to the air, the London clay changed from a bright cobalt blue to an orangey colour. She rode by invitation on the contractor's locomotive *The Fox*, bumping along the temporary way between Winchmore Hill and Palmers Green in the evening light through cuttings soon to be ablaze with poppies thriving on the newly-excavated clay. At last:

> It was the night of the 31st March 1871, the permanent way was completed, the station was finished and smelled strongly of fresh paint, everything was ready. It was late in the evening, all was very quiet, the familiar sound of the working engine and attendant trucks attracted no attention, but suddenly the village was startled by a loud explosion, a perfect volley of explosions!

The last work train was departing over a chain of detonators. Next morning regular passenger and freight working started. About 16 trains arrived and departed daily at Enfield on weekdays (five on Sundays), most of them after 1st May running to and from Moorgate Street, a few to Victoria via Ludgate Hill; two additional trains terminated at Palmers Green. North London Railway trains provided extra journeys from 1st February 1875 between Broad Street and Enfield or Palmers Green, while from the same day the Victoria service was worked by LCDR locomotives and coaches. Further variety was available from 1st June 1878 when some GNR trains began to work between Enfield and Woolwich via Ludgate Hill and Blackheath. SER locomotives and stock took these over from 1st August 1880, some workings then calling at Cannon Street on the way. By then the combined services at Enfield totalled over 27 each way, departures starting at 07.42 and finishing at 23.10. There was no workmen's traffic as yet, but Palmers Green had two extra early morning trains. From the early 1880s the GNR Stirling Radial 0–4–2T with their bumpy little four-wheel coaches were replaced by small Stirling 0–4–4T. The latter were in turn succeeded about 1890 by the larger Stirling tanks of the same wheel arrangement, known as 'Wolves' from their staccato bark.

Bacon's map of 1880 shows Wood Green starting to grow between Green Lanes and the railway to Enfield with some other new housing in and around Brownlow Road, Bounds Green. For the latter, the GNR opened a station called Bowes Park on 1st November 1880, with an island platform linked by footbridge to new roads either side of the line. A centre track at the country end, controlled from a small signal box, provided for rush-hour reversals. By the end of the 1890s this station was extremely busy, with new streets extending from the railway to the Enfield Road almost all the way to Palmers Green and also about a quarter-mile depth of new housing on the west side of the line. Patronage justified the extension in 1911 from Wood Green of five Up trains in the morning and nine Down in the evening.

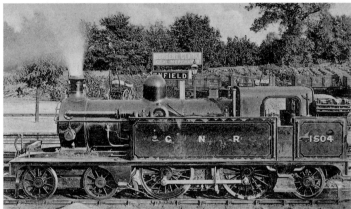

Above: North London Railway 4-4-0T No.58 on a Broad Street–Enfield train (six four-wheel coaches and two four-wheel brake vans) at Palmers Green, c.1910
H. Gordon Tidey

Left: GNR 4-4-2T 1504 at Enfield station, c.1905
Commercial postcard

The first GNR station at Enfield, looking to buffers, c.1905.
Commercial postcard

Palmers Green & Southgate station GNR, looking to London c.1905. *Lens of Sutton*

Villa development at Palmers Green was less rapid until about 1900, when side streets sprouted out each side of the Enfield Road from Wood Green to Winchmore Hill, encouraged much more by the new electric tramway than the railway. The Metropolitan Electric Tramways' 1907 opening from Wood Green to Palmers Green and on to Winchmore Hill in 1908 and Enfield a year later caused much damage to the GNR short-distance traffic whilst increasing the railway's commuter loadings. As much of the new housing was directed at the middle-class market, the new traffic was lucrative, with a high proportion of first- and second-class bookings. In 1905 the *Evening News* saw Palmers Green and Southgate, 30 minutes journey from the City, as the places where the bank clerk or the man with a responsible position in a merchant's office could find the home he desired. A typical house had five bedrooms, two reception rooms, study, kitchen and scullery, with a long garden, all for a rent of £70 a year. By 1914 the combined efforts of railway, electric tramcar and willing builders had brought the frontier of London a good half-mile north of Winchmore Hill station, touching Enfield itself. That place, however, was only very slowly losing its small country town atmosphere. At Bycullah Park, north of the terminus, where in the 1870s a special 15-minute train service had brought thousands to Easter steeplechases and fairs, a large villa estate was laid out in the following decade. There was very little else before 1900 to produce traffic for the GNR, apart from some streets of artisans' cottages on the north side of the town. Schemes in the 1870s to encourage suburban development by extending both the GNR and GER towards Forty Hill and a junction with the Lea Valley line got no support.

At the beginning of the twentieth century Enfield had 49 arrivals and a similar number of departures, including 16 NLR journeys each way to and from Broad Street and two SER trains each way on the Woolwich service. The latter were hauled by brass-domed dark green 0–4–4T but, rendered redundant by electric tube railways and motor buses, lasted only until 30th April 1907, the Enfield–Victoria trains following them into oblivion on 30th September. In late Victorian and Edwardian years the GNR locals were hauled by Ivatt's 4–4–2T running Down chimney-first and returning bunker-first. Just before 1914 these were replaced by Ivatt N1 0–6–2T then a few years later the squat-chimneyed Gresley N2 0–6–2T arrived to monopolise the service for the rest of the steam era. From 1912 the old close-coupled sets of 11 or 12 GNR four-wheelers gave way to eight-coach rakes of the first Gresley articulated coaches, known as 'Bogie Locals'. North London trains were easily distinguished by their scarlet-ended guards' brakes fitted with 'birdcage' observation glasses, one at each end of the rake. The gas-lit NLR four-wheelers were first-, second- and third-class, the last being semi-open, with wooden seats. In the 1890s there were usually three first-class coaches (96 seats), four seconds (200) and three thirds (150), an allocation which gives some indication of the type of traffic carried. These trains were hauled by black Adams/Park outside-cylinder 4–4–0T, which always found some difficulty with full trains on the Down flyover at Wood Green, so much so that their exhausts were easily heard over two miles away at Palmers Green. Not until the late 1920s were they retired in favour of Fowler's sprightly 'Jinty' 0–6–0T.

Increasingly concerned with the problem of operating a congested main line south of Hitchin, especially during emergencies and engineering work, the GNR board finally decided to make the long-considered loop, securing an act in 1898 for an Enfield–Stevenage line. Whilst this was a more costly solution than quadrupling the two double-track sections of two and 2½ miles on the Wood Green–Stevenage section of the main line, it was hoped that the loop would generate additional business, especially suburban traffic of good class between Enfield and Hertford, in an area well beyond the reach of the electric trams. Yet, as we shall see, once the line was built, this aspect was virtually ignored by the railway operators.

After much discussion and indecision, contracts were let in January 1906 to the Stockton-on-Tees firm of H. M. Nowell for the first 4¾ miles of the 20 miles north of the terminus. In undulating clay country, the engineers faced construction of cuttings up to 42ft deep and embankments of similar height, which required angles of rest as low as 1 in 3.

As extension from the original terminus would have involved a level-crossing, a junction was made about half a mile to the south, at the country end of a new station called Grange Park. Perched on a wind-swept embankment with a view east to cuckoo-haunted woods, the timber platforms of the latter were reached by gas-lit slopes connected by an underline subway to a single-storey slate and brick booking office at road level on the Down side. Suburban activity here started boldly in 1909 with the erection of three impressive shopping parades and the first villas in roads called the Chine and the Grangeway, all on the Grange Park estate east of the line.

North of the station three sidings, later to be used for storing passenger stock, ran parallel to the new double line on the Down side. A new station for Enfield was provided just east of the old, immediately south of the bridge over Windmill Hill. In red and engineering bricks, its large booking hall at street level on the Down side was connected to the well-canopied wooden platforms by ample staircases. With the opening of the extension the old terminus became the general merchandise and coal depot for the area, including the new suburb of Grange Park; its passenger platform, which remained intact for many years, returned to use briefly in October 1940 when an unexploded bomb fell on to the through line.

Curving slightly north-west from Enfield station, the new line traversed the western edge of the town on a long embankment planted with 'plane and other suitable trees' on both sides, its bridges over side roads decorated with stone copings and red facing bricks; the cosmetic treatment was required by clauses in the 1898 Act 'for the protection of Enfield Urban District Council'. At Gordon Hill, on its outermost northern edge, Enfield got its third GNR station. Very much at the brim of London, this place retained a frontier atmosphere until the end of the 1960s. In a wide cutting, spanned at the northern end by a massive five-arch road bridge, were two well-canopied island platforms, with spacious waiting rooms and other brick-built offices. A covered footbridge and walkway led to a single storey brick ticket office building at the top of the eastern cutting slope; nearby on Gordon Hill itself stood a two storey house for the stationmaster (now demolished). It was clear the GNR envisaged development into a terminus for suburban services, but only the Up island was used as such and the outer road on the Down side, connected to the through lines only at its northern end, accommodated berthed carriages and vans and was fenced off from the Down platform to avoid any misunderstandings. In 1973, when this road was connected to the Down line at the southern end, the original connection was removed. We shall return to the fate of these bay roads later. Terraced villas and cottages had reached the top of Gordon Hill by 1895–8 and in 1911, just south of the station, on the Up side, the GNR opened an 11-acre staff sports ground to which special cheap tickets were available from all its London area stations.

Beyond Gordon Hill the alignment was across undulating countryside, entering an area still remote and free from urban taint, destined to remain unspoiled for many years after the opening of the railway, its stations seeing only golfers, walkers and lovers. Before reaching Crews Hill station, the tracks were carried 70ft above a tributary of the river Lea on the 495ft Rendlesham Viaduct with its 14 graceful brick-and-concrete arches. Higher ground was now encountered, and the station, at the transition from embankment to cutting, was a simple affair with small uncanopied brick buildings on wooden platforms, covered stairs leading from the London end to a subway beneath the embankment, and a small wooden booking office on the Up side. A modest goods yard was sited on the Up side north of the station. Crews Hill served a golf course, a scattering of nurserymen's greenhouses and a stud farm which provided some horsebox traffic.

Crews Hill, looking to Hertford, 1963. The freight yard is behind the country end of the Up plat-form. Apart from the electric lighting, upper quadrant sema-phores and the screen of poplars, this scene shows no substantial change since the station was opened 53 years earlier.
Stations UK

Entering Hertfordshire, the line emerged from deep cutting on to another embankment, crossing 30ft above a side valley of the Cuffley Brook on the 390ft 11-arch Soper's Farm Viaduct before running into its temporary terminus at Cuffley. This station, on the north side of the road between the two villages of Cuffley and Goff's Oak, was similar to Crews Hill in all respects, including the siting of its goods yard.

Passenger service to Cuffley started on 4th April 1910, calling at all the new stations, with over 50 arrivals daily at Gordon Hill, the last as late as 00.44, and a similar provision in the Up direction. Cuffley however closed early (19.30) and had only 16 trains each way including a solitary North London Railway train* to and from Broad Street. On Sundays there were but three trains in and out of Cuffley, increased to five in the summer of 1910. There was some excursionist traffic at Cuffley in the summer; the local newspaper reported 6,000 arriving over the Whitsun holiday weekend in 1911. As traffic built up, service was increased, so that by 1914 there were about 69 each way, 20 going through to Cuffley, the rest reversing at Gordon Hill. A 1913 scheme for a garden city at Cuffley, 2,750 houses on 550 acres, got little further than planning stage, but Cuffley's great moment came with the war, when it gave earthly rest to the scorched steel tracery of SL21, the first bombing airship to be shot down over England. On the following day, Sunday 3rd September 1916, the little station saw a level of traffic never repeated until the area finally became suburbanised in the 1960s.

Some difficulty was encountered in raising capital for the remainder of the loop, but construction was eventually begun in 1911 by Robert McAlpine & Sons (Cuffley to Hertford), followed a little later by H. Arnold & Sons (Hertford to Langley Junction). Work continued slowly until labour and material shortages brought it to a virtual halt late in 1916. Activity was resumed in the following year, and by December a single running line was available without stations or signals. Regular freight workings, at first of empty wagons only, started on 4th March 1918, the whole 14¾ miles from Cuffley to Langley Junction under the control of Tyer's No. 5 Absolute and Permissive single line tablet instruments. This system, used for the first time in Britain, allowed a limited number of trains to follow each other, those in the rear being duly warned as to time intervals, and of course there was no question of any working in the opposite direction until all the tablets had been returned to the instrument at the far end of the single line section. Lineside telephones were available for emergency use.

The partially completed loop, in all 23 miles, and only 1½ miles longer than the main line between the two junctions, came into its own on the morning of 6th February 1920 when passenger trains were diverted over it for the first time after two freight trains had collided, blocking the only two roads in Welwyn North tunnel. To avoid the appalling delays which use of the single line section produced on this occasion, the GNR quickly installed the second track and normal signalling, including a flyunder for the Down road at Langley Junction. This work was brought into use on 23rd December 1920 but the only regular traffic over the northern section was four or five freight trains daily, mainly coal Up and empties Down.

---

* This train was withdrawn from 1st May 1918 together with other off-peak NLR workings. An LMSR train ran in weekday rush-hours between Broad Street and Cuffley from 2nd May 1938 to 9th September 1939 inclusive.

Stations at Hertford and Bayford had been substantially completed by 1917 but the GNR was incredibly slow in making use of its new investment, not operating regular passenger trains north of Cuffley until 2nd June 1924. The London service, worked by N2 0–6–2T and Gresley 'quad-art' bogie compartment coaches, terminated at the new Hertford North station, which was also used by the Hatfield–Hertford branch service, the old terminus at Hertford (Cowbridge) closing the previous evening. North of Hertford about four trains ran each way daily, terminating at Hitchin and calling at new halts at Stapleford and Watton as well as at Stevenage. Watton (Watton-at-Stone from July 1924 to avoid confusion with Watton in Norfolk) was Sir Nigel Gresley's local station. This service did not lack interest, as for much of its pre-war existence it was worked by steam railmotors and steam railcars, but it really lies outside the scope of this book.

Between Cuffley and Hertford the line penetrated a remote part of Hertfordshire which remained thinly populated for many years after the start of the train service. Reaching the head of the valley of the Cuffley Brook, the tracks passed through the north eastern outcrop of the Barnet Ridge in the lonely 1½-mile Ponsbourne Tunnel, the longest on the GNR. Five 10ft diameter shafts (one of them 140ft deep) carried engine smoke to erupt incongruously into the quietness of Wormley Wood. Half a mile from the northern portal was Bayford station, reached only by a bridle path from the scattered village of some 400 people west of the railway. Small waiting huts on the platform and a slightly larger booking hut at road level on the Up side above the line were the only buildings. A little-used goods yard was sited on the Up side north of the station.

After Bayford, the tracks descended into the valleys of the Mimram and Lea, running over two viaducts, Horns Mill, 50ft high with seven arches above the Hatfield Road and the river Lea, and the Hertford viaduct, with 20 brick arches and a skew girder span over the Hatfield branch and the river Mimram. Coming out on the east side, the Hatfield branch kept company with the new line into the station, which was on the west side of the town. This station, only half-finished and left so for over 50 years, was intended to have four roads and two island platforms, but only the western island had tracks either side; the other, which was without buildings, had a track on its western flank. The main island which was normally the one used, had a substantial building with pleasant brickwork, terra cotta detailing and moulded corbels for its large awning. A subway to a miserable little booking office at street level completed the station, altogether a very poor thing compared with the elegant and impressive GER terminus on the other side of the town. At the south end of the platforms were connections to the Hatfield line and some sorting and carriage sidings; general merchandise and coal traffic continued to be handled at the original GNR station at Cowbridge, nearer the centre of the town.

To complete the loop, the GNR proposed to quadruple south of Gordon Hill, with improved junctions at Wood Green burrowing below the main lines. This work was authorised in 1914, but finance could not be found by the impoverished LNER which kept the powers for the Wood Green junctions alive into the 1940s. Another unfulfilled proposal was a north to east spur at Hertford for through running between Langley Junction, Cowbridge and the GER Hertford branch.

Hertford now had a route to London 1½ miles shorter than that of the GER, but neither the GNR nor the LNER ever showed any inclination to develop traffic on this costly line. The fastest time for the 19¼ miles between Kings Cross and the county town was never reduced below an unremarkable 44 to 47 minutes minimum, achieved by only two trains a day, the rest taking ten or more minutes longer. On the inner section, train services showed no significant improvement in the 1930s over those of 1914, 24 trains a day to and from Hertford North, a further 22 to and from Cuffley and another 41 at Gordon Hill; additionally two trains terminated at Grange Park and another two at Bowes Park. The only non-stop workings of any note were one daily from Finsbury Park to Enfield Chase, and another Up from Gordon Hill to Finsbury Park in 15 minutes. Other factors were of course at work, including the attitude of major landowners to selling their property north of Gordon Hill for building, but the unenterprising train service undoubtedly played its part in preserving this lovely corner of London's country from the inter-war speculative building boom. Virtually nothing happened north of Gordon Hill apart from some 1930s bungaloid accretions at Goff's Oak and Cuffley. Passenger traffic on this section consisted almost entirely of summer pleasure-seekers coming out from urban north London at weekends to enjoy the countryside, often taking advantage of ticket facilities which allowed them to travel either by the Cuffley or the Lea Valley lines and return by the other. Steadier revenue came from the greenhouse nurserymen east of the line at Crews Hill and Goff's Oak who provided business in coal and fertilisers inwards and tomatoes, flowers and other garden products outwards.

Things were a little more lively south of Gordon Hill, where building went on steadily through the 1920s and 1930s until Grange Park, Winchmore Hill and Southgate coagulated into a continuous mass of small red-roofed houses. This development was not stimulated or enjoyed by the LNER alone; in 1932 the Piccadilly tube was extended from Finsbury Park to Arnos Grove, Southgate, with a station on the main road at Bounds Green only a few hundred yards from backstreet Bowes Park. the latter, once one of the busiest on the GNR suburban system, lost almost all its traffic overnight. Nor was that the end of the pillage. A further extension of the tube to Cockfosters was completed in 1933 with stations at Southgate village centre and west of Enfield. Bus services with favourable fare facilities ensured that not only was almost all the available traffic brought into these new stations, but a goodly picking also from the steam railway's catchment area at Palmers Green, Winchmore Hill and Enfield itself. Financially weak and unable to obtain government assistance for suburban electrification in this area, the LNER did nothing; indeed the outbreak of war provided excuse for reducing services which were not to be restored to their former level for many years. Broad Street trains, which had run in rush hours only throughout the 1920s and 1930s, generally terminating at Gordon Hill, ceased altogether on 4th October 1940 after temporary suspension from 11th September to 3rd December 1939 inclusive. Some peak-hour operation between Broad Street and the Hertford loop was resumed on 30th July 1945 with stock and locomotives provided by the LNER. Moorgate services, suspended from 11th September to 31st December 1939 and again, after bomb damage, from 30th December 1940, were resumed on an attenuated basis to Aldersgate on 1st October 1945 and to Moorgate on 6th May 1946. The basic service to and from Hertford was reduced to approximately hourly throughout the war and for some time afterwards, although there were extra workings at peak periods.

War years saw the line carrying a good deal of special freight and passenger movement, some of it using the connection to the Palace Gates line at Bounds Green, mentioned earlier. Operations suffered major disruption on 26th October

1944 when a German V2 missile severed both tracks at the country end of Palmers Green station, but with some remarkable organisation and hard work, the tremendous hole was filled and traffic resumed after only 24 hours. In the meantime shuttle services with a locomotive at each end of the train had kept passengers moving.

The late 1940s and early 1950s were doldrum years for a line which smelt of decay and decline as grotty 'quad-arts' were trundled to and from Hertford North by filthy and now wheezing N2 tanks. Towards the end of the 1950s the coaches were being repainted and repanelled, while from 1954 onwards some five-car sets of new standard BR suburban stock were seen on the line. A variety of locomotives appeared on the through and local freights from ex-GNR 0–6–0 upwards, and in the 1950s L1 2–6–4T shared local passenger working with the N2 0–6–2T.

Electrification, first proposed by the GNR before 1914, was announced in the BR Modernisation Plan of 1955, but even now there was to be a long delay before anything happened. In the meantime, in 1959 the tracks on the loop were rebuilt to allow maximum speeds to be raised from 40/50mph to 70mph and on 15th June that year diesel-hauled passenger trains and railcars were introduced with a much improved timetable which provided a basic half-hourly service with extra skip-stop workings in the peak periods. Around the same time builders at last began to make some progress at Cuffley, erecting several estates of small houses for commuter families between the railway and the old village on the hill.

The Hertford–Hitchin trains, which had ceased after traffic on 9th September 1939, were restored on 5th March 1962 with about four or five journeys each way at peak hours Mondays to Fridays and approximately hourly for part of Saturdays and Bank Holiday Mondays. The two intermediate stations remained closed but their yards continued to deal with public goods traffic until 1965. After that, at Watton, a Cory oil tanker siding was active until the end of 1991.

N2 0-6-2T 69547 on an Up train at Grange Park station, looking to Enfield Chase, 24th March 1958, a scene showing little change over the previous 40 years, and virtually none to the buildings and fittings since the station was opened in 1910. *Alan A Jackson*

Under the Beeching regime freight working was rationalised, the yards at Palmers Green, Winchmore Hill, Crews Hill, Cuffley and Bayford all closing from 1st October 1962 to be replaced by a new centralised solid fuel depot in the old station yard at Enfield Chase. Here rail hopper wagons discharged about 59,000 tons of fuel annually into road trucks standing below them. These then took the fuel to the old goods yards where the local merchants retained their rented staithes. But domestic heating was at the brink of a major change and it was not long before the Enfield depot saw its traffic falling as solid fuels gave way to gas and oil. The inevitable closure took place from 1st July 1974, BR advising helpfully that the nearest public freight stations would then be St Pancras or Welwyn. The tracks at Enfield yard were taken up in 1975 and the carriage sidings on the Down side here were lifted four years later. This enabled the whole area to be sold off for residential development in 1983.

As the Hertford North–Cowbridge connection had been closed in 1963, after 1974 local freight was confined to the oil tankers mentioned above. Through freight working had also diminished perceptibly in the 1960s and early 1970s, particularly after closure of the large Ferme Park yards at Hornsey between 1968 and 1973. And the loop's role as an emergency by-pass to the main line was less in demand after the 1959 completion of quadrupling between Greenwood (New Barnet) and Potters Bar.

In preparation for electrification, the manual lock-and-block signalling on the loop was replaced by colour lights in 1971–2 (the last of the picturesque GNR somersault semaphores, at Palmers Green, had disappeared in 1955). All movements came under the Kings Cross Signalling Control Centre from 4th July 1976 and the modernisation scheme was finally completed in 1977. Most signals were three-aspect, with some four aspect ones between Wood Green and Gordon Hill and two aspect displays between Hertford and Langley Junction, where minimum headway lengthened out to five minutes.

Work on the electrification started in 1973, only 70 years after the GNR's first moves in that direction. Electric services between Moorgate and Hertford North began on 8th November 1976, using the former GNCR inwards from Drayton Park, where a change was made from 25kV overhead catenary to 750V dc conductor rail for the tube tunnel section. Initially the service provided nine trains per hour at peak periods to and from Hertford North, three per hour off peak, two per hour on Sundays, and additional workings as far as Gordon Hill. With the introduction of electric trains, the diesel car shuttle to and from Stevenage was augmented at peak hours, running hourly at other times, always with convenient connections at Hertford North. A full electric service beyond Hertford started on 14th May 1979, operating at hourly intervals (two an hour in the peaks) and calling at Watton at Stone after that station was reopened on 17th May 1982. Modifications subsequently somewhat diluted the generous initial electric services; in particular Bowes Park, still suffering from tube competition, was reduced to an hourly train off peak in 1995 and Watton at Stone, Grange Park and Bowes Park were closed on Sundays after 3rd October 1993.

Apart from its own equipment, electrification brought few visual changes but there was some modernisation of lighting and modest tidying up and replacement of neglected structures, notably at Bowes Park, where in 1975 the footbridge was replaced and a new ticket office provided on the island platform. At Gordon Hill,

Intermediate suburban terminus: Gordon Hill sleeps in the afternoon summer sun, 21st July 1973; looking towards Hertford. The closed-off Down bay is being used for storing empty stock.
Alan A Jackson

where the Down side buildings were demolished and replaced with a wooden waiting hut, both bay roads were electrified, giving this station the appearance its GNR planners may well have envisaged. But this was to be a brief hour of glory. From May 1981 the Down bay was taken out of use; its track subsequently removed, the area quickly became totally overgrown. From 5th October 1981 the Up bay saw only emergency workings until 11th January 1987, after which it again housed a handful of peak hour departures and arrivals. Sadly in recent years this once dignified station has suffered much punishment at rail level from vandals whilst above, its spacious forecourt is untidily cluttered with parked cars and bottle banks.

Acting as an ancillary to the East Coast Main Line south of Stevenage seems now very much a secondary role for what is primarily a suburban and outer suburban electric railway with a buoyant traffic although still very much in competition with LT's Piccadilly tube line south of Enfield. Even so, electrification, along with modernisation of signalling and trackwork do render any necessary main line diversions a far less onerous proceeding than was once the case. For the railway-minded explorer, the GNR atmosphere still lingers here and there, perhaps to be tasted most strongly at Enfield Chase, where the generously-canopied timber platforms are approached through an entrance hall with beamed ceiling and leaded glass fenestration. The once peaceful remoteness of Crews Hill between trains, punctuated only by the whispering of the poplars behind the platform, is now severely degraded by the restless noise of the nearby M25 motorway. Further out still, the bare, isolated platforms of Bayford and the somewhat forbidding Pons-bourne tunnel (where during the German air assaults on London, the royal train would sometimes take shelter for the night) have since electrification lost much but not quite all of their mystery and romance.

Ex LNER N7 0-6-2T 69665 leaving Liverpool Street with a train for Enfield Town in September 1958. *R.C. Riley*

The Enfield Town Branches (map page 350)

Moving east from the GNR main line, we find a through route following the west bank of the river Lea out of London. This was opened in 1840 from a junction with the Eastern Counties Railway at Stratford by a company known as the Northern & Eastern. In its anxiety to keep to the easy flatness of the valley floor, it neglected the old market town of Enfield, which had to make do with a station at Ponders End, a good two miles east of its centre. Only a little more fortunate were the middle-class residential villages of Tottenham and Edmonton, strung along the Hertford road, an early example of ribbon development. Popular rural retreats for City merchants, professional men and artists, these places got stations on their easternmost fringes (the present Angel Road and Tottenham Hale).

Enfield and Edmonton, with populations of over 9,000, soon demanded more direct railway accommodation. Local pressures led to the deposit in 1845 of an Enfield, Edmonton & Eastern Counties Railway Bill (the N&ER had been leased to the ECR in 1844), and in 1846 of an Enfield & Edmonton Railway Bill. The latter was successful, with arrangements made for the ECR to take over the project and build the line.

Thomas Earle began work on the contract in 1848. From just north of the N&ER Edmonton station the 3m 7ch single track traversed market gardens on an almost level and direct north-westerly course to terminate east of the crossroads at the centre of Enfield, where a three-storey late seventeenth-century mansion, latterly a school attended by John Keats, was conveniently available to become the station house and offices. At Lower Edmonton, a single platform occupied a central position at the edge of the village green, with C. F. Cheffins' sober two-storey house behind it, on the west side of the line. Although the main turnpike road had been diverted to cross above the line south of the station, there was a level-crossing at the south end of the platform and a footpath was cut through the platform itself. This was at ground level and when a train was due, it was covered with an iron plate.

Without 'formal or public demonstrations', the line opened on 1st March 1849. An infrequent service, often involving a change at the junction, and the long way round through Stratford to the Bishopsgate terminus offered little competition to the horse coaches and buses which continued to ply along the direct main road from Edmonton through Tottenham to the City. But for anyone with a sense of fun and adventure there was always the possibility of a ride on the rather splendid little steam railmotor *Enfield*, which appeared on the branch soon after its opening. This was a 2–2–0 locomotive and a 36-seat, four-compartment coach on one frame, built at Fairfield Works, Bow, by W. B. Adams, and was normally attached to a nine-ton 116-seat carriage and used for the through journeys between Enfield and London. With its 5ft driving wheels, the ungainly *Enfield* could cover the 10¾ miles from Edmonton to Bishopsgate in 27 to 30 minutes, touching 50mph and using only 12lb of coke a mile compared with a normal locomotive's consumption of 30–33lb. But despite this brilliant performance *Enfield* was not a consistent success and was eventually converted to a 2–2–2T.

After the formation of the Great Eastern Railway in August 1862 there was some improvement in the London service, with 14 trains each way daily in 1864, but the long way round through Stratford tried everyone's patience and the dissatisfaction of all the communities along the high road led to schemes for improved access to the City. Several proposals for a direct line along the road route emerged in the early 1860s: from Angel Road to the NLR near the present Dalston Junction station in 1861, from Edmonton to Finsbury Circus in 1863, and a scheme for a NLR branch from Dalston to Edmonton in 1864. None was successful, but when planning new facilities in connection with its proposed City terminus, the GER took the precaution of filling this now obvious gap. This was done by projecting a line south from the Enfield branch at Edmonton, parallel to the main road, but far enough west of it to avoid major property demolitions. At Stamford Hill it crossed under the main road, running south east to Hackney along the western edge of the open land at Hackney Downs. At Hackney, a junction was made with a second new line coming

Workmen's train for Liverpool Street at Lower Edmonton Low Level in the 1880s. *Enfield Libraries*

from the N&ER at Copper Mill, the two then running together to join the ECR main line at Bethnal Green, thus forming a much more direct route from the City not only to Enfield, but to Hertford and Cambridge. A brick viaduct between Hackney Downs and Bethnal Green minimised the destruction of property in the inner area. Other features of the scheme included doubling of the original Enfield branch outwards from Lower Edmonton and links at Tottenham with the proposed Tottenham & Hampstead Junction Railway, and at Hackney with the NLR. Although the last was never built, a footway connection was established between Hackney Downs GER and Hackney NLR stations on 1st December 1885, remaining in use until the Broad Street-Poplar service ceased on the evening of 13th May 1944.

These proposals were included in the GER (Metropolitan Station & Railways) Act of 29th July 1864, but their realisation was much delayed by the GER's financial problems, work on the Hackney Downs to Lower Edmonton section not starting until early in 1870. Other associated new lines appearing in the GER (Additional Powers) Act of 19th June 1865 and never started were a branch from Tottenham to Winchmore Hill and a loop from Lower Edmonton to the N&ER at Ordnance Factory (Enfield Lock).

Although Liverpool Street was delayed by the financial situation and still unfinished, the section from Bethnal Green Junction to Stoke Newington opened on 27th May 1872. This had intermediate stations very closely spaced: at Cambridge Heath, just south of the bridge over the Regents Canal; at London Fields, serving south Hackney; Hackney Downs, immediately on the London side of the junction with the Copper Mill line; and Rectory Road, serving the southern part of Stoke Newington. At Stoke Newington the station was well-placed on the main road, at the east side, close to what was to become an important retail centre. As will be appreciated when details of the train service are studied, the section south of Hackney was soon to become very congested. Quadrupling between Hackney Downs and Bethnal Green was completed in June 1894, the new fast lines on the east side of the viaduct serving only Hackney Downs and Bethnal Green stations.

The 1872 underline bridge over West Green Road, Tottenham looking west, c.1906. The entrance to Seven Sisters station is on the far side of the bridge behind the left abutment. The message blazoned on the bridge plates reads: 'GREAT EASTERN RAILWAY/ SEVEN SISTERS STATION/ TRAINS TO THE CITY EVERY FEW MINUTES/ WEEKLY PACKETS OF TICKETS EQUAL TO 4D PER DAY.'

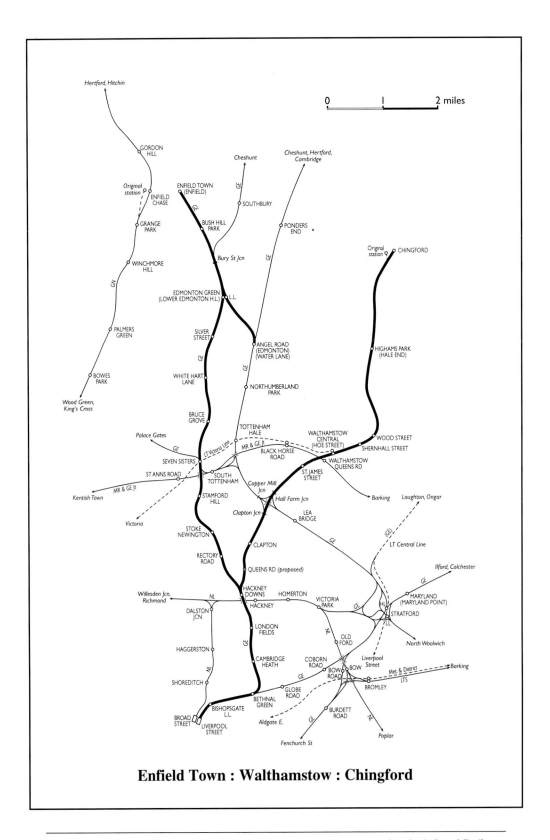

Enfield Town : Walthamstow : Chingford

The remainder of the new route to Enfield opened to Lower Edmonton on 22nd July 1872 and to Edmonton Junction on 1st August 1872, when trains ran to Enfield over a new double line. At Enfield, now only 10m 55ch from Liverpool Street, the mansion 'with its beautiful façade and tracery-work of carved brick (probably unrivalled in England)' was demolished, but the central part of the frontage went to what is now the Victoria & Albert Museum. In its place there appeared a rather dull single-storey building, two gabled sections linked by a lantern-roofed entrance hall, facing a small yard surrounded by substantial iron railings and flanked by a two-story cottage for the stationmaster. Within there was an island platform.

Intermediate stations on the northern section were: Stamford Hill, in the initially very select Amhurst Park residential district, and just west of the main road; Seven Sisters, serving south Tottenham and sited just north of the bridge over the 1868 Tottenham & Hampstead Junction Railway; Bruce Grove, almost on the main road in the centre of Tottenham; White Hart Lane, serving the still rural northern edge of Tottenham; Silver Street, in Upper Edmonton; and Lower Edmonton, west of Edmonton Green and just south of the junction with the old branch. The original Edmonton station, renamed Lower Edmonton Low Level, remained open as a terminus for a few workmen's trains to London, some of which went via Stratford, the rest via Copper Mill Junction and Hackney Downs. The single track of the original line between Lower Edmonton and Angel Road, now worked on the electric train tablet system, was also traversed by some freight trains.

GREAT EASTERN RAILWAY.

OPENING OF THE NEW LINE TO EDMONTON.

On **MONDAY, 22nd JULY, 1872**, a further portion of the New Railway extending from Stoke Newington to Edmonton will be OPENED for PASSENGER TRAFFIC, and Ordinary Trains will run between Bishopsgate, Stamford Hill, Seven Sisters, Bruce Grove, White Hart Lane, Silver Street, and Edmonton

EVERY HALF-HOUR.

DOWN.		UP.	
Every Half-hour from 7.15 a.m. to 11.45 p.m. on WEEK DAYS; and on SUNDAYS from 7.45 a.m. to 10.15 a.m., and from 1.15 p.m. to 11.15 p.m., as under:—		Every Half-hour from 7.2 a.m. to 11.32 p.m. on WEEK DAYS; and on SUNDAYS from 7.32 a.m. to 10.32 a.m., and 12.32 p.m. to 11.2 p.m., as under:—	
Bishopsgate ...... dep. 15 & 45 min. after every Hour.		Edmonton .... dep. 2 & 32 min. after every Hour.	
Bethnal Green ···	„ 18 & 48 „ „ „	Silver Street......	„ 5 & 35 „ „ „
Cambridge Heath	„ 21 & 51 „ „ „	White Hart Lane	„ 8 & 38 „ „ „
London Fields ···	„ 23 & 53 „ „ „	Bruce Grove ···	„ 11 & 41 „ „ „
Hackney Downs	„ 26 & 56 „ „ „	Seven Sisters ···	„ 14 & 44 „ „ „
Rectory Road ···	„ 29 & 59 „ „ „	Stamford Hill ···	„ 17 & 47 „ „ „
Stoke Newington	„ 31 & 1 „ „ „	Stoke Newington	„ 20 & 50 „ „ „
Stamford Hill ···	„ 34 & 4 „ „ „	Rectory Road ···	„ 22 & 52 „ „ „
Seven Sisters ···	„ 37 & 7 „ „ „	Hackney Downs	„ 25 & 55 „ „ „
Bruce Grove ···	„ 40 & 10 „ „ „	London Fields ···	„ 28 & 58 „ „ „
White Hart Lane	„ 43 & 13 „ „ „	Cambridge Heath	„ Even Hours and Half-hours.
Silver Street......	„ 46 & 16 „ „ „	Bethnal Green···	„ 33 & 3 min. after every Hour.
Edmonton	arr. 49 & 19 „ „ „	Bishopsgate	arr. 36 & 6 „ „ „

TRAINS RUN BETWEEN LONDON AND STOKE NEWINGTON—
From BISHOPSGATE every Quarter of an Hour from 7.0 a.m. to 12.0 night on WEEK DAYS; and on SUNDAYS from 7.30 a.m. to 10.30 a.m., and from 1.0 p.m. to 11.30 p.m.
From STOKE NEWINGTON every Quarter of an Hour from 6.50 a.m. to 11.35 p.m. on WEEK DAYS; and on SUNDAYS from 7.35 a.m. to 10.35 a.m. and 12.50 p.m. to 11.5 p.m.

FARES:

BISHOPSGATE TO	SINGLE.			RETURN.		
	1	2	3	1	2	3
Bethnal Green..................	3d.	2d.	1d.	4d.	3d.	2d.
Cambridge Heath ....} London Fields................}	4d.	3d.	2d.	6d.	4d.	3d.
Hackney Downs................} Rectory Road ....} Stoke Newington.............}	6d.	4d.	3d.	8d.	6d.	4d.
Stamford Hill	7d.	5d.	4d.	10d.	7d.	5d.
Seven Sisters ....} Bruce Grove ....}	8d.	6d.	4d.	1s. 0d.	9d.	6d.
White Hart Lane	9d.	7d.	5d.	1s. 2d.	10d.	8d.
Silver Street	10d.	8d.	6d.	1s. 3d.	1s. 0d.	10d.
Edmonton	1s. 0d.	10d.	8d.	1s. 6d.	1s. 3d.	1s. 0d.

WORKMENS TRAINS leave Edmonton for Bishopsgate, on Week Days, at 5.2 and 6.2 a.m., calling at the intermediate Stations.
WORKMENS WEEKLY TICKETS AT ONE SHILLING EACH are issued by these Trains.—For particulars see Hand Bills.

Bishopsgate, July, 1872.　　　　　**S. SWARBRICK, General Manager.**

PRINTED AT THE COMPANY'S WORKS, STRATFORD.

Timetable and Fares poster issued for the opening of the line between Stoke Newington and Edmonton (Lower Edmonton), Monday 22nd July 1872. *Alan A Jackson*

Stamford Hill station entrance building on the overline bridge in Amhurst Park, looking west, c.1904. *Commercial postcard*

Substantial and moderately spacious, but exceedingly plain, the standard pattern intermediate stations of yellow brick were enlivened only by their pretty saw-tooth platform canopies of matching length, trimmed with wooden valancing. As far out as Lower Edmonton, none was as much as a mile from its neighbour. Freight facilities were provided at Manor Road Sidings (on the Down side between Stoke Newington and Stamford Hill); at White Hart Lane (on the Up side, with a refuge siding opposite); and on the Up side at Enfield. At the turn of the century another yard was built at Lower Edmonton between the old Low Level station and Edmonton Junction.

At Seven Sisters there was no junction with the Tottenham & Hampstead Junction Railway until 1st January 1880, after which trains could run between Seven Sisters and South Tottenham stations. Although an embankment was built to form a Stamford Hill–St Ann's Road connection, this was never completed, and the Seven Sisters–St Ann's Road north western curve authorised in the GER (General Powers) Act of 1890 was not even started. A flimsy-looking bridge over the T&HJR here was an afterthought authorised in an act of 1866 in place of the level-crossing envisaged in the 1864 act, which was just as well, in view of the intensive traffic eventually generated on both lines.

In releasing the GER from any obligation to rehouse the large number of unfortunates displaced by the construction of the Liverpool Street terminus and the new lines serving it, Parliament had inserted in the 1864 act a requirement for a 2d return train to be run daily for workmen between Lower Edmonton and London. There were no great colonies of horny-handed sons of toil beyond Bethnal Green; Hackney Downs still had a rural air, breezy Stamford Hill only a few large tree-shrouded villas in huge gardens, while Tottenham and Edmonton were semi-rural and largely middle class. Writing four years after the opening of the new Enfield line, James Thorne remarked that Tottenham had 'many outlying farms and much of the land still under the plough . . . flowers are grown for the London market'. Edmonton was noted for its market gardens at this time. Not surprisingly there was some resistance in these districts to the proposed workmen's trains; in 1869 the local newspaper suggested they would only encourage a large body of people who could not fail to add to poverty and mortality and bring an increase in local rates.

But the GER did not renege. On the contrary, from the very first day of operation the statutory requirement was interpreted generously and there were two 2d return trains from the temporary terminus at Stoke Newington to Bishopsgate, leaving at 05.20 and 06.20, calling at all stations. When the remainder of the line was opened these were extended to start from Enfield, which was operationally more convenient than Lower Edmonton. Until 1920 this provided the remarkable bargain of a daily return run of 21½ miles for 2d (under 1p).

The introduction of the full train service to Enfield was delayed by the inadequacy of the London terminal arrangements. Although the opening of the new approach tracks as far as Bishopsgate Low Level station on 4th November 1872 helped a little, it was not possible to add more trains until the West Side suburban platforms of Liverpool Street were ready on 2nd February 1874. Within two years from then the Enfield line had a basic frequency of four trains an hour (two of these reversing at White Hart Lane) with strengthening in peak hours. Supplementing the statutory 2d returns were fares only slightly more costly for early morning users and the frequent cheap service from closely-spaced stations rapidly changed the whole character of the district as far north as Lower Edmonton. Whilst elevated Stamford Hill retained its middle class aspect, the market gardens and little bourgeois demesnes either side of the main road through Tottenham and Edmonton were quickly covered with thousands of low-rent houses set in serried ranks. Twelve years after the opening of the line, the GER general manager, William Birt, described what happened to the Royal Commission on the Housing of the Working Class:

> . . . speculative builders went down into the neighbourhood and, as a consequence, each good house was one after another pulled down, and the district is given up entirely, I may say, now to the working man. I lived down there myself and I waited until most of my neighbours had gone; and then, at last, I was obliged to go.

Census returns for Edmonton serve to illustrate the rate of growth. From 14,000 when the line opened, the population increased 70 per cent by 1881 to 23,463 and by 1901 had reached almost 62,000. As we have noted, the workmen's 2d trains were not the only ones offering cheap travel, but 2d trains were increased to three daily in 1883, to five in 1890 and by 1898 there were seven, all this a simple response to overcrowding rather than benevolence on the part of the GER. The 2d trains all ran before 07.00, return journeys being possible by any train after 16.00 or noon on Saturdays. In an attempt to get some more revenue, the GER had twelve 3d trains running by 1900 between 07.00 and 07.30 followed by half-fare trains arriving at Liverpool Street between 07.30 and 08.00, the latter used by 'the better class of workmen, warehousemen, shopmen, and not a few poorly-paid clerks'. After 08.00 ordinary fares applied, and as there were no third-class season tickets, the second-class accommodation was generously provided.

Rectory Road, looking to Enfield Town, Up train entering. The newspaper placards at the bookstall indicate a date of 1904. This station exhibits the almost standardised platform canopies used on the Enfield Town and Chingford branches. *Commercial postcard*

At the turn of the century these Enfield line trains were hauled by 0–6–0T of a design dating back to 1886 and nicknamed 'Jubilee Jumpers' or 'Buck Jumpers'. There were also a few Holden 0–4–4T dating from 1898–1901 to be seen on Enfield trains. All coaches were four-wheelers and the workmen's trains usually consisted of 15 compartment coaches offering a total of 852 seats. First class was upholstered in blue cloth, second in red, but third-class passengers got hard sprung seats covered with American cloth, backed by partitions open above luggage rack level. This last feature was much exploited by itinerant musicians playing mouth organs, concertinas, or merely giving voice. In an atmosphere of cheap shag and inadequately washed bodies, men of strong character also attempted to conduct hymn singing and prayers over the tops of the partitions, although these were by no means universally appreciated. A letter in the *Tottenham Herald* in June 1894 complained of 'religious fanatics' on the 06.19 from Seven Sisters to Liverpool Street.

For some years the GER alleged that the 2d trains were covering their working expenses, but this was evidently no longer the case in 1904 when the general manager, J. F. S. Gooday, gave figures to the Royal Commission on London Traffic. He also refuted the suggestion that the GER gained something from the freight traffic that the ingress of population had brought with it. As Acworth had noted some years earlier, the Enfield line was certainly not a cheap one to work with steam traction; the 45lb of coal gobbled up each mile by the engines on the 46-minute all-stations run compared with the 30lb or so per mile necessary to keep them moving at around 40mph for a similar non-stop journey.

Although he had no particular responsibility for the situation he described, having been general manager only since 1899, Gooday expressed some concern at the social effects of his company's policy, remarking at one point to the Royal Commission, apparently in all seriousness, that 'the aggregation of so vast a population of one class in one locality seems likely to be productive of social danger'. But this was England, and the red belt created by his blue engines was to prove no more of a social danger than the upper class concentration in Mayfair.

In any case, the territory served was not exclusively plebeian. Enfield had always supplied a leavening of first- and second-class traffic. In the late 1860s and early 1870s a subscription list 'for the attention of gentlemen passengers' was pinned-up in a newsagent's shop next to the station each Christmas to the benefit of drivers and firemen. Efforts were made to develop this lucrative middle-class business in the late 1870s. The 700-acre Bush Hill Park Estate west of the line just south of the terminus was sold in 1872 to the Bush Hill Park Land Company for conversion to a villa colony for which a station in the GER's best suburban style was opened on 1st November 1880. In the following decade housing of the terrace type appeared east of the new station, some 600 cottages existing by 1892, mostly of five-room design. An *Evening News* advertisement of July 1901 mentions 'cottages for working men at Bush Hill Park (2d or 3d return), 6s 9d rent.' A second booking office was opened in 1894 to serve this artisan area, Bush Hill Park becoming one of those places where the railway formed a social boundary, with both classes using the same station, but rarely meeting because they passed through it at quite different times of the day. Even in the 1950s, Bush Hill Park appeared better cared-for than most other stations on the line, with plenty of clean seats on the platforms and well-kept gardens.

Bush Hill Park, GER, Down side entrance block and stationmaster's house, c.1905.

Main entrance block and station-master's house, Enfield Town station c.1908.
Commercial postcard

On the remnant of the original Enfield branch, workmen's trains continued to be the only passenger service. Loadings were sufficient to justify an additional platform at Lower Edmonton in 1899, built alongside the original but south of the level crossing. A small booking office here issued weekly or fortnightly blocks of the special workmen's tickets, in numbers restricted to the accommodation available – rather better treatment than today's air passengers get. There were five trains each way between here and Stratford in 1908, another five to Liverpool Street, one via Stratford. Seven years later, there were two fast 2d trains and two fast 3d trains via Angel Road and Stratford or via Hackney Downs. Patronage fell sharply after 1919 as local employment opportunities increased and competition from road services consolidated; the remaining single morning train disappeared in 1931 but one train ran to the Low Level on Monday to Friday evenings until 8th September 1939. Occasional passenger diversions and freights continued to use the line until close of traffic on 5th December 1964.

Passenger traffic decline was also evident on the newer line. During 1905 electric trams replaced the former horse and steam service along the main road parallel to the railway between Stamford Hill and Edmonton and two years later the LCC's electric cars were plying from Stamford Hill to the City near Liverpool Street station. With motor buses joining in from about 1910, the road services drained away much of the railway's off-peak traffic. There was also some erosion at rush hours, especially after the introduction of through tramcar service to the West End and City via Finsbury Park in August 1912 and from Edmonton to the City via Stamford Hill in June 1920. Evidence of the effect of electric tramcar competition was the reduction in basic service to half-hourly 12-coach trains (quarter-hourly inwards from Seven Sisters) by 1907. Peak hour working remained intensive, and in that year the line was carrying ten trains (usually of 17 coaches) between 07.00 and 08.00, six from Enfield, one from Bush Hill Park, one from Cheshunt (via the Churchbury Loop and Lower Edmonton High Level) and two from Palace Gates (via Seven Sisters). Some of these ran semi-fast reducing the 40-minutes all-stations timing for the $10\frac{3}{4}$ miles Enfield run to 27 minutes. At this period, Enfield Town, with its locomotive depot and carriage sidings, had a daily provision of 56 Up trains and 63 Down, whilst Seven Sisters had 97 Up and 98 Down. The traffic day extended from 04.00 to 01.00. Seven Sisters, the busy junction with the Palace Gates branch, was given an additional entrance and ticket office in Birstall Road, for passengers from the west side in 1906, no doubt another response to tramway competition. This remained open for issue of workmen's tickets until 6th July 1942.

Stoke Newington station main entrance building in High Street, c.1908. No fewer than seven railway staff are posed by the doorway and there are two horse cabs in the yard. *Commercial postcard*

It was the existence of parallel electric tramway facilities which enabled the GER, in response to government pressure, to close the inner area stations London Fields and Cambridge Heath to effect manpower economies in World War I. Somewhat surprisingly, and unlike similarly-placed stations in south London, both reopened in 1919 and remain in use today, though since 1992 at peak hours only.

Tramcars and motor buses, if slower, were certainly no less comfortable than the severely spartan third-class accommodation provided by the GER. Although a train of bogie carriages had been tried out in 1900, four-wheelers were the rule until after the end of World War I. In them, the workmen's ticket-holders and third-class passengers sat five-a-side on hard seats covered with a shiny dirt-resisting cloth. Second-class buttocks enjoyed sprung cushions, whilst first-class passengers got more leg room and sat only four each side. In 1899 James Holden, the locomotive, carriage and wagon superintendent, introduced six-a-side four-wheelers and later rebuilt the older carriages to this width, thus providing a 21 per cent increase in carrying capacity at low cost. A prototype train composed of four-wheeler bogies mounted on bogie frames was produced in 1913 for suburban traffic.

These changes were in part designed to meet the problem of increasingly concentrated rush hours, which were causing severe overcrowding on some trains. Consideration was given to electrification of suburban routes to improve the service and build-up off-peak traffic, but the capital required for this frightened the GER board. Instead the company adopted a scheme put forward by its superintendent of operations, Frederick V Russell, which for one-fortieth the cost of electrification promised a 75 per cent increase in inward rush-hour trains and a 50 per cent increase in evening departures from Liverpool Street. This was to be achieved by making certain minor alterations, principally in terminal and track arrangements at Liverpool Street and Bethnal Green. At Enfield Town, where the platforms had been lengthened in 1903/05 to take more coaches, a third platform was added on the east side. Introduced on 12th July 1920 and soon known by its newspaper title, the 'Jazz Service' gave 12 trains an hour in the evening peak as far as Seven Sisters and nine thence to Enfield Town. Off-peak, weekdays and Sundays there were four-coach trains every ten minutes. Standard rush-hour trains were composed of 16 gas-lit four-wheelers offering 848 seats, still mostly hauled by the 'Buck Jumpers'. Stopping patterns, indicated by coloured headcodes, were varied.

Good as it was, the Jazz did little to revive declining patronage. Competition from road transport was only one of the factors now operating. Industry had established itself in the Lea Valley before 1914, and encouraged by the construction of new

---

Bruce Grove station, looking east to High Road, Tottenham, c.1910. Note the deliberate attempt to bring the architecture of the signal box into keeping with the other station buildings.
Commercial postcard

motor roads and the post-war boom in road transport, factories proliferated in the 1920s and 1930s, creating a whole new pattern of journeys to work by bus, tram, bicycle or on foot. After the 1926 general strike, the slack-hours timetable was thinned out and loadings on the Enfield line suffered further losses after the opening of the Piccadilly Line tube from Finsbury Park to Arnos Grove on 19th September 1932. As this offered a much more attractive service to Kings Cross and the West End, its stations at Manor House, Turnpike Lane and Wood Green were soon winning many former Enfield line passengers from the district between Stamford Hill and White Hart Lane, some coming on buses and trams, others walking across.

Like its predecessor, the LNER found difficulty in obtaining capital for electrification and was disheartened when the Underground was favoured for the assistance that various governments devised to counter mass unemployment. Small improvements were made. From 1926 all trains were hauled by the more powerful N7 0–6–2T introduced by the GER in 1915, and beginning in 1925, the old GER four-wheel 'cattle trucks' gave way to Nigel Gresley's articulated bogie sets, known as 'quint-arts', two per train of ten separate bodies. Ten-minute interval departures from each terminus in the slack hours were maintained until 1939, though by then the practice of running alternate trains fast between Liverpool Street and Stoke Newington with a connection at Seven Sisters for Palace Gates had disappeared. Sunday trains were only half-hourly by 1939. During 1934–5 all manual signals except those at Seven Sisters were replaced by three- and four-aspect Westinghouse Brake & Signal Co. colour-lights controlled by track circuits. Together with the improved performance given by the N7s, this reduced the all-stations time from end to end to 34 minutes. In the early 1940s, with the war closing City offices and workshops, the frequency was widened to half-hourly (ten minutes at rush hours), whilst train lengths were reduced respectively to five and six coaches.

A visit to the line in 1955 found it little changed from the railway so familiar to the author in schooldays twenty years before. At Liverpool Street, platforms 1 and 2 were buffered with N7s, Westinghouse pumps busily panting. There too were the familiar Gresley carriages, as drably uninviting as ever, each compartment with its dusty, severely straight-backed, hard-padded benches and limited knee-room. First-class compartments were still available, though the fares had been withdrawn on 6th October 1941 (second had gone at the end of 1937). This weekday mid-morning train carried an average of half-a-dozen passengers and although its station stops of some 20 seconds were almost up to Southern Electric standard, the ambling jogtrot between stations was another matter. At White Hart Lane, the porter disobligingly refused a proffered ticket, instructing that it should be left at the street level passimeter booth which had been installed here and at some other stations on the line by the LNER in the early 1930s to economise in staff.

White Hart Lane still had the wide exit doors which the GER had installed for the crowds attracted to home matches at the nearby Tottenham Hotspur football ground. At its height, this traffic had brought as many as 10,000 to the station on trains running at intervals of rather less than five minutes, the closest possible headway whilst this line was operated with steam. A returning crowd of this size would be cleared in little over half an hour. After electrification, the football business remained at a high level for some years and in 1961, in the period just before the start of a home match, trains would be arriving every four minutes from Liverpool Street, with others coming in from Hertford East and Bishops Stortford via the Churchbury Loop. A new entrance for returning spectators was added in 1962. At this time a railway officer informed the author that to limit damage and hooliganism, it was the policy to load the new electric trains so tightly at White Hart Lane and Liverpool Street that the football supporters were unable to move their arms and legs during the brief journey to and from the match.

Bush Hill Park on 13th September 1958, looking to London, with a Liverpool Street–Enfield Town train entering, hauled by N7 0-6-2T 69667. *Alan A Jackson*

A word should be said about the decline and extinction of the freight facilities, never an important feature of this line. The private sidings on the Up side just north of Seven Sisters station, installed for a lager brewery and ice factory in 1882 and later used by the Tottenham Council, had fallen out of use by the late 1940s. Closures elsewhere began with Enfield Town yard, whose traffic was diverted to Enfield Chase and Churchbury from 14th September 1959 ahead of electrification. The site, east of the passenger platforms, was then leased for the erection of a seven-storey office block with shops at ground level, which was completed in 1964 as Bovril House. Bush Hill Park Sidings, north of the station on the Down side, were put out of use in May 1964 and the depots at Manor Road, Stoke Newington and Lower Edmonton (high and low level) were shut the following 7th December. General freight facilities were withdrawn from White Hart Lane in January 1968 but the yard remained open for solid fuel traffic to merchants' staithes until 2nd July 1977.

When it seemed almost too late (and indeed in a sense it was) the Enfield Town service was at long last electrified; resignalling in preparation for this had been completed in May 1960. Fed from a 6.25kV 50-cycle ac overhead wire system (converted to 25kV in 1980/83) the new trains appeared in public service on 14th November 1960, working to the steam timetable. The full electric service was started on the 21st of that month but such was the complexity and intensity of the technical troubles encountered with the new stock that it was not possible to achieve the planned timetable until 18th June 1962. From that date a ten-minute slack hour frequency was implemented, with all-stations trains reaching Enfield in only 29 min from Liverpool Street, semi-fasts in 25 min. Between 17.00 and 18.00 there were six trains to Enfield, three more calling only at Lower Edmonton on their way to Hertford East and Bishops Stortford over the reopened Churchbury (Southbury) line, which we shall consider later. A similarly generous frequency applied in the Up direction in the morning peak.

The ten-minute slack hour service proved incapable of generating additional traffic in what was a fully-built up area where most short journeys were easily and conveniently achieved by excellent bus services. Few people wished to travel to or towards Liverpool Street during the day. The headway was therefore widened out to 20 min from June 1965. When the Victoria line tube railway opened through south Tottenham to Walthamstow on 1st September 1968 it very quickly attracted passengers from stations to the north of Seven Sisters, where a convenient inter-change was available from 1st December 1968. On that date the original West Green Road entrance of Seven Sisters station was replaced by a new combined BR and LT ticket hall in Seven Sisters Road, reached from the south ends of the Enfield line platforms by making use of part of the old Birstall Road subway. Fast trains on the Bishops Stortford and Hertford East services were then stopped at Seven Sisters and passengers quickly adopted this new and more direct route to Kings Cross and the West End. The Seven Sisters interchange was a major factor in the scaling-down of peak hours services which followed its opening.

The Enfield line's inner London stations presented a particular problem; their peak hours traffic fell away steeply in the early 1970s and the off-peak patronage was low. Sunday trains had been withdrawn from Cambridge Heath, London Fields and Rectory Road in June 1965 and the decline continued through the 1970s. Stamford Hill was closed on Sundays from October 1981. From 5th October 1981 calls at stations south of the Seven Sisters (apart from Hackney Downs) were restricted to the half hourly all-stations Southbury line services (Enfield Town Trains ran semi-fast, stopping at Hackney Downs, Seven Sisters and then all stations). A 1983 survey of Hackney residents in the line's catchment area showed that a high proportion were unaware of the destinations served or the frequency of the Enfield line services.

In an experiment funded by the GLC and marketed as the 'Jazz Service' (again) from 3rd October 1983, the frequency at all stations to Enfield was raised to four an hour between 10.00 and 16.00 (19.00 on Saturdays). With the Southbury line services, this gave a ten minute service at these times as far as Lower Edmonton. A brave try, it failed miserably, having little or no effect on the low level of off-peak traffic south of Seven Sisters. After over 2½ years, reality was recognised in the timetable applicable from 12th May 1986, which gave Enfield Town only two trains an hour off peak, four an hour to stations between Bethnal Green and Lower Edmonton; Sunday services became hourly. 1991 saw an attempt to close the Enfield line stations entirely on Sundays, a proposal quickly withdrawn in the face of strong protests. Business at the inner area stations continued to be disappointing and despite expensive rebuilding in 1985–86, Cambridge Heath and London Fields were closed except at peak hours from 11th May 1992.

It would be an exaggeration to say that electrification changed the line's image overnight; it was too ingrained into the north London urban scene for that. The change in traction brought with it only two major new structures; a quite presentable new station for Enfield Town, officially opened on 25th April 1958 and a power-operated signal box with a conspicuous sun baffle, erected at the north end of platforms 2 and 3 at Hackney Downs in 1959. For some years the electric trains ran over a line which retained much of its GER atmosphere. Between trains, the closely-spaced stations, with their soot-stained brickwork, their platforms gloomy under rotting saw-tooth canopies and their cavernous stairways and underline subways, still seemed to be haunted by the ghosts of corduroy-trousered artisans and consumptive clerks clutching their cheap tickets.

BR eventually found the money to initiate a modest programme of station modernisation in 1974–80, making a start at Stoke Newington and Stamford Hill. A second phase of rebuilding, which saw the disappearance of a great deal of the remaining GER structures, followed in 1981–86, launched with substantial assistance from central and local government funds. The two most notable rebuildings were at Seven Sisters and Rectory Road; details of these and the other works are given in the list overleaf, which also records the quite remarkable number of contemporary fires. No fewer than six of the 12 intermediate stations were seriously damaged in this way, between December 1972 and July 1984, often overnight, in suspicious circumstances. At Silver Street a fire made a second rebuilding necessary. Lack of supervision also ensured that almost as soon as new construction work was completed it was defaced by the wall-scrawling fraternity and vandalised in other ways.

A journey in the summer of 1996 found punctual four-car trains well-filled north of Seven Sisters with Edmonton Green particularly busy in early afternoon. Little activity was however evident at Silver Street, Bruce Grove, Stamford Hill, Stoke Newington, Bethnal Green and Rectory Road, where the costly GLC reconstruction of 1985 exhibited sad signs of persistent vandalism. Inwards from Edmonton Green, the railway environment was depressing, with tracks weedgrown, accumulations of uncleared litter between platforms and unwelcoming and tatty street entrances often failing to give prominence to their purpose. Station premises appeared neglected and unwelcoming, in strong contrast to those of London Transport in similar inner suburban locations. The time may be approaching when a drastic reappraisal would be appropriate for a line which has since the late 1950s absorbed such a very large amount of capital investment without much tangible return either to railway revenue or urban renewal. One possible development could be a thinning out of the stations, which are spaced far too close together for modern needs.

Enfield Town Line: Station Fires and Reconstruction

(Since c. 1960 all platforms have been extended to take 8-car electric trains).

Bethnal Green: Rebuilt 1985–86, platforms reduced to two (on north side); all GER structures at rail level removed. Crude metal covers over stairwells, simple pitch-roofed waiting pavilion on Down platform.

Cambridge Heath: Gutted by fire 27th July 1984: GER canopies destroyed, station closed until September 1984. Closed again, for rebuilding, 17th February – 16th March 1986. New street frontage and ticket hall. All platform buildings demolished and small shelters substituted.

London Fields: Gutted by fire 13th November 1981, closed and neglected. Rebuilt 1985–86, all GER structures demolished, new waiting shelters; entrance, subway and staircases refurbished. Reopened 25th September 1986.

Hackney Downs: New street entrance hall and ticket office by BR architect Sandy Boal, funded by Urban Aid Programme and GLC grant, 1981. New waiting rooms, platform awnings and train indicators funded from same sources 1982–85. GER canopies preserved on Down Enfield platform.

Rectory Road: Closed by fire early morning 9th December 1972, reopened 17th January 1973. Completely rebuilt 1984–85. Street level building (opened 1st May 1985) in brick under a tiled roof; BR double arrow logo in brickwork. New footbridge, small tiled-roof, glass and brick pavilion shelters on each platform; all GER structures demolished. Three quarters of the cost met under Urban Aid Programme.

Stoke Newington: Ticket hall and office modernised. New and much smaller canopies along walls of cutting replacing GER structures. Completed 1974–75.

Stamford Hill: New ticket office in refurbished street level building 1979. Platform improvements with new shelters 1984 with GLC funds. All GER structures demolished.

Seven Sisters: Rebuilt 1979–80. GER platform structures demolished, new heated waiting rooms with lavatories at each end of Down platform, new 300ft awning, stairs to Seven Sisters Road covered over. From May 1985 escalator connection and retiled subway from combined BR/LT ticket hall to Down platform, funded by GLC.

Bruce Grove: Rebuilt 1979. Down side canopies and structures demolished, roofing over stairs removed. GER canopies retained on Up side. Ticket hall in arch under the line rebuilt.

White Hart Lane: Gated exit/entrance on Down side for football crowds, 1962. Station gutted by fire c. 1977. Ticket hall, entrance and ticket office rebuilt on Up side. New steel staircases (unroofed) on both sides. Work completed 1978–79. GER canopies remain on both platforms but valancing cut away.

Silver Street: New ticket hall and entrance building; GER structures on Down platform demolished, work completed 1979. Gutted by fire 12th June 1984. Ticket hall and entrance again rebuilt 1985–86. GER canopies remain on Up side.

Lower Edmonton/Edmonton Green: New flat-roofed ticket hall and entrance building on Up side facing Edmonton Green shopping centre. GER buildings and entrance in Church Street (Down side) closed. GER platform canopies remain on both platforms. Work completed 1977–78. Renamed Edmonton Green 28th September 1992.

Bush Hill Park: Ticket hall and entrance on Down side gutted by fire August 1981. Rebuilt in brick with flat roof 1982. GER canopy retained on Up side.

Enfield Town: Rebuilt 1957–58 by BR architect H H Powell. Flat-roofed structure in brownish-red facing bricks across end of line with large entrance hall lit by clerestory, mechanised ticket office, parcels office, cycle store, ladies' waiting room and men's lavatories. Concourse area re-roofed with asbestos cement decking. Platforms 1 & 2 (island) given a central canopy 418ft long, glazed for 6ft back from edges each side. Side platform 3 unaltered, no shelters. All GER structures removed (except signal box).

The Churchbury or Southbury Loop (map page 365)

Well before the arrival of railways in London, the Hertford road along the Lea Valley showed signs of ribbon development, a growth nurtured by the business of the road, adjacent market gardens supplying the needs of London and the popularity of the valley for holiday trips and retirement homes. As early as 1864, the GER, considering a second line up the western side of the valley near London might bear some fruit, included in its Additional Powers Act of 1865 an 'Ordnance Factory Railway' which was to leave the Bethnal Green-Edmonton line authorised the previous year at Lower Edmonton, proceed along the west side of the Hertford road and cross it to make a junction with the 1840 Northern & Eastern line near Ordnance Factory station (now Enfield Lock). Perhaps the promoters also hoped that the 1850s enlargement of the Royal Small Arms Factory would lead to further developments, but industrial expansion in the Lea valley was thirty years away, and the powers for the loop were wisely abandoned in an act of 1869. Proposals of the 1870s to link the GNR and GER Enfield branches to the Lea Valley line also came to nothing.

Noting that its direct line from Enfield to Liverpool Street with its cheap trains and frequent service had worked wondrously to enlarge Tottenham and Edmonton, the board reconsidered the position at the beginning of the 1880s, reviving the old dream in an act of 1882, which provided for a 5m 7.5ch line from north of Lower Edmonton to Cheshunt on the Cambridge line. With stations much closer to the main Hertford road than those on the older line, this loop was expected to open up a first- and second-class ticket-holder district which seemed ready for building development. Construction was however deferred until 1889/90 and it was not until 1st October 1891 that passenger and freight operation could start. There were 17 Down passenger workings and 18 Up, with five each way on Sundays, the service running only between White Hart Lane on the Enfield line and Cheshunt, calling at all intermediate stations and taking about 23 minutes.

Construction through the comparatively level land of the valley was not costly in terms of engineering works but the GER chose to spend lavishly on stations designed for heavy suburban traffic. Substantially-built in stone, red brick and tiles, with distinctly urban elevations, their long, well-canopied platforms looked quite out of place amid the market gardens and brickfields. Each had a full set of offices, including 'Waiting Rooms, First-Class, Ladies', a facility unlikely to be much in demand in what was a distinctly artisan and working-class area, although it was perhaps indicative of the company's hopes for the district. Features displayed by these pleasing buildings were ridge tiles, ogee gables, chimney buttresses, false pediments, tile-hung gables and windows with segmented arches with glazing bars reminiscent of Bedford Park. They were clearly intended to blend in with the large middle-class villas that they were expected to serve.

From Bury Street Junction, 60ch north of Lower Edmonton, named after a hamlet west of the line, the double track veered north-east, soon reaching a station called Churchbury on the south side of the bridge carrying the Ponders End-Enfield road over the railway and about a quarter-mile west of Ponders End High Street. Its main building, sitting over the line, was the most impressive of the three intermediate stations, presumably because as the nearest to London, it was expected to reap the greatest measure of suburban business. Covered staircases led down from it to platforms at each side of the line, well-canopied for much of their length. On the Up side at the London end, the small goods yard had ample room for expansion.

GER Station Forty Hill,
entrance block at right.
Up train at platform,
c. 1905.
Enfield Libraries

There were only a few cottages between the station and the Hertford road, whilst on the west side there was nothing but two brick works, using the brick earth that lay on the gravel terrace to make yellow stock bricks for the houses at Tottenham, Edmonton and other places in north London. The southernmost of this pair was to be served by a long siding off the Down line.

Keeping fairly close to the west side of the valley road, the line entered Forty Hill station at the point of transition from a low embankment to a very shallow cutting. The platforms stood on the north side of the bridge over a narrow country road called Turkey Street which connected Enfield Wash with Forty Hill, a northern outpost of Enfield town. Covered staircases led to a tiled subway under the line and the main building, a square pavilion on the Up side in the approach road to the goods yard at the country end of the station. A small entrance on the Down side was close to the half-dozen cottages and inn that constituted the hamlet called Turkey Street. Another handful of workers' cottages built in the 1850s was all that existed between the east side of the station and the main road a quarter of a mile away.

From Forty Hill, the general direction was north-east towards Waltham Cross, but to avoid property demolition in this already large village it was necessary to go to its extreme northern end before crossing above the Hertford road to reach the Lea valley line. At this point, on the west side of the bridge over the main road, were platforms on a curve built over arches in blue engineering brick which carried the tracks to the elaborate plate girder bridge with its brick arch abutments and six supporting iron columns. Entrances were made on each side of the line, the main one on the south side with a covered staircase leading to the solid red brick main building on the Up side. As there was already a station named Waltham Cross on the old line, half a mile to the south-east, this one was called Theobalds Grove after the former royal palace and park and the eighteenth century mansion about ¾-mile west of the railway. The goods yard, at the London end of the station on ground level, was reached by a steeply-graded 15ch single track from the Up road. From the road bridge the embankment dwindled down on to the marshes bringing the tracks to Cheshunt Junction about ¾-mile south of Cheshunt station, where a bay platform was provided on the Down side, 5m 15ch from Bury Street Junction.

No improvements were made, or were necessary in the first ten years apart from

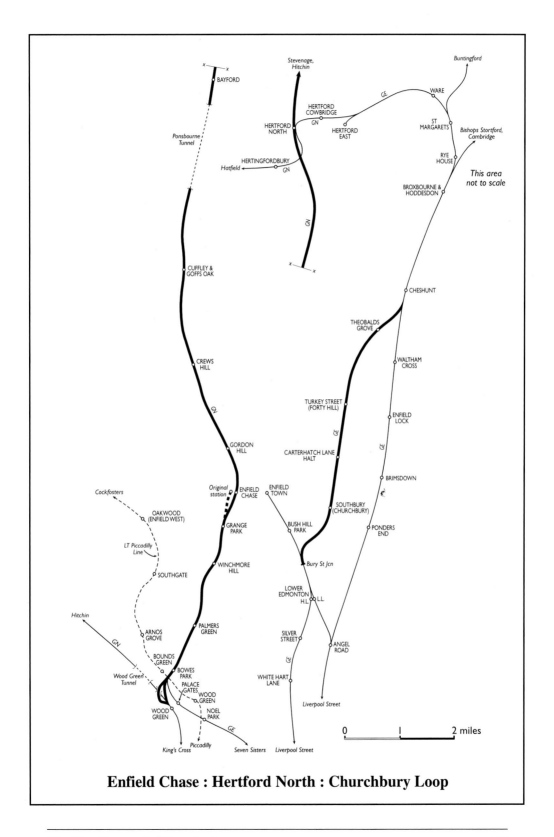

Enfield Chase : Hertford North : Churchbury Loop

the addition of one or two trains. Doubtless the unenterprising character of the service, with the requirement to change to reach London on all but a few morning trains did much to discourage such traffic potential as existed, but the fact was that at this time the district served lacked residential attractions and was too far from town to entice season-ticket holders. Builders showed no inclination to buy up the nurseries, market gardens and brickfields along the line except in penny packets along the main road.

In 1907 there were 21 Down journeys and 23 Up, all but three morning rush-hour workings running between Cheshunt and White Hart Lane. Sunday service remained at five each way between those stations. Why White Hart Lane? Brian Perren has suggested it was chosen because it was the maximum distance the single train used for the service could work up the Liverpool Street line, given the constraints of an hourly interval and adequate running-round time at termini. Freight business was possibly slightly more remunerative than passenger; the brickworks and nurseries needed coal and coke, the nurseries and market gardens took in fertilisers, and all three provided some outward traffic. Through freights were seen on the line as well as the daily pick-up working.

Low passenger revenue was seriously eroded after the opening of the Metropolitan Electric Tramways from Lower Edmonton to Enfield Lock (Freezywater) on 11th December 1907 and onwards to Waltham Cross centre on 17th April 1908. Not only did the electric cars provide a cheaper and much more frequent service for the local journeys that had made up most of the new line's business; they offered the great boon of accessibility, passing as they did through the very centre of the then thinly built-up area each side of the main road. Almost overnight the GER receipts fell to half what they had been, which in any case was not much. Forty Hill and Churchbury, within a quarter-mile of the tramway, fared the worst, with Theobalds Grove, half a mile north of the tram terminus slightly less affected. After pausing, as if they were unable to comprehend what had happened, the GER decided upon complete abandonment of the passenger service, the last trains running on 30th September 1909. Reluctance to act promptly was understandable, for this was something quite new for the GER, and was the first passenger closure in the county of Middlesex. There was something of a minor sensation over it, with Winston Churchill, then President of the Board of Trade, called upon to answer a question in the Commons. He gave the now familiar reply that this was the undertaking's business, no concern of central government, passing on to Branch, the local MP, a copy of a letter from the GER general manager. This explained that the district had not developed as expected, its principal occupations were market gardening and nurseries, with most of the population locally employed, but the electric trams were to blame, for they had abstracted such traffic as existed.

Freight working continued, no doubt just covering costs, though much of it, equally well handled by the Lea valley line yards, showed no net gain to the GER. A brighter era briefly dawned when from 1915 the Lea valley became a centre of war industries. This activity was principally sited around Angel Road, Edmonton, at the Royal Gunpowder and Royal Small Arms Factories at Waltham Abbey and Enfield Lock, and at the Ponders End Shell Works. Production requirements were such that the factories could not subsist on local 'walking' labour, and although most of the workforce came in by tram or the existing train services from the London end of the Lea valley, the GER was called upon by the government to re-open the loop for passengers. This it did on 1st March 1915, using A. J. Hill's new auto-train, the first on its system. After trials on the Southend-Shenfield line in 1913, a Y65/F7 2–4–2T had been fitted with a compressed-air control system for auto-working, with subsequent trials on the Mildenhall and Ramsey branches; the accommodation consisted of two clerestory-roofed coaches, a first- and third-class composite, and a third-class driving trailer. It was this unit, providing 76 third-class and nine first-class seats, which was moved to the Churchbury loop. The conductor issued tickets on the train, tramcar-style. A second and similar train arrived on the loop in December 1915 when the service was built up from an initial 15 journeys each way between Cheshunt and Lower Edmonton (where passengers changed for Angel Road) to 18, six of the latter going on to White Hart Lane. For this service, which operated on weekdays only, a timber halt was opened at Carterhatch Lane, 69ch north of Churchbury, on 12th June 1916. Wartime traffic was not substantial, declining rapidly with the rundown of the war factories, so the GER withdrew the service again after the last train on 30th June 1919. The halt was demolished, the auto-units sent south to work the Palace Gates shuttle. Towards the end, their place had sometimes been taken by normal trains hauled by 0–6–0T or 0–6–2T.

Its main interests concentrated on long-distance passenger and freight, the GER's successor, the LNER, unlike its southern neighbour, lacked incentive for developing London suburban business. Thus when the area served by the loop was opened-up by the completion of the Great Cambridge Arterial Road (now the A10) from Tottenham to Wormley in 1924, the board remained impervious to suggestions that because the new housing the GER had looked for seemed likely to arrive at last the railway should be re-opened. And the houses came; with their ready-made drainage, services, and all-weather access for delivery of materials, combined with considerable publicity value, the London arterial roads completed as unemployment relief in the 1920s proved a strong magnet for speculative builders, and the Great Cambridge Road was no exception. If further encouragement were needed, this was given by the extension of a 12-minute motor bus service along the new road as far as Southbury Road in April 1934, and on to Turkey Street two years later. By this time, row after row of small houses had appeared to line the new road, soon followed by estates filling in much of the area crossed by the railway between the Cambridge Road and the old Hertford road. Close behind came industrial development, attracted by easy road transport access and low land costs in an era when the economic situation favoured industrial growth in the London region. Some extra business came to the goods yards, but the LNER remained inflexible on restoration of passenger service. Its attitude was not wholly inexplicable; any addition to the 58 trains an hour passing Hackney Downs in the peak was unthinkable without electrification or other major works for which capital could not be raised without government assistance, and that assistance tended to favour the Underground until around 1935. Nor did the LNER see much popularity to be gained from decanting passengers from the loop at Lower Edmonton or White Hart Lane to join already crowded Enfield Town trains. Nevertheless one feels that had this been south of the Thames, the loop, with hundreds of new houses and many new factories closing in on it, especially at the London end, would not have been left to stagnate.

After World War 1, coal and goods yards were still served daily by freight trains working in both directions over the Down line, the other track being used for wagon storage. Most of the traffic was in solid fuels and building materials but through the

1930s and 1940s some of the factories made use of the rail service. In 1927, when there were three through Down freights in the early hours and three local workings on Tuesdays to Fridays, the signal boxes at Bury Street Junction, Churchbury and Theobalds Grove stations were open from 03.00 to 19.00, 07.00 to 15.00, and 05.00 to 13.00 respectively. Forty Hill box was switched out, to be opened only for shunting operations without use of the block instruments. Subsequently Bury Street box was closed, the points then being worked from a two-lever ground frame controlled from Edmonton Junction box. Churchbury station box also closed, as did Forty Hill, which was demolished. After these economies, the signalman for Theobalds Grove box travelled with the Down pick-up goods. Some of the GER signals were replaced by LNER upper-quadrants. but the GER track on its ash and gravel ballast was left undisturbed until 1950 apart from essential replacements.

Leased out for non-railway purposes, the three stations remained more or less intact. Forty Hill and Theobalds Grove were used as domestic accommodation, occasionally visited by press photographers in the silly season when the occupants were persuaded to take tea on the tracks or to string washing between the platforms. Churchbury was for many years a joinery works, its platform canopies boarded in. Later it acted as a store for a builders' merchant, whose stock of wc pans, piping, tiles and other goods could be seen stacked under the canopies.

When there were interruptions between Cheshunt and Clapton, the loop provided a valuable diversionary route. Examples of such use occurred in February 1919 when melting snow submerged the Lea valley line at Tottenham to a depth of 3ft; in January 1928, when a small underline bridge at Angel Road collapsed after a cloudburst; in October 1929 after a collision at Tottenham; and in 1940 and 1944 when the Lea valley route was blocked by enemy action. The 1928 diversions lasted for several days and it is recorded that on this occasion if on no other, the three stations were temporarily re-opened, (no doubt at some inconvenience to the tenants), their names chalked on blackboards, and with hurricane lamp illumination after dark. Double-line working was usually the rule during these diversions, after the empty wagons had been dragged out. In 1947 double-line running was restored permanently.

The British Transport Commission's Railway Modernisation Plan of December 1954 included a promise that train services from Liverpool Street to Hertford East and Bishops Stortford would be electrified, and it soon became clear that this was to include resumption of passenger services over the loop, now to be known as the 'Southbury Line', following consultations between the BTC and the local authorities in which it had been agreed that Churchbury and Forty Hill stations would be respectively renamed Southbury and Turkey Street after the roads they served. Whilst the decision to re-open was a recognition of further development in the area since 1945 and of the strength of local pressures for rail service, maintained for at least a decade, a major factor evident in the upgrading of track and signalling to main line status was the part the loop could play in increasing the flexibility of Eastern Region operations in the London area.

Work on rebuilding the right of way to main line standards started in the early summer of 1956 when the six-year-old track and concrete sleepers were uprooted, together with all the ballast. Bridges were rebuilt or strengthened and junctions realigned to allow 50mph running instead of the previous 20mph. When this work was finished, the overall speed limit was raised to 60mph from 40mph. At first it was thought the stations might be rebuilt, but financial pressures and the discovery

Unit 296 on Up special train at Theobald's Grove station on 20th November 1960, the day before reopening for public service. *Alan A Jackson*

that their substantial construction remained sound led to a decision simply to refurbish, bringing platforms to standard height, and fitting-out with cold cathode lighting which exhibited the station name along the platform. At Southbury the old canopies were repaired and the original buildings thoroughly cleaned up. Turkey Street lost its canopies and platform buildings, receiving instead only two small brick shelters. Theobalds Grove retained all its buildings although the canopies were reduced to less than one car's length each side. A pleasant touch was the appointment to stationmaster here of the son of the first booking clerk. Three- and four-aspect searchlight signalling with continuous track circuiting replaced the old double-line block system. Finally the line was wired for 6.25kV* overhead traction supply (25kV from a point north of Theobalds Grove). Some through diesel-hauled trains worked over the loop non-stop from 2nd November 1959.

The three stations opened for enquiries on 14th November 1960, an official ceremony followed on 16th November, and public service, using 19 four-car sets of new multiple-unit stock, started on 21st November. The eight-car trains which included composite first- and second-class trailers, operated every 30 minutes every day of the week between Liverpool Street and Broxbourne, where they divided for Hertford East and Bishops Stortford. Liverpool Street to Lower Edmonton was covered non-stop in 15 minutes, half the time taken by the all-stations steam service, with calls at every station beyond. Extra trains at peak hours provided approximately 20-minute intervals. As noted earlier, the planned level of service was not reached for some time owing to serious technical difficulties with the new rolling stock.

With the opening of the Victoria Tube line in 1968 an additional stop was made by the Southbury Loop trains to allow interchange at Seven Sisters. Electrification of the Lea Valley route between Cheshunt and Clapton on 5th May 1969 brought further change; the normal pattern of service then became Lea Valley trains via Tottenham Hale between Liverpool Street and Hertford East and Bishops Stortford–Liverpool Street electrics via the Southbury Loop with interchange connections between the two at Broxbourne.

* Uprated to 25kV in 1983–84

The reopened GER station at Southbury on 20th November 1960 when tickets were being sold for the restored public service from the following day. *Alan A Jackson*

Freight traffic faded away during the first decade of the loop's renaissance. Theobalds Grove yard, closed to all except coal on 3rd January 1966, saw its last train at the end of the following May and was leased to a scrap metal merchant. Turkey Street depot was shut from 1st June the same year, but Southbury lasted until December 1970. As commuter traffic at the three stations was not substantial there was no immediate pressure to convert these yards to car parks. At first it seemed that the very long period of passenger closure, combined with the continuing growth in local employment opportunities in the post war years was making it very difficult to build up traffic for the electric service. Southbury and Turkey Street each saw only about 500 joining trains each day in 1974 but at Theobalds Grove the figure was around 1,500. Thanks to a considerable amount of new housing in its catchment area, this was also the busiest commuter station, with season ticket holders increasing from 456 in 1961 to 706 in 1974. At the other two stations, the number of season ticket holders, about 250 at each, showed little or no growth in the same period.

As elsewhere, vandalism and security measures were principal agents in stimulating station works. In 1978 Theobalds Grove was given a modernised ticket office and ticket hall, and new entrance doors protected by a canopy. Further work here in 1987–88 involved demolition of some GER structures and erection of new waiting shelters and awnings. In the same period Turkey Street's heavily-vandalised GER street level building was demolished and replaced with more secure accommodation built into an arch next to the subway; new waiting shelters were erected on the platforms here and at Southbury.

To one who knew this line during its long period of closure a journey over it in an electric train at first assumed an almost dreamlike quality. It was difficult to realise that the romantic sight of a deserted railway which so stirred childhood imagination had really been breathed back to life. That feeling has now gone, as has that strange half rural, half suburban, almost pioneer atmosphere that could be sensed around the stations; such open land as now remains is very largely taken up with sterile playing fields and motor roads, including, across the northern end of this railway, the ineluctable, all-enclosing, all-roaring M25.

Chingford Station, c. 1903, main entrance block and stationmaster's house Down Side, and cab yard, facing Station Road. *Chingford Historical Society Collection*

The Chingford Branch (map page 350)

The Chingford line's history shares much with that of its Enfield sister, for it was another of the feeders for the new Liverpool Street terminus, destined to receive cheap trains which were to lead to social development of very similar pattern.

Although Chingford was to remain a very small and unimportant place for another 70 years, Walthamstow already had some 5,000 inhabitants by the middle of the nineteenth century. Like Tottenham, Edmonton and Enfield, it was a place of rural retreat for London businessmen; it too depended on the Northern & Eastern Railway for access to the City, a horse bus connecting with all trains at Lea Bridge station.

The 1860s saw the first stirrings of organised suburban development in the area. This was essentially directed at the middle-class market, so that when Parliament insisted on a workmen's train obligation for proposed GER lines through Walthamstow, James Higham, one of the developers, rose up in anger at the threat of plebeian invasion. So anxious was he that the right sort of people came to Walthamstow that in conjunction with other developers, he promoted his own line, alongside the GER scheme of 1864. But it was the GER which got parliamentary approval in that year for lines which were part of the new suburban system associated with their City terminus at Liverpool Street. The first of these, in a separate act, was a branch from Leyton (Loughton Branch Junction) to a point three quarters of a mile south of High Beach, a holiday resort in the Epping Forest, passing through east Walthamstow and Chingford Green. This was intended to carry good class residential traffic as well as the excursionists to and from the Forest. As mentioned earlier, the main act – the GER (Metropolitan Station and Railway) Act, 1864 – included a line from Bethnal Green to Hackney Downs, where one section continued north to Lower

Edmonton and another forked north east to join the N&ER at Copper Mill Junction. This act also contained powers to extend the latter line across the N&ER through Walthamstow to a junction with the proposed High Beach branch. It was in this main act that Parliament included the obligation to run one 2d return workmen's train daily between Walthamstow and the City as some recompense for the destruction of working-class housing in inner London. Thus the GER had two proposed lines through the area, each likely to nurture a different class of housing development.

The ambitious plans of the youthful GER were soon overshadowed by a difficult financial situation, which was to lead to the appointment of a receiver in 1867. An embankment had been built from west Walthamstow down into the Lea valley, but work ceased when the GER found itself unable to pay the contractors. In 1868 it was necessary to obtain an extension of time for the 1864 lines. Houses were now appearing in some quantity and Higham had been hammering at the GER board-room door, even offering to muster cash to secure a railway as far as Walthamstow. All this no doubt influenced Parliament, for in granting the extension of time, it insisted the GER build a branch into Walthamstow from its Lea valley line.

Money was somehow scraped together for this, a single track over the alignment used by the contractors for the embankment mentioned earlier, and trains began to run between Lea Bridge station and a temporary terminus called Shern Hall Street on 26th April 1870. Situated in the centre of the chain of small villages that formed Walthamstow, this station had an earth bank platform on the south side of the railway in the cutting between the 60yd Nag's Head tunnel and Shern Hall Street itself. Two other stations were provided in Walthamstow. The west end was served by a single wooden platform on the south side just east of the bridge over St James's Street, which gave it its name; at Hoe Street, just half-a-mile from the terminus, there were substantial buildings on a platform on the south side, facing open fields. Hoe Street station was destined to become the main traffic centre of the new suburb, and there were already some small houses under construction immediately south of it.

Trains worked the branch hourly, connecting with the Bishopsgate via Stratford service on the main line. This lasted for just over two years, during which time the GER managed to complete an important part of its 1864 proposals. From 1st August 1872 it was possible to work a half-hourly service between Shern Hall Street and Bishopsgate over the newly-completed double track between Hall Farm Junction and Hackney Downs. This had one intermediate station, opened on 1st July 1872 following the completion of the Hackney Downs–Copper Mill Junction line on 22nd June. Clapton station, on the east side of the Upper Clapton Road, served what was then the north-eastern edge of continuously built-up London. It had no goods yard until 2nd July 1900 when one was opened on the Up side, south of the bridge over the river Lea. Between Clapton and Hackney Downs stations were two short tunnels, the southerly one passing under the Downs. During the 1890s, against an intermediate signal box called Queen's Road between the tunnels, the GER erected a platform, but never completed the proposed station.

Powers to abandon the planned branch from Leyton to High Beach Green were obtained in 1869 subject to the presentation in the following session of a bill to extend from Shern Hall Street over the northern end of the High Beach Green alignment as far as Chingford Green. This was duly sanctioned in 1870, together with the Lea Bridge–St James's Street spur, which had been built in advance of parliamentary authority. At Wood Street, Walthamstow, the extension deviated to the east of the 1864 alignment, probably for reasons connected with land purchase. Passenger trains served the Chingford terminus in Bull Lane (now Kings Road) over a single track opened on 17th November 1873. As a further attempt was to be made in the next parliamentary session to obtain an extension to High Beach, the building on the single platform was a temporary wooden structure and locomotives slaked their thirst at an old farm pond.

From the opening day, trains ran from Chingford to Bishopsgate (and from 2nd November 1874 to the new Liverpool Street station) via Hackney Downs over a newly-doubled line between Shern Hall Street and Hall Farm Junction. With the extension, Shern Hall Street platform was closed, to be replaced by a permanent station at Wood Street serving the eastern part of Walthamstow. This had substantial buildings in yellow stock brick and two platforms from which stairs led down to a street-level booking hall. Hale End (now Highams Park), a second intermediate station between here and Chingford, was a less solid structure.

On 2nd September 1878, the branch reached its final form with the opening of a permanent terminus at Chingford, some distance north of the original. At the very edge of the Forest, 10m 37ch from Liverpool Street, it possessed a large station house on the Down side, and two main platforms with bays at their outer edges; the track leading to it was the only piece of a High Beach extension sought in 1874 which parliament had allowed. As was sometimes the case with such parliamentary pruning, the original plans were followed and the centre was a through station, its two roads going on for some 75yd beyond the platforms to be used as an engine dock and watering point pending further progress northwards. An extension bill deposited in 1882 for a line via Sewardstone to a point a quarter of a mile north of High Beach was badly timed. On 6th May 1882, Queen Victoria came to Chingford in the GWR royal train (hauled by the GER's first blue locomotive, a modest 0–4–4T) to declare the Forest open to the public. In the excitement, opposition to the desecration of the Forest by a railway was easily aroused, killing the extension then and for all time.

Although the temporary station at Bull Lane, Chingford was shut, it was not demolished until the early 1950s. Its approach tracks served for many years to store wagons moving in and out of the goods yard built in 1878 between the old and new stations.

Until the turn of the century, pleasure traffic formed the main business at Chingford and a buffet, directed to its needs, survived on the Down side until 1972. Residential trade was apparent by 1910 when £375 semi-detached houses were ready on the Forest Estate, east of the station, and an entrance was opened on that side to Beresford Road.

During the last decades of the nineteenth century very strong housing growth in Walthamstow required expansion and improvement of the somewhat sparse accommodation installed in 1870 and 1873. Pressure first became apparent at St James's Street, the nearest point to London. A Down platform had been erected here with the doubling of the line in 1873, and it received a waiting room two years later. From 27th May 1890 a second ticket office and entrance were in use at the eastern end of the Up platform, a facility which survived (although latterly with very restricted opening hours) until October 1967.

Hoe Street also acquired a Down platform in the 1873 doubling but there was no booking office or entrance on that side until 1897, a belated response to the northward growth of the suburb. The original small goods yard on the Down side was virtually replaced by a larger one opened south of the line on 15th July 1880. A footpath across this linked the GER platforms with the adjacent Walthamstow station of the Midland's Tottenham & Forest Gate line after its opening from South Tottenham to Woodgrange Park on 9th July 1894. That line, with its services to Moorgate and East Ham, passed below the Chingford branch west of Hoe Street station. With the completion of the Walthamstow Council electric power station off the inappropriately-named Sylvan Road in 1901, coal was delivered to its private sidings via Hoe Street yard. Immediately north of Wood Street station, carriage sidings were laid out together with a small engine shed, facilities later expanded to meet the needs of an increased train service. From 20th April 1893 a goods and coal depot was available on the Up side south of Wood Street station, its business consisting largely of domestic fuels and building materials.

As on the Enfield line, the crowds presenting themselves for the 2d trains soon obliged the GER to provide more accommodation. The number of such trains increased from three in 1883 to six in 1890, seven in 1897, eight in 1899 and finally ten in 1904, all reaching Bishopsgate Low Level or Liverpool Street between 05.00 and 07.00. Many of their patrons, obliged to save every penny they could, preferred to use them even if they had to wait for their place of employment to open at 08.30 or even 09.00. Despite pleas about the consequent distress to young girls, especially in winter, the GER resisted all pressures to extend the 2d concession to a later hour, but it did start half-fare (4d return) trains in 1885 which arrived in London between 07.30 and 08.00. This rate was also available from midnight to 05.00 on the all-night service started between Wood Street and Liverpool Street on 21st June 1897. Unique in London, these half-hourly trains, which gave the line a continuous service from very early Monday morning until very late Saturday night, brought many printers, newspaper workers and other night toilers to live in the west Walthamstow area. Reduced to hourly as a wartime economy from 15th January 1917, the trains continued to run until 1966, when for the first time since 1897 there was a prolonged interval at night.

The half-fare trains, marginally profitable provided they were full, were especially popular in Walthamstow, patronage so increasing around the turn of the century that the GER general manager could tell the 1904 Royal Commission on London Traffic 'Walthamstow is largely the home of the half-fare traveller and at this place the half-fare forms the principal traffic'. At this time there were nine half-fare trains, offering a total of 7,400 seats, but the last two were severely overcrowded. By 1920 the loadings on these trains were more than double those of the 2d trains, with as many as 20 to 30 passengers crammed into third-class compartments meant to seat 12. In May that year the general manager admitted loadings in excess of 1,460 on evening peak trains to Chingford, over four-fifths in the third-class accommodation. Probably in an endeavour to recover its losses on some of the sub-standard fare trains, the GER set Chingford line third-class fares season ticket rates at an abnormally high level. Most rush-hour trains had at least eight of their 15 cars allocated to first- and second-class passengers; the latter cars, always subject to invasion by third-class ticket holders, were patronised by the higher-paid clerks, civil servants and junior managers who boarded at Highams Park and Wood Street.

As far as Wood Street frequency had reached half-hourly by early in 1874, but at peak periods there were trains every 15 minutes. On the country section beyond, a two-hourly off-peak and hourly peak service sufficed, strengthened at summer weekends and holiday times. By 1902 there were seven trains an hour to and from the three Walthamstow stations in the rush hours and although the basic half-hourly frequency in the off peak was unchanged, it had been extended to Chingford to meet the tentative emergence of residential traffic there and at Highams Park. Soon after this, the rush-hour service was built up to 12 an hour in the morning (07.00 to 08.00), ten from Wood Street, and between 18.00 and 20.00 there were 15 Down trains, five of them terminating at Wood Street. An all day slack-hour interval of 15 minutes applied from July 1909. Most rush-hour trains consisted of 15 gaslit four-wheelers offering a total of 768 seats, but there were also a few 16- and 17-car sets, some all thirds. Motive power was normally a 'Buck Jumper' o–6–oT.

As at Tottenham and Edmonton, the combination of cheap and frequent trains from closely-spaced stations led speculators to erect low-rent housing in quantity, which was filled almost as soon as it was ready. East of the Lea valley, each side of the line as far as Wood Street, there was by 1901 a mass of tightly-packed streets half a mile or more deep. From just over 11,000 inhabitants when the railway first opened, Walthamstow's population grew by 95 per cent in the subsequent decade and by 113 per cent in the 1880s. The figure had reached 95,131 in 1901 with almost 50 per cent of the working adults in the UDC area travelling by train to workplaces in inner London. To an even greater degree than at Tottenham and Edmonton, the colonisers were the upper strata of the working class: junior clerks, artisans, uniformed public servants, shopworkers and warehousemen. Not until around 1910 was large-scale industry established here.

One of the most prominent developers in the 1890–1914 period was Thomas C. T. Warner, who told a parliamentary committee in 1901 that he had covered some 300 acres with houses and half-houses (maisonettes) let at rents of 6s 6d and 7s 0d (32½p and 35p) a week, his 2,184 weekly tenants mostly 'artisans and clerks working in London'. Giving evidence to another parliamentary committee two years later, Walthamstow UDC bemoaned the fact that of 18,600 houses in its area, 11,654 were let at rents up to 9s 6d (47½p) and 3,421 up to 11s 6d (57½p), none producing enough rate income to cover the cost of the local authority's services.

Not everyone worked in London. Until electric tramcars rendered it redundant there was some patronage for a Walthamstow to Stratford service. This was started on 7th June 1880 at two-hourly intervals, with some trains going through to Chingford for pleasure seekers, but with the arrival of the electric trams, midday trains were cut back to Wood Street in 1910 and the service ceased on 3rd October 1914. This was not the end of passenger working over the Lea Bridge–St James's Street spur, as from 1914 there were summer services between North Woolwich and Chingford and between Lea Bridge and Chingford.

Another cross-town facility was from Chingford or Wood Street to Highgate Road from 1st August 1885, using the curve opened in that year between Hall Farm Junction and Copper Mill Junction. At first there were some 12 trains daily each way weekdays and Sundays in summer; to encourage pleasure traffic, ordinary returns were issued at a fraction over the single fare. These trains were extended on 4th June 1888 to a single platform at Gospel Oak, from which passengers could transfer to the North London Railway or go out to Parliament Hill Fields. Patronage,

Liverpool Street train leaving Highams Park station c. 1905 watched by some young trainspotters. *Commercial postcard*

never very great except at summer weekends and public holidays, fell-off badly with the intensive bus and tram competition from 1910 and there were only two trains a day each way by the end of 1918; the service ran for the last time on Sunday 5th September 1926. After that until August 1939 trains ran between Gospel Oak and Chingford only at Easter, Whitsun and August Bank Holidays, nor were they restored after World War 2.

For some years the little wooden station at Hale End was the quietest on the Chingford line, although it gained some pleasure traffic after Highams Park and its lake were added to the public area of Epping Forest in 1891. To mark this, the station, which had received a second platform in 1878, was renamed Highams Park (Hale End) on 1st October 1894. During the 1890s some terraced housing appeared south and west of the station, whilst west of the line a distinctly urban encroachment was the arrival in 1898 of the British Xylonite Company from Homerton. This had a fairly neutral effect on passenger flow, but was to provide some business for the goods yard on the Down side. With the construction of more houses, traffic at the station slowly increased and in 1900 it was rebuilt in more substantial form. Further development followed east of the line, so that by 1908 some 5,000 new residents were established around the station. In 1922 J. F. Gairns described Highams Park as 'a busy station for residential traffic of a good class'. Here again the social layering of the branch showed similarities with the Enfield line.

The overcrowding of the Liverpool Street trains which followed the increasing concentration of peak-hour traffic in the 1910s and early 1920s was no less evident on the Chingford branch, making the line a worthy candidate for the 1920 'Jazz Service' improvements. To accommodate the additional trains, Chingford's platforms were lengthened and a new signal box and four more carriage sidings were

Clapton main entrance block, on the overline bridge in Upper Clapton Road, looking north, c. 1905. *Commercial postcard*

erected there. The Wood Street carriage sidings and locomotive shed were expanded and additional signalling appeared at various points along the line. Track circuiting was installed at Chingford station, also between Wood Street and St James's Street. From 12th July 1920 the new arrangements allowed rush-hour trains to run at approximately five-minute intervals, alternate workings terminating at Wood Street where, to facilitate quick turnarounds, an Up side siding was converted into the Up running line, the original line becoming a terminal road with spurs to both Up and Down tracks. Many Wood Street trains now ran non-stop between St James's Street and Liverpool Street. To save time at the terminals, locomotives were coaled from baskets. There were 848 seats in the rush-hour trains of 16 four-wheelers, but slack-hour service was given by 318-seat trains (six four-wheelers) running every ten minutes instead of 15. Stopping at all seven stations, the Jazz reached Chingford in 33 minutes from Liverpool Street, or 29 when running semi-fast.

Whilst the Chingford branch was not exposed to the parallel electric tramcar and motorbus competition which afflicted the Enfield line, there was some decline in patronage from the early 1920s. This could be attributed to increasing employment opportunities in the Lea valley industrial zone and the growth of commercial institutions in and around Walthamstow. It was to some extent counterbalanced by steady growth in middle-class commuter traffic associated with new private enterprise housing at Chingford, South Chingford and Highams Park designed to attract the inner London white-collar worker. Population at Chingford rose from 9,482 in 1921 to 22,076 ten years later. For its new season-ticket holders, the LNER rebuilt the booking hall at Chingford and provided a Down side exit at Highams Park in 1934.

As former users of the inner stations went by bicycle, bus or tram or on foot to the new factories, industrial troubles in the 1920s forced the reduction of the slack-hour service to 20-minute intervals on several occasions, causing many casual travellers to desert the railway for bus or tram when making local journeys in Walthamstow and Chingford.

Nor was the peak-hour Jazz a popular success. It was a poor substitute for electrification; the combination of ageing, uncomfortable four-wheel coaches and the inability of the overloaded 0–6–0T and 0–4–4T to maintain time brought many complaints. Much of this dissatisfaction was dissipated by the arrival of the pugnacious N7 0–6–2T (hauling virtually all trains by 1928) and new Gresley 'quint-art' sets. The latter, marshalled into ten-car (872-seat) trains ousted the GER 'cattle trucks' between 1927 and 1931 and were to last until electrification 30 years later. Their second-class seats became thirds after the end of 1937; first-class tickets were withdrawn in October 1941. Apart from the troubles mentioned, off-peak services between the wars were at ten-minute intervals, alternate trains fast between Clapton and Liverpool Street.

Another improvement made by the LNER was the replacement of the 1891 Sykes' lock-and-block manual signalling with Westinghouse Brake & Signal Co. three-aspect colour lights and track circuits. Hackney Downs to Clapton Junction was so converted on 24th February 1935, the rest on 30th January 1938, worked from the boxes at Hackney Downs, Clapton Junction and Chingford, instead of the six formerly used. The existing mechanical frames in the retained boxes were fitted with electric locks and circuit controllers.

Wartime conditions reduced off-peak service to half-hourly but rush-hour loading still required about nine trains an hour inwards in the 1950s, by which time a 20-minute slack-hour frequency was operating. In this last decade of steam traction a semi-fast train stopping only at four stations took 26½ minutes for the 10½-mile run from Chingford to Liverpool Street; those trains calling at all nine stations required 34½ minutes. Five-car sets, half the length of rush hour trains, were the rule in the off peak. As the ageing 'quint-arts' and N7 locomotives were suffering from lower standards of maintenance, service deteriorated, sorely trying the patience of the regular passengers. A town meeting at Chingford in 1955 heard protests about dirty carriages and mechanical breakdowns, the MP for Epping suggesting that the branch had 'the most decrepit engines and the most ramshackle rolling stock imaginable'. Following this up in the House of Commons, he described how one train had been held up two hours when a door fell off at Clapton whilst another stopped in the Bishopsgate tunnel for half an hour, its passengers gradually becoming smoke-dried. He complained that despite increasing population since 1939, Chingford had only 84 trains a day compared with 125 then, and 50 on Sundays compared with 68.

Business was still quite buoyant in the mid 1950s, when Highams Park was dealing with around 1,000 tons of freight and 5,000 parcels monthly. Ticket issues each month at this station totalled some 50,000 with another 1,500 seasons. But with the return of road transport to a peacetime scale, freight traffic fell off. Most was inwards, coal, coke, timber, building materials and general merchandise, but in the early days there had been some milk taken out from the farms at Highams Park and Chingford. Yard closures started under the Beeching regime with the withdrawal of coal facilities at Hoe Street, the yard there closing finally in November 1964

One of 'the most decrepit engines', so described by the MP for Epping in 1955, N7 69604 on an Up train from Chingford entering Liverpool Street on 23rd September 1958. *R C Riley*

although coal traffic to the power station continued until December 1967. No goods facilities were available at Highams Park and Chingford from 4th October 1965. At Clapton, freight traffic ceased from 7th December 1964, while Wood Street yard closed from 6th May 1968.

Unusually for a London line, the Chingford branch saw pleasure traffic both inwards and outwards for many years; until the more prosperous 1930s, Chingford was a popular resort for north Londoners at summer weekends and Bank Holidays, demanding extra trains to carry the crowds out to the Forest. As late as 1920 up to 100,000 used the station on a Bank Holiday and 46 additional staff were on duty to handle the traffic. Summer excursion fares from the branch stations to east coast resorts were introduced by the GER in 1890, and the LNER ran special seaside trains in the summer months, a practice continued by BR. There were also special through workings, to Lea Bridge for the motorcycle speedway events, and to Northumberland Park for matches at Tottenham Hotspur football ground. These last used the Copper Mill curve, continuing until that was rather suddenly taken up in 1960.

In the BR Modernisation Plan of 1955 the branch was listed for electrification. Work began early in the following year to prepare for operation from overhead lines carrying 6.25kV ac at 50c/s (this was to be uprated to 25kV from 20th November 1983). Three-car multiple-unit sets, seating 272 made up the trains which entered service on 14th November 1960 but as on the Enfield line, these were soon in trouble from technical problems and needed to be helped out by steam traction until the end of 1961 (steam continued even longer for freight trains, not giving way entirely to diesel locos until well into 1962). After a greatly prolonged breaking-in period, the technical problems with electric traction were finally overcome, full electric service starting on 18th June 1962 with a ten minute basic frequency, supplemented at peak hours. Between 08.00 and 10.00, 18 trains from the branch arrived at Liverpool Street and there was a similar number of return workings in the evening peak. Semi-fasts from Liverpool Street reached Chingford in 22 min, all-stations trains taking two minutes longer. It soon became obvious that this provision was absurdly over generous; as on the Enfield line, traffic patterns had long since changed and inwards from Walthamstow Central much had been permanently lost to road transport. In 1965 the basic frequency was widened out to 20 min and the long-established all-night trains were withdrawn. Although the curve to Lea Bridge had been wired for electric working it was never so used, and the rails were taken up in 1967.

Some minor changes were made with electrification. At Chingford, the two main platforms were linked by a path across the outer ends, sealing off the 'extension' and allowing the subway to be closed. The eastern platform face (No. 4) was not electrified and fell out of use. Wood Street Sidings were rearranged. Hoe Street station, renamed Walthamstow Central on 6th May 1968, underwent partial re-building to accommodate the terminal traffic of the Victoria line tube which was opened to here on 1st September 1968. It had at first been intended to bring the tube to the surface at the London side of Wood Street, making that station the terminus, but this had been dropped as an economy. At Walthamstow Central, a combined LT/BR ticket hall on the Down side, with covered access to a new bus station, was soon much busier than the original Up side entrance. Reached by stairs from the platforms, the top landing of the escalators serving the tube station was beneath the BR tracks.

In 1974–75 St James's Street and Wood Street stations were rebuilt in glass reinforced plastics, brick and aluminium, the result seeming to be designed more to deter vandals than attract the eye. Waiting rooms, staff accommodation and ticket offices were all replaced; platform shelters took the form of light steel-framed canopies and the ample GER awnings were swept away. By the 1990s, the main entrance hall at St James's Street, long unstaffed, bore a wounded, sad look. Chingford received a new ticket hall and ticket office under a suspended ceiling in 1978, all within the existing building. At Highams Park a new ticket office and enlarged Up side waiting room were provided in 1979, again using the GER structure. Clapton benefited from injections of finance by the GLC and other local authority sources; in 1982–83 a modern glass-fronted ticket office, a new station bridge from the ticket hall to the Up platform and a rebuilt and enlarged waiting room were all completed without entirely destroying the GER atmosphere. Some of the latter also remained on the platforms at Walthamstow Central. The carriage sidings at Wood Street, declared redundant, were taken up and the site was sold for development in 1986.

As on the Enfield Town line, the tube service was soon diverting much traffic from stations inwards from the interchange point. This caused BR peak hour frequencies to be reduced, beginning in May 1974. Weaving through the drab workaday districts it had helped to create to reach lower middle class suburbia at Highams Park and Chingford on the edge of Epping Forest, the branch now presents difficult problems for transport planners. Its outer section remains busy, but the loadings between Liverpool Street and Walthamstow Central are light for exactly the same reasons as those on the Enfield Town line south of Seven Sisters. This decline, and schemes for a new south west/north east tube railway could eventually lead to a significant reshaping of the present infrastructure and transport mode on both routes.

The level crossing and station at Woodford, where the original building was on the Down side but a substantial ticket office and additional entrance has by this time been provided on the Up side. Looking south to London, c. 1910. *Commercial postcard*

The Loughton, Epping & Ongar Branch   (map page 386)

We now enter GER suburban territory offering strong contrasts to that just considered. Except at its two innermost stations, the line to Loughton and beyond served a favoured residential area along the eastern edges of Epping Forest, ending in what was until quite recent times a country branch of the quietest kind. Writing in 1920, George Potter commented that although much of the route passed through residential districts, '. . . these are well wooded, and the traveller does not have the feeling that all the available land has been completely swallowed up by the erection of modern houses'. First- and second-class business was encouraged and more first-class seasons were sold on this than on any other GER suburban service. Often as many as one-third of the seats on the trains were first class. No workmen's tickets were ever issued by the GER beyond Leytonstone. This shaped the nature of the development just as much as the cheap fare policy on the Enfield and Chingford lines. Returning to Potter, we find him expressing the view that among London's many suburban lines, few could take 'a higher place for prettiness of scenery and outlook as seen from the carriage windows'; once Loughton was passed, he viewed only 'pastures and cornfields interspersed with woods and coppices . . . there is beauty indeed in Essex'. Some of this survives; there are not many other places where one can see sheep and pheasants scattering over fields at the approach of a tube train.

An early scheme for a line to Epping from the London & Blackwall Railway and the ECR at Ilford came to nothing. Subsequent proposals for the area were at least partly inspired by hopes of residential development. The Woodford Railway, promoted in 1852 to run from a junction with the NLR at Victoria Park to Woodford had on its board Edward Warner, a prominent landowner who had plans drawn up for building over his estates at Woodford and Hale End. Coming to Parliament alongside an ECR bill for a Woodford and Loughton branch, the independent scheme lost out, but the ECR Act of 1853 stipulated that the Loughton branch could not be opened until 'an additional line of rails' had been laid between the ECR and Woolwich Railway junction at Stratford and the junction at Bow between the ECR and the London & Blackwall Railway.

Leaving the old N&ER about half a mile north of Stratford, the ECR Loughton branch ran north-east between the small villages of Leyton and Leytonstone, reaching the Roding valley at Wanstead. Turning north and keeping to the west side of the valley, it terminated on the south side of the High Street in the centre of Loughton, then a village of 1,500 people on the eastern fringe of the Forest, 12 railway miles from Fenchurch Street. Cheaply-built, the double track followed ground contours fairly closely, rising steadily to a modest summit at Buckhurst Hill, crossing four public roads on the level in four miles south of that station. A 1 in 110 descent from the summit to Loughton was the steepest gradient on the line. Indicative of the expectations was the generous provision of stations, although when the line opened on 22nd August 1856 there was little sign of pending changes in the rural and semi-rural nature of the territory traversed. No goods facilities appear to have been available initially, nor was there a telegraph until 1858.

Low Leyton station, just north of the junction, at the southern tip of the village, was to be renamed Leyton on 27th November 1867. It was closely followed by Leytonstone, conveniently adjacent to the centre of that settlement. The new manifestation of the Devil was well kept at bay here, a section of the 1853 act stipulating that no trains were to stop at stations within the parish of St Mary Leyton between the Sunday church hours of 10.30 – 13.00.

About half a mile north of Leytonstone, the tracks passed beneath two roads in a cut-and-cover tunnel, the only one on the branch. Snaresbrook & Wanstead the next station, was about midway between those places, but Woodford, a straggling village extending for about three miles along the Stratford to Loughton road, got two stations. The first, called George Lane, Woodford served the extreme southern end, whilst Woodford station was just east of Woodford Green and Woodford Wells. Buckhurst Hill, the last of the intermediate stations, was about a mile east of the small community either side of the Loughton road. At the terminus of the 11m 39ch branch in Loughton High Road, (Lopping Hall) a goods yard had appeared by 1858 and at the extreme end of the line, fed by three tracks, was a small engine turntable. Soon after the opening, at the suggestion of Horatio Love, the ECR chairman, a field on the east side of the line here was let to an operator to provide 'a place of refreshment and amusement for the excursionists'.

Most of the level-crossings were sited at stations. The platforms at Buckhurst Hill and Leytonstone were staggered either side of the crossing gates so that trains halted with their locomotives at the roadway's edge. Woodford also had staggered platforms, the Up south of the Down, both south of the crossing.

Opposite top: Eagle Lane level crossing and signal box, between Snaresbrook and George Lane (South Woodford) stations, c. 1905. The train is on a Down service. *Commercial postcard*

Opposite centre: George Lane (now South Woodford) station and level crossing, looking south east, c. 1905. In this predominantly middle class area, a weatherproof footbridge was considered a justifiable extravagance. *Commercial postcard*

Opposite bottom: Loughton, looking north, 1911. The original approach to the 1856 terminus is seen on the left, in use as carriage sidings. The 1865 extension to Epping and Ongar diverges to the right through the re-sited Loughton station completed in that year.

Epping station and signal box, looking to Ongar, c. 1910. *Lens of Sutton*

Epping, a small agricultural and market town of just over 2,000 inhabitants, stood along the Newmarket road clear of the northern tip of the Forest, remote from metropolitan influence. About five miles to the east, on the Dunmow road was the similar but smaller town of Chipping Ongar. Both places were objectives of an independently promoted scheme of 1858 for an 11¼-mile extension beyond Loughton. The Epping Railways Bill, which contained the stern provision that signals were to be erected 'to prevent Danger at the point of Junction with the Eastern Counties Railway', received royal assent in 1859. Three years later the little company was absorbed by the ECR as had been foreseen in the act, but construction had to await the birth of the Great Eastern Railway. That company opened a single line from Loughton through Epping to Ongar on 24th April 1865.

Theydon Bois station and goods yard, looking towards Epping, 1911. *NRM*

To avoid the higher ground, the extension left the older line about a quarter-mile south of the terminus, swerving east through a new two-platform Loughton station very close to the junction. With the opening of the Ongar line the old terminus was closed and the approaches were used to extend the goods yard and carriage sidings; excursion sidings were also later erected on the site for the considerable holiday traffic to the Forest and such trains seem to have terminated here (Chingford station was not yet open). Following the west side of the Roding valley, the extension ran north east through the remotely-situated station of Chigwell Road which was a good mile north of Chigwell village. This passing place, which originally had only one platform, on the Down side, was quiet enough to justify closure in the manpower shortage of World War 1 and was still lit by oil lamps after the end of World War 2. Just beyond it, the line turned into the uplands north of the Roding valley, a long stretch of 1 in 86 bringing it to Theydon (Theydon Bois from 1st December 1865), a station serving the several communities bearing that name either side of the line. In 1885 this station was rebuilt with a passing loop and given an Up platform. After a short traverse of the valley of a stream feeding the Roding, the track started the long climb at 1 in 78 to its summit between Epping and North Weald stations, a dizzy 340ft, which until the opening of the Thaxted branch in 1913 remained the highest point on the somewhat undramatically engineered GER. At Epping, the station, which was a good quarter of a mile south of the town centre, had a passing loop, and served as an intermediate terminus. There was also a goods yard at the London end on the Down side; an engine shed was added in 1892.

Beyond here the railway entered thinly-populated countryside, served by two small stations, North Weald, close to the small village north of the line, and Blake Hall, with not so much as a hamlet within half a mile, its namesake two miles away. The terminus at Ongar, with its single long platform on the south side and goods yard behind, was at the north end of the High Street which formed the major part of the town.

Down train about to leave Ongar, c. 1903, looking to Epping. *Commercial postcard*

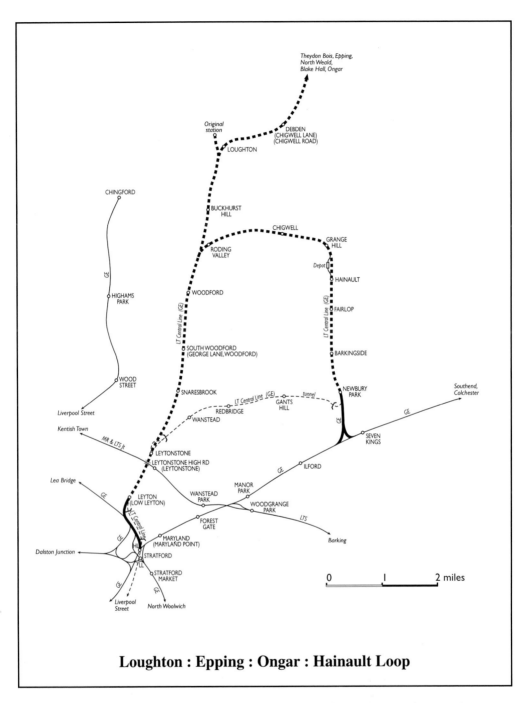

Loughton : Epping : Ongar : Hainault Loop

Extensions beyond Ongar were promoted on several occasions, and mooted more often. The Epping Railways (Dunmow Extension) Act of 1860 would have taken the line north to Great Dunmow along the upper valley of the Roding, but powers lapsed when capital could not be raised. Twenty-eight years later there was an ambitious scheme to build from Ongar through Great Dunmow to Bury St Edmunds. Subsequent proposals were made under the Light Railways Acts: the

25-mile Central Essex Light Railway (1901), with interchange stations at Ongar, Great Dunmow and Yeldham; the Ongar & Shenfield Light Railway, promoted in 1919 by the Essex Light Railways Syndicate; and the Mid-Essex Light Railway (Ongar-Dunmow) of the Essex Light Railway & Property Co. Ltd (1920). None of these was able to acquire the capital to make a start, and with the arrival of the rural motorbus in the early 1920s the need for further railway provision in remotest Essex faded fast. For its part, the GER nursed an idea for completing a link between Ongar and Chelmsford, forming a strategic loop for its main line, but this was never formalised.

At the opening of the Loughton branch, the ECR provided nine trains each way daily, all but one using Fenchurch Street (Sunday trains terminated at Bishopsgate). Even at this early date there was some recognition of residential needs in that two of the only three semi-fast workings were timed to run Up at 09.15 from Loughton and Down at 17.10 from Fenchurch Street. Most of the trains were diverted to Liverpool Street when the new terminus opened in 1874, but a rush-hour service, mostly semi-fast, continued to and from Fenchurch Street. By that year Loughton had gained some 40 trains each way daily, whilst Epping had 18 and Ongar 12. In the 1890s steady suburban growth at the inner end justified 62 Down trains daily as far as Snaresbrook (where 11 terminated). A further train finished its run at Woodford, 28 ended their journeys at Loughton, eight at Epping, the remaining 14 running through to Ongar. After the opening of the Ilford to Woodford loop, the service south of Woodford was augmented by trains which ran on and off the loop. Thus in 1907 we find that Leytonstone had 70 Down trains and 63 Up, whilst at Woodford there were 72 and 67. In that year Loughton had 50 Down and 48 Up workings, Epping had 22 each way and Ongar still had 14 arrivals and 14 departures. The best time among these trains for the nine miles from Liverpool Street to Woodford was 21 minutes, all-stations trains taking 33 minutes. Loughton, 11½ miles, was reached in 25 minutes by semi-fasts, but stopping trains took 40 minutes; 35 minutes was the best time for the 16½ miles to Epping (53 minutes for all stations), whilst Ongar, at 22½ miles, was gained in 56 minutes by the best trains, 77 by the slow ones. In the peak hour from 08.24 to 09.24 there were 14 trains off the branch to London, four of them into Fenchurch Street; two of the total originated at Ongar, one at Epping, six at Loughton, one at Buckhurst Hill, two at Snaresbrook, while the remaining two came off the loop at Woodford.

With the growth in residential traffic, the GER rebuilt stations on the inner section and made other improvements. At Leyton in 1878–9 a new main entrance on the High Road overline bridge replaced that on the Down platform which became an exit only. In 1888 the entire station was reconstructed, while another exit and entrance was added at the country end in Union (now Langthorne) Road in 1901. A very commendable rebuilding at Leytonstone in 1891–2 saw the end of the staggered platforms and included a public pedestrian subway which became a scene of carnage in a 1944 rush-hour air raid. Snaresbrook got a bay platform for Up trains in 1893, and ten years later an entrance for ticket-holders was added on the Up side in response to building development. George Lane, given a footbridge in 1881, was rebuilt two years later. Woodford was reconstructed with a bay and booking office on the Up side in 1892 as middle-class housing was spreading around the station. A new Buckhurst Hill station with parallel platforms was opened north of Queens Road in 1892. Additional carriage sidings were provided at Loughton and new sidings made at Woodford. Sykes' lock-and-block signalling was installed between Loughton and the junction at Leyton in 1901–2, and about the same time an intermediate box called Leytonstone South was added on the London side of Leytonstone station. To relieve overcrowding at South Woodford, another goods depot was established at Eagle Lane. This yard and signal box, on the Up side, just over a quarter-mile south of George Lane station, was opened on 15th May 1899.

Beyond Loughton, the main change before 1914 was the completion of a double track as far as Epping in January 1893, the work including a second platform for Chigwell Lane on the Up side together with a footbridge.

The GER worked the line with 15-car trains of four-wheelers, which normally included five first-class cars compared with three per train on the Romford line and only two in the 15-car Enfield Town and Chingford trains. Ten of the 15 coaches were usually detached at Loughton or Epping as not only was the traffic on the outer section very much lighter, but stations beyond Epping were too short to take 15 without drawing-up. From 1911 bogie carriages, some of them new, others constructed from pairs of the old four-wheelers, were brought on to the line in eight-car sets (reduced to two on the outer section). These trains were customarily hauled by S. D. Holden's class G69 2–4–2T, introduced in the same year. Other locomotives seen on passenger trains in the last years of the GER were 1100 class 0–4–4T and the ubiquitous 'Buck-Jumper' 0–6–0T. Gresley articulated sets finally saw off the four-wheelers in 1928, and although the LNER brought the more powerful N7 0–6–2T on to the Ongar line, the 2–4–2T did not entirely disappear until the completion of electrification in 1957.

As already suggested, the business traffic was probably the most remunerative of any on the GER system. Under pressure from the LCC, the Railway & Canal Commissioners allowed workmen's fares at Leyton and Leytonstone in 1911 on the grounds that the areas served were similar in character to that around Maryland Point on the main line, where workmen's rates had always been available. However, the GER sturdily and successfully resisted all other attempts to impose workmen's facilities on the branch; only at these two innermost stations did the housing and social mix show any similarity to that at Tottenham and Walthamstow, though even then the main growth between 1870 and 1900 contained a strong leavening of white-collar families – one witness to a Royal Commission in 1904 thought the area 'practically a dormitory'. Between 1882 and 1902, season ticket issues at Leyton and Leytonstone increased by 303 per cent, including a notable 171 per cent growth in first-class seasons. There was no large-scale suburban building from Snaresbrook to Loughton until the early 1900s, when new villas and shopping parades began to appear near the stations. Until the mid-1920s almost every house built in this sector was in the higher price range, for middle-class occupation; thus in 1911, rather more than 44¼ per cent of Wanstead's housing stock had seven or more rooms and almost 11 per cent of the population were in the professional classes.

Suburban expansion here continued at an accelerated pace in the late 1920s and 1930s, spreading out to Loughton, even to Theydon Bois, where there were some new streets west of the station. Much of this later growth was of cheap speculatively-built houses selling at £600 or less, situated on the low-lying land to the east of the line. One large estate off Snakes Lane Woodford was built so near the Roding that it was under water in January 1939. By the outbreak of World War 2, much of the land between the Roding and the Forest, bisected by the railway, was covered with houses as far out as Loughton. Discontent with the LNER steam service, strained by the extra traffic, began to boil up in the early 1930s. A public meeting held at Loughton in May 1935 heard a railway official confess that the facilities offered were not up to requirements. As we shall see in a moment, a promise of something better was about to appear.

On the outer section, the peace remained almost undisturbed during the LNER régime. There had been some extra activity during World War 1, mainly from the construction of army camps and at North Weald an airfield for the defence of London, but in 1921 the GER was able to introduce conductor-guard working as a Sunday economy and the two coaches used on weekdays were never overcrowded. There was some housebuilding between the wars at Epping, but in general the country beyond Theydon Bois remained untouched by suburban influences. World War 2 saw a revival of activity at North Weald, where the Royal Air Force station was expanded.

Penetrating as it did into deepest Essex, the outer end of the branch carried a lot of farm produce, particularly milk. This latter traffic grew large enough to justify daily milk trains on Mondays to Fridays to and from Ongar in 1911, with Saturday workings added in 1916. Full churns were loaded at each station as far as Theydon Bois on the Up run and empties were unloaded on the return working. Although some of the milk was put out at stations south of Loughton, most of it went through to Stratford for distribution in inner London. In 1918 some 5,000 17-gallon churns were reaching Stratford from the branch weekly, and at Ongar alone, farm carts, some travelling up to eight miles in all weathers, fed 1,300 churns a week to the railway. Inwards freight, much of it solid fuels and building materials, flowed steadily until BR diesels arrived to replace the GER and LNER 0–6–0s after World War 2. Snaresbrook Yard was closed from 1st August 1949 and Leytonstone from 2nd September 1955. The remainder went under the Beeching axe: South Woodford from 25th November 1963, North Weald from 6th January 1964, Buckhurst Hill from 10th April 1964, Eagle Lane, Woodford, Loughton, Debden, Theydon Bois, Epping, Blake Hall and Ongar all closing from 18th April 1966, and Leyton, Goodall Road, served by trains from Temple Mills, from 6th May 1968 when it was converted into an engineer's depot.

With the Forest so close to the line on the west side, summer pleasure traffic remained an important feature at stations between Buckhurst Hill and Epping until the 1950s, both the GER and the LNER encouraging it with cheap fares. Large tea rooms and pleasure gardens were placed strategically on the roads from the stations to the Forest, as at Coppice Row, near Theydon Bois station. Children came in their hundreds in special trains chartered by Sunday Schools and other organisations, including Dr Barnardo's Homes, whose trains from Stepney to Theydon Bois continued into the LNER era. In the opposite direction, excursions were worked through to east and south coast resorts, the latter via the East London line. These continued, steam-hauled, and later diesel-powered, well into the 1960s, long after tube trains had taken over the ordinary workings.

Tube train operation of the branch was first mooted in the early 1930s. A major objective of the 1935–40 London Railways New Works Programme was to bring the eastern suburbs of London into more direct communication with the West End, at the same time relieving the very heavy pressure on the LNER lines through Stratford. Much of the overloading arose from the hundreds of acres of cheap houses which by the late 1930s had filled the area bounded by the Loughton line, the Woodford-Ilford loop, and the main line. To meet the needs of this new population, it was proposed to extend the Central London tube railway below ground to Leyton via Stratford, where it would briefly surface for cross-platform interchange with the LNER main line. At Leyton, the tube trains were to surface and take over the working of the Ongar line and the Hainault loop (to be reached by a new tube railway below Eastern Avenue as far as Newbury Park). Work on this part of the Programme, financed at 2½ per cent interest, with interest and capital guaranteed by the Treasury, began in October 1936 but the exigencies of war brought it to a halt in 1940.

A new station at Loughton, slightly east of the old, was sufficiently advanced to allow it to open on 28th April 1940. Its two island platforms on the embankment served three roads, and although decorated with London Transport totems and designed for the new service, it saw nothing but the drab LNER steam trains for the first 8½ years of its life. To emphasise its continuing ownership, the LNER instructed the architects, J. Murray Easton and Robertson Fellows, deliberately to avoid undue similarity with contemporary London Transport stations. A barrel vault theme was adopted for the core block and the centrally-supported platform canopies had a bold sweep seldom before seen in concrete work, combining grace and strength in a most impressive manner.

Such was the importance attached to easing the congestion on the eastern suburban services that the post-war Labour government allowed work to resume in 1945 despite economic and supply problems. Tube trains reached Stratford on 4th December 1946 and Leytonstone on 5th May 1947. The new tracks reached the surface about a quarter-mile south of Leyton station, where a new frontage was constructed for the High Road entrance. Leytonstone received substantial rebuilding with a sub-surface booking hall, pedestrian subways beneath the platforms and an island platform on the east side to allow two Up trains to stand in the station at the same time. As elsewhere on the line, the level-crossing was abolished before the tube service started. Steam trains shuttled between Leytonstone and Ongar until 14th December 1947 when they were cut back to Woodford to make way for the

N7 0-6-2T 9630 working a Leytonstone–Epping steam shuttle service after the arrival of Central Line tube trains at Leytonstone on 5th May 1947. *Lens of Sutton*

London's Local Railways

Top: Ex GER F5 2-4-2T 67203 accelerates out of Ongar station bound for Epping on 18th May 1957. *R C Riley*

Below: Ex GER F5 2-4-2T 67202 and 67218 on Up and Down trains passing on the loop at North Weald, 16th November 1957 looking to Ongar. *R C Riley*

extension of tube working. For this, Snaresbrook, South Woodford, and Woodford received new ticket halls and restyled frontages. At Snaresbrook the site of the bay road and goods yard became a car park, opened in September 1949. Leytonstone's yard went the same way. Additional ticket halls were provided on the Up (now 'Westbound') side at Snaresbrook and South Woodford in 1948. Loughton's new station received its electric trains at last on 21st November 1948, with a service every four minutes in peak periods and every ten at other times. At Buckhurst Hill, the GER station of 1892 remained virtually unchanged.

Commuters who had been looking forward to electrification found it a not unmixed blessing. They lost the semi-fast workings and suffered a substantial reduction in seats. A tube passenger from Woodford in 1948 faced a journey to Oxford Circus taking up to 30 minutes longer, despite the elimination of the transfer at Liverpool Street, and at peak hours was much more likely to stand for part of the journey, even if the trains were cleaner. This discrepancy remained significant when more modern tube stock was introduced; before electrification there were 11 steam trains leaving Liverpool Street for Woodford and beyond between 17.00 and 18.00 on Mondays to Fridays, offering a total of 9,952 seats, but in 1961, in the same period of the peak, the 18 tube trains had only 5,904 seats.

Although there were misgivings in some quarters about extending tube operation into the London Green Belt, the electrification was carried through to Epping on 25th September 1949. A substantial business was expected at Chigwell Lane, renamed Debden on that day, after a large LCC housing and industrial estate already opened there. Two reversing and storage roads were placed between the running lines just east of the platforms to give a terminal facility, trains running to and from London every ten or twelve minutes, and every six in the peak periods. Between here and Epping there were through workings to and from London only at 40-minute intervals (12 to 15 minutes in the rush hours) but a shuttle between Loughton and Epping gave the stations on this outer section a 20-minute headway.

For another eight years, GER tank engines and drab LNER coaches shuttled between Epping and Ongar whilst the authorities weighed the difficult balance between operating convenience and the poor traffic potential. Finally it was decided to electrify the single line, operating it as economically as possible. No substation was provided, that at Epping producing just sufficient power to enable two four-car trains to run simultaneously between Epping and Ongar, passing at North Weald, this being enough to give what was considered a reasonable peak hour frequency. Tube trains made their appearance at the remote-seeming Ongar platform on 18th November 1957, looking like fish out of water. Since 14th August 1949 the Epping–North Weald section had been track-circuited and this system had replaced train staff and ticket on the remaining stretch of the single line from the following 25th September. With it, BR had provided a passing loop and second platform at North Weald. There were no changes to the typically GER rural stations for the arrival of the tube trains, apart from replacement of oil lamps by electric light and installation of standard LT signs and totems.

With electrification, the whole line south of Epping had been track-circuited and signalled to LT surface line standards, the principal indications given by two-aspect long range colour lights with repeaters. Signal cabins with power frames and miniature levers were opened for the tube service at Leytonstone, South Woodford, Woodford, Loughton, Debden and Epping, but the old GER boxes remained at North Weald and Ongar with the modifications just mentioned. Ongar box and shunting neck were eventually abandoned from 23rd March 1969.

Steam locos and later, diesels, continued to run over the line north of Leyton with freights and passenger excursions until 1966. Even then LT did not have the line entirely to itself; some passenger workings were still worked each way between Epping/Loughton and Liverpool Street/Stratford. Operated for the convenience of railway workers, these trains were available to the public, running outside tube traffic hours until finally withdrawn on 31st May 1970. The diesel car sets used on these services in their last years provided a useful fall-back when the exposed Epping–Ongar tube trains were defeated by bad weather, though this flexibility was lost when the original junction at Leyton was removed on 29th October 1972 in response to London Transport's rigid policy of isolating itself from the national rail network.

Almost the only special traffic available on the Ongar line was that generated by the Air Shows at North Weald airfield. For some years London Transport operated a special 15 min service to and from Loughton on these occasions, with alternate trains going through to Ongar. This involved the use of five four-car trains and special care and vigilance to avoid overloading Epping substation or excessive voltage drops. Latterly there was a shuttle service between Epping and North Weald.

London's Local Railways

As far as regular patronage was concerned, Epping showed some signs of residential expansion after the arrival of the tube service. Debden became very busy as we shall see shortly and from the late 1950s onwards, the planning authorities allowed Ongar a considerable measure of additional housing.

But the outermost section remained a problem. Despite the growth at Ongar, traffic never justified the electrification. North Weald and Blake Hall soon secured for themselves the unenviable position of the least-used stations on the LT system; Blake Hall, which attracted only some 260 passengers a week, lost its Sunday trains from Sunday 23rd October 1966. Facing heavy costs for track works, LT sought complete closure beyond Epping in 1970, when off peak trains were said to be carrying an average of less than ten passengers each (although some peak hour services loaded up to 200). As no alternative bus service could be arranged, the Transport Users' Consultative Committee recommended retention, a finding endorsed by the Minister, though no grant was offered. Essex County Council agreed in 1976 to meet a quarter of the annual loss if costs were cut by operating only one train at a time instead of the normal two. This was accepted and applied from 18th October 1976, producing a somewhat ludicrous 35/40 min peak hour interval for a tube railway service. With the passing place no longer required, the North Weald signal box and loop were taken out of use in 1977 (the level crossing there had been closed to vehicles in May 1962).

When the Essex Council subsidy was withdrawn, fares were boosted to a high level and in 1979–80 passengers using the Ongar trains endured five increases in eight months. This and the speed restriction of 30 mph over the whole line imposed by the poor state of track and engineering works discouraged traffic so much that by 1980 the annual loss was over £0.6m on a service carrying only 650 passengers daily each way. After a second formal application to close the line in 1980 had failed, in a search for further savings, the isolated and little-used Blake Hall station was closed completely after traffic on Saturday 31st October 1981 and from 6th December 1982 (after withdrawal of a temporary District Council subsidy) trains ran only Mondays to Fridays at morning and evening peaks (five and six services each way respectively).

From 30th October 1989 in a sudden outburst of light headedness ('to evaluate demand') an all day (including Sundays) service was restored, with an initial week of free travel and a large illuminated Underground sign at Ongar station. This did no good at all and the Monday–Friday peak hours only pattern was resumed on 8th April 1991 (just three morning trains each way plus one each way at North Weald, and four each way in the evening). But even the commuters had found other alternatives, using their cars to reach better-served LT or BR stations, and by 1993, in the evening rush hour, some departures for Ongar from Epping were loading as few as 12 passengers, with none at all on the inward return runs. Ongar was then producing only 85 passengers a day, North Weald a mere 50. A third formal application to close the line in 1993 was successful, and the end came with the last train offering the now very lively and bumpy ride from and back to Epping's platform 2 on 30th September 1994. Attempts were then to be made to operate the line privately, but with heavy engineering works overdue, a refusal by LT to have the private trains in its Epping station, frequently unreliable Central Line connections at Epping, and the line's history of low traffic, any such enterprise would seem to need a great deal of faith and good fortune.

Some changes south of Epping since the introduction of Central Line tube services remain to be mentioned. North of the line around Chigwell Lane the LCC had opened its Debden Estate in 1947, a major project which eventually included a total of almost 4,500 dwellings accommodating a population of some 16,000. Then there was development south of the line in the 1950s and later an extensive industrial estate which included the Bank of England Printing Works; offices followed in the early 1970s. All this activity brought a great increase in traffic to what had been a very quiet rural station. Direct access from the industrial estate to the westbound platform was opened in 1956, a new station footbridge in 1957. Then, in 1974–75, with half the cost met by the government, a major rebuilding scheme was undertaken, involving a larger ticket hall, new canopies on both platforms and new lighting.

In connection with the architecturally-disastrous Underground Ticketing Scheme, Snaresbrook received a new ticket office and associated buildings in the late 1980s, with sad consequences for its GER heritage. Elsewhere this pleasing aspect of most of the line's stations received more consideration, as at Buckhurst Hill, where in 1995 damaged windows were replaced and expertly etched in replica GER style; in the retention of GER seats; and in the sympathetic preservation of the GER buildings and canopies at Leyton and elsewhere. Alas, Leyton did suffer some desecration from an external predator. A start was made in 1991 with construction of the M11 Link road, which was to run alongside the railway on the west side from a point just north of Leytonstone station to the site of the former Leyton goods yard west of Leyton High Road. This was to cut a great swathe through back gardens and little side roads and at Leyton station required closure of the 1901 Langthorne Road entrance from 3rd March 1995. No compensation was offered by the government for its replacement.

After the closure of Eagle Lane goods yard in 1966 the site had been used for dumping tube tunnel segments. These were removed in 1986 preparatory to sale of the land to Wimpey for erection of small houses.

Signalling was modernised as part of a major programme covering the whole of the Central Line. Stratford–Leytonstone, including a lengthened westbound loop at Leytonstone, was completed on 1st May 1995 but the remainder of the scheme was not in use until 9th November 1997.

By the mid 1980s off peak patronage north of Loughton had fallen substantially and the service of five trains an hour in the middle of the day was accordingly reduced to three in 1986. Commuters living near stations north of Woodford were now using their cars to reach stations closer to central London, where residents were soon complaining of the street parking around the station areas. This change in travelling patterns, facilitated by wider car ownership, was in part a response to the higher fares operating in the Essex County Council area, but it also reflected an increasing lack of tolerance with the long and slow journeys to outer stations in rolling stock expressly designed for high load capacity short distance travel. This last aspect received greater emphasis when the new Central Line stock entered service in 1993–95. All-stations travel out to Buckhurst Hill and beyond in nasty little longitudinal seats with upright backs, listening to irritating repetitive automatic announcements and in summer, noisy ventilation fans, then became even more of an acquired taste. The 1930s policy mistake of extending costly all-stations urban tube service deep into outer suburbia (and beyond) is nowhere more apparent than on these eastern extremities of the Central Line, which unlike those of the tube lines in north and north west London, lack any faster and more comfortable alternative rail routes.

The Fairlop or Hainault Loop (map page 386)

As early as 1846 the Eastern Counties Railway obtained powers for an Epping Extension which was to have left the main line at Ilford, following the Roding valley as far as Woodford where it would join the route subsequently constructed from Stratford, which has already been noticed. Nothing happened; for many years the district north of Ilford slumbered in rural peace, London influence showing only in some retirement and other middle-class development at Chigwell and Woodford from around 1865. When Ilford's rapid suburban growth began during the last quarter of the century much of it spread northwards from the main line, prompting the 1895 promotion of an independent Ilford, Barkingside & Chigwell Row Railway. Although the bill for this was deposited for the 1896 session, it was withdrawn when the GER promised to build a similar line itself, an end result which may well have been the real intention of the promoters. True to its word, the GER secured parliamentary authority in its 1897 General Powers Act for a 5m 7f 7ch loop from Ilford through Barkingside, Fairlop and Chigwell to join the Epping and Ongar line at Woodford. A 1f 8.7ch eastern curve completed the triangular junction at Ilford.

Some of the Churchbury optimism still remained. Fairlop loop stations were built to similar high standard, but unlike Churchbury, this was also an expensive line to make, its route lying across the grain of the country through gravel overlaid with clay, requiring 15 steel girder and four brick arch bridges, a short tunnel, cuttings up to 50ft deep and long stretches of embankment. Construction started in 1900 under the Manchester contractor C. J. Wills, working to the plans of the GER chief engineer, John Wilson. Much difficulty was experienced in stabilising the clay earthworks and when the line was at last ready, through freight trains were worked over it from 20th April 1903 to consolidate the formation. After the deep cuttings at Chigwell and Grange Hill had been shaped, hundreds of old sleepers were set alight, smouldering for weeks in an attempt to burn and settle the unstable clay.

Chigwell station, LNER, c. 1931, looking east. The station master's house (left) is on the Down side of the line, which passes under the Chigwell Road. Barclay's Bank appear to occupy rather vulnerable premises shared with a tobacconist and confectioner; and is that the bank manager's Baby Austin? *Commercial postcard*

Passenger and local freight operations started on 1st May 1903. At first the service worked from either Fenchurch Street or Liverpool Street and then back to London, both ways round the loop. Trains stopped a short time at Fairlop before returning to town, the complete tour taking about 1½ hours or about 30 minutes on the loop itself. Trains at Ilford to and from loop stations numbered about 20 daily each way, nine each way on Sundays. Composition was normally Holden 0–6–0T or 2–4–2T with up to 16 four-wheel coaches.

Either side of the summit at Grange Hill, the loop had long stretches of 1 in 100 and the sharpest curve was 10-chain radius. Direction was designated Down from Ilford to Chigwell, Up from Chigwell to Woodford. From Woodford Junction, which was facing for Down trains, the double track curved east on a high embankment across the Roding valley, spanning the river on a three-arch brick viaduct. On the north side, a quarter of a mile from the junction, Chigwell Bank box broke up the long stretch between two stations. On the other side of the river, the line entered a cutting in which Chigwell station was situated, its site about half a mile south of the village centre, on the east side of the main London road. Two well-canopied platforms were reached by covered staircases from a handsome brick booking office building on the road bridge and both platforms had waiting rooms and lavatories in the same red brick. There was no goods yard, but a short distance to the east, a ground frame gave access to a siding and wharf on the north side of the line, used for loading fruit grown in an adjacent orchard owned by the GER for supplying its hotels. This facility had been removed by the end of the 1920s. On the south side near Chigwell was a refuge siding, later to be buried by an earth slip.

Soon after Chigwell the line entered a 260yd tunnel followed by a cutting which led into Grange Hill station. This cutting, 50ft deep at the tunnel end, gave much trouble during construction and subsequently, until London Transport built retaining walls. Grange Hill was almost the twin of Chigwell with its booking office building on the south side of the bridge carrying the Woodford–Lambourne End road over the line, but in addition there was a goods yard here, on the west side, behind the platform, with connection at the London end.

From Grange Hill the tracks ran south for about two miles, mostly on embankment across the western fringe of Fairlop Plain. Stations here were very closely spaced in anticipation of continuing northern expansion of Ilford. Hainault, the first of the series, sat on a brick arch viaduct, its small entrance pavilion at road level on the west side. Within half a mile radius there were hardly half a dozen houses, but the passenger accommodation was no less lavish than elsewhere on the line. The small goods yard was on the west side just south of the platforms. Separated by only 30ch from its neighbour, Fairlop station was almost identical, except that the goods yard was at the north end on the east side, complemented by a cattle dock and siding on the opposite side. This was the nearest station to the huge Claybury mental hospital which the LCC had opened in 1893, but there was little else within its catchment area apart from a farmhouse and a mission room.

Barkingside station, at the end of the embankment, at least had a village and Dr Barnardo Girls' Home to serve, both a quarter-mile west of its platforms. The main building was on the level at the west side, and in front of it the goods yard extended from its connection south of the platforms almost up to the approach road. Newbury Park, the last of this trio of putative suburban stations, was in a cutting, 1m 61ch north of Ilford. At the time of its opening, new houses were being erected near here at the north-eastern edge of burgeoning Ilford, and the population had grown enough to justify the opening of an Infants' School close to the new station in 1895. In general design and appearance very similar to Chigwell and Grange Hill, Newbury Park had a booking office building on the road bridge at the southern end of the platforms. Goods facilities were provided on the west side of the line at the north end of the station. The cutting continued southwards to Newbury Park Junction, where double-track curves branched towards Ilford (Ilford Carriage Sidings Junction) and towards Seven Kings (Seven Kings West Junction) on the main London–Colchester line.

At the planning stage, the GER had envisaged the loop not only as opening up a new area for residential development, but also as a freight by-pass for the congested main line between Ilford and Stratford, but in practice very little use was made of the eastern curve, with through freight trains and passenger services over it limited to the occasional seaside excursion or special. As constructed, the loop presented difficulties to heavy goods trains and there was no attempt to make connections for direct working between trains off the Loughton line and Temple Mills yard or between that line and the strategic cross-London link at Victoria Park.

Instead, everything was done to prepare for heavy passenger traffic, misplaced optimism in this direction being most evident in the location and design of the stations, all of which had substantial buildings and 640ft platforms graded level and capable of accommodating 1,000-seater trains of 20 four-wheelers. Architect and civil engineer, briefed to allow for heavy season ticket traffic, provided adequate weather protection in the form of long canopies, covered footbridges or subways, rail-level buildings in red brick and tiles with lavish waiting and lavatory accommodation each side of the line. With the intention of creating buildings worthy of the new districts they were to serve, decoration was elaborated with curves and cupolas, gables and curly ironwork carrying the GER monogram. Barkingside was indisputably the most handsome of the six stations, its main west side structure featuring stone-arched windows, stone quoins and a deep stone plinth under hipped roofs, the central portion crowned with a dainty Baroque cupola carrying a weather vane. The reason for the extra expenditure is obscure but may have been connected with its proximity to Doctor Barnardo's Homes and VIP visits thereto. This station and Newbury Park were within the Ilford Council's electric lighting district, but the other four had to make do with gas and oil lamps.

Indicative of the undeveloped nature of the areas served were the three pairs of semi-detached garden-city style cottages for railway staff placed near each station. Set a little apart from them was a small detached villa for the stationmaster with a pillared porch and larger garden. Wooden houses, some still in use at Grange Hill, were erected for the navvies constructing the line.

Once again the GER had badly misjudged. After a frenzy of activity from about 1890, the market for London suburban houses declined, bringing a noticeable slowing down in the northward growth of Ilford. Had it not been for the Ilford Council's electric tramcars, unkindly started on 14th March 1903 just before the railway was ready, there might have been a little business at Barkingside and Newbury Park stations, but the trams, which ran parallel to the line through the centres of the existing settlements, not only stole all the local traffic between Barkingside and Ilford, but carried much of the commuter load direct to Ilford station, leaving the railway with a pitiful trickle from the still thinly-populated new roads south east of Newbury Park station. North of Barkingside, with the exception of Chigwell, the new stations stood isolated in open country, their massive urban forms looking uncomfortable and misplaced. With no housebuilders in sight, the GER board contributed in 1904 to the cost of acquiring Grange Park Forest, Hainault, as a public open space, a desperate gesture which was to do it little good. Writing at the end of 1907, Cecil J. Allen, then a GER employee, painted a truthful picture. After remarking that the growth of North Ilford was very slow, he continued,

> and now the extraordinary sight may be seen of two palatial stations – Hainault and Fairlop – within a quarter of a mile of each other and yet with scarcely a house in sight, while the daily number of passengers to and from them could often be counted on the fingers.

Soon after these words appeared in *The Railway Magazine*, the GER accepted the inevitable, closing Hainault and its goods yard to all traffic after the last train on 30th September 1908. This move failed to stem the loss on working, calculated in 1911 at £8,000 a year.

Further retrenchment occurred in World War 1, when Barkingside was selected as the most suitable candidate on this line for a list of stations to be closed to release more railwaymen for the army. Passenger and goods trains called here for the last time on 21st May 1916, the few regular patrons no doubt finding the frequent and cheap Council tramcars to Ilford station a tolerable alternative. When the station reopened (on weekdays only) on 1st July 1919 little business was done, and all year round Sunday service was not restored until August 1934.

World War 1 brought new and unusual traffics. Wounded soldiers came in long ambulance trains to Newbury Park for transfer to the 1912 Ilford Emergency Hospital at the west side of the station, whilst at Hainault Farm and Fairlop Plain men and materials arrived to form and maintain a fighter air station for the defence of London. After the war, with the departure of the Sopwith Camels, the grass airfield remained open for civil flying, becoming the focus of a 1936 City of London Corporation scheme for a 948-acre six-runway London airport to replace Croydon. But for the onset of World War 2, this would have been built and with it a planned new Fairlop station, some 500yd south of the old, linked to the terminal buildings by covered ways. And Heathrow might have been left in peace . . .

Towards the end of the GER era, train services over the loop were modified to eliminate most of the through workings to and from London apart from rush hours and on Saturday afternoons, when there was some sports ground and other pleasure traffic. At other times trains then mostly ran between Ilford and Woodford with a few London to Ilford services extended to Fairlop and some Down Woodford via Stratford workings going through to Chigwell, Grange Hill or Fairlop. Sunday trains, generally confined to the loop, were approximately hourly before World War 1, then, as a wartime economy, were reduced to two-hourly. On 1st May 1921 the hourly interval was resumed, and with the growth of the residential areas served and the popularity of country excursions, some extras were introduced in 1932. A half-hourly frequency followed a year later.

During the building boom of the late 1920s and early 1930s, Ilford's growth entered a second more powerful phase, covering over the area crossed by the Eastern Avenue motor road which had been opened in March 1924. Between that year and 1936 almost all the land between the eastern bank of the Roding and the loop was

Roding Valley halt, LNER, north side, fronting Station Way, January 1937. In the background is some of the new housing (Cherry Tree Rise) that prompted its opening.
London Transport Museum

filled with small houses up to a point well north of Barkingside. East of the railway, Fairlop Plain remained untouched and elsewhere on this side, apart from some building at Newbury Park from 1931 onwards, and some lighter activity either side of Hainault station, there was no development of any consequence before 1940. Fairlop's immediate surroundings were still free of housing estates in that year although there was some building towards Claybury along the Chigwell Road a quarter-mile west.

The activity at Hainault caused the LNER to re-open the station for passenger and parcels traffic on weekdays from 3rd March 1930, but it had been in use some time before then. A note in the working timetable for March 1927 mentions that tickets available at Hainault were issued to the employees of Messrs Hughes' works and also to the public at Hainault and from certain suburban stations 'on application'. It was also possible for holders of season or ordinary tickets available at Fairlop from the Woodford direction and at Grange Hill from the south to alight or join trains at Hainault. The freight yard there remained closed, never to be restored.

In the 1900s Woodford had started to grow northwards from the station either side of the Loughton line, expansion which was resumed with greater vigour in the early 1930s, soon reaching and passing Woodford Junction. Responding to agitation from estate owners and others, the LNER opened a halt on the loop a short distance from the junction, on 3rd February 1936. Named Roding Valley, it was equipped only with simple shelters and an open iron footbridge – the LNER lacked the enthusiastic approach to suburban business envinced by the Southern Railway, and clearly had no wish to emulate the confident optimism of its GER predecessor.

Some improvements were made to the train service for the new residents, many of whom were London season-ticket holders. From 22 trains each way round the loop (a few running through to London or other points en route) and about 15 each way on Sundays in 1927, the service was built up in ten years to 44 round the loop to Woodford and beyond and the same number to Ilford and beyond, plus three from Newbury Park to Ilford and beyond, with half-hourly service each way for most of Sunday.

The Fairlop or Hainault Loop

Much more than this was however required to improve the lot of the thousands of central London workers who had been enticed to purchase low-cost new houses either side of Eastern Avenue between Newbury Park and Wanstead and who depended on crowded buses to get to Ilford and other stations. Of those within easy access of the loop stations, something like 40 per cent wanted a direct transit to points west of St Pauls. Backed by the local MPs, a powerful pressure group arose to represent this discontented mass, whose number grew each day as more houses were built, crowding into congested trains at Ilford, and obliged to make a second transport change at Liverpool Street.

Even the long-distance oriented and impoverished LNER could not continue to ignore the highly unsatisfactory situation which had arisen by 1929. Early the following year the company commissioned a consultants' study of an Ilford–Liverpool Street tube railway, but shied away when told of the capital cost and low return this would bring. Not that the Ilford & District Railway Users' Association had much interest in the usefulness of an LNER tube; it was campaigning for an extension of the Central London Line from Liverpool Street to Romford via Eastern Avenue, with a branch to Claybury. Continued lobbying eventually brought LNER and Underground heads together, but the lack of return on capital remained a problem. After the formation of the London Passenger Transport Board there were further joint consultations under increasing pressure from central government, resulting in the inclusion of Underground extensions into North Ilford in the 1935–40 London Railway New Works Programme, which was to be financed by government-guaranteed loans in recognition of its contribution to the relief of unemployment.

Under this proposal, the Central London Line was to be projected from its terminus beneath Liverpool Street station to Stratford, where the trains were to come to the surface to afford easy interchange with LNER suburban services to Shenfield, to be electrified at the same time. Descending again to deep-level tube, the Underground trains would go on to Leyton where they were to surface to join the Loughton line and provide the service on it, as described earlier. From Leytonstone, a new tube would be made under Eastern Avenue as far as Newbury Park, where the Underground trains would take over service on the Fairlop loop (London Transport named it the Hainault loop after deciding to use the latter place as the terminal). Work on these projects, which began in October 1936, was well advanced when stopped under wartime constraints in 1940.

At that time tube tunnels had been completed beneath Eastern Avenue and following an initiative of Lord Beaverbrook, these were converted to a 2½-mile long factory for the Plessey Company, producing aircraft components. In the air-conditioned atmosphere of a brisk spring day, safe from bombing, it accommodated 2,000 workers, mostly girls, at any one time in the 24 hours. Transport within the 12ft diameter tunnel was by means of an 18in gauge tramway operated by electric battery locomotives. Another almost-finished installation found wartime use. The Underground depot on the west side of the loop between Grange Hill and Hainault stations served from June 1943 to January 1945 as an assembly point for railway rolling stock operated by the US Army Transportation Corps. Earlier some tube cars had been stored there. Fairlop Plain again provided a military airfield, completing the strange assortment of new traffics brought on to the loop in wartime conditions.

After the war, at a time when there were very severe restrictions on capital expenditure, the government gave priority to completion of the Central Line eastern extensions. Much work was needed in the tunnels after Plessey's departure, but tube trains were operated along the 4.11-mile new section between Leytonstone and Newbury Park from Sunday 14th December 1947, calling at three tunnel stations, Wanstead, Redbridge, and Gants Hill, each of them well placed to serve the inter-war housing. LNER steam trains between Ilford, Newbury Park and Woodford ran for the last time on Saturday 29th November, allowing engineering work to proceed unhindered in the interim, when passengers used a special bus service calling at all loop stations except Roding Valley. A new western spur to the main line at Ilford, opened in September 1947 to serve the loop and the new electric car sheds for the Shenfield main line electrification, was used only briefly by passenger trains. This curve was severed by an extension of the depot in 1948, but as we shall see, the eastern curve remained in use for a little longer.

At Newbury Park, the tube tracks emerged either side of the old GER line south of the station, which was not substantially altered apart from the opening of a temporary ticket office in what was to be the bus forecourt on the east side. On 6th July 1949 a permanent ticket hall, entrance, and staff canteen were opened here, passengers reaching the GER platforms by a new concrete footbridge across the centre of the station. These new buildings were flanked by a combined bus station and car park. The former, used by eastbound buses on routes 66 and 139 (now 296) had been designed by Oliver Hill in 1937 and included a coppered barrel vault roof in reinforced concrete of 60ft span, 30ft high and 150ft long, apparently inspired by airship sheds of the 1930s. This new work, on the site of the seven GER staff houses, was but a part of the complete rebuilding envisaged in 1937, and still not undertaken over 60 years on. Only one further change was made here; in 1956 the GER street building, with its covered staircases to the platforms (where the old ticket office had apparently remained open until late in 1954) was demolished to make way for the new road bridge carrying the widened Eastern Avenue. Despite the dualling of the road, no provision was included in the roadworks to allow the Oliver Hill bus station to be used by westbound buses, as had been intended before World War 2.

With the arrival of the tube trains at Newbury Park, Hainault depot, designed for 344 cars, came into partial use, with the tracks as far north as Grange Hill electrified to permit empty stock movements. Nine-car sidings also provided at Newbury Park north of the goods depot on the west side were subsequently removed.

London Transport designated Leytonstone–Newbury Park–Woodford as *Inner Rail* and the other track as *Outer Rail*, following Inner Circle practice. Trains ran to and from Newbury Park about every four minutes at peak periods, every 7½-minutes at other times. Steam passenger trains had disappeared entirely from the loop and passengers for stations beyond Newbury Park used a truncated version of the bus service already mentioned.

Despite the provision of the much requested link to the West End, the new facility proved a mixed blessing, especially in the early days. Passengers soon found that the total capacity offered in the trains was less than in steam days, especially as regards the number of seats. The addition of many who had formerly travelled by bus direct or to and from Ilford station made things worse and there was added discomfort in frequent breakdowns of the 20-year-old rolling stock, which had been stored in the open during the war years. Until the new depots at Hainault and Ruislip were fully operational, maintenance could not be organised to provide a sufficient quantity of fault-free trains.

Hainault was reached by Underground trains on 31st May 1948, Woodford on 21st November. Little alteration was made to Barkingside and Fairlop stations other than retiling of booking halls and installation of LT signs and lighting. Originally scheduled for complete rebuilding, Hainault received a new island platform on the west side, and a passimeter booking hall built into the embankment at road level blended into the old GER subway between the platforms; like Newbury Park, it was destined to exhibit two conflicting architectural styles for at least another 50 years. At Grange Hill, where the street level overline building had been demolished by a German VI missile on 12th July 1944, there was a reconstruction in the rather arid late 1940s style, but the GER stationmaster's house survived. Chigwell saw little change apart from rebuilding of the ticket office but Roding Valley lost its halt status and underwent some rearrangement in 1949.

With the extension to Hainault, peak-hour service was increased by four trains an hour to Leytonstone, two of which continued to Hainault, giving that section 17 trains an hour at the busiest times. Otherwise Hainault had a 7½- to 10-minute frequency according to the time of day. Between Hainault and Woodford a shuttle of three-car trains worked every 7½ minutes at peak hours, 24 to 30 minutes otherwise. This replaced the original concept, found to cause operating problems, of working trains right round the loop in both directions to and from the rest of the Central Line.

Standard LT open-air signalling was installed, with train stops, two-aspect long-range colour-lights, repeaters and fog repeaters, most of it controlled by track circuits. To allow the requisite stopping distances for steam-hauled freight and excursion trains, distant signals of the externally-lit disc type, showing a swallow-tailed bar on a yellow ground, were placed along the open-air section. New signal cabins were opened at Newbury Park (59 levers), Hainault (83 levers) on 12th May 1948, and a subsidiary cabin at Grange Hill controlled from Hainault on 29th October 1948. Fairlop LNER box closed on 20th April 1948, after which all the goods yards were controlled by ground frames. At Newbury Park, the Outer Rail tunnel mouth was protected by electric train detectors in the station platform.

For the first decade or so of tube operation, the frequent electric services to both City and West End, with easy connections to the remainder of the Underground system drew out the maximum available patronage but there was very little scope for generating new traffic. Much of the uncovered land adjacent to the line to the east and north was by that time in the postwar London Green Belt, statutorily protected from housing development. It is true that the LCC had sited a large new estate just east of Grange Hill station but this was on land bought for the purpose in the 1930s and had been opened in 1947. Covering some 247 acres, it was eventually to house about 11,000 and much increase business at Grange Hill and Hainault stations. A large area of open land on the west side of the line between Hainault and Grange Hill was also later built over, some of it sold surplus to LT depot requirements in 1976. There were smaller infilling developments elsewhere.

Freight trains, hauled from the early 1960s by diesel locos, at first worked in and out via the eastern curve at Ilford but this was disconnected on 17th March 1956 to provide space for a BR new electric train depot. Thereafter the freights entered via Woodford, reversing on a short length of the original line south of Newbury Park road bridge. Although the road overbridges south of that point provided clues, the GER alignment was soon obscured, with much of the original formation filled to ground level to form allotment gardens. Freight traffic on lines such as this was now doomed; Fairlop's sidings closed on 24th March 1958 and the late evening path for the working disappeared entirely from the timetable from 4th October 1965 with the abandonment of the yards at Newbury Park, Barkingside and Grange Hill. As elsewhere, the sites of the old goods yards made useful station car parks. The stub line south of Newbury Park remained in place until 1992 when major track and signalling changes were made in the area in connection with the Central Line resignalling scheme.

Few changes have been made to the stations in recent years and significant signs of the GER origins survive to please the eye, notably at Barkingside, though in 1987 the lofty entrance hall of that station suffered considerable desecration in the name of the Underground Ticketing System. Near New Barns Farm, rather under halfway from Chigwell to Roding Valley, the M11 motorway was aligned to pass beneath the railway, which from September 1972 was carried over it by a 152ft span concrete bridge. This new road would soon be feeding car commuters from remoter Essex and East Anglia into the Central Line at stations nearer London.

By the late 1950s, television and wider car ownership were eating deeply into off-peak traffic; a little later, office dispersal was also draining off the London commuter flows. Weekend business, much of it to sports grounds, was lost to the car. Fairlop, penalised by its proximity to Hainault, and still with virtually no houses nearby, was closed on Sundays after Sunday 28th September 1958 and on Saturdays after Saturday 24th January 1970. It was considered for total closure in 1982 but was reopened again at weekends from 21st April 1990 in the hope of attracting some traffic bound for Fairlop Waters, a nearby leisure complex east of the line. In 1969 Saturday receipts at Roding Valley averaged only £24, Sundays £9, and after a short period of local authority subsidy, this station was closed at weekends from 2nd August 1970. London Transport restored weekend calls from Saturday 13th April 1991 but since this was achieved by dispensing with staff, the effects on revenue and the condition of station structures seemed likely to be counter-productive. At some of the other stations between Newbury Park and Woodford, ticket clerk attendance has been reduced to a single shift basis in recent years.

The quiet nature of the Woodford–Hainault section made it an obvious choice for testing the automatic train equipment devised for the new Victoria line tube and the shuttle service between these points was operated with this refinement for an extensive period from 5th April 1964. Poor loadings on this section caused it to be considered for complete closure in 1970 and again in 1982. From 6th December in the latter year trains ceased to run north of Hainault after about 20.00 each evening.

After a 1991 attempt to widen intervals up to 45/46 min, even at peak periods, some improvement followed local complaints: from 2nd November 1992 the whole service terminated at Woodford, running across Hainault, with intervals of 18–24 min at peak hours, 20 min at other times and mostly 30 min at weekends.

By the mid 1970s Fairlop, Roding Valley, Barkingside and Grange Hill were respectively the third, fourth, eighth and eleventh least-used stations on the whole London Underground system, none of them gathering as many as 1,000 passengers a week. Indeed north of Newbury Park, the line still forms the outer boundary of continuously-built up London, its semi-rural aspect emphasised when tube trains are occasionally delayed by horses and deer straying over the tracks.

The LTSR station building at South Street, Romford, c. 1905 (right), looking north. The GER station entrance can be seen at the left. The connecting footway between the two stations is visible above the arch of the underline bridge. *Commercial postcard*

Romford, Upminster & Grays (map page 406)

On the north side of the Thames Estuary, nineteenth century railway objectives were three in number; Tilbury, where a ferry would carry passengers to the Londoners' favourite river resort of Gravesend and its Rosherville Gardens, destination of well over a million steamboat passengers a year in the 1830s and 1840s; the inlet at Thames Haven (which had potential for development as import docks); and Southend, which had begun to develop as a bathing resort at the end of the eighteenth century. Foreshadowing events, a scheme of 1833 had proposed a link between the planned Eastern Counties Railway at Romford and Thames Haven. This 16-mile line was authorised in July 1836 as the Thames Haven Railway & Dock Company but although the powers were renewed in 1846, construction was never started.

After the London Tilbury & Southend Railway had acquired its full independence in 1880, the Great Eastern Railway felt tempted to exploit the developing residential and pleasure resort of Southend and the deep water docks at Tilbury, whose construction had been authorised to the East & West India Dock Company by an act of 1882. Apprehension about the GER's intentions played a part in the LTSR's promotion of a cut-off line between Barking and Pitsea, which would provide a faster route to the seaside town, leaving the original LTSR line via Grays free for the Tilbury Dock traffic. This direct line through Upminster, authorised in 1882, was opened throughout on 1st June 1888. The year 1882 also saw a move to break the LTSR monopoly of the Tilbury Dock traffic in the form of an independent Romford & Tilbury Railway, supported by local landowners. This envisaged a 12-mile double track from the GER at Romford to the LTSR at Grays, with a branch into the new Tilbury Docks. An associated scheme proposed a Tilbury & Gravesend Railway, tunnelling beneath the river. This was sanctioned in August 1882 but the considerable amount of capital required was not attracted and powers were abandoned in

1885. Despite GER support, the Romford & Tilbury also sank, defeated in the Lords but the GER, determination unalloyed, launched its own Tilbury branch in its General Powers Bill of 1883. This line was to branch off from the east end of Romford station, passing west of Upminster and east of South Ockendon before running directly into the Tilbury Docks, then under construction. Failing in its attempt to negotiate with the GER over this challenge, the LTSR put in its own bill, seeking running powers into Romford station for a 2m 5f 5ch line from a junction on the west side of Upminster station on the new cut-off line. South of Upminster the LTSR proposed a line to connect with its main line at West Thurrock about a quarter mile west of Grays station. The GER scheme received support from the Romford Local Board and the Dock Company, the latter no doubt hoping that a little competition would reduce freight rates. Landowners on the other hand saw the LTSR schemes as marginally more helpful to residential development around Upminster. It was the LTSR which emerged as the victor, its two cross country lines receiving sanction on 20th August 1883. This effectively blocked any opportunity for others to grab a share of the Tilbury Dock business. But, once completed in 1886, the Tilbury Docks failed to attract traffic. By 1888 the Dock Co was bankrupt. Cautiously, the LTSR made no start on the Romford-Grays links whilst keeping the powers alive. Eventually fears of GER intentions nagging, a decision was made to build, but as cheaply as possible, laying only a single line. Despite the generally flat nature of the countryside traversed, there were some unavoidable engineering works; a heavy retaining wall to provide space for a separate station at Romford; a 105ft span brick bridge over the Ingrebourne west of Upminster; and the Stifford Viaduct over The Mar Dyke south of Ockendon. The 6¾ mile southern section opened first, on 1st July 1892. It had one intermediate station at Ockendon, 3¼ miles from Upminster, serving the only community of any size along the route. Situated at the west end of the village of South Ockendon, it had two platforms on a passing loop and a small goods yard on the east side. On that side there were substantial brick built ticket and other offices with a two storey house at the south end.

Apprehensive about LTSR trains coming on to its main line to enter Romford station the GER made difficulties, seeking to ease its frustration by offering to lease the Romford-Upminster line from the LTSR at three per cent of its capital cost in return for running powers from Upminster to Tilbury. When this dubious proposition was spurned by the LTSR, the two companies eventually agreed to a separate LTSR station at Romford east of the GER platforms, subject to the GER receiving a small rent for the site. It was also agreed the GER would provide freight facilities at Romford for three years, after which the question of independent accommodation could be raised.

This agreement necessitated a widening of the GER embankment on the south side to provide room for the LTSR's single wooden platform and a run-round loop, the infill held by a 1,260ft retaining wall parallel with Victoria Road. At the west end, the LTSR erected a three-storey building with a 40ft frontage to South Street facing the main entrance to the GER station across the road. This building accommodated the street level ticket office (later moved to platform level), waiting rooms, parcels and other offices as well as the stationmaster's residential quarters. Up above there was no weather protection on the platform apart from some canopied circulating space behind the buffer stops. At a point five chains east of the platform, a connection was laid to the GER Up line for exchange of freight traffic.

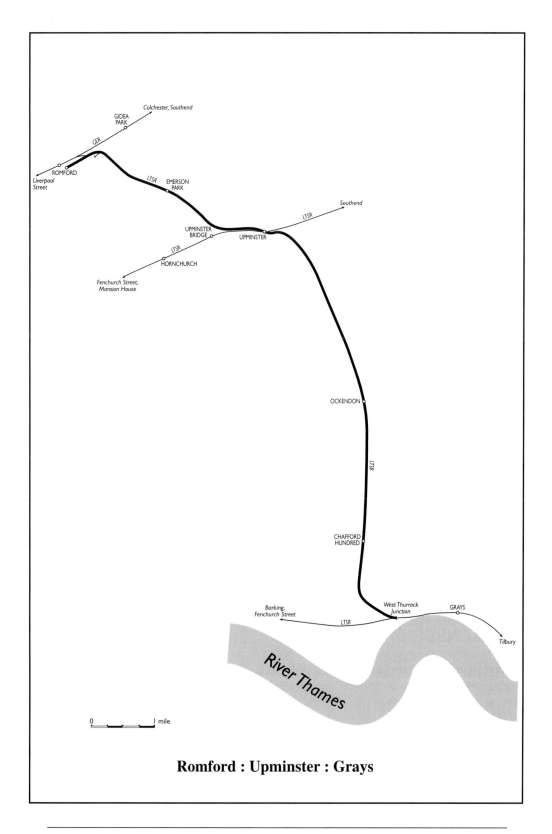

Romford : Upminster : Grays

At Upminster station, east of the platforms on the north side, a small engine shed was built for the branch locomotives. Train services between Upminster and Romford began on 7th June 1893, numbering eight each way daily between Romford and Grays plus one between Romford and Upminster. On Sundays there were five each way over the whole length and short workings on each section. From Romford to Grays, the LTSR's oil-lit four-wheelers were hauled by Sharp Stewart 4–4–2T in 32–38 minutes but it seems likely there were few through passengers. Signalling arrangements, supplied by the Railway Signal Co, allowed only one train at a time on the three sections controlled by the boxes at Romford, Upminster, Ockendon and West Thurrock Junction.

Leaving behind the eastern edges of Romford town, the line ran across open country to join the LTSR main line just west of the separate bridges over the Ingrebourne. Residential development was just starting around the old agricultural village of Upminster, where the Romford–Grays trains used the northern face of the Down island platform, which was connected to the Up side by a subway.

In July 1896 under the Romford station agreement, the LTSR opened a separate freight yard in Victoria Road, Romford near the point where the two lines diverged. After this, the connection to the GER fell into almost total disuse. From the new yard, one train daily worked through to Tilbury Docks whilst a second, on Wednesdays only, carried animals bound for Romford Market. Freight trains were hauled by LTSR 0–6–2T or the company's only two tender engines, the Sharp, Stewart 0–6–0s built in 1898 for the Ottoman Railways. Poultry and calves in sacks for the Market were also accepted as passenger train traffic, most of this business coming off main line trains at Upminster.

An ancestor of Monsieur Hulot walks along the LTSR platform to board an Upminster train in charge of a Midland Railway tank engine; looking north east, 1921. *H J Patterson Rutherford*

After the Midland Railway had taken over the LTSR in 1912, the freight side was actively developed and further business arose when Hall & Co. of Croydon opened private sidings for building materials on the west side of the line off Manor Road, Romford in 1923. Hall's enterprise was well placed for the resumption of the residential construction which had begun in the district between Romford and Upminster in the 1890s, mostly on the higher ground between the GER main line and the LTSR branch west of the Ingrebourne. An estate called Emerson Park, 220 acres in extent, situated east of Butts Green Road, was purchased for development in 1895. Four years later, the first houses were being advertised. Estates known as Heath Park (near the confluence of the LTSR and GER) and Great Nelmes (adjoining Emerson Park to the north) were advertising house plots in 1904 and 1908 respectively. At Great Nelmes, plots 60ft by 300ft were offered for detached houses with the privilege of 'exclusive use' of Great Nelmes Woods. These developments, along with the Gidea Park Garden City on the north eastern edge of Romford from about 1910 and the Upminster Garden Suburb, north of Upminster station, from about 1903, were all designed to attract the comfortably-off middle class. Though they did not settle hereabouts in any great number, those that did were very articulate and were soon badgering the rival railway managements for additional passenger facilities.

The LTSR responded by opening a single platform on the north side of the cutting just east of the Butts Green Road bridge over the Romford–Upminster line. Protected by a lengthy and prettily-valanced umbrella canopy for much of its length which seemed to anticipate a future island platform, this facility was opened on 1st October 1909. A large wooden nameboard announced it as 'Emerson Park and Great Nelmes' but tickets referred to 'Emerson Park Halt'. A fortnight after its opening, a short loop of about four car length was provided on the north side of the running line a quarter mile west to facilitate reversal of 11 additional trains to and from Upminster. Within five years, the privileged residents of the new area were enjoying another facility: a connection off the 00.10 theatre train out of Fenchurch Street, which delivered them at Emerson Park Halt at 00.54, ready for a hot cocoa and bed.

Generous provision for a Romford–Upminster service; a seven-coach train pauses at Emerson Park and Great Nelmes Halt, LTSR c. 1910. *Commercial postcard*

The GER reaction to all this was to start a horse-bus service between the Emerson Park Estate and Romford station, following up with what was to be its last suburban station in the London area: Squirrels Heath & Gidea Park, opened on 1st December 1910 (the two place names were reversed from 1st October 1913 and 'Squirrels Heath' was later dropped altogether). By diverting its buses to run Hornchurch–Emerson Park–Heath Park–Gidea Park station, and wording its station nameboards 'Alight Here for Great Nelmes and Emerson Park', the GER did its level best to draw off the new residential revenue, much of it first or second class.

Such was the confidence in development of traffic that the Midland Railway Bill for the 1914 parliamentary session included a loop from a widened Barking–Upminster line to connect with the Romford branch, which would be doubled. But this was not to be; as World War 1 intensified, the railways had more urgent concerns; the housebuilding around Emerson Park came to a stop; and afterwards life around Upminster would never be quite the same again.

Residential development in the area certainly resumed in the early 1920s but most of the new properties were now small and designed for those further down the social scale than the Edwardian pioneers. By the early 1930s, the triangular area formed by the two railways and the Ingrebourne was almost completely built over with small houses and bungalows and between 1928 and 1939 hundreds more in similar style were erected north of the Hornchurch and Upminster Roads, covering the land between them and the railways. All this brought many new passengers to Emerson Park Halt but their tickets were almost all third class.

Apart from a few new roads at Cranham in the fork between the two lines east of Upminster station, the flatlands around the Upminster–Grays railway remained undeveloped between the wars. Had this been the GWR, there would have been pagoda halts at Cranham and West Thurrock to develop what trade was to be had but the LMSR was little interested in promoting lightly-remunerative local passenger traffic. Although Upminster itself spread south as far as Corbets Tey, this development did not touch the Ockendon line and the new residents found their way north to Upminster station.

On the Ockendon line, most journeys were between Upminster, Grays, Tilbury and Gravesend, the latter encouraged by the availability of through tickets covering both rail and ferryboats. As for freight, the expected use of the line for dock traffic did not materialise, most of it passing to the former GER via Barking and Forest Gate Junction. The statutory requirement to run two freight trains a day via Ockendon was strictly followed but since the Dock traffic did not achieve the guaranteed tonnage prescribed in the legislation, the PLA was obliged to pay compensation to the LTSR. Occasionally the route's strategic value was demonstrated when flooding or other emergencies blocked the LTSR main lines.

The rapid suburban expansion of London between the wars provided the outdated steam railways with increasing problems in handling commuter traffic and when government financial assistance was made available for projects likely to reduce unemployment both the LMSR and the LNER seized the opportunity. The LMSR dug out the Midland's 1914 plans and widened Barking–Upminster to four tracks, electrifying two to carry District line trains as far as Upminster but the Romford branch was left untouched. This scheme involved a major rebuilding of Upminster station, including extension of the LTSR island platform; the provision of a second island to the north for the new Down Local road and the Romford–Grays trains;

improvements on the former Up platform with bay for terminating Grays trains at the eastern end; and a large new entrance and ticket office building on the overline road bridge at the London end. All this work was substantially completed in time for the extension of the District line services on 12th September 1932. Traffic was there for the taking, and on 17th December 1934, on the new local lines a little west of the point where the Romford branch diverted, Upminster acquired a second station, named Upminster Bridge, an island platform serving new housing either side of the Ingrebourne.

The LNER also quadrupled the former GER main line, first as far as Gidea Park, then on to Shenfield. When four new 650ft platforms were provided at Romford in 1931, the former LTSR arrangements were not altered, but from 2nd April 1934 the old LTSR station building was closed for public use except at rail level. This followed an agreement between the LMSR and LNER to rationalise at places where they were in competition and the former LTSR platform now came under LNER control, all passengers passing in and out of the main station via the wooden footway which ran along the south side of the underline road bridge. Although this facility had been provided with the LTSR station in 1893, until 1934 its use had been restricted – there were no through fares via Romford GER/LTSR. The LTSR street building survived until July 1986, when it was demolished following a fire.

By the end of the 1930s the Romford–Upminster line was surrounded by a fully built-up area, though trees and bushes hid much of it from the eyes of passengers, giving quite a false impression. In particular the rural atmosphere of Emerson Park, buried in its dell, was now totally deceptive. Such was the growth of traffic from the new housing north west of Upminster that even the pinch-penny LMSR was moved to introduce some improvement. This came on 1st August 1934 with the arrival of push and pull units powered by former Midland Railway Johnson 0–4–4T (affectionately known as 'One Lung Charlies') which provided some 36 trains a day each way compared with the former 29, four of the new workings shuttling between the Halt and Upminster. Sunday service on the line remained at nine each way, about half working to and from Grays. At this time there were 12 weekday departures from Upminster for Grays or Tilbury, about 14 the other way. Some of these trains ran to and from Romford. With push and pull operation now total, the loop north of Emerson Park was dismantled early in 1936 and from 1st March that year a 'key token' replaced the old train staff.

Wartime brought no major changes apart from a reduction in the number of short workings to and from Emerson Park and these disappeared altogether in 1948. To increase flexibility of working Tilbury Dock traffic should normal paths be damaged by air attack, a running connection was put in between the LNER and LMSR east of Romford station on 21st July 1940. This replaced the original junction, which, together with the LTSR signal box, had been removed in the 1930s, but it was little used until the arrival of diesel cars on the Upminster line.

After the war, the Romford–Upminster line faced a series of threats. Its vulnerability was first indicated in February 1951, when at a time of serious coal shortages, the service was reduced to 16 each way daily and from the end of the following August, when Sunday trains were withdrawn permanently. Steam traction in the form of the remaining 'One Lung Charlies' and N7 0–6–2T, last ran on Saturday, 15th September 1956. On the following Monday diesel railcars doubled the frequency to 32 each way daily, basically half hourly, from 06.05 to 21.22, reducing

BR 42504 on Upminster–Grays–Southend service at Ockendon, 8th May 1960. The signalman is waiting to hand the single line staff to the driver. *Frank Church*

the running time from Romford to Upminster to eight minutes and ending through running on to the Grays line. In connection with provision of a new Underground car depot east of the platforms, Upminster station underwent further reconstruction at this time. With platform faces 4 and 5 allocated exclusively to District Line trains, a new platform 6 was carved out of the cutting slope on the north side for the Romford trains, coming into use on 20th May 1957. Another consequence of the LT depot was the removal of the crossing west of Upminster station in 1959, which left the wartime connection at Romford the only outlet; this was regularly used by the diesel cars when proceeding from and to their depot at Stratford.

Following a census taken in the summer of 1964, the Romford–Upminster line was included in the notorious Beeching list of proposed passenger closures. Formal notice of abandonment from 4th January 1965 appeared in August 1964 along with details of proposed new and augmented bus services. Beeching's census-takers had counted 588 passengers joining Upminster trains between 06.05 and 21.10, 321 of them alighting at Emerson Park, where 139 boarded, making a total of 406 arriving at Upminster through the day. In the reverse direction, the corresponding figures for the same June Monday were 397, 121, 346 and 622. Maximum activity at Emerson Park focussed on the 08.24, which took up 101 commuters for Romford and the 08.37, which loaded 37 for Upminster. Some trains in the middle of the day were found to be carrying but three or four passengers.

Opposition to closure was well organised; hearings before the Transport Users' Consultative Committee established hardship, and in October 1965 the Minister issued a reprieve, recognising that the line's contribution to commuter travel outweighed the net gain on closure calculated by the accountants. Despite this, a second attempt at the kill was mounted in 1969, prompted by identification of an annual cash deficit of £70,000 and a net saving from abandonment of £40,000. Again the defence was successful; another reprieve was granted in 1972 after it had been noted traffic was responding to local publicity and that savings were to be had by restricting the trains to two-car sets.

Freight traffic was no exception to the general trend at London local stations. Upminster lost its yard from 7th December 1964 and freight trains disappeared from the line with the closure of Hall's Romford sidings and the former LTS yard in Victoria Road, Romford from 4th May 1970.

Diesel car working became increasingly unreliable, causing many cancellations and it was with some relief that users heard in August 1984 of the intention to electrify this 3¼ mile line as part of a programme to eliminate the anomaly of diesel car sets working out of Stratford depot to operate three lines* within what was otherwise a totally-electrified zone. The conversion was done at minimum cost: between the outer end of Romford station and the point of divergence the gantries on the main line were used to support the 25kV overhead traction supply; a cheaper method of mast erection, used on the East Coast main line was adopted; and reconstruction of two low overline bridges was avoided by inserting neutral sections. Emerson Park's platform was extended to accommodate the three-car Class 305 electric sets to be used. Resignalling eliminated the last of the semaphore signals in the area, and electric working started on 12th May 1986. Driver-only operation was introduced in the following year.

A few years before the electrification, juvenile vandalism had emerged as a serious problem. In an effort to protect drivers and passengers from injury arising from collisions with objects placed between the rails, some of the diesel units had been fitted with powerful headlights in 1980. Emerson Park became a centre for the perpetrators. Its little ticket office, burnt out in 1987, was replaced with an ugly structure at considerable cost and the automatic ticket and permit to travel machines subsequently installed were soon totally wrecked. On the trains, manned only by a driver, the interiors were defaced by paint sprays or the contents of fire extinguishers. When exhausted, the extinguishers were thrown on the track, which was also used as a dump for torn-out train seats, supermarket trolleys or anything else that might cause satisfying noise or damage. Some drivers refused to work after dark. In 1993 and again in 1994, the harassed management announced that they were considering withdrawing all but a few commuter trains and the service was sometimes stopped as a result of vandalism. Police action restored calm but a police presence could not be continuously maintained. On a service already making a cash loss, the depletion in off-peak travel and revenue arising from such events was a serious matter which, if they persisted, seemed likely to once again bring closure into focus.

On the other side of Upminster, the single line railway enjoyed something of change of fortune in the immediate post-war years. The LCC Aveley Estate, at South Ockendon, opened in 1950, was to cover 391.25 acres, accommodating a population of almost 22,000. This development clothed the railway on both sides with houses and industrial buildings for about 1½ miles south of Ockendon station. Ideally the station should have been moved to a more central position in the new community to stimulate maximum patronage of the train service but no funds for this were made available by the authorities. Whilst many of the adult residents at Aveley found employment locally, or soon enough acquired cars to reach workplaces along the Thames Estuary, there was some increase in traffic through the day, from shopping and entertainment travel and from youngsters commuting to shop and office employment further afield.

* The other two were the Southminster and North Woolwich branches.

After the introduction of diesel cars on the Romford section. Grays trains worked in and out of the Up side bay at Upminster, at first powered by a variety of steam locos: N7 0–6–2T, LTSR 4–4–2T and 0–6–2T, ex GNR C12 4–4–2T and BR 2–6–4T. Most trains were formed of three-car push-pull sets. Then from 6th January 1958, diesel cars were introduced, providing a basic half hourly service (hourly on Sundays) with a journey time of 15 min and additional workings in the peak period. Some trains ran through to Tilbury Riverside.

Sustained by the new industries of Aveley, Ockendon yard remained open until May 1968. Freight did not entirely disappear from the line even then as oil and cement trains were diverted over it as occasion required.

It was this strategic value and possibly the extra traffic brought by Aveley that caused BR to include the line in its LTS electrification scheme. The conversion was completed in time to allow the four-coach electric sets to work hourly (every 30 min between Ockendon and Upminster) from 17th June 1963. On Sundays there were hourly trains between Fenchurch Street and Tilbury Riverside via Ockendon. Between West Thurrock Junction and Grays station (where they could terminate in a Down side bay) the electric trains were able to use a new third track, worked by tokenless track circuit block. Trains continued to pass at the Ockendon loop in peak hours until the signal box there was gutted by fire on Christmas Eve 1977. After a period of working with one train on line, the new signalling was commissioned in November 1978. There were colour light signals at Ockendon, where use of the loop was restored and the whole line was worked with tokenless track circuit block under control of Upminster box. Both the Grays and the Romford lines came under the new Upminster Integrated Electronic Control Centre when this was opened on 17th April 1995, replacing all the manual boxes in the area. This change, which included a new track layout between West Thurrock Junction and Grays, was completed on 8th April 1996. Off peak traffic between Upminster and Grays has declined since the 1960s but some increase may be expected from more recent developments. First to appear was the Lakeside retail centre, with its 250 shops, opened in October 1990. Sited south of Aveley, below the level of the railway and west of it, Lakeside is close to the M25 motorway and with its huge car parks, is primarily succoured by road transport. Closely behind and still in progress at the time of writing was Chafford Hundred, a new community of 5,000 homes between the railway and Grays. Planning permission for this was granted on condition the developers provided a new station and this came into public use on 30th May 1995. Using 'traditional' design and materials in the hope of achieving what was described as 'a welcoming, comfortable feel to complement the growing new community', it had a single 12-car length platform on the Down side, a brick building featuring a gabled glass-walled atrium as its centre piece, a forecourt and a 150-space car park. Bus services provided a link to the Lakeside Shopping Centre.

In preparation for traffic growth, the peak service was doubled in September 1995, with some trains running through to and from Fenchurch Street via Ockendon and Chafford Hundred. This may be a portent. Certainly this section of the former LTSR cross-country line does seem likely to have a more assured future than the northern part and various options have been discussed, including doubling throughout and diversion of all the services between Fenchurch Street and Grays–Pitsea stations over it, perhaps leaving the stations between Barking and Grays to an extension of the Gospel Oak–Barking service.

Millwall Extension Railway Manning Wardle 2-4-0T No.6 on North Greenwich train of two ex-GER oil-lit four-wheel coaches at Millwall Junction station, c. 1905.

Railways to Blackwall & North Greenwich   (map page 416)

'It will be apparent even to the most sceptical, that few undertakings embrace more important advantages than the present'. A potential investor, reading these words in the 1835 prospectus for a railway between the City of London and Blackwall learned that the 'advantages' were those to be derived from constructing a short cut to the meandering and dangerous river passage round the Isle of Dogs; it was claimed that not only would this reduce the cost of transporting goods to and from the East and West India Docks, but would cut an hour each way from the journey of those using the numerous Thames estuary steamer services, all of which called at Brunswick Wharf, Blackwall. Pickings from this river steamer traffic between London and the estuary towns and beyond were certainly worth having in the early 1830s when around 1,750,000 passengers a year were travelling this way to Gravesend, Margate and Ramsgate alone. Brunswick Wharf was also an embarkation point for the numerous emigrants to the colonies. Along the Commercial Road there were almost 100 return bus journeys daily between London and Blackwall, some of them operated by the West India Dock Company.

Proposals for improving communications between the West India Docks and the City of London dated back to 1825, when an iron flange tramway along the Commercial Road had been suggested. Although this was formulated into a parliamentary bill in 1828, it failed for lack of support. Two schemes for railways between the City and the West India Docks were evolved in 1835, one, whose prospectus is quoted above, with George Stephenson as engineer, the other, engineered by Sir John Rennie, having the title The Commercial Railway. It was the latter which succeeded in obtaining an act on 28th July 1836. Just over 3½ miles of line were proposed from the Minories at the eastern edge of the City, to Brunswick Wharf, Blackwall, running south of the Commercial Road; if the dock companies requested, there were to be branches into both the East and West India Docks. Since the inner part of the area was already built over, the width of the formation was restricted to 25 yards, except where there were railway installations, passing places or loading points. The railway company was authorised to use locomotives, stationary engines or 'other power', but any steam engines employed were to 'consume their own smoke' and their funnels were to be fitted with a 'gauze of wires' at a maximum of one eighth of an inch apart, to reduce the fire risk to the sails and timber of vessels. The West India Dock Co. was empowered to hold shares in the railway and the chairmen and deputy chairmen of both the East & West India Dock Companies were to be given seats on the railway's board.

A further act in 1837 extended time for acquisition of land and allowed the East India Dock Company to subscribe, correcting what appears to have been an error of drafting in the original statute. Both dock companies did in the event subscribe capital, but were limited by the second act to a maximum of £50,000. Another part of the 1837 bill did not succeed. All along, the promoters had wished to have a worthwhile entry into the City but were obstructed in this intent by the Corporation. A proposed terminus in Lime Street was rejected by the Corporation on the grounds that it would increase street congestion.

Realising that the success of its passenger business depended on a convenient City terminus, the company made another attempt in 1839, when a less ambitious invasion of only 415 yards across the boundary to a terminus 'at or near' Fenchurch Street was allowed. This 1839 act also changed the name of the undertaking to the London & Blackwall Railway. In return for the use of its hallowed territory, the City Corporation obtained many protections, amongst them a ban on stationary and other steam engines within its boundary, except on the east side of the Minories. Another section of this act allowed the railway company to negotiate with the newly-amalgamated East & West India Docks Company over the use of Brunswick Wharf.

This was to be the first railway to cross an area of London already fully built over with streets and houses. Not until the Isle of Dogs was approached was there any open land, so on the western section, as far as the West India Dock, the tracks were placed on a brick viaduct of 285 arches, mostly of 30ft span, to eliminate level crossings and minimise demolition. Streets and water were spanned by iron girder bridges, the Limehouse Basin and Limehouse Cut of the Regent's Canal by structures of three and one 87ft spans respectively. There was very considerable scope for compensation in the 1836 act, so much so that despite the restricted width, land owners and property owners waited upon the directors daily with demands 'compared with which the exactions of the country gentry were liberal arrangements'. After leaving this costly viaduct, the line was in cutting for most of the distance to the Blackwall terminus.

William Tite designed for Blackwall a handsome brick and Portland stone two-storey building presenting a 105ft long, 45ft high frontage of 'Roman-Doric character' to the river. Parallel to the railway on the south side, but partly extending beyond the buffers, the accommodation included ladies' and gentlemen's waiting rooms and lavatories, a booking hall, and above it, a large room borrowed by the customs men when ships serving foreign and colonial ports berthed here. Along much of the length of the platform the frontage was extended in the form of a blind arcaded brick wall supporting one side of the 'light and elegant' all-over roof which offered some protection to carriages stored in the station overnight until it fell into disrepair and was replaced around the turn of the century by the usual umbrella-type valanced awnings. At first there was but one track, with a wide platform bounded by the brick wall mentioned, but the introduction of steam traction in 1849 required alterations in the layout. Three tracks were then made, with a narrow island platform between two of them, its northern face much longer than the southern one. The third road was used as a carriage siding until eventually a platform took its place. No such extravagance was shown at Minories, a temporary terminus pending further advance into the City. A two-track, side-platform station, this had an overall roof which provided less protection than the one at Blackwall. Five small stations were erected to serve the populous district traversed: Shadwell, Stepney, Limehouse, West India Dock and Poplar (re-sited in 1845). Others were subsequently added at Cannon Street Road (21st August 1842), Leman Street (1st June 1877) and Millwall Junction (18th December 1871), but the first of these lasted only six years and the others closed from 7th July 1941 and from 4th May 1926 respectively. With stations so closely-spaced and the potential fire danger to the timber and ropeyards clustered against the viaduct and to the vast expanse of sailcloth and rigging in Limehouse Basin, it was thought wise to avoid the use of steam locomotives. This advice, given to the directors in an 1837 report by the engineer George Parker Bidder, was endorsed by both George and Robert Stephenson, the latter suggesting that rope-haulage would also be cheaper as space was restricted and land costs were very high. Robert told the parliamentary committee in 1836 that considering the 'immense value of the property on every side' he thought the railway would have to be abandoned rather than use steam engines.

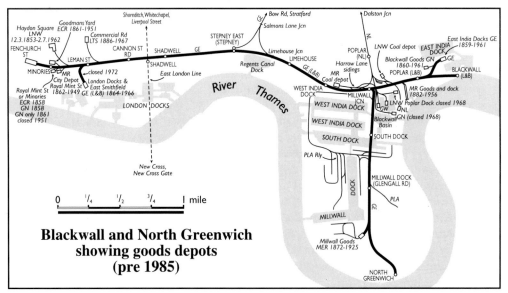

**Blackwall and North Greenwich
showing goods depots
(pre 1985)**

Bidder and George Stephenson were appointed engineers for the line in January 1838, a decision having been made for a 5ft gauge rope-hauled system. The gauge was that of the neighbouring Eastern Counties Railway which was to open about the same time, and with which future connection for traffic exchange was expected.

Public service on one track only started on 6th July 1840, the second line following on 3rd August. From the latter date, a 15-minute frequency was worked every day of the week between 08.30 and 20.45. Widened out to earlier starts and later finishes, this frequency was to remain unaltered until 1883. The intermediate stations at Limehouse, West India Dock and Poplar opened with the line on 6th July; Stepney was not ready until August and Shadwell came into use from 1st October.* Two classes of accommodation were offered in the blue-painted six-wheeled coaches but some of the inferior class had open sides and no seats under the rudimentary roof.

At each end of the line were a pair of steam winding engines. Minories had Maudsley & Field marine condensing engines developing 110–115hp, but the engines sited between Poplar and Blackwall were only 70–75hp machines as the line fell some 68ft from the viaduct to its eastern end. Two hemp ropes, each about seven miles long, wound on to one drum as they were uncoiled from the drum at the opposite end of the line, guided at about 30mph along the tracks by cast-iron sheaves of 3ft diameter spaced 33ft apart. Both the 'north line' and the 'south line' were equipped in this fashion and used alternately for traffic in each direction.

The method of working was rather curious. At the start of each day there would be one coach standing at each intermediate station. As the rope began to move, these would be attached to it, proceeding as one-car 'trains' to Blackwall without further stops. Also, as the rope moved, a complete train attached to the same rope left Minories, detaching a single coach at each station it passed. When the residue of two coaches reached Blackwall, it would be marshalled with the collection of single coaches already arrived there to form a return train. The whole operation was then carried out in reverse, using the same track; the single coaches dropped at each intermediate station on the outward journey returned one by one to Minories, followed by the train, which again discarded a single coach at each station on its way. A similar sequence was performed on the other line. By this means an end-to-end journey could be made in 10 to 15 minutes, compared with about one hour on the river when conditions were favourable. Modifications were made to the rope working from time to time but there were always some journeys that could not be completed without going to a terminus and working back along the line. All movements of the ropes were controlled by signals on Cooke & Wheatstone's single needle telegraph instruments, used here for the first time on a public railway. Blackwall station, beyond the engine house, was entered on a slight upward gradient, enabling the incoming coaches to be detached from the rope and sent in on a slowing momentum. This feature also allowed a gravity-assisted departure, with some muscular contribution by the staff. A similar arrangement existed at Fenchurch Street, in conformity with the City's ban on steam engines.

The City terminus, just south of Fenchurch Street, and named after it, was opened on 2nd August 1841. Behind an unassuming frontage by William Tite was a modest two-platform train-shed. In deference to the City's collective conscience, a provision

---

* Shadwell closed after traffic on 21st May 1916, reopened from 5th May 1919 and was permanently closed from 7th July 1941.

in the 1839 act forbade railway operations here on Sundays, Good Fridays and Christmas Days, but the Sunday trains which had always worked to and from Minories came into Fenchurch Street from Sunday 5th June 1842, the ban having been lifted by the act of that year, which noted that the extension had been totally enclosed. With the sinful railway working decently obscured behind fenestrated walls and a roof of slate and iron, the God-fearing City Corporation went to church with a clear conscience. In his evidence to the 1846 Royal Commission on Metropolitan Railway Termini, the superintendent of the London & Blackwall Railway averred that the short extension into Fenchurch Street which had cost £250,000, had increased its business by 50 per cent. It also caused the collapse of traffic at Minories, which was closed permanently after the last train on 23rd October 1853.

Although rope haulage provided speeds which were high for the period and was clean and relatively safe, it proved expensive and troublesome in operation. Manpower requirements were high, with two men on each coach to attend to the speedy conclusion of rope-gripping and slipping, and maintenance costs were also heavy. When after a very short time the original ropes wore down, they were replaced by steel wire rope which caused much distress by twisting. Travel on the Blackwall in this period was always something of an adventure, demanding patience and a well-developed sense of humour. The directors were soon regretting their decision, longing to break out of their isolation and attract the traffic of other lines to their well-situated City terminus. In 1845 they supported a London & Blackwall Railway Extension Bill seeking powers for a line from Stepney to join the Eastern Counties Railway near the River Lea at Old Ford; from here the promoters cheekily proposed running powers over the ECR as far as Stratford, whence they would build their own line northwards to Epping. These suggestions were vigorously resisted by the ECR, which was also not keen on the idea that some of its trains might be diverted from the Shoreditch terminus into Fenchurch Street. But during the passage of the bill, the ECR opposition was withdrawn on condition that the running powers were dropped and the Epping line be left to the ECR to build as the company thought fit. The London & Blackwall Railway Extension Act of 1845 gave the London & Blackwall company power to lease the Extension and to purchase it, which was done in February 1846.

To allow the expected through running, the act required the Extension to be built to standard gauge (the Eastern Counties had been converted to standard by October 1844), and in preparation, the original line was narrowed to standard gauge and worked with steam locomotives from 15th February 1849. Between 1848 and 1860 the Blackwall company acquired nine handsome passenger locomotives, all 2–2–2 well tanks by Jones, Potts & Co or George England & Co, also two England 2–4–0T for freight working. All were painted blue and shedded at Blackwall. The last one survived until 1883. The old 5ft gauge Blackwall coaches, retrucked for standard gauge working, were still in use in the mid-1860s when complaints were being made about their condition. Residual fears of fire led to the erection of a light iron roof to trap sparks and hot cinders on the section of viaduct through Limehouse Basin. Speeds were generally better than in cable days, and from 22nd June 1849 until 5th November 1854 a service was run non-stop between Fenchurch Street and Blackwall in five minutes, in connection with the Gravesend steamers, a time which could not be matched by public transport today or by car, except perhaps on a clear road at dead of night.

The Extension opened on 2nd April 1849, but was of limited use as the ECR continued to create difficulties. Although exchange platforms had been built, few ECR trains called and the ECR facility was closed from 6th January 1851. Regular traffic over a junction here between the two railways did not pass until 13th April 1854. Meanwhile, the Blackwall worked a 15-minute service between Fenchurch Street and its new station at Bow Road (known as Bow & Bromley), apparently going forward to the exchange platforms (Victoria Park & Bow) only on the rare occasions when it was possible to make a connection with the ECR trains.

The Blackwall was eventually released from its isolation by the arrival of the East & West India Docks & Birmingham Junction Railway (later more neatly renamed the North London Railway). This line, partly subsidised by the East & West India Dock Company, opened between Islington (later Highbury & Islington) and a junction with the London & Blackwall Extension at Bow near what was known later as Gas Factory Junction) on 26th September 1850. From that date, a 15-minute service was worked between Fenchurch Street and Islington, extended, with the opening of the line to Camden Town (now Camden Road) on 7th December. These trains, which brought a substantial accretion of traffic to the Blackwall, much of it of a commuter nature despite the roundabout route, were extended west to Hampstead Road (now Primrose Hill) on 9th June 1851. Until physical connection was made with the LNWR on 15th February 1851, some rolling stock and train crews were temporarily hired from the Blackwall Company. With the start of the North London service, Blackwall Railway trains between Fenchurch Street and Bow & Bromley were withdrawn and the latter station was closed.

As both parties came to realise the advantages of co-operation, relations between the Blackwall and the ECR gradually improved, so much so that the two companies sponsored a railway called the London, Tilbury & Southend, designed to secure the pleasure traffic to Gravesend and Southend and make better use of the western section of the Blackwall. The first section of the LTSR, from Forest Gate Junction on the ECR to Tilbury was opened on 13th April 1854, the trains running through to Fenchurch Street via Stratford and the 1848 link at Bow. From this time, the section of the Blackwall between Bow Junction and Fenchurch Street falls outside our terms of reference and the reader needing its later history must look to histories of the London, Tilbury & Southend.

The new friendliness between the Blackwall and its neighbour was sustained after the ECR's absorption into the GER from 1st July 1862. Negotiations followed which led to the London & Blackwall Lease Act, 1865 which authorised the L&BR to lease its undertaking to the GER, a lease which was to operate from 1st January 1866 for 999 years, with the GER guaranteeing the Blackwall dividends of 4½ per cent on its ordinary capital. The small company retained a nominally independent existence until finally absorbed into the LNER in 1923. Another part of the 1865 act opened up the Blackwall to much heavier freight use by granting running powers to the Midland, the LNWR and the GNR (the NLR was merely assured of the passenger running powers enjoyed since 1850 and the goods powers of 1853, in return for which it undertook to run into Fenchurch Street every 15 minutes, an obligation removed by the 1865 act).

Two more links were made between the eastern end of the Blackwall and other lines. In October 1851 for coal, and on 1st January 1852 for all freight, the East & West India Docks & Birmingham Junction Railway was extended from Bow to West

India Docks, with a coal depot at Poplar and a spur to the Blackwall line. Use was at first confined to freight, but after the opening of Broad Street station, a passenger service was started on 1st August 1866 between that terminus and a new NLR station at Poplar. North London trains ceased to run into Fenchurch Street after traffic on 31st December 1868, the GER substituting a passenger service between Fenchurch Street and the NLR at Bow which ran from the following day, lasting until close of traffic on 3rd April 1892. A more convenient connection for passenger trains between the Blackwall and the NLR at Poplar opened on 1st September 1870 and was used until 30th June 1890 by an extension of the Broad Street–Poplar (NLR) service to Blackwall in connection with river steamers. This Poplar connection lost much of its former value after the opening of the Limehouse Curve on 5th April 1880; seeing little use after the cessation of the NLR trains to Blackwall, it was removed in August 1890. The double-track Limehouse Curve, first authorised in 1865, completed the triangle at Stepney, enabling trains to run direct from Blackwall to the GER at Bow Junction and, via Gas Factory Junction, on to the NLR at Bow. Extending from Salmons Lane Junction on the Stepney–Bow line to Limehouse Junction, just west of Limehouse station, it was used from 1st September 1880 by a Palace Gates–Stratford–Blackwall service, but this was unsuccessful and ceased after traffic on 28th February 1881. Passenger trains were seen again on the Curve in the summers of 1890 and 1891 when a Sunday service carried dockers and their families to a few hours' cheap excitement at Southend.

Although the Blackwall Railway promoters had envisaged freight movement between the docks and the City, the reasons why this had not materialised are not difficult to find. Double transhipment over such a short distance, with mixed rope and animal haulage would be unduly costly compared with the traditional lighterage, and in any case the layout of the two-horse cartage dock complexes was not conducive to the provision of an adequate railway layout without major rearrangement.* This last factor continued to limit freight activity to and from the old docks even after the Blackwall had been linked to the main railway system and converted to steam traction. But despite this disappointment, the location of the Blackwall line assured it of a strong growth in freight traffic once it had been connected to the other railways. Using the running powers established in 1865, other companies added their own goods depots and yards to those built by the Blackwall. Between 1853 and 1866 ten installations appeared along the L&BR at the City end and between West India Dock station and Blackwall,† owned by five different companies (LNWR, GER, Midland, GNR and LTSR), all but one of which worked their own locomotives to and from their depots (Haydon Square, LNWR, was served by NLR locomotives). As early as 1862 the GNR and Midland depots at Royal Mint Street were alone handling some 310,000 tons of freight a year.

Passenger business in the early years was not unsatisfactory, although many

---

* Although the Blackwall Railway built a branch from near Leman Street to the Wool Warehouse of the London Docks in 1864 (the Dock Company guaranteed 5 per cent on the capital) it did not prove possible to lay further tracks in the dock area. A second branch from near Poplar (L&BR) station into the East India Docks served mainly a GNR goods depot, extending only for a very short distance on to the North Quay of the Export Dock.

† The locations and dates of these depots are shown on the map on page 416.

Millwall Extension Railway train for Millwall Junction at North Greenwich, with unidentified Manning Wardle 2-4-0T, c. 1905. *Lens of Sutton*

steamboat users continued to go on board in the City despite the saving in time that the train offered. Seeking to capture some of the river trade, the Blackwall Railway in 1843 bought from Thames Ironworks steam vessels *The Railway*, *The Brunswick* and *The Blackwall* to start an hourly through-fare service between Fenchurch Street, Woolwich and Gravesend. But the once-thriving regular steamer services between London and the estuary towns collapsed as soon as railways were opened along the river, and the Blackwall turned its energies, as we have seen, to attracting other railways on to its system. On the river, pleasure sailings continued to bring uncertain and seasonal grist to the Blackwall mill until 1914.

Almost from the opening, rather more than half the passengers carried between Fenchurch Street and Blackwall were local as distinct from river users, and in the early years there was a considerable amount of Sunday pleasure traffic to Blackwall, where the crowds strolled by the river, watching the shipping and refreshing themselves at the *Railway Tavern* and the *Brunswick Hotel*. Through the nineteenth century the line was used mostly by workmen moving between the intermediate stations and the docks, sailors, craftsmen and others with business at the docks, and, until the telephone came into general use in offices in the 1890s and 1900s, messengers between the City shipping offices and ships. About the time the latter traffic started to fade, the Blackwall really began to feel the tramway competition which had begun with a horse-drawn service along the Commercial and East India Dock Roads in December 1872. Reductions of the Blackwall service were initiated as early as October 1883 when Sunday intervals were extended from 15 to 30 minutes. In 1902 the weekday frequency became 20 minutes instead of 15, and the Sunday trains ceased altogether from 4th October 1908, probably a direct result of the opening of the electric tramway from Aldgate to Poplar on 15th December 1906. A further cut to half-hourly on weekdays was offered as part of the GER contribution to manpower economies at the height of World War 1. It is unlikely that these reductions caused much hardship, so it is surprising to find that quarter-hourly intervals were restored in 1919 even though the traffic day was shortened from around 07.00 to 20.00 (07.00 to 15.00 on Saturdays). For years these trains were handled by the 150 class, the smallest of the GER's 0–6–0T, with 1300 class 2–4–2T sometimes appearing.

The newly-formed LNER was not long in deciding that the Blackwall service was expendable, announcing in 1926 that the passenger service would be withdrawn after 30th June. However the issue was decided by the coal shortages caused by the miners' strike and by the General Strike that year, so that in practice no trains were run after the last working on the evening of 3rd May.

Goods traffic kept the line busy for another decade or so, but quickly diminished when both docks and railway installations suffered severe damage from German air attacks early in World War 2. From 1949, as the map on page 416 shows, all remaining depots and yards were closed. At Blackwall the scene was radically changed in 1947 by the erection of a huge electric power station on the site of the passenger terminus and the East India Export Dock. The few freight movements that remained in the early 1950s were being worked on and off the line via the Limehouse curve; the old London & Blackwall Railway viaduct across the base of the triangle between Stepney East station and Limehouse carried only the former Up line, used as a siding since 1951 from the Limehouse end for occasional transhipments of crane-lifted scrap metal between railway wagons and lighters in the Basin below. This section, together with Limehouse curve, went out of use on 5th November 1962.

Poplar Dock was silted up when visited by a party of railway students in November 1954, but a fine specimen of a Midland Railway signal box and Midland signals were discovered intact, one of the latter with no role other than that of warning drivers not to take their trains over the edge of the dock into the mist-shrouded river. Although not officially closed until 1956, all activity here had ceased long before that date. Connections into the docks at Millwall Junction remained in use until the early 1960s, as did the extensive sidings west of that station, but most of the docks traffic, including the bulk grain moving out to Welwyn Garden City to be made into the breakfast cereal called 'Shredded Wheat', was routed via the old NLR line and Bow. Tracks east of Millwall were taken up in 1967 and a direct line was built from Poplar NLR yard to the western Poplar docks across the bed of the Blackwall Railway. This link, opened in May 1968 to replace the old high-level NLR access lines, was used by trains entering via Victoria Park over the former NLR line, which was singled from 19th August 1979. Connected to it were some remnants of the Blackwall Railway tracks which extended through the site of Millwall Junction as far west as Ming Street. These lines were visited by freight trains (latterly carrying scrap metal) until 1981, the last movement into Poplar docks taking place on 30th August that year. The track between Poplar and Victoria Park was lifted in 1984.

To the west, the London & Blackwall and the Extension Railway formation between Fenchurch Street and Bow continued to be very busy with fast and frequent electric passenger trains to Barking, Tilbury and Southend.

For many years the old London & Blackwall viaduct east of Limehouse remained, neglected, weed grown and trackless, but its usefulness was far from over, for as we shall see at the end of this chapter, it was destined for a second life, carrying a new railway to Blackwall and beyond.

Poplar station, London & Blackwall Railway, looking west, 20th November 1954. The track on the right leads to the former GNR Blackwall and GER East India Dock goods depots. *Alan A Jackson*

Millwall Junction signalbox and station, looking east, 20th November 1954. The North Greenwich line diverges right, where the goods brake van is standing; the London & Blackwall Railway to Blackwall runs straight ahead, and the connection to the North London Railway is at the left. *Alan A Jackson*

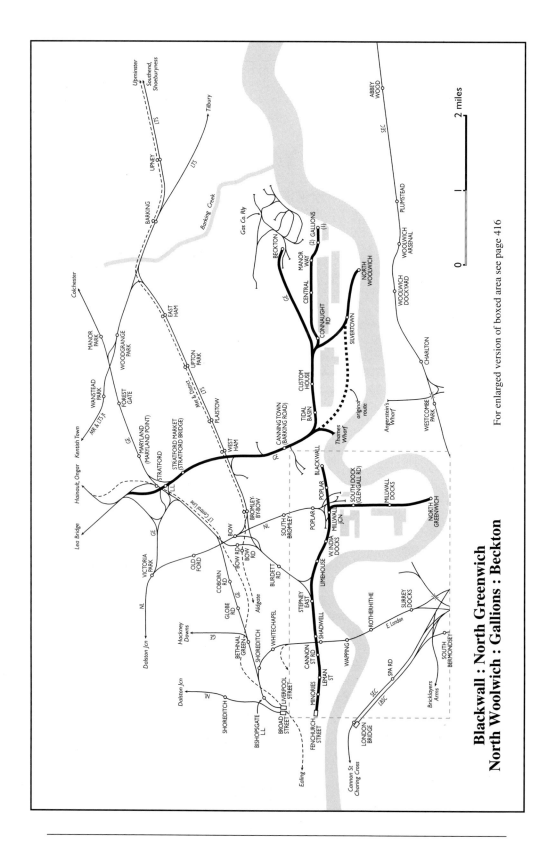

Blackwall : North Greenwich
North Woolwich : Gallions : Beckton

For enlarged version of boxed area see page 416

0 — 1 — 2 miles

A somewhat curious offshoot of the London & Blackwall was the Millwall Extension Railway, a single track authorised by the London, Blackwall & Millwall Extension Railway Act of 19th June 1865 and which, although a mere 1m 49ch in length was initially split amongst three companies and operated in four separately-owned sections. Its main task was to serve the Millwall Docks which had been opened in the southern part of the Isle of Dogs on 14th March 1868, the first docks in London to be provided with a complete internal railway system, much of it with sharp radius curves. In the hope of securing some of the traffic between central London and the town on the opposite bank, the MER was extended beyond the Docks to the southern tip of the Isle of Dogs to terminate at a station accurately, if somewhat misleadingly called North Greenwich.

The Millwall Canal Company (Millwall Dock Company from 1870) was of course the principal party in promoting the MER, but it was actively assisted by the London & Blackwall, and later, the GER. This collaboration was immeasurably eased by the fraternal relationship of the respective general managers of the dock company and the GER, a happy state of affairs only matched by the ill-feeling of the East & West India Docks Co., which saw the project as encouraging a rival by making use of its land for a railway 'prejudicial and injurious to their undertaking and calculated seriously to interfere with the Trade and Shipping Interest of the Port of London in connexion therewith'. However, agreement was eventually reached with the London & Blackwall on 21st March 1865 by which E&WID opposition was withdrawn provided the railway through its premises was built, owned and controlled by the company and not worked with locomotive power. It was stipulated that if the London & Blackwall wished to operate a locomotive-hauled passenger service on the Isle of Dogs, another line would have to be built under the Dock company's property instead of the proposed surface railway. Both dock companies eventually contributed to the construction and working of the line, controlling it through a joint committee on which the GER was also represented.

From Millwall Junction, a new station between West India Dock and Poplar (L&BR) stations, the first five chains of the North Greenwich branch were owned by the L&BR, the next 41ch were the property of the London & India Docks Co. and were followed by 52ch owned by the Millwall Dock Co. The final 31ch were again part of the L&BR. Three swing bridges of rather flimsy construction combined with light track and the vast quantity of tarred wood and sail near the line caused the dock companies to reject the use of steam locomotives within their boundaries, and when the line opened for goods traffic from Millwall Junction to Millwall Dock on 18th December 1871, horses were used. From the same day, a half-hourly service was worked, using single cars hauled by two Millwall Dock Co. horses, calling at the intermediate station and crossing place, South Dock, and a station named Millwall Dock on the south side of Glengall Road, serving the workmen's colony of Cubitt Town. The original passenger vehicles were four large Starbuck tramcars which later went to the Wisbech & Upwell Tramway. Millwall Junction had three platforms, those from the Up Fenchurch Street line and branch splaying into the fork of the junction. Brick station offices occupied the wider part of the triangle and connection with the outside world was by footbridge. The other two stations, built partly in brick, but mainly in wood, had only one platform. From June 1872 the passenger service was increased to four journeys an hour, starting at 07.30 and ending at 16.30.

With the opening of the Millwall Dock–North Greenwich section on 29th July 1872 a full passenger service was started with GER locomotives taking over the single car from the horses at the southern boundary of Millwall Docks. The locomotives had been moved on to the line with their fires out, hauled by horses. This final part of the branch was on a 682yd brick viaduct terminating at a single wooden platform at North Greenwich where there was an engine run-round road, a small engine shed and carriage sidings, but no goods facilities. The tracks finished at a substantial barrier just above the river's edge.

The first locomotive was *Ariel's Girdle*, built by Kitson's and shown at the Great Exhibition of 1851 before being purchased by the ECR. Originally a 2–2–0 well tank, it was rebuilt in 1868 as a 2–4–0T with 4ft driving wheels. Its place on the North Greenwich line was taken in 1878 by a Kitson four-wheeled tram engine with a vertical boiler.

Doing its best to secure a Greenwich traffic, the GER transferred its Blackwall–Greenwich steam ferry service to the pier at North Greenwich in 1874 after purchasing the ferry rights from the Poplar & Greenwich Ferry Co. The latter's pier, about 200yd from the railway, was replaced in 1877 by a new pier near the station. Through bookings were arranged between Fenchurch Street and what the GER was pleased to call 'South Greenwich' at an advertised journey time of 36 minutes. This gave the Millwall Dock Company the ability to draw on labour south of the river, leading in time to a substantial traffic in workmen. In accordance with the terms of the 1865 act, a penny fare workmen's train had been run since 1872. Another feature was the carriage of crowds to see Millwall Rovers Football Club after its formation in 1885. On occasion these trains loaded up to five crowded coaches, placing considerable strain on the tiny locomotives of what was virtually a light railway. This problem disappeared after 1910 when the football club moved to its present New Cross ground.

Anxious to provide an alternative to the dangerous and uncertain ferry operations in winter fogs, the LCC built a pedestrian and cyclist tunnel between Greenwich Church Street and North Greenwich. This opened on 4th August 1902, the GER agreeing to close its ferry (after 31st October) when offered £8,000 of the ratepayers' money as compensation.

Horse operation through the dock area continued for eight years after opening, when, with some strengthening of the swing bridges and a change of attitude by the dock companies' insurers, steam traction was introduced. The Millwall Dock Company purchased three small Manning Wardle 2–4–0T with 3ft 6in driving

North Greenwich train of three ex-GER coaches at Millwall Dock station, Glengall Road, Millwall Extension Railway. 'Coffee Pot' Manning Wardle 2-4-0T bears its PLA number 29 (ex MER 4), c. 1910.

wheels. Of a type used by civil engineering contractors on temporary railways, these engines imposed minimal strains on the flimsy track and were used for all passenger trains together with hired GER coaches from 23rd August 1880. Known locally as 'coffee pots' from their tall smokestacks and spark arresters, they were first painted dark yellow, later altered to brick red, lined in black. Rebuilt in 1905, they passed into Port of London Authority ownership when that body was formed in 1909, continuing to haul the branch trains of two or three oil-lit four-wheel GER coaches until November 1922.

For most of the period a 15-minute service was operated from about 07.00 until 18.00, then half-hourly until about 22.00. Sunday trains, usually half-hourly with a church interval from 10.00 to 13.00, did not call at South Dock, and ran from 29th August 1880 to 28th December 1913. Some workmen's trains and other early morning workings were started in July 1883. Operation was by train staff and ticket, with staffs exchanged at each end and at South Dock.

All the rolling stock was stored at North Greenwich, and although the GER provided guards, the drivers, firemen and cleaners were all dock employees. According to Thomas Peacock, two cleaners 'paid unremitting attention to the brasswork, washed the engines down with soft soap every fortnight and once a week scoured the couplings and buffers with emery paper'. It is not clear whether this commendable endeavour was in any way associated, financially or otherwise, with the fact that these engines carried advertisements for Pears Soap affixed to their tanks and smokeboxes.

In a rash attempt at modernisation, the PLA purchased in 1922 three redundant steam railmotors from the GWR to replace the little Manning Wardles. Two of the cars had four-coupled driving units and were Swindon products of 1904, the other had a six-coupled driving unit (later converted to 2-4-0) and was originally built for the Port Talbot Railway Co in 1906. These vehicles, specially fitted with electric light and reduced in weight, were not an unqualified success on the Millwall Extension. Some bridges had to be strengthened before their arrival and facing points had to be equipped with locking bars; they were tight on curves, and to loading gauge, rendering anything close to the track vulnerable to damage. Their introduction did little to revive the flagging fortunes of the passenger service, which had been reduced to half-hourly in 1915 and was now a victim of motor bus competition. The PLA and the LNER took a long hard look, deciding to abandon from 30th June 1926, but as on the Blackwall line, the date was fixed by the General Strike, the last trains running on 3rd May.

Between North Greenwich and Glengall Road the line was completely closed. Parts of the viaduct were demolished ten years later, but the station at North Greenwich, in use as a store, remained more or less intact until the mid-1960s. During 1929, the PLA completed a new entrance to the south West India Dock from Blackwall Reach which severed the central section of the railway, but a link to Millwall Dock was retained by constructing a diversion round the west side of the Dock, which was opened in January 1929. Although their importance decreased with the growth of road motor transport and the later decline of the inner dock system, the dock railways, connected to the Blackwall line at Millwall Junction and thence to the former North London lines, remained in use until 1970. With the subsequent removal of tracks and equipment, the death of the Millwall Extension Railway seemed complete, but as we shall see later, it was to reappear in a new guise.

An Up train leaving North Woolwich behind N7 0-6-2T 69640 on 24th June 1961. The 1847 terminal building can be seen, to the left of the goods yard, still busy at this time. *R C Riley*

The North Woolwich Branch (map page 424)

There are some similarities between the lines we have just considered and the North Woolwich line and its appendages. Both started life as alternatives to river passenger services, handling pleasure traffic before becoming servants of the dock complexes and riverside industry. Sub branches were necessary in each case to reach dock extensions and industrial installations. Both systems for some years provided service to important places on the south bank of the river in connection with ferries and river steamers.

A proposal of 1833 for a railway from Commercial Road, Limehouse to a point in East Ham opposite Woolwich came to nothing but ten years later another scheme, promoted primarily to move seaborne coal from the riverside to places on the ECR, was more successful. The Eastern Counties & Thames Junction Railway, which obtained its act on 4th July 1844, was to be about 2¾ miles long, running from Stratford, ECR (Eastern Junction) to the mouth of the river Lea (Bow Creek) opposite Blackwall. Included in the act were a junction with the Northern & Eastern Railway 'near the engine house thereof' at Stratford and a passenger and goods pier in the Thames at the southern terminus. This site, at Bugsby's Reach, became known as Thames Wharf; to the north of it, between the Lea and the new railway, was the shipbuilding and ironworks of C J Mare & Co, which opened in 1846 becoming the Thames Ironworks & Shipbuilding Co in 1857.

Construction of the single line was delayed by flooding of Plaistow Marsh and other land east of Bow Creek, but it was eventually opened for freight on 29th April 1846. Business built up quickly and the track was to be doubled in conjunction with the extension to North Woolwich, to be mentioned in a moment. Coke ovens were set up at Thames Wharf to convert sea coal into locomotive fuel for the ECR and the N&ER.

Although somewhat indirect, the new line came closer to the important military and market town of Woolwich than any other railway and a 2½-mile extension across the marshes to a point immediately opposite this desirable objective could be cheaply built. This scheme, backed by George Parker Bidder, Samuel Morton Peto and the original Eastern Counties & Thames Junction directors, received sanction in an act of 21st July 1845 after meeting no opposition in Parliament, although the Board of Trade had suggested with some lack of foresight that it was unwarranted on grounds of public need.

Whilst preparations for the North Woolwich extension were going ahead the Eastern Counties & Thames Junction obtained powers to build a branch across the river Lea to the pepper warehouses of the East India Dock Co, and also a quarter-mile curve to the main line at Stratford, pointing towards London. The preamble to this 1846 act noted that the Eastern Counties Railway had purchased the EC&TJR, using the powers given in the original act of 1844. A year later, with the North Woolwich line under construction, the ECR also bought that undertaking, paying £2.10s (£2.50) for each of its 1,200 £25 shares.

Both the double track extension to North Woolwich and the new curve at Stratford were opened on 14th June 1847, together with the second track on the original section. An hourly passenger service ran between Bishopsgate and North Woolwich, supplemented after a few years by summer extras. From the junction at Thames Wharf, the route kept close to the river as far as its terminus opposite Woolwich, where at first there was nothing but the station, a hostelry known as the *Barge House*, some empty and decaying houses and the ferry pier built by the ECR. A contemporary writer though it 'singular to hear the whistle of the locomotive and the clatter of the iron wheels where, twelve months since, the heron, the plover, and the bittern roamed in undisturbed solitude'. Intermediate stations named Stratford Bridge and Barking Road were built where the Stratford and Barking roads crossed the line. Both were subsequently resited, but the sober and dignified Italianate building across the end of the tracks at North Woolwich survived to be damaged by German bombs in World War 2.

A small housing development, harbinger of many miles of mean streets, was soon in progress between the railway and Bow Creek, north of the Barking Road. Only a year after the opening of the line to passengers, a directory records:

> A new town called CANNING TOWN, is being formed; the streets being laid out, about 200 houses already erected. The neat cottages erected here each have a garden back and front, an entrance porch, a sitting room, kitchen, and wash house, fitted up with oven, boiler &c; and three chambers fitted up with handsome painted iron bedsteads. They possess that grand desideratum for the working classes, the maximum of comfort with the minimum of expense.

One street was named after Bidder, principal promoter of the North Woolwich Railway. Barking Road station was duly renamed Canning Town, although not until 1st July 1873. Its removal to the north of Barking Road took place in 1888, by which time the densely packed workers' houses were well established east of the railway at this point.

Two steam ferries came from a Barking shipyard to transport ECR passengers to and from Woolwich town while a third vessel was added later. Those not holding railway tickets were charged one penny to cross the water. Gravesend Steam Packet

Company steamers also called at the ECR pier and much of the early traffic on the railway was to and from the river services. At Bishopsgate, Woolwich passengers were allocated a special booking office, whence they proceeded to trains with rolling stock superior to that on most other ECR lines, 8-wheel coaches 40ft long and 9ft wide. From 1st June 1854 a second ECR service was worked half-hourly between Fenchurch Street and North Woolwich via Stratford Bridge. By that time the Bishopsgate trains were also half-hourly, and both services worked on Sundays, with the usual church intervals. The 1862 timetable showed North Woolwich as having the most lavish GER suburban service, with 81 trains daily (31 to and from Bishopsgate, 50 to and from Fenchurch Street).

The half-mile freight branch to the Blackwall pepper warehouses opened in June 1848 was soon to prove a useful support to the revenues from the North Woolwich passenger service. Using powers obtained in the 1847 Act, the ECR leased the warehouses from the Dock Company to form the Blackwall goods depot. Access to the bridge over the Lea involved a climb at 1 in 30 while there were further hazards including the 180ft-radius curves which restricted the line to four-coupled locomotives for much of its life.

Before the North Woolwich line had been completed, Bidder and his associates formed a land company which secured most of the riverside marsh all the way from Bow Creek to Gallions Reach and from the Barking Road to the river. At this time it was mostly pasture with only two or three houses, and could be obtained for a few pounds an acre. This was an astute move which was to help cushion the severe loss of passenger traffic following the opening of the South Eastern Railway's line from London to Woolwich and Gravesend on the south bank in July 1849. One of the early moves – the offer of reduced-rate season tickets to anyone caring to rent a house on the lonely and malarious marshes – was a complete failure, but the opening of pleasure gardens opposite North Woolwich station in May 1851, brought some business to the line at weekends and holidays. The facilities offered included bowling greens and a dancing saloon which, it was carefully noted, was readily convertible to a locomotive shed should the need arise. With the passing of years these gardens deteriorated to a vulgar resort, with standards of behaviour which shocked Victorian busybodies. A voluntary committee 'rescued' them to be placed in the care of the LCC, which in 1890 converted them to the Royal Victoria Gardens, the public park they remain today. Although a row of cottages appeared at North Woolwich about the time the line opened, White's *Essex Gazetteer* shows that in 1848 the stationmaster still found it necessary to live at East Ham. Efforts to attract industry to sites alongside the railway were rewarded in 1851 by the establishment of a glass factory and wharf, followed a year later by the arrival from Greenwich of S W Silver & Co's waterproofing works. Expanding its activities to the manufacturing of cable, ebonite and other rubber-based products, this firm gave its name to the small new community (Silvertown) which grew up around the works, about a mile west of North Woolwich. Towards the end of the nineteenth century, Silver's works were taken over by the India Rubber, Gutta Percha & Telegraph Works Co. Similar products were manufactured by W. T. Henley, who in 1853 bought 12 acres at North Woolwich, where a submarine cable and electrical works were erected.

Perhaps the most enterprising and ambitious of all the proposals to develop the area held by the land company was the scheme to build alongside the railway a deep water dock larger than any other in London, and the first to be adequately served by rail. These plans, in which Bidder, Peto, Kennard, and David Waddington, the chairman of the ECR, were all closely involved, were announced in 1849, Bidder was appointed chief engineer of what was to be named the Victoria Dock. As the entrance to the dock was to be formed near Bow Creek, it was necessary to carry the railway over it on a swing bridge. Because traffic would be interrupted as ships moved in and out, an avoiding line was built at the dock company's expense along the northern and eastern edges of the dock, branching from the original route at Thames Wharf Junction and joining it again at Silvertown, about three quarters of a mile west of the terminus. Under its statutory title of 'The Woolwich Abandoned Line', the discarded section around the south side of the dock passed to the dock company. Eventually the swing bridge, which had become something of a nuisance, was dismantled, leaving the remainder of this section to be worked as a long siding from the Silvertown end. Known as the Silvertown Tramway, this performed a useful role for many years in serving the numerous industrial installations which appeared between the dock and the river edge.

The Victoria Dock was opened on 26th November 1855, the avoiding line with its intermediate station of Victoria Dock, Custom House, carrying its first traffic at the end of that month. Industrial and dock development eventually required the provision of further stations: Victoria Docks, Tidal Basin in 1858 at the north western corner of the dock; and Silvertown, at the junction between the old and new lines, on 19th June 1863. By 1900 the latter was an important industrial centre with some 20 large firms and many smaller ones, chemicals, creosoting, and manure manufacturing brushing shoulders with jam, soup, candle, cocoa, and sugar factories. (Tate & Co. had established itself here in 1871, Lyle & Sons ten years later.)

To service the new dock, the ECR opened on 15th August 1854 a 1½-mile link between the NLR at Victoria Park and the North Woolwich line at Stratford. At first used only for freight, this carried passengers from 16th October, when the NLR started a service between Victoria Park and Stratford Bridge.*

Interchange with ECR main line trains was achieved through a new Low Level station at Stratford on the south side of the main line, which became known to travellers as the 'North London Station'.

Another connection was established with the construction of the LTSR between Barking and Bow. This opened on 31st March 1858, crossing above the North Woolwich branch about half-way between Canning Town and Stratford Bridge, the two lines connected by a curve between Lower and Upper Abbey Mills Junctions, allowing direct running between North Woolwich and Fenchurch Street via Bromley. A service over this route was started on 1st June 1858 in part replacement of the old one via Stratford Bridge.†

By 1864 the North Woolwich branch was carrying a total of about 40 passenger trains a day each way.

* The Victoria Park–Stratford Bridge service, popularly known as 'Stratford Jack', was taken over by the GER from 1st November 1866, reverting to the NLR a year later. This working by each company in alternate years continued until 1st November 1874 from which date the GER maintained it. On 1st October 1895 it was extended over a newly-provided additional track to a new third platform at Canning Town, some trains going through to North Woolwich.

† The Fenchurch Street–Stratford Bridge–North Woolwich service had operated between 1st June and 15th October 1854 and again from 1st May 1855. From 1st June 1858 alternate trains from Fenchurch Street went via Bromley.

A second large dock, called inevitably the Royal Albert, was opened to the east of what had now become the Royal Victoria on 6th May 1880 by the London & St Katharine's Dock Company (which had absorbed the Victoria Dock Company in 1864). This new dock was entered from Gallions Reach but was connected by a cut to its predecessor, requiring a second diversion of the North Woolwich branch. Work on the new line started with the construction of the dock in 1875, a cut-and-cover operation in dry ground which presented no difficulty. Known in the acts as the 'Substituted Line' and opened for traffic in June 1876 it passed through a 1,800ft brick-lined subway, partly double and partly twin tunnels, beneath what was to be the water channel between the two docks. Built at the cost of the dock company, it was vested in the GER, the dock company taking in return the old surface route (the 'Transferred Portion'), the severed sections of which they later rejoined by making the Connaught Road rail and road swing bridge over the shipping channel. The GER retained power to use the old route free of payment, and for many years freight trains too heavy to tackle the 1 in 50 tunnel ramps came this way, their speed restricted to 15mph. The small dimensions of the tunnels later prevented the GER from using its six-a-side passenger stock on the North Woolwich services.

After some 50 years the somewhat alarming discovery was made that ships were scraping the top of the tunnels as they passed through the cut. The subway was lowered and while the work was proceeding, from 30th September 1935 to 28th March 1936, passenger trains passed over the old surface line.

The new Albert Dock was served by a passenger railway running along its north side as far as the river bank at Gallions, to which we shall return later. On the south side of the dock was a goods line, branching from the 'Transferred Portion' and turning east over the top of the subway at its southern end.

F5 2-4-2T 7095 on a Palace Gates train at North Woolwich, c. 1938, looking to buffers.
Lens of Sutton

The street frontage of Canning Town station, c. 1904. Separate booking offices are indicated for Up and Down trains, and 'Trains every half hour' with 'Through bookings to Stations on the North London Line' are advertised. *Commercial postcard*

'Stratford Jack', the GER service from Victoria Park to Canning Town (some workings went on to North Woolwich) at the GER platform, Victoria Park Station, c. 1905. *Commercial postcard*

A third dock in the group, opened on 8th July 1921 by the Port of London Authority (which had taken over the dock companies in 1909), was named after King George V. Entered from Gallions Reach, it had water connection to the Royal Albert, which was parallel to it on the north, but this time no alterations were required in the North Woolwich lines. The dockside quays and warehouses were amply served by lines connected to the Royal Albert Dock south side railway.

This substantial provision of dock facilities, with the continuing industrial development largely associated with the docks and riverside wharves, assured the North Woolwich line of a steady flow of freight. Passenger liners using the docks also brought traffic, not only for their fuelling and provisioning, but boat trains, often as many as four for each ship.

Many hundreds of workmen crossed the Thames twice daily, many of them using North Woolwich station to get to and from their workplaces. After the introduction of the LCC Free Ferry on 23rd March 1889, most used this in preference to the penny GER ferries, which somewhat surprisingly survived until 30th September 1908. Electric tramways opened by the West Ham Corporation to a terminus at the north side of the Victoria Dock in 1904 and 1912 secured some of the railway's traffic from this direction but left it still an important passenger carrier. At this time a generous and varied train service was available. Thus in 1907 there were journeys to and from Fenchurch Street at 15-minute intervals all day including Saturdays; one of the four trains each hour worked via Abbey Mills Junctions and Bromley, another ran via Stratford Market and Bow Road, calling at all stations, whilst the third and fourth ran to and from Custom House, serving the Gallions line. One of these last two worked fast between Fenchurch Street and Canning Town. There was also an hourly train each way between Liverpool Street and North Woolwich via Stratford Market, calling at all stations; an approximately hourly service between Palace Gates and North Woolwich; seven trains each way daily between Stratford Market and Custom House on the Beckton service; and the shuttle between Victoria Park and Canning Town via Stratford Low Level about every half-hour. The latter carried bookings between GER and NLR stations.

The 1910 timetable shows no less than 96 trains each way daily at Canning Town, Mondays to Saturdays inclusive. Of these 52 ran to and from Fenchurch Street by both routes and 11 between North Woolwich and Palace Gates. On Sundays there were 46 trains each way, including six on the Palace Gates service and 24 to and from Fenchurch Street. The Canning Town–Victoria Park trains, not included in these totals, ran 35 journeys each way on weekdays and 27 on Sundays. Ten years later Canning Town had some 110 trains each way daily, 86 to and from North Woolwich (15 Palace Gates, 34 Fenchurch Street, four Victoria Park, seven Liverpool Street, 26 Stratford or Stratford Market). Stratford Market, a very busy station, was substantially rebuilt in 1894 with dormer windowed offices at street level and four platform faces including a central island.

Discouraged by the many level crossings and swing bridges, motor bus operators left the area alone, apart from a service between East Ham and Woolwich Ferry, which had little effect on the railway. Sunday trains to and from Victoria Park ceased after 30th September 1923, but the lavish provision on weekdays was maintained through the 1920s and 1930s, with Canning Town reaching a peak of activity just after World War 1, when there were over 130 trains each way including those terminating. This station, which had a bay platform on the Down side for the shuttle service to Victoria Park, was rebuilt at street level in 1932–33. The new brick building with hipped roof on the overline bridge included a spacious entrance hall with a three-windowed ticket office.

A new road through the dock area eventually brought a challenge to the railway's passenger business. Constructed under an unemployment relief programme, this Canning Town–Silvertown link included impressive concrete viaducts to span the railway and water barriers. Its eastern end was opened on 21st April 1934 and it was completed with the Silvertown viaduct and approaches in July 1935. Three years later, London Transport established a trolleybus service along this Silvertown Way, extending the existing Stratford–Canning Town route to the North Woolwich ferry terminal. Offering a decided contrast to the cramped and gas-lit GER carriages, the quiet, smooth-running electric buses made serious inroads into the railway revenue; this now entered a decline from which it never recovered, and which was to be accelerated by the effects of World War 2.

At the end of the 1930s there were still over 90 weekday trains to and from North Woolwich (15 Palace Gates, 37 Fenchurch Street via Bromley, four Victoria Park, 35 Stratford or Stratford Market) and 14 to and from Gallions (seven of them running through to and from Fenchurch Street). The Custom House–Stratford section also got four trains each way to and from Beckton. On Sundays there was an approximately hourly service between Chingford and North Woolwich (summer only) and a train about every hour between Fenchurch Street and North Woolwich. Sundays also saw 13 trains each way to and from Palace Gates.

The importance of freight has already been noticed. As dock traffic grew, the line between Stratford Bridge and Tidal Basin was quadrupled to allow the many goods trains to work alongside the intensive passenger service. A small beginning was made with this widening in 1860 and there were extensions in 1879–1883, and in 1890, the work reaching completion in 1892. By the turn of the century the branch served numerous goods depots, some operated by 'foreign' companies, as well as many riverside wharves and factory sidings. On the west side just south of Stratford Market station, the forage, fruit and vegetable market opened by the GER on 1st October 1879 was fed by an extensive layout. Traffic here reached over 52,000 tons in 1897. Immediately to the south of this was a GER coal depot. On the Down side, just south of Abbey Mills Lower Junction the West Ham and Plaistow Goods Depot was opened by the GER on 1st October 1906, extending as far east as Pretoria Road. On the opposite side, from connections with the Up and Down goods roads 270yd south of Abbey Mills Lower Junction, were reception and outward sidings linked with a branch of over half a mile which ran north and then south to serve the gas and electricity works on the east bank of the Lea. Canning Town Down side was the site of an LNWR goods yard opened in 1880. Beyond here, south of the Barking Road, was a GER depot dating from the opening of the line and rebuilt in 1904. Nearby, also on the Up side, the lines to the GER depot at East India Dock, Blackwall, branched off. To the south of this, off the old Silvertown alignment, were the GER Thames Wharf coal sidings on the site of the 1847 depot and also a Midland Railway Thames Wharf depot of 1870. In the latter year the Midland established a depot at Victoria Dock where there were also GER (c.1855), GNR (c.1885) and GWR (1902) depots. The Victoria Dock lines were reached through Port of London Authority sorting sidings south of the line between Tidal Basin and Custom House stations where movements were made by the PLA's own locomotives. There were

LNER F6 2-4-2T 7790 at Custom House, looking west, c. 1937. The indicator board on the loco-motive reads 'ALBERT DOCK'; there is no station of that name, but the train is destined for the PLA branch to Gallions, which ran along the north side of the Royal Albert Dock.

also two other GER depots, dating from the opening of the line, west of Silvertown station, and at North Woolwich. Private sidings abounded off the Silvertown Tramway and between Silvertown and North Woolwich. Apart from the Midland's Victoria Dock depot which had closed on 3rd April 1939, all these freight facilities were active at the outbreak of World War 2.

In the 1920s the weight of the goods and passenger traffic was such that the level-crossing gates on the branch were closed against road movement for about nine hours out of the 24 and at the busiest time of the day for 47 minutes in each hour. Rail was supreme as long queues of road trucks formed, waiting to enter or leave the docks area. At this time most freight was worked between Temple Mills Yard, Stratford and the yards and sidings at Thames Wharf and Silvertown or the PLA sidings at Victoria Dock. There were also through trains between the latter points and the LNER main line at Clarence Yard, Finsbury Park, and between the PLA sidings and the former LNWR yard at Canning Town and destinations on the LMSR. Locomotives of the latter company worked trains either via South Totten-ham or via Victoria Park, also carrying traffic to and from the GWR and SR systems. So serious was the congestion that when the railway companies received government encouragement to produce new works schemes for the relief of unemployment, the LMSR presented a Bill for an independent line between Wanstead (on the Totten-ham & Forest Gate line) and the PLA sidings at Custom House, alleging that this would avoid delays in negotiating 12 junctions on the 6¾-mile LNER route between South Tottenham and the docks. Needless to say this 1930 Bill was vigorously opposed by the LNER, and although it passed the Commons committee in modified form, it was thrown out by the Lords. Promising improvements, the LNER got its way, but did little or nothing before war came.

A northbound train in charge of LNER L1 2-6-4T 67701 leaving Stratford Low Level on 16th February 1957 after passing beneath the main line platforms. The two tracks on the right are now used by the Richmond–North Woolwich electric services. *R C Riley*

Almost from the start of World War 2, freight and passenger movement fell steeply. In accordance with contingency plans, labour and plant were sent from London docks to the provincial seaports, and in the late summer of 1940 the Royal group of docks were viciously attacked by the German air force. Damage was so great that from 7th September 1940 all passenger trains were terminated at Custom House, not reaching North Woolwich again until 1st January 1941. Wartime destruction and reductions in traffic caused the abandonment of the Fenchurch Street services in October 1940. Passenger loadings at Tidal Basin, a station badly mauled by bombing, were down to four per cent of the 1939 total in 1942, when receipts were less than £1 a day, and it was closed from 15th August 1943. Another wartime casualty was the remnant of the once busy service to and from Victoria Park, latterly cut back to Stratford Low Level; the old GER platforms at Victoria Park were used for the last time on 31st October 1942.

Some life returned to the docks in 1942 when they and the railways became busy with preparations for the invasion of North Africa; this was followed by similar activity for D-Day. Once again the PLA sorting sidings were bustling; freight train movements reached 40 a day, with up to 1,500 wagons handled.

Throughout the war the passenger service consisted of a shuttle between North Woolwich and Stratford with a few peak-hour workings to and from Palace Gates. A Sunday workmen's service ran until close of traffic on 16th March 1947. LNER N7 0–6–2T or GER 2–4–2T hauling Gresley 'quint-art' sets were now the usual rule.

Traffic patterns were changing. The mean little houses which crowded up to the line at Canning Town and between Silvertown and North Woolwich were sadly reduced or smashed about by the German bombs, forcing many of the dock workers to seek accommodation further afield. After the war they did not return to the trains, most of them coming in daily by road. For another 20 years the train service remained more than sufficient for the business offering. In 1960 for example, an hourly service with 10-minute frequency in the peak periods had replaced what had been a very largely peak-hours only service of only 26 trains a day each way. In 1962 there were 37 Down trains (six starting from Palace Gates, one from Cheshunt, the rest from Stratford Low Level) and 38 Up (nine through to Palace Gates, the rest terminating at Stratford Low Level). Other through workings had been withdrawn from 21st November 1960 with the introduction of electric service to Chingford and Enfield. Steam locomotives (N7 0-6-2T and L1 2-6-4T) hauled the indestructible quint-arts on all services until Rolls-Royce 3-car diesel sets were introduced on some workings from 1st January 1962. For a few more months the N7s continued on this their last regular assignment. These trains no longer called at Stratford Market, which had finally succumbed to road competition on the night of 4th May 1957, but in the 1950s and for a time in the 1960s, the branch still saw up to five boat trains a week between Liverpool Street and the docks, with BR locomotives working to and from the quayside over the PLA system. Saturday trains on the branch ceased after traffic on 4th January 1969, but in 1974 three-car diesel sets were still working 37 journeys each way daily, one third of them to and from Tottenham Hale.

Stratford Market station on its last day, 4th May 1957, with a North Woolwich train hauled by BR N7 0-6-2T 69661. War damage to the canopies remains unrepaired. *Lens of Sutton*

Stratford Southern Junction and signal box, looking north to Stratford Low Level station, 10th August 1979. The curve to the left of the picture allowed a direct run from the North Woolwich line to Liverpool Street or Fenchurch Street (via Bow Jc). Another curve to the right, beyond a signal box already dismantled by this date, gave direct access to the Colchester and Loughton lines. *Alan A Jackson*

For some years after the war, goods traffic remained buoyant with about 60 trains a day running on and off the branch at Stratford. After Bishopsgate depot was destroyed by fire in December 1964, Stratford Market depot assumed new life, taking all perishable traffic from the Continent via Harwich, with customs clearance on the spot. Some thousand tons of fruit and vegetables were then handled every week at the 660ft platform. Thames and Blackwall Wharves were modernised in 1961, each receiving two new electrically-operated rail-mounted cranes to transfer freight to and from the 10 barge berths, rail, and road vehicles. Freight to and from the docks declined slowly until the early 1960s, then very rapidly as the containerisation revolution had its effect. Seasonal traffic included the movement of East Anglian sugar beet into Tate & Lyle's sugar refinery at Silvertown, which required as many as four trains daily at the peak. The yards and sidings at Thames Wharf, Bow Creek, Blackwall, Silvertown and Canning Town (LNWR) each still had enough traffic in the 1950s to justify allocated shunting pilot locomotives, which were sub-shedded at Bow Creek and Silvertown. Stratford Market, West Ham & Plaistow , West Ham electricity works, Berk Chemicals, and Cohen's private sidings were all worked by pick-up freight trains. All goods workings were diesel hauled by 1965.

Most of the remaining freight facilities were closed as the 1960s came to an end: Thames Wharf (Midland) on 4th October 1965, Canning Town (LNWR) and the Blackwall and East India depots on 6th March 1967, Canning Town (GER) on 1st July 1968, and North Woolwich on 7th December 1970. After a century of use the connection to the former LTSR line was taken out in 1958 and the eastern curve at Stratford Low Level went in 1973. The 'top line' between Custom House and Silvertown, last worked in October 1967, was dismantled soon afterwards. From 25th August 1969, passenger trains used only one track (the former Down line) east of Custom House; the other was allocated to the much reduced freight workings to the Silvertown factories and Ward's scrapyard. With this change, North Woolwich and Silvertown signal boxes were closed. All freight movements ceased early in 1993 and the former Up line was taken out of use on 29th March that year. At Stratford Market, full load freight facilities and coal traffic were withdrawn from 5th November 1984 but the GER fruit and vegetable market lingered on, road-served, until May 1991 when it was transferred, together with historic Spitalfields, to a purpose-built complex at the edge of Hackney Marshes on the site of the former GER wagon works at Ruckhold Road, Leyton. After some use by engineer's trains, the Stratford Market sidings were lifted in 1988 and the whole site, together with its pub, licensed to open between 07.00 and 10.00, was taken for the rolling stock depot completed in 1996 ready for the Stratford extension of the Jubilee Line tube.

BR N7 0-6-2T 69608 on North Woolwich train at Stratford Low Level station, 21st May 1955, looking north west. The bridge carrying the main lines out of Liverpool Street and the Central Line tube tracks runs across the picture above the locomotive. Note the wartime pillbox at the right. *Alan A Jackson*

Much affected by the decay of activity at the Docks, passenger traffic between Stratford and North Woolwich continued to decline in the late 1960s and early 1970s. When BR was driven to suggest further service cuts in 1976, the Greater London Council, already much involved with planning redevelopment of the rundown Docklands areas, came to the rescue with a grant which enabled a Monday to Friday half hourly frequency to be maintained between Tottenham Hale (or Stratford Low Level) and North Woolwich until early evening.

But the GLC had more ambitious plans and what followed owed much to its initiatives. From 14th May 1979 the train service was rearranged with diesel railcar sets operating Mondays to Fridays at 20 min intervals at peak hours and half-hourly off peak between North Woolwich and Camden Road, reopening to passengers the former GER line between Stratford Low Level and Victoria Park (closed 1942) and the former NLR line thence to Dalston Junction (closed 1944). These trains over what was renamed the 'Crosstown Link Line' called at a new island platform station at West Ham under the LT station and later connected to it by a covered way. With GLC funding, Silvertown, Custom House and Canning Town stations were all rebuilt during 1979. At Silvertown the former Up platform was completely demolished and the rebuilt platform and waiting room were on the north side. Canning Town's dreary war-damaged platforms were replaced by an island with a glass-walled waiting shelter. This was reached by open stairs from the road overline bridge, where a little later a flat-roofed ticket office and entrance building replaced the much more attractive LNER station of 1933. Few changes were made at Stratford Low Level apart from a new waiting room on the Up platform and a new subsidiary ticket office for passengers interchanging between the main line or the Underground and the North Woolwich line.

Entirely new stations funded by the GLC and the Docklands Partnership were opened near former NLR station sites on 12th May 1980 at Hackney Central and Hackney Wick (just east of the former Victoria Park platforms). Both were of similar design with a sloping walkway to a brick building housing ticket hall, waiting and staff room. An open footbridge provided access to the Up platforms, which had an enclosed waiting room. Local opinion formers ungratefully commented that the stations were 'open, wind swept and inhospitable places with open footbridges and minimal platform cover'. At the formal opening ceremony, Sir Peter Parker drew attention to the lack of lavatories, commenting enigmatically that to have none at all was better than offering vandalised facilities.

During the first year of operation, the quality of the new diesel car service was seriously eroded by staff shortages, the resulting cancellations doing much to discourage new traffic; as a driver explained when the line was visited in August 1979 and we watched a disappointed man tear up his free promotional ticket in disgust at the absence of an advertised train, 'we have the drivers, we have the train sets, but we can't get enough guards'. He went on to explain how hapless passengers were left stranded at the unstaffed stations east of Stratford, unaware when, if ever, their timetabled train would arrive. A half-hourly Saturday service was introduced on 16th July 1983 but did not run east of Stratford. Some notice seems to have been taken of the criticism of the low-cost new stations of 1980; Dalston Kingsland, opened on 16th May 1983 to replace the old Dalston Junction station, was a much better job, given a pleasing appearance by large areas of red brick and adequately sheltering the passenger's path from street to the canopied waiting areas. This station

North Woolwich station exterior, fronting Pier Road, 7th December 1974. This fine building, which escaped destruction in the punishing 1940 German air attacks on the docklands, is now restored as a museum of the Great Eastern Railway. The sole remaining platform, used by the electrified service to Stratford and Richmond, is reached through a replacement building to the left.
Alan A Jackson

stood exactly on the site of the original NLR Kingsland station (9th November 1850–31st October 1865) and generated a satisfying degree of traffic from its very convenient position in a busy retail centre on Kingsland High Street opposite Ridley Road Street Market.

At North Woolwich, where the layout was reduced to one track, the rebuilt platform on the south side was served by a new single-storey ticket office building with a heated waiting room which was completed on the former freight yard site early in 1980. With funding from the London Docklands Development Corporation, the heavily-vandalised and war damaged 1847 terminal building was acquired by the Passmore Edwards Museum Trust and handsomely restored to house a well-arranged museum of the Great Eastern Railway. Opened in September 1984, this was sustained by revenue funding from the London Borough of Newham.

Signalling was modernised in 1984; the remaining manual boxes, at Custom House, Abbey Mills and Stratford Southern Junction, were closed and from 18th November the whole line was controlled from the Stratford Panel, with track circuit block working to Custom House and one-train working thence over the single line to North Woolwich. Around the same time the old semaphore signalling between Stratford and Dalston was also replaced with three aspect colour lights controlled from Stratford, allowing closure of the two existing boxes.

This work prepared the way for the introduction from 13th May 1985 of 750V dc third rail two-car electric trains working weekdays and Sundays at basic 20 min intervals between North Woolwich and Richmond, taking 61/62 min. Designated 'North London Link', this amounted to an almost total diversion through north east London of the former NLR services to the City terminus at Broad Street station, leaving the Dalston Junction–City line to rush hour Watford services only. Funded by the GLC, the electrification completed the Council's bold plans of the late 1970s with one exception: a tunnel under the Thames from Silvertown to Woolwich Arsenal station. Not everyone was pleased; there was some grumbling in the Hampstead area at the loss of direct access to the City, exacerbated by the unsatisfactory interchange with Moorgate trains at Highbury but it soon became apparent that the new service was going to produce a higher level of traffic than before.

The newly-electrified section over the 8½ miles between Dalston Western Junction and North Woolwich included a station at Homerton, on the site of one which had last seen passenger trains on the same day of the month 41 years earlier. Long-planned, it was said that this station, funded by the GLC and the Department of the Environment, had to await electrification because the diesel sets could not be given an additional stop without creating pathing problems west of Dalston Junction. Sited in a densely populated and deprived area with two large hospitals, Homerton was soon generating a satisfactory traffic. Dalston Kingsland and Hackney Central also did well. Less successful was Hackney Wick, which had a very thin catchment area consisting mainly of industrial units and recreational open land. By mid 1987 it was reported that over the North London line as a whole there had been an increase of some 2,400 passenger journeys a day, a figure which exceeded that used by the GLC in making a case for electrification. In October 1989 the former Southern Region slam-door electric stock first used was replaced with sliding door Class 313 units which gave a smoother ride and an increase of 50 per cent in capacity. But there was a down side: plagued by cancellations, unpunctuality and a low standard of car cleaning, service quality remained poor well into the 1990s.

For a second time, Silvertown station was rebuilt in 1990, given a new ticket office and waiting area as 'Silvertown & London City Airport'. Immediately to its north, the two single track tunnels beneath the channel connecting the Victoria and Albert Docks had long been prone to flooding (at times up to 5ft above the rails) but with the high level lines now closed and electric working, almost any depth of water brought an interruption to rail services and this nuisance could no longer be tolerated. It was finally tackled in 1994–95 when major structural repairs and waterproofing were undertaken, backed up by a modern drainage and pumping system; the cost was funded by the owners, the London Dockland Development Corporation.

The opportunity to carry out this improvement arose when the line had to be closed for another reason. Substantial works in the Canning Town area in connection with the extension of the Jubilee tube line from Green Park to Stratford required suspension of the train service between Stratford and North Woolwich from close of traffic on 28th May 1994 until 29th October 1995. With the reopening on the latter date, Canning Town station was resited on the south side of the road bridge to provide convenient interchange facilities with the new tube, bus and DLR stations at this point. West Ham emerged from this closure with a rebuilt platform and improved interchange facilities with the LT services to the City and Barking/Upminster.

Long periods of closure, operating problems and a poor public image have combined to seriously erode the impact of the electric services on this line, discouraging maximum traffic development; at the time of writing they present a challenge to management as the second decade of electric working begins. Beyond those matters capable of internal solution, the line's future will depend very much on the successful regeneration of what is still a very run-down area for the time being somewhat overprovided with public transport, and also perhaps upon the completion of the rail crossing of the Thames at this point.

The Beckton Branch

(map page 424)

The North Woolwich line sprouted two branches of its own, the first of these serving the huge riverside works of the Gaslight & Coke Company, one of those splendid manifestations of Victorian energy hidden away in unfashionable corners of the metropolis. Sited on desolate marsh to the south-west of Barking Creek, the works were well placed to receive sea-borne coal, but poorly served by land – nothing more at first than a rough road from Barking. Construction started in November 1868, the first gas was produced on 25th November 1870, and full production began the following month. A 'village' of some 130 workmen's cottages, houses for foremen and officials, a church, chapel and recreation ground was built nearby and what Thorne called 'this busy if not altogether lovely colony', which was often cocooned in its own private fog, received the name Beckton after the first Governor of the company. By 1900, it was contributing half the rateable value of Barking.

A Gaslight & Coke Company Act of 1871 authorised the construction at the company's expense of a single line from the North Woolwich branch at Custom House Junction, about a quarter-mile east of Custom House station. Other than the level-crossings of Connaught Road and East Ham Manor Way there were no intermediate stations or special features on the 1m 56ch across the marsh. Beyond East Ham Manor Way, the track was double on the company's own land.

Freight traffic started on 14th October 1872, followed on 17th March 1873 by workmen's trains operated by the gas company, but the line was leased to and worked by the GER from 18th March 1874. A clause in the 1871 Act required the operation of a penny workmen's train each way on weekdays between Barking Road and Beckton before 06.00 (Down) and after 18.00 (Up), but in practice these and other passenger trains worked to and from Stratford Market or Stratford Low Level at times suited to the shift changes at the gas works. Throughout the line's history all passenger trains were in fact workmen's trains, tickets issued in the afternoon being available for return the following morning. It is doubtful whether the small booking office at Beckton saw much use, except perhaps in the early years. Latterly, tickets were always collected from Down trains at Custom House.

At Beckton station, 2m 1ch from Custom House, the long and (of course) gas-lit platform, with its wooden shelter and small signalbox, was on the north side of the line about a half-mile inland from the river wall. From here the tracks continued into the works, which were sited east and north of the station, and were eventually to occupy about 360 acres. They were served by about 40 miles of internal standard gauge lines, fully signalled and latterly worked by over thirty 0–4–0T steam locomotives (replaced by Planet diesels from 1959). Most journeys were to carry coal between the two collier piers and the retort houses. A full-scale locomotive works and erecting shop was maintained by the gas company for many years.

Freight on the branch comprised gasworks supplies and materials inwards and some coke outward, but the bulk of the coke went by water. Around 1892 the GER opened a freight yard (West Ham South Depot) on the north side of the branch just east of Connaught Road level crossing.

Access to the gasworks for employees not living at Beckton was much improved by the opening of two electric tramways in the 1900s. East Ham Corporation's line from the Town Hall to New Beckton (Cyprus) via East Ham Manor Way was inaugurated on 22nd June 1901 and extended to the Royal Albert Dock on 25th March 1903. At the level-crossing with the railway both tramcars and trains were

Beckton station
looking west,
1948.
Mowat Collection

controlled by semaphore signals worked from Beckton Tramway Crossing box. A second tramway, coming south from Barking to terminate close to the northern boundary of the gasworks, opened on 1st December 1903, to be extended to the centre of Barking on 15th December. Whilst these tramway facilities must have had some effect on the travel patterns of Beckton workers, some of the journeys would be entirely new as the demand for labour increased with the continuing expansion of the works. The railway remained the most convenient route for those who lived at Canning Town or Stratford.

At this time there were seven trains each way, originating at Stratford Market; by 1918 the terminus was Stratford Low Level, but the number of trains was unaltered. Weekday arrivals at Beckton were 05.37, 06.58, 13.33, 16.11 and 21.33. Departures were at 06.20, 12.28 (Saturdays), 14.31, 16.18, 17.24, and 22.15. Sundays saw arrivals at Beckton at 05.38 and 21.33, with departures at 06.27, and 21.42. It will be seen that although office workers had a convenient afternoon departure they had to rise early or make a more circuitous journey via Gallions and the East Ham tramcar. In 1939 the branch had only four trains each way and still the two on Sundays, the journey time being 20 minutes for the five miles from Stratford, calling at all stations. Both tramcar services had by then been replaced by motor buses and bus journeys from Stratford and Canning Town were possible via the Barking by-pass built in 1927. Few now used the trains, and it was no great hardship when the LNER closed the line after severe bomb damage in September 1940. Service was briefly resumed after repairs, but passenger trains ran for the last time on 28th December that year.

Freight traffic continued at much the same level as previously for another two decades, but there were a few brief hours of wartime glory. A shortage of fuel to heat huts and water at the many airfields and camps in eastern England during the winter of 1943–44 brought Beckton to the rescue with 21 trains a week carrying off its coke mountain to 113 sites via 86 wayside goods yards.

West Ham South yard was closed on 7th December 1964, leaving the branch to the much diminished freight requirements of the gasworks, by then only a dozen wagons a day, even though the working timetable included an unaltered layover of one hour, relic of busier days long before. As coal gas production was run down, rail traffic faded to nothing, bringing complete closure in February 1971.

The Gallions Branch (map page 424)

The Rudyard Kipling character who asked 'Is it Tilbury and a tender, or Gallions and the Dock?' neatly summarised one function of the second shoot from the North Woolwich branch. When the London & St Katharine Docks Company planned to build the Royal Albert Dock in the misty uninhabited marshes east of Canning Town, it was realised that the normal dock railways for freight would not be enough. Some sort of passenger facilities would be required to serve the liners expected to berth in the dock. The dock company therefore built on its land a 1m 61ch double-track line between the North Woolwich branch at Connaught Road and the river edge at Gallions, punctuating it with four closely-spaced stations. This 'Royal Albert Dock Railway', which passed close to the northern boundary of the new dock area, was not ready in time for the opening of the dock on 6th May 1880, but a limited train service worked from 3rd August. Having brought the line into the world, the dock company decided to make an honest woman of itself, belatedly turning to Parliament in 1882 for authority 'to maintain and use' the railway 'as if the same had been authorised by this act'. The act also gave powers to make working arrangements with the GER, restricted the line's traffic to passengers and parcels, and required a penny workmen's train in the Down direction before 07.00 and back again after 18.00 each day.

At Custom House station the GER built a bay on the up side for the Gallions trains, renting it out to the dock company. The new line began 34ch east of here at Royal Albert Dock Junction, whose signal box also controlled Connaught Road, the first station, another 220yd further east. Like all others on the dock railway, this was fully staffed by the dock company, which issued its own tickets, and it had all the signalling and amenities of a normal passenger station. Beyond it, the tracks swung north-east before running almost dead straight eastwards as far as Manor Way. About half-way along this straight section was the second station, simply and aptly named Central. At Manor Way, the station (which did not open until July 1881 and was called Manor Road until 1882) was at first on the west side of the road bridge over the line. Gallions station followed very quickly, sited about half-way along the north side of the dock entrance basin. Here the dock company erected a pleasant-looking hotel in the style of a large country house (described by Baedeker as 'small, but first class') for the use of liner passengers and their relatives and friends. Beyond the platforms the tracks went on to join the dock freight lines, eventually passing on to a pier which in later years was used as a coaling jetty by William Cory & Son Ltd, who had their own locomotives.

As already mentioned, the first trains ran on 3rd August 1880, probably in the first few weeks to and from Central only but Bradshaw, showing the service for the first time in November 1880, indicated an approximately half-hourly frequency between Gallions and Custom House, taking 10 minutes, with the last train of the day leaving Gallions at 19.00. The service first appeared in GER timetables in April 1881 when 33 trains a day were shown, but only to and from Central. By July that year, both Bradshaw and the GER timetables were agreed on 33 trains a day each way between Custom House and Gallions, including eight each way to and from Fenchurch Street. This service, which probably began on 1st July 1881, included 13 each way on Sundays (four running to and from Fenchurch Street). All local trains were worked by three 2–4–0T bought by the dock company from the LNWR, these continuing in use until the GER took over all workings on 1st July 1896. Fares, first,

Royal Albert Dock Co 2-4-0T loco No.7 on Custom House train at Gallions terminus c. 1900. *Lens of Sutton*

second, and third class, to all stations on the dock line were the same in each case and tickets were collected at Connaught Road. During the early part of the twentieth century, the railway was at its busiest; there were in 1900 about 53 trains each way, 35 locals between Custom House and Gallions, 16 to and from Fenchurch Street (two via Stratford Market), the others to and from Stratford Market or Stratford Low Level. Two Down workings from Liverpool Street were not balanced. Sundays saw only a shuttle between Custom House and Gallions. The heavy weekday provision catered primarily for dock workers, overseers and office staff, many of whom returned to their Canning Town homes for midday dinner, thus creating four peaks daily.

Sunday trains ceased after 27th June 1915; from the end of 1917 there was no service on bank holidays. From early 1918 until the end of World War 1 a special service was worked over the branch in connection with a ferry carrying munitions workers between Gallions pier and the northern installations at Woolwich Arsenal. At this period the basic service on the line was about half-hourly, but only seven trains worked to and from Fenchurch Street.

With the change in traffic patterns created by the electric tramcar and motor bus services already mentioned, the need for a local service diminished and it was discontinued from 6th July 1932. As successor to the GER, the LNER maintained through workings to and from Stratford or London, while PLA staff and signalmen continued to work the line.

In 1938 there were 15 Down trains, eight from Fenchurch Street (two via Stratford), four from Victoria Park and three from Stratford Low Level. Eight Up trains worked to Fenchurch Street (one via Stratford), two to Victoria Park and six to Stratford Low Level. This service provided trains spread throughout the day, concentrated at rush hours, but there was nothing from Saturday lunchtime until Monday morning.

Over the years some changes were made in the stations. Gallions was replaced from 12th December 1886 by a larger station of the same name, sited 275yd east. This had an island platform, the south face for the dock company's local trains, the north for the GER workings. About a year later, Manor Way station was moved to the east side of the road bridge and underwent further rebuilding when the old wooden bridge was replaced by a more substantial structure in 1926. Around the same time the somewhat elaborate wooden building at Gallions was demolished and a smaller one put in its place. Central, the least used of the stations, was reduced to halt status form 1st November 1933.

When German aircraft swarmed over the docks on Saturday afternoon 7th September 1940, passenger service had ceased for the week. A stick of bombs put the line completely out of action, and although repaired and used for wagon and van storage, it never carried passenger trains again. Formal abandonment was authorised by the PLA Act of 1950, but Cory's used the tracks for some time after.

The DLR: or New Life for the Old

Brief reference* must now be made to London's latest local railway. Happily this provides a fitting conclusion to both chapter and book since, for all the controversy and criticism it has generated, the Docklands Light Railway, in the extent to which it has made use of the formations of the several lines just described, nicely illustrates the abiding nature of London's railnet.

Planned as a transport system expressly to further the regeneration of London's North Bank docklands, the DLR had a chequered childhood. Its initial underfunding, apparently based on an investment appraisal that totally ignored its ability to turn negative land values to extremely positive ones, produced a railway unable to cope with the crowds arriving on its opening day. Almost at once, if it were to be of any use at all, its capacity had to be upgraded at very considerable further cost and it was later considered politically expedient to back it up by the very expensive extension through its catchment area of the Jubilee Line, a conventional tube railway.

Something of a curiosity amongst railways, the DLR, despite its name, has long seemed to share more characteristics with a full-scale urban electric railway than with the modern light rail systems of the USA and Western Europe. Though enthusiasts will point to its sharp curves, steep gradients and rolling stock as evidence to the contrary, this impression has grown stronger as the system has developed. Necessarily, by the choice of a conductor rail traction supply, its right of way is rigidly segregated throughout; even when it uses a road (Royal Albert Way) its central reservation is very convincingly isolated from it. The inner portion to the Bank involved extremely costly deep level tube construction; all its stops are at high-platform stations, some of them surprisingly elaborate. Nor is there anything 'light' about its civil engineering or its sophisticated signalling and control systems.

But our main theme here is the manner in which the DLR in large part runs alongside, above, and in some cases actually on the roadbeds of the London & Blackwall, the London & Blackwall Extension, the Millwall Extension, the North London Railway through Poplar and Bow, and the North Woolwich, Gallions and Beckton branches. This feature is important in the way it influenced the pattern of the DLR layout and even the planning of the northern Docklands development as a whole, shaping these just as strongly as the topography of the principal docks. Knowledge of the DLR's relationship with its predecessors can also enrich the interest of a journey over it. A careful student will wish to unravel this topographical puzzle by comparing large scale maps of various dates but here we shall do our best with verbal description.

The first stage of the DLR, seven and a half miles of line and 15 stations, electrified at 750V dc, with bottom contact third rail, was opened to the public on 31st August 1987. Shortly after leaving the little Tower Gateway terminus, close by Fenchurch Street station, the double track occupies the southern side of the widened London & Blackwall viaduct (formerly occupied by two of the four approach tracks to Fenchurch Street), passing through the DLR Shadwell station, which is about 220yd/201 metres west of the L&BR's Shadwell. At Limehouse station, the DLR parts from the main line, taking over the original roadbed of the L&BR, using its

---

* Brief because its origins and development are fully treated in the publishers' *Docklands Light Rail Official Handbook* (Bibliography section 6).

1840 viaduct as far as a point on the east side of West India Dock Road. From here, it rises steeply but, eastwards, does not deviate much from the course of the L&BR. Beyond the DLR Poplar station, the new railway, again at ground level, turns sharply north to join the roadbed of the former NLR to Bow, passing beneath Poplar High Street. The DLR's All Saints station occupies the precise site of the NLR Poplar station but its next stop, Bow Church, is on the south side of Bow Road whilst the NLR's impressive station abutted the north side of the overline bridge. Having passed under Bow Road, the DLR now veers east to climb up alongside the northernmost part of the Blackwall Extension Railway before running along the south side of the former Eastern Counties Railway main line into Stratford station, making use of one of the two tracks formerly connecting the latter to the Fenchurch Street line.

South of its junction at Poplar, the Isle of Dogs section of the initial DLR at first follows a completely new alignment across the West India Docks before veering east to join the formation of the Millwall Extension Railway at a point just under a quarter mile north of the DLR Crossharbour station. There the platforms are more or less on the same site as the MER's Millwall Docks (Glengall Road) station of 1871, which was also above street level. Continuing south, the DLR then follows the MER roadbed through Mudchute DLR to the Island Gardens terminus. This last section is laid on the 27-brick arch 1872 viaduct of the MER but the DLR ends slightly to the north of the original North Greenwich terminus, which was very close to the water's edge, its site now occupied by a boat club.

The second above ground section of the DLR, from Poplar eastwards to Beckton, five route miles, with ten new stations, was opened on 28th March 1994. This takes up the approximate line of the London & Blackwall Railway almost as far as the site of that company's Poplar station, but is carried above it at a higher level. It then veers north east, crossing Bow Creek on a new alignment before turning south and east to accompany the North Woolwich branch to a point just beyond Custom House station. The Canning Town DLR station is slightly south of the original 1847 station site but at a higher level and the DLR's Royal Victoria is about 300yd/274 metres east of the Tidal Basin station of 1858–1943. At Custom House, the old and new station sites are alongside. Just beyond Royal Albert station, the DLR takes up the approximate line of the Gallions branch, with Beckton Park DLR virtually on the site of the latter's Central station of 1880–1940. After this the DLR diverges north away from the Gallions branch at a point near the site of the former Manor Way station, allowing the passenger a glimpse of the Gallions Hotel, which still stands, looking somewhat lonely and neglected at the time of writing. Soon turning west, as if it had lost its way, the DLR runs for a short distance parallel with Winsor Terrace, following if not precisely over the roadbed of the terminal section of the former Beckton branch. However the DLR's Beckton terminus is just under half a mile west of its namesake's former platform, Away to the east, the new DLR Beckton depot occupies part of the extensive gas works site.

So it is that some of London's oldest local railways have played an important part in the planning and realisation of one of its newest, and as we have seen earlier in this book, this process is also occurring in south London with Croydon Tramlink. In this way, even those local lines that have been abandoned live on in another guise and there will no doubt be more examples as the London rail system adapts and develops to meet twenty-first century needs.

SOURCES AND BIBLIOGRAPHY

Note: This bibliography is not comprehensive but will give an indication of the sources used and also where the reader can find further information and background. Only some of the secondary sources listed in sections 5–7 were consulted in the preparation of this book.

1: GENERAL AND PRIMARY SOURCES

Parliamentary papers, private bills and acts and evidence before parliamentary committees (House of Lords Record Office).

Railway companies' minute books, reports and other papers (Public Record Office and, for London Transport and predecessors, the Greater London Record Office).

Railway companies', BR and LT public and working timetables and appendices.

Passenger statistics and freight loadings supplied to the author by BR.

Traffic Circulars, London Transport Railways and predecessors.

2: NEWSPAPERS AND PERIODICALS

Contemporary accounts and reports in:

Branch Line News, British Railways Magazine, Daily Telegraph, Edgware Gazette, Electric Railway, Electric Railway Society Journal, Estates Gazette, Evening News (London), *Great Western Railway Magazine, Herapath's Railway & Commercial Journal, Illustrated London News, Law Reports, Railnews, Railway & Travel Monthly, Railway Gazette, Railway Magazine, Railway News, Railway Observer, Railway Times, Southern Railway Magazine, Surrey Advertiser, Times, TOT Magazine, Tottenham & Edmonton Advertiser, Transport & Travel Monthly, Underground News.*

3: MAPS AND PLANS

Ordnance Survey maps, various editions and scales, pre 1940

Edward Stanford's *New Map of Metropolitan Railways and Improvements sanctioned in 1866*, 1866.

New Large Scale Atlas of London & Suburbs . . ., George W Bacon, 1880 and 1888

Stanford's map of the County of London, 1905

Stanford's Indexed Atlas of the County of London, 1911

Bacon's Atlas of London & Suburbs 1904, 1912, 1928

Bartholomew's Reference Atlas of Greater London, Seventh Edition 1940, Ninth Edition, 1954, Eleventh Edition, 1961.

Geographia Ltd, *The Authentic Map Directory of London & Suburbs*, First Edition 1924, Third Edition 1933.

Geographia Ltd, *London Map Directory . . .*, First post war Edition, 1964

Nicholson Greater London Street Atlas, Comprehensive Edition, 1995

4: STATE PAPERS

The Royal Commission on London Traffic, Report, Evidence, Appendices (eight vols), 1905–06

Reports of the London Traffic Branch, Board of Trade, 1908–15

London & Home Counties Traffic Advisory Committee, Report upon the Public Inquiry held in October 1925 with respect to the Travelling Facilities to and from North and North East London, HMSO, 1926

London & Home Counties Traffic Advisory Committee, Public Inquiry with regard to the alleged inadequacy of travelling facilities to, from, and within, certain areas of East London, Minutes of Evidence and Report, HMSO, 1926

London & Home Counties Traffic Advisory Committee, Public Inquiry with regard to the alleged inadequacy of travelling facilities to, from, and within, certain areas South East of London, Minutes of Evidence and Report, HMSO, 1926

5: SECONDARY SOURCES: GENERAL

Acworth, W M, *The Railways of England*, various editions from 1888

Allerton, R J, *London County Council Housing Service Handbook*, 1962

Anon, *The Country at London's Door*, 1926 (Southern Rly)

 Country Homes at London's Door, 1927 (Southern Rly)

 Southern Homes, 1932 (Southern Railway)

Improving London's Transport, 1946 (*Railway Gazette* Supplement)

North London Railway, A Pictorial Record, 1979 (HMSO)

Barker, T C and Robbins, Michael, *A History of London Transport, Vol 1, The Nineteenth Century*, 1963, and *Vol. 2 The Twentieth Century to 1970*, 1974

Barran, Sir David, *London Rail Study*, 1974

Bayman, Bob and Connor, Piers, *Underground Official Handbook*, Third Edition, 1994

Borley, H V, *Chronology of London Railways*, 1982

Brown, David and Jackson, Alan A, *Network South East Handbook*, 1990

Clark, R H, *A Southern Region Chronology and Record 1803–1965*, 1964

Connor, Piers, *Going Green: The Story of the District Line*, Second Edition, 1994.

Course, E A, *London Railways*, 1962

London's Railways Then & Now, 1987

Croome Desmond F, and Jackson, Alan A, *Rails Through the Clay, A History of London's Tube Railways*, Second Edition, 1993

Crump, Norman, *By Rail to Victory*, 1947

Darwin, Bernard, *War on the Line*, 1946

Dickens's Dictionary of London, 1896

Dobson, C G, *A Century and A Quarter*, 1951 (Hall & Co.)

Edmonds, Alexander, *History of the Metropolitan District Railway Company to June 1908*, 1973

Faulkner, J N and Williams, R A, *The London & South Western Railway in the Twentieth Century*, 1988

Gray, Adrian, *The London, Chatham & Dover Railway*, 1984

South Eastern Railway, 1990

Howard Turner, J T, *The London Brighton & South Coast Railway* (three vols, 1977, 1978, 1979

Jackson, Alan A, *London's Termini*, Second Edition, 1985

London's Metropolitan Railway, 1986

'London Transport under the Greater London Council', in *Modern Railways*, February, 1986

'BR in London: the GLC contribution' in *Modern Railways*, April 1986

Semi-Detached London, Suburban Development, Life & Transport, 1900–39, Second Edition, 1991

(ed.) *The Memories & Writings of a London Railwayman . . .*, 1993

Jeafferson, J C, *Life of Robert Stephenson*, 1864

Klapper, C F, *Sir Herbert Walker's Southern Railway*, 1973

Lawrence, David, *Underground Architecture*, 1994

Leboff, David, *London Underground Stations*, 1984

Lee, Charles E, *Workmen's Fares . . .*, 1944

The Metropolitan District Railway, 1988

London County Council, *Housing . . .*, 1928

Housing 1928–30, 1931

London Housing, 1937

Moody, G T, *Southern Electric 1909–79*, Fifth Edition, 1979

Peacock, Thomas P, *Great Western London Suburban Services*, New Edition, 1978

Pratt, Edwin A, *British Railways & The Great War* (two vols), 1921

Robbins, Michael, *The North London Railway*, Seventh Edition, 1974

Surrey County Council, *Rail Line Improvements in Surrey (SWT Operating Area), Final Report*, 1995

Taylor, Derek and Bush, David, *The Golden Age of British Hotels*, 1974

Thornbury, W and Walford, Edward, *Old & New London* (six vols.), 1897

Thorne, James, *Handbook to the Environs of London* (two volumes) 1876

Waters, Lawrence, *Britain's Rail Super Centres: London – The Great Western Lines*, 1993

Welch, H D, *The London, Tilbury & Southend Railway*, 1963

White, H P, *A Regional History of the Railways of Great Britain: Vol 3 Greater London*, 1987

Williams, R A, *The London & South Western Railway*, (two vols) 1968, 1973

6: SECONDARY SOURCES: LOCAL STUDIES

Anon, *A Short History of the Plessey Tunnel Factory 1941–2*, 1942

Return to North Woolwich: The North Woolwich Railway and Transport Around the Royal Docks, 1987

Bayliss, Derek A, *Retracing The First Public Railway*, 1981

Blake, Jim and James, Jonathan, *Northern Wastes: The Story of the Uncompleted Northern Line Extensions*, 1987

Body, Geoffrey, *The Blackwall and Millwall Extension Railways*, nd
Connor, J E, *All Stations to Poplar*, 1980
  Stepney's Own Railway: A History of The London & Blackwall System 1984
Course, Edwin, *The Bexleyheath Line*, 1980
Cresswell, Henrietta, *Winchmore Hill, Memories of a Lost Village*, 1907
Davies, Reg and Bevan, David, *Rails to the People's Palace and the Parkland Walk*, Third Edition, 1994
Elliot, Alan, *Wimbledon's Railways*, 1982
Frost, K A, *The Romford-Upminster Branch*, 1964
Frost, Ken, 'Grays-Upminster-Romford', in *Railways South East: The Album*, 1994
Goode, C T, *The Railways of Uxbridge*, 1983
  The Hertford Loop Line, 1984
  To The Crystal Palace, 1984
Goudie, F W, *Metropolitan to Jubilee: Wembley Park to Stanmore*, 1986
Hamilton, J E, *The Industries of Crayford*, 1980
Heselton, Kenneth Y, *Sunbury and the Thames Valley Railway*, 1975
Hodge, Peter, *The Hertford Loop . . .,*1976
Horsburgh, E L S, *Bromley, Kent, From the Earliest Times to the Present Century*, 1929
Jowett, E M, *Raynes Park: A Social History*, 1987
Kidner, R W, *The Dartford Loop Line 1866–1966*, 1966
  The North Kent Line, 1977
Lake, G H, *The Railways of Tottenham*, 1946
Lee, Charles E, *Early Railways in Surrey, The Surrey Iron Railway . . .*, 1944
Peacock, Thomas B, *PLA Railways*, 1952
Pearce, Alan; Jolly, Stephen and Hardy, Brian, *Docklands Light Rail Official Handbook*, 1994
Pond, C C, *The Walthamstow and Chingford Railway*, 1982
Robbins, Michael, *Railway Development in South West London*, Transactions London & Middlesex
    Archaeological Society, vol 34 (1983), 259–269
Ruegg, R, *Summer Rambles Round Woolwich*, 1847
Scott, Peter G, *Harrow & Stanmore Railway*, Second Edition, 1981
Sherwood, Tim, *Change at Clapham Junction: The Railways of Wandsworth and South West London*, 1994
Skinner, M W G, *Croydon's Railways*, 1985
Spence, Jeoffry, *The Caterham Railway*, 1952
Thomas, R H G, *London's First Railway: The London & Greenwich*, 1972
Townsend, Charles E C, *Further Notes on Early Railways in Surrey*, Newcomen Society, 1950
Wilmot, G F A, *The Railway in Finchley: A Study in Suburban Development*, Second Edition, 1973
Woodman, Trevor, *The Railways to Hayes . . ., Kent*, 1982
Young, John N, *Great Northern Suburban*, 1977

7: MAGAZINE ARTICLES ON SPECIFIC LINES & LOCATIONS

BRJ = *British Railway Journal**, ER = *Essex Review*, GEJ = *Great Eastern Journal**,
GWRJ = *Great Western Railway Journal**, LRR = *London Railway Record**, R = *Railways*,
RM = *Railway Magazine**, RSE = *Railways South East*, RTM = *Railway & Travel Monthly*,
RW = *Railway World*, U = *Underground*, UN = *Underground News**

Anon, (Lee, Charles E?), 'The Gauge of the Surrey Iron Railway', RM August 1967
Anon, 'The Expansion of the Great Eastern Railway: The New Line from Woodford to Ilford', RM
    June 1903,
  'Milk Traffic on the Ongar Branch, Great Eastern Railway', RM November 1918
Baker, Ian, 'Railways Around Tooting', LRR January 1955
  'North of Wood Green', LRR April 1995
  'From Harrow to Uxbridge', LRR July 1995
  'Tracing the Line to Alexandra Palace', LRR April 1996
Braidley, Philip W, 'Construction of the Metropolitan Stanmore Branch', U vol 1, 12
Burnham, T G, 'Branch to Bromley North', RM February 1975
Connor, J E, 'The Railways of Beckton', LRR November 1994, January 1995
  'The Gallions Branch of the PLA', LRR April 1995
  'The Palace Gates Branch', LRR July, October 1995

'The Greenwich Park Branch', LRR April, July 1996

Croome, Desmond, 'The Strange Story of Northfields (Weymouth Avenue)', UN 406 (October 1995)

Davis, P R, 'A Long-Forgotten Airport Scheme', U vol 10, 3

Derrick, J, 'The Woodside & South Croydon Joint Line', LRR July 1995

  'The Alexandra Palace Line', LRR January 1996

Edwards, W E, 'The Stanmore Railway', RM February 1922

Faulkner, J N, 'The Shepperton Branch of the Southern Region', RW February 1964

  'Easter Monday at Kempton Park', RM April 1955

  'To Guildford via Cobham', RM September 1959

Frost, K A, 'Railways Around Romford', RSE Winter 1988/89

Gairns, J F, 'The Ealing & Shepherds Bush Railway, RM July 1920

  'The Hackney Downs Group of Lines, Great Eastern Railway', RM October 1922

Gillham, J C, 'The Railways of Kew and Gunnersbury', RM September 1956

Holmes, J G, 'The North Woolwich Branch', RM May-June 1946

Hopwood, H L, 'The Enfield-Stevenage Loop Line', RM July 1920

  'The London & Blackwall Railway', RM May 1927

Jackson, Alan A, 'The South Acton Branch', RM December 1958

  'North-West from Ealing', RM September 1959, October 1959

  'The Wimbledon & Sutton Railway', RM December 1966

  'Beyond Edgware', RM February 1967

  'Almost A Tube', (Alexandra Palace Branch), RM May 1973, June 1973

  'Chessington: Southern Electric Swansong', RM January 1974

  'Rails to Tattenham Corner', RM June 1975

  'Brent Valley Railcars', RW May 1979

  'Racing to Residential: the Wimbledon & Epsom Line', RW July 1980

  'Romford to Grays', RW December 1979

  'The Horton Light Railway', RM October 1981

  'Central Line to the West', RSE Winter 1987–88

  'Northern to Morden', RSE Winter 1988–89

  'Newbury Park: Not Quite What It Was Meant To Be', LRR April 1996

Jenkins Stanley C, 'Denham to Uxbridge (High Street)', GWRJ 1, 1992

Jenkins, Stanley and Turner, Chris, 'Uxbridge Vine Street', GWRJ 13, 1995

Kirkby, Dick, 'Derby Day', RSE 12, Summer 1993

Kirkland, R K, 'The Great Western and Brentford Railway', RM February 1960

  'The Staines Branch Western Region', RM April 1955

Morss, Jeffrey, 'The Palace Gates to North Woolwich Line', RM September 1962

Norris, P J, 'The Bromley North Branch', RW February 1957

Paar, Harry, 'Hidden Aspects of The Fairlop Loop Line', GEJ, 81, January 1995

Potter, G W J, 'The New GER Loop Line', [Fairlop Loop] ER vol 12, 1903

  'The Loughton and Ongar Branch of the Great Eastern Railway', RM September 1920

Riley, R C, 'The Steam Railmotors of the SECR', R January-February 1951

  'Railmotors of the LBSCR', R August 1952

Sams, J G B, 'The West Croydon and Wimbledon Railway', RM March 1927

Sekon, G A, 'The First Railway With Non-Stop Trains: The London & Blackwall Railway', RTM
  April 1912

Smith, William H, 'The Crystal Palace (High Level) Branch, BRJ 28 (1989)

Treby, Edward, 'The Edmonton-Cheshunt Line', RM March 1958

  'By Central line to Ongar', RM September 1968

  'The Central Croydon Branch', RW March 1974

  'From Custom House to Gallions', RM February 1975

Turner, Chris, 'Uxbridge High Street', GWRJ 10 (1994)

Webster, V R, 'Railway Byways in East London', BRJ 27 (1989)

Wilson, B G, 'The Railway Development of Wimbledon', RW March 1961

Wilson, P W, 'By Railway to Tattenham Corner', RM July 1901

INDEX

Note: Stations are indexed under their most recent names. For train services refer to entries for main stations; for signalling details, refer to individual lines and stations; for locomotives and rolling stock, refer to the individual lines. Page numbers in *italics* indicate illustrations. There may be more than one reference on the page indicated.